RESEARCH METHODS

RESEARCH METHODS

LEARNING TO BECOME A CRITICAL RESEARCH CONSUMER

RONALD C. MARTELLA
Eastern Washington University

RONALD NELSON
Arizona State University

NANCY E. MARCHAND-MARTELLA
Eastern Washington University

ALLYN and BACON
Boston London Toronto Sydney Tokyo Singapore

Series Editorial Assistant: Jessica Barnard
Director of Education Programs: Ellen Mann Dolberg
Marketing Manager: Brad Parkins
Composition and Prepress Buyer: Linda Cox
Manufacturing Buyer: Megan Cochran
Production Editor: Christopher H. Rawlings
Editorial-Production Service: Omegatype Typography, Inc.
Electronic Composition: Omegatype Typography, Inc.
Cover Administrator: Linda Knowles

A Viacom Company
160 Gould Street
Needham Heights, MA 02494

Internet: www.abacon.com

Library of Congress Cataloging-in-Publication Data
Martella, Ronald C.
Research methods : learning to become a critical research consumer / Ronald C. Martella, J. Ron Nelson, Nancy E. Marchand-Martella.
p. cm.
ISBN 0-205-27125-1
1. Research–Methodology. 2. Science–Methodology. I. Nelson, J. Ron. II. Marchand-Martella, Nancy E. III. Title.
Q180.55.M4M34 1999
001.4′2–dc21 98-7617
CIP

Text credits appear on page 587, which is considered an extension of the copyright page.

Printed in the United States of America
10 9 8 7 6 5 07 06 05 04

Contents

PREFACE xvii

PART ONE
UNDERSTANDING RESEARCH 1

CHAPTER 1 THINKING CRITICALLY ABOUT RESEARCH 3

Objectives 1
Overview 1
What Is Science and the Scientific Method? 5
What Are the Purposes of Science? 6
Description 6
Prediction 6
Improvement 7
Explanation 8
What Is a Scientific Theory? 8
Good Versus Bad Scientific Theories 10
Testability of a Theory 10
What Are the Types of Scientific Logic? 11
Inductive Logic 11
Deductive Logic 12
Combination of Logic Forms 13
In What Ways Do We Gain Information? 14
Tenacity 14
Intuition 15
Authority 15
Empiricism 16
Rationalism 16
What Are Constraint Levels in Educational and Psychological Research? 17
Experimental Research 18
Causal-Comparative Research 20
Correlational Research 20
Case Study Research 20
Naturalistic or Descriptive Research 21
What Are the Differences between Basic and Applied Research? 22
Basic Research 22
Applied Research 22
What Is Replication Research? 23
Reasons for Replications 23
Types of Replications 27

Replication as the "Big Picture" 29
Summary 29
Discussion Questions 29

PART TWO
CRITICAL ISSUES IN RESEARCH 33

CHAPTER 2 FUNDAMENTAL ISSUES FOR INTERPRETING RESEARCH 35

Objectives 35
Overview 35
What Is Variability? 36
Sources of Variability 36
What Is Internal Validity? 38
Maturation 38
Selection 40
Selection by Maturation Interaction 41
Statistical Regression 41
Mortality 42
Instrumentation 43
Testing 43
History 44
Resentful Demoralization of the Control Group 44
Diffusion of Treatment 45
Compensatory Rivalry by the Control Group 45
Compensatory Equalization of Treatments 46
What Is External Validity? 46
Population Validity 47
Ecological Validity 49
What Are Statistical and Social Validities? 56
Statistical Validity 56
Social Validity 57
Summary 58
Discussion Questions 59
Interpretation Exercises 59

CHAPTER 3 RELIABILITY, VALIDITY, AND INTEROBSERVER AGREEMENT 63

Objectives 63
Overview 63
What Are Reliability and Validity Issues in Quantitative Research? 65
How Do Researchers Assess the Reliability of Measurement Devices? 66
Types of Reliability Coefficients 66
Standard Error of Measurement 71

How Do Researchers Determine the Validity of Measurement Devices? 73
Types of Validity 74
What Are Reliability and Validity Issues in Qualitative Research? 77
Reliability Issues 78
Validity Issues 78
Illustrative Example of Reliability and Validity Procedures 78
What Is Interobserver Agreement? 79
What Are the Methods of Establishing Interobserver Agreement? 80
Measures of Permanent Products 81
Event Recording 82
Latency and Duration Recording 82
Interval Recording 83
What Are the Factors that Influence Interobserver Agreement? 85
Reactivity 85
Observer Drift 85
Complexity of the Measurement System 86
Observer Expectations 86
What Are the Factors to Consider when Assessing Measurement Devices in the Context of a Study? 86
Description of the Measurement Device 86
Adjustments to the Measurement Device 86
Appropriateness of the Measurement Device 87
Cooperation of Participants 87
Summary 87
Discussion Questions 88
Practice Exercises 89

PART THREE
QUANTITATIVE RESEARCH METHODS 91

CHAPTER 4 BASIC STATISTICAL CONCEPTS AND SAMPLING PROCEDURES 93

Objectives 93
Overview 93
What Are the Scales of Measurement? 94
Nominal Scale 94
Ordinal Scale 94
Interval Scale 94
Ratio Scale 95
What Is a Univariate Frequency Distribution? 95
How Can We Describe Data Sets? 95
Measures of Central Tendency 95
Measures of Variation 96

Shape of the Distribution *97*
What Role Do Hypotheses Play in Research? 98
Inferential Statistics *98*
Role of Hypotheses *99*
Null and Alternative Hypotheses *99*
Directional and Nondirectional Alternative Hypotheses *100*
What Are Parametric and Nonparametric Tests of Statistical Significance? 102
Parametric Tests *102*
Nonparametric Tests *102*
What Is Statistical Significance? 102
Errors Made in Interpretations of the Significance Level *104*
What Are Type I and Type II Errors and Power? 105
Type I Errors *105*
Type II Errors *106*
Relative Seriousness of Type I or Type II Errors *107*
Power *108*
Five Methods of Increasing Power *108*
What Are the Types of Statistical Significance Testing Methods? 111
Parametric Tests of Statistical Significance *111*
Nonparametric Tests of Statistical Significance *116*
What Are the Different Sampling Methods? 119
Probability Sampling *120*
Nonprobability Sampling *124*
What Are the Sampling Decisions Researchers Make? 125
What Is Sampling Error? 126
Summary 127
Discussion Questions 128

CHAPTER 5 EXPERIMENTAL DESIGNS 130

Objectives 130
Overview 130
What Are True Experimental Designs? 132
What Are the Most Common True Experimental Designs? 133
Pretest–Posttest Control-Group Design *133*
Posttest-Only Control-Group Design *136*
Solomon Four-Group Design *138*
What Are Factorial Experimental Designs? 141
Analysis of Data *141*
What Are Quasi-Experimental Designs? 144
What Are the Common Quasi-Experimental Designs? 144
Static-Group Comparison *144*
Nonequivalent Control-Group Designs *146*
Counterbalanced Designs *149*
Time-Series Designs *151*

What Are Preexperimental Designs? 153
What Are the Types of Preexperimental Designs? 153
One-Shot Case Study 153
One-Group Pretest–Posttest Design 155
When Should Researchers Use Each Experimental Research Design? 156
Discussion Questions 157
Sample Article: "The Effects of Learning Strategy Instruction on the Completion of Job Applications by Students with Learning Disabilities," by J. Ron Nelson, Deborah J. Smith, and John M. Dodd 158

CHAPTER 6 CAUSAL-COMPARATIVE RESEARCH 174

Objectives 174
Overview 174
What Is the Causal-Comparative Research Method? 175
What Should Researchers Consider when Designing a Causal-Comparative Study? 176
Development of Hypotheses 176
Selection of Groups 176
Analysis of Data 177
Research Examples 180
When Should Researchers Use the Causal-Comparative Research Design? 182
Discussion Questions 182
Sample Article: "The Current and Future Outcomes of Interpersonal Social Interactions: The Views of Students with Behavioral Disorders," by J. Ron Nelson, Marcy Drummond, Ron Martella, and Nancy Marchand-Martella 183

CHAPTER 7 CORRELATIONAL RESEARCH 200

Objectives 200
Overview 200
What Is the Correlational Research Method? 201
What Are the Issues in Designing a Correlational Study? 201
Types of Variables in Correlational Research 201
Critical Issues in Correlational Research 202
Analysis of Data 203
Research Examples 227
When Should Researchers Use the Correlational Research Method? 230
Discussion Questions 231
Sample Article: "Peer Victimization: Cause or Consequence of School Maladjustment?" by Becky J. Kochenderfer and Gary W. Ladd 232

PART FOUR
QUALITATIVE RESEARCH METHODS 253

CHAPTER 8 QUALITATIVE RESEARCH: METHODS 255

Objectives 255
Overview 255
What Are the Characteristics of Qualitative Research? 257
What Are the Differences between Qualitative and Quantitative Research? 258
Source of Data 258
Nature of Data 263
Process of Change 264
Type of Reasoning 264
Focus of Research 265
What Are Qualitative Research Procedures? 265
Phases 265
Sampling 267
What Is Understanding in Qualitative Research? 270
Descriptive Validity 270
Interpretive Validity 271
Theoretical Validity 271
Generalizability 272
Evaluative Validity 273
What Are the Evaluative Criteria for Judging the Reliability and Validity of Qualitative Research? 273
Criterion 1: Completeness of Information 274
Criterion 2: Adequacy of Interpretation 274
Criterion 3: Determination of Inconsistencies in Data 274
Criterion 4: Adequacy of Metaphors, Pictures, or Diagrams 274
Criterion 5: Collaboration with Participants 274
Criterion 6: Multiple Methods to Gather Data 274
Criterion 7: Disqualification of Interpretations 276
What Are the Types of Triangulation Methods? 277
Data Sources Triangulation 277
Analyst Triangulation 277
Theory/Perspective Triangulation 278
Methods Triangulation 278
Summary 279
Discussion Questions 279

CHAPTER 9 QUALITATIVE RESEARCH: DATA COLLECTION AND DESIGNS 281

Objectives 281
Overview 281

What Are Field-Oriented Studies? 282
Case Study *282*
Observation Studies *282*
Participant Observation Study *285*
Nonparticipant Observation Study *286*
Natualistic Observation Study *287*
Simulations *287*
Interview Studies *288*
Ethnography *291*
Document Analysis *293*
Analysis of Data *294*
Research Examples *298*
When Should Researchers Use Each Qualitative Research Design? 300
Discussion Questions 301
Sample Article: "Successful Mainstreaming in Elementary Science Classes: A Qualitative Study of Three Reputational Cases," by Thomas E. Scruggs and Margo A. Mastropieri 302

PART FIVE
SINGLE-CASE RESEARCH METHODS 325

CHAPTER 10 WITHDRAWAL AND ASSOCIATED DESIGNS 327
Objectives 327
Overview 327
What Are Graphing Methods in Withdrawal Designs? 330
What Are Withdrawal and Associated Designs? 331
A-B Design *331*
Withdrawal Design *333*
A-B-A-B Design *334*
B-A-B Design *334*
A-B-C-B Design *335*
Analysis of Data *337*
Research Examples *340*
When Should Researchers Use Each Withdrawal and Associated Design? 347
Discussion Questions 350
Sample Article: "Reducing Negative Comments through Self-Monitoring and Contingency Contracting," by Pamela S. Courson-Krause, Nancy Marchand-Martella, Ronald C. Martella, and Brenda Schmitt 351

CHAPTER 11 MULTIPLE-BASELINE DESIGNS 363
Objectives 363
Overview 363
What Are Graphing Methods in Multiple-Baseline Designs? 364

What Are Multiple-Baseline Designs? 364
Multiple-Baseline Design across Behaviors 366
Multiple-Baseline Design across Participants 366
Multiple-Baseline Design across Settings 366
Multiple-Probe Design 367
Analysis of Data 369
Research Examples 379
When Should Researchers Use Each Multiple-Baseline Design? 385
Discussion Questions 387
Sample Article: "Generalized Effects of a Peer-Delivered First Aid Program for Students with Moderate Intellectual Disabilities," by Nancy E. Marchand-Martella, Ronald C. Martella, Martin Agran, Charles L. Salzberg, K. Richard Young, and Daniel Morgan 388

CHAPTER 12 ADDITIONAL SINGLE-CASE DESIGNS 405

Objectives 405
Overview 405
What Is a Changing-Criterion Design? 405
Analysis of Data 407
Research Example 412
What Is a Multitreatment Design? 413
Analysis of Data 416
Research Example 418
What Is an Alternating Treatments Design? 418
Analysis of Data 422
Research Example 423
What Are Combination Designs? 424
Analysis of Data 428
Research Example 428
When Should Researchers Use Each of the Additional Single-Case Designs? 428
Discussion Questions 430
Sample Article: "Problem Solving to Prevent Work Injuries in Supported Employment," by Ronald C. Martella, Martin Agran, and Nancy E. Marchand-Martella 431

PART SIX
ADDITIONAL RESEARCH METHODS 447

CHAPTER 13 SURVEY, HISTORICAL, AND PROGRAM EVALUATION RESEARCH METHODS 449

SURVEY RESEARCH 449
Objectives 449
Overview 449

What Are the Purposes of Survey Research? 450

Description *450*

Explanation *450*

Exploration *451*

What Are the Different Types of Surveys? 451

What Are the Factors in Choosing a Survey Method? 451

Sampling Procedures *451*

Sampling Population *451*

Question Format *452*

Content of Questions *453*

Response Rate *453*

Time and Money *453*

How Is Survey Research Designed? 453

Sampling *453*

Developing the Survey Instrument *456*

Analysis of Data *458*

Research Example *459*

When Should Researchers Use Survey Research? 459

HISTORICAL RESEARCH 460

Objectives 460

Overview 460

What Are the Characteristics and Purposes of Historical Research? 461

Characteristics *461*

Purposes *461*

How Is Historical Research Designed? 462

Research Question or Hypothesis *462*

Data Collection *463*

Analysis of Data *464*

Research Example *468*

When Should Researchers Use Historical Research? 469

PROGRAM EVALUATION 469

Objectives 469

Overview 469

What Are the Goal and Objectives of Program Evaluation? 470

Goal *470*

Objectives *470*

What Are the Types of Program Evaluations? 471

Needs Assessments *472*

Process Evaluations *473*

Outcome Evaluations *474*

Efficiency Evaluations *474*

How Is a Program Evaluation Conducted? 475

Establishing Boundaries *475*

Selecting Evaluation Methods *475*

Collecting and Analyzing Data *476*
Reporting of Findings *476*
Analysis of Data *476*
Evaluation Example *476*
When Should Program Evaluations Be Conducted? 477
Discussion Questions 477
Sample Article: "Faculty Willingness to Accommodate Students with Learning Disabilities: A Comparison among Academic Divisions," by J. Ron Nelson, John M. Dodd, and Deborah J. Smith 478

CHAPTER 14 CONDUCTING RESEARCH SYNTHESES 489

Objectives 489
Overview 489
What Are the Purposes of Research Syntheses? 490
Establishing Cause-and-Effect Relationships *490*
Determining the Degree of Relationship between Two Variables *490*
Developing Theories *490*
Assessing the External Validity of Findings *491*
What Are Systematic and Unsystematic Research Syntheses? 491
Unsystematic Research Syntheses *491*
Systematic Research Syntheses *491*
Comparison of Unsystematic and Systematic Research Syntheses *492*
What Are the Considerations for Conducting Research Syntheses? 493
Identifying Primary Sources *493*
Identifying Secondary Sources *493*
Overcoming Selection Biases *494*
Focusing the Literature Search *494*
How Do Researchers Plan and Execute Research Syntheses? 494
Formulating a Precise Research Question *494*
Defining Critical Terms *495*
Formulating a Literature Search Framework *497*
Searching the Literature *497*
Coding Study Characteristics *500*
Determining the Magnitude of Intervention Outcomes *502*
Relating Study Characteristics to Intervention Outcomes *508*
Reporting the Results *512*
Analysis of Data *513*
When Should Researchers Conduct Research Syntheses? 515
Discussion Questions 515
Sample Article: "The Moral Reasoning of Juvenile Delinquents: A Meta-Analysis," by J. Ron Nelson, Deborah J. Smith, and John Dodd 516

PART SEVEN ACTION RESEARCH 523

CHAPTER 15 ACTION RESEARCH: MOVING FROM CRITICAL RESEARCH CONSUMER TO RESEARCHER 525

Objectives 525
Overview 525
What Is Action Research? 526
Dimensions of Action Research 527
What Are the Characteristics of Action Research? 527
Purposes and Value Choice 527
Contextual Focus 527
Change-Based Data and Sense Making 528
Participation in the Research Process 528
Knowledge Diffusion 528
How Are Quantitative Methods Used in Action Research? 528
Research Example 529
How Are Qualitative Methods Used in Action Research? 529
Research Example 530
How Are Single-Case Methods Used in Action Research? 531
Research Example 531
How Are Survey, Historical, and Program Evaluation Methods Used in Action Research? 531
Survey Research 532
Historical Research 532
Program Evaluation 532
What Are the Ethical Principles and Codes of Conduct for Research? 532
American Educational Research Association 533
American Psychological Association 533
Ethical Conduct of Action Researchers 538
How Does One Write a Research Article? 538
Contents 538
A Cautionary Note 541
How Are Articles Submitted for Publication? 542
When Should One Conduct Action Research? 542
Discussion Questions 543
Sample Article: "Dyads and Data in Peer Coaching," by Cynthia O. Vail, Jennifer M. Tschantz, and Alicia Bevill 544

GLOSSARY 553

REFERENCES 565

INDEX 575

PREFACE

Today we are seeing more scientific breakthroughs than ever before. It would have been difficult even 10 years ago to predict the advances in computer science we see now. Medical technology is becoming more advanced in treating diseases and injuries. The use of the laser beam has transformed everything from the way many operations are performed to how we play music. Compact disc drives are almost as common as floppy disk drives on computers. High-definition televisions are on the horizon, as are the mass production of electric automobiles and the cloning of animals. Science touches us every day in almost every way. Every one of us has been greatly affected by science in some manner. But, how has science changed how we educate our youth? Sure, there are more computers in the classroom, but have they improved our instruction? Has the way we approach educating students in the classroom been affected by educational and psychological research? Of course, you will find many professionals saying that research has not affected educational practice, and you will find other professionals saying that research has improved educational practice.

Although there is not a definitive answer to the question of the impact of educational and psychological research on educational practice, we could conclude that educational and psychological research can have a larger effect on educational practice. We still have a growing problem of illiteracy, and many professionals believe that our students are not achieving in math and science at an acceptable level. So, what is needed to ensure that educational and psychological research can help with the problems faced by teachers and practitioners? There are certainly enough research journals available to inform the public on research findings. There are certainly enough researchers to conduct research, especially in colleges and universities. There are also ample participants to be studied. One way of increasing the impact of research on educational practice is to teach educational and psychological professionals how to think critically about research so they become critical research consumers.

This text is designed differently from most research texts. We designed a text that would help the professor teach students to think critically about research rather than to actually conduct research. The first step in creating a good researcher is the same as that in creating a good professional; that is, we must first teach them how to think about research. Once this goal is accomplished, we can then set out to teach future researchers how to actually conduct research.

Students studying this text will learn the skills associated with thinking critically about research. Students will also learn how to conduct their own research to answer future research questions. Our goal is to develop scientist/practitioners. This goal will be achieved by having students learn information in a sequenced fashion; thus, chapters will build off of previous ones. The chapters are divided into seven parts.

CONTENTS

Part 1 discusses skills in learning how to become critical research consumers (Chapter 1). Information needed to think critically about research is presented, including descriptions of science, what science is, the process of science, and the purpose of science.

Part 2 covers the concept and sources of variability. Internal and external validity are keys to understanding much of the educational and psychological research produced. Therefore, a great deal of time is spent on these concepts. Statistical and social validity are also described. A discussion of the differences in these important forms of validity is presented (Chapter 2). The concepts of reliability and validity from quantitative and qualitative perspectives are also discussed in Part 2. A special form of reliability and validity (i.e., interobserver agreement) is presented. Interobserver agreement is used in single-case research. Finally, factors to consider when assessing measurement devices in the context of an investigation are presented (Chapter 3). Several examples and nonexamples are presented throughout the chapter to help students learn key concepts.

Part 3 begins with a presentation of some basic statistical concepts. A knowledge of these concepts is critical for an understanding of many quantitative designs. Sampling methods are also discussed at length. The method of sampling is important in determining the type of design used as well as claims that can be made of the generalizability of the results (Chapter 4). The different methodologies are covered including true experimental designs, factorial designs, quasi-experimental, and preexperimental designs (Chapter 5). Additionally, causal-comparative research methods (Chapter 6) and correlational research methods (Chapter 7) are presented. At the end of each chapter, we describe when each form of research method is used. Finally, Chapters 5 through 7 present sample articles for students to critique that include rating forms to analyze various aspects of the studies.

Part 4 focuses on qualitative research methods (Chapter 8), data collection, and designs (Chapter 9). Methods of sampling are discussed. Chapter 9 closes with a section on when different qualitative research methods should be used. A sample article for students to analyze and an analysis form are included in the chapter.

Part 5 presents a detailed discussion of single-case methods. We show how single-case methods may be thought of as a combination of quantitative and qualitative methods. Methods of graphing and withdrawal and associated designs are discussed in Chapter 10. Multiple-baseline designs (Chapter 11) and additional single-case designs (Chapter 12) are presented. Each chapter discusses when to use the various types of single-case designs. A sample article for critique along with a rating form are presented at the end of each of the chapters.

Part 6 focuses on additional types of designs including survey and historical research and program evaluations (Chapter 13). A detailed discussion of research syntheses is presented (Chapter 14). We discuss when each form of research is conducted. We also present a sample article for critique and a rating form at the end of each chapter.

Part 7 covers issues to consider when planning and conducting a research project (Chapter 15). Recall that the text is designed to teach students to think critically about research; however, we also want to produce scientist/practitioners. Practitioners can, and in some instances should, produce data to make informed decisions. When practitioners produce such data, they are engaging in action research. A discussion of how to conduct action research is presented. When a decision is made to conduct an investigation, ethical issues must then be considered. These ethical issues are described. These "action researchers" should also know the process one goes through to write and submit an article for publication. We describe such a process. Finally, a sample article to critique is presented at the end of the chapter.

We realize that the amount of information contained in the text is vast. Therefore, we present objectives at the beginning of each chapter and discussion questions at the end of each chapter. In addition, many chapters end with sample articles that illustrate the techniques and methodology discussed, along with questions and forms for the student to use in evaluating these articles.

We have also prepared an instructor's resource manual to accompany this book. Please contact your local Allyn and Bacon representative for more information about this useful supplement.

ACKNOWLEDGMENTS

We would be remiss if we did not acknowledge the individuals who have affected our educational careers. First and foremost, we wish to thank our families for their support. We should also thank our children for allowing us to take the time to complete the project. We wish to thank those teachers who helped guide us to this point in our careers—Professors Richard Foxx, Robert Wageman, Harold Mansfield, David Santogrossi, Alan Hofmeister, John Nicholls, Martin Agran, K. Richard Young, Benjamin Lignugaris/Kraft, Charles Salzberg, James Shaver, and Carl Cheney.

In order to complete this text, several individuals were involved. We wish to thank everyone at Allyn & Bacon for their continued support throughout the project, especially Nancy Forsyth, without whom this project would not have come to fruition. To the students who helped with the article searches and managerial tasks—Tara Ebey, Trish McGrath, Jenni Reilly, and Donald Stenhoff—we extend our sincere thanks. And finally, our thanks to the reviewers who provided invaluable feedback and suggestions to keep us on track and helped us produce a better product that would have been impossible without their expertise: Steven M. Brown, Northeastern Illinois University; Tracy Lee Cross, Ball State University; Gary Greer, University of Houston, Downtown; Barbara Lounsbury, Rhode Island College; Suzanne MacDonald, The University of Akron; Joanna Martin, University of Texas–Tyler; Thomas A. Romberg, University of Wisconsin–Madison; Theresa Siskind, The Citadel; B. James Starr, Howard University; Paul Westmeyer, University of Texas, San Antonio; and Gary H. Zarter, Seattle University.

PART ONE

UNDERSTANDING RESEARCH

CHAPTER 1 THINKING CRITICALLY ABOUT RESEARCH

Chapter 1

THINKING CRITICALLY ABOUT RESEARCH

OBJECTIVES

After studying this chapter, you should be able to:

1. Explain the importance of thinking critically about research.
2. Explain what is meant by the term "science."
3. Describe the scientific process.
4. Describe each of the four purposes of science.
5. Explain what makes a theory a scientific one.
6. Describe how one can determine if a theory is a good one.
7. Explain the difference in how science is conducted when using inductive or deductive logic.
8. Explain the criticisms of each form of logic and explain how science can be seen as essentially a combination of each form of logic.
9. Describe the five ways of gaining information.
10. Explain why only two of the methods of gaining information are used in science.
11. Describe the five constraint levels of research.
12. Explain the difference between basic and applied research.
13. Describe what is meant by action research.
14. Describe what is meant by replication research.
15. Explain why replication research is important in science.
16. Describe the three major categories of replication research.

OVERVIEW

One of the most important skill areas in research that needs to be developed is learning to think critically. Critical thinking is the ability to take a topic, consider both sides of the issue, and make an informed decision on the topic. For example, when reading educational and psychological research, one must read what the researcher has written, consider how the research was conducted, determine if there were any plausible alternative explanations, and make a decision on the believability of the claims made by the researcher. Unfortunately, many professionals seem to skip the middle steps. They read what the researcher has written and accept the conclusions made by the researcher as fact. This scenario does not represent critical thinking.

Due to the possible difficulties in making an impact on education through educational and psychological research, we should teach educational and psychological professionals how to become critical research consumers. Professionals who learn to consume research will learn some important information on how to conduct research. Educational and psychological professionals should be able to read and understand what research is and how to interpret research findings. Thus, the primary purpose of teaching about research is to develop *critical thinking skills*.

In order to develop these skills, several elements must be included and learned. Different research methods must be known. However, it is not enough to know the different designs. A critical research consumer knows why different designs are used and what types of research questions are answered.

First, a critical research consumer must learn what science is, how it works, and why it works. Science means different things to different people. Therefore, it is critical to come to some understanding of what we mean by the term "science." We will present a definition of science, describe how science works, and discuss the purposes of science.

Second, the critical research consumer should know what constitutes a scientific theory. There are many theories put forth almost on a daily basis. In order to discriminate between a scientific theory and one that is not, one must understand the distinctions between the two types. We will discuss what constitutes scientific theories.

Third, it is important to understand the different types of logic used in science. The method of logic one uses will determine how the study of a particular phenomenon is approached. We will provide a description of the two types of scientific logic along with a discussion of how the logic forms can be combined.

Fourth, certain methods of knowing fit within a scientific framework and others do not. Unfortunately, many people do not understand how to discriminate scientific sources of information from other sources that are not scientific. In fact, Sagan (1996) indicates that up to 95% of individuals in the United States are "scientific illiterates." In other words, most individuals cannot make a distinction between valid sources of information and sources that are suspect. We will present various sources of information and explain which are considered scientific and which are not.

Fifth, the critical research consumer must know how to discriminate between research methods that use more control (i.e., high constraint levels) from those that use less control (i.e., low constraint levels). Variables that can affect the interpretation of research must be clear to the consumer. Issues of reliability and validity are critical aspects of research and will be presented in this chapter.

Sixth, the differences between research that focuses on more theoretical issues (i.e., basic) as compared to research that addresses educational/psychological problems (i.e., applied) should be understood as well. Some research findings may not have an immediate impact on society; however, whether research findings have an immediate impact or not or whether the application of the research findings to society is obvious or not does not make the research valuable or not valuable. The differences between basic and applied research will be discussed in this chapter.

Seventh, science does not advance with single, isolated research findings. In order to make advances in a field of inquiry, one must see the same results several times through different research investigations. Thus, the critical research consumer must know what replications are, why they are conducted, and how they can help to advance our knowledge. Replication research will be discussed in this chapter.

We want professionals to learn how to think about research differently. They will not see research as something that must be avoided and feared, but something that is exciting and can make them better and more informed professionals.

WHAT IS SCIENCE AND THE SCIENTIFIC METHOD?

As with most topics, we will never find one completely agreed upon definition of science. Consider the following from Marx and Hillix (1963):

> *Science is a many-sided social enterprise that has been defined in several ways. Some prefer to emphasize a way of thinking*—the scientific attitude—*as the major characteristic. For others, science is primarily a way of doing; the* scientific method *is seen as the most important feature. Still others prefer to emphasize the product of this method—the systematically ordered* body of knowledge *that scientists have produced. None of these emphases can be accepted to the exclusion of the others. The safest procedure is to accept them all and consider science as the total enterprise: men thinking with a certain attitude, using scientific methods to produce facts and theories that are ordered descriptions and explanations of the world. (p. 3)*

Generally, science is the search for understanding of the world around us. Science is the attempt to find order and lawful relations in the world. It is a method of viewing the world. Finally, science is the testing of our ideas in a public forum that takes a series of five steps. These steps are considered the scientific method to gaining an understanding of our world. They include (a) identify a problem, (b) define the problem, (c) formulate a hypothesis or research question, (d) determine the observable consequences of the hypothesis or research question, and (e) test the hypothesis or attempt to answer the research question.

The first step, identify a problem, is an awareness on the part of the researcher that something is missing in a knowledge base. The desire, then, is to find information to fill the gap. For example, there may be a gap of knowledge in how a teacher's reaction to disruptive behavior encourages future disruptive behavior.

Second, the researcher must define the problem. The attempt here is to become clear about what exactly the problem is. For example, a problem such as having disruptive behavior in the classroom is not well defined. The students can be engaging in serious problems such as fighting or more minor problems like whispering or exchanging notes to one another. The term "disruption" must be defined in such a way that a clear picture of what is meant by it is developed. Therefore, the problem must be identified and defined.

Third, the researcher must formulate either hypotheses or research questions. Hypotheses are statements about the relation between two or more concepts. For example, we can make a hypothesis that if a teacher attends to disruptive behavior, the disruptive behavior will get worse. Research questions are queries about events but are not attempts at predicting what will occur. For example, instead of the hypothesis stated before, we could ask, "What would happen if a teacher attends to disruptive behavior?"

The fourth step in the scientific method is to determine the observable consequences of the hypothesis or research question. For example, for the preceding hypothesis and research question, we could conclude that teachers who do not provide attention to disruptive behaviors will have better classroom management than teachers who attend to such behavior.

The final step is to test the hypothesis or attempt to answer the research question. This step requires the actual collection of data. Once the data are gathered, they are analyzed to determine if the hypothesis was correct or if they answer the research question. For example, the data indicated that when teachers attended to disruptive behaviors in the classroom, higher levels of disruptions occurred as compared to when teachers did not attend to such disruptive behaviors.

Although the scientific method is powerful in filling gaps in knowledge, the critical research consumer must understand that even though the data are gathered and the hypothesis is tested or the research question is answered, errors will likely occur in the investigation, and some of those errors will put the researcher's conclusions into question. Additionally, any isolated observable event obtained from a single investigation can support several theories, some even conflicting. Therefore, as will be seen later in the chapter, one can never prove a theory but can only provide support for it due to errors made by researchers or the possibility that isolated observable events that may show only chance findings are present.

WHAT ARE THE PURPOSES OF SCIENCE?

Generally, we can assume that science has several purposes—to describe and predict (Caldwell, 1994; Chiesa, 1994; Gall, Borg, & Gall, 1996), to improve or manipulate the world around us, and to explain our world (Chiesa, 1994; Gall, Borg, & Gall, 1996).

Description

Throughout the scientific process, we attempt to provide a description of an event or phenomenon. Piaget did precisely this. He described certain abilities in children at different points in their lives. From these observations, he developed a theory of development that has different developmental levels, each with a set of abilities present. Description is something that we all do on a daily basis. We describe how others dress, how classrooms are situated, and how students attend to the teacher. The descriptions we make allow us to make some conclusions such as students dress differently today than they did 10 years ago, students' desks are generally placed in rows facing the front of the classroom, and students seem to attend to teachers who are more dynamic than to teachers who are less lively. One could think of description as the first step in science. Scientific inquiry begins with the description of the phenomenon. These descriptions can lead to interesting future research questions such as if we placed students at tables in a circle, would they be more likely to attend to the teachers or can we increase student attention by teaching the teachers how to be more dynamic? Descriptions can also lead to important discoveries such as every time the teacher turns away from the student, the student begins to disrupt the class. It seems as if the student is displaying the disruptive behavior to get the teacher's attention.

Descriptive information has provided a large amount of information about our schools and how they are doing. For example, information such as the levels of reading our students are achieving is descriptive information. The percentages of students who drop out of school, take drugs, and commit crimes are also descriptive. This descriptive information can be used by policy makers to make future decisions. The federal government, state, and/or local school districts may use this information to set priorities for grant funds or instructional programs. Whether the funded interventions (e.g., instructional programs) work is a question for another purpose (i.e., improvement).

Essentially, all research conducted provides us some form of a description. However, certain research methods are geared only to provide descriptive information. These methods are presented in Chapters 8 and 9. These methods generally come under the heading of qualitative research methods. These methods are ideally suited for providing a description of the observed phenomenon.

Prediction

A second purpose of science is to make predictions about what will happen in the future. If you are studying this text, you no doubt have been subject to this purpose. College students take a standardized test such as the *American College Testing* Program (ACT) or *Scholastic Aptitude Test* (SAT); if you want to go on to graduate school, you may take the *Graduate Record Exam* (GRE); if you go to law school, you will most likely take the *Law School Aptitude Test* (LSAT); and if you want to go on to get an advanced degree in business, you may need to take the *Graduate Miller Analogies Test* (GMAT). The purpose of all of these tests is to help predict how you will do in school. The results of these tests along with other information such as grades in high school or college are used to select students who will most likely achieve in the program.

Professionals also use predictions to identify students who are more likely to do poorly in school. Children who come from low socioeconomic backgrounds may be admitted into Head Start Programs. These programs are aimed at increasing the chances for success of students from backgrounds that might decrease their chances of succeeding in school. Variables that may place children at a higher level of risk of failure include coming from a single-parent household, having parents with a lack of educational background, being a member of a minority group, coming from a family with few economic resources, and coming from the inner city. When these risk factors are combined, the risk of school failure is increased. A caution here is in order. With prediction studies, the probability of something such as school failure is increased when variables are combined; however, the probability will not reach 100%. In other words, an African American child may come from a single-parent household, where the parent has a fifth-grade education, earns less than $9,000 a year, and lives in the inner city and he or she may not fail in school. The prediction simply means that proportionally more children from this background fail in school compared to, for example, a Caucasian child who lives in the suburbs with two college-graduate, middle-class parents. Thus, the importance of making predictions of this sort is to provide at-risk children with skills that can aid in their school success before they actually enter school.

As with descriptive research, most research methods allow for the prediction of something in the future. The more we know about a phenomenon, the better able we are to make future predictions. However, specific research methods are developed to provide predictions; these methods are presented in Chapters 6 and 7. These methods include causal-comparative and correlational research methods. These methods provide an indication of the strength of relationship between or among variables.

Improvement

The third purpose of science is to make improvements in the subject matter. When discussing these improvements, interventions are at issue. Essentially, one purpose of science is to determine the best or most effective interventions to bring about desirable changes. For example, when we are concerned with determining how best to instruct students, we are attempting to determine what interventions are most appropriate. This purpose is the basis for the effective teaching literature that has been developed over a number of years. Inherent in the quest for improvement, researchers are also attempting to determine the variables (e.g., type of instruction, method of behavior management) that control phenomena (e.g., amount of material learned, on-task behavior). These variables are called *independent variables* (we also will use the terms "interventions" and "treatments" throughout the text to refer to independent variables) and the phenomena are *dependent variables*. The question becomes, "What causes this to occur, or how can we control this phenomenon to bring about changes we would like to see?"

Unlike the previous two purposes of science, the goal of making improvements is somewhat more difficult to achieve in that there are variables that can interfere with accurate conclusions based on the obtained data. These variables are presented in Chapter 2. Three research method categories allow for the investigation of improvement methods. First, experimental research requires a manipulation of the independent variable to determine the effects on the participants' behavior (also called the dependent variable) (e.g., changing the type of instruction or comparing groups receiving different types of instruction). Experimental research allows for the demonstration of cause-and-effect relationships. Experimental methodologies are presented in Chapter 5.

Second, causal-comparative methods provide a comparison of participants on some existing condition such as the academic achievement of high socioeconomic status (SES) students compared to low SES students. The independent variable (i.e., SES) is predetermined in that it is not really possible to make some students low SES status and other high SES status at random (see Chapter 6).

Third, correlational research can provide information on how to make improvements as the relationship between or among two or more variables is measured. Similar to causal-comparative research methods, correlational methods can help to determine how different levels of SES students perform in school. Correlational research takes advantage of how natural variations in one variable (e.g., not all children come from identical SES backgrounds) are related to natural variations on a second variable (e.g., not all children have the same achievement levels). Correlational research is presented in Chapter 7.

Explanation

The final purpose of research is to explain why a phenomenon occurs. To achieve this purpose, researchers develop theories. However, not everyone agrees we will ever be able to explain why phenomena occur fully because there are an infinite number of possible reasons why something occurs or does not occur. We can never really isolate all of the potential variables that are potential causes of an event. Therefore, some researchers argue that we can demonstrate relationships among variables but never truly know what causes something to occur. Whether we can truly explain a phenomenon is up for debate, but researchers use scientific theories as an attempt to do just that.

Explanation of a phenomenon requires knowledge from the other three purposes of science. To explain a phenomenon, we must first describe it, then predict when it will and will not occur, and finally be able to change the direction of the phenomenon. Once we are able to do all three of these things, we can begin to explain why something occurs. Again, our explanation is not necessarily correct since we could make a mistake along the way. We can only gain a sufficient amount of confidence in our explanation since we can never prove that the explanation is correct. Not being able to prove that our explanation is correct can be better understood by knowing what a scientific theory is.

WHAT IS A SCIENTIFIC THEORY?

Scientific philosophies help to guide us in how to collect and interpret our data. We also must have to understand what the data mean. Scientific theories aid us in understanding our data in a more general context. Unfortunately, the term "theory" has taken on several different connotations. When speaking of theories, we may be speaking of three different things (Chiesa, 1994). First, a theory may be a simple guess where the person stating the theory is making some prediction or explanation. The person may be indicating an expected outcome such as, "I have a theory about the outcome of Goals 2000," or a causal relation such as, "I believe that the whole-language approach to teaching reading produces better readers."

Second, a theory may refer to a model derived to help understand a phenomenon. The model may involve hypothetical constructs such as the id, ego, and superego to account for unexplained phenomena. "This type of theory proposes a speculative explanation which, for scientific purposes, requires experimental testing to establish to what degree the model fits empirical data it attempts to explain" (Chiesa, 1994, p. 136).

Third, a theory may refer to an explanatory system that describes the data gathered before the theory was developed. These theories attempt to determine regularities in the phenomenon. For example, data are gathered, then the researcher takes all of the data into consideration and looks for uniformities in the data. Once these uniformities are found, the theory is constructed or is formed from these uniformities. These theories do not rely on guessing nor do they rely on hypothetical constructs. These theories are derived *from* experimentation; they do not come *before* experimentation. These theories are grounded in the data that came before them.

Now that we see there are three different types of theories, we must determine if a theory is a scientific one. According to Popper (1957/1996), a scientific theory is one that is falsifiable or refutable. In other words, a scientific theory must be able to be disproven. This sounds almost counterintuitive at first until one realizes that technically, a scientific theory cannot be proven, only disproven. The reason for not being able to prove a theory is that we will never know all of the variables that can affect the results of an experiment that supports the theory or from which the theory was developed. Simply stated, errors are always made in scientific research conclusions. We do not know where or when those errors will occur only that they can occur at some point. If an error in a research conclusion is made and we say that we have proven a theory, we would be placing trust in a potentially false theory. Thus, we say that we have confidence in a theory. For instance, we could have 100 studies that were used to help develop a theory or that support an existing theory, but if we gather data from one additional study that does not fit with the theory, the theory could be disproven.

So, we set out to disprove theories, not to prove them; in order to disprove a theory, we must be able to test the theory. Many psychological theories do not fit within this criterion. For example, Popper (1957/1996) indicates that the psychoanalytic theories of Freud and Adler were not testable, not irrefutable. It is not possible, for example, to disprove the existence of the id, ego, and superego. Thus, Popper indicates that we must look to refute a theory rather than confirm a theory. As stated by Popper,

1. *It is easy to obtain confirmations, or verifications, for nearly every theory—if we look for confirmations.*
2. *Confirmations should count only if they are the result of* risky predictions; *that is to say, if, unenlightened by the theory in question, we should have expected an event which was incompatible with the theory—an event which, had it happened, would have refuted the theory.*
3. *Every "good" scientific theory is one which forbids certain things to happen; the more a theory forbids, the better.*
4. *A theory which is not refutable by any conceivable event is nonscientific. Irrefutability is not a virtue of a theory (as people often think) but a vice.*
5. *Every genuine* test *of a theory is an attempt to falsify it, or to refute it. Testability is falsifiability, but there are degrees of testability: some theories are more testable, more exposed to refutation, than others; they take, as it were, greater risks.*
6. *Confirming evidence does not count* except when it is the result of a genuine test of the theory; *and this means that it can be presented as an unsuccessful but serious attempt to falsify the theory.*
7. *Some genuinely testable theories, when found to be false, are still upheld by their admirers—for example, by introducing* ad hoc *some auxiliary assumption, or by re-interpreting the theory* ad hoc *in such a way that it escapes refutation. Such a procedure is always possible, but it rescues the theory from refutation only at the price of destroying or at least lowering its scientific status. (pp. 159–160)*

Consider each of these statements. The first statement refers to what many people do today. We can find research to support virtually every theory (Caldwell, 1994). However, this is not critical thinking. Thinking critically about science is attempting to find alternative explanations for research findings, and, thus, theories.

The second statement is a caution of accepting research that supports a theory as a confirmation of the theory. Confirmations may occur when we are not looking for them. If we are looking for confirmation, we can usually find them in any set of data.

The third statement refers to placing restrictions on what is expected based on the theory. For example, if we have a prediction that instructing students based on a discovery format will result in improved skills but we do not specify these skills, the theory is weaker than one that predicts that the instruction will improve specific skills. The more specific one is, the easier it is to refute the theory.

The fourth through seventh statements allude to the fact that scientific theories must be disprovable. Essentially, we must not look for confirmations since we will usually find them. We must look for falsifications instead. However, many will attempt to protect their theories from being disproven or attempt to rescue a theory from being disproven. These attempts do not constitute science. The critical research consumer should attempt to determine whether the theory described can be tested and disproven. If a theory cannot be tested or disproven, it does not fall under the category of a scientific one.

Good Versus Bad Scientific Theories

Thomas (1996) discusses how to determine a good theory from a bad one. He describes 14 different standards with which to compare theories in child development. Table 1.1 summarizes each of these standards from Thomas (pp. 17–26). The importance of these standards is that a critical research consumer can use them to make a determination of the utility of the theory. Essentially, all theories that impact education, such as those proposed by Skinner, Piaget, Vygotsky, Freud, Goodman, Goodlad, Gardner, and Rogers, can be assessed in terms of their utility by considering these standards.

Testability of a Theory

The ability of a scientific theory to be tested is the most important criterion to be met (Schlinger, 1995). The requirement for a theory being testable is, like other areas of philosophy, one that can be interpreted in a number of ways. For example, can a person's intelligence be tested directly? Some researchers would say that intelligence is a theoretical construct used to explain how people behave in different contexts. Others see intelligence as something that is real but cannot be directly measured. However, intelligence can be indirectly measured through intelligence

TABLE 1.1 Standards to Determine if a Theory is Good or Bad

A THEORY IS BETTER IF IT:	
Standard 1.	accurately reflects the facts of the real world.
Standard 2.	is stated in a way that makes it clearly understandable to anyone who is reasonably competent (i.e., *anyone who has an adequate command of language, mathematics, and logical analysis*).
Standard 3.	not only explains why past events occurred but also accurately predicts future events.
Standard 4.	offers practical guidance in solving daily problems.
Standard 5.	is internally consistent (i.e., *all of the parts fit together logically*).
Standard 6.	is founded on as few unproven assumptions as possible and requiring the simplest possible mechanisms to explain all the phenomena it encompasses.
Standard 7.	*can be disproven.*
Standard 8.	the evidence supporting it is convincing.
Standard 9.	is able to accommodate new data.
Standard 10.	provides a *novel* or original view of the phenomenon.
Standard 11.	offers reasonable answers to questions about all *educational* phenomena.
Standard 12.	stimulates the creation of new research techniques and the discovery of new knowledge.
Standard 13.	continues to attract attention and enlist adherents over an extended period of time.
Standard 14.	explains *the phenomenon in a manner that fits with one's way of viewing the world (e.g., behaviorally, cognitively, humanistically).*

Note: The *italicized* words are modifications of Thomas (1996).

tests. The responses to questions on intelligence tests are measures that allow for the testing of intelligence. What about long-term memory? A theory for long-term memory may not be testable according to some researchers since long-term memory is a term for being able to remember something at a given point in time. Others see long-term memory as something that exists and can store information for later recall. However, can we test long-term memory directly? At the present time, we may lack the physiological measurement instruments to allow for directly testing long-term memory. However, we may be able to test what the long-term memory is able to do indirectly. At issue, then, is the thing that is being tested. With a theory of long-term memory, we must be testing long-term memory. Others may argue that long-term memory is not being tested, only responses to certain environmental events at a later time. Thus, there is a lack of agreement as to what constitutes the testing of a theory. Ultimately, it is left up to the critical research consumer to determine if the theory was tested.

WHAT ARE THE TYPES OF SCIENTIFIC LOGIC?

Simply, scientific theories are constructed one of two ways depending on the scientific logic one uses. First, they are constructed after a large number of investigations are conducted that allow researchers to develop a theory based on past research results. Second, theories are constructed and then used to predict what will occur in following investigations. In other words, theories may be conducted after data have been collected (induction) or before data are collected (deduction). Thus, scientific logic takes two basic forms—induction and deduction. There are also combinations of the logic forms, and these constitute how most theories are constructed.

Inductive Logic

Inductive logic involves moving from the specific to the general. For example, every student who has taken this class has learned how to think critically about research; therefore, all students in future classes will also learn how to think critically about research. Inductive logic is used in the formulation of theories. These theories are developed after supporting research data are collected in a systematic fashion. For example, some researchers see the scientific method as consisting of three steps (Kitchener, 1983). The first step involves the collection of data. Data that are to be collected are based on observable events. The second step involves the formation of scientific regularities. Scientific regularities lead to the development of generalizations and laws. For example, Thorndike's Law of Effect involved the collection of observable data across a large range of organisms and finding consistencies. The Law of Effect states that the effects of our actions will determine if the actions will be repeated. Third, theories are formulated that are collections of earlier laws and include data previously collected. Several investigations are required that lead to the demonstration of scientific regularities, which then lead to the development of a theory. Thus, the development of a theory takes a great deal of time to develop. The critical aspect of inductive logic is that theories are grounded in the data, and investigations are not guided by a theory.

Inductive logic has the advantage of grounding the theory in data. Once a theory is constructed, it will have a great deal of empirical support. Proponents of inductive logic also argue that it allows for research to be conducted that is not theory-laden. In other words, there are no hypotheses that the researcher is attempting to disprove. There are only research questions that allow the researcher to move in a number of directions due to a lack of constraint by hypotheses. Johnston and Pennypacker (1980) stated the following:

> *We have already alluded to the fact that the inductive strategy forces the accumulation of facts and that this activity is essential to any empirical approach to understanding. Moreover, induction stimulates a relatively thorough search for similarities among facts or phenomena that initially are very different. The discovery of a unifying principle*

> *underlying a set of diverse observations is always a major event in science, for it has the effect of systematizing large amounts of information. Showing that any two events are different (given that one indulges in sufficiently sensitive observation) is relatively easy, but identifying the dimension along which they are similar and illustrative of a common, lawful process is quite another matter. Achievements of that order require demonstrating orderly, repeatable, usually functional relations and a powerful induction, such as Darwin's proposal that the unifying principles of diversity and selection account for the observed morphological disparities among species. (p. 30)*

Therefore, we see that inductive logic is an important aspect of the scientific method. Being able to demonstrate lawful relations is a critical aspect of a science of human learning.

Although inductive logic sounds "logical," not everyone agrees with inductive logic. For example, in 1977, Suppe stated that "the importance of induction and confirmation is coming to be sharply downgraded in contemporary philosophical thinking about the scientific enterprise and the knowledge it provides" (cited in Caldwell, 1994, pp. 36–37). Among the arguments brought against induction are the following: (a) the future will not likely be exactly like the past, (b) a limited number of tests or observations will not provide enough evidence that a universal theory is true, and (c) there is no justification for inductive inferences (i.e., making generalized statements based on limited data). The first concern, for many researchers, is that the assumption that human learning is consistent and orderly is not likely true. There is a great deal of variation between and among individuals. The second concern involves the amount of evidence needed to develop a theory. In essence, there will never be enough evidence to show that a theory is true. Thus, when do we move from collecting data to constructing a theory? The final concern is that that there is no real justification for induction since induction cannot be shown to be correct on logical grounds nor on the basis of the success it has shown (Feigl, 1934/1996).

Deductive Logic

Deductive logic moves from the general to the specific. For example, all students who take this class become proficient critical research consumers; this student took the class, therefore this student is a proficient critical research consumer. Deduction in research essentially involves the construction of a theory containing a set of postulates (i.e., assumptions), making predictions or hypotheses based on the theory, and then the testing of parts of the theory to determine if the results of the testings uphold the theory. If the results of an investigation do not support the theory, the theory may need to be either discarded or modified when taking into consideration the results. As stated by Johnston and Pennypacker (1980):

> *To the extent that experimental outcomes verify the predictions, confidence in the validity of the postulate set is augmented. If the experimental results fail to support the prediction, and the prediction is a logically valid consequence of the postulates, then one or more of the postulates have been falsified.... The appropriate strategy under these circumstances is to revise the postulate set until the obtained results could have been predicted, and then to confirm the new prediction by experimental replication. (pp. 30–31)*

Therefore, the difference between inductive and deductive logic is that the theory is developed last in inductive logic and first with deductive logic. The assumption is that with inductive logic, the theory is correct or valid due to the empirical evidence built up before the theory construction. With deductive logic, the assumption is that the theory is valid, or confidence in the validity of the theory is increased, due to the data collected that support the theory or were predicted by the theory.

The primary advantage of deductive logic according to its proponents is that deductive logic has explanatory power. A major purpose of science is to explain phenomena. Theory development helps with the development of explaining why or how something occurs. Deductive logic also enables researchers to provide evidence that can increase the confidence in a theory. If, upon successive testings, the theory is not refuted, the confidence in that theory is heightened. Deductive logic also allows the researcher to make predictions based on the existing theory of what should be observed in the future, guiding the researcher in making and testing constructs or ideas. Finally, deductive logic allows for the production of hypotheses, which is a critical part of scientific inquiry. In educational and psychological research, the majority of research relies on the development of hypotheses.

Although deductive logic has several advantages, several limitations are also noted by critics. First, deductive logic essentially "locks" a researcher into testing certain constructs or ideas. For example, a researcher may in general be interested in testing the statement, "When less teacher-directed structure is implemented in a classroom setting, more in-depth learning will result." Unfortunately, if more in-depth learning does not result, little note is taken as to what occurred instead (Johnston & Pennypacker, 1980). Inductive logic, on the other hand, requires asking questions rather than making deductive statements. Rather than making a prediction of what will occur when discovery learning is implemented, an inductionist would ask, "What is the relation between teacher directedness and learning?"

Second, a deductive approach to science cannot be conducted by itself. Deductive conclusions are essentially elaborations on previous knowledge. Deductive logic takes what is already known and can point to new relationships among known variables but cannot be a source for new truth.

Finally, a deductive approach has the tendency to make researchers more interested in "proving" their hypotheses or predictions rather than exploring new information that was previously unknown.

Combination of Logic Forms

Induction and deduction actually do not occur in isolation, but some combination does occur (Johnston & Pennypacker, 1980). Johnston and Pennypacker called this combination a fusion of induction and deduction, and Graziano and Raulin (1993) call the combination a functional theory. Science essentially involves the combination of the two and does not advance using a single strategy of logic (Johnston & Pennypacker, 1980). Think of it this way. When one engages in deductive logic, the source of the original formulation of the theory comes from induction. In other words, the researcher must build on something when formulating the theory. This something involves the experiences and prior knowledge about the phenomenon under consideration. Once the theory is constructed, the researcher can make hypothesis statements or predictions about expected results in future investigations of the phenomenon. This hypothesis testing is deductive. However, when we are attempting to affirm the original hypothesis, we verify that in-depth learning did occur. Once we determine that in-depth learning occurred, we then engage again in induction by concluding that teacher-directed instruction is critical for more in-depth learning to result. As stated by Johnston and Pennypacker:

> *If the hypothesis (A) is true, then a certain result (B) will be observed (deduction). Upon investigation, B is indeed observed. It is therefore concluded that A is true (induction). From the standpoint of formal deductive logic, such reasoning is clearly faulty—so faulty, in fact that it is referred to by logicians as the* Fallacy of Affirming the Consequent. *From the standpoint of inductive reasoning, however, no fallacy exists, since the (probable) truth of the antecedent, A, can be established* only *by observation of the consequent, B. (p. 32)*

Johnston and Pennypacker bring up an important point. Whenever we test a hypothesis, the research findings will always be used to make conclusions of the theory. These conclusions are arrived at through the process of induction.

Affirming the consequent, however, is a difficult area. A number of paradoxes and problems have been demonstrated over the years, such as the paradox of the raven by Carl Hempel and the Goodman paradox (Caldwell, 1994). A discussion of the problems and paradoxes of confirming theories is beyond the scope of this book; however, suffice it to say that not all agree with the use of induction since it requires regularities observed today to be projected into the future. A consensus on either side of the debate will most likely never occur. Therefore, the main concern for the critical research consumer is probably less on what type of logic a researcher uses and more on what the research was attempting to do. If a researcher sets out to "prove" a theory and finds supporting evidence for the theory, the critical research consumer should be cautious. It is not difficult to find support for one's theory; it is much more difficult to show how incremental findings add to the confidence in the theory, or to show that upon many serious attempts, falsification of the theory has not been achieved. In other words, before a critical research consumer accepts the validity of claims about a theory, large amounts, not isolated bits, of data must be taken into consideration.

IN WHAT WAYS DO WE GAIN INFORMATION?

Try to answer the following question: "You are teaching fourth-grade students and an administrator approaches you and asks, 'Are your students learning?' You answer the question with a *yes*. From where will you get your information?" We are asked questions all the time about many topics such as, Will the economy get better or worse in the next 5 years? What are the best methods to teach reading or math? What is the possibility of life on Mars? Do we have a good relationship with our family? and What is the effectiveness of the death penalty in deterring violent crimes? We usually answer these questions readily and in some instances automatically. But where does the information come from that allows us to answer these questions? And, are the sources of this information valid? Finally, depending on the sources of information you use, how sure are you that your answers are correct?

We all use various sources of information at different points in time usually without actually being aware of these sources. The sources of information come at us and most of us readily accept the information or do away with the information without much thought. Whether we accept the information we receive or not depends on our experiences throughout our lives including our educational, familial, religious, and social backgrounds. To be a critical research consumer entails questioning sources of information that we once accepted and accepting information from sources we once refused to consider. In a sense, we will be providing experiences throughout this textbook that will change how you gain information and what you do with the information once it is in your possession. To this end, there are five ways of obtaining information we must consider—tenacity, intuition, authority, empiricism, and rationalism.

Tenacity

The first way we acquire knowledge is through tenacity. Tenacity is the persistence of a certain belief or way of thought for a long period of time. We essentially accept the information as being correct since, if it were not correct, it would not have lasted such a long time. For example, we may ask people about what they consider to be the best method of child discipline. Many people would indicate that it is preferable to spank children when they behave poorly. Most of us believe in this method of child discipline because it has been around for as long as we can remember. Arguments such as "I was spanked, my parents were spanked, and my grandparents were spanked, and we all turned out okay" are used to defend the practice. Spanking may be the most effective disciplinary method devised, but do we really know this from tenacity? The answer is "no." Just because beliefs have been around for a long time do not make them correct. Recall that the belief that individuals from African decent were inferior in intellect persisted for centuries, even among some people today. Just because the belief was held by many for so long does not make the information correct, any more so than the belief that Germans were a superior race a half century ago. These beliefs are not supported by scientific data, although some will still claim that there is scientific support for the superiority of one race over another in terms of intellect (e.g., Herrnstein & Murray, 1994). At some point, research will either support or refute long-held beliefs. However, long-held beliefs tend to be resistant to contrary evidence. Tenacity is not considered a source of scientific information. Tenacity can aid us in asking research questions, such as "What is the best way of disciplining children?" It is not an adequate source of confirming or refuting information.

Intuition

The second way we acquire knowledge is through so called intuition. Intuition is a "feeling" one gets about a topic. For example, suppose we are exposed to two options in teaching a child how to spell. One method is through teaching about morphographs (i.e., the smallest unit of language that carries meaning) and the other is a sight-word-only method. We look at both methods and have a feeling that the sight-word method would be more successful because it seems easier to teach. We made our decision based on our intuition in this case. Intuition most likely comes from our past and current experiences rather than some form of extrasensory perception. We may have been taught via the sight-word method or had more familiarity with it. Thus, our decisions based on intuition are supported by previous information on the same or similar topics.

Some curriculum developers have indicated to us that intuition is the most important source of information. One writer in particular indicated that curricula she writes do not need to be field-tested to assess their effectiveness since she just knows it will work. However, if intuition is based on past experiences, our intuition may not be altogether accurate since accuracy depends on the occurrence of past information. Possibly more problematic with intuition is that its accuracy is usually not assessed in any meaningful manner. Therefore, there is a lack of feedback regarding the accuracy of our intuition. If we do not get feedback, there is no way to adjust our intuition. In other words, if our intuition is based on faulty information from the past, our intuition will always be based on this faulty information unless we have feedback to let us know the information is incorrect. If this feedback does not occur, our intuition will continue to be incorrect. Intuition is not a way to obtain scientific information. As with tenacity, intuition can help us raise research questions, but it is not a way of confirming or refuting information.

Authority

One of the skills college students should develop is critical thinking. Critical thinking means taking into consideration all available information and making an informed decision about a topic. Unfortunately, college educators may be faced with a dilemma. On one hand, it would be wonderful if students developed critical thinking skills. On the other hand, the development of critical thinking skills may mean that information provided by the educator is challenged by the student. If we want students to accept everything we tell them, students will be relying on authority for information. Authority is the third method of acquiring information.

For example, students are frequently confused about the best way to teach reading to elementary-aged children. Unfortunately, the debate has created an "us versus them" mentality. Some college faculty may tell students to use a whole-language or literature-based approach to reading. Other faculty tell students to use a systematic approach that emphasizes teaching phonics first. Students come away unclear and wonder who is correct. Many students align themselves with the faculty they like the best. Thus, information that is accepted is based on the person or persons providing the information. But what are the pitfalls with acquiring information through authority? First, many authorities may simply be wrong in the information they are providing. Second, authorities provide information based on their particular biases. Therefore, the information is rarely objective. Third, even if the information provided by an authority is correct, you would have to rely on that authority or other authorities to tell you so. Critical research consumers may rely on authority but also attempt to search out confirming evidence. Again, as with tenacity and intuition, authority requires an active attempt on the part of the critical research consumer to gather supporting or refuting evidence of the obtained information. Authority is a source for developing research questions, but it cannot provide us with information to help confirm or refute a scientific theory.

Empiricism

The three aforementioned ways of acquiring information all have the same weakness; that is, they do not require a level of rigor that is needed in scientific inquiry. This level of rigor is what separates science from other endeavors; science requires a level of evidence that is not required in every day life. The fourth source of information is one that we all use in our lives but most likely not to the extent and systematic manner in which a scientist uses it. This source is called empiricism. Empiricism is querying knowledge through the observation of our world. It is the information we gain from our senses. If we say that a student of ours is sad, we most likely made an inference of an emotional state based on what we observed such as a frown. If we wished to test the effectiveness of a reading program, we would observe how well students read before and after the program. Empiricism, then, is the foundation on which science functions. Instead of relying on what has been around for a long time, what we feel to be correct, and what others tell us, we actually go out and see for ourselves. It is like saying, "Show me that it works."

Empiricism must meet a higher level of rigor than the previous three ways of obtaining information simply because it is public. Others must observe the same phenomenon before we can come to any acceptable conclusions in regard to our research results. However, empiricism is not infallible. Mistakes can be, and often are, made. Observations require some repeatability over a period of time. In other words, if we observe something as occurring only once, we cannot be sure that there is a real phenomenon taking place unless we see it again. If we observe something only once and make conclusions based on some isolated incident, we run the risk of making incorrect conclusions since an isolated incident does not provide enough evidence to allow us to make correct or adequate conclusions.

Rationalism

Rationalism is interpreting or understanding the world around us through our reasoning processes. An example of this is the process of deductive logic described earlier. We first begin with a general statement such as, All students who read this book will learn how to think critically about research. Then, we have a second statement such as, This student just finished reading the book. Finally, we make a logical conclusion based on our previous statements such as, This student has learned how to think critically about research. Unfortunately, we cannot know from rationalism alone if the statement is true. For instance, in the example about reading the textbook on research, we will not actually know if every student who reads the book will be able to think critically about research. We must make some type of assessment to determine whether indeed every student who did read the book learned how to think critically about research. Thus, what is needed is the addition of rationalism to empiricism. Thus, when we add the two together, we have a method of gathering information in a scientific context.

Rationalism and empiricism can be used together in three ways. First, we can use deductive reasoning in which we first make a general statement, then make observations, and finally conclude whether the general statement was supported. Thus, rationalism was used in making the general statement, empiricism was used in making the observations, and rationalism was again used in making the conclusion.

Second, we can use the combination of rationalism and empiricism when we are engaged in inductive reasoning in which we make observations and then develop general statements about the phenomenon. In this case, we first used empiricism when making the observations, and then we used rationalism when taking the research findings into consideration, to make general statements about the phenomenon.

Third, we can use the combination of the two when we fuse induction with deduction. First we make observations, then we develop general statements based on these observations, and then we continue to make observations to test the accuracy of the general statements. Empiricism was used to make the initial observations, rationalism was used to make general conclusions about the phenomenon, empiricism was used to make further observations of the phenomenon, and finally rationalism was used to determine whether the observations supported the general statements.

WHAT ARE CONSTRAINT LEVELS IN EDUCATIONAL AND PSYCHOLOGICAL RESEARCH?

One potentially confusing aspect of scientific research is the methods used to gain information using empiricism. All research methods are not created equal, and as will be shown throughout the text, all research methods do not address the same questions or serve the same purposes. A major difference between or among research methods is the level of constraint placed on the participant and/or setting. Level of constraint is "the degree to which the researcher imposes limits or controls on any part of the research process" (Graziano & Raulin, 1993, p. 44). The level of constraint in research does not make a particular research method good or bad. The questions asked by the researcher or the purpose of the research should determine the level of constraints placed on the participants. For example, if we wanted to determine if "X" (the independent variable) caused "Y" (the dependent variable), we would need to use high constraint research since we are attempting to determine the effects of one variable on another excluding the effects of other variables on the dependent variable. (*Note:* Cause can mean one thing resulted due to something else; cause can also mean that there is a functional relationship between variables such as when "X" occurs, it is reliably followed by "Y.") For example, suppose we wanted to determine whether the arrangement of a classroom (independent variable) affected the on-task time (dependent variable) of students. We would need some way to remove or at least control for the effects of other variables such as the type of task the students were engaged in, the way the teacher presented the task, or the level of distractions in the hallway. In other words, this research would have a high level of constraint.

If we used a research method that did not control for these other variables, we would have a difficult time determining the effects of the classroom arrangement on student behavior independent of everything else. On the other hand, if we wished to measure how students felt when engaged in a classroom activity, we could use a lower constraint type of research.

The advantage of high constraint research is that it allows us to make cause-and-effect determinations. The main disadvantage is that high constraints make the context artificial. Thus, to say variable "X" causes "Y" is not to say that variable "X" will cause "Y" in a different or normal situation. The ability to generalize the results of high constraint research to other contexts is limited. Low constraint research can tell us what will happen in a normal or seminormal context. We can say that in this situation, this happened or that happened. However, we cannot say that variable "X" will cause "Y" in that or any other context. Thus, there are trade-offs in research. If you want to know what occurs in a participant's life, you could use low constraint research. If you want to know what causes the participant to do what she does, you could use high constraint research.

A description of the constraint levels in educational and psychological research follows. Generally, there are five levels of constraint—experimental, causal-comparative, correlational, case study, and naturalistic or descriptive research (see Figure 1.1 for a continuum of constraint levels). We will consider each of these constraint levels in turn, moving from the highest constraint level research to the lowest. Additionally, each of the five constraint levels will be described in more detail throughout the text.

Experimental Research

Experimental research methods are quantitative in nature. The designs typically require a number of participants placed into one or several groups. Thus, these designs can also be called *group designs.* Experimental methods are considered the highest level of constraint research due to the attempt to isolate the causal variable. In order to do this, the impact of all other variables outside of the investigation must be kept to a minimum so the researcher can determine whether the independent variable caused the changes in a participant's behavior and not some other uncontrolled variable. Thus, an investigation with the highest level of constraint would be one that is conducted in a laboratory setting. In this type of setting, sights, sounds, smells, etc., can be controlled, thus ensuring that as many outside variables as possible are eliminated. As investigations move from artificial settings such as laboratories to more natural settings such as classrooms, the constraint level decreases due to an inability to control for many of the variables outside of the investigation that could impact the participant. Therefore, there is a continuum of constraint levels within experimental research methods.

Although experimental research methods differ in terms of their respective level of constraint, they all have several things in common. First, experimental research methods involve attempting to gather information in an objective manner. Second, experimental researchers most likely come

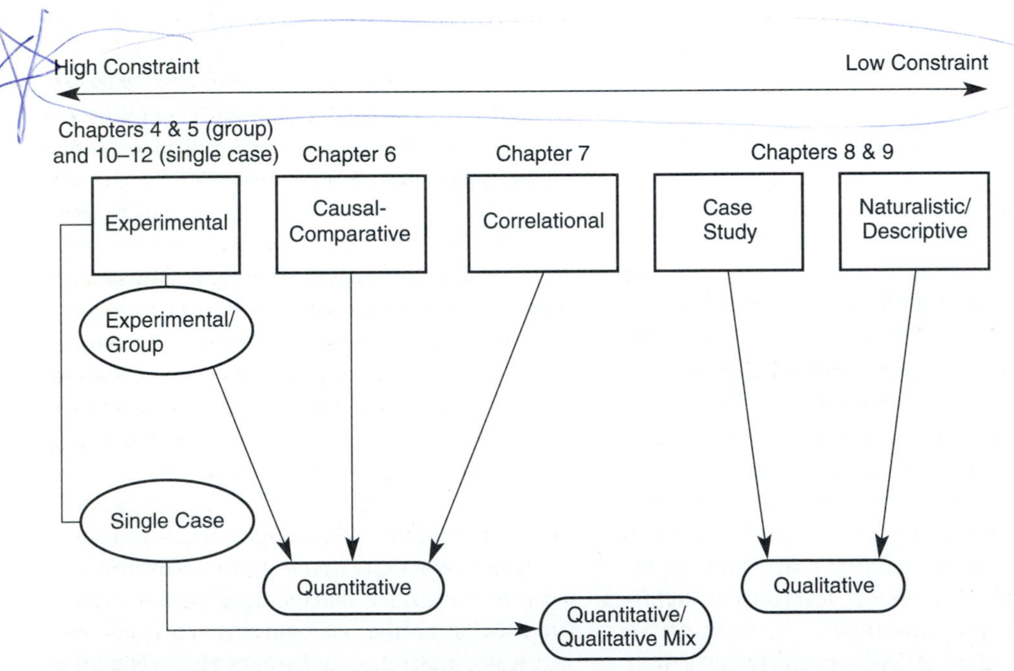

FIGURE 1.1 Continuum of constraint levels for different research methods.
(*Note:* The categories of quantitative and qualitative methods are meant to be for general guidance only since case study and naturalistic and descriptive research methods can also fall under the category of quantitative research depending on how the data are collected and analyzed.)

from a scientific-rational perspective. Finally, the method of gathering data is strictly prescribed. The researcher attempts to remain as separate from the participants as possible, only interacting with the participants when it is absolutely necessary. The data that are gathered are operationally defined. In other words, the dependent variable (what is being measured) is defined in an observable manner. Numbers are attached to those observations such as the percentage of math questions answered correctly or the score achieved on a standardized test.

Researchers using experimental methods usually believe that the results of an investigation can be generalized to a larger number of individuals. Thus, they see that there is variability between and within each individual but assume that as a whole, the group, culture, or population is relatively consistent. Experimental researchers typically deal with variability among individuals by gaining an average score for the group. The average score is then used to make conclusions. The goal of many experimental researchers is to find general laws that will hold true for large numbers of people. Thus, the attempt is to gather a sample of participants for an investigation that is representative of the entire population or some target population. (*Note:* Sampling methods will be discussed in Chapter 4.)

Experimental Methods. A major feature of much of experimental or group research is the attempt to find cause-and-effect relationships. In order to do this, researchers will manipulate the independent variable. Recall that an independent variable is the variable that has an effect on the dependent variable. For example, a computer tutorial used in your class can be considered an independent variable and the knowledge the students gain is the dependent variable. Experimental researchers may provide the computer tutorial to your class and not to another and make comparisons on a test at the end of some specified period of time. Thus, the assumption is that the researcher can determine whether the independent variable (i.e., computer tutorial) caused changes in the dependent variable (i.e., knowledge gained). There are several different experimental research designs. Chapter 5 discusses these experimental designs.

Single-Case Methods. Although some professionals may see experimental research as requiring random assignment of participants (e.g., each participant selected for a sample has an equal chance of being assigned to experimental and control groups), experimental designs really do not have to include this. Experimental designs are experimental because they are designed to control for variables outside of the experiment. That is, experimental designs attempt to find cause-and-effect relationships. Single-case designs do just this. Although experimental designs are typically quantitative, single-case designs may be thought of as a combination of quantitative and qualitative designs (see Chapters 10 to 12). Single-case designs rely on the intensive investigation of a single individual or a group of individuals. They develop as the study progresses. Single-case methods rely on objective rather than subjective data collection methods, and the experimenter does not attempt to interact with the participants in a manner that would affect their performance. Finally, the data collected are quantified and are based on direct observation of the subject matter.

Single-case researchers conduct single-case research for many reasons. These reasons fall into two general categories—limitations of group research and the research question under investigation. First, many single-case researchers consider group designs to have ethical problems (because one group of participants does not get an intervention), practical problems (it is difficult if not impossible to randomly assign students in a classroom to two groups or to obtain a large enough sample of students), averaging of results (loss of information on the outcomes for individual participants), generality of findings (it is difficult to generalize results to individual students with particular characteristics), and intersubject variability (some participants improve whereas others deteriorate) (Barlow & Hersen, 1984).

Second, single-case researchers view the variability seen in individuals as being important from a scientific viewpoint. That is, single-case researchers assume that much of the variability seen within participants is due to environmental or contextual circumstances. Single-case designs will be presented in Chapters 10 through 12.

Causal-Comparative Research

Causal-comparative research looks very similar to experimental research (i.e., group research) with two main differences. First, participants are not randomly assigned to one of at least two groups. Second, the independent variable is not manipulated. Causal-comparative research is conducted for one of two reasons—(1) if the independent variable of interest cannot be manipulated such as comparing an instructional technique for students with and without Down syndrome (independent variable), since it is not possible to make someone have Down syndrome; or (2) when it would be unethical to manipulate the independent variable such as the effects on students who receive proper and improper nutrition (independent variable) since it would not be appropriate to place a student on a poor diet to see what happens. With causal-comparative research, the main independent variable is called a classification, subject, or organismic variable since it is something that resides within the individual or is due to some characteristic the individual possesses (e.g., ethnicity, disability, gender). Thus, participants are already assigned to a group due to some innate characteristic. Independent variables may be presented such as instruction, but the comparisons are based on the nonmanipulated independent variable (e.g., how individuals with and without Down syndrome respond to the same instruction). The main function of causal-comparative research is to determine relationships between or among variables. Causal-comparative research will be discussed further in Chapter 6.

Causal-comparative research is considered to have a lower constraint level than experimental research because no attempt is made to isolate the effects of a manipulable independent variable on the dependent variable. Thus, the level of control or the ability to determine the effects of an independent variable is more limited than for experimental research.

Correlational Research

Correlational research has the same goal as causal-comparative research in that relationships between or among variables are sought. There is no manipulation of an independent variable. Unlike causal-comparative research, there is usually just one group, or at least groups are not compared. For this reason, correlational research has a lower constraint level than causal-comparative research. There is not an active attempt to determine the effects of the independent variable in any direct way.

With correlational research, measurements are taken in a single group of two variables such as grades and Scholastic Aptitude Test scores. One of the variables is called the independent variable and the other the dependent variable, although the distinction many times is not critical. Correlational research is discussed further in Chapter 7.

Case Study Research

Case study research may be considered to be qualitative in nature since the effort is to study a single participant or group of participants in depth. Qualitative researchers do not believe that everything to be studied can be operationally defined to permit observation. Therefore, it is critical to get to know the context in which the individuals interact and to become acquainted with the individuals themselves to study them adequately. Qualitative researchers do not attempt to reduce the phenomenon under study to operational definitions that limit what can be studied. They believe that if one were to count the number of math problems correct, for example, a great deal of other information regarding the process of learning would be overlooked. Thus, in order to get a comprehensive picture of the participants, one must not be limited to specific and precise definitions of what is being observed.

Case studies are not the same as single-case research. With single-case research, there is an attempt to manipulate the independent variable. With qualitative research, an active attempt to manipulate variables is not undertaken. Case studies have a lower constraint level than correlational research since there is no attempt to determine how variables are related systematically to one another. Case studies may be conducted in more artificial settings such as a therapist's office or in the community. The most important characteristic of a case study, however, is the attempt to learn about individuals in an in-depth manner.

Naturalistic or Descriptive Research

Naturalistic or descriptive research can also be considered qualitative; however, some may argue that descriptive research can also be quantitative depending on how the data are collected (i.e., in a qualitative manner, such as through field notes [see Chapter 9], or quantitative, such as counting the number of occurrences of a particular behavior). For our purposes, we will consider descriptive research to be primarily qualitative in nature. Since descriptive research is typically conducted in the natural setting, we will use the term "naturalistic research" for the remainder of the chapter.

Qualitative research makes no attempt to determine cause-and-effect relationships. However, qualitative researchers are not always in total agreement as to what one can and cannot study with this approach. Some believe that cause-and-effect relationships can be drawn from qualitative research, and others believe that qualitative research only provides descriptions of what one observes. There may not be an attempt to generalize the findings of naturalistic research since the participants under study are observed in their context, which will not exactly match the context of other individuals. However, some qualitative researchers believe that it is possible to generalize the findings of research studies to a larger population (see Chapter 8).

Although quantitative research has defined designs, qualitative research may not have specified design types since the research design develops throughout the investigation. Thus, the definition of qualitative research is more difficult to agree upon than is quantitative research. Philosophical discussions of qualitative research methods are presented in Chapter 8.

Naturalistic research is considered to have the lowest level of the constraint since an independent variable is not defined and manipulated in any manner, and identifying a cause-and-effect relationship is not the purpose of the research. The research is conducted in the participants' natural setting; case study research may be conducted in an artificial setting that raises the amount of control over the participants' environment, thereby raising the level of constraint.

Ethnographic Research. Another type of qualitative research is ethnographic research in education. Ethnographic research involves the intense and in-depth study of a culture. Thus, ethnographic research is a type of naturalistic research that is more intense than other forms of qualitative research. A culture can be as wide as a nation or as narrow as a classroom. A key feature of ethnographic research is that a multitude of data collection methods are used to obtain as complete a picture as possible of the phenomenon under study. For example, interviews and observations may be used in combination or information may come from a variety of sources such as the teacher, researcher, student, and administrator. Several types of interview methods are available as are participant and nonparticipant observation methods. The major difficulty with ethnographic research is summarizing and interpreting the vast amounts of data that are generated. Ethnographic research has a low constraint level due to the natural setting in which it is conducted and the lack of attempt to isolate the effects of an independent variable on a dependent variable. Ethnographic research, types of observation research, and types of interview methods are presented in Chapter 9.

WHAT ARE THE DIFFERENCES BETWEEN BASIC AND APPLIED RESEARCH?

It is important to understand the difference between basic and applied research. Recall that basic research focuses on more theoretical issues as compared to applied research, which focuses on educational/psychological problems. It is especially important to understand the importance of each for educators.

Basic Research

Unfortunately, there seems to be somewhat of a movement away from valuing basic research. People in the community want to know how this research study impacts society now. However, basic research does not work this way. Basic research may not even seem to have any relevance for us at all since its primary purpose is the development of a theory. Consider early research on behavioral principles when much of the data were collected on rats in a small experimental chamber called a Skinner Box. What relevance does a rat pressing a bar to receive a piece of food have for children learning to read in the classroom? Other types of basic research may have more obvious links with the applied setting. Consider the research conducted by Gardner (1993) on multiple intelligences. Gardner proposes that there are seven intelligences and that instruction should build from the type of intelligence that a particular child may have. Similarly, Piaget's research led to a theory of human development. Initially, Piaget set out to describe the development of children. He did not set out to see the best way of facilitating student learning. However, later research by developmentalists was aimed at developing educational practices based on Piaget's theory of human development (Bybee & Sund, 1990). This later research was of the applied nature. The point of basic research is that the research is conducted to help develop a new theory or refine an existing one. The immediate relevance of the research results may not be obvious or even known for a number of years. However, basic research is critical for applied research to survive. Basic research provides the foundation for applied researchers in future endeavors.

Applied Research

Applied research is exactly what it says—it is applied. Researchers in the applied arena attempt to solve real-life problems or study phenomena that directly impact what practitioners or lay people do by using a theory that was developed through basic research. For example, in education, a phenomenon such as how to teach mathematics in a manner that is efficient and facilitates problem solving may be studied. The results of the research can have a direct impact on how we educate children in mathematics. A few years ago, two of the authors of this textbook and their colleagues began to study the best method of teaching problem solving that would result in the participants' ability to use the skill in other contexts. The participants were adults with traumatic brain injuries who were to be placed in independent or semi-independent living arrangements. The difficulty these individuals encountered was an inability to solve everyday problems that we may take for granted such as what to do when the electricity goes out. The first step was to find out what had been done in the past with regard to teaching problem solving. Next, the typical method of teaching problem solving had to be modified since the participants had limited memory abilities. A problem-solving program was developed and tested. The results of the investigation led to further investigations that would ultimately improve and refine the teaching method. The problem-solving investigations were applied. They sought to improve the lives of individuals who were having difficulties.

One of the other authors of this textbook has recently been involved in applied research on a different topic. A major problem today in schools is the level of student disruption in and out of the classroom. Thus, current research has focused on how to improve the school climate by setting up a schoolwide management system to decrease the level of disruptive behaviors. Therefore, applied research attempts to gather information on human behavior but also attempts to provide information that is immediately useful to practitioners in applied settings.

Action Research. Action research is probably the purest form of applied research. Action research involves the application of the scientific method to everyday problems in the classroom. The difference between action research and other research is that the research is conducted in real-life settings with less control than one may have in a more artificial setting, school personnel are involved directly with the implementation of the research, and there is less impact on the field as a whole than is possible with other methodologies. Think of action research as research on a micro level. Suppose that a teacher was having difficulty gaining the attention of some members of her class. An action research study would involve implementing a different instructional technique, for example, and measuring the effects. The results of the research are limited to the classroom since there is a lack of information on how the class is similar to other classes and how the students are similar to other students. This limitation does not imply that action research is less important than other research; in fact, for that teacher, action research may be more important since the findings can lead to improvement in her classroom. Action research promotes the use of the scientific method to improve the classroom environment so that teachers can find out for themselves what works and what does not work for them.

The exciting aspect of action research is that teachers and practitioners can conduct research and not only learn more about their settings and those with whom they serve, but can also help to inform other educational and psychological professionals on what was found. There are opportunities for teachers and practitioners to publish written accounts of their action research investigations. Action research, ethical research practices, and information on how to write a research report are presented in Chapter 15.

WHAT IS REPLICATION RESEARCH?

Throughout this textbook, we will discuss different research methods, how research is conducted, and for what purposes. However, you will not likely become a critical research consumer unless you understand the importance and purpose of replications. Unfortunately, many research textbooks allocate a few pages to replication and do not typically discuss its importance to science.

Reasons for Replications

Replications have been called a critical aspect in the advancement of science (Allen & Preiss, 1993; Barlow & Hersen, 1984; Lamal, 1990; Meier, 1997; Neuliep & Crandall, 1993b; Sidman, 1960). Thus, replications are necessary when investigating a phenomenon. Essentially, replicating a research study involves doing it over again. There are two primary reasons for the importance of replications—reliability and generalizability.

Reliability. Replications allow us to determine the reliability or consistency of previous findings (Barlow & Hersen, 1984). As stated by Lamal (1990), "We are, other things being equal, more persuaded by evidence that is reliable, and the best empirical test of reliability of evidence is provided by replication" (p. 32). Suppose that you were reading a study regarding the effectiveness of using manipulatives in teaching mathematics. Say there were no other studies at that time regarding the use of manipulatives. The investigators indicate that the improvement of the students was significant and that teachers should use manipulatives when teaching mathematics. What would your reaction be? If you had finished this textbook before reading the study, but did not read this section on replications, you most likely would have considered the type of design used. You would have considered how the researchers measured the dependent variable (i.e., math skills such as counting) and what the independent variable (i.e., manipulatives) was. You would have also considered whether there were possible reasons for the improvement in the math skills of the students other than the independent variable. Once you made all of these considerations, you may have concluded that the study was well conceived and designed. You may have also concluded that the study was able to show that the manipulatives had the desired effect on the math skills. Still further, you may have even concluded that the conclusions made by the researchers were valid or at least supported by the results of the study. However, would your conclusion have been correct?

In most, if not all, applied research, there are mistakes made or there are things that researchers are forced into that weaken the investigation. These weaknesses are seen by the critical research consumer and begin the questions surrounding the validity of the claims made. The concern here is whether an aspect of the investigation made the research's claim incorrect. Will you know that based on one investigation? Most likely not. Unfortunately, not everyone thinks critically about research. A great deal of money and professional respect has been lost due to people not considering the importance of replicating previous research. Consider the following passage from Rosenthal (1990).

> *On April 13, 1989, the daily newspapers and the television network news programs were filled with the theme of replication in science. The day before there had been an extraordinary symposium with an audience of 7,000 attendees of the Dallas meeting of the American Chemical Society, at which the replicability of "cold fusion" was a major topic. Professors B. Stanley Pons of the University of Utah and Martin Fleischmann of the University of Southampton reported a large excess of energy produced at room temperature from a simple electrolytic cell. There had been a number of failures to replicate this "cold fusion" effect but, by the time of this symposium, successful replications had apparently been conducted at Texas A&M and at Moscow University. (pp. 1–2)*

The news of cold fusion was exciting. Think of having as much energy as we wanted. We could generate energy essentially from a glass of water. If the results were correct, our lives would be forever changed. The state of Utah moved to help fund further research as did the federal government. But then the replication process began. Why were there successful and unsuccessful replications? If we take the scientific assumption that we can find order in natural phenomena, we would expect the original results to be reliable. But they weren't. Over the period of a few years, the general conclusion was that the researchers who discovered an excess of energy misinterpreted their readings. The excitement over cold fusion died. It looked as if money was wasted because people did not wait until successful replications were conducted.

Another reason why one should not place too much confidence in the results of one investigation is what Rosenthal (1990) called the "file drawer problem." In order to understand this problem, one should consider what articles become published. The articles that are generally published are those that are about successful research. The investigations that are not successful rarely make it into print. Also, consider the percentage of articles that are selected for publication. It may surprise some students that not all articles written by researchers are published. Some journals publish fewer than 10% of all articles submitted for publication. Therefore, the articles that are published represent a biased sample of all studies actually conducted. So the concern is that if the articles that are printed represent a biased sample, and if unsuccessful investigations are rarely published, then how is one to know if the article published represents data that are reliable? The answer is, you can't. The only way to determine the reliability of the findings of an investigation is to conduct replications. Rosenthal describes how researchers can "cope" with the problem statistically. However, the statistical method advocated by Rosenthal is beyond the scope of this text. The interested reader should read Rosenthal (1990).

We all hope that researchers are honest. It is probably safe to assume that the overwhelming majority of researchers are honest. However, as stated by Bornstein (1990), "It is clear that scientists are as likely as everyone else to use illogical—even circular—reasoning in evaluating empirical data. They distort scientific information—consciously or unconsciously—to render that information consistent with their *a priori* beliefs" (p. 71). Additionally, Lamal (1990) indicated that based on a study conducted by the America Psychological Association's Board of Scientific Affairs, "scientific fraud is more widespread than generally acknowledged" (Board of Scientific Affairs, 1984, p. 3, cited in Lamal, 1990, p. 33). Whether there is a great deal of scientific fraud seems to be a moot point since scientific fraud is difficult to detect even when there are replications of others' works. The critical point is that when replications are conducted by other researchers, and when the results support the original research, we can be more confident that scientific fraud did not occur.

Generalizability. The second general reason that replications are important is that information on the generalizability or transferability of the results of one investigation is enhanced. Chapter 2 will discuss in more detail the concern of generalizability of research results. Suffice it to say now that a single investigation, no matter how complex or how many individuals are included in it, cannot equal the weight of several investigations of the same phenomenon.

Hendrick (1990) indicates that there are eight aspects that must be considered in defining replications. Seven of these aspects are important in understanding the concern over generalizability of a study's results. The following is a discussion of each of the seven aspects.

Participant Characteristics. Researchers and critical research consumers must be aware of the participant characteristics. Suppose that you are a teacher working with children in the fourth grade. You read an investigation on the effectiveness of a curriculum aimed at improving the self-esteem of students. You are interested in using the curriculum in your class. What should you consider? The first question you must ask yourself is, "Are these participants similar to my students?" If there are differences, you should consider whether the differences are serious enough to make the curriculum ineffective for your students. Students differ in terms of age, gender, socioeconomic background, and personality characteristics. You must be aware of the differences among your students and determine whether the participants represent your students. Replications aid in this determination if multiple investigations have been conducted with students of different ages, from different socioeconomic backgrounds, and with different behavioral or personality characteristics.

Research Histories of Participants. A second concern that teachers and practitioners as critical research consumers should have involves the histories of the participants. For example, if participants were volunteers, they may be very different from your students. Participants may have also received enticements to participate such as payment, which may make them more willing to continue in the program as compared to students who are not paid. Participants may also have been involved in other investigations. This involvement is not unusual with laboratory schools associated with universities. Students involved in investigations may be fairly sophisticated in research as participants and may respond to an independent variable differently than naive students. Replications can help to decrease this concern by involving students with varying histories. If you were to see an intervention that was effective with a wide range of students with different histories, you might be more confident that the investigation's results could hold true with your students.

Historical Context. Historical context refers to the particular social-cultural settings that the participants involved in research represent. The concern is that if research is conducted with participants from the inner city, for example, will the results hold true for participants who live in the suburbs? However, historical context is not limited to the geographic setting. In fact, the geographic setting is less important than social experiences or the cultural backgrounds of the participants. For example, suppose that you worked on a Native American reservation teaching secondary-aged youth. You determine that the students must learn social skills to increase the chances they will be successful once they get out of school and/or leave the reservation. You select a social skills curriculum that was shown to be effective in developing social skills in one research investigation. The investigation contained mostly European American students from a large city. One skill taught is to establish eye contact when interacting with others. The problem here is that in some cultures, such as many Native American tribes, making eye contact with elders or persons of authority is a sign of disrespect. The social skills curriculum would have a difficult time achieving the same type of outcomes as in the research study. Replications can aid by determining the effectiveness of interventions or independent variables across many cultures or social situations.

Physical Setting of the Research. The physical setting of the research is not considered as much as the other aspects described here. Although researchers may describe the physical settings such as the size of the room and the placement of tables and chairs, there is little systematic research detailing how the physical variables of the room or setting can differentially affect the outcomes of interventions. Variables such as the amount of light in the room, the level of noise, the familiarity with the surroundings on the part of the participants, and the color of the setting may affect the interventions. In classrooms, variables such as the room arrangement and whether there are windows may differentially affect what works in the classroom. An example would be if the participants in the original investigation were in a classroom without windows. The level of distraction would be minimal. However, a teacher's concern might pertain to how windows in her classroom affect her students' classroom performance. Would the students respond to the same type of instruction the participants in the study received even when they have the added distraction of windows? Replications can help to answer this question to a certain extent if the physical surroundings of different investigations were varied.

Control Agent. We know that the characteristics of different teachers can interact with student characteristics. One student may be difficult to teach for one teacher but fairly easy for another even when both use the same instructional techniques. Consider what would happen to you if you had someone (i.e., control agent) come into a setting in which you were working to observe what you were doing. If you liked, trusted, and knew the person well, you may be relaxed. If, on the other hand, you were being observed by someone you disliked (i.e., control agent) or someone you did not know, you may act differently. Another potential difficulty is the level of skill the person involved in the research may have. Many investigations are not going to use poor teachers when attempting to determine the effectiveness of an instructional technique. Teachers or control agents may be, and often times are, very well trained and are masters at what they do. A critical research consumer should be concerned with the skill level and characteristics (such as gender) of the person actually interacting with the participants in an investigation. The question we should ask is, "Do my skills (or characteristics) match those of the persons involved in the study?" Replications involving different control agents can provide valuable information on the effectiveness of the intervention when persons with varying skills levels and characteristics are involved.

Specific Task Variables. As with several of these other aspects, the effect of different task variables is not always known. Specific task variables involve the details of the methods used in research. Variables such as the format in which information is presented (e.g., two separate pages or double-sided), the formatting of materials (e.g., font sizes and styles), and the "look" of the materials (e.g., gray cover without designs or colorful covers with appealing artwork, type of paper). Interestingly, business marketers have known for years about the importance of specific details. The manner in which items are packaged can determine the success or failure of a new product, for example. Unfortunately, educational and psychological researchers are not as sophisticated in these small details. For example, suppose that you had to select a textbook and you had two choices—one that had few or no pictures and a bland cover and another with pictures throughout and a sparkly cover. Chances are, you would be more likely to select the one that is more appealing to you (i.e., the flashy one). Participants can also be affected the same way. They may respond differently to the way materials are designed and/or presented. Successful replications that use materials that are formatted differently and are presented in a number of different ways can increase our confidence that these small details are not critical. However, if replications reveal that the participants responded differently to how the material was presented, we have information that is critical to our success.

Primary Information Focus. A final concern with generalizability is the methods by which information is transmitted to participants. This information is the independent variable. Essentially, primary information focus involves the methods in which the independent variable is implemented. For example, suppose that you are teaching a class on sexual education and wished to teach secondary students about disease prevention techniques during sexual activity. You read an article explaining how to teach about "safe sex." The results of the investigation showed that the instruction was successful in changing the students' opinions about abstinence and disease prevention techniques (i.e., they were more likely to refrain from sexual activity or, if they were going to become or stay sexually active, they stated they would be more likely to use "safe sex" techniques). The authors described the intervention, which included verbal information on the problem of teenage pregnancies and AIDS, a film showing the negative effects of sexually transmitted diseases, and class discussions. Based on the information, you decide to implement the intervention with your class. You acquire the written documents used in the study as well as the film. You implement the independent variable exactly as it was described in the investigation. The question is, "Will your students acquire the same information as the participants in the investigation?" Students will interpret the information differently based on their past and present experiences, their characteristics, the person leading the discussion, or the manner in which they are seated.

Another potential problem is that the researchers did not fully describe the independent variable, or a historical event that could have affected the independent variable was left out of the description. Details can be left out if they are considered to be unimportant or if the researchers were unaware of information such as a student in the class who had a family member with AIDS and the other participants were aware of this. In this case, the effects of the independent variable or the information received by your students may not be the same as was shown in the investigation. Replications can increase our confidence in the primary information focus if the results across investigations are consistent even though there are possible additions or deletions to or from the independent variable.

Types of Replications

Now that we know why replications should be conducted, we should learn about the different types of replications that are done. Sidman (1960) described two types of replications—direct and systematic—and Barlow and Hersen (1984) described a third—clinical.

Direct Replications. Probably the most straightforward type of replication is the direct replication (which is similar to what Hendrick [1990] called an "exact replication" and Neuliep and Crandall [1993a] called a "literal replication"). Simply stated, direct replications are investigations that conduct an experiment in the same manner as a previous experiment. The replication is also conducted by the same researcher. Obviously, one difference in the replication study and the original study is the change of participants; however, the participants in the two investigations are homogeneous (i.e., essentially alike on critical attributes such as achievement levels). All other variables remain essentially unchanged. For example, suppose that a researcher wanted to determine the effectiveness of a safety program at the elementary level. The researcher would define who the participants were, set up the assessment methods, present the independent variable, and so on. The same researcher would then do the same procedures during a second investigation with students who were similar in all important respects (e.g., age, grade level, previous safety training).

The information gained from a direct replication reflects generality across other individuals. Essentially, all that direct replications do is add to the total number of participants who have been exposed to the intervention. Thus, if the results of the replication are consistent with the original study, we gain more confidence that the same procedures will work with other individuals with the same or similar characteristics as the participants in the investigation. Therefore, the utility of direct replications is somewhat limited. In order for replications to provide us the largest amount of information possible, the replications should be independent of one another. As stated by Rosenthal (1990):

> *But what does independence mean? The usual minimum requirement for independence is that the subjects of the replications be different persons. But what about the independence of replicators? Are ten replications conducted by a single investigator as independent of one another as ten replications each of which is conducted by a different investigator? (p. 8)*

Clearly the answer is "no." Direct replications are important in that they allow us to determine whether the same results will be found under the same conditions. Unfortunately, direct replications are not independent replications in that they rely on the same researcher to conduct the investigation.

Systematic Replications. Systematic replications can be thought of as a method that extends the advantage of direct replications. Systematic replications allow for the generalization of a procedure to other individuals as does direct replications but also allow for the generalization across other situations. Thus, systematic replications are investigations that are conducted by different researchers and/or different people implementing the independent variable, involve participants with different characteristics than those in the original investigation (e.g., secondary students without disabilities versus students with disabilities), and/or are conducted in different settings (e.g., in the classroom versus in the community). For example, suppose that a researcher wanted to determine the efficacy of a problem-solving program designed for individuals with traumatic brain injuries when individuals with mild mental retardation serve as the participants. The researcher is different, but the independent and dependent variables are the same. Additionally, the participants differ on important characteristics. First of all, the participants from the two investigations do not have the same impairments. The participants may also be of different ages. We could change the example by stating that there were different teachers involved in the investigations. We could also say that different measures of the dependent variable were used (called an "operational replication" by Neuliep and Crandall [1993a]). We could use a different variation of the independent variable such as using peer tutors to present the problem-solving program instead of having a teacher present it (called an "instrumental replication" by Neuliep and Crandall [1993a] and a "conceptual replication" by Hendrick [1990]). We could also replicate the original investigation's procedures exactly with the exception of making some change in part of the procedures such as spending 5 days per week to teach children a skill rather than 2 days per week as in the original investigation to speed up the program (called a "partial replication" by Hendrick [1990]).

Systematic replications aid in the independence of investigations that Rosenthal (1990) described. Their obvious advantage over direct replications is that the generalization of the original study's results can be demonstrated across more variables than only the number of participants.

Clinical Replications. Clinical replications essentially come about as a result of direct and systematic replications. As explained by Barlow and Hersen (1984), direct and systematic replications essentially involve one independent variable, whereas clinical replications involve the combination of two or more independent variables to form an intervention package. Barlow and Hersen have also used the term *field testing* to describe the same process. For example, suppose that we wanted to study the most effective method of classroom management. Some direct replications conducted over the years have shown the effectiveness of using a procedure called "time-out" with elementary-aged children. Systematic research has also shown that time-out is effective in settings other than the classroom and with different teachers. Children from different age groups have shown improved behavior due to the procedure. Other investigations have shown that classroom structure and procedures such as rules and routines also can have a positive impact on student behavior. Investigations have been replicated with both direct and systematic approaches. If we took these independent variables and combined them (i.e., time-out and classroom structure), we would have an intervention package that teachers could use. Clinical replications, then, would be applying the intervention package to elementary-aged children.

The obvious advantage of clinical replications is that they allow a researcher to build on previous replications in a manner that is more representative of what actually occurs outside of the typical research setting. In a research setting, one independent variable may be provided to the participants. However, in real life, many things are going on that can affect the student. Thus, combining variables and assessing their combined effect more closely represents the dynamics that occur in an applied setting.

Replication as the "Big Picture"

The purpose of presenting this information on replication research early in the text is to stress the importance of looking at the "big picture." Throughout the text, issues and concerns of research investigations and types of research methods will be presented. The presentation of these issues, concerns, and methods is similar to looking at each tree in a forest. We can tell how healthy each tree is in isolation. However, if we look at only one tree, we cannot determine the overall health of the forest. The remainder of this textbook will aid you in determining the health of individual trees, but you must remember that the goal of science is to determine the overall health of the forest.

SUMMARY

There are several methods of science that guide researchers in their endeavor to describe, predict, explain, and improve the world around us. Researchers will use either inductive or deductive logic or a combination of the two when moving through the scientific method. The logic used will determine ultimately how one will approach, utilize, and explain the findings of research. Additionally, the development and testing of a scientific theory will also be affected by the type of logic one uses in research.

Unfortunately, the differences in how one views the scientific endeavor tend to create a schism among researchers. The tendency among some researchers is to ignore the research that does not fit within their particular orientation.

This tendency is not an aspect of thinking critically about research. The critical research consumer should understand the differences among researchers and appreciate those differences. One does not always have to agree with another research orientation, only have respect for it. Thinking critically involves understanding the type of logic one is using and the implications of the data generated. Critical research consumers do not reject research that does not fit within their particular orientation; they attempt to integrate results from other science orientations to be more fully informed.

The term "research" does not signify the complexity of the nature of the research endeavor. Researchers gather their information through the use of rationalism and empiricism. They attempt to stay away from other methods of gaining information such as tenacity, intuition, and authority not because these methods are inadequate, but because these methods do not call for the level of rigor that rationalism and empiricism do.

The research endeavor also requires a decision made by researchers in terms of the constraint level they wish to use based on the research question. High constraint research has the advantage of aiding in determining cause-and-effect relationships. The primary disadvantage is that high constraint research restricts our ability to generalize to others in other situations outside of an investigation. On the other hand, low constraint research allows us to see what is normally occurring in the "natural world" but does not allow us to isolate causal variables. The decision made by the researcher in terms of constraint level will determine whether the research question can be answered or not.

The research endeavor requires researchers to choose between basic or applied research. The line separating each type of research is blurred many times; however, basic research allows us to develop a theory and applied research allows us to apply a theory to everyday life such as solving an educational problem. However, it must be remembered that each research endeavor falls on a continuum between basic and applied research. Possibly, an extreme example of applied research is action research. Action research allows teachers and practitioners to become researchers themselves to solve their own problems in the classroom or to determine the most effective methods of teaching their students.

Finally, although we tend to place a great deal of emphasis on single investigations, it must be remembered that single investigations can be prone to error. If we place too much confidence in single investigations, we will frequently be wrong. Science advances and we gain confidence in the results of investigations when those results can be replicated. Replications are critical in the research endeavor.

DISCUSSION QUESTIONS

1. You hear an interesting lecture on the impact of science on education. The lecturer indicates that one reason why educators are not much affected by scientific research is that they have not developed critical thinking skills about research. Do you agree with this statement? Indicate how we can develop critical thinking skills about research.
2. A friend of yours tells you that she keeps hearing about this "scientific method" in her class on research, but she is unclear as to its meaning. Describe to your friend the steps taken in the scientific method.
3. You are watching television and hear someone say that science is a meaningless attempt to understand the world. Researchers can "prove" any scientific theory by finding evidence in support of the theory. Do you see anything wrong with this statement? Explain.
4. A student in an education course does not think much of science because, as he says, its

only purpose is to find ways to control people's minds. You respond by explaining to the student what science is and the different purposes of science. What would you say?

5. The student tells you that she is not sure of the difference between inductive and deductive logic. Describe what the terms mean and how a researcher approaches theory development and testing through each logic form, and explain how they can be combined.
6. You are reading a newspaper account about educational reform. You see the following quote from a teacher: "I know intuitively that children learn best if they are self-directed." Although the teacher may be correct with her assumption, is her method of gaining information a scientific one? Why or why not?
7. You are in a class discussing effective instructional procedures. The topic of quantitative and qualitative research arises. A student in class asked the professor to describe briefly what quantitative and qualitative research are. The professor asks for volunteers to answer the question. Of course, being the high achieving student that you are, you volunteer. How would you describe quantitative and qualitative research?
8. You're watching the news when you hear the following: "Lately, there has been some concern over using public money to support basic research. It seems as if the public would rather see applied research funded at a higher level instead." What is your conclusion about basic and applied research? In other words, what is the importance of each type of research, the purpose of each, and the ability of applied research to exist without basic research?
9. You go to an educational class and hear the professor say that she was excited about the increased use of action research. Another student in the class, knowing that you are taking a research course, asks you what the professor means by action research. What would you say?
10. A friend of yours comes to you excited about an article she read in an educational psychology class. The article described a study that demonstrated that if you teach children based on their respective learning styles (e.g., visual, tactile, auditory) you can be more effective as a teacher. Not wanting to burst the student's bubble, but also wanting to caution her about taking single studies too seriously, describe the importance of replications in a scientific endeavor. How would you explain replications to your friend?

PART TWO

CRITICAL ISSUES IN RESEARCH

CHAPTER 2 FUNDAMENTAL ISSUES FOR INTERPRETING RESEARCH

CHAPTER 3 RELIABILITY, VALIDITY, AND INTEROBSERVER AGREEMENT

CHAPTER 2

FUNDAMENTAL ISSUES FOR INTERPRETING RESEARCH

OBJECTIVES

After studying this chapter you should be able to:

1. Describe what is meant by unsystematic variance.
2. Indicate the major sources of unsystematic variance.
3. Describe what is meant by systematic variance.
4. Indicate the major sources of systematic variance.
5. Describe the term *internal validity.*
6. Explain each of the 12 possible threats to the internal validity of a study.
7. Describe the term *external validity.*
8. Describe the term *population validity.*
9. Explain each of the two types of population validity.
10. Describe the term *ecological validity.*
11. Explain each of the 10 types of ecological validity.
12. Describe what is meant by statistical and social validity and explain how they are different.

OVERVIEW

Researchers face several methodological issues when conducting research. These issues vary depending on the type of research conducted; however, we will discuss general methodological issues in this chapter and revisit them as we move through the text.

We will focus on two primary roles of individuals involved with research. The first role involves that of the researcher. Researchers' roles include developing the research question(s) they will attempt to answer and/or the research hypothesis (i.e., a test of the assumptions made by researchers), using an appropriate methodology to answer the research question and/or test the hypothesis, interpreting the results, and making conclusions based on the results of the study. Researchers attempt to use the most appropriate methodology to form their conclusions. However, some researchers will make a mistake in the selection or implementation of the methodology. Applied researchers have an additional problem. Applied research is difficult to conduct in many instances because there are some things we simply may not be able to do in applied situations that we can do in a laboratory setting (e.g., randomly assigning a classroom of students to two different instructional procedures). Therefore, many limitations to the methodology of a study are the result of the constraints placed on researchers.

The second role of individuals involved in research includes that of the critical research consumer. The critical research consumer's role includes reviewing the methodology used to determine if it was appropriate, determining if the methodology had any weaknesses, and determining if the researcher's conclusions were valid. The critical research consumer must also understand that some methodological flaws are the result of the applied environment rather than a mistake or omission made by a researcher. (This issue will be discussed throughout the text.)

The purpose of this chapter is to provide a general framework of information necessary for the chapters that follow. In doing so, this chapter will give the critical research consumer the necessary skills to think critically about various types of research methodologies and to make decisions with regard to the validity of the researchers' conclusions. Of course, the types of skills used to critique a study will depend on the methodology used; in some cases, the tools will not be appropriate for the task, and in other cases, the tools will be absolutely critical. Methodological issues faced by researchers fall into at least five general categories: variability, internal validity, external validity, statistical validity, and social validity. These five general categories will be discussed throughout this chapter.

WHAT IS VARIABILITY?

Variability is in every part of daily life. We do not always feel the same every day. Some days we are happy, and other days we are sad. Those around us also vary in the way they feel. However, variability is not restricted to the way we feel. When we play basketball, we do not shoot the ball the same way every time. When we write a paper, we do not use the same words each time nor do we even hold the pencil the same way. There is variability in every thing we do. This variability can have many different effects on research results. In some cases, we want variability to occur; in other cases, variability can have a negative effect on our research results. Thus, variability can be either friend or foe. When it is our friend, we want to encourage and support it. When it is our foe, we want to reduce or eliminate it. The methods by which researchers attempt to encourage some sources of variability or reduce other sources of variability associated with each specific design will be discussed in detail in later chapters.

Sources of Variability

There are several sources of variability in research. If researchers can learn where these sources are, they can attempt to control them. Sources of variability can be placed in two general categories—unsystematic variance and systematic variance.

Unsystematic Variance. Unsystematic variance is variability within individuals and/or groups of individuals. This variability is essentially random; some individuals change in one direction, others in another direction, and some do not change at all. For example, some individuals may feel better than they did yesterday, others feel worse than they did yesterday, and some feel the same as they did yesterday. Another example would be in taking tests. Some individuals see test improvement the next day, others see their performance decline, and still others see essentially the same test performance. When taken together, the overall result of this variance is little overall change. Most researchers would consider unsystematic variance a fact of life that cannot be totally eliminated or accounted for at this time. However, it may be possible to account for some unsystematic variance at a later time when our understanding of human behavior and our measurement systems evolve to allow for such accountability (Sidman, 1960). There are two major sources of unsystematic variance—*measurement error* and *individual differences.*

Measurement Error. Measurement error exists because a measurement device (e.g., a test, a person doing an observation) does not measure an attribute the same way every time. Measurement error occurs frequently. In fact, we could assume that all measurements have some measurement error. For example, if you weighed 150 pounds but the scale weighed you at 148 pounds, there would be measurement error on that scale of 2 pounds. In other words, the scale has an error of measurement built into it. In order for this measurement error to be considered unsystematic, the scale would weigh you at 148 pounds at one time, 153 pounds at another, and 150 pounds a third time. The sum of all your weight differences from the average weight (the sum of all weighings divided by the number of weighings) would be zero if we did an infinite number of weighings. In the end, the measurement error would be a wash, and that average would be the best estimate of your true weight.

We can never weigh ourselves an infinite number of times. Therefore, measurement error must be estimated. Measurement error is directly related to the reliability of the measurement instrument (i.e., how consistent the device measures an attribute)—the less reliable the measurement device, the larger the measurement error. Researchers are concerned with the reliability of their measurement devices since they desire to reduce their measurement error. This issue will be discussed in more detail in Chapter 3.

Individual Differences. Another source of unsystematic variance is individual differences. Most researchers assume that intrinsic factors, or factors unaccounted for, cause people to be different from one another. For example, one reason why you do well in math and a peer does not may be due to an inborn ability to achieve at math or to factors of which the researcher is unaware such as past learning histories. Therefore, some people may respond favorably to math instruction whereas others may not.

Systematic Variance. Systematic variance is variability that we can account for between or among groups of people. That is, something is occurring that makes a group of individuals move in the same direction. Some individuals may improve, some may worsen, and still others may remain approximately the same; however, on the whole, the group's performance will change. On the other hand, all individuals may move in the same direction with the amount of change differing among the individuals. Think of systematic variance as moving your hand through water. You cup your hand and push the water in a certain direction. Some water will escape and not move in the direction you wish it to move. Some water may move in the opposite direction. But on the whole, much of the water will move in the direction you desire. Using the same example, if you move your hand through a narrow trough, you may be able to move virtually all of the water. If you attempt to move water in a lake, the amount of water you move may be small. The amount of water you move on the whole depends to a large extent on the amount of control you can exert on the body of water. This occurrence is similar to what researchers attempt to do. They want to see what moves individuals in a certain direction. They understand that some individuals will not be affected as intended, but on the whole, the group will be affected. In order to have a larger effect on individuals, researchers may attempt to exert as much control over the environment of those individuals as possible.

Take the example of weighing yourself on a scale. If you were to get on the scale an infinite number of times and the scale weighed you at 148 pounds every time you stood on it, you would have an example of systematic measurement error. In order to find your actual weight you would simply add 2 pounds to the scale reading. Thus, if you were to measure a group of individuals on some attribute and were to measure them consistently lower on that attribute, you would have systematic variance. Now take two groups of individuals. If you consistently measured one group lower on an attribute and the other group higher on the attribute, you would see differences between the two groups. Unlike unsystematic variance where researchers attempt to decrease its influence, researchers attempt to increase one source of systematic variance. The difference between the two groups would be due to this type of systematic variance.

Researchers are primarily concerned with two sources of systematic variance—the *independent variable* and *extraneous variables.* The systematic variance associated with the independent variable is desirable to quantitative researchers; the systematic variance associated with extraneous variables is not desirable to quantitative researchers and an attempt is usually made to decrease the impact of extraneous variables on the dependent variable (i.e., what we are trying to impact or change).

Independent Variable. The method that quantitative researchers use to achieve systematic variance is to manipulate (e.g., present then withdraw) the independent variable or to have at least two levels or forms of the independent variable (i.e., presence and absence). Qualitative researchers do not attempt to manipulate the independent variable as do quantitative researchers but nevertheless have a concern for detecting the source(s) of systematic variance. The approach used by qualitative researchers differs from that used by quantitative researchers (Marshall & Rossman, 1995; Silverman, 1993) and will be discussed in Chapter 8.

Extraneous Variables. A second source of systematic variance is from factors that are not designed (i.e., unplanned) to be in a study. Researchers frequently refer to these extraneous variables as threats to internal validity.

WHAT IS INTERNAL VALIDITY?

Internal validity indicates that we are confident that there was a functional relationship (i.e., a change in the dependent variable was associated or correlated with the implementation of the independent variable) between the independent variable and the dependent variable. Internal validity simply addresses the question, "Did the individual change as a result of what I did/observed, or was the change due to something else?" Extraneous variables, like independent variables, may affect individuals in a similar manner.

The effects of extraneous variables on the dependent variable are a major concern of researchers and constitute threats to the internal validity of a study. One purpose of the research design chosen in a study is to control for these extraneous variables. Thus, it is important for critical research consumers to determine if threats to the internal validity of the study are present, and if they are, what their affect on the results of the study may be. Think of the critical research consumer's role as one of a detective. The critical research consumer's job is to find what else may have accounted for the results. It is important to realize that few research studies have no threats to internal validity; thus, the critical research consumer must assess the results of a study and the conclusions made by the researcher based on those results since those conclusions may be faulty. The critical research consumer must weigh these factors before drawing any conclusions about the significance or importance of the study.

There are several possible threats to the internal validity of a study (see Campbell & Stanley, 1963; Cook & Campbell, 1979). These threats are shown in Table 2.1 and can be separated into two categories: (a) threats that result in differences within or between individuals (i.e., maturation, selection, selection by maturation interaction, statistical regression, mortality, instrumentation, testing, history, and resentful demoralization of the control group), and (b) threats that result in similarities within and between individuals (i.e., diffusion of treatment, compensatory rivalry by the control group, and compensatory equalization of treatments). Each threat will be described in detail with examples and nonexamples and their effects on a study.

Maturation

Maturation may threaten the internal validity of a study when there is a passage of time where bio-

TABLE 2.1 Threats to Internal Validity

RESULTS IN DIFFERENCES WITHIN OR BETWEEN INDIVIDUALS
Maturation—Changes in the dependent variable may be due to biological or psychological processes.
Selection—Differences between groups may be due to differential selection or assignment to groups.
Selection by Maturation Interaction—Similar to selection, but the main focus is the maturation of the participants.
Statistical Regression—Changes in the dependent variable may be due to the movement of an attribute to the mean of that attribute.
Mortality—Differences between groups may be due to a differential loss of participants.
Instrumentation—Changes in the dependent variable may be due to changes in how the dependent variable is measured.
Testing—Changes in the dependent variable may be due to the effect of the first testing on the second.
History—Changes in the dependent variable may be due to events other than the independent variable that occur between the first and second measurement or during the application of the independent variable.
Resentful Demoralization of the Control Group—Differences between groups may be inflated due to a lack of effort on the part of the control group.
RESULTS IN SIMILARITIES WITHIN OR BETWEEN INDIVIDUALS
Diffusion of Treatment—Differences between or within groups may be decreased due to unintended exposure to the independent variable.
Compensatory Rivalry by the Control Group—Differences between groups may be decreased due to increased effort on the part of the control group to keep pace with the experimental group.
Compensatory Equalization of Treatments—Differences between groups may be decreased due to unintended compensation of the control group for not receiving the independent variable.

logical or psychological changes take place. For example, suppose we wanted to improve the motor abilities of a group of 4-year-old children with physical limitations through a technique called patterning. Patterning involves using exercises to help individuals relearn each stage of motor learning. We gave a pretest to measure the children's motor abilities and compared these results to a posttest measurement taken 2 years after the application of the pretest. The findings indicate that the motor abilities of the children improved markedly. It would be difficult to claim that the improvement was due *only* to the patterning; it may have been affected by the natural maturation of the children due to the time lapse between the pretest and posttest assessment.

Maturation may also be a threat depending on the time at which measures were taken. For example, if we were to take measures early in the morning and again in the afternoon, we may see changes in the individuals' responses simply due to the passage of time. Likewise, if we took measures prior to lunch and then after lunch, we may see that changes had taken place. Maturation is always a concern when we see that measures were taken at different times for two different groups. Say we wanted to test the effectiveness of a new curriculum. The difference between two groups of students in fourth grade was measured. One group received the new curriculum and the other received the standard curriculum. We noticed that the group who received the new curriculum outperformed the group who received the standard curriculum. However, the time the measurement was applied must be taken into account. The measurement was given to the students who received the standard curriculum just before they left for home and was given to the students who received the new curriculum the next morning. Therefore, we made the conclusion that at least some of those observed differences may have been because students are usually tired at the end of the day as compared to when they arrive at school in the morning.

A nonexample of this threat can be illustrated by the following. Suppose we wanted to determine if the types of instructions (i.e., phrased as questions versus directives) provided to children with a high level of noncompliance affect the probability of following directions. Students were provided with instructions in the form of questions (e.g., "Can you put the book on the shelf?") the same time each morning. Then, after some period of time had elapsed, the form of instructions changed to directives (e.g., "Please put the book on the shelf"). These instructions were presented at the same time each morning as before. The time of measurement of compliance was important since the passage of time (i.e., morning versus afternoon) could have differentially affected the probability of following instructions. Thus, maturation is not a threat in this example since the time at which instruction was provided was the same before and after the implementation of the independent variable.

Selection

Selection may threaten the internal validity of a study if groups of individuals are selected in a differential manner. The key word here is *differential.* What makes groups of individuals different from one another is how they were selected in the first place. This threat is common when we select preexisting groups to be involved in an experiment and do not attempt to demonstrate how they are similar on critical variables. Even if we can demonstrate that the groups were equivalent on critical variables, we may still have a selection threat since it would be hard to imagine an instance where we would be aware of all of the critical variables that could account for group differences.

Say we wanted to compare two types of mathematics curricula. To do this, one group of individuals who received the standard curriculum was compared to individuals who received the new curriculum. Now suppose that the first group of students was in a remedial classroom for students who had difficulty in mathematics and the second group of students was in a classroom for gifted and talented children in mathematics. After the instruction was provided, we found that the second group who received the new curriculum outscored the first group. Obviously, the second group would be expected to outscore the first group because the students were initially better at mathematics. In this case, we would be unable to assess which curriculum was more effective because the groups were different from the outset.

An instance where selection would not be a threat might involve a situation where we wanted to study the effects of play therapy on the aggressive behavior of students with behavior disorders. Students were randomly assigned to two groups (see Chapter 4). The experimental group received play therapy, and the control group received the normal classroom routine. The experimental group's level of aggressive behavior was compared to that of the control group. After the play therapy intervention was finished, we found that the experimental group's level of aggressive behavior was considerably lower than the level for the control group. Selection would not be a strong threat since we assumed that the two groups were equivalent on important variables before the implementation of the independent variable. In other words, the only difference between the two groups should have been the independent variable.

Selection by Maturation Interaction

This threat to the internal validity of a study is similar to the maturation and selection threats described before; however, the main concern here is the maturation of the individuals selected for involvement in the study.

For example, say we worked with several individuals with articulation problems. Participants were assigned to two groups (i.e., experimental and control) on a nonrandom basis. The average age of the experimental group was 5 years, and the average age for the control group was 8 years. The experimental group was provided with an independent variable that was designed to improve articulation by teaching the participants how to emit specific speech sounds. The control group received group support. The articulation skills of participants in both groups were measured 1 year later; we found that the experimental group made greater gains in its articulation abilities when compared to the control group. Our conclusion that the independent variable improved the experimental participants' articulation may have been erroneous since we failed to see if the groups were initially equivalent on critical variables. They were similar to each other except on the basis of age. We would expect that younger children would make greater gains as compared to the older children simply by growing older and having more experience with language. Thus, much of the gains made may have been due to the maturation of the participants in the experimental group and not due to the independent variable.

Selection by maturation interaction would not be a threat in the following investigation. Suppose we wanted to measure the attitudes of students toward their teachers after a grading period. Two groups of students were selected and compared. The first group of students was enrolled in a discovery learning classroom, and the second group was enrolled in a skills-based classroom. The students were of the same age (12 years) and were in the same grade (7th grade). They came from similar socioeconomic backgrounds and had parents with similar educational levels. We compared the attitudes of the two groups after the grading period and detected a major difference between their attitudes. The skills-based group had more positive overall attitudes of its educational experiences as compared to the discovery learning group. Based on this information, it was concluded that students favored the skills-based classroom. The students were measured within the same period of time after the study. The equalization of time of measurement was important since attitudes can change over time. Thus, we can rule out a selection by maturation interaction as a threat since both groups were similar on all critical variables and were exposed to the same passage of time.

Statistical Regression

Statistical regression may be a threat to the internal validity of a study if we select participants who are extreme on some attribute. Statistical regression is a phenomenon that occurs when individuals deviate from the norm. When individuals who deviate from the norm are selected, a change in that attribute toward the mean can be expected. The greater or more pronounced the difference between the participants and the norm, the greater the expected change in some attribute toward the mean. Consider the following: If your parents are taller than the mean height (e.g., father is 6'9" mother is 6'2", we would expect you to be shorter, on average, than your parents. The opposite is also true. If your parents are shorter than the mean height (e.g., father is 5'3" mother is 4'7", we would expect you to be taller than your parents. This phenomenon also occurs with other human attributes such as intelligence. For example, if your mother is gifted, say, with an IQ of 150, we would expect your IQ to be less than 150. Your IQ would move back toward the mean IQ of the population, which is 100.

Statistical regression is a threat to the internal validity of an experiment if a group of participants was chosen based on extreme scores (e.g., mental retardation) and you see a change from one test to the next. For example, suppose that we gave a pretest, such as an intelligence test, to a group of children and found that the average IQ for the group was 65. After a metacognitive strategy was implemented to improve mental processing, the group's average IQ increased to 75. We could not conclude that the metacognitive strategy was effective in improving IQs since an increase in the group's posttest average intelligence would be expected to move toward 100 simply because of statistical regression to the mean. (*Note:* Regression toward the mean would be expected here since 75% to 80% of all mental retardation is considered to be due to socioeconomic disadvantage, not inherited traits; Hardman, Drew, & Egan, 1996; Heward, 1996; Smith & Luckasson, 1995.) We would have likely seen an improvement in the group's scores without any independent variable being implemented. If we were not aware of statistical regression, we may have mistakenly concluded that the independent variable was effective when, in reality, it may not have been effective at all.

A nonexample of this threat would be if we compared two groups of participants who had low IQ scores (i.e., 50). One group was exposed to the independent variable, and the second group was not exposed to the independent variable. The only difference between the two groups should have been the independent variable. Then, if any differences were noticed between the groups, we could safely conclude that statistical regression did not contribute to the cause of the change since any statistical regression to the mean would have occurred with both groups. Any noticeable difference could be attributed to the independent variable.

Mortality

Mortality can be a threat to the internal validity of a study when there is a differential loss of participants. This differential loss could be from death (thankfully an unusual occurrence), selectively eliminating scores of some group members, or the withdrawal of participants. The key to the definition of mortality is the term *differential.*

Consider the following example. Suppose we were attempting to see if a new metacognitive skill could enhance the learning rates of students. We set out to determine the learning rates of students through timed trials of oral responses to mathematics facts. Twenty students were randomly assigned to one of two groups. The metacognitive skill was taught to one group of students (experimental) but not to the second group (control). On the pretest, we saw that both groups of students had an average time of getting through all of their required math facts in 90 seconds. Upon posttesting, we saw that the experimental group made it through the math facts in 75 seconds on average; the control group answered the math facts in 88 seconds on average. At this point, we concluded that the metacognitive skills enhanced learning. However, only seven students were left in the experimental group after the posttest, whereas the control group had all 10 students. Therefore, the experimental group's change from pre- to posttest was attributed to mortality, not the metacognitive skills. We concluded mortality as a threat because the students who dropped out of the experimental group were the slower students in the first place. So, if we remove the slower students from the group, the learning times should decrease. Now suppose that on seeing that the number of students in both groups differed, the data of three students in the control group were thrown out randomly. There is still a problem with mortality since three is still a differential loss of participants. Thus, it really does not matter if the number of participants lost from both groups is the same; whether or not the participants who were lost from each group are similar to each other is the critical question.

Mortality is not a threat in the following scenario. Suppose there were two groups of individuals who were involved in a study of short-term memory. On the pretest, the two groups scored similarly on the number of nonsense symbols they could remember after a passage of 5 seconds from the time they saw the symbols to when they were requested to recall the symbols. The experimental group was provided with a newly discovered memory strategy aimed at enhancing short-term memory. At posttest, it was discovered that the experimental group retained 50% more words than did the control group. However, 10% of the participants were lost from each group. Information on the characteristics of those lost from each group was gathered, and it was determined that the individuals lost in each group had similar characteristics on variables considered important for the study (e.g., intelligence, age, experience). Thus, there probably was not a differential loss of participants, and mortality was an unlikely threat.

Instrumentation

Instrumentation can be a threat to the internal validity of a study when there are changes in the calibration of the instrument(s) used in measurement. If the measurement device changes throughout or anytime during the study, we cannot be sure if the change was due to the independent variable or due to changes in the way the dependent variable was measured.

For example, suppose we wanted to see how a certain behavior management procedure works to decrease the self-injurious behavior of a young child. A frequency count (i.e., tally of every instance of a behavior) was used for 4 hours before the independent variable was implemented; then we changed the way we measured the dependent variable to count only if the behavior occurred at least once in eight half-hour intervals. We presented data to suggest that the behavior decreased from an average frequency of 100 behaviors in a 4-hour period before the independent variable was implemented to eight behaviors in 4 hours while the independent variable was in effect. Although this result was impressive, changes in the measurement device accounted for the results rather than the independent variable. Consider that the maximum number of behaviors (i.e., at least once per half-hour interval) was eight.

A nonexample of instrumentation as a threat would involve using observers who did not know if the independent variable (i.e., assertiveness skills) was in effect for each participant. During a period in which the normal occurrence of the behavior was observed, we saw that there was a somewhat stable response pattern of low assertiveness skills. The participants were taught how and when to be assertive; the observers continued to measure the level of assertiveness being demonstrated by the participants. Throughout this time, the observers did not know if we were teaching the skills to the participants. We saw that during the assertiveness training, the participants' skills improved significantly. In this case, instrumentation is less likely to be a concern since any change in the manner of measurement would not likely be the result of knowledge the observer possessed about how the participant(s) should respond. Likewise, if we made sure that the dependent variable was measured in a consistent fashion (i.e., no major changes took place in how the device was used in measuring the dependent variable or in how behaviors were counted), instrumentation would be less of a threat to the internal validity of the study.

Testing

Testing threatens the internal validity of a study when participants show improvement on a posttest simply due to the effects of taking the pretest. If the two tests are alike, participants may have learned some things from the first test (i.e., had become test wise) that helped improve their scores on the second testing. In other words, the independent variable may not have accounted for a change in participant behavior; the change may have been due to pretest exposure.

For example, say we wanted to compare two groups. The experimental group was provided with a pretest and a posttest; the control group was provided with only a posttest. We saw that the experimental group outperformed the control group. Testing may be a major problem here. The two groups were not only different with regard to the independent variable, but they were also different with regard to the exposure to the test. The experimental group had an advantage over the control group since the experimental group had the opportunity to learn about how the test was conducted and was able to perform at a higher level because of previous experience with the test.

Testing would not be a threat in the following situation. Suppose a pretest measuring concern for multicultural issues was provided to an experimental group and also to a control group. In this instance, the two groups were equated on all variables including the past exposure to the pretest. A training seminar was provided to the experimental group on multicultural awareness, whereas the control group was provided a seminar of equal length on social skills. If previous exposure to the test on multicultural issues resulted in improved performance on the posttest, we would have seen an improvement in the control group's performance. The difference between the control group and the experimental group on the posttest would most likely have been due to the independent variable since the threat of testing was removed as an alternative explanation. (A simpler solution would be to randomly assign participants to two groups and give both groups only the posttest. By removing the pretest altogether, we would remove testing as a threat to the internal validity of the study.)

History

History may well be one of the threats to the internal validity of a study that gives researchers the most concern. History is defined as anything other than the independent variable that is occurring between the pretest and posttest or during the implementation of the independent variable that may affect the participants' performance.

For example, suppose we wished to teach students how to perform CPR. A CPR training program was developed to teach the students this important skill. We conducted a pretest to determine if the students knew how to do CPR. The CPR training program was implemented and then the posttest was conducted. We found that the students' posttest performance improved and concluded that the program was successful. However, we did not realize that the students were involved in the Boy Scouts at the same time as our training program. It was also learned that as part of their experiences in the Boy Scouts, the students received first-aid training that included CPR around the same time that we were teaching them how to perform CPR. There is a problem of history in this scenario. We cannot conclude that our program was successful—that is, that changes were due to the independent variable (the training that we provided).

A nonexample of history as a threat follows. Suppose we wanted to decrease the hyperactivity of several students. Half of the students were randomly assigned to an experimental group and half to a control group. For the experimental group, we used a self-management program to teach the students how to control their own behavior. The control group received time on a computer equal to the amount of time the control group was involved in the program. Upon completion of the study, we determined that the experimental group had a significantly lower level of hyperactivity than did the control group. History was less of a threat to the internal validity of this study since the control group was exposed to the same history as the experimental group. Thus, any change in the experimental group as a result of history would have also be seen in the control group.

Resentful Demoralization of the Control Group

Resentful demoralization could be a threat to the internal validity of a study when a group of individuals believes that another group of individuals is receiving something desirable that is not given to everyone involved. Thus, the individuals not receiving that "something" may feel resentful and demoralized toward the other individuals since they believe that something desirable is being withheld from them. They may put forth less effort into tasks such as a posttest than they would have ordinarily.

For example, suppose that a number of low-performing students were assigned to an experimental group to receive help in math that incorporated a new remedial instructional technique. Other low-performing students did not receive the special remediation (control). When the students in the control group realized that the other students had access to special help, they felt cheated. Their effort in completing homework diminished as did their efforts in class. At the end of the grading period, these individuals had fallen behind the experimental group participants. The results seemed to indicate that the independent variable was more powerful than it actually was. If the control group participants had continued trying as they did before the study, they may not have fallen as far behind.

The following investigation illustrates a non-example of this threat. Say we had two groups of individuals who were involved in a program designed to decrease their episodes of depression. The experimental group received a new drug, and the control group received a placebo. Since the control group was blind to the type of "drug" it was receiving, it was unlikely that the group would become demoralized by not receiving the new drug. We saw large differences between the two groups in their responses to the independent variable; thus, it was unlikely that the difference was due to the control group becoming upset with what they could have considered an inequity that might have led to further depression.

Diffusion of Treatment

Diffusion of treatment is a threat to the internal validity of a study when the independent variable was applied when it was not intended. If this occurs, the effectiveness of the independent variable may be diminished.

For example, suppose we had an experimental group that received the independent variable and a control group that did not. The experimental and control group participants were in close proximity to one another (i.e., they were in the same class). During the delivery of the independent variable, the experimental group participants noticed that they were learning new and exciting things. They called their friends, who also included some of the control group participants, and told them what they were learning. The control participants wanted to change just as much as the experimental group participants so they tried doing what their counterparts were doing. The control participants also began to learn these new and exciting things based on discussions with their friends who were exposed to the independent variable. Given the posttest, we noted that the differences between the two groups were minimal. We concluded that the independent variable was not very effective, when, in fact, it may have been very effective.

Diffusion of treatment would not be a threat in the following situation. We counseled a participant in his marital relationship. The participant was taught a set of interpersonal skills that we thought would help his marriage. His social interactions with peers were also assessed, and we planned to teach other skills to help him get along with others. We noticed that his relationship with his wife improved, but his relationships with friends did not improve. The independent variable seemed to have been effective since the other relationships did not change. Later, he was taught how to improve other relationships and noticed that these improved as well. In this case, we ruled out diffusion as an alternative explanation for the results of the study since his relationships with others did not improve until the independent variable was implemented.

Compensatory Rivalry by the Control Group

This internal validity threat is also called the *John Henry effect.* If you remember the story of John Henry, you will recall that he fought against the use of a steam-powered railroad spike driver. John Henry increased his efforts to keep up with the power tool. A similar thing may happen in studies. If individuals who are not exposed to the independent variable believe they are in competition with the experimental group, they may increase their effort to keep up with or surpass their peers. The results of this increased effort could be the masking of the effects of the independent variable.

For example, suppose we took two classrooms and decided to implement a new form of reading instruction in one of them (experimental). The other classroom (control) received a standard reading curriculum. The teacher in the control classroom, wanting to look as competent as the other teacher, increased the intensity of her instruction. At the end of the term, the students in both classes took a standardized reading test. We found that the differences between the classrooms were minimal. This lack of difference may not have been due to an ineffective independent variable but due to the increased effort exercised by the teacher in the control classroom.

A nonexample of compensatory rivalry by the control group would involve a situation where we wished to study the effects of a new math curriculum in one of two classes. The first class (experimental) received the new curriculum, and the other class (control) received the standard curriculum. Before the independent variable was in effect, several observations were conducted in both classes to determine the normal routine in each class. Then, the independent variable was implemented and the routines in both classrooms continued to be observed. The observations confirmed that the teacher in the control classroom did not alter her routine. There was only minimal differences between the two groups at posttest; thus, we were fairly confident that there was no compensatory rivalry by the teacher in the control classroom.

Compensatory Equalization of Treatments

This threat to internal validity may occur if individuals not receiving the independent variable received something additional from people within or outside of the study as compensation compared to what is normally received.

For example, say we provided special counseling services to a group of individuals with depression (experimental) and provided no counseling services to others with depression (control). The groups' scores were compared on a depression inventory; it was found that the two groups were not much different from one another. It seemed that the special counseling was ineffective. However, additional information was received that the case worker for those in the control group received money for a special outing once a week since these individuals were not afforded the opportunity to receive counseling. Essentially, we were comparing counseling to special outings as compared to counseling versus no counseling. Both groups received different independent variables. Both variables may have been effective or ineffective. The problem arises from making conclusions based on the understanding that the control group did not receive a special intervention.

Compensatory equalization of treatments would not be a threat in the following study. Say we studied the effects of the pretraining of job skills to on-the-job training. The group that received the pretraining met two times a week for approximately 1 hour. An attempt was made to ensure that the other group received the prescribed independent variable and did not receive additional training. This additional training could have occurred if the second group received two workshops per week lasting 1 hour each to supplement the on-the-job training. The implementation of the prescribed independent variable was monitored. Little difference between the two training methods was noticed; thus, it was concluded that there was little difference between pretraining and on-the-job training of vocational skills. We were confident that there was little chance for a compensatory equalization of treatments threat.

WHAT IS EXTERNAL VALIDITY?

We may never know exactly if a particular threat to internal validity affected the results of a study.

However, there must always be an attempt to determine all of the possible causes or functional relationships that exist between the independent and dependent variables. Once the possible extraneous variables that may affect the outcomes of a study are determined, our attention must then turn to the generalizability of the results. Critical research consumers must ask the question, "What does this mean for me and the individuals with whom I work, in my setting, at this particular point in time?" This question refers to *external* validity.

External validity asks, "What is the generalizability of the results of a study?" This question is a crucial one for those of us who are concerned with translating research into practice. If a study has sound internal validity but little external validity, we might consider the results to be of little value to us at this point in time. Having limited external validity does not mean that the results are not important. Basic research may seem to have little relevance for practitioners; however, basic research is critical to us at later times. Applied researchers take findings from basic research studies and attempt to apply the information gained to everyday situations.

Practitioners are especially concerned with external validity because their situation dictates that they apply the best practices from research. If research results cannot be generalized from the laboratory to the field, they have little relevance to practitioners. Thus, applied researchers must be especially concerned with the external validity of their results if those results are to be generalized to other individuals and situations. There are two general categories of external validity (Bracht & Glass, 1968)—*population* and *ecological validity* (see Table 2.2).

Population Validity

Population validity concerns the ability to generalize the results of a study from a sample to a larger group of individuals. Population validity answers the question, "Will the independent variable change the performance of the individuals with whom I work?" Population validity is usually what one thinks of as external validity. Population validity can be separated into two types—*generalization across participants and interaction of personological variables* and *treatment effects*.

Generalization Across Participants. When we speak of generalization across participants, we must define the participants targeted for generalization. Bracht and Glass (1968) address this point when they discuss two levels of generalization. First, there is generalization from the study participants (e.g., 50 students with attention deficits in a school district) to the accessible population (e.g., all students with attention deficits in a school district). The accessible population is the population from which the participants were selected who are accessible to the researcher. Second, there is the generalization from the accessible population to the target population. The target population is a much larger group of individuals such as all individuals with attention deficits in the country. This type of validity is difficult to achieve since the accessible population must be similar in all respects to, or representative of, the larger population.

Generalizing across participants usually involves the generalization of results from the study participants to the accessible population. The best and possibly only valid way to achieve generalization from the accessible population to the target population is through several replications of a study (see Chapter 1).

For example, say we wanted to compare a drug intervention for middle school students with attention deficit disorders with no drug intervention. An advertisement was placed in the local newspaper for volunteers to become involved in the study, and a total of 50 such individuals responded. These volunteers were randomly assigned to one of the two groups. At the end of the study, the group that received the drug was compared to the no-drug control. It was concluded that the drug had some positive effects. A concern arose as to whether these results could be

TABLE 2.2 Threats to External Validity

POPULATION
Generalization Across Subjects—The extent to which we can generalize from the experimental sample to the accessible population.
Interaction of Personological Variables and Treatment Effects—The extent to which the intervention differentially affects experimental participants based on their characteristics.
ECOLOGICAL
Verification of the Independent Variable—The extent to which one can reproduce the exact implementation of the independent variable.
Multiple Treatment Interference—The extent to which one can generalize the effects of a single independent variable when participants are exposed to several independent variables.
Hawthorne Effect—The extent to which the extra attention provided to the participants during the study limits generalization to situations where the extra attention is not present.
Novelty and Disruption Effects—The extent to which the novelty or disruptive aspects of an independent variable limit generalization to situations where these novelty or disruptive aspects are not present or fade away.
Experimenter Effects—The extent to which the study's results are limited to the individual(s) implementing the independent variable.
Pretest Sensitization—The extent to which the study's results are limited to situations where only a pretest is utilized.
Posttest Sensitization—The extent to which the study's results are limited to situations where only a posttest is utilized.
Interaction of Time of Measurement and Treatment Effects—The extent to which the effects of the independent variable on the dependent variable will maintain through time.
Measurement of the Dependent Variable—The extent to which the generalizability of the study's results are limited to the particular dependent measure used.
Interaction of History and Treatment Effects—The extent to which the study's results can be generalized to a future time period.

generalized to other individuals within the same area where the advertisements were placed (accessible population). Because we knew that volunteer participants differ in some important respects to nonvolunteer individuals (Rosnow & Rosenthal, 1976), we concluded that generalization across participants was a threat to the external validity of the study.

A nonexample of this threat would be randomly sampling individuals from an accessible population. Random sampling would allow us to generalize the results from the sample to the accessible population because everyone in the accessible population would have an equal chance of being selected to participate in the study. Say we wished to find out the working memory capacity of individuals with attention problems. The target population was defined as all individuals who were diagnosed as having an attention deficit disorder as defined by the *Diagnostic and Statistical Manual,* fourth edition (DSM-IV). Next, those individuals who were accessible for the study were selected. Once this was done, the number of individuals to include in the study was determined. Finally, this number was randomly selected from the accessible population. When the results were interpreted, we were better able to generalize these results to others who were in the accessible population since we assumed that the study's participants were representative of the accessible population.

Interaction of Personological Variables and Treatment Effects. An interaction of personological variables and treatment effects exists when the independent variable has differential effects on the members of the experimental group depending on the characteristics (personological variables) of each group member.

For example, suppose we paid participants in an experimental group $1 for every book read (independent variable). The number of books read was measured; it was found that the experimental group read three more books on average than a group of individuals who did not receive payment (the control group). We decided to take a closer look at the members of the experimental group and found that there were some members from high socioeconomic families and others from low socioeconomic families. Thus, an additional question was asked of whether the money paid for reading books was more or less effective depending on the socioeconomic status of the group members. If there was an interaction, we would have had to be careful with our claims of the generalizability of the results to the accessible population since the socioeconomic status of participants may differentially affect how they responded to the independent variable.

A nonexample of interaction of personological variables and treatment effects as a threat involves one type of interaction—aptitude-by-treatment interaction. A popular theory in education is that of learning styles. This theory indicates that if we match styles of teaching (e.g., lecture, use of media, hands-on activities) to each student's unique style of learning (e.g., auditory, visual, tactile/kinesthetic), we can teach students more effectively. This theory rests on the interaction of a student's aptitude (i.e., style of learning) and the intervention used. We set up a study with an experimental and control group. Two independent variables were defined—(a) the style of teaching, and (b) the style of learning. This illustration is an example of a factorial design (see Chapter 5). The results indicated that the style of teaching had strong effects on the achievement of students; hands-on activities seemed to produce higher levels of academic achievement as compared to the other methods of instruction. The style of learning was also shown to interact with the type of instruction (e.g., auditory learners outperformed other learners when the lecture format was used; visual learners outperformed other learners when instructional media was used; tactile/kinesthetic learners out performed other learners when hand-on activities were used). We made conclusions with regard to the type of instruction that was most effective with each type of learner. (*Note:* Such an interaction has not been consistently demonstrated; Slavin, 1994.)

Ecological Validity

As population validity is concerned with the generalization of results to others in the accessible and target populations, ecological validity is concerned with the generalization of results to other environmental conditions (Bracht & Glass, 1968). When reading a research report, one must be concerned with the ability to generalize the results of the investigation to other situations outside of the investigation. Ecological validity is concerned with 10 threats to the external validity of a study—verification of the independent variable, multiple treatment interference, the Hawthorne effect, novelty and disruption effects, experimenter effects, pretest sensitization, posttest sensitization, interaction of history and treatment effects, measurement of the dependent variable, and interaction of time of measurement and treatment effects.

Verification of the Independent Variable. A frequently ignored, but important concern of ecological validity is whether the independent variable was implemented as described (Shaver, 1983). Researchers spend a great deal of time making sure that the dependent variable is measured consistently but may fail to ensure that the independent variable is implemented consistently. If the independent variable is not implemented in a consistent fashion, we cannot determine what was done to produce a change in the dependent variable. A critical aspect of science is replicating the findings of previous research. One cannot replicate a study when the independent variable has not been implemented as intended.

For example, suppose we attempted to find the effects of specific praise on the motivation of a student. Specific praise was defined as a verbal indication of desirable behaviors that the student exhibited (e.g., "Good job, Billy. You put the book on the shelf" versus "Good job"). The praise was provided for every fifth desirable behavior on average. However, the implementation of the independent variable was not documented. Our results indicated that the student's motivation improved; this improvement seemed to be due to the independent variable. However, if you were to take this study and implement the same techniques in another setting, you may obtain different results. The person implementing the independent variable may have praised every desirable behavior, not every fifth behavior on average. If this occurred, you would need to know about it to replicate the study and understand the results of the study.

The following scenario provides a nonexample of this threat. Suppose we wanted to determine the effects of problem-solving training on a group of individuals with cognitive delays. A teacher implemented the independent variable, and the effects on the dependent variable were measured. At the same time, data were collected on whether or not the teacher provided appropriate praise and appropriate error correction procedures. Thus, we were more confident that the independent variable was implemented as described, and we increased the chances that if others implemented problem-solving training in the same manner, they would obtain similar results.

Multiple Treatment Interference. Multiple treatment interference occurs when there are multiple independent variables used together. This situation prevents us from claiming that any one independent variable produced the effects. We would have to take into consideration that all independent variables were used together. To make any claims for ecological validity, we would have to describe the combined effects of the independent variables.

For example, say we exposed a group of students to a phonics-based reading program and measured their decoding and reading comprehension performance. The same participants were then assessed on how they performed when taught with a whole-language approach. The results indicated that the whole-language approach was superior to the phonics approach. However, the two independent variables were not separated. The results may have been different if the approaches had been implemented in isolation or if the whole-language approach had been implemented before the phonics approach.

If only one level of the independent variable was implemented with each group, multiple treatment interference would not be a threat. Suppose we wanted to initiate counseling for individuals with eating disorders and to determine the impact of three counseling techniques (e.g., behavioral, cognitive, familial counseling). Participants were assigned to one of three groups, and one of the techniques was implemented with each group. The behavioral technique was found to be more effective in reducing the occurrence of the behaviors associated with eating disorders. Notice that we did not expose each group to more than one technique since we wanted to generalize the results to situations where only one technique would be used.

Hawthorne Effect. The Hawthorne effect gets its name from several studies carried out at the Hawthorne Plant of the Western Electric Company (Roethlisberger & Dickson, 1939). Essentially, when the experimenters increased the lighting in the plant, the productivity of the workers increased over time. However, in later studies, when the lights were turned down, the productivity increased. In fact, no matter what the researchers did, the productivity of the workers increased. It seemed that the critical variable was not what the researchers did but was the extra attention the employees were receiving. The Hawthorne effect is a potential problem whenever the participants are aware that they are in an experiment and/or are being assessed.

For example, say we wanted to assess the effects of lowering the sugar intake of individuals considered to be hyperactive. Two groups of individuals who had been diagnosed as having an attention deficit disorder (ADD) were formed. The individuals were randomly assigned to one of two groups. One group (experimental) had its diet planned and was strictly monitored, whereas the other group (control) was allowed to eat in a normal fashion. The control group's diet was not planned nor was the group's diet monitored as closely as was the experimental group's diet. A large reduction in the experimental group's level of hyperactivity was observed; however, there was not a change in the control group's behavior. We concluded that the sugar restriction aided in the decrease of hyperactive behavior. However, this decrease may not be replicated in situations where we were not present or where the individuals did not receive the level of monitoring the experimental group received.

If a control group was provided with the same amount of attention as the experimental group, then the Hawthorne effect would not be a threat to the external validity of the study. Suppose we wanted to see the results of family counseling on the levels of physical and emotional abuse suffered by family members. Rural families who had little contact with others were included in the investigation. Instructors went into some homes and provided training on effective behavior management techniques. A goal was to find out if the training sessions were effective; therefore, the level of abuse of families exposed to the training was compared to families who did not receive the training. One possible difficulty encountered was that the families visited and trained improved simply due to greater outside contact. Thus, to decrease this threat, we made visits to the other families for approximately the same length of time but provided no training. If the Hawthorne effect was present, we would have likely seen it with the second group of families.

Novelty and Disruption Effects. Novelty and disruption effects may occur when the experimental variables introduced into an investigation change the situation in such a manner that the participants react to the changes in the situation in general versus reacting to the presentation of the independent variable in particular. In other words, being part of an investigation itself may change the impact of the independent variable. When novelty effects are present, the effect of the independent variable may be enhanced. Thus, it is difficult to generalize the initial results of an investigation if the investigation brings something into the environment (in addition to the independent variable such as more people, recording instruments) that is different from the ordinary routine. The initial effects may not hold true if the novelty wears off or the independent variable is assimilated into the normal routine. The opposite is true for a disruption threat. When the experimental variables of an investigation are implemented, the investigation may disrupt the normal routine of the participants. If this occurs, the effectiveness of the independent variable may be suppressed if the participants fail to respond to the independent variable or respond to it negatively due to having their routine broken or disrupted.

For example, suppose we wanted to study the effects of teaching styles on students in a high school class. The teaching styles used in the classroom were evaluated, and the teacher was questioned on what she was doing and why. The teacher was given feedback and made some changes in how she was instructing her students. The students responded positively (i.e., their academic progress accelerated) to the change in teaching style. We left the classroom confident that what we taught the teacher was effective and could generalize to other classrooms. If our presence and/or the novelty of the independent variable affected the students, we would have had a problem with the external validity of the study. When other teachers attempt to use the new teaching style, they may not get the same results because novelty effects may not be in effect. The opposite would hold for disruption effects. Our presence in the classroom may have caused a disruption in the class routine, thereby making the independent variable less effective. In this example, the disruption caused by the study may have interfered with the students' concentration and, thus, decreased the academic progress they were making before we became involved with the class.

A nonexample of these threats involves investigating the effects of an instructional procedure that produces high rates of responding on the disruptive behaviors of students in a middle school classroom. Say we entered the classroom for 2 weeks before the implementation of the independent variable. During this time, the level of disruptions decreased and then returned to the level before we were present. After the students became accustomed to our presence, the independent variable was implemented. The data revealed that the independent variable was effective in decreasing the students' disruptions. Since we stayed in the class for an extended period of time to allow students to get used to our presence, novelty and disruption threats were reduced.

Experimenter Effects. Experimenter effects are also referred to as *generalization across behavior change agents.* Just because we have certain findings with one person implementing the independent variable does not mean that others implementing the independent variable will have the same success. Studies are usually well planned, and the individuals conducting the studies are usually well trained and typically have some expertise in the area they are investigating. Thus, it may be difficult to claim the results of a study will generalize to other individuals who implement the independent variable without the same level of training, the same motivation, or the same personological variables that were not present in the original experiment.

Consider the following example. Teaching is a profession that is affected by a variety of factors. What makes one teacher effective and another teacher ineffective does not only depend on the curriculum they are using but also depends on other factors such as the excitement they exhibit toward the subject matter. Suppose we developed a better way of teaching social interaction skills to students with behavior disorders. The new technique used scenarios in which the participants had to respond (e.g., "You see a person that you dislike at a store and that person approaches you. How would you react?"). Our findings on the new program indicated that we were effective in teaching social skills to students with behavior disorders. A teacher purchased the program to use with her students who also had difficulties interacting with others. She began the program but believed that the scenarios were too juvenile for her students. She took them through the program but did so in a very subdued and unexcited fashion. After the program, she found that the students did not improve and concluded that the program did not work. Critical research consumers must be concerned with the possibility that the manner in which the independent variable is presented and by whom may make a difference in the replicability of the results.

A nonexample of experimenter effects involves implementing a program to improve the productivity levels of employees at an assembly plant. The plant was one division of a large corporation. The plant managers brought in a motivational speaker. The speaker discussed the importance of a productive workforce, the improvement in self-esteem for workers, and the increased pride of being associated with a productive workforce. The managers measured the productivity levels of the workforce before and after the speaker. They found that the productivity level increased significantly. The managers recommended that other divisions of the corporation bring in motivational speakers. The other divisions brought in other speakers who focused on the same topics as the first speaker and measured the reaction of the workforce. They too found that productivity levels increased after each speaker. Experimenter effects are not a strong threat since other speakers exhibiting different presentation styles but speaking on the same topics had similar results.

Pretest Sensitization. Many times researchers will provide a pretest when attempting to determine the effects of the independent variable on the dependent variable. After this pretest, they will provide the independent variable followed by the posttest. The difference between the pretest and the posttest may then be determined to be the result of the independent variable. However, the pretest may make the independent variable more effective than it would have been without the pretest.

For example, suppose we wanted to see the effects of a class on developing one's self-esteem. A questionnaire was provided before the class to determine how each individual felt about himself or herself in terms of popularity, ability, and physical appearance. The independent variable was then implemented that involved teaching how each student was unique and how each could have an impact on other people. The class lasted approximately 2 weeks. At the end of the 2-week period, a posttest was conducted. The data indicated that the participants' self-esteem improved from the pretest to posttest assessment. A teacher read about the study and decided to replicate the procedure in her classroom. She taught the self-esteem class and conducted a posttest to determine the effects. She found that the students still had relatively low levels of self-esteem. One possible reason for her failure to replicate the results of the previous study would be that she did not implement a pretest. When a pretest is implemented, that pretest may become part of the independent variable. The pretest may have altered the participants' perceptions of the oncoming class and made the class more effective. Although researchers frequently use a pretest to assess the effectiveness of an independent variable, practitioners may not do so.

Pretest sensitization would not be a threat if a pretest was not provided. Suppose we tested the effectiveness of a drug prevention/drug awareness program. Sixty participants from an accessible population of middle school children were randomly selected. The children were then matched based on age, socioeconomic status of their parents, parental educational level, and whether the children had been previously exposed to drugs. Matching on these variables helped ensure that the groups were equal or similar on what we considered to be important variables. A pretest was not provided since there is less of a need to see if there were initial differences between the groups. The experimental group was exposed to the drug prevention/drug awareness program; the control group was not exposed to the program. A posttest was provided that measured the attitudes about the acceptability of experimenting with illegal drugs. The results indicated that the experimental group participants were less inclined to experiment with drugs than were the control group participants. Since a pretest was not used, this threat was removed.

Posttest Sensitization. Posttest sensitization is similar to the pretest sensitization threat. The application of a posttest may make the independent variable more effective since the posttest is essentially a synthesizing of the previously learned material.

For example, suppose we wanted to find out how much information students in a statistics class remembered. A pretest was given, and the results indicated that the students' knowledge level was low, scoring an average of 20% on the test. The students were instructed throughout the semester. They were then given a posttest at the end of the term. Students taking the test indicated that they began to realize how to put together all of the information they learned during the semester; that is, they realized how to use statistics to answer research questions and saw the "big picture." The students did well on the posttest by answering an average of 85% of the questions correctly. We concluded that the independent variable was effective. However, the extent to which the posttest improved the effectiveness of the independent variable was not known.

Posttest sensitization would not be a threat in the following study. Say we were interested in researching the effectiveness of teaching cognitive skills to adults with learning disabilities. The independent variable involved helping the adults become aware of how they go about solving a problem and teaching personal speech or self-talk. A group of adults diagnosed as having a specific learning disability in reading comprehension was selected. Half of the adults were randomly assigned to an experimental group and the other half to a control group. The independent variable (cognitive skill instruction) was implemented, and a posttest was conducted after 10 weeks of instruction. The posttest measured the ability to comprehend a series of written passages. The posttest revealed that the experimental group outperformed the control group. In this example, the posttest may have helped bring everything learned in training to the surface or helped the information fall into place. Since this was a potential problem, we indicated that the posttest was part of the independent variable, and if others were to implement the same procedure, the posttest should be added to the intervention package.

Interaction of History and Treatment Effects. All research is conducted in some time frame. This time frame can affect the generalization of the findings if the environment has changed. We live in a different world as compared to when a study was conducted, no matter how slight the difference is between the world of today and the world of yesterday. If these differences are major, we would have an especially difficult time in making external validity claims. This difficulty is why researchers attempt to use the most up-to-date references available to set up the purpose or importance of their study. If we see a researcher who cites a study from 1900, for example, we may be very concerned about the generalizability of those results. However, if there is a particular need to set the context for the present investigation (e.g., set an historical context) and an investigation conducted long ago is of such importance that it is needed to set such a context, an older reference may be appropriate. The key here is to determine the purpose of such a reference and how it is used. If the reference has historical significance, it is probably appropriate; if the reference is not used for such a purpose, it may be not appropriate.

For example, suppose we assessed the effect of condom use for adolescents in a particular high school. The use of condoms was promoted, and free samples were provided to all who requested them. A survey was conducted before and after the program. The results indicated that safe sex practices increased during the program. We concluded that our intervention had the desired effect and promoted the program on a wider scale. However, there may have been any number of events that occurred at the same time as the program that enhanced its effectiveness. Say we found that just after the program began, reports of an increase in the number of individuals diagnosed with HIV were made public. There was also a nationwide media campaign on the importance of safe sex. The program's effectiveness probably increased as a result of this event. That event may or may not be repeated again in other high schools. Therefore, the generalizability of the results would be limited to certain historical events.

A nonexample of interaction of history and treatment effects might involve the following. Suppose we wanted to demonstrate the efficacy of a group counseling procedure with adults with depression. Six individuals who met the criteria for clinical depression were recruited. Self-reports of their level of depression were measured on a rating scale before and after group counseling. Before the group counseling began, the average self-rating for feelings of depression was 7 out of 10 (with 10 being very severe and 1 being no depression). After 2 months of group counseling, we administered a posttest to measure the effects of group counseling. The average self-rating decreased to 4. However, the events in each person's life (e.g., illnesses of family members, employment) as well as the general environment (e.g., economy, weather) were also tracked. We noticed that at the same time as our counseling, a general feeling of optimism hits the country. The economy improves, the job outlook is very positive, and Congress is discussing increased funding for rehabilitative services that may impact the participants directly. These events are documented, and conclusions are made with these factors in mind. We did not claim that counseling *alone* was effective, but stated that counseling seemed to be effective during this particular time in history (i.e., describing what was occurring at the time). Since our claims were restricted to a limited time span, the threat of history and treatment is minimized.

Measurement of the Dependent Variable. When reviewing a study, the method of measuring the dependent variable must be viewed closely. There should be some assurances that the results were not limited to particular measures. A concern arises as to whether the results may differ if other measures were used.

For example, suppose we were teaching individuals how to engage in problem solving. They are taught how to go through a series of problem-solving steps. At the end of the sequence of steps, the individuals generate a possible solution to a given problem. The individuals' problem-solving abilities are assessed by asking them to describe problem situations and to say how they would solve the problem. We found that the problem-solving abilities of these individuals improved as a result of the independent variable. We claimed that these results could be generalized to the actual environment and that these individuals were prepared to solve real problems when they were faced with them in everyday life. However, a problem existed in that we could not be sure what happened when these individuals were faced with real-life problems. There was no way of knowing whether they could respond to situations that were similar to or different from the problems used in training. The generalizability of the results would be restricted only to those measures used in the study.

Measurement of the dependent variable would not be a threat in the next scenario. Say we wanted to determine the effects of self-instructional training on adults with developmental disabilities involved in supported employment situations. It was commonly believed that self-instructions would aid these employees in completing work tasks. The employees were taught how to talk themselves through a work task. During the assessments, employees were asked to describe how they would verbally complete a work task. The employees' self-instructions were measured by having them emit the self-instructions aloud. After the program ended, it was found that the level of self-instructions improved. However, a more critical measurement is whether each person's actual correct completion of work tasks improved during training. Thus, the ability to complete work tasks appropriately before and after the self-instructional training was assessed. We found that the correct completion of work tasks improved during self-instructional training. Measurement of the dependent variable was less of a threat since we assessed not only the employee's self-instructional abilities, but also the actual completion of work tasks.

Interaction of Time of Measurement and Treatment Effects. The interaction of time of measurement and treatment effects is a problem when we consider that the time the measurements are taken may determine the outcomes of a study. Most skills taught to individuals may be expected to deteriorate over time if these individuals are not given sufficient opportunities to perform or practice the behavior. However, the effect of the independent variable could diminish, stay the same, or even be enhanced over time (Bracht & Glass, 1968). Most researchers take posttest measures immediately after the completion of the study. Critical research consumers must also be concerned with the maintenance of the independent variable's effects or the generalization across time. If maintenance is assessed, it is usually short-term (e.g., less than 6 months). Long-term maintenance (often more than 6 months) occurs much less frequently.

For example, suppose we wanted to assess the effects of a weight-loss program. Several individuals were weighed before and after the program was completed. The results indicated that those individuals who completed the program lost more weight than those who were not involved in the program. It seemed as if the program was successful in reducing the weight of individuals who were overweight. However, program effects must stand the test of time. Thus, we should have continued to assess if the participants maintained their weight loss for an extended period of time.

A nonexample of this threat might involve investigating the efficacy of teaching abduction prevention skills to children. The independent variable was implemented that involved teaching the children to say "no" when approached by a stranger attempting to lure them away from a park, to walk or run away from the stranger, and to tell an adult of the encounter. A posttest was then conducted that involved having a "stranger" approach the children and attempt to lure them away from a park. All of the children were found to perform the skills at the criterion level (i.e., they said "no," walked or ran away, and told an adult of the encounter). The interaction of time of measurement and treatment effects is an important consideration when teaching such skills. Thus, maintenance data were taken at 1 month, 3 months, 6 months, and 1 year after the program ended. The children's skills were found to maintain at acceptable levels through the 3-month assessment but deteriorated during the 6-month and 1-year assessments. We concluded that ongoing booster training is required for abduction prevention skills to maintain for more than 3 months. Our claims of external validity were enhanced since we were able to determine the interaction between the time of measurement and treatment effects.

WHAT ARE STATISTICAL AND SOCIAL VALIDITIES?

Researchers are concerned about the validity (i.e., the degree to which *accurate* inferences can be made based on the results of a study) of their work. If a study is valid, it will be deemed important by others in the field. One may even say that the ultimate purpose of any study is to achieve a high level of validity. There are different types of validity that must be considered. Two critical types of validity are *statistical* and *social*. In education and psychology, most research is determined to have statistical validity if the results reach a certain level of confidence (e.g., .05) (i.e., the probability of obtaining the results of the investigation by chance—not due to a systematic variable). With social validity, researchers must determine if the results of a study are important to society.

Statistical Validity

Statistics are mathematical models that are used to provide evidence of some types of research questions. Suppose we use the analogy of digging a hole. A shovel is a tool that would be appropriate for such an activity. With a shovel, we can dig a deep hole and do so efficiently. However, if we wish to rake the yard, a shovel would not be the most appropriate tool to use. If we attempt to use a shovel to rake the yard, we will be faced with a rather difficult task. A shovel is not an efficient tool any more than using a rake to dig a hole. The same thing happens in research. Statistics should be used in a manner that is consistent with their purpose. For example, if one wished to find the average score for a group of students, a descriptive statistic called the arithmetic mean would be used. If one wished to find out how individual scores on a dependent measure were distributed around the mean, a descriptive statistic called a standard deviation would be used. If one wanted to make inferences back to the accessible population, inferential statistics would be used. Likewise, inferential statistics would be used if one wanted to determine the probability that our results occurred due to chance. Statistics are not mysterious devices; they are simply tools that help us both to determine the effect of systematic variables on the dependent variable and to make interpretations of our data.

Inferential statistics can be used to argue against one special threat to internal validity—*chance*. Suppose we took a sample of two groups from a target population to use in an investigation. Both groups were found to be the same at the beginning of the study but were found to be different at the end of the study. It was assumed that this difference was due to chance. If our results reached a level of statistical significance (e.g., .05), we would be able to determine how likely that chance finding is. The difference between the groups was an unlikely chance finding (e.g., less than 5 times in 100), so we concluded that the results were statistically significant. In other words, the probability of committing a Type I error (i.e., incorrectly concluding that there was systematic variance that affected the dependent variable when there was no systematic variance—the results were a chance finding) was 5%.

Suppose we implemented a process to increase the intellectual functioning of individuals with mental retardation. On the pretest, the experimental and control groups had average IQs of 60. The independent variable was implemented with the experimental group. A statistically significant difference (at the .05 level) was found in the IQs of the experimental group (mean = 65) as compared to the control group (mean = 60) on the posttest. That is, the probability of getting differences this large or larger, assuming that all results were due to chance, was about 5 out of 100. However, we did not conclude that this statistically significant finding was important. Another statistic could have been used to help us determine this. For example, an *effect size* (see Chapter 14) could have been used. An effect size can tell us how large the change in the independent variable was compared to another group of participants who did not receive the independent variable. Researchers should not only be concerned with statistical significance but should also concern themselves with the effect size of the results.

Social Validity

If our research results are to be used outside of the research setting, we must achieve some level of social validity. Before the results from a study make a contribution to society, they must be deemed important by society (Wolf, 1978). (*Note:* We are talking about applied versus basic research.) According to Wolf, social validity was once seen as a difficult area of inquiry for those who wished to use only objective measurement in research. Social validity is subjective since it cannot be operationally defined in a manner that allows it to be observable. However, social validity is ultimately a critical aspect of any research study, especially in applied research.

There are three concerns of social validity (Wolf, 1978). First, critical research consumers must determine the social validity of the goals of a study. If the goals are not socially relevant, the purpose of our research is suspect. For example, suppose we had the goal of determining if students in a mathematics classroom acquired and maintained information better if the teacher used only a drill and practice format as compared to a discovery learning format. This research question seemed desirable since the acquisition of mathematics knowledge is critical for future success. On the other hand, suppose we had a goal of determining if children can be taught to read before the age of 4 years. Many educators may not see this as a desirable goal. Thus, even if we were able to demonstrate reading ability before the age of 4 years, the techniques used to teach these children (and the age at which instruction begins) may not be adopted by educators since the outcomes are not seen as socially desirable and, to some, counterproductive.

Second, critical research consumers must determine if the procedures used in the study were worth the findings that resulted. That is, do the ends justify the means? Suppose we wanted to improve the independent living skills of adults with traumatic brain injuries. The cost of rehabilitation may add up to hundreds of thousands of dollars. Since the long-term outlook of these individuals is likely dim without such services, the long-term costs may outweigh the short-term costs. Society may value the rights of individuals to receive the most appropriate services available no matter the cost; therefore, the high cost of rehabilitation may be justified. On the other hand, suppose that our goal was to get students to not disturb others during instruction. We set out to determine whether having the students wear mouthpieces decreases the disruptions they make during instruction. We may have a desirable goal, but the procedures we used to achieve that goal are likely to be less than socially acceptable.

Third, critical research consumers should determine the social validity of the study's effects. For example, we again had the goal of keeping students from disrupting others during instruction. In order to achieve this, students were taught how to monitor their own disruptive behavior. Upon completion of the study, the students' level of disruptive behavior decreased from being disruptive during 80% of the instructional session to 5% of the instructional session (which was the average level of comparison students). We probably would consider this to be a large improvement. On the other hand, suppose we wanted to improve the intelligence (as measured by an IQ test) of 7-year-old children with mental retardation. The children's academic stimulation in the home was enhanced by asking parents to read selected children's books to their children every evening. The children's IQs were measured 6 months after the program began. The results indicated the children's IQs improved by an average of 5 points (from an average of 62 to 67). This finding may not be seen as important since such a small improvement probably will not result in improved academic performance.

SUMMARY

There are many methodological issues that are potentially present in research that the critical research consumer must consider. Of course, these issues will take on more or less of a role in the design and interpretation of research depending on the research question and methodology used. As critical research consumers, we should be able to identify methodological issues and to determine if a researcher has addressed them. If there are unresolved issues, critical research consumers should determine how serious these issues are and how they might affect our confidence in the conclusions made by the authors.

These research issues include several major issues. First, quantitative and qualitative researchers are concerned with the unsystematic variance found in their data and the methods used to decrease this unwanted variance. Second, quantitative researchers are concerned with systematic variance and the methods used to increase one source of systematic variance and decrease another source. Along these lines, quantitative researchers are concerned with the internal validity of their study. They want to answer the question, "Did the independent variable produce the results?" An attempt should be made to decrease threats to the internal validity of a quantitative study. Third, quantitative and qualitative researchers are concerned with the external validity of the study. They are concerned with the ability to generalize the results of the study to other individuals and situations. Thus, researchers should attempt to control for threats to the external validity of the study. Fourth, quantitative and qualitative researchers are concerned with the social validity of their study. An attempt should be made to determine to what extent society deems the goals, procedures, and outcomes of a study to be desirable. Finally, quantitative researchers are concerned with the statistical validity (if used) of their data.

They attempt to increase the opportunity of detecting systematic effects on the dependent variable (called power—discussed in Chapter 4).

Critical research consumers should look at each of these issues (if applicable) and determine if the conclusions made by the researchers are warranted or if other conclusions are more appropriate. Critical research consumers should also determine when and how to apply the results of a study. The remainder of the text will aid you in becoming critical research consumers by helping you become informed about how to analyze and interpret the research literature. Each chapter after Chapter 3 will document a research methodology, the questions each can answer, the steps taken in conducting each, how results are analyzed, and how each methodology controls for threats to the internal and external validity of a study, if applicable.

DISCUSSION QUESTIONS

1. Explain variance and provide an example of how you demonstrate variability in your daily life.
2. Explain how unsystematic and systematic variance are related.
3. Systematic variance moves a group in the same direction. Do all individuals in a group move in the same direction with systematic variance? Explain your response.
4. Suppose you are a practitioner working with individuals with a particular need. What would be more important to you, internal validity or external validity? Why?
5. Is it possible to have external validity without internal validity? Explain your response.
6. You read in the newspaper that a new intervention for stress has been developed. The treatment works based on rapid eye movements controlled by a therapist. The report indicates that a preliminary study has found positive effects. Provide two possible alternative explanations for these results.
7. For each of the threats to internal validity, indicate which threats are likely to make individuals exposed to the independent variable different from those who were not exposed to the independent variable. Which threats are likely to make the groups more like each other?
8. Is it true that the larger the number of participants in a group, the greater the ability to generalize to the target population? Why or why not?
9. If statistical validity only controls for chance events, why do people still place so much emphasis on it?
10. Should applied researchers be required to report some form of social validity in their research? Why or why not?

INTERPRETATION EXERCISES

Internal Validity

For the following scenarios, indicate the major threat to internal validity that is present and provide a justification for your answer. (*Hint:* Use a process of elimination to determine the major threat.) There may be more than one correct response; what is important here is the justification.

1. Fifty infants born to mothers on welfare who were receiving child care services were randomly assigned to either an enrichment (experimental) group or to a group receiving a normal regime of child care (control). The experimental group was tested monthly to follow the progress of the children. The groups were tested by examiners who did not know

the group affiliations of the children. Both groups were assessed at the end of the study at age 2. The mean IQ scores of the experimental and control groups were 130 and 90, respectively. It was concluded that the enrichment program was effective in raising IQ scores.

2. Students involved in extracurricular activities were compared to children who were not involved in such activities at the end of 12th grade. The SAT was used for comparison purposes. It was found that students who were involved in extracurricular activities scored 100 points on average above those who were not involved in the activities. The school principal decided that she would implement a schoolwide program to get more students involved in extracurricular activities since involvement can increase SAT scores by an average of 100 points.

3. A psychologist investigating the incidence of child abuse trends realizes that the incidence of physical abuse is increasing at an alarming rate. The psychologist believes that the cause of this increase must be due to the increased amount of stress parents are under as a result of economic pressures. He decides to implement a counseling program to reduce the stress on parents.

4. Children who were born to mothers with IQs less than 70 were placed in an early intervention center that offered special sensory stimulation. At 3 years of age, the children were found to have an average IQ of 85 (15 points higher on average than their mothers). The examiners were not aware of the purpose of the study. The researchers pointed out that children born to mothers with low IQs will also likely have low IQs themselves. Thus, the researchers concluded that the special sensory stimulation was effective, and all early intervention centers should implement this program.

5. Ten children with articulation problems were placed in a special speech development program at 4 years of age. They were assessed with a reliable instrument before the program began. After a period of 4 years, the children were again assessed with a parallel form of the first assessment. The researchers found that the level of articulation problems decreased substantially from the pretest. They concluded that the program should be implemented on a wide-scale basis due to the positive results of this study.

6. Twenty individuals with head injuries and memory difficulties were matched on age, length of time since injury, educational level, and socioeconomic status. Each pair was randomly assigned to one of two groups and provided a pretest. One group (experimental) was given a memory-enhancing drug and the other group (control) received a placebo drug. Both groups received 10 hours of rehabilitation services (e.g., vocational, independent living skills) per week during the study; the experimental group received an additional 2 hours of memory training per week. At the end of 3 months, the groups were tested again. The researchers found that the experimental group outperformed the control group by 25%; this result was statistically significant. The researchers argued for the use of the drug with all individuals with head injuries who also had memory difficulties.

7. A sociologist studying the effects of a government program designed to get homeless people off the street and into shelters followed a random sample of 100 homeless individuals. At the beginning of the study, 20% of the individuals regularly used shelters, 50% used the shelters at times of cold weather only, and 30% of the individuals never used the shelters. After a period of 2 years during the program, the sociologist could only contact 80 of the individuals and found that 25% of the individuals regularly used the shelters, 60% of the individuals used the shelters only during cold weather, and only 15% of the individuals never used the

shelters. The sociologist indicated that the program increased the regular use of the shelters by 5%, and 85% of the individuals used the shelters during cold weather as compared to 70% before the implementation of the program. The sociologist concluded that the program was successful.

External Validity

For the following scenarios, indicate the major threat to external validity and provide a justification for your answer. (*Hint:* Use a process of elimination to determine the major threat.) There may be more than one correct response; what is important here is the justification.

1. A psychologist decided to study the effects of the cognitive ability of college students when faced with a task with and without someone watching. It was hypothesized that the response rate of individuals would be slower when they were being watched. The results of the study confirmed the hypothesis, and the psychologist claimed that these results were important to supervisors of employees and student teachers. He indicated that if we expect individuals to perform at their best, we must not interfere by using obtrusive observation methods. He believed that since there is no reason to suggest that college students in an introduction to psychology class who volunteer to become participants in the study are any different than others, we can generalize these findings to others in the target population.

2. A researcher demonstrated that the best way to teach individuals how to use covert verbalizations to control their respective phobias was through direct instruction of the skills. The results of the study indicated that individuals who go through this direct instruction learn how to engage in covert verbalizations and are better able to reduce their phobias. The individual doing the teaching was a PhD-level therapist who had 20 years of experience working with individuals with phobias. The person was the co-developer of the direct instruction method and was very excited about its potential. The researcher claimed that almost any person working with individuals with phobias could experience success with this method of intervention.

3. A health psychologist was interested in increasing the use of seat belts among high school student drivers. She provided a driver training workshop and discussed the possible benefits and dangers of driving without a seat belt. She provided the participants a pretest that included watching films depicting cars that were in serious accidents. After watching the film, she asked participants to rate the likelihood that they would use a seat belt. She also provided a posttest in the same manner as the pretest. She found that the participants were much more likely to indicate they would wear seat belts after the workshop than before. She concluded that the results of the study indicate that a similar *workshop* should be provided in high schools around the country (she mentioned nothing about the pretest and posttest).

4. An educator researched the best way to teach young children sight words. She compared two training programs. One program was based on learning words in context and the other program was a phonics-based program. After the students learned all of the words, she provided a posttest where all of the words were presented in context; however, she did not test the words out of context. She found that the students who learned the words in context outperformed the students who learned the words through a phonics-based approach. She concluded that teaching words in context was superior to teaching words through phonics.

5. An educational psychologist attempted to show the best way to set up a classroom to

promote appropriate behavior. He met with the teacher before going into the classroom and taught her several effective teaching techniques. The teacher indicated that she hoped the new techniques would work since she was having increasing difficulty with the class. After the first week of implementing the new technique, the teacher recorded a 90% decrease in disruptive behavior. The psychologist suggested that all of the teachers in the school should try the new technique since it was so effective.

6. An educator was frustrated with the limited amount of retention of information his students demonstrated. He noticed that the students remembered little after the summer break and he spent too much time reviewing what students had learned the previous year. Thus, during the new school year, he decided to use less lecture in classes and more hands-on experiences. He used this teaching style up to Christmas break and tested how much of the material students retained over the break. To his delight, the students retained nearly 80% of the information they had learned (he estimated that students only retained 50% of the information over the summer break). He concluded that the hands-on approach was far superior to the lecture method in helping students retain learned information, and that his colleagues should use the same technique.

7. A school counselor working with depressed students decided to find out what the effects of a comprehensive counseling package would have on feelings of committing suicide. As part of the counseling, she began a support group for not only students but also their families. She also gave the students homework that involved finding reinforcing activities or hobbies. Additionally, she used group counseling techniques and one-on-one counseling in an attempt to change their negative thinking processes. At the end of a year, she found suicidal thinking had decreased. She believed that the critical part of the package was the group and individual counseling. She indicated that other school counselors should use these procedures if they wish to decrease the suicidal thoughts of students suffering from depression.

CHAPTER 3

RELIABILITY, VALIDITY, AND INTEROBSERVER AGREEMENT

OBJECTIVES

After studying this chapter you should be able to:

1. Define reliability, validity, and interobserver agreement.
2. Describe differences in how quantitative and qualitative researchers view reliability and validity.
3. Describe three types of test reliability and identify the type of test reliability related to different research problems.
4. Interpret the reliability coefficient.
5. Interpret the standard error of measurement and describe how it relates to reliability.
6. Describe four types of test validity and the types of test validity related to different research problems.
7. Define interobserver agreement.
8. Describe the relationship between interobserver agreement, reliability, and accuracy.
9. Interpret measures of interobserver agreement.
10. Describe procedures used to reduce observer effects.

OVERVIEW

Of all the decisions made by researchers, determining how to measure the matter of interest may be the most important. The goal of measurement in research is to turn the complexity of the environment in which the study is being conducted into a set of data that represent only those features in which the researcher is interested. All features of the participants as well as all aspects of the environment not key to the purpose of the research are intentionally ignored as far as measurement is concerned. In this way, measurement is a process in which targeted features of the participants and study environment are selected from among all possible features and recorded. This process involves generating a set of numerical data for quantitative researchers and a narrative description for qualitative researchers.

The primary goal of measurement is to obtain a complete and accurate record of the targeted features of the participants and study. The ideal goal of measurement is that the resulting data represent all instances of these targeted features. Implicit in the idea of completeness is that the recorded data should reflect what has actually happened. If the measurement procedures used by researchers do not detect all instances of the targeted features of the participants and study environment, the resulting data cannot be said to be accurate. On the other hand, even if the measurement procedures provided a complete record of these targeted features, the data may still be inaccurate through the recording of nontargeted features. Thus, it is impossible to obtain a totally accurate record of the targeted features of the participants and study environment—measurement procedures or devices provide estimates of these targeted features.

It should be clear that a primary concern of quantitative researchers is the completeness and accuracy of their findings. The concepts of reliability, validity, and interobserver agreement (in the case of the direct observation of behavior) not only constitute the framework to guide the design and implementation of measurement procedures, but also the framework to judge the trustworthiness of the findings.

The concepts of reliability and validity are interrelated. Reliability centers on the question of whether the measurement device produces consistent results across observations, providing the researcher a way of assessing the trustworthiness of the findings. Validity generally focuses on the question of whether the measurement device indicates what it purports to measure. More accurately, it is not the measurement device that is valid, but the inference made by the researcher based on this measurement device (Popham, 1981). It may be helpful to remember that the word *validity* has the same root as valor and value, referring to strength or worth. Interobserver agreement can be considered a special case of reliability in which the degree of agreement between independent observers is used to provide a measure of the trustworthiness of the data.

Reliability and validity have traditionally been defined in educational and psychological research concerned with the indirect measurement (e.g., rating scales, checklists, interviews that rely on informants) of the targeted features of the participants and study environment. For example, an indirect assessment of children's conduct problems in the classroom would be the *Behavior Rating Profile* (2nd ed.), which requires informants to rate students on their school, home, and interpersonal relationships (Brown & Hammill, 1990), whereas interobserver agreement has been defined in educational and psychological research concerned with the direct measurement (e.g., observations of actual participant performance) of the targeted features of the participants and study environment. For example, a direct assessment of children's conduct problems in the classroom would be the frequency (number) of conduct problems exhibited in the classroom rather than a teacher's rating of conduct problems on a checklist or rating scale.

Questions about the validity of a measurement device and the resulting data are not typically a concern when researchers directly measure the behavior about which they intend to draw conclusions. For example, although validity would be an issue if a researcher used a questionnaire to measure the study habits of students who are at risk for school failure, it would not be a concern if the researcher directly observed how these students study. In other words, validity is inherent in direct observations.

In the case of qualitative research, reliability is viewed differently than it is in quantitative research. This difference arises primarily because qualitative researchers produce a narrative record rather than a numerical record of the targeted features of the participants and study environment. Qualitative researchers view reliability as the fit between what actually occurs in the setting under study and what is recorded as data, whereas quantitative researchers view reliability as the consistency across different observations. Both qualitative and quantitative researchers consider their findings valid if the inferences they draw about the matter under study are accurate.

This chapter begins with a discussion of the concepts of reliability and validity within the context of quantitative research. This discussion includes a description of three methods used for determining reliability including their relationship to standard error of measurement as well as four types of validity. Next, the concepts of reliability and validity within the context of qualitative research are discussed, including the procedures used to determine them. This chapter concludes with a presentation of interobserver agreement and a discussion of guidelines on how to assess measurement device(s) in the context of a research study.

WHAT ARE RELIABILITY AND VALIDITY ISSUES IN QUANTITATIVE RESEARCH?

There are different types of reliability that vary based on the evidence gathered. Similarly, there are different types of validity, the choice of which depends on the intended function of the measurement device used by the researcher. Most researchers view reliability as the consistency of the results over time. In other words, most researchers believe that reliability indicates whether the participants would essentially respond the same way at different times. This type of reliability is referred to as "stability," and constitutes only one of three ways used by researchers to secure estimates of the stability of measurement devices. However, critical research consumers should consider the relationship between reliability and validity before looking more closely at the three procedures for estimating the reliability of measurement devices.

If a measurement device is reliable, does that mean that it is valid? If a measurement device is valid, is it also reliable? Answers to these questions depend on the relationship between reliability and validity. Reliability has traditionally been considered a necessary but insufficient condition in measurement use (e.g., AERA et al., 1985; Feldt & Brennan, 1989). In order for a measurement device to be valid, it must be reliable. Unreliable measurement devices cannot be valid. Yet a measurement device that is reliable does not guarantee that it is valid. For example, a highly reliable standardized academic achievement test might be valid for assessing children's academic competence but not for predicting their success in college.

Again, it is not the measurement device that is valid, but the inferences made by the researcher based on this measurement device. Put another way, a measurement device could yield both valid and invalid scores depending on the inferences drawn by the researcher. On one hand, the measurement device may be considered valid if the researcher drew inferences for which the device was designed. On the other hand, the measurement device would be considered invalid if the researcher drew inferences for which the device was not designed. The measurement device would also be considered invalid if the researcher drew inaccurate conclusions.

The validity of inferences drawn from tests is sometimes referred to as consequential validity (Gall, Borg, & Gall, 1996). Problems arising from these inferences are not surprising given that many of the constructs of interest within education and psychology (e.g., intelligence, personality) are value-laden. Gould (1981) chronicles the range of inappropriate inferences made in the area of intelligence. For example, in the late 1800s, some researchers believed that intelligence was a function of brain size, thereby drawing inappropriate conclusions. For example, in 1879, Gustave LeBon concluded:

> *In the most intelligent races, as among the Parisians, there are a large number of women whose brains are closer in size to those of gorillas than the most developed male brains. This inferiority is so obvious that no one can contest it for a moment; only its degree is worth discussion. All psychologists who have studied the intelligence of women, as well as poets and novelists, recognize today that they represent the most inferior forms of human evolution and that they are closer to children and savages than to an adult, civilized man. They excel in fickleness, inconstancy, absence of thought and logic, and incapacity to reason. Without doubt there exist some distinguished women, very superior to the average man, but they are as exceptional as the birth of any monstrosity, as, for*

example, of a gorilla with two heads; consequently, we may neglect them entirely. (Gould, 1981, pp. 104–105)

Gould (1981) reexamined LeBon's data. Although Gould found the numbers sound, the claim that women's intelligence was inferior to men was unfounded because gender differences in brain size can be easily explained by other factors such as height and weight. Gould concluded that the weight of the brain was just that and nothing more.

Do valid tests have to be reliable? As discussed in Chapter 2, researchers must be concerned with measurement error because it is directly related to the reliability of the measurement device. Measurement devices provide estimates (true value plus measurement error) of the attribute under study. Measurement devices that yield unreliable or inconsistent scores have large unsystematic measurement error. (Systematic error does not affect the reliability of measurement devices.) When the score fluctuates even though the attribute under study does not, the problem rests with the measurement device. The measurement device yields results that are influenced by unsystematic measurement error. Such a device cannot yield a consistent measurement of a variable. Thus, it is not possible to demonstrate the validity or accuracy of something that cannot be measured consistently.

For example, suppose we wish to make an inference of a person's intelligence with an intelligence test. We provide the test the first time and get a score of 115. A second testing produces a score of 95; a third testing produces a score of 105. What is the person's intelligence? It would not be possible to make an inference due to the inconsistency or unreliability of the scores. Thus, we cannot have validity without reliability. On the other hand, we can measure foot size fairly consistently (unless, of course, we use an elastic ruler!). We can say that the measure of foot size is reliable. However, can we then say that the size of one's foot represents that person's intelligence? We would have a problem with the inference we made or the validity of the statement. Therefore, we can have reliability without validity.

HOW DO RESEARCHERS ASSESS THE RELIABILITY OF MEASUREMENT DEVICES?

Reliability is an extremely important characteristic of measurement devices and should be examined closely. In short, we are concerned with estimating the precision with which one may generalize from one sample of behavior to other samples when considering the reliability of measurement devices.

There are different ways of securing evidence regarding the reliability of the measurement device used by quantitative researchers. We will now consider the three most commonly used approaches to assess the reliability of measurement devices. These approaches include the coefficient of stability, the coefficient of equivalence, and the coefficient of internal consistency. With the exception of the coefficient of internal consistency (where comparisons are made among the items on the measurement device), each of these approaches involves comparison of one administration of the measurement device with another administration using the same people. This comparison is followed by a calculation of a correlation coefficient that measures the degree of relationship between two sets of scores.

Types of Reliability Coefficients

Coefficient of Stability. The coefficient of stability, sometimes called test-retest reliability, is computed by administering the measurement device to a sample of individuals and then readministering the device to the same sample of individuals after some time delay. A reliable measurement device is one in which each participant's score is reasonably the same on the second assessment as on the first, relative to the rest of the group. In other words, it is not necessary for a measurement device to produce essentially the same score for each participant on the second occasion as on the first. In the case of a measurement device with a high degree of test-retest reliability, if scores change (move up or down) from one administration to another they do so in a relatively systematic manner (i.e., on average all participants' scores tend to go up or down the same degree).

The coefficient of stability is expressed numerically by determining the correlation or relationship between the scores obtained from the two administrations of the measurement device; this coefficient provides an estimate of the stability or consistency of the measurement device over time. The sequence for obtaining the coefficient of stability can be depicted as follows: Coefficient of stability = administer the measurement device—provide a time delay—re-administer the measurement device. This sequence is depicted in the following example. Say we wanted to establish the coefficient of stability for a survey of teachers' attitudes toward students with disabilities. The same survey would be administered to the same teachers on two different occasions. A reasonable time delay between the first and second administration would be approximately 4 weeks. This period of time would ensure that teachers would be unable to recall their responses on the first survey and that they would not be influenced by other factors such as training or experience. Participant scores on the first and second occasion would then be correlated to establish the coefficient of stability for the survey.

If the coefficient of stability has been used by the researcher to assess the reliability of the measurement device, it is important to consider the period of time delay used. On one hand, if the retest has been administered too quickly after the initial test, the participants may recall their responses to many of the items that will tend to produce a spuriously high-reliability coefficient. On the other hand, if the retest has been delayed for too long after the initial test, the participants' abilities may have changed producing an indeterminable effect on the reliability coefficient. Between-testing intervals of 3 to 6 weeks are common with measurement devices that can be influenced by maturation (e.g., growing older) or instruction (e.g., achievement tests). Longer between-testing intervals are often seen with intelligence or aptitude measurement devices that are not easily influenced by development or instruction.

Coefficient of Equivalence. The coefficient of equivalence, sometimes called alternate forms or parallel forms reliability, is computed by administering two analogous forms of the measurement device to the same group of individuals. A reliable measurement device using the coefficient of equivalence is one in which each participant's score is reasonably the same on the second form of the measurement device as on the first, relative to the rest of the group. Again, it is not necessary for a measurement device to produce a corresponding score for each participant on the second form of the measurement device as on the first. In the case of a measurement device with a high degree of alternate form reliability, if scores change (move up or down) from one form of the measurement device to another, they do so in a relatively systematic fashion.

The correlation coefficient is expressed numerically and is derived by correlating the two sets of scores obtained on the alternate forms of the measurement device. This correlation provides an estimate of stability or consistency of the measurement device between samples of the targeted feature under study. Alternate forms reliability is important in those cases in which there is a need to eliminate the potential influence of practice effects on participants' scores. For example, say we are interested in studying the effects of an intensive instructional approach in science over a 1-week period. In this case, it would be necessary to use parallel forms of the measurement device because there is a high probability that there will be practice effects.

The sequence for obtaining the coefficient of equivalence can be depicted as follows: Coefficient of equivalence = administer Form A of the measurement device—administer Form B of the measurement device. Additionally, researchers will sometimes include a time delay when calculating the coefficient of equivalence, essentially combining stability and equivalence. In this case, the sequence for obtaining the coefficient of equivalence can be depicted as follows: Coefficient of equivalence/stability = administer Form A of the measurement device—provide a time delay—administer Form B of the measurement device. The following example depicts this sequence. Suppose we wanted to establish the alternate forms reliability of a measurement device for the science program we wish to conduct. The first form would be administered to a group of students on Monday. Given that the study period will be 1 week, the second form of the measurement device would be administered on Friday of the same week. Participants' scores on the two forms of the measurement device would be correlated to establish the coefficient of equivalence.

If the coefficient of equivalence has been used by the researcher to assess the reliability of the measurement device, it is important to consider the equivalence of the sample items used for each form of the measurement device. Because measurement devices typically include only a small sample of all potential items, they are likely to discriminate in favor of some participants and against others. If the researcher has included items that are very similar in nature on the two forms of the measurement device, each form will discriminate in favor of the same participants, which will tend to produce a spuriously high reliability coefficient. If the researcher has included items that are not similar in nature on the two forms of the measurement device, each form will discriminate in favor of different participants, which will tend to produce a conservative reliability coefficient.

Coefficient of Internal Consistency. Internal consistency refers to the tendency of different items to evoke the same response from any given participant on a single administration of the measurement device. In contrast to the two methods discussed earlier, the coefficient of internal consistency is determined from a single administration of the measurement device. Internal consistency establishes how unified the items are in a measurement device. In other words, it provides a measure of the degree to which items on the measurement device are functioning in a homogeneous (similar) fashion. For example, say we wanted to establish the internal consistency of a personality measure containing 40 items. Because each of these items is believed to be measuring the same construct (i.e., personality), we would want each item to reflect an individual's personality. This point would also be true in the case of measurement devices that contain subscales reflecting different aspects of a construct or entirely different constructs. The sequence for obtaining the coefficient of internal consistency can be depicted as follows: Coefficient of internal consistency = administer Subtest A of the measurement device—administer Subtest B of the measurement device.

There are three commonly used methods for computing internal consistency: split-half correlation, Kuder–Richardson method of rational equivalence, and Cronbach's Coefficient Alpha. The split-half correlation is computed by administering the measurement device to a group of individuals. The measurement device is then split into two subtests to obtain two sets of comparable items. This division is typically accomplished by placing the odd-numbered items in one subtest and the even-numbered items in another subtest. The scores of the two subtests are then computed for each individual and correlated with one another. Of course, calculating split-half reliability demands that the items that compose the two subtests be as similar as possible. Otherwise, the estimate of the reliability will be complicated by a change in the content of the two subtests. This demand is more likely to be met by items on a measurement device with homogeneous items than by items on a device that are designed to measure multiple attributes. Additionally, the correlation obtained is an estimate of the reliability for only *half* the measurement device, whereas the Spearman-Brown prophecy formula is used to provide an estimate of the reliability of the *entire* measurement device.

The method of rational equivalence is the only technique used by researchers that does not require the computation of a correlation coefficient (Richardson & Kuder, 1939). This method assesses the internal consistency of the measurement device through the analysis of the individual items. As such, it requires only a single administration of the test. A number of formulas have been developed to provide an estimate of the internal consistency of measurement devices that are scored dichotomously (i.e., right or wrong) and for those that are not scored dichotomously. The Kuder–Richardson formulas (K–R20 and K–R21) are used in the case of measurement devices that are scored dichotomously and Cronbach's Coefficient Alpha is used in the case of devices that are not scored dichotomously. Each of these formulas can be thought of as representing the average correlation from all possible split-half reliability estimates.

The basic rationale underlying the measures of internal consistency is that if the items on a measurement device are relatively homogeneous, there will be a great deal of variance on the measurement device. This variance occurs on any given measurement device because there will be some participants who will score high and some who will score low if the items are measuring the same thing. The internal consistency formulas incorporate this rationale by stressing the impact of score variance, with minor adjustments made for test length.

Interpretation of Reliability Coefficients. In general, reliability coefficients provide an estimate of the effect of unsystematic measurement error on the findings. In other words, the reliability coefficient provides an estimate of the extent to which the measurement device is free of unsystematic measurement error. Reliability coefficients vary between values of 0.00 and 1.00, with 1.00 indicating perfect reliability and 0.00 indicating no reliability. The higher the reliability, the smaller the influence of measurement error. Although it is difficult to assess what constitutes high and low reliability in research, some guidance is necessary to assess the quality of the measurement device used by researchers. Reliability coefficients of .70 or above are usually considered respectable regardless of the type of reliability calculated or the method of calculation used. Reliability coefficients of .90 and above are not unusual for standardized achievement tests. Although reliability coefficients of .70 and higher are certainly desirable among many measures, lower coefficients can be tolerated; of course, this will reduce the level of confidence in the findings.

Researchers need to look closely at the reliability of commonly used measurement devices. The use of projective personality tests is a case in point. Projective personality tests such as the Rorschach Inkblot Test, the Thematic Apperception Test (TAT), the Children's Apperception Test (CAT), and the Draw-A-Person Test have been derived from the psychoanalytic model of personality in which projection is defined as a primary defense mechanism against anxiety (Weiner & Stewart, 1984). For example, the Rorschach Inkblot Test is comprised of 10 inkblot designs, five of which are black and white and five of which are in full or partial color. The cards are presented in a specific order, and the client is asked to report whatever he or she sees in the blot. The results are scored according to one of several standardized systems. Reliability studies of the Rorschach Inkblot Test have yielded low reliabilities (e.g., ranging from .20 to .64) that are similar to other projective personality tests. These low-reliability figures led Anatasi (1982) to conclude:

> *...projective techniques are clearly found wanting when evaluated in accordance with test standards. This [conclusion] is evident from the data summarized...with regard to standardization of administration and scoring procedures, adequacy of norms, reliability, and validity. The accumulation of published studies that have "failed" to demonstrate any reliability and validity for such projective techniques as the Rorschach and the D-A-P is truly impressive. (p. 589)*

Relationship among Reliability Coefficients and Sources of Unsystematic Measurement Error. Participants' responses on a measurement device are influenced by many things other than the matter under study by the researcher. These other things are called measurement error. As mentioned in Chapter 2, some measurement error is systematic and some is unsystematic. The reliability methods described before provide an estimate of the degree to which unsystematic error affects the findings, and different methods take into account different sources of error. The five primary sources of unsystematic measurement error that affect reliability include the following:

1. *Variations in individuals* such as fluctuations in mood, alertness, fatigue, and recent good or bad experiences. For example, changes in the performance of participants from the pretest to the posttest might be influenced if the pretest was given early in the day when participants were alert and the posttest was given at the end of the day when participants were fatigued.

2. *Variations in the conditions* of administration from one administration to the next such as unusual noise or inconsistencies in the administration of the measurement device. For example, differences in the pretest and posttest performance of participants might be influenced if the individual administering the tests used different administration procedures (e.g., participants read the instructions independently on the pretest while the individual administering the posttest reads the instructions and solicits questions).

3. *Biases associated with the measurement device* such as items that discriminate in favor of some individuals and against others. There are numerous biases that may be encountered in measurement devices. These biases include those based on gender, religion, geographic location, linguistic ability, and race. An example of racial bias in intelligence testing was pointed out by Robert L. Williams, a black psychologist. Williams (1974) noted, "Is it more indicative of intelligence to know Malcolm X's last name or the author of Hamlet? I ask you now, 'When is Washington's birthday?' Perhaps 99% of you thought February 22. That answer presupposes a white norm. I actually meant Booker T. Washington's birthday, not George Washington's" (p. 165). Another type of bias occurs when the researcher uses a measurement device that discriminates in favor of the experimental group and against the control group. For example, a researcher is interested in assessing the effects of a mnemonic strategy designed to help students recall science-related facts. To do so, the researcher compares the performance of the experimental group that receives the mnemonic strategy with that of the control group that receives instruction on global science concepts rather than factual information using a measurement device that includes only factual questions. In this case, it would not be surprising that the experimental group would outperform the control group because the measurement device is likely to discriminate in favor of the experimental group.

4. *Biases associated with participants* such as cheating, help given to participants by the administrator of the measurement device, guessing, marking responses without trying to understand them, practice effects, and anticipation of participants regarding the results expected by the researcher. For example, differences in the pretest and posttest performance of participants might be influenced if they were monitored closely during the pretest but not during the posttest. This lack of monitoring would provide participants the opportunity to assist one another.

5. *Biases associated with the administrator* of the measurement device such as differences in scoring or interpreting results, errors in computing scores, and errors in recording scores. These types of biases tend to occur across both experimental and control groups, introducing error variance in their scores.

These five sources of unsystematic measurement error affect the reliability of the findings by introducing unaccounted error; therefore, researchers will be unable to determine what effect sources of error have on the findings of their investigation. The effect of the first three sources of unsystematic measurement error can be estimated by applying the different methods of estimating reliability described previously. The last two sources of unsystematic measurement error cannot be accounted for by the different methods of estimating reliability. Rather, the researcher must take steps to ensure that biases associated with the participants and the administrator of the measurement device do not affect the findings.

Table 3.1 summarizes the sources of unsystematic measurement error estimated by each of the methods of estimating reliability. The different methods of estimating the reliability of measurement devices take into account different sources of error. Reliability coefficients based on a single administration of the measurement device (i.e., internal consistency) do not account for two important sources of error—variations in individuals and conditions. Individuals vary from day to day on many subtle attributes such as mood, fatigue, and attitude toward the measurement device. Similarly, it is difficult for researchers to maintain standard conditions when the measurement device is administered on different occasions.

Reliability coefficients based on the administration of the same measurement device on two different occasions (i.e., coefficient of stability) do not account for biases associated with the measurement device. The specific items on a measurement device are likely to discriminate in favor of some participants and against others because the items typically constitute a limited sample of all of the items that could be included on the device.

Each of these sources of unsystematic error are only estimated when reliability coefficients are based on the administration of two different forms of the measurement device with a time delay between administrations (i.e., coefficient of equivalence). Additionally, this method of estimating reliability tends to reflect more closely the conditions that are in place in applied settings. Critical research consumers should consider which of the aforementioned sources of unsystematic measurement error is present in the setting to which they wish to generalize the findings and take these sources of error into account when assessing the reliability of the measurement device.

Standard Error of Measurement

The methods for estimating the reliability of measurement devices have centered on providing an overall estimate of the consistency in a group of participants' scores on the measurement device. However, these methods do not tell us much about the consistency of an individual's score. The standard error of measurement is used to provide an estimate of the consistency (or accuracy) of an individual's score. The standard error of measurement can be viewed as an estimate of the

TABLE 3.1 Sources of Unsystematic Measurement Error Estimated by Each Reliability Method

METHOD OF ESTIMATING RELIABILITY	SOURCES OF UNSYSTEMATIC MEASUREMENT ERROR ESTIMATED
1. Coefficient of stability	• Variations in individuals • Variations in conditions
2. Coefficient of equivalence	
• Single administration of both forms	• Biases associated with the measurement device
• Time delay between administrations of both forms	• Variations in individuals • Variations in conditions • Biases associated with the measurement device
3. Coefficient of internal consistency	• Biases associated with the measurement device

variability of an individual's score if the measurement device was administered over and over again. This estimate of the variability of an individual's score is based on data from the group and enables the researcher to estimate the range within which an individual's true score probably falls. The formula for the standard error of measurement is as follows:

$$SEM = SD\sqrt{1 - r_{xx}}$$

where SEM = standard error of measurement

SD = standard deviation of the scores or responses

r_{xx} = reliability of the test

An example illustrating the use of the standard error of measurement follows. Suppose we are working with a measurement device that had a standard deviation of 8.0 and a reliability coefficient of .92. We would substitute in the formula and solve as follows:

$$\begin{aligned} SEM &= 8.0\sqrt{1 - .92} \\ &= 8.0\sqrt{.08} \\ &= 8.0(.28) \\ &= 2.24 \end{aligned}$$

How does one interpret what 2.24 means? Based on the properties of the normal probability curve, the value of ±2.24 can be used to make some confidence-band assertions about the accuracy of an individual's scores. The relationship between errors and the normal probability curve is depicted in Figure 3.1. About 68% of all test scores will be within plus or minus one standard error of measurement of their true score, and about 95% will be within ± two standard errors of measurement of their true score. In the preceding example, if a participant obtained a score of 50 on a mea-

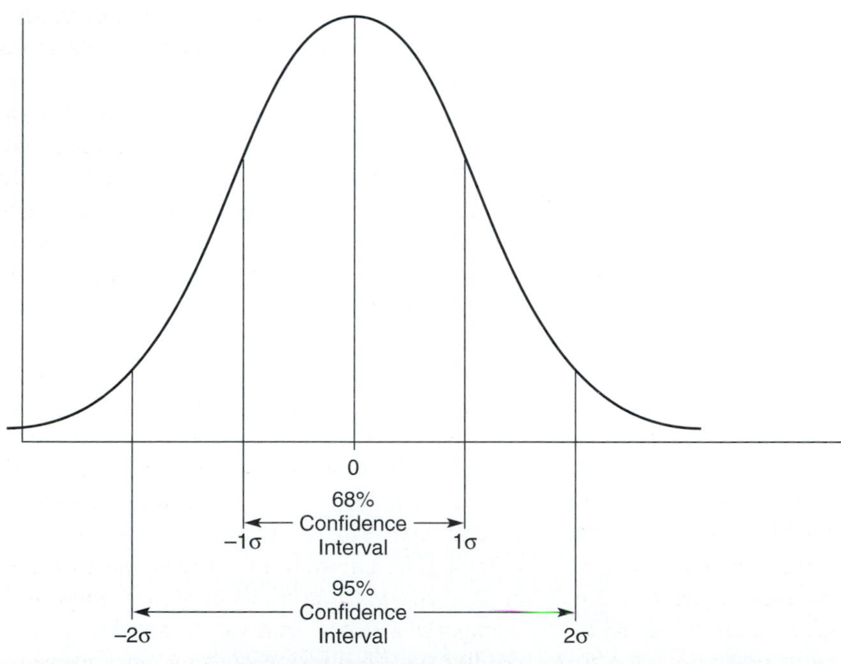

FIGURE 3.1 Normal probability curve depicting 68% and 95% confidence intervals. (σ is the population standard deviation.)

surement device, there would be 68 chances in 100 that his or her true score would be between 47.76 and 52.24 (i.e., 50 ± 2.24); and 95 chances in 100 that his or her true score would lie between 45.52 and 54.48 (i.e., 50 ± 4.48).

The size of the standard error of measurement is inversely related to the reliability coefficient. That is, as the reliability of the measurement device increases, the standard error of measurement decreases. Thus, measurement devices of low reliability are subject to large errors, whereas devices of high reliability are subject to small errors. For example, if the measurement device in the preceding example would have had a reliability of .98, the standard error of measurement would have been 1.12; whereas, if the reliability had been .52, the standard error of measurement would have been 5.52.

Although the standard error of measurement is not often reported by researchers, it can be easily calculated from the information provided (i.e., reliability of the measurement device and standard deviation). The standard error of measurement is typically more useful to the researcher because it is very stable across populations. The standard error of measurement is more useful in interpreting test scores than are reliability coefficients (AERA et al., 1985). Additionally, the standard error of measurement helps the researcher understand that the scores obtained on measurement devices are only estimates and can be considerably different from the individual's "true score."

HOW DO RESEARCHERS DETERMINE THE VALIDITY OF MEASUREMENT DEVICES?

Validity and reliability refer to different aspects of a measurement device's "believability." It should be clear by now that reliability coefficients answer the question, "Does the measurement device yield consistent results?" Judgments of validity answer the question, "Is the measurement device an appropriate one for what needs to be measured?" These are questions critical research consumers must ask about any measurement device researchers select to use.

Consider the report by Weinstein (1990) regarding the impact of teacher preparation programs on prospective teachers' beliefs about teaching. Weinstein concluded that teacher preparation programs did not change prospective teachers' beliefs about teaching—"Despite course work and field experiences, the candidates' beliefs about teaching and themselves as teachers remained unchanged throughout the semester" (p. 140). However, Weinstein found that there was a significant decrease in optimism ($p < .05$), a 13% decrease in the number of candidates who stressed caring, an 8% increase in the number of candidates enthused about teaching, a 13% increase in the number of candidates who believed they had the ability to maintain discipline, a 16% decrease in the number of candidates who believed they had the ability to motivate students, and a 14% increase in the number of candidates who believed they could meet the diverse needs of individual students. This case illustrates how researchers can misrepresent and invalidate their data. This case also punctuates the notion that there is an uncritical acceptance of researchers' conclusions by others; this lack of skepticism is extremely problematic.

Additionally, it is important to note that validity not only deals with the measurement device's representation of the construct under study, but also the circumstances of its administration. The validity of the measurement device is affected by the manner in which it is administered. If the measurement device is administered inappropriately, the interpretation of the results, and hence the validity of the measurement device, will be adversely affected.

Like reliability, there are a number of procedures used to validate a measurement device. We will deal with three types of validity—construct, content, and criterion. Each type of validity provides a different view of whether the measurement device is fulfilling its purported purpose. It is important to note that we do not discuss face validity (simply looking at items on a measurement device and judging the device to measure what it is supposed to measure) directly because it is not a *Standards* approved form of validity (AERA et al., 1985). Despite the fact that face validity is not an accepted form of validity, the validity of many measurement devices is based on it. Indeed, the *Standards* were originally developed to stifle the proliferation of the use of face validity.

Types of Validity

Construct Validity. Construct validity of a measurement device is the extent to which it can be shown to measure a hypothetical construct. The word *construct* is a term used to refer to the skills, attitudes, or characteristics of individuals that are not directly observable but are inferred on the basis of their observable effects on behavior. The extent to which it can be shown that a measurement device has construct validity depends largely on the specificity of the construct itself. Sometimes the construct measured is one for which representative items can be written with reasonable ease such as the ability to compute mathematical problems correctly. In this situation, there is a high degree of agreement about what demonstration of the construct would look like. However, there are many psychological constructs such as intelligence, attitude, and personality where there may be little agreement about what demonstration of the construct would look like. Demonstrating construct validity when there is no clear, widely accepted definition is problematic.

There is no single way to demonstrate the construct validity of a measurement device. The authors of the *Standards* make clear that the construct validity of a measurement device cannot be established with a single study. Rather, construct validity is based on an accumulation of research studies. More often than not, the construct validity of a measurement device is inappropriately based on face validity procedures. One common face validity procedure involves using the opinions of judges or experts in an area to establish the construct validity of a measurement device. The extent to which experts' individual conclusions about what the measurement device appears to be measuring agree with each other is believed to provide an indication of the construct validity of the device. Another common face validity procedure does not involve any systematic process at all. Researchers simply accept the instrument as logically related to the construct. However, as noted before, face validity, regardless of how it is established, is an unacceptable form of validity (AERA et al., 1985).

Acceptable approaches to establishing the construct validity of a measurement device include intervention studies, differential population studies, and related measures studies. Intervention studies demonstrate that participants respond differently to the measure after receiving some sort of experimental intervention. For example, to validate a new measurement device measuring an individual's test anxiety, we might take 50 college students majoring in science. Students would be randomly assigned to two groups of 25 each. One group (experimental group) is told that the science test is necessary to continue pursuing a degree in science, whereas the other group (control group) is told that the science test is only to provide professors information with which to guide the development of their courses. Then all of the students are given the test anxiety inventory. If the experimental students display significantly greater test anxiety on the inventory than the control students, this finding would provide evidence to support the construct validity of the inventory.

The differential population approach to establishing the construct validity of a measurement device involves demonstrating that individuals representing distinct populations score differently on the measure. For example, to validate a new self-report social adjustment scale, students identified as having behavioral disorders and those without behavior disorders would be administered the scale. If the students with behavioral disorders display significantly lower levels of social adjustment than the students without behavior disorders, this finding would provide evidence of the construct validity of the scale.

The related measures approach to establishing the construct validity of a measurement device involves demonstrating a correlation (either positive or negative depending on the measurement device) between participants' scores on the measurement device and their scores on another measure. For example, to validate a new measure of collaboration skills, a group of individuals would be administered the new measure along with a measure of individualism. Because one would expect individuals with collaborative skills to display less individualism and vice versa, one would expect a negative correlation between the measures. This example illustrates that the correlation can be positive or negative depending on the measure involved.

Although there are number of approaches to establish the construct validity of measurement devices, researchers rarely provide evidence to indicate that they are indeed measuring the constructs (inferences) that they purport to measure. Construct validity is a particularly important factor to consider when there is no clear, widely accepted definition of the construct of interest such as with intelligence, attitude, and personality. In some instances, construct validity is not an important factor to consider. In those cases in which the construct is clear and there is a widely accepted definition (e.g., ability to compute mathematical problems correctly), construct validity may not be important to consider. Construct validity may also not be an issue in those cases in which the concern is to identify a measurement device that has predictive validity for a particular purpose and there is not an intent to appeal to theory. In this case, researchers are most interested in whether the measurement device predicts some established outcome.

Content Validity. Content validity refers to the representativeness of the sample of items included in measurement devices. This type of validity is important because it is generally impossible for a measurement device to encompass all of the relevant items that would prompt individuals to display the behaviors characteristic of a particular construct. Content validity is primarily of importance in assessing the skills and competencies of individuals such as in achievement testing. The content validity of a measurement device is assured when it includes items that represent the entire range of skills and competencies and emphasizes each particular area of skills and competencies according to its importance in providing evidence of the construct.

There is generally one approach used to establish the content validity of measurement devices. Achieving content validity requires that the construct be translated into a set of distinctive behaviors. These behaviors are then described in terms of how people act, or occasionally in terms of what others say about these people. The measurement device is then constructed, with items that are representative in type and proportion, to prompt people to display these characteristic behaviors. Because most measurement devices measure a number of different subtypes (i.e., behaviors) in a given content area, they must include a proportionate number of items to represent each subtype. Essentially, a proportional stratified item development procedure is employed to ensure that each subtype includes the same number of items as the proportion in the given content area. This procedure helps ensure that the measurement device includes a balance of items. In contrast, a nonproportional item development procedure would involve simply selecting a specified number of items to represent each subtype regardless of its proportion in the content area.

Looking closely at the content validity of the measurement device is especially important in those cases where different intervention approaches are being studied. In such cases, the measurement device may favor one intervention over another. For example, if researchers used a mathematics achievement test that emphasized computational skills to assess the relative intervention effects of a new program emphasizing understanding of mathematical concepts, they may conclude that the new program was not any more effective than the traditional program. The outcomes might have been different if the researchers had employed a mathematics achievement test that emphasized both computational skills and understanding of mathematical concepts. The critical research consumer should carefully consider the content validity of the measurement device in cases that involve the comparison of the effects of different interventions.

Criterion-Related Validity. Criterion-related validity refers to the extent to which an individual's score on a measurement device is used to predict his or her score on another measurement device. There are two types of criterion-related validity—concurrent and predictive—that are used to infer an individual's probable standing on some criterion variable (e.g., aptitude, intelligence, work-related skills), differing only in a temporal manner. Statements of concurrent validity indicate the extent to which the measurement device may be used to estimate an individual's present standing on the criterion variable. On the other hand, statements of predictive validity indicate the extent to which the measurement device may be used to estimate an individual's future level on the criterion variable. Thus, the primary difference between concurrent and predictive validity is the time interval. Predictive validity requires that a substantial time interval occur between administration of the measurement device being validated and the gathering of the criterion data. With concurrent validity, no such time interval is present. It should be apparent that the legitimacy of the criterion measurement device is critical to both concurrent and predictive validity. The criterion measurement device must be valid if meaningful statements about the concurrent and predictive validity of a measurement device are to be made.

The concurrent or predictive validity of a measurement device is established by collecting both the scores of a group of individuals obtained with a certain measurement device and their scores from other devices administered at approximately the same time (concurrent validity) or a future date (predictive validity). The scores are then correlated to provide an estimate of the concurrent or predictive validity of the measurement device.

Interpretation of the coefficient of concurrent or predictive validity is relatively straightforward. These coefficients, like reliability coefficients, vary between values of –1.00 to 1.00. A 0.00 correlation coefficient between the scores of two measurement devices would be interpreted to mean that there is no systematic relationship to each other—scores on one measurement device tell us nothing about scores on the other measurement device. The greater the value of the coefficient, the more accurate the prediction of the scores of one measurement device to the other and vice versa. If the coefficient is either –1.00 or 1.00, a perfect prediction can be made.

Looking closely at the concurrent validity of the measurement device used by researchers is critical in those cases in which they have used a short, easily administered measurement device in place of one that is long or not easily administered. In such cases, researchers are trying to get an efficient estimate of the construct of interest. This administration is not problematic if they employed a measurement device that had a high degree of concurrent validity with a "valid" criterion measurement device. Looking closely at the predictive validity of the measurement device is critical in those cases in which researchers want to predict future performance. Predictive validity is the most commonly used form of criterion-related validity used by researchers.

Concurrent validity can be illustrated by the following example. Say a district has developed its own curriculum-based measure of academic performance. It needs to ask the question, "Does our assessment device actually measure achievement?" At this point, the district needs to find a valid criterion measure. According to Salvia and Ysseldyke (1995), there are two basic choices for this criterion measure: (a) another achievement test that is presumed to be valid, and (b) judgments of academic performance made by teachers, parents, or the students themselves. If the new curriculum-based measurement correlates significantly with the other criterion measures, the district can conclude there is evidence for the new assessment's concurrent validity with another criterion measure.

Predictive validity can be illustrated by the following example noted by Salvia and Ysseldyke (1995). If a district develops a test of reading readiness, it can ask, "Does knowledge of a student's score on the reading readiness assessment allow an accurate estimation of the student's actual readiness for instruction sometime in the future?" As noted before for concurrent validity, the district must first find a valid criterion measure such as a valid reading achievement test. If the district's test of reading readiness corresponds closely with the validated reading achievement test and accurately estimates how the student will perform in subsequent instruction, it has established a measurement device that has predictive validity.

WHAT ARE RELIABILITY AND VALIDITY ISSUES IN QUALITATIVE RESEARCH?

As mentioned before, both quantitative and qualitative researchers are concerned about the reliability and validity of the data collected. Additionally, many qualitative researchers are concerned with reliability and validity; however, it should be noted that others in the qualitative community do not view reliability and validity as necessarily important (see Chapter 8). It is difficult to establish the reliability and validity of qualitative research using quantitative methods because the researcher *is* the measurement device. There are several reasons why quantitative methods for establishing reliability and validity are generally not relevant to data collected using qualitative methods. First, qualitative researchers generate a narrative representation of the target features of the participants and study environment rather than a numerical one. The traditional methods for estimating the reliability and validity of measurement devices were developed for numerical representations of the target features of the participants and the study environment.

Second, because qualitative researchers use an emerging design approach rather than a predetermined design approach, two researchers are not likely to produce the same results (Eisner, 1991; Hillocks, 1992; Pitman & Maxwell, 1992). In essence, qualitative researchers expect that researchers will collect distinct information because their backgrounds and interests differ, which is likely to influence the design of the study. Additionally, qualitative researchers will also interpret the data differently and reach different conclusions because of their varied backgrounds and interests. Although qualitative researchers are likely to produce differences in findings and interpretations about the same inquiry area, these differences do not necessarily mean that the findings are incomplete or inaccurate.

Third, quantitative methods for establishing reliability are not generally relevant to qualitative studies because of the influence of contextual variables that operate in natural settings (Marshall & Rossman, 1995). Examples of contextual variables in a study of violence prevention efforts in schools might include community demographics and resources, school organizational procedures and practices, staff characteristics, and student and family characteristics. Different or contradictory data may be obtained by the same researcher because of these contextual variables rather than being attributable to the lack of reliability. In short, changes in the context may produce differences in the findings rather than the differences being a function of measurement error.

The final reason that quantitative methods for establishing reliability are not generally relevant to qualitative research centers on differences in the underlying theoretical stance of these two research methods (Taylor & Bogdan, 1984). Qualitative researchers collect data that are subjective, dynamic, and changeable over time. As mentioned previously, participants' views and perceptions are influenced by changes in the context. In contrast, quantitative researchers collect data that are objective, stable, and static. These researchers use predetermined designs to control or account for changes in the context.

Reliability Issues

Because of these aforementioned issues, qualitative researchers have redefined reliability in a manner more congruent with qualitative theory and methodology. Qualitative researchers view reliability as the fit between what actually occurs in the setting under study and what is recorded as data (Taylor & Bogdan, 1984). Given this view, qualitative researchers use methodological procedures in which they fully explain their procedures, verify their observations, and cross-check their sources (Bogdan & Biklen, 1992). Qualitative researchers provide the following specific evidence of reliability (Marshall & Rossman, 1995):

1. Description of the method including the underlying logic.
2. Qualifications of the researcher as participant observer.
3. Assumptions of the researcher.
4. Research questions that are stated and directly connected to the study procedures.
5. Description of the study period as well as range and cycle of activities observed.
6. Data collected from multiple sources.

Validity Issues

Although quantitative and many qualitative researchers have similar views regarding the validity of their data (i.e., accuracy of the inferences drawn from the data), they differ in the methods used to establish the validity of their data. Validity in qualitative research is relative to the researchers' purpose and the circumstances under which the data were collected. The inferences drawn by qualitative researchers will differ depending on their background and interests. In essence, qualitative researchers expect that researchers will interpret the data differently and reach different conclusions because of their varied backgrounds and interests. Although qualitative researchers are likely to produce differences in findings and interpretations about the same inquiry area, these differences do not necessarily mean that the interpretations are invalid. Qualitative researchers provide the following specific evidence of validity (Maxwell, 1992):

1. Description of how an ethical stance toward participants was maintained.
2. Description of field work and analyses including the logic and theoretical base of the data categorizations.
3. Description of cases or situations that might challenge the emerging hypotheses or conclusions.
4. Data collected from multiple sources.
5. Description of how the quality of the data was checked.
6. Description of the formulation and reformulation of the interpretations of the data.
7. Description of how the impact of value judgments was minimized.
8. Discussion of how the study is linked to a theoretical base.
9. Discussion of the limitations of the study.

Illustrative Example of Reliability and Validity Procedures

The following information obtained from a method section of a qualitative study provides an example of how qualitative researchers establish the reliability and validity of a study (this is also the illustrative study at the end of Chapter 9). The purpose of the study was to identify variables associated with successful mainstreaming in science that appeared to be robust across grade levels and specific categories of disability (Scruggs & Mastropieri, 1994).

Scruggs and Mastropieri (1994) went to great lengths to ensure that their data collection had been accurate and systematic and that their conclusions logically proceeded from the interactions of those data sources with their personal perspectives. They obtained multiple sources of evidence in support of each of their conclusions and had extended interactions with the participants. They addressed the issue of consistency by independently confirming all of their conclusions across the classrooms. A detailed description of the *Participants* section of the article is provided to show the level of detail used.

The participants were from a middle SES school district with about 50,000 students in a western metropolitan area. This district was one of four with whom the project staff collaborated as part of a larger project to study science and disability. District science education administrative personnel, building-level administrators, teachers, and special education personnel were interviewed to identify reputational cases of mainstreaming success in science. Project staff also observed three classrooms in three different schools. During the first and second project years, the project staff worked with district teachers and specialists (along with those of the three other school districts) to develop and refine guidelines for including students with disabilities in science classes. Project staff presented the teachers and specialists with draft versions of project guidelines developed from information from previous literature and previously published guidelines and solicited and received written feedback. Project staff revised the guidelines based on teacher/specialist feedback on two separate occasions throughout the 2-year period. The authors noted that the final product contained information on characteristics of specific disability categories, general mainstreaming strategies applied to science classes, and strategies for adapting specific science activities (e.g., electricity units) for students with disabilities. Copies were distributed to all cooperating teachers and administrators. Teachers in the three targeted classrooms were asked to refer to the guidelines in the final product when needed, but they were under no obligation to do so. All teachers reported informally that they had frequently referred to the guidelines.

Scruggs and Mastropieri (1994) fully described each of the three classrooms including the number of students as well as other pertinent demographic information (e.g., socioeconomic status, ethnicity, disability category). They described the teachers in terms of their training and years of experience. The curriculum was described in detail, including what was used, how it was used, and why it was used. The background of the project staff was also described in detail (e.g., staff beliefs and preparation for the project). The description of data collection included how and when data were collected. Scruggs and Mastropieri indicated that the data were analyzed for consistencies and inconsistencies. Out of the data grew a list of seven variables that seemed to be consistent and robust with respect to all data sources across the three different classrooms. Scruggs and Mastropieri further indicated that these variables also were supported by previous research literature including both convergent and divergent instances. Importantly, the conclusions made by the project staff were reexamined to ensure that they were directly supported by evidence gathered in this investigation. This reexamination is a feature sometimes missed in qualitative research on learning and behavior, as noted by the authors.

With regard to reliability and validity, Scruggs and Mastropieri reported the following:

> *Although it may have been less appropriate to address concerns of "reliability" and "validity," at least in the more traditional quantitative sense, in this investigation, we nevertheless wished to ensure that our data collection had been accurate and systematic and that our conclusions logically proceeded from the interactions of those data sources with our personal perspectives. We addressed these issues by obtaining multiple sources of evidence in support of each of our conclusions and by planning and implementing extended interactions with the participants. We also addressed the issue of consistency by confirming that all conclusions were supported by evidence from each classroom, considered independently. (1994, p. 793)*

WHAT IS INTEROBSERVER AGREEMENT?

A primary approach to measurement in educational and psychological research concerned with the direct measurement of behavior is the use of observers to record the occurrence and nonoccurrence of specific behaviors (Baer, 1977; Kratochwill & Wetzel, 1977). It is necessary to qualify the conclusions that interobserver agreement permits about data before describing the procedures used by researchers to establish interobserver agreement. This qualification is necessary because the concept of interobserver agreement or reliability of observations is not the same as the concept of reliability used in educational and psychological research that incorporates indirect measurement of behavior.

Recall that reliability centers on the precision with which one may generalize from one sample of behavior to other samples obtained with measurement devices. The other samples may be obtained at different points in time as in the case of the coefficient of stability or they may be obtained with other sets of items drawn from the universe of possible items and, in some cases, involve both different items and a different time (i.e., coefficient of equivalence). Additionally, the other samples may be obtained from sets of items on a single form of the measurement device as in the case of the coefficient of internal consistency.

In contrast, interobserver agreement says nothing about whether the observations of two independent observers are reliable. Although a high degree of agreement between two independent observers recording responses during a session enhances the believability of the data, it only allows the conclusion that their total values for a session were in agreement. It does not indicate that the observers identified the same responses because each observer may have failed to identify or had mistakenly identified different responses (albeit the same number of responses). In other words, just because two observers say that they saw something does not mean that it really happened. Establishing the degree of interobserver agreement enables the researcher to accept the believability of the data because independently verified reports often are more accurate than a single report.

Interobserver agreement is not only used to assess the occurrence and nonoccurrence of the dependent variable (Hawkins & Fabry, 1979), but also the occurrence and nonoccurrence of the independent variable (Billingsley, White, & Munson, 1980). Measures of interobserver agreement help in answering the question, "Is that what I would have seen if I had been there?"

In general, interobserver agreement serves four primary functions. First, interobserver agreement provides information regarding whether the definitional aspects of the response and intervention are replicable. Second, interobserver agreement provides information with which to assess the extent to which the definitional aspects of the response and the intervention plan are employed competently. Third, interobserver agreement provides information with which to assess the believability of the experimental effects. Finally, interobserver agreement provides information with which to assess the believability of the absolute level of responding aside from any experimental effects shown.

The first two of the preceding functions concern the replicability of the study. Adequate descriptions of the definitional aspects of the response and the measurement procedures as well as the intervention are necessary to ensure that the study can be replicated. The remaining two functions focus on the believability of the reported data. Confidence in the reported findings is enhanced when two independent observers achieve a high degree of agreement regarding the occurrence and nonoccurrence of the response and the intervention.

WHAT ARE THE METHODS OF ESTABLISHING INTEROBSERVER AGREEMENT?

Although a small number of studies have used correlation coefficients to establish the level of interobserver agreement, the percentage of agreement between two independent observers is the most common method for reporting interobserver agreement (Kelly, 1977). Thus, we will focus on the procedures used by researchers to establish the percentage of agreement between two independent observers.

There are a number of general issues that should be considered when assessing interobserver agreement information. First, it is critical that a clear, specific definition be developed to ensure that the observers are able to identify the beginning and end of the behavior. Second, the frequency with which observations are conducted that include interobserver agreement measures should be analyzed. Although there are no set rules, the frequency of interobserver measures used by researchers must fall between the ideal (every recorded response) and the minimum (once per condition such as once before intervention and once during intervention). Although there appear to be no specified standards, it is common practice to assess interobserver agreement on at least 20% to 25% of the sessions. Third, interobserver agreement should be reported for both the dependent variable and the independent variable. Further, agreement data should be reported for each behavior for each participant. Finally, the level of interobserver agreement should meet an acceptable level. Although a minimum criterion for the acceptability of interobserver agreement has not be established, the usual convention is to expect independent observers to achieve an average of at least 80% agreement (Barlow & Hersen, 1984).

Of course, the 80% rule is arbitrary and must be interpreted within the context of the study. For example, if the average interobserver agreement for a study using permanent products such as written answers to mathematics problems was 80%, one would view the data cautiously, whereas this level of interobserver agreement would be acceptable in those cases in which the researcher was measuring more complex behaviors such as the wide range of behavior associated with teaching.

The specific formulas used by researchers to establish interobserver agreement are dependent upon the observation procedure used and include measures of permanent products, event recording, latency and duration recording, and interval recording (Allessi, 1980; Sulzer-Azaroff & Mayer, 1991). The observation procedures and associated methods for calculating interobserver agreement follow.

Measures of Permanent Products

Researchers sometimes use permanent products (e.g., completed worksheets, puzzles completed, written examinations, written spelling words) to assess the effects of an intervention. With this observation procedure, the researcher observes the product of a participant's behavior. The actual behavior itself is not observed. For example, a researcher might use the number of mathematics problems completed correctly to assess the effects of a self-management intervention on the on-task behavior of students. Although it may seem unnecessary to assess the level of agreement with permanent products that are easily identified discrete responses, mistakes do occur in the scoring of permanent products. The following formula is used to establish the percentage of agreement between independent observers measuring permanent products. The percentage of agreement equals the number of agreements divided by the total number of agreements and disagreements multiplied by 100:

$$\text{Percentage of agreement} = \frac{\text{agreements}}{\text{agreements} + \text{disagreements}} \times 100$$

Inspection of the forumula reveals that as the number of disagreements goes up, the percentage of agreement goes down. For example, say that interobserver agreement was achieved on 90 of 100 math problems. In this scenario, disagreement between observers occurred on 10 problems. By substituting these numbers into the formula, the percentage of interobserver agreement would be 90% (i.e., 90 agreements/[90 agreements + 10 disagreements] with the result of .90 multiplied by 100). In contrast, if interobserver agreement had been achieved on 75 of the math problems (observer disagreed on 25 of the problems), the percentage of interobserver agreement would drop to 75%.

Event Recording

Researchers may simply tally the number of times a response (e.g., talk outs) occurs within a defined period of time to assess the effects of an intervention. Event recording establishes the numerical dimension of behavior. This observation procedure is used in those cases in which there is a discrete behavior with a clear beginning and end, and the behavior is roughly equivalent in duration. Examples of behaviors that are amenable to event recording include a tally of the number of correct oral responses a student provides, the number of times a student is tardy or absent, the number of times a student uses profanity, and the number of self-injurious behaviors of a student with autism (e.g., face slapping). Nonexamples of behaviors without a clear beginning and end include on-task behavior, out-of-seat behavior, and social engagement. Event recording is also limited with high-frequency behaviors (e.g., motor movement of a child with attention deficit disorder) because the observer becomes overwhelmed and may lose count when trying to tally behaviors. The following formula is used to establish the percentage of agreement between independent observers measuring events. The percentage of agreement equals the smaller total divided by the larger total multiplied by 100. As the discrepancy between the smaller total and larger total becomes greater the level of interobserver agreement decreases and vice versa.

$$\text{Percentage of agreement} = \frac{\text{smaller total}}{\text{larger total}} \times 100$$

The percentage of agreement with event recording should be interpreted cautiously because it does not provide any assurance that the two observers were recording the same behavior. For example, one observer recorded that a child talked out 31 times during a 40-minute observation period and a second observer recorded 30 times during the sample period. However, the first observer recorded 26 occurrences during the first 20 minutes of the observation period and 5 occurrences during the last 20 minutes, whereas the second observer recorded only 15 occurrences during the first 20 minutes of the observation period and 15 occurrences during the last 20 minutes. The calculation for this observation would be the smaller total of 30 divided by the larger total of 31, resulting in .97, which is then multiplied by 100 for a percentage agreement of 97%. Thus, the percentage of agreement would have been inflated and would not accurately reflect their actual level of agreement. A solution to this problem is to shorten the time interval within which interobserver agreement is computed. The 40-minute observation period used in the preceding example could be broken down into four 10-minute intervals. Percentage of agreement could then be calculated for each interval. Thus, it is important to look at the length of interval used to compute the percentage of agreement in the case of event recording.

Latency and Duration Recording

Latency and duration recording procedures, like event recording, are used in those cases in which there is a discrete behavior with a clear beginning and end; however, in contrast with event recording, the behaviors exhibited are not roughly equivalent in time. For example, say tantrums occur often for a young child with autism but vary in the length of time of their occurrence (e.g., one lasts 10 minutes, the next lasts 15 minutes). Simply counting these behaviors loses large amounts of information. What is worse—one tantrum or two? The answer is you really do not know because one tantrum may have lasted 45 minutes, and two tantrums lasted a total of 10 minutes.

Latency recording involves recording the time from a specified event (e.g., an instructional cue such as, "What color is this?") to the start of the targeted behavior or completion of the response (e.g., "blue"). As noted before, event recording establishes the numerical dimension of behavior; duration recording provides the temporal dimension.

Duration recording simply involves measuring the length of time a response lasts. For example, latency recording could be used to measure the time between a request from a teacher to begin work on an assignment to the actual initiation of the assignment by the child; duration recording could be used to measure the amount of time a student appropriately interacts with others on the playground. Duration recording is also used in those cases in which the behavior is emitted at high rates. For example, some individuals with severe disabilities emit high rates of self-injurious behaviors such as biting. Although event recording might be used because biting has a distinguishable start and finish, counting each occurrence if it occurred at high rates might be difficult to achieve adequate interobserver agreement. Thus, recording the total amount of time the individual is engaged in biting may not only be easier, but will also achieve a higher level of interobserver agreement. The following formula is used to establish the percentage of agreement between independent observers measuring the latency or duration of behavior.

$$\text{Percentage of agreement} = \frac{\text{shorter latency/duration}}{\text{longer latency/duration}} \times 100$$

An example of using this formula to calculate interobserver agreement follows. Say one observer recorded 50 minutes of on-task behavior of a student, and the other observer recorded 40 minutes of on-task behavior. The interobserver agreement percentage would be 40 (short duration) divided by 50 (longer duration), which equals .80. This value would then be multiplied by 100 for a percentage of agreement of 80%.

There are two problems experienced by observers that must be looked at closely when interpreting interobserver agreement using latency and duration recording. First, the procedures for ensuring that both of the observers begin the observation period at the same time must be established. Small variations between observers can distort the percentage of agreement. Second, as with event recording, high agreements do not necessarily assure that the observers reported the same latencies or durations for the same occurrences of behavior. These issues should be examined closely by the researcher when assessing the results of the study.

Interval Recording

Interval recording procedures are often used by researchers to provide an estimate of the number of occurrences and the duration of behaviors. They are useful for nondiscrete behaviors that do not have a clear beginning and end, that occur over time, and that occur at a relatively high rate. Interval recording procedures involve dividing observational periods into units of time. There are three basic types of interval recording procedures: whole-interval recording, partial interval recording, and momentary time sampling.

1. *Whole-Interval Recording.* The whole-interval procedure requires the observer to record that the target behavior occurred only if it did so throughout the entire specified time interval. This procedure provides a conservative estimate (i.e., underestimates the occurrence) of an observed behavior because it does not count a behavior unless it occurs for the entire interval.
2. *Partial-Interval Recording.* The partial-interval procedure requires the observer to record that the target behavior occurred if it did so at any point during the specified time interval. This procedure provides a more liberal estimate (i.e., overestimates the occurrence) of the observed behavior than the whole-interval procedure.
3. *Momentary Time Sampling.* The momentary time sampling procedure requires the observer to record that the target behavior occurred if it did so immediately after the end of the specified time interval. This procedure provides the most liberal estimate of the observed behavior.

The decision with regard to which of the interval recording procedures should be used is based on three factors: (a) the conditions in which the behavior is being recorded; (b) the type of behavior being recorded; and (c) the direction of the expected intervention effects. First, the whole-interval and partial-interval recording procedures will require an independent observer, whereas the momentary time sampling procedures do not necessarily require one. Thus, momentary time sampling is used in those cases in which the observer might disrupt the intervention, an independent observer is not available, or the teacher or observer does not have the time to watch the student the entire interval. Second, the types of behaviors being measured play a role in the type of interval recording procedure used. The general rule is that a more conservative interval recording procedure (e.g., whole-interval) should be used when behaviors are emitted at a high frequency or for extended periods of time; a more liberal recording procedure (e.g., partial interval) should be used when behaviors are emitted at a lower frequency or for shorter periods of time. Finally, the expected direction of the intervention effects plays a role in the type of interval recording procedures used. The general rule is that a more conservative interval recording procedure (e.g., whole-interval) should be used in those cases in which the intervention effects are expected to increase the frequency or duration of behavior; a more liberal interval (i.e., partial interval) should be used in those cases in which the intervention effects are expected to decrease the frequency or duration of behavior.

To illustrate why a partial-interval recording system should be used with behaviors we want to decrease and whole interval used for behaviors we want to increase, an example will be discussed. Say we wish to take partial-interval data on in-seat behavior. This behavior is one we would like to increase. We define this behavior as "buttocks flat on chair seat; child facing forward in seat, feet flat on floor." We set up 10-second intervals for 5 minutes. If Jerry, a student who needs to improve his in-seat behavior, stays seated for 2 seconds for each 10-second interval, he receives a "plus" for the interval because he was in-seat at least part of the time. He could do this for all 30 intervals (six 10-second intervals per minute for 5 minutes) and achieve a percentage of 100% for staying in his seat. This method obviously inflates (overestimates) Jerry's behavior. On the other hand, if we were using whole-interval recording, Jerry would receive 0% of intervals of in-seat because no intervals included a full 10 seconds of sitting in his seat.

This scenario can be changed to illustrate why whole-interval recording is used for increasing behaviors. Say we wish to decrease Marybeth's pencil-tapping behavior in the classroom during independent seat work. We set up 15-second whole intervals for 10 minutes. If Marybeth taps her pencil for 13 of the 15 seconds for each interval, she would receive a "negative" or "check" in each interval. She could do this for all of the intervals. In essence, she could be tapping her pencil quite extensively yet receive 0% of intervals of pencil tapping using whole-interval recording. Partial-interval recording would record this behavior as 100% intervals of pencil tapping.

The following formula is used to establish the percentage of agreement between independent observers for each of the interval recording procedures. The percentage of agreement equals the number of agreement intervals divided by the total number of agreement and disagreement intervals multiplied by 100.

$$\text{Percentage of agreement} = \frac{\text{agreement intervals}}{\text{agreement intervals} + \text{disagreement intervals}} \times 100$$

The basic method for establishing interobserver agreement with interval recording involves computing the level of agreement for all of the intervals (total agreement). To provide a more conservative estimate of interobserver agreement, both the scored interval (i.e., occurrence agreement) and unscored interval (i.e., nonoccurrence) methods for establishing interobserver agreement should be used (Cooper, Heron, & Heward, 1987; Hawkins & Dotson, 1975). Both the scored and unscored interval methods use the preceding formula: agreement intervals (scored or unscored) divided by the total agreement and disagreement intervals (scored or unscored) multiplied by 100.

An example of scored, unscored, and total interval interobserver agreement follows.

Look at the example of the scored intervals provided in Figure 3.2. One minute's worth of 10-second intervals will be compared. Now, total interobserver agreement can be computed. Total interobserver agreement relates to how well both observers agreed on what they saw and what they did not see. Agreement was noted for Intervals 1, 3, 4, and 5. Therefore, the number of agreements (4) is divided by the number of agreements (4) plus disagreements (2) and then multiplied by 100 for a total agreement percentage of 67%. We now can look at scored interval interobserver agreement. We have agreement on intervals that were scored (i.e., behavior occurred recorded as a plus) for Intervals 1, 3, and 5. We disagreed on when we saw the behavior occur in Intervals 2 and 6. Therefore, the number of agreements of when the behavior was scored as occurring (3) is divided by the number of agreements (3) plus disagreements (2) and then multiplied by 100 for an agreement percentage of 60% for scored intervals. Finally, we can look at unscored interval interobserver agreement. We have agreement on intervals that were unscored (i.e., agreement that the behavior did not occur recorded as a check) for Interval 4. We disagreed on when we saw the behavior occur in Intervals 2 and 6. Therefore, the number of agreements of when the behavior was scored as not occurring (1) is divided by the number of agreements (1) plus disagreements (2) and then multiplied by 100 for an agreement percentage of 33% for unscored intervals. Analyzing the data this way gives us important information. We now have information that the observers agreed on what they saw and what they didn't see. This information is helpful for data collection purposes and study replications.

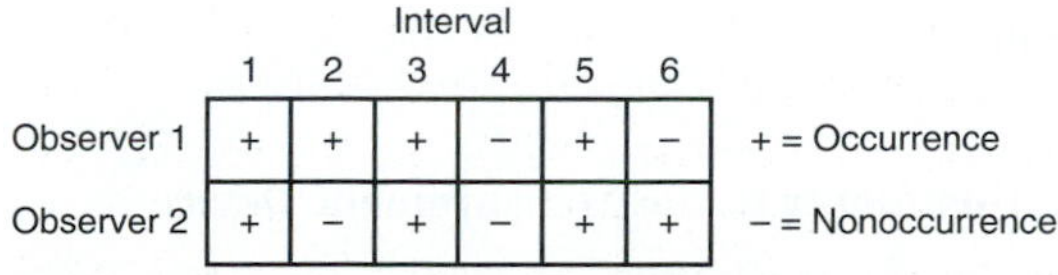

FIGURE 3.2 Example of interval recording by Observers 1 and 2.

WHAT ARE THE FACTORS THAT INFLUENCE INTEROBSERVER AGREEMENT?

There are a number of environmental conditions that can have an impact on observers and influence the quality of data collection and should be considered by both the researcher and research user. These environmental conditions include reactivity, observer drift, complexity of the measurement system, and observer expectancies (Kazdin, 1977).

Reactivity

Reactivity refers to differences in interobserver agreement that result from observers being aware that their observations will be checked. Reactivity typically results in higher levels of interobserver agreement and accuracy of observations (Reid, 1970). Reactivity can be overcome by providing random interobserver checks, audiotaping or videotaping the observations and randomly selecting those that will be scored, or conducting interobserver agreement checks 100% of time.

Observer Drift

Observer drift occurs when observers change the way they employ the definition of behavior over the course of a study. In contrast to what one may think, observer drift does not necessarily result in lower levels of interobserver agreement. Observers can develop a similar drift if they work closely together and communicate about how they record the observed behavior. This drift will affect the accuracy of the data. Conversely, observer agreement will decrease over the course of the study if observers do not work closely together and communicate about how they record the observed behavior. Observer drift can be prevented or at least diminished through booster training on the definitions of the behavior(s) and by having data collected by individuals experienced in conducting observation sessions.

Complexity of the Measurement System

The complexity of the measurement system is influenced by the number of individuals observed, the number of behaviors recorded, the duration of the observations, and the size of the time intervals in interval recording. Generally, the greater the complexity, the lower the levels of interobserver agreement. Thus, researchers must balance the complexity of the measurement system with the need to obtain reasonable levels of interobserver agreement and accuracy. Achieving this balance might involve observing fewer individuals, recording fewer behaviors, or changing the duration of the interval.

Observer Expectations

Observer expectations can influence their observations. If observers expect the intervention to have a specific effect, the observers are more likely to observe the effect if they were unaware of the intended effect. Observer expectations appear to be most problematic when the researcher provides them feedback about how the study is progressing, what the intervention is, in what condition the study is, and how the individuals are responding (Kazdin, 1977). The impact of observer expectations can be decreased by keeping the observer "blind" as to the specifics of the investigation (e.g., the intervention, condition, purpose of the investigation) and by using individuals experienced in conducting observations.

WHAT ARE THE FACTORS TO CONSIDER WHEN ASSESSING MEASUREMENT DEVICES IN THE CONTEXT OF A STUDY?

The selection of measurement devices by researchers is one of the most important decisions that they make in the design and implementation of a study. The selection of measurement devices is especially difficult for researchers because the time and resources available to assess the target features of the participants and study environment are almost always limited. Thus, critical research consumers should reflect on such issues as they assess the measurement devices used by researchers. There are four key issues that critical research consumers should consider when assessing the quality of the measurement devices selected by researchers—(a) description of the measurement device, (b) adjustments to the measurement device, (c) appropriateness of the measurement device, and (d) cooperation of participants.

Description of the Measurement Device

The first issue to consider centers on the description of the measurement device provided by researchers. The information provided by researchers regarding measurement devices varies depending on whether they are using well-known, less well-known, or unknown measurement devices. When researchers use well-known standardized measurement devices, they usually assume that we are familiar with the devices and do little more than name them because reliability and validity information on such devices are reported extensively elsewhere. Critical research consumers can rely on administration and technical information manuals and reviews of standardized measurement devices such as the Mental Measurements Year Books (e.g., Conoley & Impara, 1994) when researchers use well-known standardized measurement devices. When measurement devices are less well-known, researchers typically describe or give examples of them and give evidence of their reliability and validity or direct the reader to studies establishing the reliability. Researchers commonly provide reliability and validity information in the case of unknown measurement devices. If direct observations are conducted, researchers describe how they were done and how the observers or interviewers were trained.

Adjustments to the Measurement Device

The second issue focuses on any adjustments made to the measurement device by researchers. One of the biggest dilemmas faced by researchers in designing and implementing their research is administering adequate measurement devices of the target features of the participants and study environment. The amount of time available to assess participants is almost always limited. In these situations, researchers might administer a short form of the measurement device. In such cases, it is important for critical research consumers to assess the effects of these options on the results. Reducing the length of measurement devices reduces the reliability and may also bias its content. This reduction requires that researchers provide detailed information on the process used to shorten measurement devices as well as provide information regarding the reliability and validity of the devices. The reliability and validity data that have been developed on the original test can be applied to the shortened version only with great caution.

Appropriateness of the Measurement Device

The third issue centers on the appropriateness of the measurement device in terms of administration. On one level, critical research consumers must evaluate whether the readability of the measurement device is appropriate. Assessing the appropriateness of the readability of measurement devices is especially important when the participants are young or when there are potential language issues because the responses or scores would depend to some degree on vocabulary and reading ability rather than on the target feature of the participants for which the test is valid. On a second level, critical research consumers must evaluate the appropriateness of the administration procedures. This evaluation not only includes ensuring that the researcher appropriately administered the measurement device but also whether the administration procedure is appropriate for the participants. Generally, measurement devices can be administered individually or to groups. The age or behaviors of the participants can affect whether measurement devices can be administered individually or to groups. Very young children usually cannot be assessed as a group because their attention span is limited and they do not have the reading skills required by group tests. These findings may also be the case with other groups such as those individuals with disabilities. Delinquents and potentially recalcitrant groups may require individual assessment if there is reason to believe that their performance during group administration is unreliable.

Cooperation of Participants

The final issue focuses on whether participants' cooperation was secured. Critical research consumers must assess the procedures used by researchers to ensure the maximum performance of participants. On one level, researchers need to provide participants with a comfortable physical environment. Such an environment will enhance participants' cooperation and performance. On another level, researchers need to be familiar with the administration procedures. The performance of participants is likely to be affected if the researcher does not convey the importance of the research by being conversant with the measurement device and its administration. On still another level, researchers should try to heighten the cooperation of the participants by making the administration of the measurement device a reinforcing event.

SUMMARY

Selecting measurement devices to assess the target features of the participants and study environment is one of the most important decisions facing the researcher. There are numerous dimensions on which critical research consumers can judge the appropriateness of the measurement device and associated conclusions of the researcher. Critical research consumers should be able to identify these dimensions and to determine if and how researchers addressed them. If there are problems, critical research consumers should be able to assess their seriousness and how they might affect the results. All of this has to be done within a realistic framework because measuring the target features of the participants and study environment in educational and psychological research is almost always limited by time and resources.

Questions regarding the selection of measurement devices are relevant for both qualitative and quantitative researchers concerned with the direct and indirect measurement of the targeted features of the participants and study environment. These questions center primarily around the reliability and validity of measurement devices. Validity is typically not a concern when researchers are using direct observation procedures to assess the targeted features of the participants and study environment. Regardless of the type of research, critical research consumers need to answer questions about the measurement device used in a study such as:

1. Was the measurement device reliable and valid for collecting data on the targeted features of the participants and study environment?
2. Was the measurement device appropriate for the target population and the research participants?
3. Were the administration procedures appropriate for the target population and the research participants?
4. Are the measurement device and associated administration procedures appropriate for the situation?

DISCUSSION QUESTIONS

1. A colleague tells you that she was unaware that there were different forms of validity. She asks you how the types of validity differ. How would you respond?
2. You are part of a research team investigating emotional intelligence. The research team is attempting to select the most appropriate assessment to measure emotional intelligence. What would your recommendation be to the research team in terms of the type of validity that is most important for measuring emotional intelligence that must be taken into consideration for the selection process? Why?
3. Most, if not all, of us have taken a college entrance exam. What type of validity are colleges and universities depending on when using the test scores to make admittance decisions?
4. A friend who is studying assessment asks you why there are different reliability categories. Explain to your friend what the three basic reliability categories are and what type of error each category is attempting to control.
5. Another colleague is conducting research on students' attitudes toward smoking. Your colleague wants to use the most reliable test possible; however, your colleague is unsure of the type of reliability that is most important. What would you say to your colleague with regard to the type of reliability that is most important for a questionnaire assessing students' attitudes toward smoking? Why?
6. After you respond to your colleague in Question 5, she tells you that she is unsure of the difference between reliability coefficients and the standard error of measurement. What would you tell your colleague with regard to the relative merits of both?
7. You were reading about an investigation in which the researcher used direct observations to collect data. You notice that the researcher used a partial-interval recording method to measure the on-task behavior of the students. Is there a problem with the observational method used? Why or why not? What type of behavior would a partial-interval observational method be appropriate for and why?
8. In the investigation described in Question 7, the researcher reported total, occurrence, and nonoccurrence agreement. What is the purpose of reporting all three agreement percent-

ages? What are the other basic interobserver agreement categories, and what is the advantage of reporting interval agreement for interval measures versus the other categories?

9. A student in your class asks you after a lecture on reliability and validity if it is possible to have validity without reliability. What would you say?

10. A fellow student makes a comment in class that qualitative researchers are not concerned with the concept of reliability whereas quantitative researchers are. You indicate that this is not the case. However, you indicate that qualitative researchers view reliability differently. You go on to explain why this is so. What would you say?

PRACTICE EXERCISES

Reliability

Decide which reliability approach (stability, equivalence, or internal consistency) is described for the following five exercises.

1. A researcher develops a test to assess the effects of a new science curriculum. She computes a split-half coefficient.
2. A researcher develops a new stress inventory for teachers. He administers the inventory to a group of teachers and then readministers it 3 weeks later and correlates the teachers' scores on the two administrations.
3. A test publisher creates two forms of an academic achievement test and readministers different forms to the same group of students after a 4-week period.
4. A researcher develops a questionnaire assessing students' attitudes toward smoking. She computes a Cronbach's Coefficient Alpha.
5. A test publisher develops a new high school science achievement test and readministers it to a group of high school students after a 2-week period.

Validity

Decide which validity approach (construct, content, and criterion) is described in each of the following exercises.

1. A group of experts in social studies judges the adequacy of coverage of a test of students' knowledge of social studies.
2. A researcher administers a mathematics aptitude test to a group of high school students all of whom are enrolling in a college algebra class the following year. At the end of the students' first term of college algebra, she computes a correlation coefficient between the students' mathematics aptitude scores and their achievement scores in the college algebra class.
3. Scores on a newly developed test of self-esteem are correlated with scores on the widely used Coopersmith *Self-Esteem Inventory.*
4. A science aptitude test is administered to eighth-grade students 2 days before they take the districtwide test of science skills.
5. Scores on the Graduate Record Exam (GRE) taken during college students' senior year are correlated with their GPA in graduate school 2 years later.

PART THREE

QUANTITATIVE RESEARCH METHODS

CHAPTER 4 **BASIC STATISTICAL CONCEPTS AND SAMPLING PROCEDURES**

CHAPTER 5 **EXPERIMENTAL DESIGNS**

CHAPTER 6 **CAUSAL-COMPARATIVE RESEARCH**

CHAPTER 7 **CORRELATIONAL RESEARCH**

CHAPTER 4

BASIC STATISTICAL CONCEPTS AND SAMPLING PROCEDURES

OBJECTIVES

After studying this chapter you should be able to:

1. Describe the different scales of measurement.
2. Describe what a univariate frequency distribution is and indicate the percentage of the population within –1 and +1, –2 and +2, and –3 and +3 standard deviations from the mean.
3. Describe the purpose of null hypotheses and alternative hypotheses.
4. Describe what are directional and nondirectional alternative hypotheses and indicate the advantages and disadvantages of using each.
5. Describe the differences between parametric and nonparametric tests of statistical significance.
6. Explain what is meant by statistical significance.
7. Describe what is meant by Type I and Type II errors.
8. Explain what power is and how it can be increased.
9. Describe the types of parametric and nonparametric tests.
10. Describe the different methods of sampling.
11. Describe what is meant by sampling error and describe how sampling decisions are made.

OVERVIEW

When we begin to study research methods, especially quantitative research methods, we may find the statistical aspect of research somewhat daunting. As stated in Chapter 2, statistics should be thought of as only one tool that helps in the analysis of the data we gather. The purpose of this chapter is to introduce basic, but important, statistical concepts that should serve as a foundation for our discussion of experimental designs. After this chapter, specific statistical procedures will be described for particular designs in terms of data analysis. Our goal is not to inundate you with statistical concepts and theory. Rather, we want to provide you with enough detail regarding each of the statistical procedures to ensure that you can adequately interpret the findings of quantitative research.

In this chapter, the following basic statistical concepts will be introduced: scales of measurement, univariate frequency distribution, null hypotheses and alternative hypotheses, directional and nondirectional alternative hypotheses, statistical significance, parametric and nonparametric tests of statistical significance, and Type I and Type II errors. In addition, because there is a critical concern of how quantitative research is interpreted for purposes of internal and external validity, a comprehensive description of sampling will be included. The method of sampling will be a major determinant of the type of research design being used and what type of statistical analysis will be required. In this chapter, we describe probability and nonprobability sampling methods. Finally, a discussion of sampling error and sampling decisions will be presented.

WHAT ARE THE SCALES OF MEASUREMENT?

The process of measurement in quantitative research involves representing the targeted features of the participants and study environment with numbers. Using numbers to describe these targeted features is especially useful because it permits the targeted features represented by a sample of data to be compared to another sample of data of the same kind. There are four distinct scales of measurement that enable researchers to measure the targeted features of interest under a range of different conditions and levels of precision. The level of precision provided by the scales of measurement plays a key role in the type of tests of statistical significance that can be employed (described in what follows). These scales of measurement include the (a) nominal scale, (b) ordinal scale, (c) interval scale, and (d) ratio scale.

Nominal Scale

The nominal scale offers the lowest level of precision because numbers simply act as identifiers, names, or labels. In other words, the numbers only make identification possible; they serve no other function. Although the nominal scale appears straightforward, it is sometimes misunderstood. The question to ask yourself is whether the numbers represent a measure of any particular quality of the targeted feature of the participants or study environment. If the numbers do not represent a measure, then the numbers represent names or labels. Thus, a nominal variable permits researchers to state only that a participant is the same as, or different from, another participant with respect to the targeted feature in question. For example, by using a nominal scale to specify the gender of participants, each female participant could be represented with a "1" and each male by a "2."

Ordinal Scale

An ordinal scale is one step up in precision from the nominal scale. An ordinal scale preserves the presence or absence of differences in the targeted feature of interest but not the magnitude. Data represented on an ordinal scale will indicate whether two values are equal or whether one is greater than the other. Thus, the values can be ordered in relation to each other. For example, if a teacher ranked a group of students in order of their ability in mathematics, this ranking would be an example of data representing an ordinal scale. Although one could conclude that the first student has greater ability in mathematics than the 10th-ranked student, it cannot be further inferred that he or she has, for example, twice the ability as another student.

Interval Scale

The interval scale is one step up in precision from the ordinal scale. The interval scale, like the ordinal scale, not only preserves the presence or absence of differences in the targeted feature of interest but also the magnitude. The interval scale provides equal intervals between equidistant points on the scale. For example, a 5-point difference between 5 and 10 on a 50-point scale would be considered the same as the difference between the scores of 45 and 50. Thus, one cannot only infer which participant has "more of" or "less of" some targeted feature but also "how much more of" or "how much less of." However, interval scales do not have an absolute-zero point; thus, we cannot state that the difference between a 45 and 55 is twice the amount of the difference between 45 and 50.

Ratio Scale

The ratio scale is the most robust of the four scales of measurement. The ratio scale not only possesses all of the attributes of the other three scales, but it also possesses a true zero point or the absence of the variable being measured. Possessing a zero point is important because, as the name of the scale indicates, it means that any measure of a variable made on a ratio scale can be described in terms of its ratio to other measures. For example, a ruler is comprised of a ratio scale because it has a true zero or the absence of length. The ratio scale enables one to say that a piece of wood that is 20 inches in length is twice as long as one that is 10 inches in length.

It is important to note that in education and psychology, ratio scales are not used as frequently as other scales of measurement. A problem for social scientists arises because although a measurement device may represent a ratio scale, it cannot be interpreted as such. An example will clarify this point. In the field of educational assessment, an academic achievement score of zero is clearly possible. However, obtaining a zero cannot be interpreted to mean the complete absence of achievement in the individual being tested. Thus, the scores must be treated as if they were derived from an interval scale.

WHAT IS A UNIVARIATE FREQUENCY DISTRIBUTION?

When we measure certain attributes of participants, we may wish to make certain assumptions about the population to help with the interpretation of our data. Thus, one assumption we make is the shape of the population distribution (i.e., how individuals within a population compare to others within that population) on the measured attribute. One type of distribution is called the univariate distribution. The normal distribution is one of the most common univariate distributions. The normal distribution is used extensively by researchers to interpret research findings. (*Note:* This is not the case for qualitative and single-case researchers.)

A distribution is the name given to any set of scores that has been organized in such a way as to enable the shape of the data to be seen. A univariate frequency distribution entails counting the number of times each different score occurs in a data set. A univariate distribution is obtained by plotting the frequency of each different score along the horizontal (x) axis. Figure 4.1 presents a set of scores and the corresponding frequency distribution.

HOW CAN WE DESCRIBE DATA SETS?

The frequency distribution represents how a data set can be represented graphically. Consider how data sets can be described (called *descriptive statistics*). Researchers use descriptive statistics, a very simple and parsimonious system, to describe any data set mathematically. This system includes describing the central tendency, the variation, and the shape of the distribution. Researchers typically use three measures of central tendency to describe a central reference value that is usually close to the point of greatest concentration in a set of scores. In many aspects of research, the measure of central tendency is thought to best represent the whole data set.

Measures of Central Tendency

Arithmetic Mean. The most common measure of central tendency is the arithmetic mean. The arithmetic mean is obtained by summing the scores for a data set and dividing by the number of participants or entities in that data set. Consider the following scores on an exam:

80 75 90 95 65 86 97 50

We sum the scores (638) and divide by the number of scores (8) in the data set. The arithmetic mean is 79.8. Although it is beyond the scope of this book to detail the properties of the arithmetic mean and the importance of these properties to many statistical procedures used in research, it is important to note that the arithmetic mean provides the best estimate of a population parameter than any other measure of central tendency because it takes into account *all* scores in the data set.

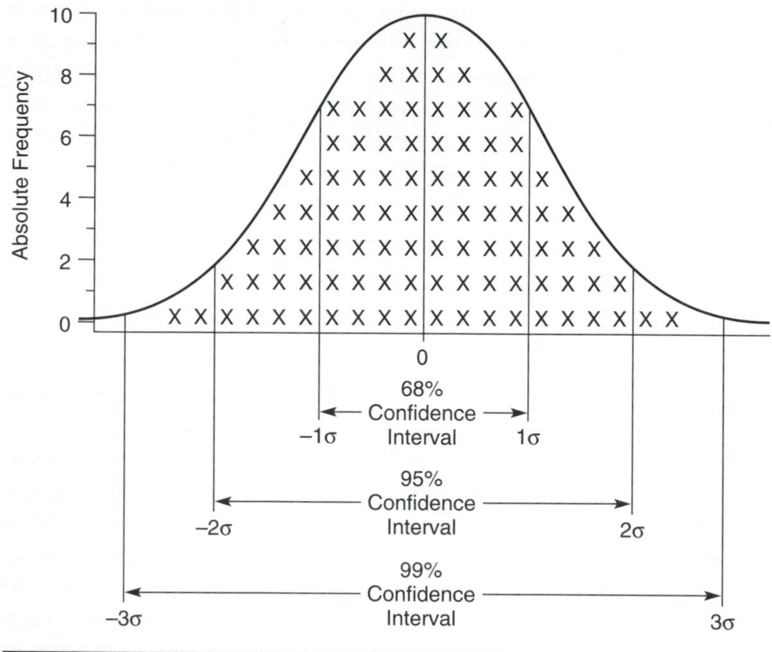

FIGURE 4.1 Frequency distribution of 100 scores depicting 68%, 95%, and 99% confidence intervals. (σ is the population standard deviation.)

Median and Mode. Two other commonly used measures of central tendency are the median and the mode. The median is the point above and below which half of the scores fall. Consider the following scores arranged in rank order:

2 5 8 8 12 14 15 17 19

In this example, the median is 12. Four scores fall above it and four scores fall below it. If another observation is added, then the number of scores is an even number. The common convention for dealing with an even number of scores is to take the arithmetic mean of the two middle values. For example, if we were to add the value 20 to the preceding set of scores, the median would be 13, (12 + 14) divided by 2. The median is a measure that is *not* influenced by extreme scores like the arithmetic mean. Finally, the mode is the most frequently occurring score in a data set. In the previous data set, the mode is 8 (it occurs twice).

When to Use the Different Measures of Central Tendency. The arithmetic mean is an appropriate measure of central tendency for interval and ratio-scale variables. The median is an appropriate measure for central tendency with ordinal variables, where the mode is used with nominal variables. Comparisons can be made using the mean, median, and mode with interval and ratio-scale variables. If the frequency distribution is symmetrical, the mean, median, and mode will be relatively the same. If the frequency distribution is skewed, these three measures of central tendency will differ substantially. The shape of the distributions is discussed more fully in what follows.

Measures of Variation

In addition to describing the central distribution of a data set, researchers should describe variation within it. Variation of the characteristic under study is always important to consider. Researchers commonly use three statistics to describe the variation in a data set including the range, the standard deviation, and variance.

Range. The range is the simplest measure of variation. The range is the difference between the largest and smallest scores. Consider the following scores:

12 9 15 24 20 8 11 21 22 14

The range for this set of scores is 24 minus 8, or 16. (*Note:* Some statisticians consider the range to be defined as the difference between the largest and smallest numbers plus one; e.g., 24 – 8 + 1 = 17.) The use of the range as an indicator of the variation in a data set is appropriate only in those cases in which the sample is small. When sample sizes increase, the range becomes increasingly unstable as a measure of variation since it only takes into consideration two scores from the total number of scores.

Standard Deviation and Sample Variance. The standard deviation and sample variance are the most commonly used statistics for describing the variation in the responses or scores in a data set. The standard deviation can be best understood by considering the meaning of the word "deviation." In research, a deviation is the distance of a score from the mean for the data set. If the mean of a data set is 10, then the deviation for a score of 12 is 2 (i.e., 12 – 10). The deviation of a score of 6 is –4 (i.e., 6 – 10). Twelve is above the mean and 6 is below the mean. The standard deviation is symbolized as "*SD*" and is a statistic that describes how much the scores are spread out around the mean. The larger the standard deviation, the more "spread out" the scores.

The sample variance is simply the square of the standard deviation. That is, the standard deviation is multiplied by itself. For example, if the standard deviation for a set of scores was 3, the variance would be 9. The standard deviation and the sample variance are not only used to indicate the degree of spread in a data set, but also to provide the basis for many of the statistical procedures used by researchers.

Shape of the Distribution

In addition to describing the central tendency and variation in a data set, researchers often look at the shape of the distribution. Although not commonly described in research studies, it is important to consider the shape of a distribution because it may affect interpretations of the data and distort the outcomes of some statistical procedures. Distributions of scores can take on three primary shapes: unimodal, bimodal, and skewed.

A unimodal distribution is one in which there are several average scores with fewer high and low scores on each side of the mode. The normal distribution is a unimodal distribution (described in what follows). A bimodal distribution is one in which the scores accumulate at two different parts of the scale. Skewed distributions are those in which scores are mainly high or low. A distribution is positively skewed when the scores are mainly low (i.e., most scores are low with a few high scores that stretch out the curve to the right), whereas a distribution is negatively skewed when the scores are mainly high (i.e., most scores are high with a few low scores that stretch out the curve to the left). Although the shape of a set of responses or scores can be examined graphically, there are a number of statistics available for describing the shape of a distribution. It is important to note that researchers rarely report these statistics. Rather, researchers typically examine the shape of the distribution and transform it to approximate the normal distribution prior to conducting more advanced statistical analysis procedures.

The idea of a distribution of frequencies provides the basis for the normal distribution as well as all other distributions (e.g., bivariate frequency; see Chapter 7). The normal distribution is a purely theoretical distribution obtained by plotting theoretically obtained probabilities across the whole range of possible values from minus infinity to plus infinity along the horizontal axis. The normal distribution is important in research for several reasons. First, many variables in nature can be shown to approximate the shape of the normal distribution. For example, psychological variables such as intelligence and achievement scores tend to approximate the normal distribution when plotted from an adequately large sample.

Second, the sampling distribution of the mean (i.e., the theoretical frequency distribution of means of an infinitely large number of samples drawn from any given population) will approximate a normal distribution as long as researchers have a reasonably large number of sample means. This phenomenon is even the case when the population from which the scores have been drawn is not normally distributed.

Finally, the unique properties of the normal distribution mean that it provides a way of assigning probabilities to scores so that the association between the sample data and the population can be clearly expressed. This association between sample data and the population is especially important because researchers in education and psychology rarely have access to the entire population and because researchers can never be certain of what is actually occurring in the population.

The normal distribution, like all distributions, is really a family of distributions that always possesses the following five key characteristics. First, the normal distribution is perfectly symmetrical about its mean. This distribution allows for the exact division of the area under the curve. Second, the total area under the normal distribution includes all possible values of a given variable. This distribution enables researchers to make precise predictions regarding the probability of a given true score falling within a specified range of scores. Third, the mean, median, and mode of the distribution, are the same. That is, the arithmetic average is equal to the central value in the normal distribution, which is equal to the most frequently occurring score. Fourth, the tails of the distribution extend out infinitely in both directions. This phenomenon means that although the tails of the normal distribution continue forever to grow closer and closer to the horizontal or *x* axis, they never actually touch the axis (i.e., reach a zero frequency). Finally, there is a consistent relationship between the shape of the normal distribution and the standard deviation from the mean (i.e., the statistic that shows how much scores are spread out around the mean). This consistent relationship enables researchers to identify the area in which a given score falls under the normal curve.

Given the latter characteristic of the normal distribution (i.e., there is a consistent relationship between the shape of the normal distribution and the standard deviation from the mean), we will examine the types of statements that can be made from it. Figure 4.1 presents 100 scores distributed normally. By counting the "X's," you can confirm the following statements:

1. Approximately 68% of the scores will fall within 1 standard deviation above and below the mean.
2. Approximately 95% of the scores will fall within 2 standard deviations above and below the mean (approximately 2.5% of the scores in each tail). (Note: We are rounding up from 1.96 standard deviations.)
3. Approximately 99% (again, we are rounding) of the scores will fall 3 standard deviations above and below the mean (approximately .5% in each tail).
4. A percentile score indicates what percentage of the group had scores as low or lower than the given score.

WHAT ROLE DO HYPOTHESES PLAY IN RESEARCH?

Taking into consideration how scores of the population on an attribute are distributed, quantitative researchers make predictions about the outcome of any study before data are collected. These predictions are termed hypotheses. Hypotheses represent statements about what findings are expected and are used in inferential statistics.

Inferential Statistics

Unlike descriptive statistics which allow researchers to describe their data sets, inferential statistics allow for statistical inference; that is, researchers are able to generalize their results to the larger population or make an "inference" about the population based on the responses of the experimental sample. This ability to generalize to the population is critical since researchers rarely have the opportunity to study an entire population. Thus, we attempt to learn about the population by studying a representative sample of that population.

Role of Hypotheses

We will look at the role hypotheses play in assessing whether two groups differ from one another. As we have discussed, most educational and psychological research begins with the development of hypotheses that predict, on the basis of theory and what has already been found, what the results of the investigation will be. Suppose that two sets of data are collected that represent behavior under two different conditions. The hypotheses constructed before the collection of data will assert that a difference is expected between the two conditions. Recall that the problem addressed by statistical significance testing is whether the difference between the two sets of data can be attributed to the effects of a given variable (systematic variance) rather than chance factors (i.e., sampling and measurement errors). Even in tightly controlled experiments, visual inspection does not allow for a sound decision because any differences that can be seen in the data may merely reflect chance or random influences rather than the effect of one variable on another. It is clear from our discussion of statistical significance that what is needed is an objective process of determining whether the prediction is, at least at some level, supported by the data. At this point, hypotheses come into play, having a critical role in inferential statistics.

Null and Alternative Hypotheses

There are two types of hypotheses that are developed by researchers. These hypotheses are called the null (pertaining to nullifiable) hypothesis and the alternative or experimental (in the case of an experimental study) hypothesis. Null hypotheses are statements of valueless statistically significant relationships between variables being studied or differences between the values of a population parameter. Alternative hypotheses are statements of statistically significant relationships between variables being studied or differences between values of a population parameter. Null hypotheses and alternative hypotheses are always used in conjunction with one another in tests of statistical significance. For example, the null hypothesis and associated alternative hypothesis illustrated in what follows show how they are used in conjunction with one another. Additionally, hypotheses should be concise statements of the relationship or difference that is expected. Not only are brief and concise hypotheses easier for the researcher to test, but they are also easier for us to understand. The following are examples of null and associated alternative hypotheses:

Null: There will be statistically nonsignificant differences in the achievement scores of students with learning disabilities in ability-grouped classrooms and those in heterogeneous-grouped classrooms.

Alternative: There will be statistically significant differences in the achievement scores of students with learning disabilities in ability-grouped classrooms and those in heterogeneous-grouped classrooms.

The function of null hypotheses and alternative hypotheses is to express statements about differences between parameters of the population from which the samples are taken. Why are researchers interested in hypotheses about possible differences between population parameters rather than possible differences between samples? The reason centers on the notion that researchers are generally interested in sample data only to the extent to which it can tell them something about the population from which it was drawn. In other words, differences between the means of two samples are largely trivial unless they suggest that the same differences would be found in the population.

The use of null and alternative hypotheses and associated statistical significance tests are an exercise in devil's advocacy. The null hypothesis provides the basis for the argument that there is no systematic difference between the scores of the experimental and control groups. Except for sampling errors and measurement errors, the performance of the two groups is indistinguishable. If, according to a formal statistical test (e.g., the *t* test) the data are consistent with this argument, then an all-chance explanation is justifiable. This explanation is typically described as "accepting the null hypothesis." On the other hand, if the data are inconsistent with the all-chance explanation, the null hypothesis is rejected and the systematic-plus-chance explanation is justifiable. Finally, it is important to note that the standard terms of "accept" or "reject" the null hypothesis are too strong. Statistical-significance testing should be viewed as an aid to judgment not a declaration of "truth." It should be clear that the null hypothesis is virtually never literally true (Cohen, 1990), and that critical research consumers should look at the results of tests of statistical significance within the context of the entire study.

Directional and Nondirectional Alternative Hypotheses

There is one final piece of information that is important to know regarding the alternative hypothesis. An alternative hypothesis is either directional or nondirectional. A directional alternative hypothesis is one in which the population parameter (e.g., mean) is stated to be greater or smaller than the other population parameter. In contrast to the example of the alternative hypothesis provided before, a directional alternative hypothesis goes beyond just stating that there will be a difference. This type of alternative hypothesis is also referred to as a one-tailed hypothesis because it specifies which end of the sampling distribution the computed value from the test of statistical significance will fall—providing evidence to reject the null hypothesis. In the case of an alpha level of $p < .05$ (i.e., the probability of obtaining a difference between groups this large or larger is less than 5%), the 5% region of rejection on the distribution is depicted in Figure 4.2. The shaded region depicts the area (5% of either end of the distribution) within which lie those *p* values obtained from tests of statistical significance that are so low as to require the rejection of the null hypothesis.

A nondirectional alternative hypothesis is one in which a difference between two population parameters is stated, but no direction is specified. The alternative hypothesis provided earlier is an example of a nondirectional alternative hypothesis. This type of alternative hypothesis is also called a two-tailed hypothesis because it does not specify which end of the sampling distribution of the test of statistical significance at which the computed value will fall providing evidence to reject the null hypothesis. In the case of an alpha level of $p < .05$, the 5% region of rejection on the distribution is depicted in Figure 4.3. The shaded regions depict the area (2.5% of both ends of the sampling distribution) within which lie those *p* values of the test of statistical significance that are so low as to require the rejection of the null hypothesis.

It should be evident that the choice of a one- rather than two-tailed hypothesis testing strategy can influence research outcomes. Indeed, this choice is a source of controversy among social scientists (Pillemer, 1991). For example, two different groups of researchers drew different conclusions regarding the effects of single-sex and coeducational secondary schools using the same data from a national survey. Lee and Bryk (1989) employed one-tailed hypothesis tests to explore whether students attending single-sex schools outperformed students attending coeducational schools. Lee and Bryk concluded that single-sex schools produced better outcomes than did coeducational schools. Marsh (1989a) found that some of the differences favoring single-sex schools in Lee and Bryk's study would have failed to reach statistical significance had two-tailed tests been used. Although Lee and Bryk (1989) defended their use of the one-tailed hypothesis tests, Marsh (1989b) stated that a

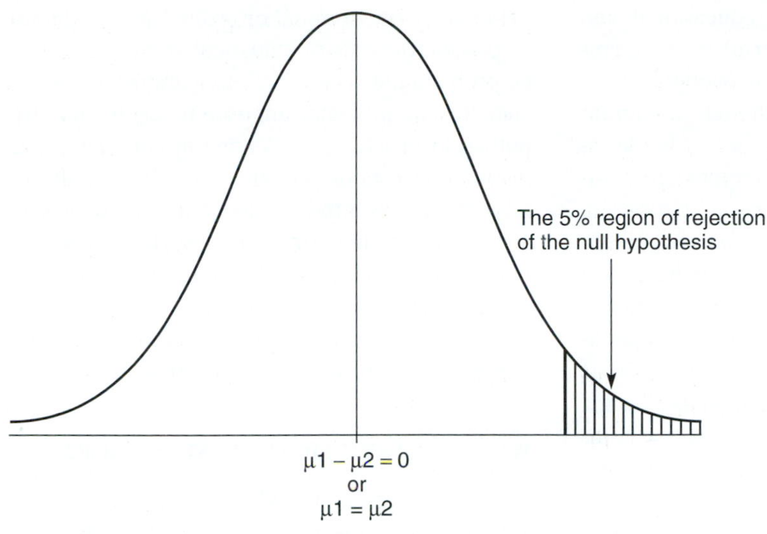

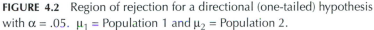

FIGURE 4.2 Region of rejection for a directional (one-tailed) hypothesis with $\alpha = .05$. μ_1 = Population 1 and μ_2 = Population 2.

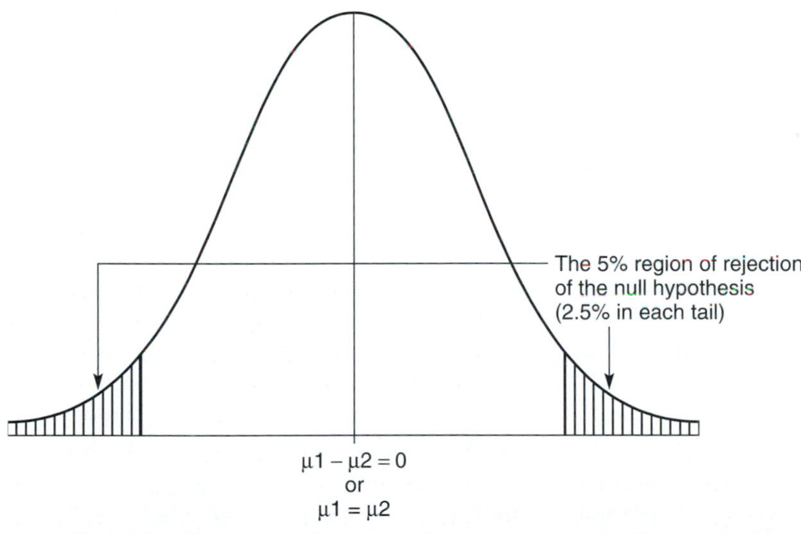

FIGURE 4.3 Region of rejection for a nondirectional (two-tailed) hypothesis with $\alpha = .05$. μ_1 = Population 1 and μ_2 = Population 2.

review of previous literature provided no clear basis for the use of a directional hypothesis.

Which type of alternative hypothesis is appropriate? There are two factors that one should consider when using a one-tailed alternative hypothesis. First, and most importantly, there should be clear evidence for the prediction made by the researchers. Unfortunately, there is good reason for questioning whether most educational and psychological theories are powerful enough, empirical generalizations are robust enough, and a priori predictions are accurate enough to warrant the use of such tests (Pillemer, 1991). Inconsistent and conflicting research outcomes are common in education and psychology (Cronbach, 1975; Hedges 1987; Light & Pillemer, 1984). Second, related to the first issue, researchers must make the decision to use a one-tailed alternative hypothesis at the outset of the study. If researchers decide on the type of alternative hypothesis after they have analyzed the data, then there is the possibility that their decision could have been influenced by the data. It is clear that this decision may introduce bias into the process.

WHAT ARE PARAMETRIC AND NONPARAMETRIC TESTS OF STATISTICAL SIGNIFICANCE?

Parametric Tests

Thus far, we have discussed the assumption that scores in a population are normally distributed. When this assumption is made and researchers conduct a test of statistical significance, they are conducting what is called a parametric test. A parameter is used to describe some aspect of a set of scores for an entire population. Thus, parametric tests of statistical significance are based on certain assumptions about population parameters. One assumption is that the scores in the population are normally distributed about the mean. Many complex human behaviors are believed to be normally distributed. Another assumption is that the population variances of the comparison groups in a study are equal (homogeneity of variance). Yet another assumption involves having at least interval or ratio-scale data.

Nonparametric Tests

When large deviations from the assumptions of parametric tests of statistical significance are present in the research data and when the data are generated from nominal or ordinal scales, the use of parametric tests of statistical significance may be problematic. Therefore, nonparametric tests of statistical significance are used to test the null hypothesis in such cases. As one might guess, nonparametric tests of statistical significance do not rely on any assumptions about the shape or variance of the population scores. Such tests also do not rely on data derived from a measure that has equal intervals (interval and ratio scales). We will discuss the advantage of parametric tests over nonparametric tests later in the chapter.

WHAT IS STATISTICAL SIGNIFICANCE?

Educational research and psychological research are best described as probabilistic endeavors rather than truly deterministic. What this means is that the findings from educational and psychological research cannot yet do, and may never achieve, the ability to predict exactly what will happen in any particular situation. Human behavior is far too variable to make perfect predictions of future behavior. We only have to reflect on our own lives to understand the range of events that affect our behavior. Thus, researchers must determine whether a difference (e.g., between the means of two samples) may be so great that there is a likelihood, at some level of probability, that it is the result of one variable influencing another rather than a function of chance due to sampling or measurement error. This is why the significance test of a null hypothesis has become a staple procedure in education and psychology. The use of statistical significance dates back almost 300 years to studies of birth rates by John Arbuthnot in 1710 and was popularized in the social sciences by Sir Ronald Fisher and by Jerzy Neyman and Egon Pearson (Huberty, 1987, 1993).

Before looking more closely at what statistical significance means, we should explore the issue of systematic versus chance explanations for findings. Exploring these types of explanations is necessary to understand the nature of statistical significance. As stated in Chapter 2, a systematic factor (independent variable or an extraneous variable) is an influence that contributes in an orderly fashion to another factor (dependent variable), for example, the reduction in heart disease (dependent variable) by individuals who watch their diet and stay active (independent variables). A chance factor is an influence that contributes haphazardly to another factor, with the amount of influence being unspecifiable. Unfortunately, researchers tend to overestimate the influence of systematic factors relative to chance factors. The upshot of this tendency is to jump naturally to systematic conclusions in preference to using chance as an explanation. This tendency is why researchers test for statistical significance.

Researchers need a way to protect themselves from favoring systematic conclusions over data that could have been the function of chance factors. Each of these individuals needs to understand that although statistical calculations have an aura of being exact, they are always conducted against a background of uncertainty. A major step in making reasonable conclusions for data is to make a judgment about the relative influences of systematic and chance factors.

Statistical significance enables researchers to make such a judgment because a statistically significant difference is one that is so great as to be unlikely to have occurred by chance factors alone (i.e., sampling error and measurement error). Consider a simple research study in which the participants are assigned randomly to either an experimental or a control group. Members of the two groups perform the identical experimental task, except for the additional manipulation of a single factor of interest in the experimental group, the receipt of training. The researcher wishes to test whether the experimental factor makes a systematic difference on a participant's performance on a specific task.

In this case, performance measures on the task will vary from individual to individual. The question is, "Why does performance vary from individual to individual?" The systematic explanatory factor is that the experimental factor, on average, improved (or damaged) the task performance in the experimental group by some unknown amount over and above the performance of the control group. Calculating the mean difference provides an estimate of the magnitude of this systematic effect. However, there are also chance factors in this situation that influence the performance measures of individuals.

Sampling and measurement errors are two of the primary chance factors about which researchers must be concerned. Sampling errors (e.g., a group's mean may be different each time it was sampled) might arise from the "luck of the draw" in randomly assigning participants to the experimental and control groups. For example, the control group may contain a predominance of participants with somewhat lower (or higher) abilities than members of the experimental group. Thus, the mean difference could be a function of a sampling error rather than a function of an experimental factor. Measurement errors refer to unknown and unrepeatable causes of variability in task performance over time and context. (Recall our discussion of reliability in Chapter 3.)

There are three possible accounts for the differences between the performance of the experimental and control groups. These accounts include (a) the variability of performance from individual to individual can be completely explained by the experimental factor, (b) the variability of performance from individual to individual can be completely explained by chance factors (sampling and measurement errors), or (c) the variability of performance from individual to individual is a function of both the experimental factor and chance factors (i.e., sampling and measurement errors).

Accepting the first account would require that variability in the scores of the experimental group would be different from all the scores in the control group. Although such a finding might occur in the physical sciences where chance variability can be small, this outcome is quite rare in education and psychology and would not require statistical inference (Skinner, 1963). Thus, researchers are left with a choice between the all-chance explanation and the systematic-plus-chance explanation. At this point, statistical significance testing comes into play. Statistical significance helps researchers with the decision about whether the observed difference is great enough to reject the null hypothesis (differences occurred due to chance factors alone); it also helps researchers accept the alternative hypothesis (differences occurred due to systematic and chance factors). The systematic and chance factors explanation must be used if chance factors do not adequately account for the findings.

Of course, referring to the statistical significance of any difference in itself is not very revealing unless a specific level of probability is set. This probability enables researchers to interpret how unlikely the difference might be due to sampling or measurement errors. The significance level can range from 0.0 to 1.0 and is specified by researchers. This significance level provides researchers a basis for accepting or rejecting their hypotheses. However, because the aim is always to have the smallest possible risk of rejecting the null hypothesis incorrectly, the probability values always lie close to zero.

The $p < .05$, $p < .01$, or $p < .001$ are the most commonly used values in educational and psychological research. The significance level sets the maximum acceptable probability of rejecting the null hypothesis because the difference is great enough to conclude that it did not occur by chance when, in fact, chance did cause the results. Thus, the null hypothesis should not have been rejected.

We will clarify the concept of statistical significance through the following example. Suppose we established a significance level of $p < .05$ to reject the null hypothesis. This level indicates that the maximum desired probability of making the wrong decision about rejecting the null hypothesis when it is true should be less than 5 in 100 (i.e., the probability of getting results or differences between groups by chance is less than 5%). The significance level sets the boundary between what is and what is not an acceptable risk.

However, there is more to the significance level then we have discussed thus far. The significance level in any given study is the probability of the obtained results, given the sample size and assuming the sample was derived from a population in which the null hypothesis is true (Thompson, 1994). Thus, the significance level must be interpreted not only in the context of the population parameters (i.e., what actually exists in the entire population from which the sample was drawn) and the size of the research sample, but also in the context of some possible problems with the logic of the significance level. (See Hayes, 1981; Thompson, 1996; Tukey, 1991 for a discussion of this issue.)

Errors Made in Interpretations of the Significance Level

Although it is beyond the scope of this discussion to detail the problems in the logic of the significance level, it is important to understand two common errors in the interpretations of it. Avoiding these two errors will allow us to understand the limited but important role statistical significance plays in interpreting the results of a study.

The first error commonly made by researchers centers on the replicability of the findings of a study. It is not unusual for individuals to conclude that smaller significance levels mean that increasingly greater confidence can be vested in a conclusion and that sample results are replicable (Carver, 1978; 1993; Shaver 1993). The significance level does not tell us anything about the extent to which the findings are replicable. Carver (1978) found numerous examples, even in research textbooks, that mistakenly claimed that the significance level indicated the extent to which the findings of the study could be replicated.

The second error centers on the importance of the findings of a study. Too many of us believe that statistically significant results are inherently important. The following hypothetical dialogue between two students illustrates how significance levels are mistakenly interpreted as indicating the importance of the findings.

CHRIS: "I set the level of significance at .05, as my advisor suggested. So a difference that large would occur by chance less than 5 times in 100 if groups weren't really different. An unlikely occurrence like that surely must be important."

JEAN: "Wait a minute, Chris. Remember the other day when you went into the office to call home? Just as you completed dialing the number, your little boy picked up the phone to call someone. So you were connected and talking to one another without the phone ever ringing.... Well, that must have been a truly important occurrence then?" (Shaver, 1985, p. 58)

In short, the significance tells us nothing about the importance or magnitude of the findings (Shaver, 1993). Some scholars suggest that significance levels are informative with regard to the magnitude of the results only when the findings are counterintuitive (e.g., statistically significant results are obtained with a small sample size). Of course, interpretation of effect sizes (i.e., statistical procedure for determining the magnitude of the difference between two or more groups—see Chapter 14) would more directly inform us about the importance of the results of a study.

WHAT ARE TYPE I AND TYPE II ERRORS AND POWER?

It is important that critical research consumers understand three concepts related to statistical significance—Type I error, Type II error, and power. If critical research consumers can understand these three related concepts, they will be well on their way toward understanding the logic behind statistical significance testing. The logic of statistical significance tests requires that researchers establish the level of statistical significance (usually $p < .05$ or $p < .01$) prior to the computation of the test. In other words, researchers should establish the level of statistical significance at which the null hypothesis will not be accepted at the outset of the study. This level of significance is called "alpha" (symbolized α). The level of significance actually obtained is called the "probability value" and is indicated by the symbol p. A higher level of statistical significance corresponds to a lower p value. For example, $p < .01$ is a lower p value than $p < .05$, but a difference that is statistically significant at the .01 level suggests that chance was less a likely cause of the obtained difference between the groups than a difference that was significant only at the .05 level.

Type I Errors

Given that an alpha (α) level is chosen at the outset of the study and the fact that one can never be certain whether to "accept" (i.e., fail to reject) or "reject" the null hypothesis, it should be clear that researchers will unwittingly misinterpret the results of tests of statistical significance. There are two possible misinterpretations. The first misinterpretation occurs when researchers reject the null hypothesis when it is true; that is, researchers conclude that any difference between sample groups was due to chance alone. This type of misinterpretation is called a Type I error (a false positive) or α. This type of misinterpretation occurs in tests of statistical significance when the test statistic yields a value that falls in the rejection region by chance alone. Because of the decision-making process associated with tests of statistical significance, the researcher rejects the null hypothesis and consequently accepts the alternative hypothesis. The probability of making a Type I error is set by the significance level (α). For example, a significance level of $p < .05$ means that the probability of making a Type I error is less than 5 in 100. Likewise, a significance level of $p < .01$ means that the probability of making a Type I error is less than 1 in 100 and so on. The equivalent of a Type I error (α) in criminal law is imprisoning an innocent person.

Consider the information presented in Figure 4.4. We assume that our null hypothesis is true. In other words, the differences between the groups were only due to chance factors and not due to chance. We know that if we randomly select from the population and randomly assign participants to one of two groups, we will get differences in the groups' mean scores by chance. For example, Group 1 may have a mean score of 110 and Group 2 a mean score of 105. If we repeat the same process of randomly selecting and

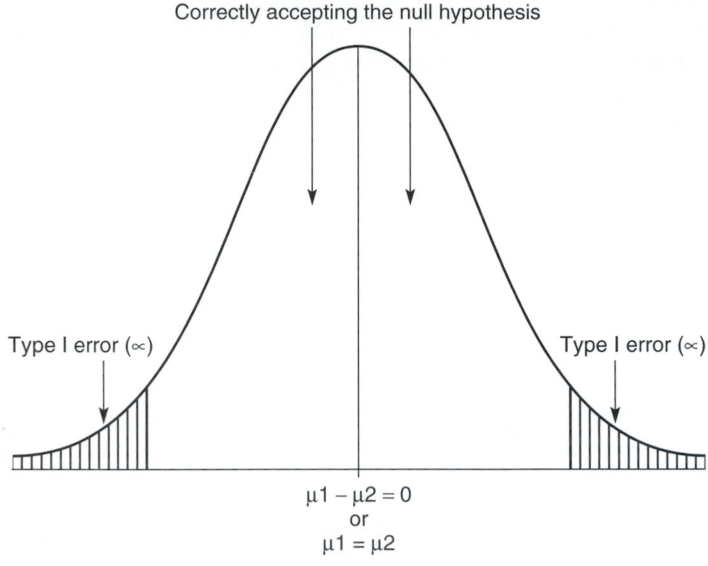

FIGURE 4.4 Normal curve with $\alpha = .05$ with $\mu_1 = \mu_2$ or $\mu_1 - \mu_2 = 0$. The vertical shaded areas represent $\alpha = .05$; a correct decision is represented when the differences between samples are between the α areas for a two-tailed test (when the null hypothesis is true, which is our assumption).

assigning participants an infinite number of times, we would get a sampling distribution of mean differences. The most frequently occurring mean difference would be 0 (i.e., Group 1 – Group 2 = 0). We would by chance have mean differences that would fall nearer and farther from this zero score by chance. Some of those differences would fall outside of the set alpha level. Thus, we would assume 5% of the scores to fall beyond the .05 level. This scenario illustrates the Type I error rate, or α.

Type II Errors

The second misinterpretation occurs when researchers accept or fail to reject the null hypothesis when, in fact, there is a difference; that is, researchers conclude that the differences between groups were due to chance and/or systematic factors. This type of misinterpretation is called a Type II error (a false negative) (symbolized β). It occurs in tests of statistical significance when the test statistic yields a value that falls outside the rejection region by chance alone. Because of the decision-making process associated with tests of statistical significance, this finding leads researchers to accept the null hypothesis when the experimental factor had a systematic influence on the dependent variable. The probability of making a Type II error (β) is influenced by a number of factors such as the significance level (i.e., as the *p* value decreases the possibility of a Type II error increases), the type of statistical test, and the sample size. To pursue the legal analogy, the equivalent of a Type II error (β) in criminal law is acquitting a guilty individual.

Consider the information contained in Figure 4.5. Suppose we had information that the samples really came from two different populations (e.g., we took a sample of participants from Population 1 and another sample from Population 2). Realize that we will never know this in a research study.

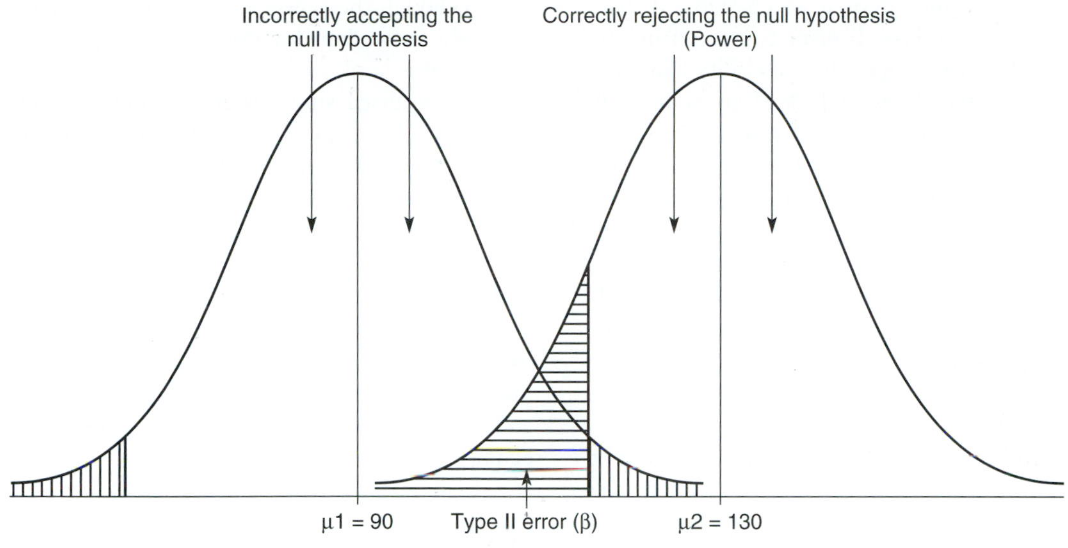

FIGURE 4.5 Normal curves with $\alpha = .05$ with $\mu_1 \neq \mu_2$. The vertical shaded areas represent $\alpha = .05$; the horizontal shaded area represents a Type II error rate, or β; an incorrect decision is represented on the left curve when the differences between samples are between the α areas for a two-tailed test; a correct decision (power) is made when the sample differences are to the left of β (when the null hypothesis is false).

In fact, we make the assumption that the samples came from the same population; this assumption is our null hypothesis. However, pretend for the moment that we had this information available. We would take a sample from each population with different means. In this example, Population 1 has a mean of 90 (symbolized μ_1) and Population 2 has a mean of 130 (symbolized μ_2). By chance, we are going to have samples with means different from the population means. These sample means will fall on either side of the population mean. Most sample means will be the same as the population means, but some will fall nearer and some farther from the population means.

If we look at Population 1 minus Population 2 ($\mu_1 - \mu_2$), we would get a score of 40. However, if we took a sample from each population and subtracted one sample mean from the other, we would get mean differences more than 40 and others less than 40. If a mean difference was sufficiently less than 40, the mean difference could fall beyond the alpha setting. If we took an infinite number of samples from each population and subtracted one from the other, we would get some mean differences that fall close to the null hypothesis (i.e., $\mu_1 - \mu_2 = 0$ or $\mu_1 = \mu_2$). If a sample mean difference falls within the alpha level, we are not going to reject the null hypothesis. We are going to conclude that the samples probably came from the same population, and the difference was likely due to chance, not a systematic variable. This scenario illustrates a Type II error, or β.

Relative Seriousness of Type I or Type II Errors

It is important to consider which of these types of errors is most serious. Making a Type I error is the most serious because it leads researchers to believe that the independent variable systematically influenced the dependent variable. This finding is especially problematic because positive results are much more likely to be reported in the research literature, leading to erroneous conclusions and misdirecting future research. On the other hand, making a Type II error is less serious because it still leaves open the possibility that a replication of the study will lead to statistically significant findings. Thus, if researchers are going to make an error, they will make a conservative one. Both types of errors point to the importance of replication studies in education and psychology. It is important for researchers to repeat their work as well as the work of others to explore the possibility that an inaccurate decision was made.

Power

Refer to Figure 4.5. Notice that when the difference falls outside of the alpha level, power is defined. Power is when we are able to detect a difference when one is actually present, or we correctly reject the null hypothesis. Mathematically, power = 1 – Type II error rate or power = 1 – β. Although the power of a test can be calculated, the procedure for doing so is beyond the scope of this book.

Before discussing power in detail, we must first discuss the four decisions that are made in a statistical significance test. Table 4.1 shows that two of these differences are correct and two are incorrect. If the null hypothesis is correct and we accept it, we will make a correct conclusion. If the null hypothesis is incorrect and we fail to accept it, we will make a Type I error (α). If the null hypothesis is incorrect and we accept it, we will make a Type II error (β). If the null is incorrect and we fail to accept it, we will make a correct decision (power).

Five Methods of Increasing Power

If power is so desirable, critical research consumers must understand what affects this probability

TABLE 4.1 Possible Decisions in Statistical Significance Testing

	ACCEPT NULL HYPOTHESIS	FAIL TO ACCEPT NULL HYPOTHESIS (or reject the null hypothesis)
Null Hypothesis True (our assumption)	Correct Decision	Type I Error (∞)
Null Hypothesis False	Type II Error (β)	Correct Decision (Power)

of detecting differences due to systematic variables when they are present (i.e., rejecting the null hypothesis). There are five basic methods of increasing the power of a test.

Use Parametric Tests. First, researchers can use parametric tests of statistical significance since they are always more powerful than nonparametric tests. Again, it is beyond the scope of this book to discuss the reasons why this is the case. However, suffice it to say that it is recommended that parametric tests of statistical significance be used even in those cases in which the data do not meet the assumptions of normal distribution or homogeneity of variance (sameness of the fluctuation of scores) but are derived from interval or ratio scores. This recommendation is made because moderate departures from the theoretical assumption about shape and variance have had little effect on parametric tests of statistical significance (Gall, Borg, & Gall, 1996). Additionally, because nonparametric tests of statistical significance are less powerful, they require larger sample sizes to yield the same level of statistical significance as parametric tests of statistical significance. That is, they are less likely to provide evidence that the null hypothesis should be rejected. Finally, suitable nonparametric tests of statistical significance are not always available for problems encountered in educational and psychological research.

Decrease Sources of Error Variance. A second method of affecting the power of a test is by decreasing sources of error variance from the sampling and measurement process. Recall that scores are going to change from one time to another because, among other things, there is a lack of 100% reliability in the measurement device. If we have a test that is 50% reliable and we make an infinite number of sample comparisons, the variability of the mean differences will increase. On the other hand, if we have a test that was 100% reliable, we would have lower variability of sample mean differences. Put another way, unsystematic variance makes it more difficult to detect systematic variance. If we can decrease the unsystematic variance in a study, we would be more likely to detect the presence of systematic variance and correctly reject the null hypothesis (power). One source of unsystematic variance is error variance for the sampling and measurement process.

Relax the Alpha Level. The third way that the power of a test of statistical significance is affected is by increasing, and thereby relaxing, the significance or alpha level. For example, the power of a given statistical test of significance will be greater if a researcher requires an alpha level of $p < .10$ rather than $p < .05$ to reject the null hypothesis. Consider the information in Figure 4.6. If the alpha level is increased, the Type I error rate increases, the Type II error rate decreases, and power increases. We move from having a Type I error rate of 2.5% in each tail to 5% in each tail. The advantage is that researchers are better able to detect systematic variance; the disadvantage is that researchers will commit more Type I errors if the differences between the groups occur by chance.

Make a Directional Alternative Hypothesis. The fourth method of affecting power is by making a directional alternative hypothesis. Figure 4.7 demonstrates what occurs when a one-tailed versus a two-tailed hypothesis is made. As shown in the figure, the Type I error rate for each tail of a two-tailed test is 2.5% with alpha set at .05. With a one-tailed hypothesis, the error rate increases to 5% on the single tail. Thus, if the Type I error rate increases, the Type II error rate decreases, thereby increasing power. Additionally, it is much harder to obtain the evidence needed to accept a two-tailed alternative hypothesis than it is to accept a one-tailed alternative hypothesis. The probability of making a Type I error decreases in this case. However, as stated previously, there should be clear evidence for the prediction of the direction of the findings made by researchers, and the prediction should be made at the outset of the study. The decision to use a one-tailed test should not be made solely on the wish to increase power.

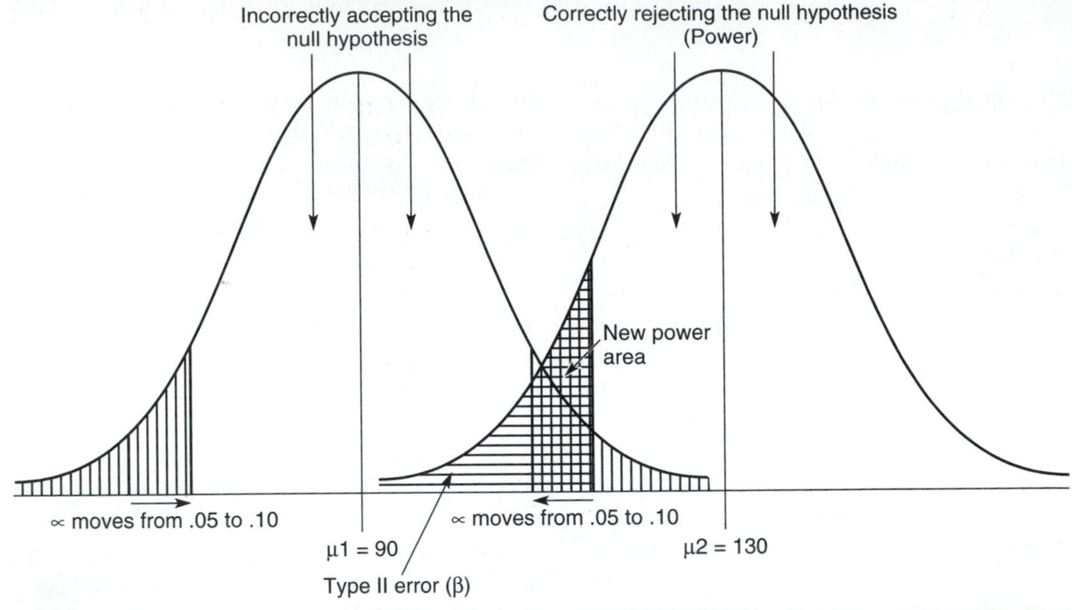

FIGURE 4.6 Normal curves with $\alpha = .10$ with $\mu_1 \neq \mu_2$. The vertical shaded areas represent $\alpha = .10$; the horizontal shaded area represents a Type II error rate, or β; an incorrect decision is represented on the left curve when the differences between samples are between the α areas for a two-tailed test; a correct decision (power) is made when the sample differences are to the right of β (when the null hypothesis is false).

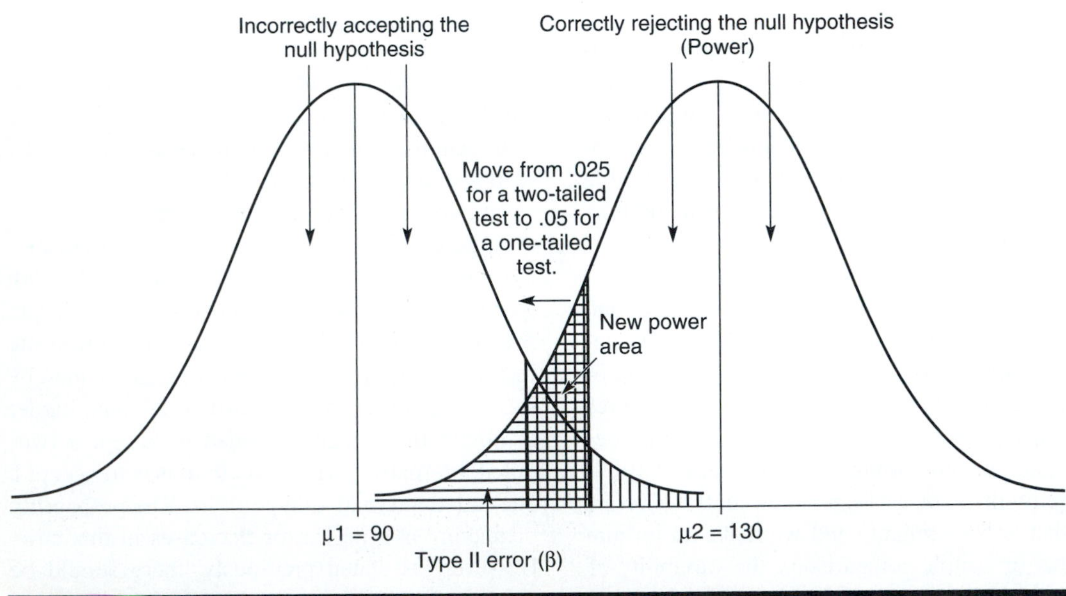

FIGURE 4.7 Normal curves with $\alpha = .05$ with $\mu_1 \neq \mu_2$. The vertical shaded areas represent $\alpha = .05$; the horizontal shaded area represents a Type II error rate, or β; an incorrect decision is represented on the left curve when the differences between samples are to the left of the α area for a one-tailed test; a correct decision (power) is made when the sample differences are to the right of β (when the null hypothesis is false).

Increase Sample Size. The final method of affecting the power of a test is by increasing sample size. As the sample size increases, so does the probability of a correct rejection of the null hypothesis. Here is the reason why. As the sample size increases, the sample begins to be a better representation of the population. The deviation of the sample mean from the population mean decreases on successive sampling. For example, if we take two samples from two different populations with different means and those samples represent 20% of each population, there will be much smaller deviations in successive comparisons of the groups than if each sample represented only 10% of each population. Figure 4.8 demonstrates this hypothetical example. If you compare Figure 4.8 to Figure 4.5, you will notice that the variability is smaller. There is also considerably less overlap of the distributions. What happens to the power then is that it increases. The Type II error rate decreases. The Type I error rate remains at .05.

WHAT ARE THE TYPES OF STATISTICAL SIGNIFICANCE TESTING METHODS?

Parametric Tests of Statistical Significance

Figures 4.9 and 4.10 display flow charts showing when to use specific inferential statistical analysis procedures. Figure 4.9 shows which procedures to use when there are two means (i.e., one or two groups), and Figure 4.10 shows which procedures to use when there are two or more means (i.e., one, two, or three or more groups). Refer to these figures throughout this section as well as throughout the analysis of data sections in Chapters 5 and 6.

Comparison of Two Means. The *t* test is a powerful parametric test of statistical significance that compares the means of two sets of scores to determine whether the difference between them is statistically significant at the chosen alpha level. Recall that in any situation, some degree of difference will always be observed. Thus, the question to be asked is not simply whether the two means

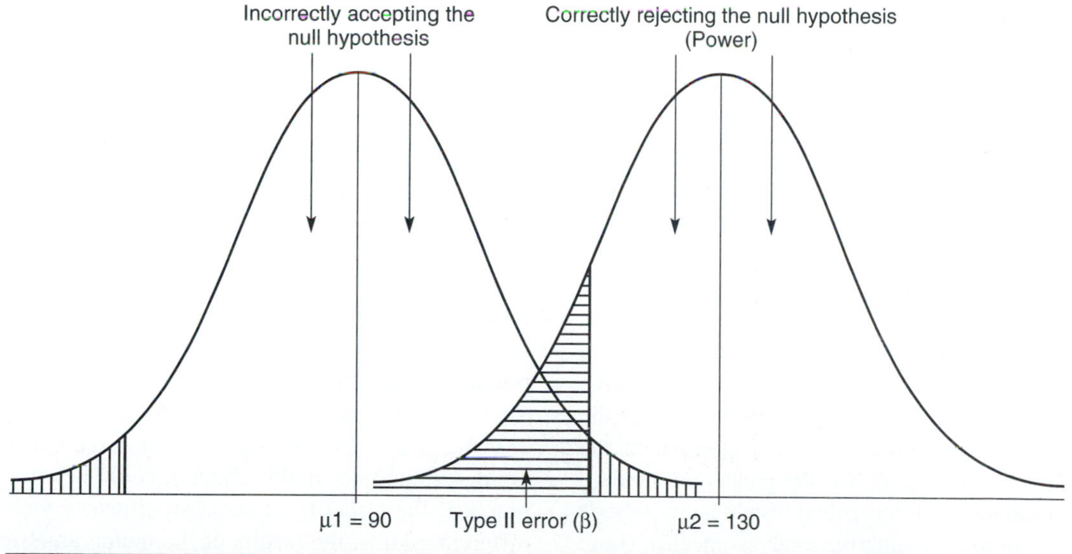

FIGURE 4.8 Normal curves with $\alpha = .05$ with $\mu_1 \neq \mu_2$. The vertical shaded areas represent $\alpha = .05$; the horizontal shaded area represents a Type II error rate, or β; an incorrect decision is represented on the left curve when the differences between samples are between the α areas for a two-tailed test; a correct decision (power) is made when the sample differences are to the right of β (when the null hypothesis is false).

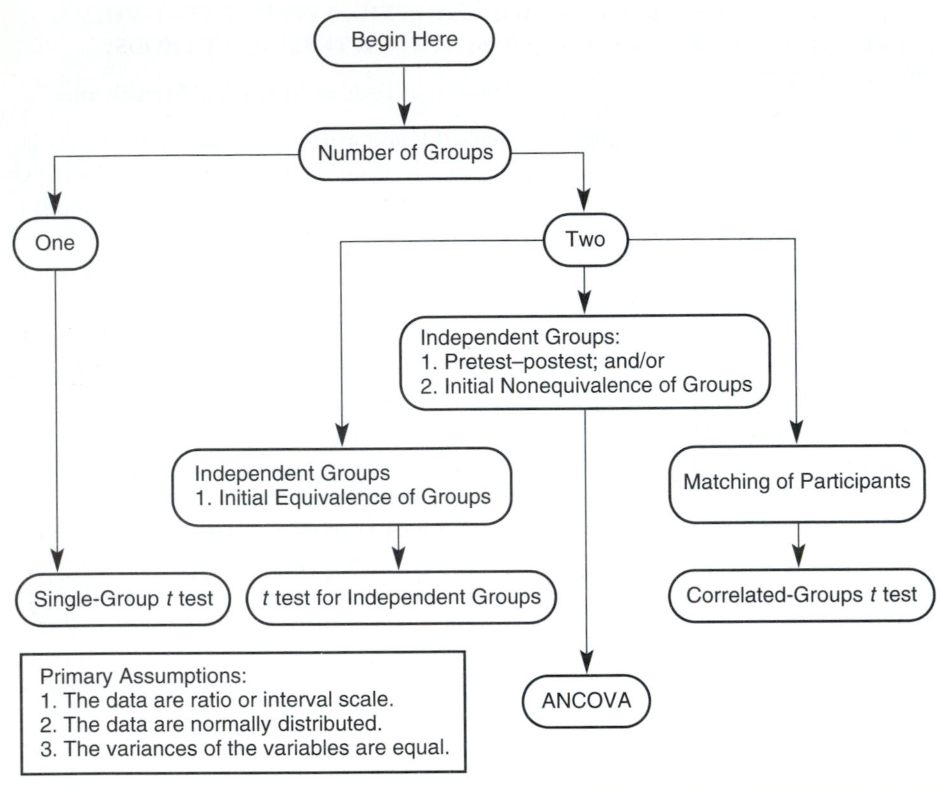

FIGURE 4.9 Selecting inferential statistical analysis procedures: Comparing two means.

are different, but whether the difference is so great as to be unlikely to have occurred by chance factors (i.e., sampling and measurement errors). If the result of the *t* test indicates that the difference is statistically significant, it provides evidence enabling researchers to conclude that it is unlikely that the obtained difference between the means is great enough to have occurred by chance factors alone. Additionally, it is important that the results of the *t* test be reported along with the summary statistics such as the mean and standard deviation to assist the critical research consumer's understanding of what the analysis means. These summary statistics should be reported for any findings from statistical inference testing.

The use of *t* tests depends on no major violations in the three assumptions about the obtained scores of parametric tests detailed before (Boneau, 1960). Again, these assumptions are (a) the scores are from an interval or ratio scale of measurement, (b) the scores of the populations under study are normally distributed (normal distribution), and (c) the score variances for the populations under study are equivalent (homogeneity of variance). Of course, if one is concerned about possible violations to these assumptions, one of the nonparametric tests (i.e., the Mann–Whitney *U* test or the Wilcoxon Signed Rank test), which are described later in this chapter, could be computed. If the tests of statistical significance yield different results, the results of the nonparametric test should be reported.

It is not uncommon for researchers to compare two groups or the same group on a number of dependent variables, each requiring a separate *t* test. Given the logic of tests of statistical signifi-

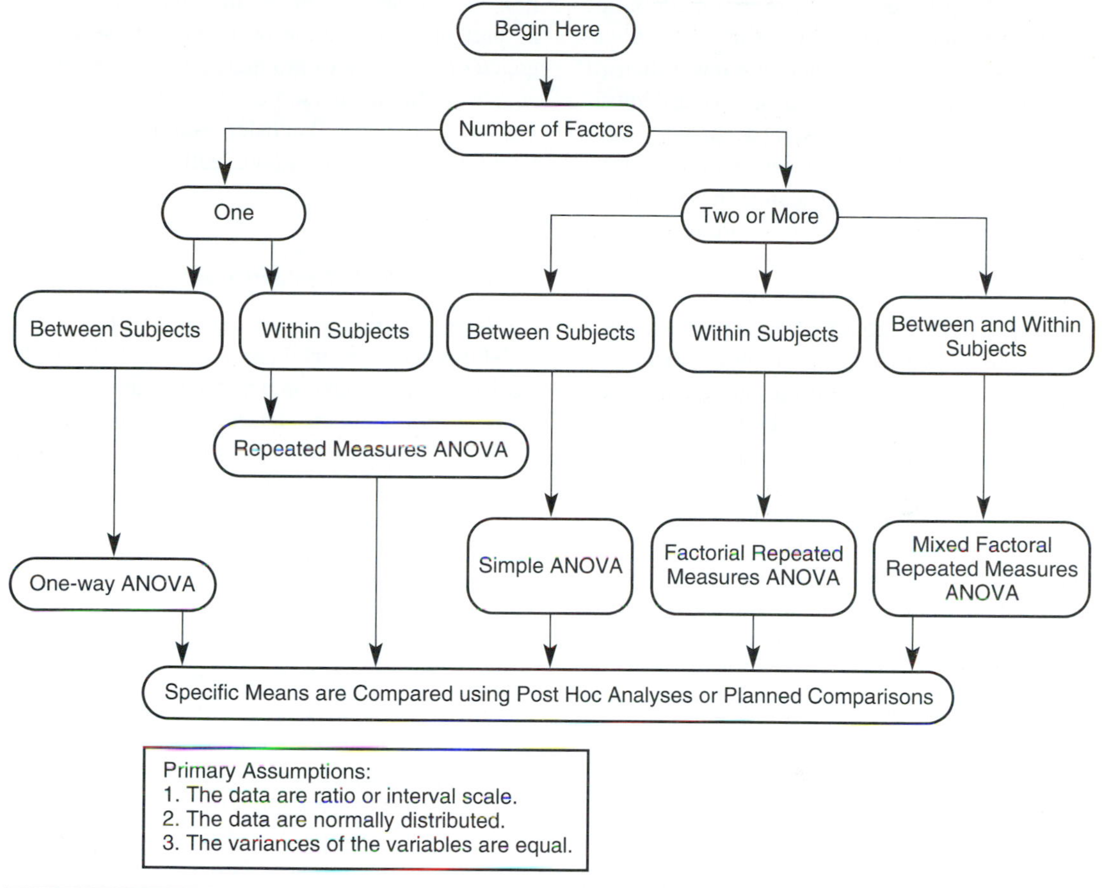

FIGURE 4.10 Selecting inferential analysis procedures: Comparing two or more means.

cance, each comparison increases the chances of finding a statistically significant difference between the means of groups on a dependent variable by comparing the groups on many dependent variables. That is, the risk of making a Type I error increases as the number of *t* test comparisons increases. For example, a researcher compares two groups on 20 different variables (this requires 20 separate *t* tests) and has set alpha at $p < .05$. Even if there are no systematic differences in the groups on any of the variables, one would expect to find at least one statistically significant finding.

The use of multiple *t* tests is much less a problem if the direction of the group difference on each variable has been predicted based on some theoretical model and/or previous research findings. If the predictions are confirmed, the null hypothesis that the findings are the result of chance factors has low plausibility. On the other hand, if the predictions are not confirmed, the null hypothesis that the findings are the result of chance factors has high plausibility. Of course, it is important to recall our discussion of the problems associated with making predications in education and psychology.

There are three types of *t* tests commonly used by researchers. They all are fairly powerful and robust tests of statistical significance. As a result, the *t* tests can be used with relatively small sample sizes. Although there are no set rules, *t* tests should not be used with means made up of fewer than 10 scores since the assumption of normality may be violated. If there are fewer than 10 scores, nonparametric tests of statistical significance should be used. At least theoretically, larger samples are better. Any increases in the size of the sample have to be balanced against the possibility of increasing sampling and measurement errors due to experimental factors such as fatigue. Thus, for most experiments, a moderate sample size consisting of 20 to 25 or more scores for each mean, coupled with careful attention to factors that influence sampling and measurement errors, is appropriate in most cases. The three types of *t* tests used by researchers are described next.

The t *Test for Independent Means.* The *t* test for independent means is used when the means of two samples are considered *independent* from one another (that is, one sample is not somehow related to another). This type of *t* test is the most common and is typically used in studies in which researchers are interested in comparing two independent samples on some dependent variable or variables.

The t *Test for Correlated Means.* The *t* test for correlated means is used in those cases in which the means of two samples are considered to be *related* in some fashion. There are two situations in which the *t* test for correlated means is used. The first situation involves an experimental situation in which two groups have been matched on some characteristic such that their scores on that characteristic vary systematically with their scores on the dependent variable or variables to be compared. The second situation in which the *t* test for correlated means is appropriate involves an experimental situation in which the same group of participants is studied across two different contexts or across two points in time.

The t *Test for a Single Mean.* Researchers typically compare the mean scores of two samples to determine whether the difference is statistically significant. However, there are times when researchers are interested in whether the difference between a sample mean and a specified population mean is statistically significant. For example, as part of an investigation exploring the intelligence of high school graduates with learning disabilities, the mean score of a group of these graduates on the Wechsler Adult Intelligence Scale–Revised is compared with the population mean of 100.

Comparison of Two or More Means

Analysis of Variance. The analysis of variance (ANOVA) is a powerful parametric test of statistical significance that compares the means of two or more sets of scores to determine whether the difference between them is statistically significant at the chosen alpha level. Again, the question to be asked is not simply whether the means differ from one another, but whether the difference is so great as to have unlikely occurred by chance. If the result of the ANOVA indicates that the difference is statistically significant, it provides evidence enabling us to conclude that there is a statistically significant difference among the means of three or more sets of scores. In other words, the difference is great enough to unlikely have occurred by chance factors alone (sampling and measurement errors). However, the ANOVA does not pinpoint which of the differences between the particular pairs of means are statistically significant.

In most cases, the ANOVA is an initial step in the analysis of the data. It is usually not interesting to conclude that there are statistically significant differences among the means. Researchers are often most interested in pinpointing which of the differences between the particular pairs of means are statistically significant. There are a number of multiple-comparison statistical testing procedures (e.g., Newman-Keuls, Tukey, and Scheffe) that can be used to pinpoint such pairs of means.

Multiple-comparison procedures are special *t* tests that adjust for the probability that researchers will find a significant difference between any given set of mean scores simply because many comparisons are made on the same data. Although it is beyond the scope of this book to detail each of the multiple comparison procedures, it is important to note that such procedures are typically conducted in a post hoc fashion. That is, multiple-comparison procedures are most commonly applied only if the p value obtained with the ANOVA is statistically significant. In rare cases, the researchers may make a priori comparisons (planned) based on previous findings or some sound theoretical base. In such cases, the researchers may forego the ANOVA and simply use one of the multiple-comparison procedures. This scenario is rarely played out because, as we mentioned before, there are few (if any) theoretical bases in education and psychology that would provide researchers with the level of precision necessary to make a priori predictions.

The use of ANOVA depends on no major violations in the same three assumptions about the obtained scores of parametric tests detailed previously. Of course, if one is concerned about possible violations to these assumptions, one of its nonparametric counterparts (e.g., chi-square) could be computed. If the tests of statistical significance yield different results, the results of the nonparametric test should be reported. Three variants of ANOVA are described in what follows.

Analysis of Covariance. Analysis of covariance (ANCOVA) is used by researchers in those cases in which they need to determine whether a difference between two or more groups on a particular variable can be explained, at least in part, by differences in the groups on another variable. ANCOVA is used to control for initial differences between or among groups statistically before a comparison is made. The effect of ANCOVA is to make the groups equivalent with respect to one or more control variables (potential explanatory variables). If a statistically significant difference is obtained while controlling for the influence of the control variable(s), this provides evidence that the control variables do not systematically influence the dependent variable or explain the obtained effect.

Repeated Measures Analysis of Variance. Repeated measures ANOVA is used by researchers in those cases in which they need to determine whether two or more groups differ on some dependent variable. Determining this difference is common in causal-comparative research when examining developmental changes in children.

As in the case of the general ANOVA procedure, the repeated measures ANOVA is an initial step in the analysis of the data. Post hoc multiple-comparison tests must be conducted to pinpoint which of the differences between the particular pairs of means are statistically significant. Additionally, multiple-comparison procedures might be used to answer such questions as: Do the group means increase significantly in a linear fashion? Is a straight line a good fit to the group means, or do significant deviations from linearity exist? or Do the group means increase and then decrease in an inverted U fashion? Multiple-comparison procedures can be used to answer such questions.

Multivariate Analysis of Variance. Multivariate analysis of variance (MANOVA) is used by researchers in those cases in which they need to determine whether two or more groups differ on more than one dependent variable. In other words, the MANOVA differs from the t test and ANOVA (which can determine only whether groups differ on one dependent variable) in that it allows researchers to determine whether groups differ on more than one dependent variable. If the result of the MANOVA indicates that the difference is statistically significant, it provides evidence enabling the conclusion that there is a statistically significant difference among the groups on one or more of the dependent variables. However, the MANOVA does not pinpoint the dependent variable(s) in which the groups differ.

In most cases, the MANOVA is an initial step in the analysis of data. It is usually not enough to conclude that there are statistically significant differences between the groups on one or more of the dependent measures. Researchers are often most interested in pinpointing which dependent measure as well as which particular pairs of means are statistically significant. Thus, if the results of the MANOVA are statistically significant, researchers do an ANOVA on each of the dependent variables to determine which of them produce statistically significant differences between or among the mean scores of the groups being studied. If more then two groups are included in the study, researchers then analyze differences in the mean scores of groups using post hoc multiple-comparison procedures (described earlier). It is important to note that it is possible (albeit highly unlikely) to obtain a statistically significant MANOVA without a statistically significant finding with any of the ANOVAs. It is not necessary to include all of the dependent variables in a single MANOVA. Rather, the dependent variables should be grouped into meaningful clusters and analyzed with separate MANOVAs.

Tests for Difference between Variances. Occasions may arise in which researchers want to test the statistical significance of the difference between the variances in scores for two or more samples. A variable may reflect itself not only in a mean difference between two groups but also in a variance difference. There are two primary reasons for testing the statistical significance of the difference between variances in scores. Given our discussion of the assumptions underlying parametric tests of statistical significance, the first reason is that most commonly used statistical tests are based on the assumption of homogeneity of variances. Although these tests are not greatly affected by minor violations of this assumption (as well as the other assumptions), if there are marked differences in the score variances, one of the nonparametric procedures should be employed.

The second reason for testing the statistical significance of the difference between variances in scores is to test a hypothesis concerning the variability of sample scores. The statistical procedure used to test whether the observed difference between variances of these groups is statistically significant is the *t* test for independent means.

If two sets of scores are obtained from independent samples, the test for homogeneity of independent variances is used to test the statistical significance of the difference between the variance in two sets of scores. In contrast, the test for homogeneity of related variances is used to test the statistical significance of the difference between the variance in two sets of scores obtained from matched samples or from repeated measures on a single sample. The *F* maximum test for homogeneity of variance is used in those cases in which there is a need to test the statistical significance of the variance of three or more sets of scores.

Nonparametric Tests of Statistical Significance

Figure 4.11 displays a flow chart showing when to use specific nonparametric statistical analysis procedures when there are one, two, or three or more groups and nominal or ordinal scales. Refer to this figure throughout this section as well as throughout the analysis of data sections in Chapters 5 and 6.

Comparisons of Relative Frequencies. The chi-square (χ^2) test is a nonparametric test of statistical significance. It compares the number of participants, objects, or responses, which fall into two or more categories, each with two sets of data, to determine whether the difference in the relative frequency of the two sets of data in a given category is statistically significant at the chosen alpha level.

There are two types of chi-square tests. In essence, chi-square tests conduct a comparison between the data that have been obtained and a set of expected frequencies. If the observed difference between the observed and expected frequencies is small, the value for chi-square will also be small and vice versa. The greater the value of the chi-square test, then the lower the probability that the difference between observed and expected frequencies could have been observed by chance factors alone. Additionally, the chi-square tests do not allow for the use of directional hypotheses.

Recall that the use of nonparametric tests such as the chi-square test does not rely on any assumptions regarding the population (i.e., normal distribution and homogeneity of variance). The chi-square test can be used under the following

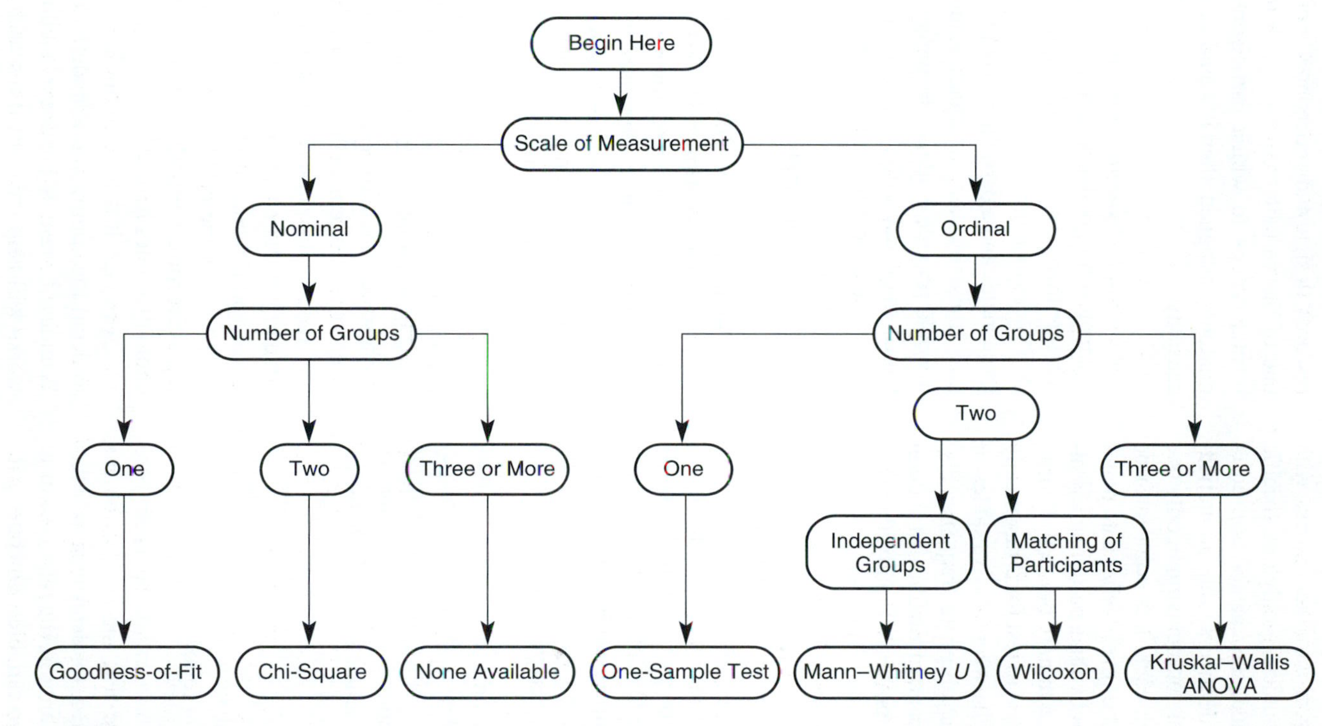

FIGURE 4.11 Selecting nonparametric statistical analysis procedures: Comparing two or more scores.

conditions. First, the data to be analyzed consist of frequencies organized into the matrix, with each cell of a matrix containing only one specific category of data. Second, the categories used in the chi-square test are defined so that an individual observation qualifies for inclusion in only one of the categories. Third, each data point must be completely independent of every other data point; this means that each individual participant is allowed to contribute once to only one cell. Fourth, the purpose of the study is to test for a statistically significant association between two variables or to determine whether an observed frequency distribution differs significantly from the distribution predicted by the null hypothesis. Finally, there are two stipulations to be made concerning the total size of the sample.

1. The sample must contain a minimum of 20 scores when there are only two categories.
2. The sample size must be such that the expected frequency for each cell of the matrix should be a least five observations. Yate's Correction Procedure or the Fisher Exact Test is employed in those cases in which the expected frequency is less than five.

Chi-square is not only necessary in those cases in which the data consist of frequency counts, but also in those cases in which there are major violation assumptions of the population parameters underlying a parametric test of statistical significance. For this latter reason, chi-square provides a way of dealing with imperfect interval scale data by converting the data into frequencies. The two types of chi-square tests used by researchers are described in what follows.

Chi-Square Test for Association between Variables. The chi-square test for association between variables is used to determine whether there is a statistically significant relationship or association between two variables. Of course, one cannot conclude that one variable has caused the observed pattern of frequencies on the other. The association may be due to the existence of some other variable. The establishment of a causal link would be primarily a function of the quality of the research design and procedures. For example, if one of the variables consists of different experimental groups to which participants have been randomly assigned, then it would be valid to infer causality.

The Chi-Square Goodness of Fit Test. The chi-square test for goodness of fit is used to determine whether there is a statistically significant relationship or association between an observed set of frequencies and a particular hypothetical distribution. If a significant chi-square value is obtained, it would provide evidence to suggest that the obtained frequency differs significantly from what one would expect from chance. Again, one cannot conclude that one variable has caused the observed pattern of frequencies on the other.

Comparisons of Two Independent Medians or Means: Mann–Whitney* U *Test. The Mann–Whitney U test is a nonparametric test of statistical significance that compares the medians or means of two sets of scores to determine whether the difference between them is statistically significant at the chosen alpha level. The Mann–Whitney U test is one of the most powerful nonparametric tests available, and it provides an alternative to the parametric t test when the researcher wants to avoid its assumptions. The Mann–Whitney U test can also be used in those cases in which an ordinal scale of measurement has been used. Additionally, the Mann–Whitney U test, like its parametric counterpart the t test, allows for both nondirectional and directional hypothesis. Of course, our discussion of the problems associated with making a directional hypothesis in education and psychology applies here.

Although it is beyond the scope of this book to detail the computations underlying the Mann–Whitney U test, a brief explanation of how it works will help the critical research consumer to understand it. The Mann–Whitney U test works by first merging the two sets of data to obtain a single rank ordering that is independent of the exact magnitude of the difference between values.

Because high values in the rankings indicate higher scores in the data, the set for which the sum is larger will contain the higher relative scores. The Mann–Whitney *U* test uses these rankings to generate a measure of the difference between the two sets of scores called a *U*. The value of *U* is determined by the number of times that a score from one set of data precedes (i.e., has been given a lower ranking) a score from the other set.

Comparisons of Two Related Medians or Means: Wilcoxon Signed Rank Test. The Wilcoxon Signed Rank test is a nonparametric test of statistical significance that compares the medians or means of two sets of scores that are considered to be related in some fashion. Recall that there are two situations in which the Wilcoxon Signed Rank test is used. The first situation involves an experiment in which two groups have been matched on some other characteristic such that their scores on that characteristic vary systematically with their scores on the dependent variable or variables to be compared.

The second situation in which the Wilcoxon Signed Rank test is appropriate involves an experiment in which the same group of participants is studied across two different contexts or two points in time. The Wilcoxon Signed Rank test provides an alternative to the parametric *t* test for correlated means when researchers want to avoid the assumptions of the *t* test. The Wilcoxon Signed Rank test can also be used in those cases in which an ordinal scale of measurement has been used. Additionally, the Wilcoxon Signed Rank test, like its parametric counterpart the *t* test, allows for both a nondirectional and directional hypothesis. Of course, our discussion of the problems associated with making directional hypotheses in education and psychology applies here.

The Wilcoxon Signed Rank test works by first determining the magnitude of the difference between the two scores generated by each participant. The differences are then rank-ordered, with the larger differences receiving higher rankings and vice versa. Each ranking is given a "+" or "–" sign to indicate the direction of differences. It is these signed rankings that provide the means for determining whether the differences between two sets of data are statistically significant. If chance factors alone are responsible for the differences between the two sets of data, then one would expect that these differences would be equally divided between positive and negative directions. In contrast, if the differences between the two sets of data are the result of the systematic influence of the variable under study, then one would expect that these differences would be unequally distributed between positive and negative directions.

Comparisons of Three or More Medians or Means: Kruskal–Wallis ANOVA. The Kruskal–Wallis ANOVA is a nonparametric test of statistical significance that compares the medians or means of three or more sets of scores (at least ordinal scale). It parallels the parametric ANOVA described earlier. The Kruskal–Wallis ANOVA is used when assumptions for a parametric test are violated.

WHAT ARE THE DIFFERENT SAMPLING METHODS?

In Chapter 2, we described the importance of population validity (i.e., inferring the results of a study from a sample to a population). Sampling provides the basis for experimental research. If everyone in the population cannot be included in the study, then researchers must select a sample. A sample is a subset of the population. The quality of the sampling technique employed by researchers conducting experimental studies enables them to maximize the degree to which the selected sample represents the population. Indeed, the quality of the sampling technique employed by researchers plays a large role in all research methods. However, the method of sampling will differ depending on the type of research conducted. For example, qualitative and single-case researchers do not rely on probability sampling methods, but on nonprobability methods in their selection of participants. (*Note:* Probability and nonprobability sampling methods will be discussed later in the chapter.)

A population is a group of potential participants, objects, or events to whom or to which researchers want to generalize the results of a study derived from a sample drawn from the population. The generalizability of the results of the study is one of the most important aspects of a study if the findings are to have any meaning beyond the limited setting in which the results were obtained. When results are generalizable, they can be applied to groups of individuals with the same characteristics in different settings.

It should be clear that the role of a sample is to represent a much larger, but typically inaccessible, population of individuals. The extent to which researchers can demonstrate that the sample is representative of the population enhances the generalizability of the findings from a study. Regardless of how large a sample is obtained or how carefully the data are collected, researchers' efforts will be wasted if the sampling technique they employed produced a sample that is unrepresentative of the population.

We will look at a number of sampling issues before describing some of the most common sampling techniques employed by researchers. The first issue centers on the types of samples. There are two types of samples: probability sample and nonprobability sample. A probability sample is one in which the likelihood of any one individual, object, or event of the population being selected is known. For example, if there are 8,000 students enrolled in a 2-year community college, and if there are 3,500 second-year students, the odds of selecting one second-year student as part of a sample is 3,500 divided by 8,000, or .44. A nonprobability sample is one in which the likelihood of any individual, object, or event of the population being selected is unknown. For example, if we did not know the total enrollment or the number of second-year students in our community college example, the likelihood of one being selected cannot be determined.

Probability Sampling

Probability sampling techniques are most commonly used by researchers because the selection of individuals, objects, or events is determined by random rules or chance. Before describing the different probability sampling techniques, we will look at the three meanings of the word *random* because it is tied directly to probability sampling techniques. First, the word *random* is used to refer to our subjective experiences that certain events occur haphazardly. This meaning has no relevance to sampling techniques in experimental research. Second, random is used in an operational way to describe techniques or methods for ensuring that individuals, objects, or events are selected in an unsystematic way. Drawing numbers from a drum after they have been thoroughly mixed is an example of a random technique. Finally, random is used to refer to the theoretical assumption about the equiprobability of events. Thus, a random sample is a sample in which every individual, object, or event has an equiprobability of being included in the sample. Of course, the probability sampling techniques that are described later do not truly ensure that every individual, object, or event has an equiprobability of being included in the sample. Rather, probability sampling techniques ensure that the determination of who will end up in the sample is determined by nonsystematic means. Now we will look at some of the most common probability sampling techniques.

Simple Random Sampling. Simple random sampling is the only probability sampling technique that ensures that each individual, object, or event has an equiprobability of being included in the sample. Indeed, simple random sampling is the standard against which all other probability and nonprobability sampling techniques can be compared. With simple random sampling, each individual, object, or event is taken from a defined population in such a way to ensure that (a) every individual, object, or event has an unknown chance of being included in the sample; and (b) the inclusion of every individual, object, or event is independent from the inclusion of any of the others (i.e., the choice of one does not influence the choice of another).

The process of simple random sampling consists of three steps. The first step involves listing all members of the population. Simple random sampling requires researchers to have complete access to the population. Having complete access to the population means that every individual, object, or event of the defined population is known. For example, suppose a researcher wants to take a random sample from the students enrolled in a high school. The defined population would be the students enrolled at that particular high school. The exact number of students enrolled in the school is known.

The second step in the process of simple random sampling involves assigning each individual, object, or event an identifying number. Researchers typically start with "1" and continue in order, number by number, until all of the individuals, objects, or events have been assigned a number. Of course, there is no reason for doing so other than logic. As long as every individual, object, or event has a different number and the range of numbers is known, any number can be used.

The third step in simple random sampling involves using a criterion to choose the sample that ensures that every individual, object, or event has an equiprobability and independent chance of being selected. To accomplish this, researchers typically use either statistical analysis packages or a table of random numbers. We will look at an illustrative example to help us understand how simple random sampling works.

Table 4.2 shows a list of 60 names and associated assigned numbers (Steps 1 and 2) that represents a population. Say we are interested in selecting 10 individuals randomly from this population using the table of random numbers. The table of random numbers consists of a large number of integers generated by means of a computer procedure (same procedure used to select a random sampling using statistical analysis packages) that virtually guarantees that as every integer is selected, it is entirely independent of those that preceded it. Therefore, no systematic patterns leading to bias or error are evident when the table of random numbers is used. For example, in Table 4.3 there is an equal number of 1's, 2's, 3's, and so on. As a result, the likelihood of selecting a number ending in a 1 or a 2 or a 3 is equal. When names are attached to numbers, the likelihood of selecting any particular name is also equal.

Before proceeding with our example, we will look at how a table of random numbers is used. Tables of random numbers include integers generated independently from one another that are

TABLE 4.2 List of 60 Names and Associated Assigned Numbers

1. Jeff P.	13. Alfred R.	25. Melia L.	37. Luke N.	49. Mario B.
2. Mary Jean M.	14. Carolyn E.	26. Wei-Ping L.	38. Shelbee O.	50. Juan V.
3. Tara E.	15. Cory M.	27. Manuel G.	39. Steven S.	51. Bethany S.
4. Don S.	16. Elfie M.	28. Lindo T.	40. Eric N.	52. Tom C.
5. Terry L.	17. George W.	29. Botheina M.	41. Jean S.	53. Malcolm M.
6. Melvin J.	18. John C.	30. Elona S.	42. Emily B.	54. Abraham L.
7. Fred E.1	19. Marilyn C.	31. Hobart C.	43. Liesel L.	55. Raymond H.
8. Stacy P.	20. Mary Jo B.	32. Tamara A.	44. Joan M.	56. Rigger W.
9. Aaron S.	21. Meredith L.	33. Telisha P.	45. Linda M.	57. Albert S.
10. Tran W.	22. Rueben W.	34. Bob D.	46. Olaf H.	58. Bernard O.
11. Bear R.	23. Saul A.	35. Richard N.	47. Leisha S.	59. Matthew P.
12. Lance E.	24. Winston C.	36. Mark M.	48. Barbara M.	60. Jamal C.

then placed into groups of four numbers (see Table 4.3). Tables of random numbers can be used to obtain one-, two-, three-, or four-digit random numbers with equal ease by simply reading across the required number of digits. We can begin to read off numbers at any point on the table and then proceed in any direction we want from that starting point. For example, taking a starting point somewhere in the middle of a table of random numbers and then continuing up the column will give just as random a sample as starting at the top left-hand corner and reading from left to right. Additionally, the number of digits considered is dependent on the total number of individuals, objects, or events included in the population. For example, if the population included 1,500 individuals, one would consider four digits at a time, whereas if the population included 50 individuals, one would consider two digits at a time.

Now we will select 10 names using the partial table of random numbers in Table 4.2. The first step is to pick a starting point. Again, it does not matter where you begin with a table of random numbers. We can begin at the start of a group of integers or anywhere within a group of integers. For this example, the starting point will be the first number 2 (4**2**40: bottom right-hand corner of the table); we will read the table from right to left. The first two-digit number considered is 24 (reading right to left). Because the population is composed of 60 individuals, and there is a name (Winston C.) associated with the number 24, this individual becomes the first to be included in the sample. Reading from right to left, the next number considered is 47. Leisha S. becomes the second individual to be included in the sample. We would then continue to select two-digit numbers in this manner until 10 values between 01 and 60 are chosen. We now have a sample of 10 names, selected by chance, from our original population of 60 individuals. The 10 individuals would be Winston C., Leisha S., Emily B., Don S., Lance E., Jeff P., Alfred R., Eric N., Bernard O., and Botheina M. following numbers 24, ~~63~~, 47, 42, 04, 12, ~~67~~, ~~70~~, ~~98~~, 01, 13, 40, 58, ~~24~~, and 29.

Systematic Sampling. Systematic sampling is an alternative to simple random sampling as a means of ensuring that each individual, object, or event has an equiprobability of being included in the sample. Systematic sampling involves the selection of every *k*th individual, object, or event on the list is chosen. The term *k*th stands for a number between 0 and the size of the sample that we want to select. Like simple random sampling, systematic sampling requires a complete listing of every member of the population. Unlike simple random sampling, systematic sampling involves drawing members of sample at a regular, prede-

TABLE 4.3 Table of Random Numbers

2889	6587	0813	5063	0423	2547	5791	1352	6224	1994	9167	4857
1030	2943	6542	7866	2855	8047	4610	9008	5598	7810	7049	9205
1207	9574	6260	5351	5732	2227	1272	7227	7744	6732	2313	6795
0776	3001	8554	9692	7266	8665	6460	5659	7536	7546	4433	6371
5450	0644	7510	9146	9686	1983	5247	5365	0051	9351	3080	0519
2956	2327	1903	0533	1808	5151	7857	2617	3487	9623	9589	9993
3979	1128	9415	5204	4313	3700	7968	9626	6070	3983	6656	6203
5586	5777	5533	6202	0585	4025	2473	5293	7050	4821	4774	6317
2727	5126	3596	2900	4584	9090	6577	6399	2569	0209	0403	3578
1979	9507	2102	8448	5197	2855	5309	4886	2830	0235	7030	3206
4793	7421	8633	4990	2169	7489	8340	6980	9796	4759	9756	3324
8736	1718	1690	4675	2728	5213	7320	9605	6893	4169	9607	9750
8179	5942	3713	8183	9242	8504	3110	8907	7621	4024	7436	4240

termined interval from the population rather than using a table of random numbers.

The process of systematic sampling consists of three steps: first, listing every member of the population; second, assigning a number to each member; and third, determining the criterion used to draw members of the sample from the population. The criterion is determined by (a) establishing the *k*th number by dividing the size of the population by the size of the desired sample, (b) selecting a starting point randomly from which to start drawing members of the sample from the population, and (c) drawing members of the sample from the population using the sampling fraction.

Consider the illustrative sample used earlier in which 10 individuals were to be selected randomly from a population containing 60 members. To establish the *k*th number, we would divide 60 by 10. Thus, we will select every 6th individual from the list. We would then randomly select a starting point. For example, we might close our eyes and point to a name. In this example, the starting point is number 22 (Rueben W.). Once the starting point is determined, every sixth name is then selected (e.g., Lindo T., Bob D, etc.).

Stratified Random Sampling. Simple random sampling and systematic sampling are used when variables of interest (e.g., IQ, socioeconomic status) are distributed evenly across the population. In other words, using the previous illustrative example, if another set of 10 names were selected, we would assume that because both groups were chosen randomly, they would be equal on the variable of interest. However, researchers are often faced with situations in which they are interested in sampling from a population that is not homogenous on variables that may influence the data. For example, the findings of an experimental study of the effects of an intervention on the reading performance of students, which does not take into account the fact that students from different socioeconomic levels have different learning histories, may not be representative of the population at large. The problem in such cases is to select a sample that is representative of a heterogeneous population.

Stratified random sampling is used in those cases in which the population to be sampled is heterogeneous with respect to one or more variables that may affect the outcomes of the study. For example, if the population includes 60% Caucasians, 30% Hispanics, and 10% African Americans, the sample should have the same ethnic breakdown if ethnicity is an important variable in the first place. A representative ethnic sample would not be necessary if ethnicity were not considered an important variable.

The process of systematic sampling consists of three steps. The first step involves listing every member of the subgroups of a population separately. The second step involves assigning a number to each member of the subgroups. The final step involves randomly drawing a proportionate number of members for each of the subgroups using a statistical analysis package or a table of random numbers.

Going back to our illustrative example, assume that the list of 60 names in Table 4.2 represents a stratified population of males and females, and attitude toward sex education in public schools is of interest. Because gender differences would be important, we would want a sample that is representative of gender differences in the population. The list of 60 names contains 35 females and 25 males, or approximately 60% female and 40% male. To mirror the population, a stratified random sample of 10 would include six females and four males.

Although simple stratified random samples such as this are relatively common in research in education and psychology, we may encounter situations in which there is a need to stratify a population on more than one variable or characteristic. For example, in a study of the effects of a science curriculum, researchers may stratify the population by gender, grade, and IQ to ensure the representiveness of the sample.

Cluster Sampling. The last type of probability sampling is cluster sampling. Cluster sampling involves selecting units of individuals, objects, or events rather than individual members themselves. Cluster sampling is often used when an exhaustive listing of the population cannot be obtained or it is possible to subdivide the population according to some logical structure or principle. Cluster sampling involves subdividing the population into a relatively large number of units and then sampling from these units to obtain a further group of smaller units, and so on until the members of the final sample are identified. For example, cluster sampling could be used to conduct a survey of students regarding the quality of library services at a university. In this case, undergraduate and graduate courses representative of each major would be identified. Then one undergraduate and one graduate course would be randomly selected from the identified courses. Students in these courses would constitute the sample. This process could be taken even further by randomly selecting students from these identified courses.

Nonprobability Sampling

Nonprobability sampling techniques involve selecting a sample where the probability of selecting a single individual, object, or event is not known. In essence, nonprobability sampling techniques provide researchers a way of selecting individuals, objects, or events when it is not possible to specify exactly how many members are in the population. Nonprobability sampling techniques are less desirable than probability sampling techniques in quantitative research because they tend to produce samples that are not representative of the population. Nevertheless, nonprobability sampling techniques are used extensively by researchers in education and psychology. We will now look at some of the most common nonprobability sampling techniques.

Quota Sampling. In many respects, quota sampling is similar to the stratified sampling technique previously described. The intent of quota sampling is to derive a sample from a heterogeneous population for which researchers do not have an exhaustive list of the members of the population. Quota sampling can result in a relatively representative sample if the population can be subdivided on one or more variables, if the subdivisions constitute known proportions of the population, and if these relationships are maintained within the sample taken from each subdivision. For example, if a population is known to be made up of 75% males and 25% females, then the proportion of males and females in the final samples should also be 75% and 25%, respectively. Of course, the samples derived from quota sampling will be representative of the population only in relation to the variable on which the population is initially divided. Researchers have no way of knowing whether the derived samples are representative of the population in relation to other variables. This situation is not a problem if researchers have subdivided the group on all of the key variables.

The process of quota sampling involves three steps. The first step involves identifying the key variable or variables on which the sample is required to be representative of the population and determining what proportion of the population falls into each of the different categories to be used. For example, if a population of at-risk students is to be subdivided on the basis of gender, then the population would need to be subdivided into the proportion of males and females identified as at-risk. The desired sample size and associated quota for each category is determined in the second step. In the final step, the members of each subdivision are selected using one of the nonprobabilistic sampling procedures described in what follows.

Convenience Sampling. Convenience sampling involves using those individuals, objects, or events that are available to the researcher. Although convenience sampling is an easy way for researchers to generate samples, the samples tend not to be representative of the population. The usual method of putting together a convenience sample is for researchers to use members of a population who are available. For example, a professor in psychology includes all of the students enrolled in an introduction to psychology class to explore some psychological phenomenon. Convenience sampling results in a sample that is representative of the population if the group of individuals, events, or objects available to the researcher is representative of a population. If this is not the case, generalizing beyond the members of the sample would be problematic.

Opportunity Sampling. Opportunity sampling is similar to convenience sampling in that researchers use individuals, objects, or events that are readily available. However, opportunity sampling consists of using members of the population who are willing to take part in the research. For example, using our college example, the professor includes those students enrolled in an introduction to psychology class who are willing to participate in the research study. In contrast to convenience sampling, opportunity sampling rarely results in representative samples. Thus, any inferences made beyond the members of the sample are problematic.

Volunteer Sampling. Volunteer sampling involves directly advertising for those who will participate in a research study. The distinguishing aspect of volunteer sampling is that the participants are self-selected. That is, rather than researchers approaching each member of the population to ask if he or she wants to be included in the sample, the volunteer approaches the researchers and asks to participate in the study. It is important to note that members of self-selected samples tend to be different from the population. Thus, any inferences made beyond the members of the sample must be done cautiously.

WHAT ARE THE SAMPLING DECISIONS RESEARCHERS MAKE?

There are a number of decisions that researchers must make with regard to selecting the particular sampling technique they will use in a study. The first, and most important, decision that researchers must consider centers on the issue of how important is it for the sample to be representative of the population of interest. If it is critical that the results of the study generalize to a particular population, researchers must use a probabilistic sampling techniques such as simple random sampling. A nonprobabilistic sampling technique may be appropriate if it is not critical that the results of the study generalize to a particular population. As we mentioned, it is plausible that samples derived from nonprobabilistic sampling techniques such as convenience sampling can be representative of a particular population. The important point to keep in mind is that the use of nonprobabilistic sampling techniques does not render a study useless. Rather, such sampling techniques limit the extent to which inferences regarding the results of the study generalize to a particular population.

The second decision that researchers must consider with regard to selecting a particular sampling technique centers on two basic issues. The first issue is whether or not researchers have access to an exhaustive list of the members of the population. If not, researchers will not be able to use simple random or systematic sampling techniques. In such cases, quota sampling may be an alternative that will result in a reasonably representative sample. The second issue centers on what resources (e.g., time, money, and assistance) are available to researchers. Probabilistic sampling techniques tend to require more resources than do nonprobabilistic sampling techniques.

The final decision that researchers must make centers on the size of the sample—just how many members of the population should researchers select to ensure that the sample is representative of the population? The less representative a sample is of the population, the more sampling error is present, and the less generalizable the results will be to the population. In general, the larger the sample is, the more likely it is representative of the population. However, it is important to keep in mind that there is a point of diminishing returns. That is, increasing the amount of resources needed to collect data from large samples does not result in greater precision. The method used by researchers to calculate the sample size that is needed to be representative of a particular population for an experimental study is as follows:

$$n = \frac{2(SD)^2 \times t^2}{D^2}$$

where n = size of sample

SD = standard deviation of the dependent variable in the population

t = critical value needed for rejection of the null hypothesis

D = estimate of the average difference between the two groups

We will now look at an illustrative example to see how researchers can determine the size of sample needed to be reasonably representative of a particular population. The goal of this study is to determine the effects of a behavioral intervention on the social adjustment of students with behavioral disorders. The researcher is using a pretest and posttest design with an experimental group and a control group. The standard deviation is estimated by looking at previous studies. In our example, a social adjustment scale is used, and the standard deviation in the population is 10. The researcher then considers the critical value associated with the particular test of statistical significance that reflects the difference between groups that would be obtained by chance alone (and not any intervention effects). Critical values can be obtained from tables included in statistics textbooks. In our example, the critical value associated with the t test is 2.00. Finally, the researcher estimates what she expects the magnitude of the difference to be. This estimate is based on previous studies using similar interventions. In our example, say that the researcher expects a 5-point increase. The values for our example are as follows.

$$SD = 10$$

$$t = 2.00$$

$$D = 5$$

Substituting these values into the preceding formula reveals that the researcher would need about 16 members each in the experimental and control groups.

$$n = \frac{(2 \times 10^2) \times 2.00^2}{5^2} = \frac{400}{25} = 16$$

Substituting different values into the formula reveals that the expected difference between groups plays the largest role in determining the size of the sample. For example, if the researcher changed the estimated expected difference in her sample to 2, she would need about 100 members in each group. Accordingly, the larger the difference between groups, the less representative the groups have to be of the population to detect the experimental effect if it exists.

Finally, there are some general issues to keep in mind with regard to the size of the sample. The first issue that should be considered is the size of the sample. Generally, the larger the sample, the smaller the sampling error. Of course, the level of precision achieved with even larger sample sizes decreases dramatically. The second issue centers on how the sample will eventually be broken down for analysis. The initial selection of participants should be large enough to account for the final breaking down of participant groups. The final issue focuses on choosing an appropriate sample of participants based on the purpose of the research. If a sample is inappropriate for the purpose of the research, it will not matter how many participants were included in the sample.

WHAT IS SAMPLING ERROR?

We discussed the notion of sampling error in our discussion of tests of statistical significance. As you might expect, it is virtually impossible for researchers to select samples that are truly representative of the population of interest. In other words, regardless of the sampling technique used by the researcher, the characteristics of the sample will differ to some degree from those of the population. The difference between the characteristics of the sample and those of the population is referred to as sampling error. For example, the average IQ in the population is 100. If we were to select 20 samples of 100 individuals selected randomly and compute the mean IQ scores for each group of individuals, we would end up with 20 averages. If all those averages were exactly 100, there would be no sampling error. Of course, this scenario would never happen. The average IQ scores for the group would vary to some degree from 100. Some would be above 100 (e.g., 100.6, 100.2) and others would be below 100 (e.g., 99.9, 99.4). The amount of variability in these values provides an indicator of the amount of sampling error present.

Although the exact computations of sampling error are beyond the scope of this book, the critical research consumer should understand that the researchers' main goal is to minimize this value. The smaller the value, the smaller the sampling error. We already know that the larger the sample, the smaller the sampling error and, consequently, the more representative the sample is of the population. The more representative the sample, the more accurate the tests of statistical significance will be. That is, better sampling leads to more accurate tests of population differences.

It should be clear that minimizing sampling error requires researchers to focus on two key aspects. The first aspect centers on ensuring the use of sampling techniques that result in samples that are representative of the population. The second aspect focuses on the size of the sample. Remember, in general, the larger the sample, the more likely it is to be representative of the population.

SUMMARY

Although the purpose of this text is not to present a comprehensive discussion of statistics, it is important for critical research consumers to have an understanding of basic statistical concepts. Critical research consumers should know why researchers used certain statistical techniques when analyzing their results. The first consideration is the type of scale of measurement used. Most educational and psychological research involves interval scale measurements. With such scale of measurements, researchers will use several types of statistics to describe their data such as the arithmetic mean, median, mode, range, standard deviation, and variance. Another critical concern is the shape of the distribution. Researchers assume that most variables of interest such as intelligence and achievement scores of the population are distributed in a normal fashion. However, other types of distributions are also present such as the bimodal and skewed distributions. This assumption of a normal distribution is key when using many inferential statistics methods to interpret research findings.

When using inferential statistics, quantitative researchers develop null and alternative hypotheses. The alternative hypothesis is either directional or nondirectional. The type of inferential statistics used to analyze the obtained data and, thus, make a determination of the believability of the hypotheses will depend upon the assumption of a normal distribution. Parametric statistics require such an assumption whereas nonparametric statistics do not.

Once a statistical or nonstatistical finding is obtained on the data, the critical research consumer must understand what statistically significant findings mean. Unfortunately, statistical significance is misunderstood by many in education and psychology. One misunderstanding is that the findings of statistical significance, and thus the interpretations made on such findings, are probabilistic. In other words, researchers will never know if their conclusions are correct. Two types of errors are made when making conclusions based on inferential statistics—Type I and Type II. An understanding of these errors is important for critical research consumers. Also, it is important for critical research consumers to understand the concept of power and how researchers can increase power.

Critical research consumers should also understand the types of statistical significance testing methods used in research. Additionally, decision rules that are followed by researchers should be learned.

Finally, the type of sampling method used by researchers is important in determining the types of claims researchers can make. These sampling methods rest on sampling decisions made by researchers. Probability sampling methods help to make a research sample of participants representative of the population. If the sample is representative of the population, the population validity of the investigation is increased. Nonprobability sampling methods are frequently used but decrease the opportunity to demonstrate population validity. Once the type of sampling method is determined, researchers must make a determination of the size of the sample. A simple formula can be used to aid in this determination. The critical research consumer should be knowledgeable of the different sampling methods and the concept of sampling error. Sampling error will affect the correctness of decisions made by researchers.

DISCUSSION QUESTIONS

1. Researchers use several type of scales of measurement. Provide an original example for each scale of measurement.
2. Suppose that a student took an IQ test and received a score of 130. The standard deviation for the test is 15 and the mean is 100. What proportion of the population scored the same or higher than the student? What proportion of the population scored the same or lower than the student? What score would a student need to be at the 84th percentile?
3. Another student had heard that the null hypothesis is a straw man to be knocked down. She asked you what this means. How would you answer her question? (*Note:* In your answer, describe the purpose of null hypotheses and alternative hypotheses.)
4. You read a research article and noticed that the researcher made a directional hypothesis. What does this mean, and what information would the researcher need to make such a directional hypothesis?
5. In the same article (as in Question 4), you also notice that the author used a parametric test. What is a parametric test, and how does a parametric test differ from a nonparametric test? (*Note:* Discuss assumptions of parametric tests in your answer.)
6. The same author in the article in Question 4 indicated that the results were significant at the .05 level. He concluded that this means that the results proved that the null hypothesis was false and that the independent variable caused the results. He went on to indicate that if the study was repeated 100 times, these same results would occur 95 times. Are his conclusions warranted? Why or why not?
7. The author in another article you were reading indicated that the alpha (α) level was .05. Based on this information, indicate what the Type I error rate is. Additionally, define the term Type I error. The researcher also stated that making Type I error is worse than making Type II errors. Do you agree with the statement? Why or why not? In your answer, describe what a Type II error is.
8. Another student in your research class tells you that he does not understand the concept of power. Describe what power is, illustrate how power can be increased, and explain why increasing the power of a test is worthwhile.
9. Suppose that you are working on a research project and compared the abilities of males and females in mathematics. You take a group of twins (male and female pairs) and compare the average math performance (i.e., scores on a

standardized test) of the gender groups. What type of parametric test would you use and why? What type of nonparametric test could you use and why (i.e., under what conditions)? What tests would you use if the males and females were not related to one another (i.e., separate samples)?

10. You were planning a study to determine the best method of teaching students how to spell. One of the first steps you considered was who you would include in your study. You decided to work with third graders. Your next decision is how to select the students. What sampling decisions would need to be made (i.e., how many students do you need, and should you use probability or nonprobability sampling methods and why)? Describe how sampling error could be affected by the sampling method you selected.

Chapter 5

EXPERIMENTAL DESIGNS

OBJECTIVES

After studying this chapter you should be able to:

1. Describe the basic requirements for true experimental designs.
2. Describe the basic design features of true experimental designs.
3. Describe the differences in the design features of factorial designs.
4. Describe the threats to internal validity associated with each of the experimental designs.
5. Describe the basic requirements for quasi-experimental designs.
6. Describe the basic design features of quasi-experimental designs.
7. Describe the basic requirements for preexperimental designs.
8. Describe the basic design features of preexperimental designs.
9. Describe the threats to external validity associated with each of the experimental designs.
10. Describe when one would use each of the designs.
11. Critique a research article containing an experimental design.

OVERVIEW

Researchers tend to be most interested in *why* things happen. Establishing cause-and-effect relationships among variables is typically the goal of most research. The experimental research designs described in this chapter are designed to test for the presence of a distinct cause-and-effect relationship between variables. In order to achieve this goal, experimental research must control extraneous variables. The results of a study using an experimental design indicate whether an independent variable produces changes in the dependent variable or that the independent variable does not produce these changes. For example, a simple experimental design would consist of two groups of participants randomly selected from a population in which one group (experimental group) receives the independent variable (intervention), and the other group (control group) receives no intervention. Both groups are tested at the conclusion of the study to assess whether there is a difference in their scores. Assuming that the groups were equivalent from the start of the investigation, any observed differences at the conclusion of the investigation could reasonably be attributable to the independent variable along with measurement and sampling error.

The controlled experiment has led to much of our substantive knowledge in many areas such as learning, memory, perception, and clinical psychology. The control achieved with experimental research designs enables researchers to ensure that the effects of the independent variable on the dependent variable are a direct (causal) consequence of the independent variable and not of other factors (i.e., extraneous variables or threats to internal validity). Of course, the experimental research designs used by researchers to establish cause-and-effect relationships differ widely in their ability to control for threats to internal and external validity (described in Chapter 2).

There are three categories of experimental research designs used by researchers in education and psychology: (a) true experimental, (b) quasi-experimental, and (c) preexperimental designs. These designs differ with regard to the level of experimental control they provide. Researchers must be concerned with the number of extraneous variables (threats to internal validity) that may affect changes in the performance of the experimental or control groups. Researchers must also be concerned with generalizing the results of studies to a broader population and set of conditions (external validity).

The ability of an experimental design to control for threats to internal and external validity is primarily dependent on four key features. The first key feature centers on the procedures used to select participants from a broader population. The usefulness of any given study is dependent on how well the results of that study can be generalized to a broader population and set of conditions. The second key feature involves the use of a control group or condition. Comparing the performance of an experimental group with that of a control group provides the basis for controlling many of the threats to internal and external validity. The comparison of conditions is critical for establishing whether there is a causal relationship between variables. The third key feature focuses on the initial equivalence of the experimental and control groups. Researchers must ensure this initial equivalence if they are to make relatively definitive conclusions regarding a causal relationship between the independent and dependent variables. The final key feature for experimental research centers on how effectively the investigation was conducted. Although researchers might employ a rigorous design, the results will be useless if the investigation is not conducted well.

The three categories of group experimental designs differ on these design features that account for differences in the levels of experimental control. The final key feature (i.e., quality of implementation) cuts across all three categories of experimental designs. True experimental designs include clear procedures for addressing each of the first three key design features including (a) the random selection of participants from a population (see Chapter 4), (b) the inclusion of a control group, and (c) the equivalence of the experimental and control groups. Quasi-experimental designs (with the exception of some time-series designs) include procedures for addressing the second key design feature (i.e., the inclusion of a control group). Preexperimental designs include none of these key design features. Table 5.1 summarizes the key design features associated with true, quasi-experimental, and preexperimental research designs.

TABLE 5.1 Key Design Features of True, Quasi-, and Preexperimental Research Designs

	RANDOM SELECTION OF PARTICIPANTS FROM A POPULATION	RANDOM ASSIGNMENT OF PARTICIPANTS TO CONDITIONS	CONTROL GROUP	EQUIVALENCE OF GROUPS
True	Yes	Yes	Yes	Yes
Quasi	No	No	Yes	No
Preexperimental	No	No	No	No

The remainder of this chapter includes a description of each of the true, quasi-experimental, and preexperimental research designs commonly used by researchers in education and psychology. Additionally, methods of analyzing data are described. (Refer to Figures 4.9, 4.10, and 4.11 for information regarding when to use each statistical analysis procedure to analyze data from investigations.) Finally, research examples are provided throughout the chapter, and an illustrative investigation is included at the end of the chapter for critique.

WHAT ARE TRUE EXPERIMENTAL DESIGNS?

True experimental designs are the only experimental designs that can result in relatively definitive statements about causal relationships between variables. Researchers can argue rather decisively that there is a causal relationship between variables if they have effectively used a true experimental design. The beauty of true experimental designs rests in their simplicity in achieving the three requirements identified by Cook and Campbell (1979) in saying that one variable (independent variable) causes another (dependent variable). True experimental designs ensure that (a) a change in the value of the independent variable is accompanied by a change in the value of the dependent variable, (b) how the independent variable affects the dependent variable is established a priori, and (c) the independent variable precedes the dependent variable.

There are three basic requirements for a research design to be considered a true experimental design. The first requirement is the random selection of participants from a population to form a sample. One of the probabilistic sampling techniques we discussed in Chapter 4 is used by researchers to ensure that the participants selected are representative of the population. The random selection of participants from a population is a critical issue to the external validity of a study. It is important to note that researchers tend to be much more concerned with the random assignment of participants to either the experimental or control group than they are of randomly selecting participants from a population to form a sample. This concern represents the tendency of researchers to be more mindful of the internal validity of a study rather than its external validity.

The second requirement is that research participants must be randomly assigned to the experimental and control conditions. Random assignment helps to ensure that the members of the experimental and control groups are equivalent to one another before the implementation of the independent variable. Ensuring that the experimental and control groups are equivalent is critical to the internal validity of the study. However, it is important to note that randomly assigning participants to groups does not necessarily guarantee initial equivalence between groups. Rather, random assignment only assures the absence of systematic bias in the makeup of the groups. Assigning participants to the experimental and control groups is accomplished using one of the probabilistic sampling techniques discussed previously.

The equal treatment of members of the experimental and control groups is the third requirement for a research design to be considered a true experimental design. Research participants in the experimental and control groups must be treated equally in every way except in relation to the independent variable. In other words, participants in the experimental and control groups are treated differently only in respect to the independent variable. However, note that the comparison of an independent variable (experimental group) with no independent variable (control group) is overly simplistic. The actual comparison in most true experimental studies is the comparison between the independent variable and the activities of the control group that occurred during the experimental time frame. Thus, the comparison might be better thought of as between two *different* independent variables. It is important for critical research consumers to understand the strengths and weaknesses associated with true experimental designs.

WHAT ARE THE MOST COMMON TRUE EXPERIMENTAL DESIGNS?

We will look at three of the most common true experimental designs—pretest–posttest control-group, posttest-only control-group, and Solomon four-group. All three of these designs are presented in terms of a single independent variable and dependent variable being compared with a control condition. Designs with more than one independent variable also represent true experimental designs; we will discuss these factorial designs separately.

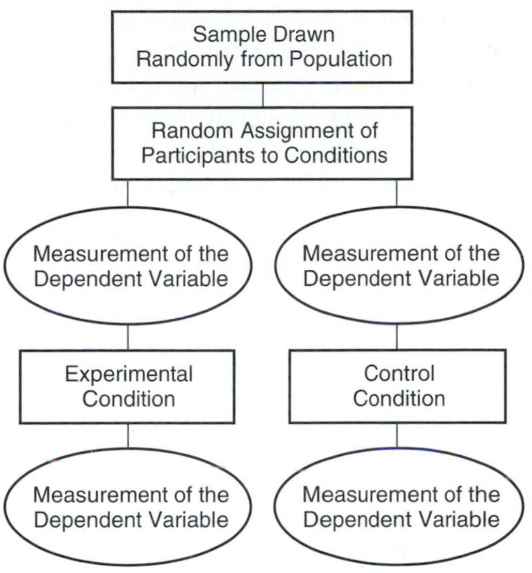

FIGURE 5.1 Pretest–posttest control-group design.

Pretest–Posttest Control-Group Design

The pretest–posttest control-group design is one of the most common designs used in education and psychology to demonstrate a causal relationship between an independent variable and a dependent variable. The pretest–posttest control-group design begins with the random selection of participants from a population to form a sample. Participants from the sample are then randomly assigned to the experimental or control groups. Measurement of the dependent variable is taken prior to the introduction of the independent variable. The independent variable is then introduced followed by postintervention measurement of the independent variable. Figure 5.1 depicts the form of the pretest–posttest control-group design.

The basic assumption of the pretest–posttest control-group design is that the participants of the experimental and control groups are equivalent prior to the introduction of the independent variable. Any differences observed at the end of the study are assumed to be due to the independent variable. The assumption that the experimental and control groups are equivalent is based on the notion that randomly assigning participants to either group will ensure that they are equivalent at the start of the study. Of course, the extent to which this assumption is met is based on the technique used to randomly assign participants to groups and the numbers of participants in each group. Additionally, recall that randomly assigning participants to groups only ensures the absence of systematic bias in the makeup of the groups, not the initial equivalence of the groups.

The goal in a pretest–posttest control-group design is to keep the experiences of the experimental and control groups as identical as possible in all respects except for the introduction of the independent variable to the experimental group. Changes in the pretest and posttest scores due to any other extraneous variables (e.g., maturation) will be reflected in the scores of the control group. In other words, any changes in the posttest scores of the experimental group beyond the changes in the control group can be reasonably attributed to the independent variable.

In some studies, using a pretest–posttest control-group design, the control group is administered only the pretest and the posttest and receives no specific intervention. In other studies using such a design, the control group is administered an equally desirable but alternative intervention or independent variable. Sometimes researchers refer to the control as a "comparison" group if the group receives an intervention rather than being in a no-intervention condition. Further, researchers may label the two groups in relation to the interventions the groups received (e.g., direct instruction group and the cooperative learning group).

Analysis of Data. Although the tests of statistical significance discussed in Chapter 4 can be used with the pretest–posttest control-group design, the analysis of covariance (ANCOVA) is preferred. With an ANCOVA, the posttest mean score of the experimental group is compared with the posttest mean score of the experimental group, with the pretest scores used as a covariate. Recall from Chapter 4 that ANCOVA statistically adjusts the posttest scores for initial differences between the experimental and control groups on the pretest. The ANCOVA is the preferred test of statistical significance because it is the most powerful. That is, ANCOVA increases the probability that researchers will detect the effects of the independent variable. Additionally, a nonparametric test such as the Mann–Whitney *U* test should be used if the data violate the assumptions underlying these parametric tests (i.e., homogeneity of variance, normal distribution of data, and interval or ratio scale data).

Internal Validity. The pretest–posttest control-group design in which the control group receives no intervention effectively controls for the eight threats to internal validity that result in changes in the performance of the experimental group. These threats to internal validity include (a) history, (b) maturation, (c) testing, (d) instrumentation, (e) statistical regression, (f) selection, (g) mortality, and (h) selection-maturation interaction. Testing may be a threat to the internal validity of the study if the pretest has a powerful effect on the intervention. The four additional threats to internal validity that cause changes in the performance of the control group are controlled if researchers provide the control group with an equally desirable but alternative intervention. These threats to internal validity include (a) experimental treatment diffusion, (b) compensatory rivalry by the control group, (c) compensatory equalization of treatments, and (d) resentful demoralization of the control group. Table 5.2 summarizes the potential threats to internal validity associated with each of the true experimental research designs.

External Validity. The pretest–posttest control-group design effectively controls for many of the threats to external validity if the study is conducted effectively. Table 5.3 summarizes the potential threats to external validity associated with each of the true experimental research designs. The threats to external validity that are controlled for include (a) multiple treatment interference, (b) novelty and disruption effects, (c) Hawthorne effect, (d) pretest sensitization, and (e) posttest sensitization. It is important to note that novelty and disruption effects and the Hawthorne effect may be threats to the external validity of a study if the researchers did not provide an equally desirable but alternative intervention. Pretest sensitization also may be a threat to the external validity of the study if the pretest has a powerful effect on the intervention. The remaining threats to the external validity of a study are dependent on the particular characteristics of the study and how well the study was conducted (see Table 5.3). For example, as discussed earlier, if the participants have not been selected randomly from a population to form a sample, then the threats to external validity associated with the population represent potential problems.

Research Example. The pretest–posttest control-group design was used to study the effects of learning strategy instruction on the job application skills of students with learning disabilities by Nelson, Smith, and Dodd (1994). The learning strategy instruction approach applied by Nelson and colleagues included the specific skills required to complete a job application accurately and neatly. Nelson and colleagues randomly assigned participants to either the experimental group (learning strategy instruction) or the con-

TABLE 5.2 Threats to Internal Validity Associated with True Experimental Designs

THREAT	RESEARCH DESIGN: PRETEST–POSTTEST CONTROL-GROUP	POSTTEST-ONLY CONTROL-GROUP	SOLOMON FOUR-GROUP
1. Maturation	Controlled	Controlled	Controlled
2. Selection	Controlled	Controlled[3]	Controlled
3. Selection by maturation interaction	Controlled	Controlled	Controlled
4. Statistical regression	Controlled	Controlled	Controlled
5. Mortality	Controlled	Controlled	Controlled
6. Instrumentation	Controlled	Controlled	Controlled
7. Testing	Controlled[1]	Controlled	Controlled
8. History	Controlled	Controlled	Controlled
9. Resentful demoralization of the control group	Possible concern[2]	Possible concern[2]	Possible concern[2]
10. Diffusion of treatment	Possible concern[2]	Possible concern[2]	Possible concern[2]
11. Compensatory rivalry by the control group	Possible concern[2]	Possible concern[2]	Possible concern[2]
12. Compensatory equalization	Possible concern[2]	Possible concern[2]	Possible concern[2]

Note: This table is meant only as a general guideline. Decisions with regard to threats to internal validity must be made after the specifics of an investigation are known and understood. Thus, interpretations of internal validity threats must be made on a study-by-study basis.

[1]Although testing is generally controlled for, it may be a potential threat to the internal validity of a study if the pretest has a powerful effect on the intervention.

[2]These threats to internal validity are controlled if the control group received an equally desirable but alternative intervention.

[3]Although selection is controlled through the random assignment of participants to groups, the lack of a pretest precludes a statistical test of the equivalence of the groups.

trol group (direct instruction). Sixteen students were taught to complete job applications using a learning strategy, and 17 students were taught to complete job applications using traditional instruction (direct instruction by the teacher of the skills necessary to complete job applications). Both the experimental and control groups received the same amount of instruction.

The dependent measures included information omissions, information location errors, and a holistic rating of overall neatness of the job application. Lower scores on the information omissions and information location errors indicated more complete and accurate job applications. Higher scores on the overall neatness of the job application indicated neater job applications. Each of the dependent measures was administered before (pretest) and after (posttest) the introduction of the independent variable.

Nelson and colleagues (1994) conducted a preliminary analysis using t tests to determine if the experimental and control groups were equivalent with regard to the dependent measures prior to the introduction of the independent variable. These results indicated that there were no statistically significant differences in the pretest scores of the experimental and control groups. Nelson and colleagues then analyzed the posttest measures with a condition (traditional, learning strategy) by gender (male, female) analysis of variance

TABLE 5.3 Threats to External Validity Associated with True Experimental Designs

	RESEARCH DESIGN		
THREAT	**PRETEST–POSTTEST CONTROL-GROUP**	**POSTTEST-ONLY CONTROL-GROUP**	**SOLOMON FOUR-GROUP**
1. Generalization across participants	Possible concern[1]	Possible concern[1]	Possible concern[1]
2. Interaction of personological variables and treatment effects	Possible concern[1]	Possible concern[1]	Possible concern[1]
3. Verification of independent variable	Possible concern	Possible concern	Possible concern
4. Multiple treatment interference	Controlled	Controlled	Controlled
5. Novelty and disruption effects	Controlled[2]	Controlled[2]	Controlled[2]
6. Hawthorne effect	Controlled[2]	Controlled[2]	Controlled[2]
7. Experimenter effects	Possible concern	Possible concern	Possible concern
8. Pretest sensitization	Possible concern	Controlled	Controlled
9. Posttest sensitization	Controlled	Possible concern	Controlled
10. Interaction of time of measurement and treatment effects	Possible concern	Possible concern	Possible concern
11. Measurement of the dependent variable	Possible concern	Possible concern	Possible concern
12. Interaction of history and treatment effects	Possible concern	Possible concern	Possible concern

Note: This table is meant only as a general guideline. Decisions with regard to threats to external validity must be made after the specifics of an investigation are known and understood. Thus, interpretations of external validity threats must be made on a study-by-study basis.

[1]Threats to external validity associated with the population are controlled if the sample has been drawn randomly from a population.

[2]These threats to external validity are controlled if the control group received an equally desirable but alternative intervention.

(ANOVA). A statistically significant effect for condition was obtained for each of the dependent measures. These statistically significant effects indicated that students who received instruction in the learning strategy condition made significantly lower numbers of information omissions errors and location errors than students under the traditional instruction condition. Additionally, students under the learning strategy condition received significantly higher overall holistic ratings on their job application than did their counterparts.

Posttest-Only Control-Group Design

The concept of applying a pretest in experimental research is very common in education and psychology. Although it is difficult for researchers to give up the comfort of knowing for sure whether the experimental and control groups are equivalent, applying a pretest is not essential to conducting a true experimental research study. Randomization typically leads to equivalent experimental and control groups (Campbell & Stanley, 1963). The posttest-only control-group design is very similar to the pretest–posttest-only control-group design with the exception that pretests of the dependent variable are not administered to the experimental and control groups. The posttest-only control-group design begins with the random selection of participants from a population to form a sample. Participants from the sample are then randomly assigned to the experimental or control groups. The independent variable is then introduced followed by postintervention measurement of the dependent variable. Figure 5.2 depicts the form of the posttest-only control-group design.

The basic assumption of the posttest-only control-group design is the same as the pretest–posttest control-group design. That is, the participants of the experimental and control groups are equivalent prior to the introduction of the independent variable. Any differences observed at the end of the study are assumed to be due to the independent variable. Of course, one of the weaknesses of the posttest-only control-group design is that researchers cannot be certain that the random assignment of participants resulted in the initial equivalence of the groups.

The goal of the posttest-only control-group design is the same as the pretest–posttest control-group design. This goal is to keep the experiences of the experimental and control groups as identical as possible in all respects except for the introduction of the independent variable to the experimental group. Changes in the posttest scores due to any other extraneous variables will be reflected in the scores of the control group. Additionally, as with pretest–posttest control-group designs, the control group in a posttest-only control-group design receives no specific intervention in some cases. In other cases, the control group is administered an equally desirable but alternative intervention.

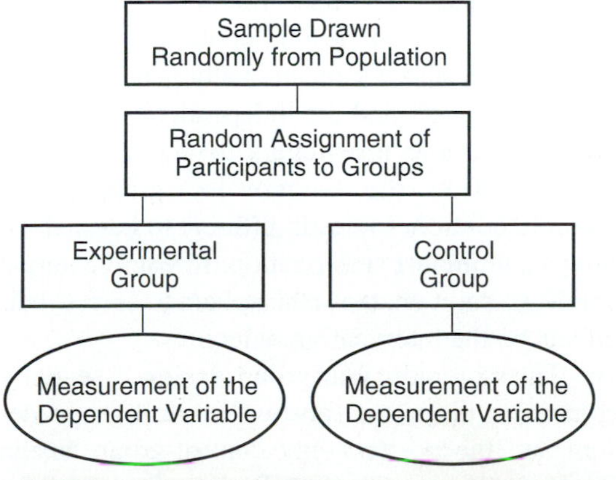

FIGURE 5.2 Posttest-only control-group design.

The posttest-only control-group design is used when there is a possibility that the pretest will have an affect on the independent variable or if researchers are unable to identify a suitable pretest measure. The posttest-only control-group design is most often used in research exploring the effects of different interventions on the beliefs or attitudes of individuals. For example, say we are interested in studying the effects of a new substance prevention program on high school students' beliefs about alcohol. A pretest in this case might influence participants' responses on the posttest. Thus, participants would be randomly assigned to either the experimental or control condition. The experimental group would receive the new substance abuse program, and the control group would receive no intervention. At the end of the intervention, a posttest would be administered to both the experimental and control groups. Any differences (statistically significant) in the responses of the experimental and control groups could then be attributed to the effects of the substance abuse program.

Analysis of Data. The data from a posttest-only control-group design is typically analyzed by doing a *t* test comparing the means of the posttest scores of the experimental and control groups. An analysis of variance (ANOVA) can be used if more than two groups have been studied. If the researcher has collected data on one or more variables unrelated to the purpose of the study such as gender or IQ, an analysis of covariance (ANCOVA) can be used. Additionally, a nonparametric test such as the Mann–Whitney *U* test should be used if the data violate the assumptions underlying these parametric tests (i.e., homogeneity of variance, normal distribution of data, and interval or ratio-scale data).

Internal Validity. The posttest-only control-group design where the control group receives no intervention effectively controls for the same eight threats to internal validity as the pretest–posttest control-group design (i.e., history, maturation, testing, instrumentation, statistical regression, selection, mortality, and selection-maturation interaction) that result in changes in the performance of the experimental group (see Table 5.2). A disadvantage of the posttest-only control-group design is that it does not enable researchers to check the initial equivalence of the experimental and control groups. Additionally, the posttest-only control-group design effectively controls for the four threats to internal validity (i.e., experimental treatment diffusion, compensatory rivalry by the control group, compensatory equalization of treatments, and resentful demoralization of the control group) that result in changes in the performance of the control group if it received an equally desirable but alternative intervention (see Table 5.2).

External Validity. As with the pretest–posttest control-group design, the posttest-only control-group design controls for many of the threats to external validity if the study is conducted effectively (see Table 5.3). A particular advantage of the posttest-only control group design is that it is able to control for pretest sensitization. Novelty and disruption effects and the Hawthorne effect may be threats to the external validity of a study if the researchers did not provide an equally desirable but alternative intervention. Posttest sensitization also may be a threat to the external validity of the study if the posttest has a powerful effect on the intervention. The remaining threats to the external validity of a study are dependent on the particular characteristics of the study and on how well it was conducted (see Table 5.3).

Research Example. The posttest-only control-group design was used by Nelson (1996a) in an evaluation study of a new smoking program designed to influence elementary-aged students' attitudes toward smoking. Because of the potential of testing effects, Nelson did not use a pretest measure of children's attitudes toward smoking. Sixty elementary-aged students in the fourth grade were randomly assigned to the experimental and control (30 children per group). The experimental group received a new antismoking program designed to reduce children's acceptance of smoking. The control group received the standard antismoking curriculum. The posttest measure consisted of a questionnaire designed to evoke children's attitudes toward smoking. The posttest scores of the experimental and control groups were analyzed with a *t* test. The results indicated that there were no statistically significant differences in the attitudes of children in the experimental and control groups.

Solomon Four-Group Design

The Solomon four-group design offers researchers the greatest amount of experimental control. Like the pretest–posttest control-group and posttest-only control-group designs, the Solomon four-group design assesses the effects of the independent variable relative to a control condition. Unlike these designs, the Solomon four-group design enables researchers to assess the presence of pretest sensitization and to assess the presence of an interaction between the pretest measures and the independent variable. Although the posttest-only control-group design controls for pretest sensitization and for an interaction between the pretest measures and the independent variable, it does not enable researchers to determine their presence. Thus, the Solomon four-group design not only controls for testing (threat to internal validity) and pretest sensitization (threat to external validity), but it enables researchers to assess their effects on the intervention outcomes.

The Solomon four-group design essentially combines the pretest–posttest control-group design and the posttest-only control-group design (compare Figure 5.3 with Figures 5.1 and 5.2). The Solomon four-group design begins with the random selection of participants from a population to form a sample. Participants from the sample are then randomly assigned to one of four groups. Two groups serve as experimental groups, and two groups serve as control groups. Measurement of the dependent variable is taken prior to the introduction of the independent variable with one of the experimental groups and one of the control groups. The independent variable is then introduced followed by post-intervention measurement of the dependent variable for all four of the groups. Figure 5.3 depicts the form of the Solomon four-group design.

The basic assumption of the Solomon four-group design is the same as the pretest–posttest control-group and posttest-only control-group designs in that the participants of the experimental and control groups are equivalent prior to the introduction of the independent variable. Any differences observed at the end of the study are assumed to be due to the independent variable and, in some cases, the preintervention measures of the dependent variable. As one might expect, the Solomon four-group design requires a great deal more effort and resources to implement than the pretest–posttest control-group and the posttest-only control-group designs. The extra effort and resources needed to implement a Solomon four-group design may be worth it in cases where it is critical to determine the effects of pretest sensitization and the interaction of the pretest and the independent variable.

The goal of the Solomon four-group design is the same as with the pretest–posttest control-group and posttest-only control-group designs; that is, the goal is to keep the experiences of the experimental and control groups as identical as possible except for the introduction of the independent variable. Changes in the posttest scores due to any other extraneous variables will be reflected in the scores of the control group.

Analysis of Data. The Solomon four-group design, in its simplest form, is essentially a 2 × 2 factorial design (i.e., two or more independent variables [called factors] affect the dependent variable either independently [main effect] or in combination with each other [interaction effect]) in which the presence or absence of a pretest is one factor (signified by the first "2"), and the

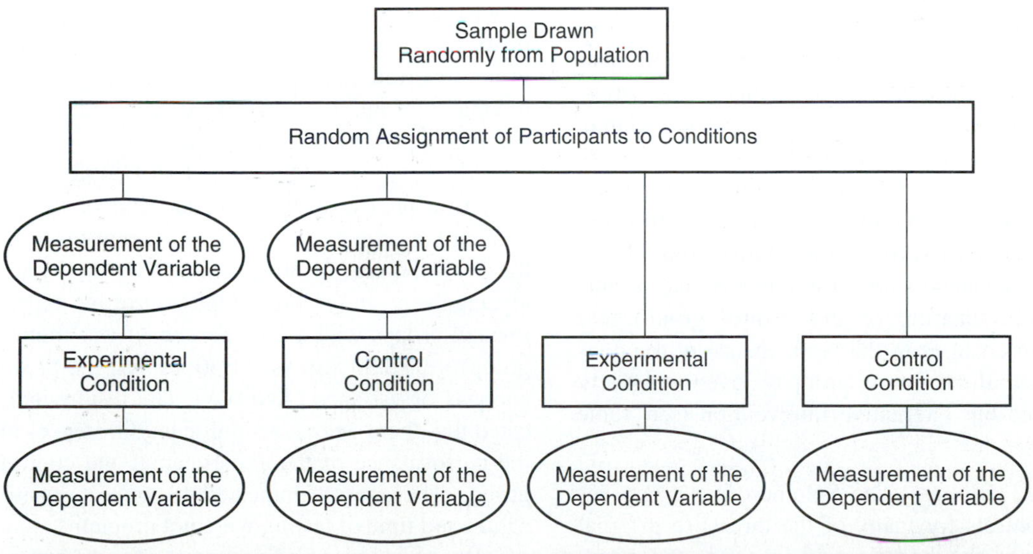

FIGURE 5.3 Solomon four-group design.

presence or absence of the independent variable is the second factor (signified by the second "2"). Thus, data from a Solomon four-group design is typically analyzed with an analysis of variance (ANOVA). Any significant main (e.g., differences between the presence or absence of the independent variable) and interaction effects (e.g., the presence or absence of the pretest differentially affects the independent variable such that the independent variable is more or less effective when the pretest is provided) are then explored using a post hoc analysis procedures such as the Scheffe test. Additionally, a nonparametric test such as the Kruskal-Wallis test should be used if the data violate the assumptions underlying parametric tests (i.e., homogeneity of variance, normal distribution of data, and interval or ratio-scale data).

Internal Validity. The Solomon four-group design controls for all eight of the threats to internal validity (i.e., history, maturation, testing, instrumentation, statistical regression, selection, mortality, and selection-maturation interaction) that result in changes in the performance of the experimental groups (see Table 5.2). As discussed before, an important advantage of the Solomon four-group design over the pretest–posttest control-group design and the posttest-only control-group design is that it enables researchers to determine the effects of the preintervention measurement of the dependent variable on the postintervention measurement of the dependent variable. Additionally, the Solomon four-group design effectively controls for the four threats to internal validity (i.e., experimental treatment diffusion, compensatory rivalry by the control group, compensatory equalization of treatments, and resentful demoralization of the control group) that result in changes in the performance of the control group if the control group received an equally desirable but alternative intervention (see Table 5.2).

External Validity. The Solomon four-group design controls for many of the threats to external validity if the investigation is conducted effectively (see Table 5.3). Novelty and disruption effects and the Hawthorne effect may be threats to the external validity of a study if researchers did not provide an equally desirable but alternative intervention. Although pretest sensitization is controlled for, posttest sensitization may be a threat to the external validity of the study if the posttest has a powerful effect on the intervention. The remaining threats to the external validity of a study are dependent on the particular characteristics of the study and how well the study was conducted.

Research Example. The Solomon four-group design was used by McNaughten and Gabbard (1993) to assess the effects of physical exertion on the mathematical performance of elementary-aged students. Participants were 120 sixth-grade students. The participants were randomly assigned to four groups (two experimental and two control). Each of the groups consisted of 15 boys and 15 girls. The independent variable was walking at a rate necessary to maintain a heart-rate range of 120 to 145 beats per minute over progressively longer durations. Walking duration was ordered at 20, 30, and 40 minutes. The dependent variable was a mathematical computation test.

Without prior exertion, one control group received a pretest and a posttest. The second control group, also without prior exertion, completed a posttest. In the same manner, one experimental group received a pretest prior to exertion and following exertion. The second experimental group received a posttest after exertion.

McNaughten and Gabbard (1993) first assessed for pretest sensitization and time of testing (testing was conducted at three different times of the day [8:30 A.M., 11:50 A.M., and 2:20 P.M.]) by analyzing the posttest scores of the control and experimental groups with a 2 (experimental vs. control group) × 3 (8:30 A.M. vs. 11:50 A.M. vs. 2:20 P.M.) analysis of variance (ANOVA). The results indicated that there were nonsignificant differences in the performance of the experimental and control groups. These results indicated that pretest sensitization and time of testing were not problems.

Based on these findings, scores for the experimental and control groups were entered into a 2 (gender) × 3 (8:30 A.M. vs. 11:50 A.M. vs. 2:20 P.M.) × 3 (duration—20 minutes vs. 30 minutes vs. 40 minutes) factorial design. There were no significant main or interaction effects for gender. A significant main effect was found for duration as well as an interaction between time and duration. Taken together, these results indicate that the mathematical computation scores of participants were significantly higher under the 30- and 40-minute duration periods during the 11:50 and 2:20 assessments but not for the 20-minute duration period. There were nonsignificant differences in the performances of the experimental and control groups under the 20-minute duration period during the 8:30 A.M. assessment.

WHAT ARE FACTORIAL EXPERIMENTAL DESIGNS?

Up to now, we have focused on experimental research designs that incorporate one independent variable (i.e., single factor). The goal in such designs is to establish a causal relationship between two variables. However, researchers are often interested in assessing the effects of two or more independent variables (factors) and in identifying which particular participants benefit most from the independent variable. Researchers use factorial experimental designs to assess the effects of two or more independent variables or the interaction of participant characteristics with the independent variable. As such, researchers use factorial designs to determine whether the effect of a particular variable studied concurrently with other variables will have the same effect as it would when studied in isolation.

Analysis of Data

The factorial designs and associated statistical analysis procedures used by researchers can be quite complex. For example, a factorial design would be used in a study in which three methods of teaching reading (i.e., direct instruction, whole language, and language experience) are compared and could be extended to include a comparison of short (i.e., periods of intensive instruction) versus massed (i.e., extended period of intensive instruction) learning conditions with a comparison of the performance of boys and girls. The effect on achievement of three methods of teaching, two learning conditions, and gender could be investigated with a 3 (direct instruction vs. whole language vs. language experience) × 2 (short vs. massed learning) × 2 (male vs. female) analysis of variance.

It is informative to look more closely at the preceeding example to identify the two primary types of factors included in factorial designs. The first and second factors were the three methods of reading instruction (i.e., direct instruction, whole language, and language experience) and the type of instruction (short vs. massed learning), respectively. These factors are considered independent variables. The last factor was gender. Although gender is considered an independent variable, it is in fact called a classification, subject, or organismic variable. In other words, these variables involve grouping participants according to a characteristic that was present prior to the start of the study and were not manipulated by researchers. Researchers typically use basic classification variables such as gender when analyzing the results of all experimental research designs. Additionally, it is important to note that factorial designs may involve repeated measurement of the same participants. The repeated measurement of participants on one or more factors can greatly complicate a factorial design.

A key advantage of factorial designs is that information is obtained about the interaction between factors. Going back to the previous example, one method of teaching reading may interact with a condition of learning and render that combination either better or worse than any other combination. Of course, one of the disadvantages of the factorial design is that the number of combinations may become quite unwieldy to conduct and difficult to interpret. In education and psychology, it is advisable to avoid overly complex factorial experiments. We direct the reader to Keppel (1973) and Ferguson (1989) for more information on factorial designs. The particular factorial design used by researchers primarily depends on the following factors:

1. The number of independent variables.
2. The attributes (i.e., classification variable) of the independent variable (referred to as a *between subjects factor* when comparing different groups).
3. Repeated measurement of participants (also referred to as a *within subjects factor*).
4. Mixing within (repeated measures) and between (comparison of group means) subjects factors.
5. Relative number of participants in each intervention group.

Internal Validity. The threats to internal validity controlled for by a factorial design is dependent on the basic underlying true experimental design (see Table 5.2). For example, if the basic underlying true experimental design is a pretest–posttest control group design, the eight threats to internal validity (i.e., history, maturation, testing, instrumentation, statistical regression, selection, mortality, and selection-maturation interaction) that result in changes in the performance of the experimental group are controlled. Additionally, the four threats to internal validity that cause changes in the performance of the control group are controlled for in factorial designs because the different experimental groups are receiving some form of the intervention.

External Validity. One of the greatest strengths of a factorial design is that it enhances the external validity of the study. Analyzing the effects of the intervention on different subsets of the sample increases the extent to which the results can be generalized to "across participants" and provides an understanding of the interaction of personological variables and treatment effects. As with all of the true experimental designs, factorial designs control for many of the threats to external validity if the investigation is conducted effectively (see Table 5.3).

Research Example. Rather than presenting an actual study in which a factorial design was employed, we will look at an example comparing a single-factor experimental design with a two-factor design to address the same research question to show how researchers use factorial designs. Suppose we are interested in assessing the effects of sentence length and number of difficult words per paragraph on the reading rates of elementary-aged students. The two independent variables of interest are sentence length and number of difficult words per paragraph. Say we choose two sentence lengths (≤ 20 words and > 20 words) and two levels of the number of difficult words per paragraph (≤ 2 and > 2). We would need to use two separate studies to assess the effects of these two independent variables using single-factor experimental designs. Table 5.4 presents what these two experimental designs might look like. The study on the top (Design 1)

TABLE 5.4 Comparison of Single-Factor and Two-Factor Experimental Designs

DESIGN 1

Sentence Length	
≤ 20 Words 20 Participants	> 20 Words 20 Participants

DESIGN 2

Average Number of Words per Paragraph	
≤ 2 Words 20 participants	> 2 Words 20 Participants

DESIGN 3

	Average Number of Words per Paragraph	
Sentence Length	≤ 2 Words	> 3 Words
≤ 20 Words	10 Participants	10 Participants
> 20 Words	10 Participants	10 Participants

is designed to assess the effects of sentence length on reading rate, and the study in the middle (Design 2) is designed to assess the effects of the number of difficult words per paragraph. In both studies, 20 participants would be assigned to each of the experimental conditions for a total of 40 participants per study (total of 80 participants). Except for the sentence length and the number of difficult words per paragraph, all of the participants would be treated the same. At the completion of the study, we would analyze the data and be able to make a statement regarding the influence of sentence length and number of difficult words per paragraph on rate of reading.

Compare these two single-factor studies with the two-factor factorial design (Design 3) presented at the bottom of Table 5.4. The two independent variables (i.e., sentence length and number of difficult words per paragraph) are manipulated simultaneously. Because both independent variables have two levels, there is a total of six (2 × 3) unique groups. This design would be called a 2 × 2 factorial design. Inspection of Table 5.4 reveals that the sample size in each of the groups is 10. This number was chosen to provide a direct comparison with the single-factor studies (i.e., we start with 40 participants and then randomly assign 10 participants to serve in each of the four groups). At the completion of the study, we would analyze the data and make a statement regarding the influence of sentence length and number of difficult words per paragraph on rate of reading (main effects). We would make a statement regarding the interaction of sentence length and number of difficult words per paragraph (interaction effects).

Our comparison of two single-factor designs with a two-factor factorial design is only correct up to a point. The factorial design will provide the same information as the two single-factor designs only when there is no interaction between the two independent variables. There are no interaction effects when the effects of one of the independent variables is the same at each of the levels of the other independent variable. Returning to our example, the effects of sentence length are the same regardless of the number of difficult words per paragraph and vice versa. On the other hand, if the effects of sentence length are different across the different levels of the number of difficult words per paragraph, there is an interaction, and the information provided by the main effect is not the same as in the single-factor designs. This finding is not problematic because the researchers would have discovered information that is not available from the single-factor designs—how the two independent variables combine to influence reading rate. Additionally, researchers will not be as interested in the main effects when there is an interaction effect because anything they say with regard to the effects of one independent variable would have to be qualified by its differential effect across the levels of the other independent variable.

Finally, it is important to address the concepts of main and interaction effects because they are key concepts associated with factorial designs. We will look at an illustrative example in which a 2 × 2 factorial design yields only main effects and in which the same 2 × 2 factorial design yields interaction effects. It is important to note that we are presenting a simplified explanation of main and interaction effects here. We direct the reader to Keppel (1973) and Ferguson (1989) for more information on main and interaction effects.

Using the same example noted before, Table 5.5 presents Study 1 in which a main effect for sentence length was obtained and Study 2 in which a interaction effect between sentence length and number of difficult words per paragraph was obtained. Inspection of the results of Study 1 reveals that changes in participants' reading rates for sentences with less than or equal to 20 words and more than 20 words were relatively (statistically the similar) consistent across the number of difficult words per paragraph. Participants generally read faster when the sentences contained less than 20 words. These results are consistent with only obtaining a main effect. On the other hand, inspection of the results of Study

TABLE 5.5 Comparison of Main Effects and Interactions Effects

STUDY 1

Sentence Length	Average Number of Words per Paragraph	
	≤ 2 Words	> 2 Words
	Mean	Mean
≤ 20 Words	112	114
> 20 Words	90	88

STUDY 2

Sentence Length	Average Number of Words per Paragraph	
	≤ 2 Words	> 2 Words
	Mean	Mean
≤ 20 Words	110	115
> 20 Words	112	85

2 reveals a different pattern. Participants' reading rates differed across the number of difficult words per paragraph. The reading rates of participants were similar regardless of sentence length if there were less than two difficult words per paragraph. However, the reading rates of participants were significantly lower when there were more than two difficult words per paragraph.

WHAT ARE QUASI-EXPERIMENTAL DESIGNS?

Quasi-experimental designs differ from true experimental designs in two ways. First, participants are not randomly selected from a specified population. Second, participants are not randomly assigned to experimental and control groups. Nevertheless, quasi-experimental designs provide a relatively high degree of experimental control in natural settings, and they clearly represent a step-up from preexperimental designs (described later) because they enable researchers to compare the performance of the experimental group with that of a control group. In other words, quasi-experimental designs enable researchers to move their experimentation out of the laboratory and into a natural context. It is important for critical research consumers to understand the strengths and weaknesses associated with quasi-experimental designs.

WHAT ARE THE COMMON QUASI-EXPERIMENTAL DESIGNS?

We will look at four common quasi-experimental designs—static-group comparison, nonequivalent control-group, counterbalanced, and time-series. Note that these four designs are presented in terms of a single independent variable and dependent variable.

Static-Group Comparison

The static-group comparison design is the same as the posttest-only control group design described before except for the absence of the random selection of participants from a population and random assignment of participants to groups. The static-group comparison design begins with the identification of two naturally assembled experimental and control groups (e.g., students in two classrooms). The naturally assembled experimental and control groups should be as similar as possible, and the assignment to one group or the other is assumed to be random. The independent variable is then introduced to the experimental group followed by the postintervention measurement of the dependent variable. Figure 5.4 depicts the form of the static-group comparison design.

Analysis of Data. The data from a static-group comparison design can be analyzed with a *t* test of the difference between the posttest mean scores of the experimental and control groups. Additionally, a nonparametric test such as the Mann–

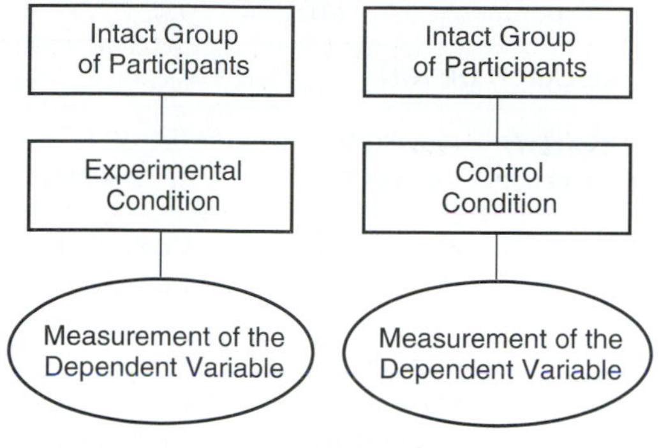

FIGURE 5.4 Static-group comparison.

Whitney *U* test should be used if the data violate the assumptions underlying these parametric tests (i.e., homogeneity of variance, normal distribution of data, and interval or ratio-scale data).

Internal Validity. The use of a comparison group in the static-group comparison design enhances its experimental control over preexperimental designs (described later). However, the lack of a pretest without the random assignment of participants to groups greatly weakens its ability to control for a number of threats to internal validity. Inspection of Table 5.6 reveals that the static-group comparison design controls for four of the threats to internal validity (i.e., statistical regression, instrumentation, testing, and history) that may result in changes in the performance of the experimental group. The remaining threats to internal validity (i.e., maturation, selection, selection by maturation interaction, mortality, resentful demoralization of the control group, diffusion of treatment, compensatory rivalry by the control group, and compensatory equalization) represent possible concerns to the internal validity of the static-group comparison design.

External Validity. Inspection of Table 5.7 reveals that the threats to external validity associated with the population (i.e., generalization across participants and interaction of personological variables and treatment effects) are a concern because participants were not randomly selected from a specified population. Novelty and disruption effects and the Hawthorne effect may be threats to the external validity of the study if the researchers did not provide an equally desirable but alternative intervention. Posttest sensitization also may be a threat to the external validity of the study if the posttest has a powerful effect on the independent variable. The remaining threats to the external validity of a study are dependent on the particular characteristics of the study and on how well the study was conducted.

Research Example. A static-group comparison design was used by Ysseldyke (1977) to assess the extent to which the student performance interacts with five independent variables or intervention conditions. The goal was to ascertain whether measures of perceptual and cognitive ability can be used to facilitate differential educational programming for children. In other words, can measures of perceptual and cognitive ability be used in diagnostic-prescriptive teaching? The five independent variables included (a) perceptual training (i.e., training in eye–hand coordination, spatial relations, position in space, figure-ground perception, and form constancy), (b) perceptual-language training (i.e., training in the discrimination, identification, and retention of the configurable properties of letter and word forms), (c) conceptual-language training (i.e., training in 16 general mental abilities such as retention), (d) Hawthorne group (i.e., teacher-provided ongoing emotional support and encouragement), and (e) control group (i.e., no intervention or special teacher contact). The dependent measures included the SRA Primary Mental Abilities Test, the Frostig Developmental Test of Visual Perception, and the Developmental Test of Visual-Motor Integration. Additionally, the Peabody Individual Achievement Test was administered prior to and after the introduction of the five independent variables to provide a measure of achievement gain over the study period. Regression analyses with

TABLE 5.6 Threats to Internal Validity Associated with Quasi-Experimental Designs

	RESEARCH DESIGN			
THREAT	STATIC-GROUP COMPARISON	NONEQUIVALENT CONTROL-GROUP	COUNTER-BALANCED	TIME-SERIES
1. Maturation	Possible concern	Controlled	Controlled	Controlled
2. Selection	Possible concern	Controlled	Controlled	Controlled
3. Selection by maturation interaction	Possible concern	Controlled	Possible concern	Controlled
4. Statistical regression	Controlled	Possible concern	Controlled	Controlled
5. Mortality	Possible concern	Controlled	Controlled	Controlled
6. Instrumentation	Controlled	Controlled	Controlled	Controlled
7. Testing	Controlled	Controlled	Controlled	Controlled
8. History	Controlled	Controlled	Controlled	Controlled
9. Resentful demoralization of the control group	Possible concern[1]	Possible concern[1]	Controlled	Not applicable
10. Diffusion of treatment	Possible concern[1]	Possible concern[1]	Controlled	Not applicable
11. Compensatory rivalry by the control group	Possible concern[1]	Possible concern[1]	Controlled	Not applicable
12. Compensatory equalization	Possible concern[1]	Possible concern[1]	Controlled	Not applicable

Note: This table is meant only as a general guideline. Decisions with regard to threats to internal validity must be made after the specifics of an investigation are known and understood. Thus, interpretations of internal validity threats must be made on a study-by-study basis.

[1]These threats to internal validity are controlled if the control group received an equally desirable but alternative intervention.

the three dependent measures serving as independent variables and the achievement gain score serving as the dependent variable were used to assess whether perceptual and cognitive ability measures can be used to provide differential educational programming.

The five independent variables were introduced to five intact groups of 118 first graders for a period of 7 months. The three dependent measures were administered at the end of the study period. In general, the results indicated that teachers' presumption that pupil performance on perceptual and cognitive ability measures provides information with which to facilitate differential educational programming is misguided. The results were consistent across the independent variables including the Hawthorne and control group conditions.

Nonequivalent Control-Group Designs

The nonequivalent control-group design is similar to the pretest–posttest control-group design described previously except for the absence of the random selection of participants from a population and the random assignment of participants to groups. The nonequivalent control-group design begins with the identification of naturally assembled experimental and control groups. Again, the naturally occurring experimental and control groups should be as similar as possible, and the assignment to one group or the other is assumed to be random. Measurement of the dependent variable is taken prior to the introduction of the independent variable. The independent variable is then introduced followed by the postintervention measurement of the dependent variable. Figure 5.5 de-

TABLE 5.7 Threats to External Validity Associated with Quasi-Experimental Designs

	RESEARCH DESIGN			
THREAT	**STATIC-GROUP COMPARISON**	**NONEQUIVALENT CONTROL-GROUP**	**COUNTER-BALANCED**	**TIME-SERIES**
1. Generalization across participants	Concern	Concern	Concern[2]	Concern
2. Interaction of personological variables and treatment effects	Concern	Concern	Concern[2]	Concern
3. Verification of independent variable	Possible concern	Possible concern	Possible concern	Possible concern
4. Multiple treatment interference	Controlled	Controlled	Controlled	Controlled
5. Novelty and disruption effects	Controlled[1]	Controlled[1]	Possible concern	Controlled
6. Hawthorne effect	Controlled[1]	Controlled[1]	Possible concern	Controlled
7. Experimenter effects	Possible concern	Possible concern	Possible concern	Controlled
8. Pretest sensitization	Controlled	Possible concern	Controlled	Controlled
9. Posttest sensitization	Possible concern	Controlled	Controlled	Controlled
10. Interaction of time of measurement and treatment effects	Possible concern	Possible concern	Possible concern	Possible concern
11. Measurement of the dependent variable	Possible concern	Possible concern	Possible concern	Possible concern
12. Interaction of history and treatment effects	Possible concern	Possible concern	Possible concern	Possible concern

Note: This table is meant only as a general guideline. Decisions with regard to threats to external validity must be made after the specifics of an investigation are known and understood. Thus, interpretations of external validity threats must be made on a study-by-study basis.

[1]These threats to external validity are controlled if the control group received an equally desirable but alternative intervention.

[2]These threats to external validity are not a concern if the researcher has randomly selected the participants from a specified population.

picts the form of the nonequivalent control-group design.

Analysis of Data. The data from a nonequivalent control-group design is analyzed using an analysis of covariance (ANCOVA). An ANCOVA is used because the primary threat to the internal validity of the nonequivalent control-group design is the possibility that differences on the posttest scores of the experimental and control groups are the result of initial differences rather than the effects of the independent variable. ANCOVA statistically equates initial differences between the experimental and control groups by adjusting the posttest means of the groups.

Internal Validity. Although the nonequivalent control-group design does not provide the same level of experimental control as the pretest–posttest control-group design, it enables researchers to address many of the threats to internal validity adequately. The effectiveness of the nonequivalent

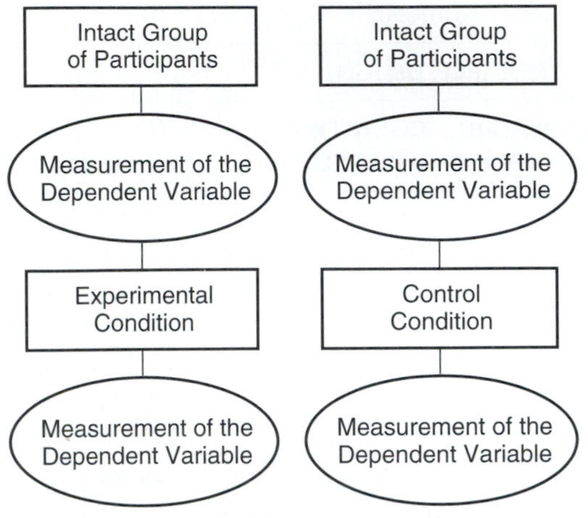

FIGURE 5.5 Nonequivalent control-group design.

control-group design in addressing the threats to internal validity increases with the similarity of the pretest scores of the experimental and control groups. Inspection of Table 5.6 reveals that the nonequivalent control-group design controls for seven of the threats to internal validity (i.e., maturation, selection, selection by maturation interaction, mortality, instrumentation, testing, and history) that result in changes in the performance of the experimental groups. The nonequivalent control-group design does not control for statistical regression that can result in changes in the performance of the experimental group. The four threats to internal validity (i.e., experimental treatment diffusion, compensatory rivalry by the control group, compensatory equalization of treatments, and resentful demoralization of the control group) that result in changes in the performance of the control group are controlled if researchers provide the control group an equally desirable but alternative intervention.

External Validity. As with the static-group comparison design, the threats to external validity associated with the population (i.e., generalization across participants and interaction of personological variables and treatment effects) are a concern because participants were not randomly selected from a specified population (see Table 5.7). Novelty and disruption effects and the Hawthorne effect may be threats to the external validity of the study if the researchers did not provide an equally desirable but alternative intervention. Pretest and posttest sensitization also may be threats to the external validity if the pretest and posttest have a powerful effect on the intervention. The remaining threats to the external validity of a study are dependent on the particular characteristics of the study and on how well the study was conducted.

Research Example. The nonequivalent control-group design was used by Nelson (1996b) to assess the effects of a schoolwide program designed to increase the institutional capacity of schools to work with elementary-aged students who exhibit disruptive behavior. The study was conducted in two experimental and two control elementary schools. The primary goal of the program was to develop universal schoolwide and classroom organizational practices that were both preventive and remedial in nature. The schoolwide practices included adjusting the ecological arrangements of the school (e.g., reducing the density of students in the lunchroom), establishing behavioral expectations for the common areas of the schools (e.g., playground, assemblies), instituting effective disciplinary responses for both minor and severe disruptive behavior, and establishing a framework for providing one-to-one consultation to teachers regarding students experiencing academic and behavioral difficulties. The classroom intervention included establishing clear behavioral expectations and instituting a universal response to disruptive behavior (i.e., the Think Time Strategy®). The control schools continued to implement typical schoolwide and classroom organizational practices.

The effects of the schoolwide program were assessed on three levels: (a) school (i.e., disciplinary responses), (b) teachers (i.e., ability to work with students experiencing behavioral difficulties, working alliance, and stress levels), and (c) students (i.e., academic performance, social adjustment, and school survival skills). Data collected on students were restricted to a selected sample of 25 target children experiencing behavioral difficulties in school and 25 criterion students who were not experiencing any difficulty (academic or behavioral) in school. The target and criterion students were enrolled in experimental schools.

Preliminary analyses were conducted to assess the initial equivalence of the experimental and control groups. The experimental and control groups were similar across all of the measures, except there were initial differences in teachers' perceived ability to work with students experiencing behavioral difficulties. This finding illustrates the nonequivalent control-group design can result in equivalence between the experimental and control groups even though the groups were assumed to be equivalent. Additionally, there were initial differences in the academic performance, social adjustment, and school survival skills of the target and criterion students. These results were expected because the criterion students were selected to provide a standard with which to assess the effects of the schoolwide program on students exhibiting disruptive behavior.

Analysis of covariance (ANCOVA) was used to assess the effects of the schoolwide program while controlling for initial differences between the experimental and control groups. The results of this analysis indicated that the schoolwide program resulted in fewer disciplinary responses. For example, suspensions decreased by almost 50% in the experimental schools, whereas they increased by over 80% in the control schools. Teachers in the experimental schools were more likely to indicate that they believed that they could work with difficult-to-teach children and that there were agreed goals among staff with regard to disciplinary matters than were teachers in the control schools. Initial differences in the academic performance, social adjustment, and school survival skills of the target and criterion students were eliminated. In other words, at the end of the study period, the academic performance, social adjustment, and school survival skills of the target and criterion students were equivalent, whereas their performance at the start of the study period was not.

Counterbalanced Designs

Counterbalanced designs encompass a wide range of designs in which the independent variable is introduced to all participants. In counterbalanced designs, two or more groups get the same independent variable(s), but the independent variable(s) is/are introduced in different orders. Counterbalanced designs are useful in those cases in which researchers are interested in studying multiple variables. Counterbalanced designs are also useful in those cases in which it is not possible to randomly assign participants to the experimental and control groups and in which participant attrition may be a problem. The level of experimental control achieved with a counterbalanced design is greater than that of the nonequivalent control-group design because each participant serves as his or her own control. Counterbalanced designs are also referred to as "rotation experiments," cross-over designs, and "switchover designs."

In its simplest form, the counterbalanced design begins with the identification of two naturally assembled groups. Measurement of the dependent variable is taken prior to the introduction of the independent variable. The independent variable is introduced to one of the groups followed by postintervention measurement of the dependent variable. The independent variable is then introduced to the other group followed by the postintervention measurement of the dependent variable. Figure 5.6 depicts the form of the two-group counterbalanced design using naturally assembled groups. (Researchers may randomly assign participants to groups.)

Analysis of Data. Although data from counterbalanced designs can be analyzed with a number of statistical tests, a repeated measure of analysis of variance (ANOVA) is most commonly used by researchers. The advantage of any repeated measurement analysis procedure is that it controls for

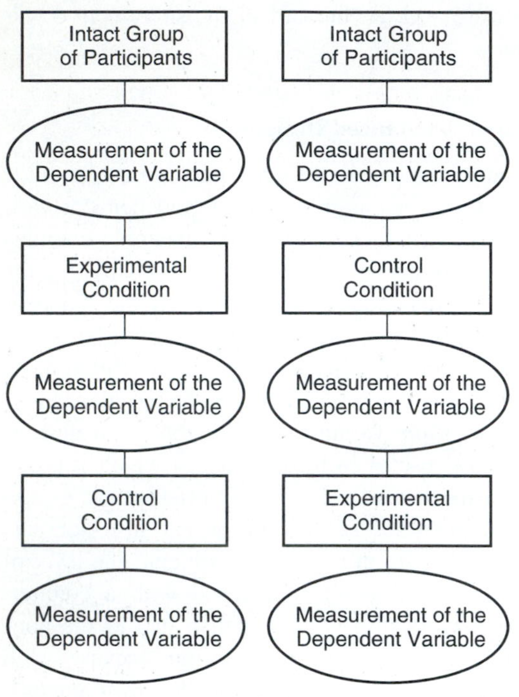

FIGURE 5.6 Two-group counterbalanced design.

differences between participants. That is, repeated measurement analyses eliminate differences between participants from the experimental error. Additionally, a nonparametric test such as the Kruskal–Wallis test should be used if the data violate the assumptions underlying parametric tests (i.e., homogeneity of variance, normal distribution of data, and interval or ratio-scale data).

Internal Validity. The counterbalanced design provides a higher level of experimental control than does the nonequivalent control-group design. This greater degree of experimental control is achieved because the counterbalancing of the independent variable enables researchers to compare participants' performance within groups rather than comparing the performance of participants in the experimental and control groups; thus, counterbalanced designs eliminate the need for groups to be equivalent.

Inspection of Table 5.6 reveals that counterbalanced designs effectively deal with seven of the threats to internal validity (i.e., maturation, selection, statistical regression, mortality, instrumentation, testing, and history) that result in changes in the performance of the experimental group. Counterbalanced designs do not effectively control for selection by maturation interaction effects because there is not a nonintervention control group with which to control for this threat to internal validity. The four threats to internal validity (i.e., experimental treatment diffusion, compensatory rivalry by the control group, compensatory equalization of treatments, and resentful demoralization by the control group) that result in changes in the performance of the control group are controlled for if researchers ensure that there is no treatment diffusion.

External Validity. The threats to external validity associated with the population (i.e., generalization across participants and interaction of personological variables and treatment effects) are not a concern when participants have been randomly selected from a specified population (see Table 5.7). If this is not the case, then these threats to external validity are of concern. Novelty and disruption, Hawthorne, and experimenter effects may be evident because of the ongoing implementation of different independent variables. Pretest and posttest sensitization are unlikely threats to the external validity of a study because of the repeated measurement of the dependent variable. The remaining threats to the external validity of a study are dependent on the particular characteristics of the study and on how well the study was conducted.

Research Example. A counterbalanced design was used by Mastropieri, Scruggs, Baken, and Brigham (1996) to assess the effects of a mnemonic strategy and a traditional instructional procedure for teaching students with learning disabilities the state capitals. The keyword method was used under the mnemonic strategy condition. The keyword method involves reconstructing unfamiliar words into familiar, acoustically similar keywords as a proxy for the unfamiliar words. For example, in learning that the Italian word fonda means bag, learners are first shown a keyword for fonda. In this case, phone is a good keyword for fonda because it sounds like fonda and is easily pictured. Next, a picture or image is constructed of the keyword and corresponding response interacting in a picture. In this case, a picture of a phone in a bag would be a good picture. When asked the definition of fonda, learners think of the keyword, phone, think of the picture with the phone in it, remember the phone was in a bag, and provide the correct response, "bag." The traditional instructional strategy consisted of presenting state and capital overheads along with instruction and practice activities.

The participants were 29 middle school students with learning disabilities. The students were enrolled in two separate social studies classes and received the mnemonic strategy instruction and traditional instruction procedures over the course of 5 weeks. The mnemonic strategy instruction and traditional instruction procedures were implemented in a counterbalanced fashion each week (i.e., one week of mnemonic strategy instruction followed by one week of traditional instruction, and so on). The primary dependent variables were scores on two recall tests of states and capitals administered at the end of each week.

Data were analyzed with a 2 condition (mnemonic vs. traditional) by 2 response (states vs. capitol) ANOVA. Statistically significant main effects for condition and response were obtained. No condition by response interaction was observed. The significant main effect for condition indicated that the mnemonic strategy was more effective in enhancing students' recall of the names of both states and capitals. The significant main effect for response indicated that students were more likely to recall the names of states than they were the names of capitals. The lack of an interaction between condition and response indicated that these effects did not vary across the experimental conditions (i.e., mnemonic vs. traditional) or responses (i.e., names of states vs. capitals).

Time-Series Designs

Time series designs involve a series of repeated measurements of a group of research participants. Any effects attributable to the independent variable are indicated by discontinuity in the preintervention and postintervention series of scores. Time-series designs differ from single-case designs (see Chapters 10 to 12) in that the unit of analysis is a group of individuals. Additionally, time-series designs can be used in an ex post facto or experimental fashion. It is important to note that there are a variety of time-series designs involving different numbers of groups, independent variables, and so on.

A time-series design begins with the identification of a naturally assembled group. Measurement of the dependent variable occurs a number of times prior to the introduction of the independent variable. The independent variable is then introduced followed by the measurement of the dependent variable a number of more times. Figure 5.7 depicts the form of time-series designs.

Analysis of Data. Data from time-series designs can be analyzed in a variety of manners. Researchers may graph the scores and look for changes in the preintervention and postintervention pattern of scores. Each score is plotted separately on the graph, and scores are connected by a line. A vertical line is inserted into the series of scores at the point the independent variable is introduced. Researchers then use the graphed data to compare the level, slope, and variation in the preintervention and postintervention scores. Visual analysis methods for assessing intervention effects are described more completely in our presentation of single-case designs (see Chapters 10 to 12). Statistical methods used with data from time-series designs can range from multiple regression to log linear analysis procedures. These statistical analysis procedures are all aimed at determining whether the preintervention and postintervention pattern of scores differs statistically from one another. We direct the reader to Box and Jenkins (1970); Glass, Willson, and

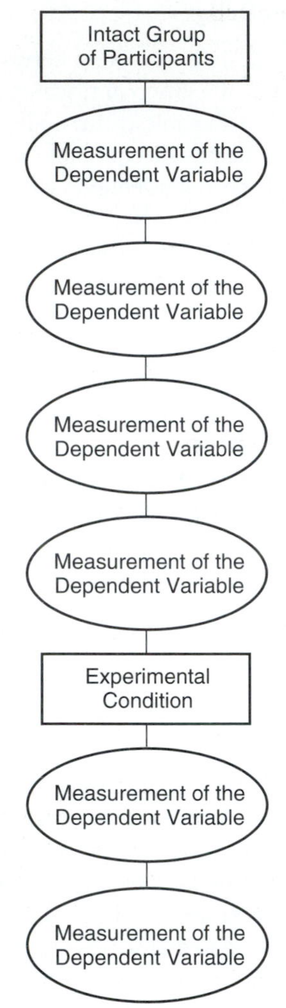

FIGURE 5.7 Time-series design.

Gottman (1975); Moran, Dumas, and Symons (1992); and Nelson (1973) for complete descriptions of statistical procedures for analyzing data from time-series studies.

Internal Validity. Time-series designs provide a high degree of experimental control even though they do not employ a control group. Inspection of Table 5.6 reveals that time-series designs control for the eight threats to internal validity (i.e., maturation, selection, selection by maturation interaction, statistical regression, mortality, instrumentation, testing, history) that result in changes in the performance of the experimental group. Instrumentation might be a concern if the calibration of the measurement device employed by the researcher changed over the course of the study. Of course, it would be unlikely for such a change to occur in direct connection with the introduction of the independent variable. The four threats to internal validity that result in changes in the performance of the control group are not applicable with time-series designs.

External Validity. As with all quasi-experimental designs, the threats to external validity associated with the population (i.e., generalization across participants and interaction of personological variables and treatment effects) are a concern because participants have not been randomly selected from a specified population (see Table 5.7). Novelty and disruption, Hawthorne, and experimenter effects tend not to be a problem because of the ongoing measurement of the dependent variable. Additionally, pretest and posttest sensitization are unlikely threats to the external validity of a study because of the repeated measurement of the dependent variable. The remaining threats to the external validity of a study are dependent on the particular characteristics of the study and on how well the study was conducted.

Research Example. A time-series design was used by Nelson (1991) to assess the effects of a state-mandated prereferral intervention process. The state of Utah mandated all schools to implement and document intervention strategies in general education classrooms prior to initiating a formal referral for special education services. The goal of the prereferral intervention mandate was to reduce the numbers of students with mild disabilities (i.e., learning disabilities, behavior disorders, and mild intellectual disabilities) receiving special education services by meeting the needs of these students in the general education classroom.

Nelson (1991) employed a time-series design with a nonequivalent control variable. The nonequivalent control variabie was used to assess potential history effects. The nonequivalent control variable was conceptually related to the dependent variables but was expected to be unaffected by the intervention. The number of students with mild disabilities served as the dependent variables, and the number of students with severe intellectual disabilities was used as the nonequivalent control variable (the prereferral intervention mandate was expected only to impact the number of students with mild disabilities).

Archival data were collected on the number of students with mild disabilities and the number with severe intellectual disabilities receiving special education services in the state of Utah 4 years prior to the implementation of the prereferral intervention mandate and 4 years after its implementation. Chow tests (a form of multiple regression analysis) were used to compare the slopes of the premandate and postmandate number of students with mild disabilities and those with severe intellectual disabilities. The results of the analysis indicated that the prereferral mandate failed to lower the number of students with mild disabilities receiving special education services in the state of Utah. Additionally, as expected, there were no changes in the number of students with severe intellectual disabilities receiving special education services.

WHAT ARE PREEXPERIMENTAL DESIGNS?

Preexperimental designs primarily differ from true experimental designs and two of the quasi-experimental designs (i.e., counterbalanced and time-series) in that they do not include a control group. The lack of a control group essentially eliminates researchers' ability to control for any of the threats to internal validity. The lack of control over possible extraneous variables that may cause changes in the dependent variable renders preexperimental designs almost useless to furthering knowledge in education and psychology. In short, researchers cannot ensure that a change in the value of the independent variable is accompanied by a change in the value of the dependent variable, which is one of the three key requirements for asserting that a causal relationship exists between two variables.

Nevertheless, we detail preexperimental designs because they are used extensively in education and psychology despite these obvious problems. It is important for critical research consumers to understand the weaknesses associated with preexperimental designs.

WHAT ARE THE TYPES OF PREEXPERIMENTAL DESIGNS?

We will look at two preexperimental designs—one-shot case study and one-group pretest–posttest. Both of these designs are presented in terms of a single independent variable and dependent variable.

One-Shot Case Study

In the one-shot case study, an independent variable is introduced to a group of participants. The one-shot case study begins with the identification of a naturally assembled group. The independent variable is then administered followed by the measurement of the dependent variable. Figure 5.8 depicts the form of the one-shot case study.

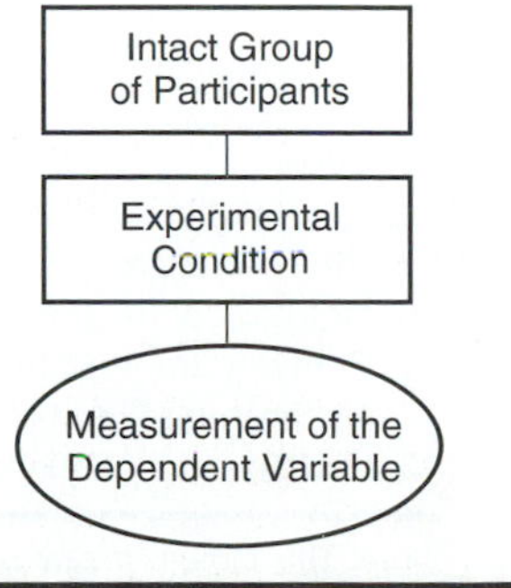

FIGURE 5.8 One-shot case study.

Analysis of Data. The data from a one-shot case study may be analyzed with the one-sample t test if there is a specified population mean. In essence, the obtained mean of the study group is compared to the specified population mean. The results of the one-sample t test will indicate whether the obtained mean of the study group differs from that of the specified population mean.

Internal Validity. Researchers utilizing one-shot case studies often collect extensive amounts of information or use standardized measures in an effort to document the effects of the independent variable. Although such efforts may seem a reasonable replacement for the experimental control associated with the true experimental designs, they do not lead to any definitive assessment of the potential extraneous variables that may have resulted in changes in the scores of individuals.

Inspection of Table 5.8 reveals that the one-shot case study has low internal validity. Four of the eight threats to internal validity (i.e., history, maturation, selection, mortality) that may result in changes in the performance of the experimental group are concerns. The remaining four threats to internal validity (i.e., selection by maturation interaction, instrumentation, testing, and statistical regression) that may result in changes in the performance of the experimental group and the four threats to internal validity (i.e., experimental treatment diffusion, compensatory rivalry by the control group, compensatory equalization of treatments, and resentful demoralization of the control group) that result in changes in the performance of the control group are not applicable.

External Validity. The one-shot case study does not control for most of the threats to external validity (see Table 5.9). Pretest sensitization is the only threat to external validity that can be controlled. Researchers who are limited to studying one group of participants should include a pretest

TABLE 5.8 Threats to the Internal Validity of Preexperimental Designs

	RESEARCH DESIGN	
THREAT	ONE-SHOT CASE STUDY	ONE-GROUP PRETEST–POSTTEST
1. Maturation	Concern	Concern
2. Selection	Concern	Controlled
3. Selection by maturation interaction	Not applicable	Concern
4. Statistical regression	Not applicable	Concern
5. Mortality	Concern	Controlled
6. Instrumentation	Not applicable	Concern
7. Testing	Not applicable	Concern
8. History	Concern	Concern
9. Resentful demoralization of the control group	Not applicable	Not applicable
10. Diffusion of treatment	Not applicable	Not applicable
11. Compensatory rivalry by the control group	Not applicable	Not applicable
12. Compensatory equalization	Not applicable	Not applicable

Note: This table is meant only as a general guideline. Decisions with regard to threats to internal validity must be made after the specifics of an investigation are known and understood. Thus, interpretations of internal validity threats must be made on a study-by-study basis.

TABLE 5.9 Threats to the External Validity of Preexperimental Designs

THREAT	RESEARCH DESIGN: ONE-SHOT CASE STUDY	RESEARCH DESIGN: ONE-GROUP PRETEST–POSTTEST
1. Generalization across participants	Possible concern	Possible concern
2. Interaction of personological variables and treatment effects	Possible concern	Possible concern
3. Verification of independent variable	Possible concern	Possible concern
4. Multiple treatment interference	Not applicable	Not applicable
5. Novelty and disruption effects	Possible concern	Possible concern
6. Hawthorne effect	Possible concern	Possible concern
7. Experimenter effects	Possible concern	Possible concern
8. Pretest sensitization	Not applicable	Possible concern
9. Posttest sensitization	Possible concern	Possible concern
10. Interaction of time of measurement and treatment effects	Possible concern	Possible concern
11. Measurement of the dependent variable	Possible concern	Possible concern
12. Interaction of history and treatment effects	Possible concern	Possible concern

Note: This table is meant only as a general guideline. Decisions with regard to threats to external validity must be made after the specifics of an investigation are known and understood. Thus, interpretations of external validity threats must be made on a study-by-study basis.

in their experimental design (this design is described in what follows).

Research Example. A one-shot case study design was used in a pilot test (preliminary study) by Nelson (1996d) to assess the effects of a universal response to disruptive behavior (The Think Time Strategy®). The Think Time strategy includes a precision request, a brief time-out (when the request is not met), and a debriefing process. Nelson assessed the effects of the Think Time strategy with 12 elementary-aged students exhibiting high rates of disruptive behaviors (e.g., off-task, verbal aggression) enrolled in four different classrooms.

The Think Time strategy was introduced over a 12-week period. For each student, teachers completed the 19-item Walker–McConnell Scale of Social Competence at the end of the study period. The results of the one-sample t test showed that teachers' ratings of the social competence of the 12 students did not deviate significantly from the norm.

One-Group Pretest–Posttest Design

The one-group pretest–posttest design differs from the one-shot case study in that a pretest measure is administered prior to the introduction of the independent variable. The effects of the independent variable are determined by comparing the pretest and posttest scores of the group of participants. The one-group pretest–posttest design begins with the identification of a naturally assembled group. Measurement of the dependent variable occurs prior to the introduction of the independent variable. The independent variable is then introduced followed by measurement of the dependent variable. Figure 5.9 depicts the form of the one-group pretest–posttest design.

Analysis of Data. The data from a one-group pretest–posttest design may be analyzed with a correlated t test. A paired set of variables is the minimum requirement for a correlated t test. The pretest scores are compared to the posttest scores. The results of the correlated t test will indicate

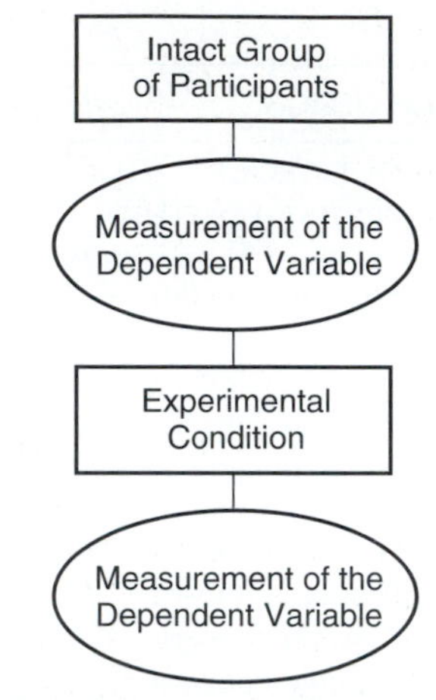

FIGURE 5.9 One-group pretest–posttest design.

whether the pretest and posttest means of the study group differ from one another. Additionally, a nonparametric test such as the Wilcoxon test should be used if the data violate the assumptions underlying these parametric tests (i.e., homogeneity of variance, normal distribution of data, and interval or ratio-scale data).

Internal Validity. Although the use of a pretest in the one-group pretest–posttest renders it better than the one-shot case study, it still does not provide much experimental control. Inspection of Table 5.8 reveals that the one-group pretest–posttest design does not control for six of the eight threats to internal validity (i.e., history, maturation, testing, instrumentation, statistical regression, and selection-maturation interaction) that may result in changes in the performance of the experimental group. The one-group pretest–posttest design does control for selection and mortality that may result in changes in the dependent variable. As with the one-shot case study, the remaining four threats to internal validity (i.e., experimental treatment diffusion, compensatory rivalry by the control group, compensatory equalization of treatments, and resentful demoralization of the control group) that result in changes in the performance of the control group are not applicable because there is no control group.

External Validity. As with the one-shot case study, researchers often provide a great deal of detail in an effort to document the effects of the dependent variable. These efforts should not alleviate concerns regarding the external validity of the one-group pretest–posttest design. Inspection of Table 5.9 shows that the one-group pretest–posttest design does not control for any of the threats to external validity.

Research Example. The one-group pretest–posttest design was used by Ebey, Marchand-Martella, Martella, and Nelson (1998) in a pilot study of a parent training program designed to help their children develop phonemic awareness. Seven families with children ranging from 3.5 to 8 years of age participated in the pilot study. Parents received training in how to implement a structured curriculum designed to enhance their child's phonemic awareness. Children were pretested with an informal reading inventory and a standardized reading assessment prior to the introduction of the parent training program and were posttested with the same assessments at the completion of the program. Changes in the pretest and posttest scores of children were analyzed. The results indicated that the posttest scores of children were higher than their pretest scores.

WHEN SHOULD RESEARCHERS USE EACH EXPERIMENTAL RESEARCH DESIGN?

Experimental research designs are used by researchers to establish causal relationships. It should be clear by now that there is a clear difference in the extent to which true experimental, quasi-experimental, and preexperimental research designs allow researchers to assert with confidence that there is a causal relationship between variables. True experimental research designs provide the highest level of confidence and are the designs of choice to establish a causal relationship between variables. The internal and external validity of true experimental designs are high because these research designs rely on the random selection of participants from a population and the random assignment of participants to the experimental and control groups. The random selection of participants from a population increases the external validity of the study, and the random assignment of participants to the experimental and control groups increases the internal validity of the study. Establishing the initial equivalence of the experimental and control groups enables the researcher to conclude confidently that any statistically significant differences are due to the independent variables. Thus, researchers who are attempting to demonstrate a cause-and-effect relationship should use a true experimental design if they can randomly select and assign participants.

Although quasi experimental research designs do not provide the same level of control as true experimental research designs, they control reasonably well for threats to the internal and external validity of studies. Quasi-experimental research designs are extremely useful because they enable researchers to conduct representative research—that is, research that replicates "real-world" conditions. Quasi-experimental research designs should be employed when it is critical for researchers to conduct a representative study. Quasi-experimental research designs may also be employed when it is impossible for researchers to randomly select participants from a population or randomly assign participants to the experimental and control groups.

The preexperimental research designs have a lack of experimental control that essentially renders them useless for establishing causal relationships between variables. Indeed, we have detailed preexperimental research designs only because they continue to be used inappropriately by researchers to infer causal relationships between variables. In contrast to true experimental and quasi-experimental research designs, preexperimental research designs do not enable reasonable comparisons to be made. Thus, any causal claims made by researchers are clearly inappropriate. Researchers should use preexperimental designs as a last resort; that is, when researchers are not able to use true experimental or quasi-experimental designs due to limitations (e.g., limited financial or human resources, teacher, administrative, or parental concerns, scheduling difficulties).

DISCUSSION QUESTIONS

1. A friend tells you that he is confused. He is taking a class in which the professor indicates that true experimental designs are critical in determining cause-and-effect relationships. Your friend indicates that he is not sure what a true experimental design is. What would you tell him? (*Note:* In your response, discuss the basic design features of true experimental designs.)

2. Your friend asks you the following question: "If all of the design features are not present, what type of research is being done?" Explain to your friend what quasi-experimental designs are. In your answer, describe how true experimental and quasi-experimental designs are similar and how they are different.

3. Your friend asks whether quasi-experimental designs can determine cause-and-effect relationships. What would you say? Why?

4. You begin to wonder how true experimental and quasi-experimental designs differ in regard to controlling threats to internal validity. How do these designs differ? If a design is quasi-experimental, are threats to the internal validity of the experiment able to be controlled? How?

5. You read a research study using a true experimental design. The research seemed well controlled (i.e., seemed to control all threats to internal validity). However, you are concerned about the generalizability of the results to your classroom. How do true experimental designs

control for threats to external validity? What are some concerns you might have?

6. In Question 5, would the use of a quasi-experimental design have been more or less useful in determining the external validity of the investigation? What information would you need to make a determination of the generalizability of the results to your classroom?

7. You are part of a research team studying the effects of math attitudes on math performance. A member of the team suggests that gender may also play a role somehow in math performance. In other words, males and females may have different attitudes toward math and may perform differently in math. What type of design would you recommend? Why?

8. You are in a situation where you have one naturally assembled group of students (i.e., your classroom). You decide to conduct an experiment to determine the effectiveness of your reading curriculum. However, you do not have access to another classroom to make a comparison. So you pretest your class, provide the instruction, and then posttest them. What type of design have you used? Are there problems with this design? What conclusions could you make in terms of internal and external validity?

9. For the example in Question 8, what would be a better design for you to use? How would you do this? How would your conclusions differ?

10. Of the designs discussed in this chapter, which design(s) seem to have the strongest control over threats to internal validity? Which design(s) do you think would be the most difficult to implement in an applied setting? Why?

THE EFFECTS OF LEARNING STRATEGY INSTRUCTION ON THE COMPLETION OF JOB APPLICATIONS BY STUDENTS WITH LEARNING DISABILITIES

J. RON NELSON, DEBORAH J. SMITH, AND JOHN M. DODD

The purpose of this study was to assess the effects of learning strategy instruction on the completion of job applications by students identified as learning disabled. Thirty-three students (average age 15 years, 6 months) were randomly assigned by grade and gender to one of two experimental conditions: learning strategy instruction or traditional instruction. The result was 16 students (10 boys and 6 girls) being placed under the learning strategy instruction condition and 17 students (10 boys and 7 girls) being placed under the traditional instruction condition. Results indicated that in addition to statistically significant lower numbers of information omissions and information location errors, holistic ratings of the overall neatness of the job applications were significantly higher for those students under the learning strategy instruction condition. In addition to these positive changes in the performance measures, social validity data suggest that students under the learning strategy condition would be more likely to receive an invitation for a job interview. The findings and future research needs are discussed.

Because employers often receive numerous applications for a single advertised position, the quality of the employment application materials has a direct effect on an individual's ability to secure employment. Employers most often use the employment application form and, when applicable, the personal résumé to decide whom to interview for a position. Regardless of otherwise equal qualifications, the content, completeness, and neatness of these employment application materials have an effect on whether an individual is given the opportunity to interview for a specific job (Field & Holley, 1976). Indeed, the skills involved in completing employment application materials may be the foundation upon which other job-finding skills, such as interviewing, are built (Azrin & Philip, 1979; Mathews, Whang, & Fawcett, 1981).

Despite the importance of a complete and accurate employment application, researchers have mostly focused on the effects of training procedures on an individual's job interview performance (e.g., Fumian, Geller, Simon, & Kelly, 1979; Hall, Sheldon-Wildgen, & Sherman, 1980; Hollansworth, Dressel, & Stevens, 1977); relatively few studies have been conducted on teaching disadvantaged individuals (Clark, Boyd, & MaCrae, 1975) or those identified as learning disabled (Mathews & Fawcett, 1984) to complete job application forms. Approaches employed in these studies were applied behavioral instruction techniques designed to teach the skills involved in completing employment applications. Mathews and Fawcett, for example, taught three high school seniors identified as having learning disabilities (LD) to complete a job application and write a résumé. The training sequence involved the student, with assistance from the experimenter, reading a set of instructional materials containing detailed written specifications for the behaviors, including a rationale and examples for each task. The student then practiced each task with feedback from the experimenter. Following training, each of the three students showed significant changes in the percentage of application items completed accurately.

Although the results of this study demonstrate that students with LD can be taught to more accurately complete job application forms, the students were reported to need assistance with reading the procedural text accompanying the employment application materials. More important, procedures required 2.5 hours of individual instructional time. This would suggest that an effective group training procedure on employment application skills should be designed to facilitate both the acquisition and the expression of information. Students must be taught to understand the procedural text included on job application forms and to provide all of the requested information accurately.

Learning strategy instruction is one instructional approach that might be used to teach students these two related skills that are necessary to independently complete job applications For the purposes of this article, a learning strategy will be defined as a collection of specific skills that one uses in a particular situation to facilitate the acquisition or expression of knowledge or skills. This type of instruction appears to be especially beneficial for students with LD because these students have been characterized as lacking active task engagement and persistence (Harris, 1986) and as lacking the skills necessary to execute and monitor the cognitive processes central to academic success (Baumann, 1986).

Although, to date, there appears to have been no empirical work conducted with learning strategies designed to facilitate both the understanding of procedural text that is included on a job application and the expression of the requested information, the present study can be placed in the context of recent work on learning strategy instruction in reading (e.g., Borkowski, Weyhing, & Carr, 1988) and writing (e.g., Englert, Raphael, Anderson, Anthony, & Stevens, 1991). Research on reading strategy instruction has focused on how to teach students to (a) determine the main idea (Baumann, 1986; Cunningham & Moore,

1986; Williams, 1986); (b) summarize the information contained in text (Day, 1980; Hare & Borchardt, 1984; Nelson, Smith, & Dodd, 1992; Palincsar & Brown, 1984; Taylor, 1982; Taylor & Beach, 1984; Taylor & Berkowitz, 1980); (c) draw inferences about what they have read (Hansen, 1981; Pearson, 1985; Raphael & McKinney, 1983; Raphael & Pearson, 1985; Raphael & Wonnacott, 1985); (d) generate questions about what they have read (Andre & Anderson, 1978–79; Brown & Palincsar, 1985); and (e) monitor their comprehension of the text (Baker & Anderson, 1982; Vosniadou, Pearson, & Rogers, 1988). In sum, this work has shown that students with LD, as well as other students, can be taught strategies to facilitate their reading and understanding of literary and expository text.

However, following written directions such as those included on job applications differs from other kinds of reading, in that the goal of the reader is to *do* something rather than to *learn about* something. In the case of procedural text or written directions, a partial understanding is insufficient—mastery of the content is required. Reading written directions is further complicated by the fact that writers of directions often overestimate the reader's experience with directions, omit intermediate steps, use technical vocabulary, and employ complex syntax (Henk & Helfeldt, 1987). Furthermore, written directions often contain unclear directional and location cues for entering information in specific places on the application form. In addition, according to Henk and Helfeldt, there is no immediate transfer of academic reading skills to following written directions. Good readers follow written directions well only 80% of the time, and poor readers achieve less than a 50% success rate (Fox & Siedow, 1980).

Paralleling work on reading comprehension, researchers have developed a number of learning strategies designed to facilitate students' abilities to generate expository text (e.g., Englert et al., 1991; Graham & Harris, 1989; Harris & Graham, 1985; Schmidt, Deshler, Schumaker, & Alley, 1988). Schmidt et al., for example, taught high school students with LD four written expression learning strategies: sentence writing, paragraph writing, error monitoring, and theme writing. The results showed improvements both in the quality of themes and in the mechanics of the written text.

Because research and theory suggest that students should be taught to apply different learning strategies to different types of situations (Brandt, 1989), students must possess specific strategies for both understanding and following procedural text or written directions. In other words, the reading and writing strategies demanded by the task requirements of a job application depart from those that students apply elsewhere. The purpose of the present study was to develop a learning strategy and study its effects on completion of job applications by students with LD. This is important because there are significant societal and personal costs associated with the unemployment and underemployment of individuals with disabilities, and, as noted, regardless of otherwise equal qualifications, the content, completeness, and neatness of a job application can determine whether an individual has an opportunity to even interview for a specific job.

METHOD

Subjects

Thirty-three students (20 boys and 13 girls) with LD served as participants in the study. All were receiving special education services in a public high school in a city in the Northwest (population 180,000) and were classified as learning disabled by a school district multidisciplinary evaluation team. Criteria for special education classification include deficits in oral expression (as measured by the Northwestern Syntax Screening Test), listening comprehension (as measured by the Carrow Test for Auditory Comprehension of Language), and/or written expression (as measured by the Comprehensive Tests of Basic Skills). Criteria also included a significant discrepancy (at least 2 years below grade placement) between the student's estimated ability and academic performance.

Students were generally from low-SES families (qualified for free and reduced lunch). Table 1 provides additional descriptions of the participants' sex, age, race, grade level, years in special education, percentage of each school day spent in special education, IQ, and achievement.

Setting

All participants were enrolled in a pre-vocational education class for students with learning disabilities. The class was taught by a certificated special education teacher with 6 years of teaching experience at the high school level. The classroom aide was a high school graduate with 8 years of classroom assistance experience. The

TABLE 1 Subject Description

	LEARNING STRATEGY INSTRUCTION (n = 16)	TRADITIONAL INSTRUCTION (n = 17)
Gender		
Male	10	10
Female	6	7
Age		
Mean	15.9	16.3
Range	14.5–17.3	14.3–17.5
Race		
White	15	17
African American	1	0
Grade Level		
12th	2	3
11th	6	7
10th	6	5
9th	2	2
Years in special education		
Mean	5.9	5.3
Range	4–8	4–9
Percentage of day in special education		
Mode	.50	.50
Range	33–83	33–83
Intelligence[a]		
Mean	98.5	96.2
Range	88–106	84–105
Reading Comprehension[b]		
Mean T	35.1	33.4
Range	22–43	25–41

[a]Stanford-Binet Intelligence Scale.
[b]Iowa Test of Basic Skills.

teacher conducted the experimental sessions during two 60-minute instructional periods. The classroom was approximately 10 m by 15 m and had 25 individual desks at which the participating students sat during the experimental sessions.

Dependent Measures

Student Performance Measures. Three mutually exclusive measures were employed to assess the effects of the learning strategy instruction on the completion of job applications by students: information omissions, information location errors, and a holistic rating of overall neatness of the job application. An omission was scored when a required item was not completed. A location error was scored when the correct information was entered in the wrong location (e.g., writing the information on the line directly below where the information was to be placed). A 5-point Likert-type scale (1 = *very messy* to 5 = *very neat*) was used to obtain a holistic rating of the overall neatness of the job application.

Interscorer agreement for omissions and location errors was determined by having two scorers independently score all of the job applications. The scorers' records were compared item by item. For omissions, agreement was noted when both scorers had marked a response as not present. Similarly, an agreement was noted when both the scorers marked the location of the information as correct or if both scorers had marked the location of the information as incorrect. Percentage of agreement for each measure was computed by dividing the number of agreements by the number of agreements plus disagreements. The percentage of agreement was 100% in both cases.

Interscorer agreement was computed for the holistic rating by having two raters independently rate all of the job applications. A Pearson product moment correlation was then calculated to estimate the reliability of the ratings. The correlation was .78, $p < .05$.

Social Validity Measure. To assess the social validity of the effects of the training, the supervisor of classified personnel at a local university employing approximately 1,200 classified staff was asked the following: "Based on this job application, if you had a position open, would you invite this person in for an interview?" The rating was completed on a 5-point Likert-type scale (1 = *very unlikely,* 3 = *undecided,* 5 = *very likely*). The supervisor rated each application and was unaware of whether it was completed under the learning strategy or traditional instruction condition.

Design

A pretest–posttest control group design was employed. Students were randomly assigned by age and gender to one of two experimental conditions learning strategy instruction or traditional instruction. This resulted in 16 students (10 boys and 6 girls) being assigned under the learning strategy instruction condition and 17 students (10 boys and 7 girls) under the traditional instruction condition. The results of a preliminary analysis revealed that there were statistically nonsignificant differences in characteristics (i.e., intelligence, achievement, age, years in special education, and percentage of each school day spent in special education) between the two groups.

Procedure

Job Applications. Job applications for entry-level jobs were obtained from eight local businesses. Two of these job applications were selected for the pretest and posttest; two additional applications were used to conduct the training sessions (demonstration and independent practice). Although these job applications were designed to elicit the same general information, the format (e.g., sequence of information and location cues) differed. The same pretest, posttest, and training job applications were used under the learning strategy instruction and traditional instruction conditions.

Preskill Instructional Module. Students under both conditions (described below) received a prepared instructional module designed to provide the relevant prerequisite vocabulary knowledge necessary to complete a job application. This instruction was conducted, and job application information collected (discussed below), prior to pretesting. The teacher presented the prerequisite vocabulary knowledge module, using a written script, to students under both conditions. The prerequisite information included definitions for the following job application vocabulary words: (a) *birth place,* (b) *nationality,* (c) *previous work experience,* (d) *references,* (e) *maiden name,* (f) *marital status,* (g) *citizenship,* (h) *salary,* and (i) *wage.* Instruction continued until all of the students earned 100% correct on a paper-and-pencil test in which the words were matched with their respective definitions.

Students under both experimental conditions also compiled the information necessary for them to complete a job application, including (a) birth date, (b) social security number, (c) complete address, (d) telephone number, (e) educational experience, (f) previous work experience, (g) references, and (h) felony convictions (if applicable). Students then constructed a job application information card containing this information.

Students under both experimental conditions then completed the pretest job application. The teacher asked them to complete the job application as if they were applying for an actual job. She also explained that typically no one is available to help people complete job applications, and they were to use their job information card for the task. Students were provided as much time as they needed to complete the application. The teacher did not provide the students any assistance during this time. The pretest session was conducted 1 day prior to the training and posttest sessions.

Learning Strategy Instruction Condition. The job application learning strategy taught in this investigation was designed after analyzing the nature of items included on standard job applications for entry-level jobs obtained from a number of local businesses, and after completing a task analysis of the steps involved in completing a job application. The strategy was also designed in accordance with the needs and skill levels of the students. The principle steps were then sequenced and a first-letter mnemonic device was developed to facilitate students' recall of the strategy steps. This resulted in a six-step strategy called "SELECT."

Students first *S*urvey the entire job application and look for the *E*mphasized words that indicate the type of information requested (e.g., previous experience) and think to themselves, "What information do I have to have to complete the job application?" and "Do I have all of the necessary information to complete the application (check job application information card)?" if not, "What additional information do I need to get?" The students then look closely at the items on the job application for *L*ocation cues that indicate where the requested information is to be entered (e.g., line immediately below the request for information) and think to themselves, "Where does the information go?" Next, they think to themselves, "How much space do I need for the information—How big should I print the information?" and then carefully *E*nter the information requested in the appropriate location. After completing the application, the students then *C*heck to see if the information is accurate (compare with job information card) and that the job application is completed, and think to themselves, "Did I put the right information in the right locations?" if not, "I need to complete another job application." Then, "Did I complete the job application?" if not, "Complete the job application." Finally, the students *T*urn the completed job application into the appropriate individual.

The special education teacher used a five-step procedure to teach the students the job application strategy during an approximately 1-hour instructional session. First, the teacher discussed the goal of the job application strategy instruction procedure (i.e., to help students accurately complete a job application) and why it is important to know how to accurately complete a job application. She also explained how they would be able to use the strategy whenever they applied for a job.

Second, an overhead transparency was used to introduce and discuss the six-step job application strategy. The teacher and students discussed the use of the strategy until it was clear that the students fully understood the steps. This was accomplished through choral responding by the students and informal checks by the teacher.

Third, using an overhead transparency, the teacher modeled the job application strategy by completing a standard job application while "thinking out loud." To actively engage the students, the teacher used prompts to encourage an interactive dialogue with the students throughout the demonstration, for example, "What is it I have to do? I need to . . ." and "How am I doing?" The students were encouraged to help the teacher. After modeling, the teacher and students discussed the importance of using self-questioning statements while completing a job application.

Fourth, students were required to verbally practice the job application strategy steps, including the self-questioning statements, until they were memorized. All of the students were able to do this correctly within a 15- to 20-minute rehearsal period. They were then required to write down the steps and associated self-questioning statements as they worked through a job application. Students were provided only one practice attempt. They were allowed to ask any questions at this time and the teacher provided corrective feedback only upon demand by the students throughout the training session.

Finally, students independently completed the posttest job application. As under the pretest condition, the teacher asked the students to complete the job application as if they were applying for an actual job. She also explained to the students that because there typically is no one there to help them complete job applications, they were to use only their job information card to complete the job application, and that they had as much time as they needed to complete the application. The teacher did not provide the students any assistance during this time. After they completed the posttest job application, the students were asked to independently describe the steps they had used, in an attempt to check whether they had employed the learning strategy. All of the students verbally stated, in sequence, the steps and associated self-questioning statements included in the learning strategy.

Traditional Instruction Condition. The same job application forms used under the learning strategy condition were used for the traditional instruction condition. During an approximately 1-hour instructional session, the special education teacher (same teacher) first discussed the goal of the job application instruction (i.e., to help students accurately complete a job application) and why it is important to know how to accurately complete a job application. She also explained how they would be able to use the things they learned whenever they applied for a job.

Next, the teacher used an overhead transparency to model how to complete a standard job application. Throughout the demonstration, the teacher explained why it was important to accurately complete job applications and instructed the students to be careful to complete all of the information and to be sure that they put the information in the correct place. To actively engage the students, the teacher used prompts throughout the demonstration, such as "What is it I have to do? I need to..." and "How am I doing?" The students were encouraged to help the teacher complete the job application. Students were then required to practice completing a job application. They were allowed only one practice attempt, and they were allowed to ask any questions during this time. The teacher provided corrective feedback only upon request throughout the session.

Finally, the students independently completed the posttest job application. The teacher did not provide the students any assistance during this time. Once again, these conditions (job application, instructions, and amount of time) were the same as those employed under the pretest and learning strategy instruction conditions.

Fidelity of Implementation. Fidelity of implementation was assessed under both experimental conditions by observing the teacher on the day of instruction to ensure that she followed the teaching steps associated with each of the experimental conditions. The primary researcher used a checklist to track whether the teacher fully completed the teaching functions described above under each condition.

RESULTS

Preliminary analyses indicated that there were nonsignificant differences between the groups on the pretest measures. Posttest measures were analyzed in condition (traditional, strategy) by gender (male, female) analyses of variance (ANOVAs). For every dependent measure, only a significant main effect for condition was obtained. The *F* values for these effects, along with the means and standard deviations for each of the dependent measures, are presented in Table 2.

TABLE 2 Mean Number of Information Omissions and Location Errors, and Mean Holistic Rating of Overall Application Neatness

DEPENDENT MEASURE	GROUP		*F*(1, 31) (CONDITION)
	A	B	
Omissions	5.35 (2.55)	0.63 (0.63)	15.29*
Location errors	1.35 (0.99)	0.25 (0.25)	5.29**
Neatness rating	3.37 (1.05)	4.48 (0.51)	7.25***

$^*p < .001$. $^{**}p < .05$. $^{**}p < .01$.

Note: Group A refers to the traditional instruction condition and Group B refers to the strategy instruction condition. Numbers in parentheses are standard deviations.

The findings indicate that students who received instruction in the learning strategy condition made statistically significant lower numbers of information omission errors and location errors than students under the job application instruction condition. Additionally, these students received statistically significant higher holistic ratings on their job applications than their counterparts. There were statistically nonsignificant main effects for gender and nonsignificant condition by gender interactions for all of the dependent measures.

Confidence in these results is strengthened by the results of the checks for fidelity of implementation conducted under both experimental conditions. These findings showed that the teacher fully completed the teaching functions described above under each condition.

The social validity measure was analyzed in a condition (traditional, strategy) by gender (male, female) ANOVA. A significant main effect for condition was obtained, $F(1,31) = 6.12$, $p < .05$. There were statistically nonsignificant main effects for gender and condition by gender interactions for the social validity measure. The effects of the job application training on the ratings (1 = *very unlikely* to 5 = *very likely*) by the supervisor of classified personnel suggest that students under the learning strategy condition (mean = 4.21; *SD* = 0.46) would be more likely to receive invitations for job interviews after training than those under the traditional condition (mean = 2.88; *SD* = 1.02).

DISCUSSION

Past research on learning strategies has focused on skills that were general in nature and that apply across subject matters (Brandt, 1989). Recent work on learning strategies, however, has focused on studying how people learn particular things in particular environments. The present study was designed to develop and assess the effects of a learning strategy designed specifically to help students with LD understand the procedural text or written directions included on a job application and provide the requested information.

The results of this study suggest that a sample of students identified as learning disabled according to the state of Washington and federal guidelines were capable of mastering a six-step job application learning strategy in a relatively short time. Because the accurate completion of job applications constitutes an important component in the job search process, these procedures may be very beneficial in facilitating successful job acquisition by students with learning disabilities.

The findings of this study support those of other researchers (e.g., Clark et al., 1975; Mathews & Fawcett, 1984), demonstrating the beneficial effects of teaching students employment application skills. In addition to statistically significant lower numbers of information omissions and information location errors, holistic ratings of the overall neatness of the job applications were much higher for those students under the learning strategy instruction condition. Confidence in the findings of this study are strengthened by the fidelity of implementation data that indicate that the experimental conditions were fully implemented under both conditions.

Most important, in addition to statistically significant positive changes m the three performance measures, the social validity data suggest that the learning strategy instruction resulted in job application forms that would be more likely to elicit invitations for job interviews. The supervisor of classified personnel at the local university indicated that he would be likely to give the students under the learning strategy condition an invitation for a job interview. In contrast, he was significantly less likely to grant a job interview to students under the traditional instruction condition.

It is important to note several limitations of the study. First, the present study provides only one comparison of many potential instructional approaches. Thus, conclusions regarding the efficacy of the learning strategy instruction over any other instructional practices must be made cautiously.

Second, because maintenance was not assessed, the long-term impact of the training is uncertain. Third, although students under the learning strategy condition verbally stated that they had employed and articulated the six-steps included in the learning strategy to complete the job applications, the subjective nature of this self-report data does not fully substantiate their claim. Fourth, the relatively small number of subjects limits conclusions regarding the effectiveness of this strategy with students from other areas of the country or, more important, students with other types of disabilities and abilities. Finally, the limited nature of the task also limits conclusions regarding the effectiveness of this type of instruction for other procedural types of texts. The skills required to understand procedural text and perform the required functions accompanying technological devices, such as videocassette recorders, personal computers, programmable microwave ovens, and so forth, differ from those required to complete a standard job application. Procedural text for these devices, with accompanying illustrations, require an individual to fully understand sequence and direction and location concepts. Readers, for example, must be sensitive to sequence cues such as "then," "next," and "finally," and complex direction and location concepts, such as "down," "outside," "against," "inside," and "up." These complex directions, when combined with manual operations and the need to monitor progress, pose an instructional dilemma.

In summary, the skills addressed in the present study, although important, are relatively simple compared to demands that students may encounter regarding the understanding of procedural text. Further research is needed not only to clarify the results of the present study, but also to address the instructional requirements for preparing students with disabilities and others to effectively manage procedural text. Given our rapidly expanding technological society, the complexity of procedural text is only going to increase. Thus, researchers and teachers must continue to develop instructional procedures to facilitate students' understanding of procedural text.

ABOUT THE AUTHORS

J. Ron Nelson, PhD, is an assistant professor in the Department of Applied Psychology at Eastern Washington University. He received his doctoral degree in special education from Utah State University. His major research interests include teaching methods for exceptional students and students at risk for school failure, as well as students' social and intellectual reasoning. Deborah J. Smith, PhD, is project director in Disabled Student Services and adjunct professor in the Department of Applied Psychology at Eastern Washington University. She received her doctoral degree in special education from Utah State University. Her major research interests include self-management strategies for classroom deportment and academic performance, as well as cognitive instructional strategies. John M. Dodd, EdD, is a professor in the Department of Reading and Special Education at Eastern Montana College. He received his doctoral degree in human development at the University of Kansas. His major research interests include culturally sensitive identification and programming for linguistically and culturally diverse students. Address: J. Ron Nelson, Department of Applied Psychology, MS/92, Eastern Washington University, Cheney, WA 99004.

REFERENCES

Andre, M. E., & Anderson, T. H. (1978–79). The development and evaluation of a self-questioning study technique. *Reading Research Quarterly, 14,* 605–623.

Azrin, N. H., & Philip, R. A. (1979). The Job Club methods vs. a lecture-discussion-role play method of obtaining employment for clients with job-finding handicaps. *Rehabilitation Counseling Bulletin, 23,* 144–155.

Baker, L., & Anderson, R. L. (1982). Effects of inconsistent information on text processing: Evidence for comprehension monitoring. *Reading Research Quarterly, 17,* 281–294.

Baumann, J. F. (1986). The direct instruction of main idea comprehension ability. In J. F. Bauman (Ed.), *Teaching main idea comprehension* (pp. 133–178). Newark, DE: International Reading Association.

Borkowski, J. G., Weyhing, R. S., & Carr, M. (1988). Effects of attributional retraining on strategy-based reading comprehension in learning-disabled students. *Journal of Educational Psychology, 80,* 46–53.

Brandt, R. (1989). On learning research: A conversation with Lauren Resnick. *Educational Leadership, 46*(4), 12–16.

Brown, A. L., & Palincsar, A. S (1985). *Reciprocal teaching of comprehension strategies: A natural history of one program to enhance learning* (Tech. Rep. No. 334). Urbana: University of Illinois, Center for the Study of Reading.

Clark, H. B., Boyd, S. B., & MaCrae, J. W. (1975). A classroom program teaching disadvantaged youths to write biographical information. *Journal of Applied Behavior Analysis, 8,* 67–75.

Cunningham, J. W., & Moore, D. W. (1986). The confused world of main idea. In J. B. Baumann (Ed.), *Teaching main idea comprehension* (pp. 1–17). Newark, DE: International Reading Association.

Day, J. D. (1980). *Teaching summarization skills: A comparison of training methods.* Unpublished doctoral dissertation, University of Illinois, Urbana-Champaign.

Englert, C. S., Raphael, T. E., Anderson, L. M., Anthony, H. M., & Stevens, D. D. (1991). Making strategies and self-talk visible: Writing instruction in regular and special education classrooms. *American Educational Research Journal, 28,* 337–372.

Field, H. S., & Holley, W. H. (1976). Resume preparation: An empirical study of personnel managers' perceptions. *Vocational Guidance Quarterly, 25,* 229–237.

Fox, B. J., & Siedow, M. D. (1980). Written directions for content area classrooms—Do students understand the teacher? *The Clearing House, 54,* 101–104.

Furman, W., Geller, M., Simon, S. J., & Kelly, J. A. (1979). The use of a behavior rehearsal procedure for teaching job-interview skills to psychiatric patients. *Behavior Therapy, 10,* 157–167.

Graham, S., & Harris, K. R. (1989). Component analysis of cognitive strategy instruction: Effects on learning disabled students' skills at composing essays: Self-instructional strategy training. *Exceptional Children, 56,* 201–214.

Hall, C., Sheldon-Wildgen, J., & Sherman, J. A. (1980). Teaching job interview skills to retarded clients. *Journal of Applied Behavior Analysis, 13,* 433–442.

Hansen, J. (1981). The effects of inference training and practice on young children's reading comprehension. *Reading Research Quarterly, 16,* 391–417.

Hare, V. C., & Borchardt, K. M. (1984). Direct instruction of summarization skills. *Reading Research Quarterly, 20,* 62–78.

Harris, K. R., & Graham, S. (1985). Improving learning disabled students' composition skills: Self-control strategy training. *Learning Disability Quarterly, 8,* 27–36.

Henk, W. A., & Helfeldt, J. P. (1987). How to develop independence in following written directions. *Journal of Reading, 30,* 602–607.

Hollansworth, J. G., Dressel, M. E., & Stevens, J. (1977). Use of behavioral versus traditional procedures for increasing job interview skills. *Journal of Counseling Psychology, 24,* 503–510.

Mathews, R. M., & Fawcett, S. B. (1984). Building the capacities of job candidates through behavioral instruction. *Journal of Community Psychology, 12,* 123–129.

Mathews, R. M., Whang, P. L., & Fawcett, S. B. (1981). Behavioral assessment of job-related skills. *Journal of Employment Counseling, 18,* 3–11.

Nelson, J. R., Smith, D. J., & Dodd, J. M. (1992). *The effects of a summary skills intervention on students' comprehension of science text.* Manuscript submitted for publication.

Palincsar, A. M., & Brown, A. L. (1984). Reciprocal teaching of comprehension-fostering and comprehension-monitoring activities. *Cognition and Instruction, 1,* 117–175.

Pearson, P. D. (1985). Changing the face of reading comprehension instruction. *The Reading Teacher, 38,* 724–738.

Raphael, T. E., & McKinney, J. (1983). An examination of 5th and 8th grade children's question answering behavior: An instructional study in metacognition. *Journal of Reading Behavior, 15*(5), 67–86.

Raphael, T. E., & Pearson, P. D. (1985). Increasing students' awareness of sources of information for answering questions. *American Educational Research Journal, 22,* 217–235.

Raphael, T. E., & Wonnacoft, C. A. (1985). Heightening fourth-grade students' sensitivity to sources of information for answering questions. *Reading Research Quarterly, 20,* 282–296.

Schmidt, J., Deshler, D., Schumaker, J., & Alley, G. (1988). The effects of generalization instruction on the written performance of adolescents with learning disabilities in the mainstream classroom. *Reading, Writing, and Learning Disabilities, 4,* 291–309.

Taylor, B. M. (1982). Text structure and children's comprehension and memory for expository materials. *Journal of Educational Psychology, 15,* 401–405.

Taylor, B. M., & Beach, R. W. (1984). The effects of text structure instruction on middle-grade students' comprehension and production of expository text. *Reading Research Quarterly, 19,* 134–146.

Taylor, B. M., & Berkowitz, B. S. (1980). Facilitating childrens' comprehension of content material. In M. L. Kamil & A. J Moe (Eds.), *Perspectives in reading research and instruction* (pp. 64–68.) Clemson, SC: National Reading Conference.

Vosniadou, S., Pearson, P. D., & Rogers, T. (1988). What causes children's failures to detect inconsistencies in text? Representation vs. comparison difficulties. *Journal of Educational Psychology, 80,* 27–39.

Williams, J. P. (1986). Extracting important information from text. In J. A. Niles & R. V. Lalik (Eds.), *Solving problems in literacy: Learners, teachers, and researchers* (pp. 11–29). Rochester, NY: National Reading Conference

FACTUAL QUESTIONS

1. According to the authors, what materials do employers rely on when selecting individuals to interview?
2. How does procedural text differ from expository text?
3. What was the stated purpose of the study?
4. Who were the participants?
5. What type of experimental design was used in the study?
6. What were the steps in the learning strategy (independent variable)?

7. What dependent measures were used to assess the effects of the learning strategy?
8. What type of intervention did the control group receive?
9. How was the fidelity of implementation assessed?
10. What were the results?

DISCUSSION QUESTIONS

1. Are there any problems with the way participants were selected and assigned to the two conditions?
2. What suggestions would you make to improve the population validity of the study?
3. Why was fidelity of implementation assessed? Does it increase your confidence in the findings? Why?
4. Why do you think it was important for the authors to use a variety of dependent measures?
5. Are there any problems with treatment diffusion, compensatory rivalry, or resentful demoralization of the traditional instruction group? Why?
6. Was it necessary for the authors to assess the initial equivalence of the two groups?
7. What other statistical analysis procedure could the authors have used to ensure the initial equivalence of the experimental and control groups?
8. What was the purpose of providing the preskill lesson to both of the groups?
9. What could the authors have done to improve the internal validity of the study?
10. What could the authors have done to improve the external validity of the study?

THREATS TO INTERNAL VALIDITY

Circle the number corresponding to the likelihood of each threat to internal validity being present in the investigation and provide a justification.

1 = definitely not a threat 2 = not a likely threat 3 = somewhat likely threat
4 = likely threat 5 = definite threat NA = Not applicable for this design

Results in Differences Within or Between Individuals

1. **Maturation** 1 2 3 4 5 NA

Justification Not enough time elapsed

2. **Selection** 1 2 3 4 5 NA

Justification analyzed subject backgrounds.

3. **Selection by Maturation Interaction** 1 2 3 4 5 NA

Justification Similar age (maturity level)

4. **Statistical Regression** 1 2 3 4 5 NA

Justification

5. **Mortality** 1 2 3 4 5 NA

Justification short term study

6. **Instrumentation** 1 2 3 4 5 NA

Justification Used standard measure - consistent

7. Testing 1 2 3 4 5 NA

Justification both groups took test

8. History 1 2 3 4 5 NA

Justification don't know about previous job [illegible] history + family assistance

9. Resentful Demoralization of the Control Group 1 2 3 4 5 NA

Justification Both received an "intervention" however if time lag occur between "intervention then, yes)

Results in Similarities Within or Between Individuals

10. Diffusion of Treatment 1 2 3 4 5 NA

Justification Had observers of teacher monitor instruct.

11. Compensatory Rivalry by the Control Group 1 2 3 4 5 NA

Justification both groups received an "intervention

12. Compensatory Equalization of Treatments 1 2 3 4 5 NA

Justification observers monitored both groups

Abstract: Write a one page abstract summarizing the overall conclusions of the authors and whether or not you feel the authors' conclusions are valid based on the internal validity of the investigation.

THREATS TO EXTERNAL VALIDITY

Circle the number corresponding to the likelihood of each threat to external validity being present in the investigation according to the following scale:

1 = definitely not a threat	2 = not a likely threat	3 = somewhat likely threat
4 = likely threat	5 = definite threat	NA = Not applicable for this design

Also, provide a justification for each rating.

Population

1. Generalization Across Subjects 1 2 3 4 5 NA

Justification Study part. not randomly selected

2. Interaction of Personological Variables and Treatment 1 2 3 4 5 NA

Justification ______________________________

Ecological

3. Verification of the Independent Variable 1 2 3 4 5 NA

Justification ______________________________

4. Multiple Treatment Interference 1 2 3 4 5 NA

Justification ______________________________

5. Hawthorne Effect 1 2 3 4 5 NA

Justification ______________________________

6. Novelty and Disruption Effects 1 2 3 4 5 NA

Justification ______________________________

7. Experimenter Effects 1 (2) 3 4 5 NA

Justification observers of teachers

8. Pretest Sensitization 1 2 (3) 4 5 NA

Justification author needs to stress use of both a pretest + a post test to prevent threats to validity

9. Posttest Sensitization 1 2 (3) 4 5 NA

Justification ?

10. Interaction of Time of Measurement and Treatment Effects 1 2 3 (4) 5 NA

Justification short time span of study. — intervention may not last

11. Measurement of the Dependent Variable 1 2 (3) 4 5 NA

Justification other studies need to use same (similar) measurement device — in study its fairly specific.

12. Interaction of History and Treatment Effects 1 2 3 4 (5) NA

Justification short study time span

Abstract: Write a one page abstract summarizing the overall conclusions of the authors and whether or not you feel the authors' conclusions are valid based on the external validity of the investigation.

CHAPTER 6

CAUSAL-COMPARATIVE RESEARCH

OBJECTIVES

After studying this chapter you should be able to:

1. Describe critical issues in designing causal-comparative research studies.
2. Describe how causal-comparative methods are similar and dissimilar to experimental methods.
3. Explain how to interpret causal-comparative research.
4. Describe parametric tests of statistical significance used in causal-comparative research.
5. Describe nonparametric tests of statistical significance used in causal-comparative research.
6. Explain the internal validity problems of the causal-comparative design.
7. Explain the external validity problems with the causal-comparative design.
8. Explain when one would use causal-comparative research.
9. Critique a research article containing a causal-comparative design.

OVERVIEW

As previously noted, one of the primary features of science is that it possesses a set of goals, principles, and procedures that provides a way of constructing knowledge that is common to both quantitative and qualitative researchers. The goals, principles, and procedures used by experimental researchers were presented in Chapter 5. This chapter focuses on the causal-comparative research method.

Although all research may share the goal of providing evidence about causal relationships (i.e., about what leads to what), a great deal of research in education and psychology only leads to descriptions of the relationships among variables. Research aimed at studying relationships between and among variables can be used to rule out causal hypotheses as well as to provide support for others. For example, if a "no relationship" finding is obtained, the credibility of a hypothesis is lessened. If a "high relationship" finding is obtained, the credibility of the hypothesis is strengthened in that it has survived disconfirmation. (The link between heavy smoking and lung cancer is a case in point.) These hypotheses can then be checked through experimental manipulation when appropriate.

Two general approaches are used by researchers to explore the relationships among variables.

The first approach is the causal-comparative method. This method involves comparing two or more samples or groups of participants that are different on a critical variable but are otherwise comparable. For example, juvenile delinquents have been compared to nondelinquents to identify whether levels of moral reasoning are related to delinquency. The causal-comparative approach is also used to compare two or more equivalent samples on a critical variable to identify changes over time. For example, young children's understanding of knowledge has been compared with that of older children to identify developmental changes in children's understanding of knowledge.

The second approach is the correlational method. This method, reduced to its barest essentials, involves collecting two sets of data and determining the extent to which these data sets covary using a correlation statistic. For example, researchers have explored the extent to which scholastic aptitude and grade-point average (GPA) are related to each other in an effort to determine if students' scores on a measure of scholastic aptitude can predict their GPAs.

This chapter begins with a general description of the causal-comparative research method. This description is followed by a discussion of how the data in the causal-comparative design are interpreted and an illustrative example of how to interpret the findings of causal-comparative research. Finally, an illustrative example of how to interpret the findings of causal-comparative research is provided for critique.

WHAT IS THE CAUSAL-COMPARATIVE RESEARCH METHOD?

As previously stated, the causal-comparative research method involves comparing two groups of individuals drawn from the same population that are different on a critical variable but are otherwise comparable. For example, we could compare students with emotional disturbance to students without emotional disturbance who are drawn from the same population to identify possible causes of emotional disturbance. In essence, the causal-comparative method is a particular way of collecting and analyzing data aimed at the discovery of possible causes for a pattern of behavior by comparing participants with whom this pattern is present to participants with whom it is absent (or present to a lesser degree). This method is sometimes referred to as ex post facto research because the causes are studied after they have presumably influenced another variable.

Causal-comparative research is similar to experimental research methods in that each compare group scores (averages) to determine relationships between the independent and dependent variables. Both experimental and causal-comparative designs use group memberships as a categorical variable. Finally, with the exception of counterbalanced and time-series designs, both compare separate groups of participants.

In essence, the causal-comparative design tends to look like experimental designs. However, there are several obvious differences. First, in experimental designs, the independent variable is manipulated, whereas in the causal-comparative design, the independent variable is not manipulated. The independent variable is not manipulated in the causal-comparative design because either it is not possible to manipulate the independent variable, as is the case with gender, or it is prohibitive due to do so, as with smoking.

For example, it is not possible to take a sample of individuals without a sexual identity and then randomly assign half to a female group and the other half to a male group to the see the effects of gender on the relative effectiveness of a mathematics curriculum. Likewise, it would be unethical to take a sample of nonsmokers and assign half to a nonsmoking group and the other half to a smoking group where they would have to smoke two packs of cigarettes a day for a year to determine the effects of smoking. The independent variables (e.g., gender, smoking status) in causal-comparative research are called *classification, subject,* or *organismic* variables, and the independent variables in experimental research are called *stimulus* variables. Note that a stimulus variable may be manipulated in a causal-comparative design, but the variable is manipulated for both groups with the intention of seeing how the classification, subject, or organismic variable affects the participants' responses.

Another difference between the causal-comparative design and experimental designs involves the issue of cause-and-effect relationships. Despite its name, the causal-comparative design demonstrates a weak indication of a cause-and-effect relationship. The experimental design can demonstrate a much stronger causal relationship. Finally, in experimental research, the participants may be assigned to groups, whereas participants in the causal-comparative design are already in preformed groups (e.g., males and females).

WHAT SHOULD RESEARCHERS CONSIDER WHEN DESIGNING A CAUSAL-COMPARATIVE STUDY?

There are a number of critical issues that researchers must consider when designing a causal-comparative study—development of hypotheses, selection of groups, and analysis of data. Critical research consumers should look closely at causal-comparative studies to ensure that these issues have been adequately considered.

Development of Hypotheses

The initial issue centers on the development of hypotheses about the causes or effects of the phenomenon under study. Although the hypotheses can initially be based on pure speculation and informal observations, it is critical that researchers look closely at theory and previous research findings to ensure that there is a basis for the hypotheses. Doing so is also critical to ensure that other possible explanatory factors that might influence the phenomenon or characteristic under study can be considered in the research design. As will become clear in our discussion of the data analysis procedures used with causal-comparative research, there are ways of determining the influence of potential explanatory factors other than those of particular interest. Indeed, it is important that researchers explore plausible alternative hypotheses about factors that might explain differences in the characteristic of interest.

Selection of Groups

The second critical issue in designing a causal-comparative study is to select the group that possesses the characteristic under study (experimental group) and a comparison group that does not have the characteristic. Selecting the group that possesses the characteristic requires a precise definition so that not only can a comparison group be selected, but also the results of the study can be interpreted meaningfully. For example, in a study of the effects of teacher attitudes on the academic performance of students at risk for school failure, it would not be precise enough to say simply that the experimental group includes at-risk students. A more precise definition would be needed such as students who are in the lower quartile in academic achievement, average 10 or more absences (excused and unexcused) a year, and average five detentions or more a year for disruptive behavior. This definition would not only enable the researchers to identify a meaningful comparison group, but also would allow the results of the study to be interpreted meaningfully.

There is a potential problem that can arise when selecting a comparison group. In the preceding example, it appears that selecting a comparison group would be rather straightforward. Researchers would select students who did not meet the specified criteria. Unfortunately, things are often not that straightforward in selecting a comparison group. In the preceding case, differences in academic performance might be due to other extraneous factors such as the type and amount of instruction they receive, intelligence level, and level of parental involvement. There are three ways to solve this problem—matching of participants, equating groups statistically, and selecting extreme groups.

Matching of Participants. Researchers could equate groups on the extraneous factors through a matching procedure to ensure that the variables do not confound the results of the study. They would match the experimental students with regard to the amount and type of instruction they receive (e.g., experimental and control students enrolled in the same class), intelligence (e.g., experimental students matched with control students having an IQ within ±8 points), and level of parental involvement (e.g., experimental students with high and low parental involvement matched with equivalent control group students).

Equating Groups Statistically. Related to the matching approach, researchers can use a statistical procedure to equate groups on the extraneous variables. This procedure is called the analysis of covariance and is described in detail later. Although some researchers question the validity of using analysis of covariance to equate groups statistically because it essentially creates an artificial or unnatural comparison group (e.g., Ferguson, 1989), it is the preferred procedure. The use of analysis of covariance to equate groups statistically is preferred for two reasons. First, there simply may not be suitable matches available for some members of the experimental group. Second, matching experimental and comparison participants on all of the extraneous factors is a time-consuming job. In most cases, it is much more efficient to measure the participants on the extraneous factors and equate them statistically using analysis of covariance.

Selecting Extreme Groups. The final approach to handling the problem of extraneous variables is called the extreme-groups method. As its name implies, this method requires researchers to select the experimental and comparison groups that are at two extremes of a score distribution on the characteristic of interest. The assumption underlying the extreme-groups methods is that the comparison group is more likely to differ on other measured factors but less dramatically so than on the variable of interest (Gall, Borg, & Gall, 1996). In the earlier study of the influence of teacher attitudes on the academic performance of students at risk for school failure, researchers could select the sample by administering a survey to 100 teachers. Then they could select the top 20 teachers who reported positive attitudes and the bottom 20 teachers who reported more negative attitudes. The remaining 60 teachers would be dropped from the study. The resulting sample of 40 teachers would most likely include a greater number of teachers with very positive and very negative attitudes than would a sample of teachers randomly selected from the population. These extreme groups are more likely to reveal an effect on the academic performance of students at risk for school failure than selecting groups that do not demonstrate extreme differences on the characteristic of interest.

Analysis of Data

The final issue focuses on the collection and analysis of the data. Researchers use a wide range of measurement devices in causal-comparative research. Standardized and criterion-referenced tests, surveys, questionnaires, interviews, and observations are all used by researchers in causal-comparative research. Thus, they must carefully consider the reliability and validity of the measurement device being used. Additionally, because inferential statistics plays a key role in interpreting the findings of causal-comparative research studies, it is critical that researchers employ the appropriate tests of statistical significance. Statistical significance testing and the statistical procedures commonly used in causal-comparative research follow.

Causal-comparative research seeks to determine whether two or more groups differ on some critical variable. Making this determination is accomplished by researchers through the use of a variety of statistical procedures. The use of these statistical procedures depends on a number of issues, including the number of groups, the type of data, and the question(s) being asked. (Refer to Figures 4.9, 4.10, and 4.11 for information regarding when to use each statistical analysis procedure to analyze data from investigations.)

Recall from Chapter 4 that there are parametric and nonparametric tests of statistical significance. Parametric tests are most commonly used in causal-comparative research studies. A *t* test is used when researchers are interested in determining whether there is a statistical significant difference between the means of two sets of scores. A *t* test for independent means is used when the means of two samples are considered independent from one another. The *t* test for correlated means is used when the samples are related to one another, whereas the *t* test for a single mean is used in those cases in which the researcher is interested in determining whether there is a statistically significant difference between a sample mean and a specified population mean. See Chapter 4 for a description of the nonparametric tests of statistical significance that parallel these *t* tests.

The analysis of variance (ANOVA) is used to compare the means of three or more sets of scores to determine whether the difference between them is statistically significant. Recall that the ANOVA does not pinpoint which of the differences is statistically significant. Thus, the ANOVA is an initial step in the analysis of data from a causal-comparative study designed to compare the means for three or more sets of scores. Researchers use multiple-comparison procedures such as the Newman–Keuls, Tukey, and Scheffe to pinpoint which pairs of means differ from one another. See Chapter 4 for a description of the nonparametric test of statistical significance that parallels the ANOVA.

Internal Validity. Although some of the threats to internal validity discussed in Chapter 2 typically do not directly apply to causal-comparative research (e.g., maturation, testing, resentful demoralization of the control group, diffusion of treatment, compensatory rivalry by the control group, compensatory equalization; see Table 6.1), researchers should look closely at the design of causal-comparative research studies to assess the potential threats to internal validity.

TABLE 6.1 Threats to the Internal Validity of the Causal-Comparative Design

THREAT	RESEARCH DESIGN CAUSAL-COMPARATIVE
1. Maturation	Not applicable
2. Selection	Concern
3. Selection by maturation interaction	Not applicable
4. Statistical regression	Not applicable
5. Mortality	Not applicable
6. Instrumentation	Not applicable
7. Testing	Not applicable
8. History	Not applicable
9. Resentful demoralization of the control group	Not applicable
10. Diffusion of treatment	Not applicable
11. Compensatory rivalry by the control group	Not applicable
12. Compensatory equalization	Not applicable

Note: This table is meant only as a general guideline. Decisions with regard to threats to internal validity must be made after the specifics of an investigation are known and understood. Thus, interpretations of internal validity threats must be made on a study-by-study basis.

There are three critical issues to consider not only in designing causal-comparative research but also in analyzing and evaluating such research. First, like all research, researchers should rely heavily on theory and previous research. The basis for exploring possible causal relationships should not be based on speculation alone. Second, the selection of the experimental and comparison group should be done with a high degree of precision. This precision is necessary for meaningful interpretations of the findings. Table 6.1 indicates that selection is the major threat to the internal validity of a causal-comparative design. Third, as with all research, the data collection and analysis procedures must be appropriate for the given focus of the study because tests of statistical significance provide the framework for interpreting the findings. This is not to say that tests of statistical significance provide the complete story; rather, they are critical for determining whether, at some established probability level, the results were a function of chance factors alone.

It should be clear that interpretations of causal-comparative findings are limited because researchers do not know whether a particular variable (i.e., subject or organismic) is a cause or a result of the pattern of behavior being studied. For example, in a study on whether students with behavioral disorders (BD) understand the cause-and-effect relationship between social interactions and educational and life outcomes, we found that students with BD did not fully understand the outcomes of negative interpersonal social interactions. We did not know the types of interpersonal social interactions patterns that were present in both groups before any of the students developed BD. Thus, it is difficult to interpret the findings.

Questions such as the following would have to be addressed in additional studies to clarify the potential cause-and-effect relationships: Do students with more serious BD have a more limited understanding of the cause-and-effect relationship between social interactions and educational and life outcomes? Does the understanding of students with BD regarding the cause-and-effect relationship between social interactions and educational and life outcomes become more limited in the process of becoming BD? or Do other factors such as level of social development or intelligence result in a limited understanding of the cause-and-effect relationship between social interactions and educational and life outcomes?

Nevertheless, the causal-comparative method is useful for identifying possible causal relationships. These tentative relationships can be explored in subsequent experimental or longitudinal studies when possible. Additionally, replications of the study that confirm the causal relationship and disconfirm other potential causal relationships can also be used to increase confidence in the existence of a causal relationship in those cases in which it is impossible to conduct experimental studies.

External Validity. As with internal validity, some of the threats to external validity do not typically apply to causal-comparative research (e.g., interaction of personological variables and treatment effects, novelty and disruption effects, pretest sensitization). However, critical research consumers should look closely at the design of causal-comparative studies to assess threats to external validity (see Table 6.2). One of the primary threats to the external validity to consider is "generalization across participants." The procedure for selecting participants is one of the most important factors to consider. It is not uncommon for researchers to use convenience sampling techniques (i.e., readily available participants) rather than random selection procedures. If this is the case, the results of the study arc unlikely to generalize across participants.

Additional threats to the external validity of causal-comparative studies to examine closely are those associated with the dependent measure and experimenter effects. For example, the "measurement of the dependent variable" is a potential threat to the external validity of causal-comparative

TABLE 6.2 Threats to the External Validity of the Causal-Comparative Design

THREAT	RESEARCH DESIGN CAUSAL-COMPARATIVE
1. Generalization across participants	Possible concern
2. Interaction of personological variables and treatment effects	Not applicable
3. Verification of independent variable	Possible concern
4. Multiple treatment interference	Not applicable
5. Novelty and disruption effects	Not applicable
6. Hawthorne effect	Not applicable
7. Experimenter effects	Not applicable
8. Pretest sensitization	Not applicable
9. Posttest sensitization	Possible concern
10. Interaction of time of measurement and treatment effects	Possible concern
11. Measurement of the dependent variable	Possible concern
12. Interaction of history and treatment effects	Possible concern

Note: This table is meant only as a general guideline. Decisions with regard to threats to external validity must be made after the specifics of an investigation are known and understood. Thus, interpretations of external validity threats must be made on a study-by-study basis.

studies because indirect measurement techniques are typically used by the researchers. Thus, critical research consumers must look closely at the dependent variable to determine whether the results would generalize beyond the dependent measure used in the study.

Finally, an interesting threat may be the verification of the independent variable. Consider the example presented previously on whether students with BD understand the cause-and-effect relationship between social interactions and educational and life outcomes. In order to be part of the investigation, students had to have a BD (the independent variable of concern). Thus, we had to rely on the BD label; more importantly, we had to rely on the validity of the assessments which aided in the labeling of students as BD. If these assessments were not valid (i.e., students without BD were labeled or students with BD were not labeled), the validity of our independent variable would be in question. It is critical to consider the methods used in categorizing participants on a subject or organismic variable. Of course, on a variable such as gender, there would be little or no concern. With other variables, especially those that leave room for error in categorization, the verification of the independent variable is important.

Research Examples

Not Possible to Manipulate Independent Variable. An example of the causal-comparative method in which it was not possible to manipulate the experimental variable is research Nelson, Drummond, Martella, and Marchand-Martella (1997) conducted with students with behavioral disorders. Nelson and colleagues were interested in exploring whether students with behavioral disorders understand the implications of different types of social interactions between adults and peers because of the bleak educational and life outcomes of such students. Specifically, Nelson and colleagues wanted to explore the hypothesis that behavior disorders, at least in part, are a function of the inability of such children to understand the cause-and-effect relationship between the social interactions they have with adults and peers and their educational and life outcomes.

To explore this hypothesis, a group of students with BD was located and had their responses compared in a structured Piagetian-type interview (i.e., students responded to specific scenarios depicting positive and negative social interactions with teachers and peers) with that of similar students without behavioral disorders. A comparative analysis of 60 students with BD and 60 students without BD across two types of interpersonal social interactions (i.e., positive and negative) and two types of social agents (i.e., teacher and peer) was conducted. There were generally no statistically significant differences in the views of students with and without BD regarding the educational and life consequences of positive social interactions. However, there were significant differences in the views of students with and without BD regarding the educational and life outcomes of negative interpersonal social interactions. This finding provided evidence, albeit limited, that suggested that students with behavior disorders do not fully understand the cause-and-effect relationships between social interactions and educational and life outcomes.

The causal-comparative method was used instead of an experimental method because the causal relationship that we wanted to explore did not permit experimental manipulation. For example, an experiment to explore the hypothesis in the preceeding example would require the random selection of two groups of students. The environment of one group of these students (experimental group) would be manipulated to induce behavioral disorders. The environment of the other group (the control group) would be manipulated to minimize the occurrence of behavioral disorders. If the hypothesis is correct, students in the behavioral disordered group should have significantly lower scores on measures of cause-and-effect relationships between social interactions and educational and life outcomes.

Prohibitive to Assess Changes in a Variable Over Time. An example of the causal-comparative research method in which it would be prohibitive to assess changes in a variable over time is the research that Nicholls and Nelson (1992) conducted to explore children's understanding of knowledge. Sixty randomly selected students (20 students each in the first, third, and sixth grades) were interviewed about parallel domains of uncontested and contested knowledge, all of which might be a part of school lessons on the topic of space. The uncontested domains of knowledge included an intellectual convention (the use of the term "shuttle" to refer to reusable space vessels), an uncontested question of morality (one should warn the astronauts of a fatal flaw with the shuttle), and an uncontested question of empirical law (the shuttle needs some type of engine to leave the ground). Paralleling the latter two matters, the contested domains of knowledge included a contested question of morality (spending priorities on space or health care) and a contested question of empirical law (whether there is sentient life in space). Children, regardless of age, were found to make adult-like distinctions between uncontested and contested knowledge and among these different types of knowledge. Thus, there were no developmental changes in students' conceptions of knowledge.

The causal-comparative method was used because it would have been prohibitive to explore the causal relationship (developmental changes) that was of interest using a longitudinal method. For example, a longitudinal study to explore the hypothesis in the preceeding example would require the random selection of one group of young students. This group of students would then be followed over 6 years with periodic assessments of their understanding of knowledge. This follow-up would require a great deal of effort to maintain contact with the same individuals and would no doubt result in a problem with the attrition of a large number of participants.

WHEN SHOULD RESEARCHERS USE THE CAUSAL-COMPARATIVE RESEARCH DESIGN?

Causal-comparative research is used to explore potential causal relationships between two or more variables. The causal-comparative research method is used under two primary conditions. The first condition is when it is not possible to manipulate the variables experimentally such as presenting or taking away behavior disorders or mental illnesses. The second condition is when it would be prohibitive to assess changes in a variable such as when there are ethical concerns as with requiring a group to smoke when there are not enough resources to conduct a study over time using a longitudinal research. Much work in developmental psychology is based on the causal-comparative research method in which the goal is to explore developmental changes over time.

Despite the intent of causal-comparative research to establish causal relationships between or among variables, such interpretations must be made with caution. Causal interpretations of causal-comparative findings are limited for two reasons. First, it is never totally clear whether a particular variable is a cause or a result of the pattern of behavior being studied or the result of some other variable. Second, the logic of statistical significance testing never results in a definitive causal statement; there is always a chance of making a Type I error. Nevertheless, the causal-comparative research is useful for identifying possible causal relationships. These tentative relationships can be explored in subsequent experimental or longitudinal studies when possible. Additionally, replications of a study that confirm the causal relationship and disconfirm other potential causal relationships can also be used to increase our confidence in the findings when it is not possible to conduct experimental studies. Our acceptance of the link between smoking and lung cancer is a case in point.

DISCUSSION QUESTIONS

1. A colleague stated that she heard that some research conducted in education and psychology is called causal-comparative research. She asks you what causal-comparative research is (i.e., how is it done). What would you say?

2. She says that since the name of the research is causal-comparative, it must mean that these are the best designs in determining cause-and-effect relationships. Is she correct? Why or why not? (*Note:* In your response, indicate what the internal validity threats are to the causal-comparative research method.)

3. Since, according to the colleague, the name of causal-comparative research implies an ability to determine cause-and-effect relationships, are these designs similar to true experimental designs? If so/not, how?

4. After you explain to your colleague what the causal-comparative design is, she asks you when it is appropriate to use it. What would you say?

5. In your answer to Question 4, explain some of the critical issues researchers should consider when they design causal-comparative research studies.

6. You find that one interesting aspect of the causal-comparative design is that the threats to internal validity that result in changes in the performance of the control group are not applicable to causal-comparative research studies. Why would this be so?

7. If a researcher used a causal-comparative design in a study you were reading, what would you look for if you were concerned with the external validity of the results?

8. Another student just finished studying quasi-experimental designs. He is now beginning a unit on the causal-comparative research method. He asks you what the differences are

between the two types of research methods. What would you say?

9. If it were possible to use an experimental design to study the subject matter studied in a causal-comparative design, what factors would have to be in place before such a study could progress (i.e., what would you have to do to the independent variable)?

10. You are talking to a student conducting a causal-comparative research study. The student indicates that she is not sure what type of statistic to use to interpret her results. What kinds of factors should the student researcher consider when selecting statistical analysis procedures to analyze data from a causal-comparative research study?

THE CURRENT AND FUTURE OUTCOMES OF INTERPERSONAL SOCIAL INTERACTIONS: THE VIEWS OF STUDENTS WITH BEHAVIORAL DISORDERS

J. RON NELSON
Arizona State University

MARCY DRUMMOND
RON MARTELLA
NANCY MARCHAND-MARTELLA
Eastern Washington University

Abstract: We examined the views of students with behavioral disorders (BD) regarding the current and future outcomes of interpersonal social interactions. A comparative analysis of 60 students with BD and 60 students without BD across positive and negative interpersonal problems with teachers and peers was conducted. In general, there were no significant differences in the views of students with and without BD regarding the current and future outcomes of positive interpersonal social interactions. However, there were significant differences in the views of students with and without BD regarding the current and future outcomes of negative interpersonal social interactions. Students with BD were more likely to support the proposition that students who have negative interpersonal social interactions would experience less negative future outcomes than were students without BD. Research needs are discussed.

The social world of students with behavioral disorders (BD) is distinguished by interpersonal problems (Coleman, 1992; Kauffman, 1997; Steinberg & Knitzer, 1992). Individuals with interpersonal problems generally experience difficulty in life including diminished motivation (Berston, 1960; Elliot & Voss, 1974; Liddle, 1962; Sando, 1952; Snepp, 1953), academic performance difficulties (Elliot & Voss, 1974), and social maladjustment (Asher, Oden, & Gottman, 1977; French, 1988; Ladd, 1983). Additionally, much literature points to the stability of interpersonal problems across settings (Loeber & Dishion, 1984; Mitchell & Rosa, 1981; Patterson, 1979, 1982; Wright, 1983) and from early childhood (approximately age 8) to late adolescence and adulthood (e.g., Blumstein, Cohen, Roth, & Visher, 1986; Farrington, 1983).

Although research on the interpersonal problems of children has yielded important information on the cognitive, social, and vocational outcomes of individuals with interpersonal problems, researchers have not fully explored students' understanding or views of the current and future outcomes of interpersonal social interactions. This information is important because an understanding of the outcomes of interpersonal problems plays a fundamental part of the extent to which individuals can understand themselves and their environment. Such research could yield important practical information with which to develop interventions for students with BD. For example, a number of scholars have discussed the importance of insight-oriented interventions to help students understand themselves and their environment (Jones, 1992). A better understanding of the extent to which students with BD recognize the outcomes or consequences of interpersonal social interactions could provide teachers and other professionals information with which to develop or refine insight-oriented interventions and to expand or refine social skills curricula approaches for students with BD.

Reviewing studies of children's social reasoning (e.g., Nicholls & Nelson, 1992; Nucci, 1981; Turiel, 1974) is informative. A number of studies have demonstrated that children make distinctions between concepts of morality and social conventions (Much & Shweder, 1978; Nucci & Nucci, 1982; Nucci & Turiel, 1978; Nucci, Turiel, & Encarnacion-Gawrych, 1983; Turiel, 1983). Moral concepts pertain to issues of welfare, justice, and rights (e.g., equitable distribution of resources), whereas social conventions are socially acceptable behaviors that regulate social interactions (e.g., modes of greeting). Children judge actions within the moral domain to be independent of existing rules (e.g., stealing would be wrong even if a rule prohibiting stealing did not exist). Conversely, children judge actions within the social convention domain to be contingent on rules (e.g., wearing a uniform to school should depend on a specific school rule) (Nucci, 1981; Nucci & Turiel, 1978; Turiel, 1974; Weston & Turiel, 1980). These distinctions parallel those made by adults on such matters (Nicholls & Nelson, 1992).

Researchers have begun to explore the relationship of self-understanding and mental health problems such as anorexia nervosa and conduct disorders (Damon & Hart, 1988). Self-understanding encompasses the full array of thoughts and attitudes that an individual uses to define the self and distinguish the self from others (Damon & Hart, 1988). Dependent upon the individual, these thoughts and attitudes may be affected by the student's physical characteristics (e.g., size) and material possessions, daily activities and capabilities (e.g., interests, academic competence), and social or psychological characteristics (e.g., interpersonal skills, disposition, and philosophical beliefs, moral values).

In 1986 Melcher explored the relationship between self-understanding and conduct disorders. In addition to developmentally immature conceptions of self as connected to social context, Melcher found that the children with conduct disorders had significantly lower developmental scores on questions concerning self over time (e.g., what the self was like in the past, what the self will be like in the future, and what one hopes the self will be like in the future). Children with conduct disorders gave little thought to the future, and when they did project the self into the future, they did so with little concern for the integration of the self into the surrounding social context. That is, children with conduct disorders did not appear to consider characteristics about themselves that would have to change in order to better match a particular social context. These findings suggest that children with interpersonal problems may have difficulty developing a sense of personal identity that allows for future planning to guide current behavior.

Exploring self-understandings of the social relationships of students with BD is important because such students face daunting odds in achieving positive educational and positive long-range success. For instance, it is common knowledge that most students with BD function below their grade level and have histories of repeated failures; and, once on the special education track, less than 10% return to the general education environment (Kauffman, Cullinan, & Epstein, 1987). Currently, research also paints a bleak picture of postschool vocational and community adjustment for students with BD who exit inclusive school programs (Edgar & Levine, 1987; Wagner & Shaver, 1989). Unemployment of these students runs between 30% to 40%; if employed, the work secured is low paying and menial. Few students with BD enter any type of postsecondary training, and many are arrested at least once in the first 2 years following their exit from school.

Taken together, research on the educational and life outcomes of students with BD and on the relationship between self-understanding and conduct disorders suggests that students with BD may not fully understand how one's thoughts, attitudes, and actions affect their current and future lives. The purpose of this study was to examine the views of students with BD regarding the impact of positive and negative interpersonal social interactions on current and future life outcomes, specifically intrapersonal (i.e., motivation) and interpersonal (i.e., responsiveness to adults and peers) factors. A comparative analysis of the responses of students with BD and without BD was conducted, and gender and age comparisons were made as appropriate.

METHOD

Participants

Two samples of students enrolled in a medium-sized school district in Washington state participated. The first sample included 60 general education students (10 boys and 10 girls from the 3rd, 6th, and 8th grades) randomly selected from one elementary school (K–6th grades) and one middle school (7–9th grades). The mean ages of the 3rd-, 6th-, and 8th-grade students were 8.45 (*SD* = .60), 11.30 (*SD* = .47), and 13.45 (*SD* = .75), respectively.

The second sample consisted of 60 students (54 boys and 6 girls from the 3rd, 6th, and 8th grades) receiving special education services under the school-related eligibility criteria for BD. The students were enrolled in eight elementary schools and two middle schools with specialized services for students with BD. Because there were limited numbers of students formally identified as BD, the sample essentially represented the entire population of such students. The mean ages of the 3rd-, 6th-, and 8th-grade students were 9.05 (*SD* = .91), 11.74 (*SD* = .88), and 14.02 (*SD* = .95), respectively. There were no statistically significant differences in the ages of the students in the first and second samples.

Interview

The interview protocol was developed by the first and second authors. The protocol was pilot tested with three students at the 3rd- and 6th-grade levels (not included in the present study) to ensure that students could distinguish the critical attributes of the interpersonal social interaction vignettes and answer the outcome questions. The students were able to make the required distinctions, and no adjustments were needed in the interview protocol.

Vignettes. Vignettes were used to introduce the four types of interpersonal social interactions to students. The vignettes consisted of black and white pictures depicting a particular type of interpersonal social interaction along with an associated description. The vignettes depicted two primary types of interpersonal social interactions (i.e., positive and negative), each of which contained two social agents (i.e., teacher and peer).

Thus, students were introduced to four possible types of interpersonal social dyads.

Pictorial cues for the vignettes of the positive and negative interpersonal social interactions were held constant to help students focus on the specific interpersonal social interaction being depicted rather than other factors (e.g., gender of the target student). Photographs for each of the vignettes used the same classroom with the picture taken at the same angle. The same classmates (i.e., four boys and four girls) were involved in the four examples of social interactions, two positive and two negative. Thus, there were two sets of two pictures. One set showed the same boy (i.e., target student) having either a positive or negative social interaction with the same teacher or peer. The other set showed the same girl (i.e., target student) having either a positive or negative social interaction with the same teacher or peer.

Negative interpersonal social interactions portrayed a teacher (or peer) and target student facing each other. The teacher displayed anger (i.e., mouth was open and finger was pointing at the target student), and the target student displayed anger (i.e., mouth open and hands downward with fists clenched). Both individuals were standing next to a group of four other students who did not display any emotion (i.e., two focused on a open book on their desktops, and two looked at the teacher or peer and the student).

The pictures depicting the positive interpersonal social interactions portrayed the teacher (or peer) kneeling down next to the target student with both individuals focused on an open book on the student's desk. The teacher (or peer) and target student were part of a group that included four other students (all were focused on open books on their desktops).

Interview sequence. All of the students were interviewed individually by the first and second authors. The interviews lasted approximately twenty minutes and were scripted to ensure consistency in the presentation of the interview. Interviewers began by introducing themselves, describing the general purpose of the study (i.e., "We are interested in finding out what students think would happen to the students who get along with their teachers and friends, and those who do not..."), and asking students their grade and age (i.e., interviewers simply noted the gender of the student). Students were told that there were no right or wrong answers, that the purpose of the interview was to understand what students think. Next, the meaning of each of the five Likert responses was discussed (e.g., ? means that you are not really sure of what you think or you do not agree or disagree with the question). The Likert response format is described following the interview sequence description.

The interview proceeded as follows:

> *Here are pictures of four students who get along differently with their teachers and other students in the classroom. We want to find out what you think will happen to these students in school and later in life.*
>
> *All of these students are in the same classroom and have the same teacher (in the case of elementary-aged students) or teachers (in the case of middle school–aged students). But these students get along very differently with their teacher(s) and other students in the classroom.*

The order of the following four paragraphs and associated pictures were presented randomly to control for order effects.

Vignette 1. This student works well with his or her teacher. He or she listens to the teacher, follows the teacher's directions, and works well with the teacher in the classroom. See how the teacher and student are working together.

Vignette 2. This student does *not* work well with his or her teacher. He or she does *not* listen to the teacher, does not follow the teacher's directions, and does *not* work well with the teacher in the classroom.

Vignette 3. This student gets along well with other students in the classroom. He/She plays well with the other students, says nice things to the other students, and works well with the other students in the classroom.

Vignette 4. This student does *not* get along well with other students in the classroom. He or she does *not* play well with the other students in the classroom, does *not* say nice things to the other students, and does *not* work well with other students in the classroom.

Next, the interviewer asked the students to explain what they saw as the main differences among the four types of interpersonal social interactions as they were presented. All recapitulated the main differences that had been outlined on a picture-by-picture basis.

After this, the interviewer verbally described one of the four types of interpersonal social interactions. The order was randomized. The participant was asked to think about the student described as the background information was presented a second time, and to think about what that student might be like. The participant was asked each of the eight questions related to the current outcomes and each of the eight questions focusing on the future outcomes of the four interactions (see Table 1). The eight parallel current and future outcomes questions included three areas:

1. Motivation.
2. Interpersonal adjustment with the teacher or boss.
3. Interpersonal adjustment with classmates or co-workers.

The question order was counterbalanced across these three areas.

Students indicated the extent to which they agreed or disagreed with each of the questions on a 5-point Likert-type scale (i.e., (1) big **NO,** indicating strong disagreement; (2) little **no,** indicating disagreement; (3) **?,** indicating uncertainty; (4) little **yes,** indicating agreement; and (5) big **YES,** indicating strong agreement). Students indicated their response by pointing to the response on the scale or by replying (e.g., 'big yes"). This format enabled us to interview both elementary and middle school students and is a response format commonly used in developmental psychology (e.g., Nelson, Nicholls, & Gleaves, 1996; Nicholls & Nelson, 1992).

TABLE 1 Parallel Questions for Current and Future Outcomes

CURRENT OUTCOMES

Would he or she be the sort of student who would:

Motivation

1. ...get good grades in school?
2. ...get their school work done on time?
3. ...try hard to understand school things?

Interpersonal Adjustment: Authority Figures

4. ...get along with their teachers?
5. ...do everything their teacher says to do?

Interpersonal Adjustment: Peers

6. ...help their classmates to understand things in school?
7. ...have a lot of friends at school?
8. ...help other students with their school work?

FUTURE OUTCOMES

Would he or she grow up to be the kind of person who would:

Motivation

1. ...get awards for doing their job well?
2. ...get their work done on time?
3. ...try hard to understand work things?

Interpersonal Adjustment: Authority Figures

4. ...do everything their boss says to do?
5. ...get along with their boss?

Interpersonal Adjustment: Peers

6. ...help others to understand things at work?
7. ...have a lot of friends at work?
8. ...help others do their work?

RESULTS

The number of female students with BD was not large enough to analyze gender effects by group. However, mean responses of male and female students (without BD) to each question were analyzed using two-tailed *t* tests. There were no statistically significant differences in the mean responses of the boys and girls (e.g., Question 1: $t(59) = 1.32, p > .05$). Thus, gender was dropped from further analysis.

To examine the views of students with and without BD regarding the current and future outcomes of interpersonal social interactions, responses to each question under the positive and negative interpersonal social interactions were analyzed with an analysis of variance (ANOVA) by student type (students without BD, students with BD), by grade (3, 6, and 8), and by social agent (teacher, classmates), with the last factor being a within-subject factor. Additionally, to determine whether students were significantly resolute, rather than indecisive or neutral about the outcomes of the positive and negative interactions, the 95% confidence interval for each mean was computed to determine whether it encompassed the midpoint of the scale. Those means in which the midpoint of the response deviated from the 95% confidence interval are underlined in Tables 2 and 3.

Positive Interpersonal Social interactions

No significant main or interaction effects were obtained. Table 2 presents the mean responses for each question for positive interpersonal social interactions and associated *F* values for the main and interaction effects. Inspection of Table 2 reveals that both students without BD and those with BD tended to believe that students who had positive social interactions with their teacher and classmates would experience positive *current* and *future* outcomes on all dimensions. Specifically, they were inclined to believe that students who had positive interactions with teachers and classmates would be motivated at school or work, be responsive to their teacher or boss, and get along well with their classmates or colleagues. The lack of statistically significant main and interaction effects indicates that students' beliefs did not differ significantly across the grades and type of social agent or between students with BD and those without BD.

Negative Interpersonal Social Interactions

There were significant main effects for student type and social agent for two questions (i.e., get along with teachers and do everything the teacher says) under the *current* outcomes of negative interpersonal social interactions. There were also significant main effects for student type for each of the eight questions under the *future* outcomes of negative interpersonal social interactions. There were no other significant main effects or interaction effects. Table 3 presents the mean responses for each question for negative interpersonal social interactions and associated *F* values for the main effects.

In the case of the *current* outcomes of negative interpersonal social interactions, students without BD and those with BD generally believed that students who had negative social interactions with their teacher and classmates would experience negative outcomes on all dimensions (see Table 3). The significant main effects for student type indicate that students with BD were more likely than their general education peers to have the opinion that students who have negative interpersonal interactions would "get along with their teacher" and "do everything their teacher says." The significant main effects for social agent indicate that both students with and without BD were more likely to believe that students would "get along with their teacher" and "do everything their teacher says" in the vignettes of negative interpersonal social interactions with *peers* than when there were negative interactions with the teacher.

In the case of the *future* outcomes of negative social interactions, students without BD generally believed that students who had negative social interactions with their teacher and classmates would experience negative future outcomes (see Table 3). In contrast, students with BD generally believed that students who had negative interactions with the teacher and their classmates would experience positive future outcomes. The significant main

TABLE 2 Mean Response to Questions for Positive Social Interactions

ITEM[2]	TEACHER WOBD[1] MEAN (SD)	TEACHER WBD MEAN (SD)	STUDENT WOBD MEAN (SD)	STUDENT WBD MEAN (SD)	F VALUES: STUDENT TYPE (A)	F VALUES: GRADE (B)	F VALUES: SOCIAL AGENT (C)	A × B	A × C	B × C
Current Outcomes										
1. Get good grades.	4.55[3] (0.65)	4.53 (0.60)	4.48 (0.79)	4.61 (0.81)	1.95	2.13	1.40	2.56	1.31	2.10
2. Do schoolwork on time.	4.13 (0.98)	4.41 (0.71)	4.53 (0.77)	4.29 (1.08)	1.08	2.37	1.41	2.79	1.40	2.12
3. Try hard.	4.32 (1.02)	4.41 (1.02)	4.63 (0.61)	4.49 (0.94)	1.67	1.40	1.72	1.38	1.29	0.48
4. Get along with teachers.	4.62 (0.60)	4.61 (0.72)	4.73 (0.55)	4.85 (0.52)	1.94	1.41	2.37	2.13	1.95	2.01
5. Do what teacher says.	4.02 (1.05)	4.10 (1.05)	4.27 (0.70)	4.32 (0.94)	1.11	1.08	2.51	2.48	1.40	1.55
6. Help classmates understand.	4.75 (0.57)	4.80 (0.41)	4.58 (0.72)	4.41 (0.76)	1.40	2.12	3.08	0.41	0.73	1.11
7. Have friends.	4.72 (0.58)	4.64 (0.64)	4.48 (0.71)	4.42 (0.83)	1.13	1.56	3.04	1.61	1.24	0.44
8. Help other students.	4.42 (0.96)	4.46 (0.75)	4.38 (0.94)	4.27 (1.00)	1.57	2.91	1.01	1.08	0.86	1.44
Future Outcomes										
1. Get awards.	4.40 (0.81)	4.53 (0.75)	4.23 (1.11)	4.41 (1.00)	1.23	1.34	3.36	2.66	1.78	2.77
2. Get work done on time.	4.62 (0.64)	4.61 (0.81)	4.63 (0.58)	4.31 (0.88)	2.53	1.03	1.32	1.56	2.14	1.44
3. Try hard to understand.	4.37 (0.84)	4.85 (0.52)	4.57 (0.74)	4.38 (0.91)	3.52	1.88	2.74	2.34	1.13	2.02
4. Get along with boss.	4.40 (0.81)	4.20 (1.03)	4.30 (0.93)	4.39 (0.85)	1.01	1.36	1.08	0.22	1.23	0.56
5. Do what boss says.	4.52 (0.70)	4.47 (0.70)	4.52 (0.79)	4.31 (1.09)	1.12	1.85	1.15	1.45	1.68	1.91
6. Have friends at work.	4.48 (0.79)	4.12 (1.12)	4.37 (0.82)	4.49 (0.75)	1.18	2.23	1.37	1.01	1.72	0.97
7. Help others with work.	4.53 (0.72)	4.41 (0.87)	4.55 (0.77)	4.58 (0.56)	1.45	2.96	1.23	1.49	1.09	0.18
8. Help others understand.	4.53 (0.72)	4.34 (0.98)	4.47 (0.75)	4.46 (0.88)	1.04	1.25	1.00	1.59	1.31	1.81

[1]WOBD = without behavioral disorders; WBD = with behavioral disorders.
[2]Questions are abbreviated. See table 1 for complete presentation of questions.
[3]Underlined means differ significantly ($p < .05$) from the midpoint of the scale.

TABLE 3 Mean Response to Questions for Negative Social Interactions

ITEM[2]	TEACHER WOBD[1] MEAN (SD)	TEACHER WBD MEAN (SD)	STUDENT WOBD MEAN (SD)	STUDENT WBD MEAN (SD)	F VALUES STUDENT TYPE (A)	F VALUES GRADE (B)	F VALUES SOCIAL AGENT (C)	A × B	A × C	B × C
Current Outcomes										
1. Get good grades.	1.93[3] (1.21)	1.87 (1.23)	1.95 (1.03)	1.63 (0.76)	3.01	1.39	3.43	2.20	2.71	1.99
2. Do schoolwork on time.	1.98 (1.30)	1.88 (1.14)	2.05 (1.17)	1.91 (0.84)	1.75	2.64	1.94	0.78	1.43	1.05
3. Try hard.	2.03 (1.25)	2.07 (1.24)	2.17 (1.28)	1.91 (1.03)	2.03	1.30	3.12	1.99	2.34	2.10
4. Get along with teachers.	2.03 (1.77)	2.67 (1.22)	1.77 (1.06)	1.44 (0.95)	9.87**	1.31	9.84**	3.12	2.78	3.01
5. Do what teacher says.	2.02 (1.04)	2.80 (1.41)	1.88 (1.04)	2.96 (0.74)	11.15**	2.30	7.29**	3.43	2.99	3.22
6. Help classmates understand.	1.88 (1.06)	1.53 (0.95)	1.80 (0.93)	1.72 (0.86)	2.96	1.67	3.51	1.40	1.67	1.63
7. Have friends.	1.77 (1.33)	1.71 (1.23)	1.67 (1.21)	1.83 (1.01)	2.63	2.05	1.38	1.82	2.06	1.02
8. Help other students.	1.90 (1.29)	1.52 (1.06)	1.78 (1.06)	1.53 (0.82)	2.20	2.55	1.17	1.23	1.24	1.66
Future Outcomes										
1. Get awards.	2.55 (1.32)	3.57 (1.68)	2.45 (1.40)	3.42 (1.43)	18.17***	1.97	1.95	2.27	1.87	2.34
2. Get work done on time.	3.12 (1.37)	3.48 (1.51)	2.75 (1.34)	3.59 (1.11)	14.30***	3.16	1.98	2.79	2.35	2.22
3. Try hard to understand.	2.70 (1.39)	3.47 (1.44)	2.28 (1.28)	3.42 (1.46)	27.79***	2.22	2.05	3.02	2.94	1.89
4. Get along with boss.	2.60 (1.33)	3.50 (1.53)	2.43 (1.24)	3.44 (1.23)	30.58***	2.30	1.26	2.23	1.37	1.92
5. Do what boss says.	2.77 (1.36)	3.57 (1.38)	2.67 (1.27)	3.49 (1.09)	20.58***	2.21	1.06	2.10	1.85	2.56
6. Have friends at work.	2.77 (1.33)	3.50 (1.43)	2.35 (1.27)	3.37 (1.34)	25.55	1.17	2.85	1.23	2.06	1.48
7. Help others with work.	2.80 (1.31)	3.57 (1.27)	2.48 (1.19)	3.47 (1.21)	19.48***	1.89	1.20	2.53	1.54	2.03
8. Help others understand.	2.47 (1.27)	3.48 (1.68)	2.43 (1.27)	3.08 (1.26)	4.31*	2.10	2.98	2.03	1.77	2.51

[1]WOBD = without behavioral disorders; WBD = with behavioral disorders.
[2]Questions are abbreviated. See table 1 for complete presentation of questions.
[3]Underlined means differ significantly ($p < .05$) from the midpoint of the scale.
$^{*}p < .05$; $^{**}p < .01$; $^{***}p < .001$

effects found for student type on all eight questions indicate that students with BD supported the proposition that even though students had negative interpersonal interactions with teachers and classmates they would be motivated at work, be responsive to their boss, and get along well with their colleagues.

DISCUSSION

Little or no research has examined the extent to which students with BD are aware of the interpersonal outcomes of positive and/or negative social interactions. This awareness, at least in part, would appear to be fundamental to an individual's self-understanding (Damon & Hart, 1988) and possibly predictive of the effectiveness with which students handle social exchanges. In the present study, examples of positive and negative social interactions with teachers and peers, all of which might occur in a classroom context, were used to gain the viewpoints of students with and without BD regarding potential current and future outcomes as related to motivation and interpersonal adjustment with authority figures and peers.

In general, both students with and without BD believed that positive interpersonal social interaction would result in positive outcomes and that negative interpersonal interactions would result in negative outcomes. Students also tended to be aware that interpersonal interactions would have an effect on motivation and interaction with authority figures and peers. For example, students with and without BD tended to believe that students who have positive interpersonal social interactions with teachers and peers would not experience motivation problems in school or work. There also tended to be no differences in the responses of children with BD and those without BD regarding the type of social agent (i.e., teacher or peer) who was interacting and future outcomes. The ability of students with and without BD to predict the outcomes of positive and negative current interpersonal interactions is consistent with previous research that has found that children make adult-like distinctions regarding moral and social matters (Much & Shweder, 1978; Nucci & Nucci, 1982; Nucci & Turiel, 1978; Nucci, Turiel, & Encarnacion-Gawrych, 1983; Turiel, 1983). Thus, it appears that as a group students with BD are able to distinguish moral and social issues.

Students with and without BD also tended to recognize that positive interpersonal social interactions are relatively stable phenomena across ages. For example, both student groups believed that students who had positive interpersonal interactions would be motivated and have few interpersonal problems with current (teacher) or future (boss) authority figures.

Consistent with studies on other populations, students with and without BD generally regarded the outcomes of negative social interactions to be associated with individuals who have interpersonal problems. That is, these individuals tend to experience difficulty in life including diminished motivation (Berston, 1960; Elliot & Voss, 1974; Liddle, 1962; Sando, 1952; Snepp, 1953), academic performance difficulties (Elliot & Voss, 1974), and social maladjustment (Asher, Oden, & Gottman, 1977; French, 1988; Ladd, 1983).

Students with and without BD differed little regarding their perceptions of the current outcomes of negative interpersonal social interactions. However, students with BD were more likely to believe that students who had negative social interactions would experience interpersonal adjustment problems with authority figures (teachers). Students with and without BD tended to believe that negative interpersonal interactions with teachers would result in greater problems with teachers than if the student had negative interactions with peers. Additionally, both groups tended to believe that students who have negative interpersonal social interactions with their peers would experience motivation and interpersonal adjustment problems. Taken together, the findings are consistent with those of Melcher (1986) who found that children with and without conduct disorders do not differ in their understanding of self in regard to the surrounding social context (i.e., authority figures and peers).

The awareness of students with BD regarding the *future* outcomes of negative interpersonal social interactions differed from their awareness of the current outcomes of such behavior. Students with BD tended to believe that negative interpersonal social interactions did not affect future intrapersonal problems (motivation) or interpersonal problems (boss and peers) negatively. In contrast, students without BD tended to see that negative interpersonal social interactions would lead to future experiences with motivation and interpersonal problems. The findings of the present study support previous research that found that children with conduct disorders tend to give little thought to the future, and when they do project the self into the future, they do so with little concern for the integration of the self appropriately into the surrounding social context (Melcher, 1986).

CONCLUSION

Self-understanding is both an individualistic and relational social concept. Self-understanding is individualistic in that it encompasses one's understanding of their physical and material qualities, interests and capabilities, social characteristics, and philosophical beliefs. Self-understanding is relational in that it encompasses the connections between one's understanding of oneself with those of others. The present study extended previous research on this latter aspect of self-understanding (Damon & Hart, 1988) by exploring the understanding of the views of children with and without BD in relation to the connection between social interactions and potential current as well as future outcomes.

Two general conclusions can be made regarding the results of this study. First, students with BD, on most accounts, do not differ from their peers without BD in their views of the outcomes of interpersonal problems. Students generally were able to discern potential positive and negative outcomes of different interpersonal interactions. This is consistent with the findings of research on social reasoning which has found that children generally make adult-like distinctions of the critical dimensions of social and intellectual matters (Nicholls & Nelson, 1992). Second, there appear to be clear differences in the views of students with and without BD regarding the future outcomes of interpersonal problems. This finding is consistent with those of Melcher (1986) who found that children with conduct disorders have significantly lower developmental scores on those questions concerning self over time.

The results of this study suggest that professionals working with students with BD should not only focus on the immediate outcomes of interpersonal problems, but also the long-term ones. This is because the results of this study suggest that students with BD make relatively accurate assessments of the potential positive and negative outcomes of different interpersonal interactions. However, students with BD tend to underestimate the outcomes of *negative* interpersonal interactions. Researchers should attempt to determine why there are differences in students' views of interpersonal problems. The environmental determinants associated with the different views are especially critical. If these determinants could be isolated, interventions could be designed at an early age in order to prevent behavioral patterns associated with BD. For example, because students with BD were able to discriminate between positive and negative social interactions, it would follow that they could be taught to make other discriminations such as how negative social interactions affect the ability to get along with their teacher. Of course, students with BD need to be taught directly how to discriminate which behaviors to use and not use under a variety of social and educational contexts. This is important because in many instances the problem for these students is not "knowing how to do X," but "doing X when it is required." Additionally, because the major difference between students with BD and those without BD is in regard to future outcomes, social skills programs should be designed to teach students with BD to predict future outcomes of negative interpersonal social interactions.

Researchers also might explore what type of curriculum approaches enhance the ability of children with BD to understand cause-and-effect relationships. For example, science curriculum aimed at exploring cause-and-effect relationships in the natural world might provide the basis for focused discussions of social relationships as experienced in future work environments. Additionally, lack of understanding vocational opportunities and expectations may account for the response of students with BD. Therefore, building career awareness of the activities and requisite skills necessary to achieve desired future employment may be a curricular issue that should be addressed early with students with BD.

There are several limitations to the present study. First, because the sample was restricted to a single school district, replication of the effects is needed. An additional confound is that the present sample met the school eligibility criteria of BD in Washington, yet these students may differ from those labeled as BD in other states. From our data, there is no basis for cause-and-effect statements to be made; thus we cannot say, for example, that differences in students' views of social interactions cause BD. However, the determining factors for the differences may be important for future researchers because preventative strategies could be implemented to address these factors. Finally, it may be that using different stimulus cues during the interviews would have led to different responses. For example, students' responses may have varied if the pictorial cues included larger numbers of students (e.g., 10 vs. 4) because the students may have viewed negative social interactions as less personal in nature. Additionally, no developmental trends were identified, yet such trends may be present. It would be interesting to determine if secondary students with BD, for instance, hold views similar to elementary students and/or their peers in general education.

REFERENCES

Asher, S. R., Oden, S. L., & Gottman, J. M. (1977). Children's friendship in school settings. In L. G. Katz (Ed.), *Current topics in early childhood education* (Vol. 1, pp. 32–61). Norwood, NJ: Ablex.

Berston, H. M. (1960). The school dropout problem. *The Clearing House, 35,* 207–210.

Blumstein, A., Cohen, J., Roth, J. A., & Visher, C. A. (Eds.). (1986). *Criminal careers and career criminals* (Vols. I and II). Washington, DC: National Academic Press.

Coleman, M. C. (1992). *Behavior disorders: Theory and practice.* Boston: Allyn & Bacon.

Damon, W., & Hart, D. (1988). *Self-understanding in childhood and adolescence.* New York: Cambridge University Press.

Edgar, E., & Levine, P. (1987). *Special education students in transition: Washington state data 1976–1986.* Seattle: University of Washington, Experimental Education Unit.

Elliot, D. S., & Voss, H. L. (1974). *Delinquency and dropout.* Lexington, MA: Lexington Books.

Farrington, D. P. (1983). Offending from 10 to 25 years of age. In K. T. Van Dusen & S. A. Mednick (Eds.), *Prospective studies of crime and delinquency* (pp. 17–37). Boston: Kluwer-Nijhoff.

French, D. C. (1988). Heterogeneity of peer-rejected boys: Aggressive and nonaggressive subtypes. *Child Development, 59,* 976–985.

Jones, V. (1992). Integrating behavioral and insight-oriented treatment in school based programs for seriously emotionally disturbed students. *Behavioral Disorders, 17,* 225–236.

Kauffman, J. M. (1997). *Characteristics of emotional and behavioral disorders of children and youth* (6th ed.). New York: Merrill.

Kauffman, J. M., Cullinan, D., & Epstein, M. H. (1987). Characteristics of students placed in special programs for the seriously emotionally disturbed. *Behavioral Disorders, 12,* 175–184.

Ladd, G. (1983). Social networks of popular, average, and rejected children in school settings. *Merrill-Palmer Quarterly, 29,* 282–307.

Liddle, G. P. (1962). Psychological factors involved in dropping out of school. *High School Journal, 45,* 276–280.

Loeber, R., & Dishion, T. J. (1984). Boys who fight at home and school: Family conditions influencing cross-setting consistency. *Journal of Consulting and Clinical Psychology, 52,* 759–768.

Melcher, B. (1986). Moral reasoning, self-identity, and moral action: A study of conduct disorder in adolescence. Unpublished doctoral dissertation, University of Pittsburgh.

Mitchell, S., & Rosa, P. (1981). Boyhood behavior problems as precursors of criminality: A fifteen-year follow-up study. *Journal of Child Psychology and Psychiatry, 22,* 19–33.

Much, N. C., & Shweder, R. A. (1978). Speaking of rules: The analysis of culture in the breach. In W. Damon (Ed.), *New directions for child development. Moral development* (pp. 19–39). San Francisco: Jossey-Bass.

Nelson, J. R., Nicholls, J. G., & Gleaves, K. (1 996). The effect of personal philosophy on African-American students' orientation toward school: Integratism versus nationalist philosophies. *Journal of Black Psychology, 22,* 340–357.

Nicholls, J. G., & Nelson, J. R. (1992). Students' conceptions of controversial and noncontroversial knowledge. *Journal of Educational Psychology, 84,* 224–230.

Nucci, L. B. (1981). The development of personal concepts: A domain distinct from moral or societal concepts. *Child Development, 52,* 114–121.

Nucci, L. P., & Nucci, M. S. (1982). Children's social interactions in the context of moral and conventional transgressions. *Child Development, 53,* 403–412.

Nucci, L. P., & Turiel, E. (1978). Social interactions and the development of social concepts in preschool children. *Child Development, 49,* 400–407.

Nucci, L. P., Turiel, E., & Encarnacion-Gawrych, G. E. (1983). Children's social interactions and social concepts: Analyses of morality and convention in the Virgin islands. *Journal of Cross-Cultural Psychology, 14,* 469–487.

Patterson, G. R. (1979). A performance theory for coercive family interaction. In R. B. Cairns (Ed.), *The analysis of social interactions: Methods, issues, and illustrations* (pp. 119–162). Hillsdale, NJ: Erlbaum.

Patterson, G. R. (1982). *A social learning approach, Vol. 3: Coercive family process.* Eugene, OR: Castalia.

Sando, R. F. (1952). How to make and utilize follow-up studies of school leavers. *Bulletin of the National Association of Secondary School Principals, 36,* 67–75.

Snepp, D. W. (I 953). Why they drop out: 8 clues to greater holding power. *The Clearing House, 27,* 492–497.

Steinberg, Z., & Knitzer, J. (1992). Classrooms for emotionally and behaviorally disturbed students: Facing the challenge. *Behavioral Disorders, 17,* 145–156.

Turiel, E. (1974). Conflict and transition in adolescent moral development. *Child Development, 45,* 14–29.

Turiel, E. (1983). *The development of social knowledge: Morality and convention.* Cambridge, MA: Cambridge University Press.

Wagner, M., & Shaver, D. (1989). *Programs and achievements of secondary special education students: Findings from the National Longitudinal Transition Study.* Menlo Park, CA: SRI International.

Weston, D., & Turiel, E. (1980). Act-rule relations: Children's concepts of social rules. *Developmental Psychology, 16,* 417–424.

Wright, J. C. (1983). The structure and perception of behavioral consistency. Unpublished doctoral dissertation, Stanford University, California.

AUTHORS' NOTE

Preparation of this manuscript was supported in part by grants (#R305F6011 & #H237D20011) from the U.S. Department of Education. Opinions expressed do not necessarily reflect the position of the U.S. Department of Education, and no endorsement should be inferred. Request for copies of this manuscript should be addressed to Dr. J. Ron Nelson, Ph.D., Department of Applied Psychology, Eastern Washington University, Cheney, WA 99004.

AUTHORS

J. Ron Nelson, Arizona State University, Tempe. Marcy Drummond, Research Associate, Applied Psychology; Ron Martella, Assistant Professor, Applied Psychology; and Nancy Marchand-Martella, Assistant Professor, Applied Psychology, Eastern Washington University, Cheney.

FACTUAL QUESTIONS

1. What was the purpose of the study?
2. In what theoretical base was the study grounded?
3. Who were the participants?
4. What types of interpersonal social interactions did the authors use in the study?
5. Describe the characteristics of the two samples of participants.
6. How did the authors present the different social interactions to children?
7. What primary statistical analysis procedure was used to analyze participants' responses?
8. What factors were included in the analysis procedures?
9. According to the authors, what general conclusions can be made about the results?
10. What limitations did the authors discuss?

DISCUSSION QUESTIONS

1. Are there any problems with the population validity of the study? Why?
2. Why did the authors present the different types of social interactions in a randomized fashion?
3. Explain the importance of assessing whether the midpoint of the response scale lies beyond the 95% confidence interval.
4. Did authors' analysis of the participants' responses address the stated purpose of the study? Why?
5. Did the authors' base the study on a strong empirical and/or theoretical base?
6. What other factors might account for differences in the views of students with and without behavior disorders?
7. What other limitations to the study might the authors have discussed.
8. Why do you think there were no developmental trends?
9. What are some potential threats to the internal validity of the study? Provide a justification for each threat.
10. What are some potential treats to the external validity of this study? Provide a justification for each threat.

THREATS TO INTERNAL VALIDITY

Circle the number corresponding to the likelihood of each threat to internal validity being present in the investigation and provide a justification.

1 = definitely not a threat	2 = not a likely threat	3 = somewhat likely threat
4 = likely threat	5 = definite threat	NA = Not applicable for this design

Results in Differences Within or Between Individuals

1. **Maturation** **1 2 3 4 5 NA**

   Justification ______________________________

   ____

2. **Selection** **1 2 3 4 5 NA**

   Justification ______________________________

   ____

3. **Selection by Maturation Interaction** **1 2 3 4 5 NA**

   Justification ______________________________

   ____

4. **Statistical Regression** **1 2 3 4 5 NA**

   Justification ______________________________

   ____

5. **Mortality** **1 2 3 4 5 NA**

   Justification ______________________________

   ____

6. **Instrumentation** **1 2 3 4 5 NA**

   Justification ______________________________

   ____

7. Testing 1 2 3 4 5 NA

Justification ____

____

8. History 1 2 3 4 5 NA

Justification ____

____

9. Resentful Demoralization of the Control Group 1 2 3 4 5 NA

Justification ____

____

Results in Similarities Within or Between Individuals

10. Diffusion of Treatment 1 2 3 4 5 NA

Justification ____

____

11. Compensatory Rivalry by the Control Group 1 2 3 4 5 NA

Justification ____

____

12. Compensatory Equalization of Treatments 1 2 3 4 5 NA

Justification ____

____

Abstract: Write a one page abstract summarizing the overall conclusions of the authors and whether or not you feel the authors' conclusions are valid based on the internal validity of the investigation.

THREATS TO EXTERNAL VALIDITY

Circle the number corresponding to the likelihood of each threat to external validity being present in the investigation according to the following scale:

1 = definitely not a threat	2 = not a likely threat	3 = somewhat likely threat
4 = likely threat	5 = definite threat	NA = Not applicable for this design

Also, provide a justification for each rating.

Population

1. **Generalization Across Subjects** **1 2 3 4 5 NA**

   Justification ____________________

   ____

2. **Interaction of Personological Variables and Treatment** **1 2 3 4 5 NA**

   Justification ____________________

   ____

Ecological

3. **Verification of the Independent Variable** **1 2 3 4 5 NA**

   Justification ____________________

   ____

4. **Multiple Treatment Interference** **1 2 3 4 5 NA**

   Justification ____________________

   ____

5. **Hawthorne Effect** **1 2 3 4 5 NA**

   Justification ____________________

   ____

6. **Novelty and Disruption Effects** **1 2 3 4 5 NA**

   Justification ____________________

   ____

7. Experimenter Effects **1 2 3 4 5 NA**

Justification ____

____

8. Pretest Sensitization **1 2 3 4 5 NA**

Justification ____

____

9. Posttest Sensitization **1 2 3 4 5 NA**

Justification ____

____

10. Interaction of Time of Measurement and Treatment Effects **1 2 3 4 5 NA**

Justification ____

____

11. Measurement of the Dependent Variable **1 2 3 4 5 NA**

Justification ____

____

12. Interaction of History and Treatment Effects **1 2 3 4 5 NA**

Justification ____

____

Abstract: Write a one page abstract summarizing the overall conclusions of the authors and whether or not you feel the authors' conclusions are valid based on the external validity of the investigation.

CHAPTER 7

CORRELATIONAL RESEARCH

OBJECTIVES

After studying this chapter you should be able to:

1. Explain the purpose of correlational research.
2. Describe the differences and similarities between causal-comparative and correlational research methods.
3. Describe critical issues in designing correlational research.
4. Explain how to interpret correlational research.
5. Describe bivariate frequency distributions.
6. Explain the logic of statistical significance testing with correlation coefficients.
7. Explain how to interpret correlation coefficients.
8. Describe the relationship between the correlation coefficient and causality.
9. Describe the three conditions that researchers must meet to infer a causal relationship between two variables using the correlational research method.
10. Describe the correlational statistical procedure applicable for each level of measurement.
11. Describe advanced correlational statistical procedures and associated applications.
12. Explain how to interpret regression and path coefficients.
13. Describe when one would use a correlational design.
14. Critique a research article containing a correlational research design.

OVERVIEW

The controlled experiment achieves control through precise manipulation of the independent variable by isolating the experiment from extraneous influences via randomization of participants to treatments. The random assignment of participants to treatments helps to ensure that all extraneous influences are equal. The integrity of the controlled experiment lies in the simplicity of its causal model; that is, randomization increases the likelihood that the effects of the independent variable are a direct causal consequence of the independent variable and not due to other causes (e.g., socioeconomic status or gender residing in initial differences between groups). Despite the simplicity of the controlled experiment for establishing causality, practical considerations (e.g., randomly select participants from the target population, randomly assign participants to groups, and actively manipulate the independent variable) have limited its use. Because of these limitations, researchers employ research methods aimed at identifying the relationships among variables such as the causal-comparative and correlational research methods.

The correlational research method is closely related to the causal-comparative research method in that the primary goal is to explore relationships among variables. Causal-comparative and correlational research also attempt to explain the subject matter of interest and attempt to identify variables that can be tested through experimental research. Neither causal-comparative or correlational research methods allow for the manipulation of the independent variable as do experimental research methods. One major difference is that the causal-comparative research method takes into consideration scores from two groups of participants, and the correlational research method takes into consideration two or more sets of scores from each participant. Thus, the comparison is between groups of participants in causal-comparative research and between scores for each participant in correlational research.

This chapter begins with a general description of the correlational research method including the analysis of data. Research examples will be included in the chapter to help illustrate many of the concepts described. The chapter concludes with an illustrative example of how to interpret the findings of correlational research for critique.

WHAT IS THE CORRELATIONAL RESEARCH METHOD?

Correlational research involves collecting two sets of data and determining the extent to which they covary or vary together. The sets of data can be obtained from the same group at the same point in time or at two or more points in time. The sets of data also can be obtained from two or more groups. In essence, the correlational method is a particular way of collecting and analyzing data aimed at the discovery of relationships between or among variables and, depending on the data analysis procedures used, the causes for a pattern of behavior.

The correlational research method can be relational or predictive in nature. Correlational research that is relational in nature explores relationships between or among variables. Correlational research that is predictive in nature predicts scores on one or more variables from a participant's scores on one or more other variables. In prediction research, the variable(s) used for prediction must be measured prior to the measurement of the variable(s) to be predicted

WHAT ARE THE ISSUES IN DESIGNING A CORRELATIONAL STUDY?

As mentioned earlier, the correlational research method is commonly used by researchers because it can be used in areas in which it is implausible to conduct experimental studies and because it offers a number of advantages over other experimental research methods. There are a wide range of statistical procedures available to not only depict the degree of relationship among variables, but also to explore the causal relationships among variables. Exploring causality is important because many variables under study in education and psychology are influenced by other variables, making it difficult to have confidence in what produced the observed effects. True experimental methods tend to limit the number of relationships that can be studied in a given research study.

Types of Variables in Correlational Research

Before discussing some of the critical issues that researchers must consider in designing a correlational research study, we should consider the types of variables used in correlational research. In correlational research there are two primary types of variables: predictor variables and criterion variables. Predictor variables are ones in which participants' scores enable prediction of their scores on some criterion variable. A criterion variable is the object of the research, the variable about which researchers seek to discover more information. Because experimental research relies primarily on distinctions between independent and dependent variables, we will refer to predictor variables as independent variables and criterion variables as dependent variables throughout the remainder of this chapter.

Critical Issues in Correlational Research

The critical issues that researchers must consider in designing a relationship or prediction correlational study parallel those used to design a causal-comparative study. These issues are (a) development of a hypothesis, (b) selection of a homogeneous group, and (c) collection and analysis of data.

Development of a Hypothesis. The first critical issue centers on the development of a hypothesis about the causes or effects of the phenomenon under study. The basis for the study should be grounded on a theoretical framework and previous research. Researchers may explore a large number of variables in those areas in which there is no viable theoretical framework or previous research. However, such a shotgun approach must be used cautiously because variables can be related to one another even if the relationship is not meaningful. For example, there is a high positive correlation between shoe size and earned income. This relationship occurs because as people reach adulthood they are more likely to earn more money than children or adolescents. Although there is a high degree of relationship between shoe size and earned income, the relationship is not a particularly meaningful one.

In addition, when two or more variables are strongly related to one another, they may not reasonably discriminate between or among the variables under study. In correlational research, it is standard practice for researchers to explore the interrelationships among the variables under study initially to ensure that they reasonably discriminate the variables of interest. Again, if variables are highly related to one another, then the measurement devices may not adequately discriminate between or among the variables of interest. Furthermore, the use of a theoretical framework and previous research is critical to ensure that all variables thought to influence the variable(s) of interest can be considered in the research design. As will become clear with our description of the statistical procedures used in correlational research, there are a number of ways of studying the overall and relative influences between or among a wide range of variables.

Selection of a Homogeneous Group. The second critical issue when designing a correlational research study is to select a homogenous group that possesses the variables under study. As with a causal-comparative study, selecting a homogenous group requires a precise definition. For example, a precise definition of peer victimization, based on self-reports and direct observation, was used by Kochenderfer and Ladd (1996) to identify children who experienced peer victimization. A precise definition will not only help ensure that the group(s) under study possesses the variables or characteristics of interest but will also aid in the interpretation of the findings. If a heterogeneous group is selected, researchers may form homogenous subgroups that possess different levels of the characteristic. The formation of homogenous subgroups is common in correlational research studies.

Collection and Analysis of Data. The final issue focuses on the collection and analysis of the data. Researchers use a wide range of measurement devices in correlational research. Standardized measurement devices, criterion-referenced tests, surveys, questionnaires, interviews, and observations are all used by researchers in correlational research. Thus, critical research consumers must carefully consider the reliability and validity of the measurement devices being used. Furthermore, because there is a wide range of correlational statistical procedures devised for various purposes, it is critical that researchers employ the appropriate statistical procedures. Statistical procedures exist for describing the relationship between two or more nominal, ordinal, interval, or ratio variables. Many of the most commonly used statistical procedures in correlational research are described in this chapter. Figure 7.1 depicts the general steps in designing a correlational research study.

Analysis of Data

Figure 7.2 presents a flow chart for the statistical analyses of correlational research data. The reader is directed to the figure for additional clarity of when each statistic is used to analyze data.

Correlational Statistical Procedures. Correlational research generally seeks to determine the relationship between or among variables. This type of research is concerned with describing the magnitude of the relationship among variables or predicting one variable from another one. Determining magnitude or predicting one variable from another is accomplished through the use of a variety of statistical procedures. As with tests of statistical significance, the use of these procedures depends on a number of issues including the number of groups and variables being studied, the type of data, and the question(s) being asked. In this section, we describe the common statistical analysis procedures used in correlational research.

Bivariate Frequency Distributions. In Chapter 3, we briefly discussed the use and interpretation of correlation coefficients with regard to the reliability and validity of measurement devices. The correlation coefficient is important because it has many applications and is the basis for many of the

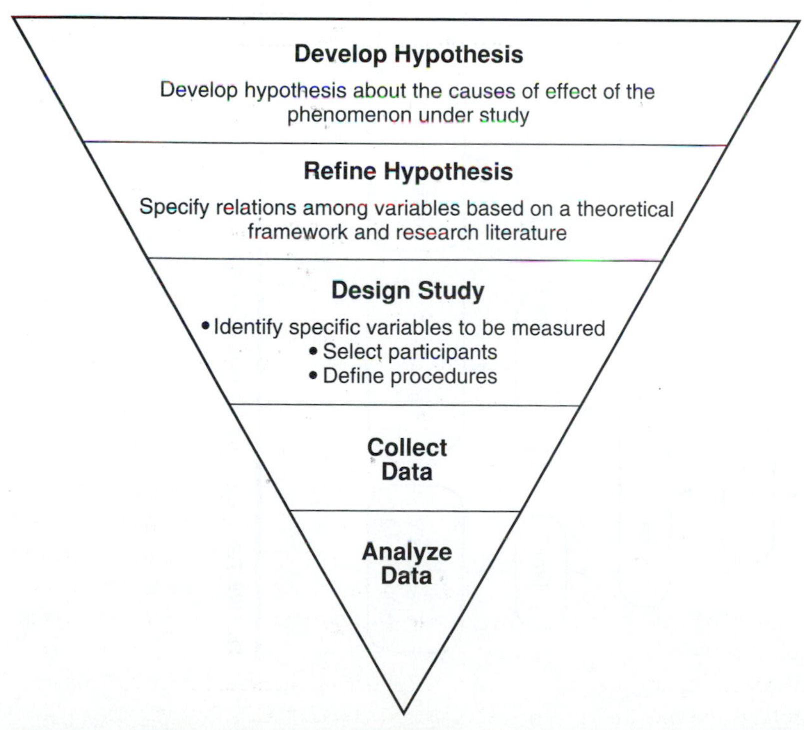

FIGURE 7.1 Steps for designing a correlational research study.

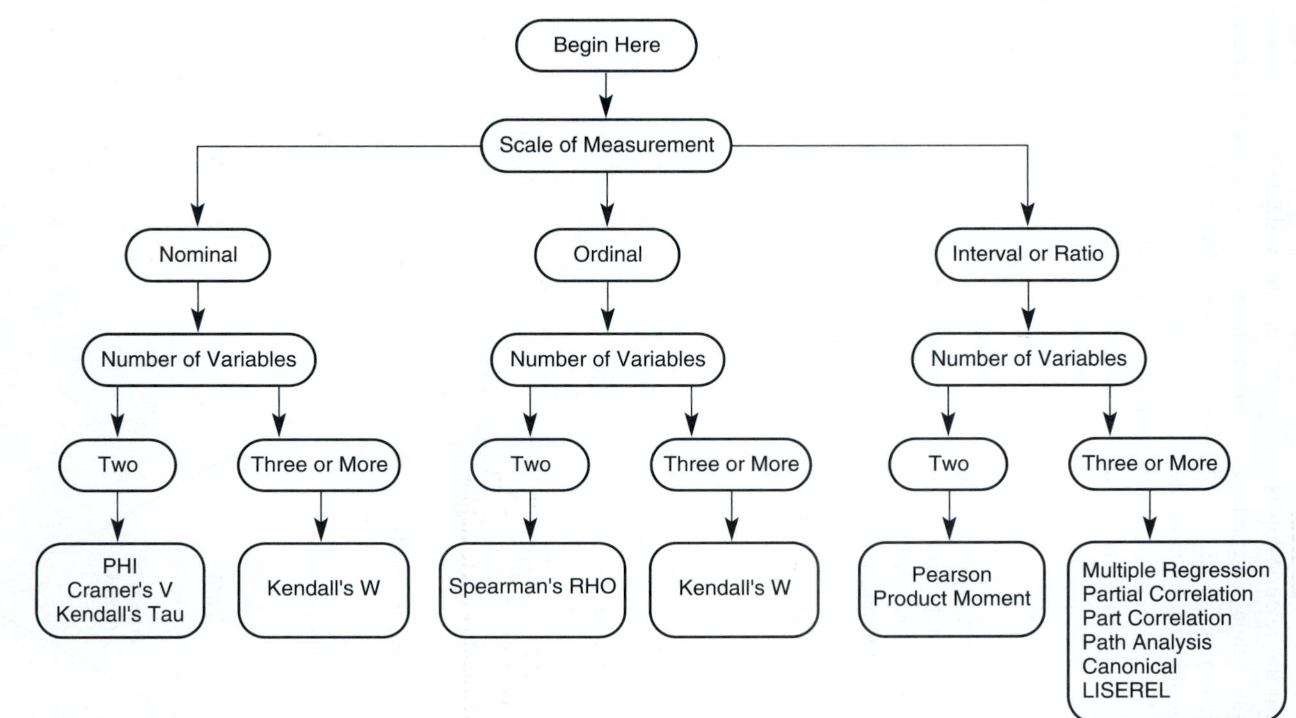

FIGURE 7.2 Selecting statistical analysis procedures: Association between or among two or more variables.

advanced statistical procedures in correlational research. The correlation coefficient is best understood by reference to the bivariate frequency distribution. A bivariate frequency distribution is an extension of the univariate frequency distribution discussed in Chapter 4 in which the scores from *two* variables are plotted either in a table or a graph. Plotting the scores of two variables on a graph (which is called a scattergram) visually depicts the degree of relationship between the two variables or the extent to which they covary. Each set of scores could be displayed separately as univariate frequency distributions. However, such graphs would not show how the variables were related. Thus, the scores for one variable are plotted on the horizontal or *x* axis and the scores for the other variable are plotted on the vertical or *y* axis. Having two variables that are graphically displayed is why it is called a bivariate frequency distribution.

A bivariate frequency distribution for a hypothetical set of scores (see Table 7.1) is presented in Figure 7.3. The scores for one variable (*A*) are plotted on the horizontal (*x*) axis and the scores for the other variable (*B*) are plotted on the vertical (*y*) axis to show they are related to one another. Reading from the table, we see that Participant 1 scored 6 on Variable *A* and 13 on Variable *B*. Follow the horizontal (x) axis (which represents Variable *A*) until the score of 6 is reached. Draw a vertical line through the score.

TABLE 7.1 Scores for Variables *X* and *Y*

PARTICIPANT	VARIABLE *A*	VARIABLE *B*
1	6	13
2	8	9
3	8	15
4	9	13
5	10	15
6	10	21
7	11	17
8	12	15
9	12	15
10	14	17

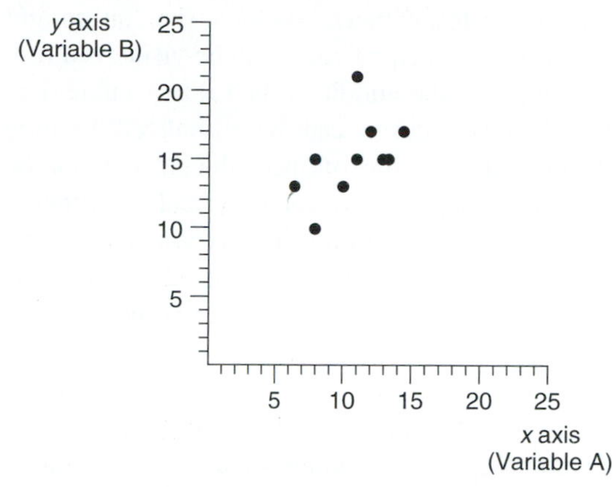

FIGURE 7.3 Scores for variables *A* and *B*.

Then go up the vertical (*y*) axis (which represents Variable *B*) until the score of 13 is reached. Draw a horizontal line through the score. Place a dot where these two lines meet. This dot represents the scores for the participant on Variables *A* and *B*. Continuing this way with each of the scores yields a bivariate frequency distribution or a scattergram. It is often convenient to draw a line on the scattergram to show the general relationship or trend in the data. This line is called a regression line.

Although it is beyond the scope of this book to discuss the computations and theoretical background for the regression line or the line of best fit, it is important to understand that the regression line provides an average statement about how a change in one variable affects another variable. In essence, the regression line describes the trend in the data and is based on all of the observations. For example, each score on Variable *A* has a corresponding score on Variable *B* and also has an estimated score corresponding to a point on the regression line. Thus, this line depicts the average estimate or prediction of scores on one variable to those scores of another variable.

Forms of Relationships. Relationships between two variables usually take four forms. These forms include linear (i.e., a straight line can be visualized in the middle of the values running from one corner to another), quadratic (i.e., an upright or inverted U-shaped curve can be visualized running through the middle of the values), cubic (i.e., an N-shaped curve can be visualized running through the middle of the values), and quartic (i.e., a W-shaped curve can be visualized running through the middle of the values) trends. A variety of statistical procedures can be used to assess the relationship between variables regardless of the form of the relationship. Finally, it is important to note that quadratic, cubic, and quartic relationships are all commonly referred to as curvilinear relationships. An example of a curvilinear relationship that is quadratic would be the correlation between age and running speed. As we grow older from infancy, our running speed increases. However, once we reach a certain age such as in our 30's, our running speed will begin to decrease. Thus, there is a relationship between the two variables but that relationships is not linear.

Correlation Coefficient. Questions such as, "Is there a relationship between maternal attachment and children's social adjustment?" "Is reading achievement related to the amount of time spent reading?" and "Is quality of child care related to infant development?" are about the relationship between two variables. The statistic that is used to describe the relationship between two variables is the correlation coefficient. Thus, correlational statistics are considered to be descriptive statistics. Correlation coefficients are used extensively in the development and validation of measurement devices as explained in Chapter 3.

There are various statistics that can be calculated to indicate the degree to which two variables are related to one another depending on the types of variables used. Recall the distinction among nominal, ordinal, interval, and ratio variables. Statistical procedures exist for describing the relationship between two nominal variables, a nominal variable and an interval/ratio variable, two ordinal variables, and two interval or ratio variables. Although we will describe each of the correlational procedures used in such cases, we will focus on the Pearson product moment correlation that is used to describe the relationship between two interval or ratio-scale variables. We will focus on this correlation because it is the most commonly used statistical procedure for deriving a correlation coefficient and because it provides the basis for many of the more advanced statistical procedures used in correlational research.

General Interpretation of Correlation Coefficients. The correlation coefficient can range from –1.00 to +1.00. Figure 7.4 presents a number of correlation coefficients and associated scattergrams. If the values for the variables plotted on the x and y axes fall on a straight line, the correlation coefficient has its largest value, +1.00 or –1.00. Graphs 7.4(a) and 7.4(b) depict a perfect positive and negative correlation between two variables, respectively. The straight diagonal line in both cases, called the regression line or line of best fit, indicates that each increment in one variable is accompanied by a corresponding increment in the other variable. A perfect correlation between two variables enables a perfect prediction to be made about one variable from the scores on the other variable. Of course, one will probably never encounter a perfect correlation in education and psychology due to factors such as measurement error.

If the two variables are not related to one another at all, then the value of the correlation coefficient is zero; see Figure 7.4(g). In such a case, knowing the value for one variable would not enable one to predict the value for the other variable. In between a perfect correlation and zero correlation, the complete range of values can be found. The larger the numbers, the more strongly the variables are related to one another. Similarly, the larger the numbers, the better the prediction of the values for one variable from the values of the other variable. Inspection of the scattergrams in Figure 7.4 shows that a strong relationship exists when the points are close to the regression line or the line of best fit; see Figures 7.4(c) and 7.4(d). Relatively confident predictions can be made when data points are close to the regression line. The actual data points are close to those predicted

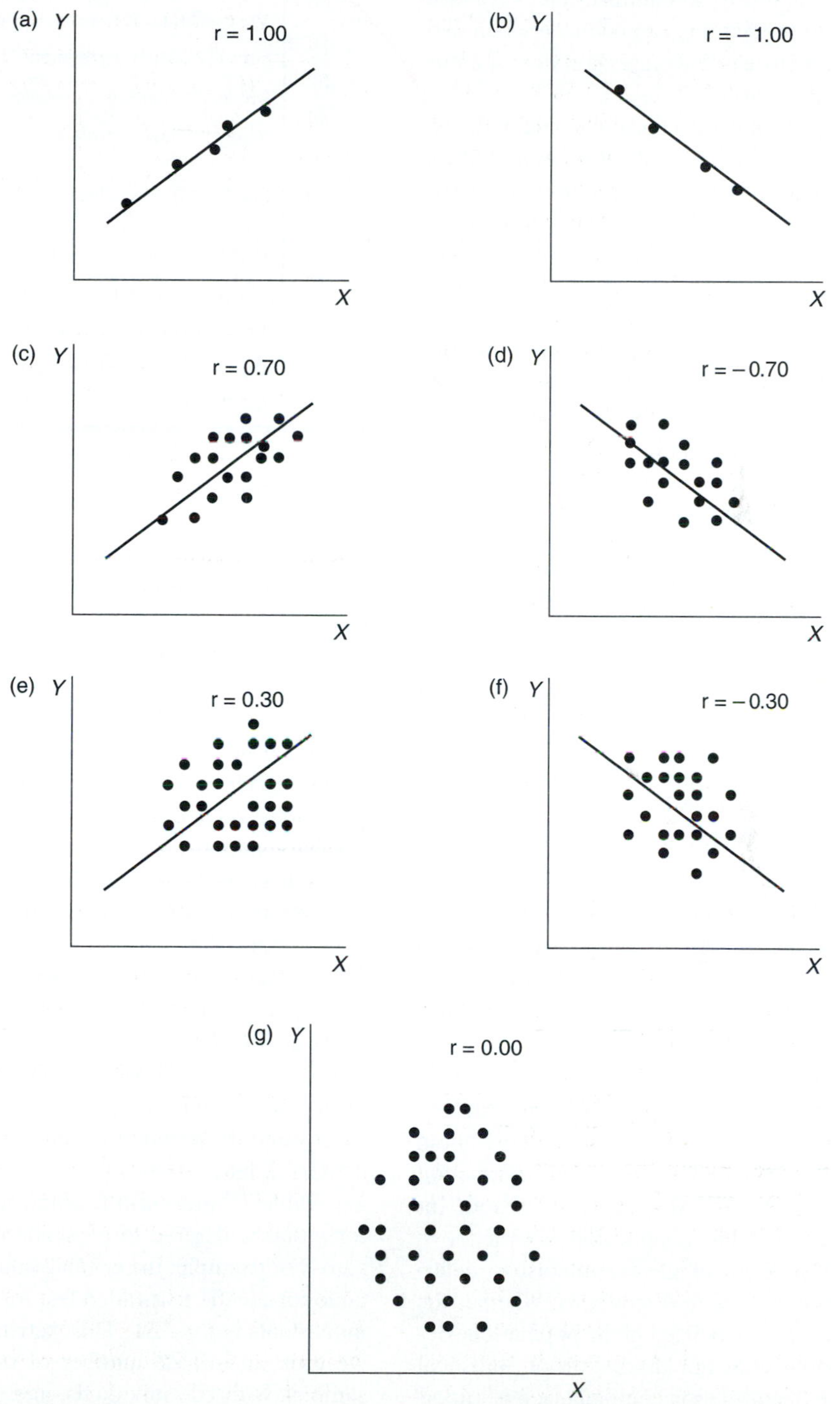

FIGURE 7.4 Positive and negative correlation coefficients.

by the regression line. In contrast, relatively little confidence in predictions can be made when data points are not close to the regression line; see Figures 7.4(e) and 7.4(f).

Figure 7.4 illustrates positive and negative correlation coefficients with the same values. What does it mean when a correlation is positive or negative? In the case of a positive correlation, individuals who scored high on one variable tend to score high on the second variable. Conversely, in the case of a negative correlation, individuals who scored high on one variable tend to score low on the second variable. In other words, the plus and minus signs determine the direction of the relationship. If the correlation coefficient is positive, then the interpretation is that individuals who had high scores on one variable tended also to have high scores on the second variable and vice versa.

Finally, as we explained in Chapter 3, it is difficult to interpret exactly what a correlation coefficient means. Whether a correlation coefficient of some particular size is important depends on the circumstances or context of the study. That is, whether a correlation coefficient is meaningful depends on the area of research and how it is to be used. Figure 7.5 presents some common interpretations for a range of possible correlations.

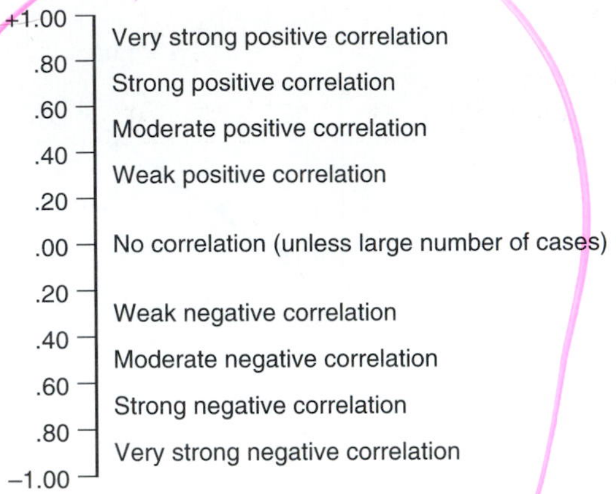

FIGURE 7.5 Rough interpretations for a range of correlations.

Statistical Significance of Correlation Coefficients. We discussed the notion that statistical significance enables researchers to draw reasonable conclusions regarding the relative influence of systematic and chance factors on the findings in Chapter 4. With regard to correlation coefficients, statistical significance testing allows researchers to draw conclusions (or make inferences) about what might be in the population from information gained from a sample. Although it is of some interest to describe the relationship between two variables, it is often of greater interest to determine, with some degree of certainty, whether the two variables are associated in the population. Before proceding with our discussion of statistical significance of correlation coefficients, it is important to know that the obtained correlation coefficient is unique to the sample of participants. In fact, if we were to examine the obtained correlation coefficients based on different samples drawn from the same population, it is highly unlikely that any two correlation coefficients would be identical. Although we would expect them to be similar to one another, there would inevitably be variations in the obtained correlation coefficients.

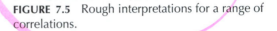

Researchers test the statistical significance of correlation coefficients because it is unlikely that a correlation coefficient of zero would be obtained from the scores for any two variables. Thus, researchers test the statistical significance of a correlation coefficient obtained from a sample to enable them to speculate about the relationship in the population. The correlation coefficient for a given sample is represented with the Roman letter r and the population value is represented by the Greek letter ρ (rho).

Table 7.2 presents the obtained critical values for r that will serve to persuade us that ρ is not zero. For example, the critical value shown in this table for the .01 two-tailed test for a sample of 20 individuals is $r = .561$. This statistic means that if we took an infinite number of randomly drawn samples with 20 individuals, and if ρ were really zero, only .01 proportion of the samples would

TABLE 7.2 Table of Critical Values

LEVEL FOR A TWO-TAIL TEST	.10	.05	.02	.01	.001
N					
6	.729	.811	.882	.917	.974
7	.669	.754	.833	.874	.951
8	.622	.707	.789	.834	.925
9	.582	.666	.750	.798	.898
10	.549	.632	.716	.765	.872
11	.521	.602	.685	.735	.847
12	.497	.576	.658	.708	.823
13	.476	.553	.634	.684	.801
14	.458	.532	.612	.661	.780
15	.441	.514	.592	.641	.760
16	.426	.497	.574	.623	.742
17	.412	.482	.558	.606	.725
18	.400	.468	.542	.590	.708
19	.389	.456	.528	.575	.693
20	.378	.444	.516	.561	.679
21	.369	.433	.503	.549	.665
22	.360	.423	.492	.537	.652
23	.352	.413	.482	.526	.640
24	.344	.404	.472	.515	.629
25	.337	.396	.462	.505	.618
26	.330	.388	.453	.496	.607
27	.323	.381	.445	.487	.597
28	.317	.374	.437	.479	.588
29	.311	.367	.430	.471	.579
30	.306	.361	.423	.463	.570
35	.282	.333	.391	.428	.531
40	.264	.312	.366	.402	.501
45	.248	.296	.349	.381	.471
50	.235	.276	.328	.361	.451
60	.214	.254	.300	.330	.414
70	.198	.235	.277	.305	.385
80	.185	.220	.260	.286	.361
90	.174	.208	.245	.270	.342
100	.165	.196	.232	.256	.324
150	.135	.161	.190	.210	.267
200	.117	.139	.164	.182	.232
LEVEL FOR A ONE-TAIL TEST	.05	.025	.01	.005	.0005

yield the obtained correlation coefficient with the sample of 20 individuals. Of course, as is always the case in education and psychology, we will never know for sure whether ρ is or is not zero.

Finally, it is important to note that whether a correlation coefficient is significant does not provide us any information regarding the magnitude of the relationship between two variables. For example, for a sample of 200, a correlation coefficient of .139 is statistically significant at the .05 alpha level; but a scattergram of a correlation of .139 illustrates that relatively accurate predictions cannot be made (see Figure 7.6). It is still a weak correlation even though it is statistically significant.

Variance Interpretation of Correlation Coefficients. It should be clear by now that the interpretation of the magnitude of a correlation coefficient is problematic. It is problematic because it is not a proportion. A correlation coefficient of .50 does not represent a degree of relationship twice as great as a correlation coefficient of .25. The difference between the correlation coefficients of .80 and .90 is not equal to the difference between the correlation coefficients of .30 and .40.

Coefficient of Determination. One of the most informative ways of interpreting the magnitude of correlation coefficients is in terms of variance or proportion of predictable variance. The proportion of predictable variance is called the coefficient of determination and is obtained by squaring the obtained correlation coefficient r^2 and multi-

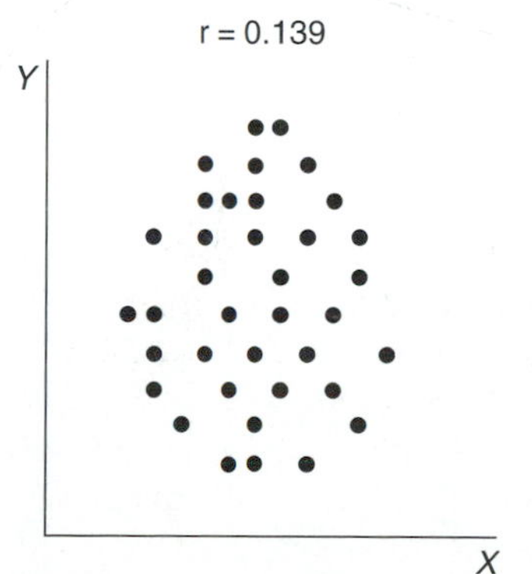

FIGURE 7.6 Scattergram of correlation of .139.

plying it by 100. The coefficient of determination is a simple proportion. For example, if $r = .90$, then $r^2 = .81$. Therefore, we can state that 81% of the variance of one variable is predictable from the variance of the other variable. In essence, we know 81% of what we would have to know to make a perfect prediction. In contrast to a correlational coefficient, a coefficient of determination of .50 represents a degree of relationship twice as great as a coefficient of determination of .25. The difference between the coefficients of determination of .80 and .90 is equal to the difference between the coefficients of determination of .30 and .40. Converting the correlation coefficient into a proportion enables us to assess the magnitude of the relationship between two variables. In our preceding example in which a correlation coefficient of .139 is statistically significant with a sample of 200 individuals, we find that we know less than 2% of what we need to know to make a perfect prediction.

It is clear that it is generally more meaningful to think in terms of the coefficient of determination rather than the correlation coefficient itself. The values for the coefficient of determination for values of r from .10 to 1.00 are presented in Table 7.3. Note that a correlation of over .80 is needed before we can state that 65% of the variance of one variable is predictable from the variance of another variable.

TABLE 7.3 Values of Coefficient of Determinations and Associated r Values

$R^2 \times 100$	r
1	.10
4	.20
9	.30
16	.40
25	.50
36	.60
49	.70
64	.80
81	.90
100	1.00

Coefficient of Alienation. Another way of viewing the magnitude of the correlation coefficient is to consider the lack of association between two variables. The coefficient of alienation (the square root of $1 - r^2$) tells us the proportion of variance of one variable that is not predictable from the variance of another variable.

Causality and Correlation. One of the things that we mentioned before about the correlation coefficient was that it could be applied to any two sets of values from two paired variables. The statistical procedures for obtaining a correlation coefficient do not assume that a meaningful relationship of any kind necessarily exists between the two variables. Thus, the correlational coefficient is only meaningful in that it permits conclusions to be made about the relationship between two variables connected in some meaningful way. Without this connection, the correlation coefficient is simply a value.

On the surface, it might appear that a strong correlation might indicate that there must be some kind of causal link between two variables. However, this is not the case. Correlation does not imply causation. Because one variable consistently increases or decreases in unison with another variable does not mean that one causes the other; this is true no matter how strong the correlation coefficient is.

Although correlation does not imply causation, a relationship between variables often provides researchers useful leads to causal relationships. Of course, if no relationship exists between two variables, a causal relationship may be ruled out. If a relationship does exist between two variables, experimental studies or the use of advanced statistical techniques and the correlational research method is required to confirm whether the variables are causally connected. Cook and Campbell (1979) identified three requirements to say that one variable (independent variable) causes another (dependent variable):

1. A change in the value of the independent value is accompanied by a change in the value of the dependent variable.
2. Some mechanism for asserting a priori how the independent variable affects the dependent variable.
3. The independent variable must precede the dependent variable. Of course, in correlational research, they may be measured at the same time.

The more advanced statistical procedures used in correlational research such as multiple regression and structural equation modeling can be used to meet these three requirements. In contrast to experimental research in which researchers control alternative explanations for changes in the dependent variable through the use of true experimental research designs, researchers using the correlational research method statistically examine the changes in the dependent variable accompanying changes in the independent variable. For example, researchers explore the effects of the alternative variables by introducing them into a regression equation and by seeing if the relationship between the two variables is affected. If the alternative variables have no effect, this indicates that the relationship may be real. If the relationship between two variables weakens or disappears with the introduction of the alternative variables, then the relationship between the two variables may not be real.

Researchers conducting correlational research typically express relationships in diagrams to assert how the causal effect behaves. Expressing relationships in diagrams is in contrast to experimental studies in which the independent variable is directly manipulated to assert how the causal effect behaves. The basic rules for representing a causal model are quite simple and must be based on a theoretical model and previous research. Figure 7.7 presents hypothetical relationships among variables. Researchers represent variables using circles or boxes. Relationships among variables that are not causal in nature are symbolized by curved lines. A single arrow on a line represents a unidirectional relationship. Arrows on both ends represent reciprocal relationships. Relationships between variables can be positive or negative. If a negative sign is not used, it is implied that the relationship is positive. Causal relationships are expressed by straight lines with an arrow on one end. The arrows show the direction of causality (i.e., independent variable to dependent variable) and usually precede from left to right. Of course, in complex models other arrangements are used to produce a clear diagram.

Inspection of Figure 7.7 reveals that Variables X_1 and X_2 are related to one another in a reciprocal fashion. The relationship between Variables X_1 and X_2 is positive. Variables X_1 and X_2 are causally related to Variable Y. Although this example only includes three variables, it demonstrates how researchers use diagrams to depict relationships under study. We will return to these diagrams when we describe the advanced statistical procedures used in correlational research.

It is important to note that it is this second requirement (i.e., the use of some mechanism for asserting a priori how the independent variable affects the dependent variable) in which researchers' conceptions of causality differ. Some researchers believe that a causal relationship can only be established through the direct manipulation of the independent variable, and others believe that such a manipulation is not necessary. It should be clear that researchers who use causal analysis in correlational research do not believe that it is necessary to manipulate the independent variable to

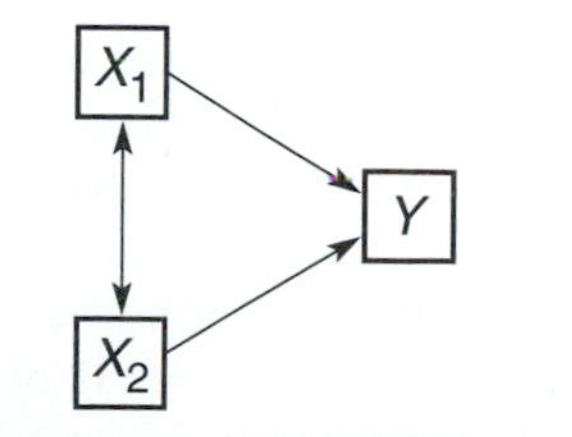

FIGURE 7.7 Reciprocal and causal relationship between variables.

assert how it effects the dependent variable. Regardless of the position researchers take on this issue, all would assert that the causal relationship between two variables cannot be established with one study. Replications of the phenomenon under study are necessary for researchers to assert with any confidence that a causal relationship exists between two variables.

Finally, researchers using the correlational research method, like those using true experimental methods, must establish the temporal order of the relationship to make causal statements. In other words, an established relationship between two variables says nothing about which one has a causal effect on the other; researchers must establish the temporal order of the relationship to accomplish this.

Factors Affecting Correlation Coefficients. There are a number of factors that affect the correlation coefficient—form of the relationship, outliers in the data, restriction of range, skewed distributions, and attenuation.

Form of the Relationship. One of the primary factors that affects the correlation coefficient is the form of the relationship between two variables. As mentioned earlier, the relationship between variables can take four different forms. The correlation coefficient is only completely satisfactory as an indicator of the relationship if the relationship is linear. The correlation coefficient is not completely satisfactory as an indicator of curvilinear (i.e., quadratic, cubic, and quartic) relationships. Of course, it is important to keep in mind that just because a relationship between two variables is curvilinear does not mean that the variables are unrelated. Rather, the use of the correlation coefficient as an indicator of the degree of relationship between the two variables is inappropriate, and a more appropriate statistical procedure should be used to determine the magnitude of the relationship between the variables.

If the relation is nonlinear, low correlations may be obtained even though a systematic relationship may exist between the two variables. Thus, researchers may underestimate the degree of relationship between two variables if the correlation coefficient is used. Although underestimating the degree of relationship between two variables is preferable to overestimating the relationship, researchers are most interested in obtaining an accurate indicator of the degree of relationship between variables. Thus, in interpreting a correlation coefficient, researchers should satisfy themselves that the relationship between two variables is linear. Any gross departure from a linear trend can readily be detected by inspection of the scattergram.

Detecting the particular type of trend through inspection of a scattergram will be difficult for small samples (less than 30 to 40 participants). The correlation ratio, also known as the eta coefficient, can be used to detect nonlinear relationships. The advantage of the correlation ratio is that it provides an indicator of the degree of relationship between two variables other than correlational methods when the relationship is considerably nonlinear. The correlation ratio is a statistical procedure used to assess the degree of relationship between a nominal variable and an interval or ratio-scale variable. If the obtained values for the correlation coefficient and correlation ratio substantially depart from one another, then it is likely that the relationship is curvilinear. Conversely, if the obtained values for the correlation coefficient and correlation ratio do not substantially depart from one another, then it is likely that the relationship is linear.

Outliers in the Data. Another factor that affects the correlation coefficient is outliers in the data set. An outlier is an individual or other entity (e.g., one or more schools out of a sample of 50) whose score differs considerably from the scores obtained by the other participants or entities of the sample. Outliers can affect the correlation coefficient. Outliers are especially problematic because they can result in an overestimate or underestimate of the relationship between variables. The scattergram can be used to identify potential outliers. If an outlier is identified, researchers must first check whether an error occurred in computing or recording the response or score. Some outliers may occur because of simple mistakes on the part of the researcher such as misplacing the decimal point. If the outlier is not a function of a computation or recording error, researchers should explore other possible explanations. For example, the particular participant may not have been exposed to the independent variable. The decision to eliminate an outlier is difficult. If outliers are left in the sample, they may distort the obtained correlation coefficient. It may be useful to compare the correlation coefficient obtained with and without the outliers included in the sample before deciding whether to include them in the analysis.

Restriction of Range. Still another factor that influences the correlation coefficient is the homogeneity or heterogeneity of the sample on which the data is collected. Suppose we consider two variables, *X* and *Y*, in which the variability (variance) of the *X* variable is restricted or abbreviated. This restriction will reduce the correlation coefficient between the two variables. This restriction is sometimes referred to as restriction of range of the correlation coefficient. Researchers should carefully consider the effect discussed here because some correlational research involves assessing the relationship between variables on highly selected samples. For example, the correlation coefficient between scores on the SAT (Scholastic Aptitude Test) and GPA in graduate school may be low because students who gain admission to graduate school are a highly selected group with little variance in performance.

Researchers can apply the correction for restriction in range when the range of scores for a sample is restricted. This correction procedure enables researchers to estimate what the relationship would be between the two variables if the variability of the responses or scores were not restricted. Use of the correction for restriction in range requires the assumption that the relationship between the two variables is linear throughout their entire range. The correction for restriction in range would not be appropriate in those cases in which the relationship is curvilinear.

Skewed Distributions. Distributions of the scores that are not normal may also affect the correlation coefficient. The use of the correlation coefficient is based on the normality assumption. That is, the distributions of the scores for the two variables are normally distributed (see the earlier discussion of the normal distribution). It is not uncommon to explore the relationships between two variables in which their distributions have different shapes. For example, the correlation coefficient will be affected if a variable with a positively skewed distribution (i.e., there are a disproportionate number of high scores) is correlated with a variable with a negatively skewed distribution (i.e., there are a disproportionate number of low scores). In such cases, the variables should be transformed to approximate a normal distribution or, depending on the scale of measurement (e.g., nominal), a nonparametric correlation statistic should be used.

Attenuation. The obtained correlation coefficient between two variables is always lower than the true correlation. The degree to which the correlation coefficient is lower is dependent on the extent to which the measurement devices are not perfectly reliable. The lowering of the correlation coefficient because of the unreliability of the measure is called attenuation. Researchers can apply the correction for attenuation to estimate the relationship between two variables if the measurement devices are perfectly reliable. Applying the correction for attenuation is useful in those cases in which the measurement devices are somewhat unreliable.

Basic Correlational Procedures. Now that we have discussed the correlation coefficient, we will look at the wide range of correlational procedures available to researchers conducting correlational research. As discussed previously, the Pearson product moment correlation coefficient is used in those cases in which the scores are interval or ratio scale. The Pearson product moment correlation coefficient is only appropriate when the two variables of interest are related in a linear fashion and are normally distributed.

There are a wide range of other correlational procedures that can be used to examine the relationship between two variables or among several variables. They can be used to examine the relationship between variables that are related in a linear or curvilinear fashion. They can be used to explore causal relationships among variables.

Part and Partial Correlation. The ability to explore the complex relationships among a wide range of variables is one of the most useful aspects of correlation research. In general, the part and partial correlation are used by researchers to explore the influence of an independent variable on the relationship between another independent variable and a dependent variable. The part correlation enables researchers to establish the relationship between two variables after the influence or effect of another variable has been removed from one of the variables but not both. The partial correlation coefficient differs from the part correlation in that it enables researchers to establish the relationship between two variables after the influence or effect of a third variable has been removed from both.

We will look at a hypothetical study to ensure our understanding of the differences between the part and partial correlation coefficient. Figure 7.8 presents a study in which the goal is to explore the relationship between family commitment to education and academic success in high school. In this study, other factors related to academic success include early achievement and socioeconomic level. The influence of these variables on academic success in high school is depicted by straight lines with an arrow. The relationships among family commitment to education, early achievement, and socioeconomic level are depicted by curved lines with arrows on both ends.

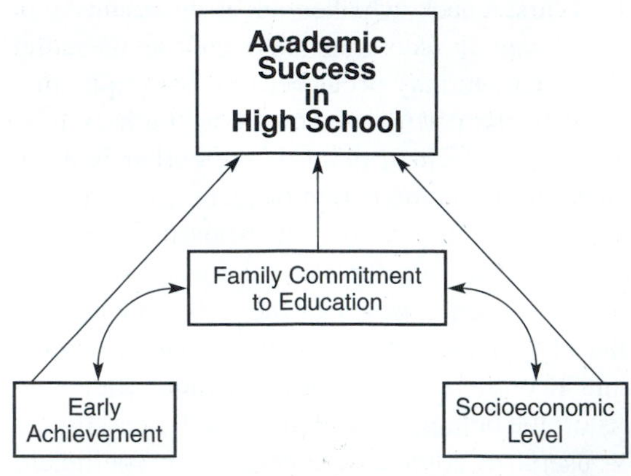

FIGURE 7.8 Determinants of academic success in high school.

The partial correlation could be used if researchers wanted to establish the relationship between family commitment and academic success in high school while controlling the influence of early achievement and socioeconomic level. Of course, the partial correlation could also be used to establish the relationship between the other variables (i.e., early achievement and socioeconomic level) and academic success while controlling the influence of two other variables.

The part correlation could be used if researchers wanted to establish the relationship between family commitment and academic success in high school while only controlling the influence of early achievement or socioeconomic level. Another use of the part correlation could be to explore the relationship between the other two variables (i.e., early achievement and socioeconomic level) and academic success in high school. The advantage of the partial correlation over the part correlation in this case is its capacity to simplify a potentially complex pattern among family commitment to education, early achievement, socioeconomic level, and academic success in high school by allowing the researcher to only look at one part of the pattern. Other more advanced statistical procedures such as path analysis, multiple regression, and structural equation modeling enable researchers to examine the complete causal pattern that is hypothesized with all of the possible influences among variables. We will describe each of these statistical procedures later in this chapter.

Correlation Ratio. We briefly mentioned the use of the correlation ratio or the eta coefficient in tandem with the correlation coefficient to determine whether two variables were related in a linear fashion. The correlation ratio is appropriate for data in which the dependent variable is measured on an interval or ratio scale and the independent variable is measured on a nominal or ordinal scale. When the correlation ratio is squared (eta^2), it can be interpreted as the proportion of the total variability in the dependent variable that can be accounted for by knowing the value of the independent variable. The correlation ratio does not require a linear relationship or require that the dependent variable be normally distributed.

Spearman Rank Correlation Coefficient and Kendall's Rank Correlation Coefficient. The Spearman rank correlation and Kendall's coefficient are appropriate when both variables are measured on at least ordinal scales. The Spearman rank correlation is referred to as ρ and Kendall's rank correlation coefficient is referred to as τ, or tau. The Spearman rank correlation coefficient and Kendall's tau essentially provide a measure of the disparity in the rankings between two variables and are computed by ranking the scores for each of the variables from smallest to largest and computing the Pearson product moment correlation coefficient on the ranks. A positive correlation exists as the ranks of one variable increase (or decrease) in conjunction with the ranks of the other variable. Conversely, a negative correlation exists as the ranks of one variable increase (or decrease) in conjunction with the ranks of the other variable. Because a large number of ties will affect the Spearman rank correlation coefficient and Kendall's tau, a corrective factor is applied in which the tied values are replaced with the average rank. If the number of ties is not large, their effect on the Spearman rank correlation coefficient and Kendall's tau is negligible.

Kendall Part Rank Correlation. Kendall part rank correlation coefficient is used in those cases in which researchers want to control the influence of a third variable on the relationship between two variables. The Kendall part rank correlation coefficient is similar to the part correlation except that it is appropriate when the variables are measured on at least ordinal scales rather than interval or ratio scales. The Kendall part rank correlation coefficient could have been used to explore the relationship between family commitment and academic success in high school while controlling for the influence of either early achievement or socioeconomic level. Unfortunately, there is no equivalent to the partial correlation coefficient for use when variables are measured in ordinal scales.

Kendall Coefficient of Concordance. The Spearman rank correlation coefficient and Kendall's tau were concerned with measuring the association between the rankings of two variables. The Kendall coefficient of concordance is used when researchers want to establish the relationship among the rankings of several variables. The Kendall coefficient of concordance is typically employed in studies of intertest reliability. For example, the Kendall coefficient of concordance might be used in a study in which the purpose was to assess the degree of agreement between college professors', principals', and mentors' rankings of the effectiveness of student teachers. A high value for the Kendall coefficient of concordance would indicate that the observers (e.g., professors, principals, and mentors) are applying similar standards in ranking the teacher effectiveness of student teachers. Conversely, a low value for the Kendall coefficient of concordance would indicate that the observers are applying different standards in ranking the teacher effectiveness of student teachers.

The Phi Coefficient and Contingency Coefficient. The phi coefficient and contingency coefficient are appropriate when both variables are measured on nominal scales. The phi coefficient and contingency coefficient are based on chi-square (as discussed in Chapter 4). The phi coefficient and the contingency coefficient are used in place of chi-square to assess the relationship between nominal variables because chi-square does not enable meaningful comparisons of chi-square values from varying tables with varying dimensions and sample sizes. In other words, chi-square does not enable researchers to make meaningful comparisons of the findings from different studies. Although the phi coefficient and the contingency coefficient enable researchers to compare differences in the relationships of variables measured on a nominal scale, they are not directly comparable to any of the other correlation coefficients we described previously. The values for the phi coefficient and the contingency coefficient range from 0 to +1. Nevertheless, the phi coefficient and contingency coefficient are useful in those cases in which none of the other measures of association that we have described are applicable.

Advanced Correlational Procedures. One of the advantages of the correlational research method over experimental methods is that researchers cannot only look at the relationships between variables, but also examine the interrelationships among variables. Additionally, researchers are increasingly using the correlational research method to establish causal relationships among variables.

The advanced correlational procedures that follow enable researchers to address a wide range of questions. It is important to note that many of these statistical procedures are not only used in correlational research, but are also used in analyzing data from experimental studies. Thus, it is important for critical research consumers to be familiar with these advanced statistical procedures. We wish to describe each of the statistical procedures in enough detail to enable you to understand them on a basic level. We encourage you to seek more information in case you encounter difficulty interpreting the results of a study.

Multiple Regression. In general, multiple regression is a highly flexible data analysis procedure that may be used whenever a quantitative variable (dependent variable) is to be studied in relationship to, or is a function of, any factors of interest (independent variables). The flexibility of multiple regression is apparent in Cohen and Cohen's (1983) description of the conditions for which it is applicable:

1. The form of the relationship under study is not constrained in any way. The relationship may be simple or complex, general or conditional, linear or curvilinear, or combinations of these possibilities.

2. The nature of the factors expressed as independent variables is also not constrained in any way. The factors may be quantitative or qualitative, main effects or interaction effects (as in the analysis of variance), or covariates (as in the analysis of covariance). The factors may be correlated with each other or uncorrelated. The factors may be naturally occurring properties such as gender, diagnosis, or IQ, or they may be the result of planned experimental manipulation (treatments). The factors may be single variables or groups of variables. The factors may be nominal, ordinal, interval, or ratio in nature. In short, virtually any information whose bearing on the dependent variable is of interest may be expressed as research factors.

3. The magnitude of the relationship of a factor to the dependent variable is not constrained in any way. The magnitude of the whole relationship or partial relationship of a variable can be determined.

4. The ability to determine the statistical significance of the relationship of a factor to the dependent variable is not constrained in any way. The statistical significance of the whole relationship or partial relationship of a variable can be determined.

It is clear that multiple regression is a versatile statistical analysis procedure for analyzing data from correlational research studies as well as for other experimental studies. Remember that the correlation coefficient determines the degree of relationship between two variables: an independent variable and a dependent variable. Multiple regression can be thought of as an extension of the correlation coefficient in which the overall and relative degree of relationship between a set of independent variables (nominal, ordinal, interval, or ratio in nature) and a dependent variable (interval or ratio in nature) is obtained. That is, multiple regression takes the same basic form as the correlation coefficient, but a set of independent variables is involved rather than just one. For example, in a hypothetical study of a set of factors (high school GPA, SAT scores, and absence rate) related to college success (college GPA), multiple regression could be used to determine the overall degree of relationship between the set of factors (high school GPA, SAT scores, and absence rate) and college GPA. Multiple regression would also be used to determine the relative degree of relationship between the set of factors (high school GPA, SAT scores, and absence rate) and college GPA.

Regression Models. A variety of regression models or equations can be constructed from the same set of independent variables to predict the dependent variable. For example, seven different regression models could be constructed from the college example described previously: three models using only one of the independent variables, three with two independent variables, and one with all three of the independent variables. As the number of independent variables increases, so does the number of potential regression models. Although researchers could examine all possible regression models, they typically use forward selection, backward elimination, and stepwise selection procedures to examine the overall and relative relationships between a set of independent variables and a dependent variable. These procedures are all included in standard statistical packages.

In forward selection, the first variable entered into the regression model is the one with the largest positive or negative relationship with the dependent variable. If the first variable selected for entry meets the established criterion (alpha level established by the researcher) for inclusion in the model, forward selection continues. If the independent variable does not meet the criterion for inclusion in the model, the procedure terminates with no variables in the regression model. In this case, none of the independent variables are predictive of the dependent variable. Once one independent variable is included in the model, the correlation between the independent variables not in the equation is used to select the next variable. In essence, the partial correlation between the dependent variable and each of the independent variables is computed. The independent variable with the largest partial correlation is the next variable considered in the model. If the established criterion is met, the variable is entered into the regression model. This process continues until there are no other independent variables that meet the established entry criteria.

In contrast to forward selection, which begins with no independent variables in the regression model, backward elimination starts with all of the independent variables in the regression model and sequentially removes them. Researchers establish removal criteria rather than entry criteria. The independent variable with the smallest partial correlation with the dependent variable is examined first. If the independent variable meets established criteria for removal, it is removed from the regression model. If the independent variable does not meet the established criteria for removal, it remains in the regression model and the procedure stops. Although backward elimination and forward selection typically result in the same regression model, this is not always the case.

Stepwise selection of independent variables for inclusion in the regression model is a combination of the forward selection and backward elimination procedures. Stepwise selection is the most commonly used procedure. The first independent variable for consideration in the regression model is selected in the same manner as in the forward selection procedure. If the independent variable does not meet the established criteria for inclusion, the procedure is terminated with no independent variables in the regression model. If the independent variable meets the established criteria for inclusion in the regression model, the second independent variable is selected based on the highest partial correlation. Stepwise selection differs from forward selection in that the first independent variable is examined to see if it should be removed based on the established removal criteria as in backward elimination. Independent variables not in the equation are then examined for removal. After each step, independent variables already in the regression model are examined for removal. Independent variables are removed until none remain that meet the established removal criteria.

Interpretation of Multiple Regression. In addition to taking the same basic form as the correlation coefficient, interpretation of the results of multiple regression is similar to that of the correlation coefficient. Recall that the correlation coefficient yields *r,* which provides an index of the degree of relationship between two variables. Similarly, multiple regression yields the coefficient of multiple correlation (*R*). The coefficient of multiple correlation can be thought of as a simple correlation coefficient between the scores of a set of independent variables and the score on the dependent variable. The *R* ranges from –1.00 to +1.00. Thus, an R value of +1.00 indicates that there is a perfect correlation between the independent variables and the dependent variable. In multiple regression, the obtained value for each of the independent variables is called a regression coefficient (*R*) and its interpretation directly parallels the multiple correlation. Thus, the correlation between a set of independent variables is called the multiple correlation (*R*), while the correlations between each of the independent variables are called regression coefficients (*R*s).

Furthermore, we indicated that the square of the correlation coefficient (coefficient of determination) tells us the percentage of the variance of the dependent variable that is predicted on the basis of the independent variable. For example, if the correlation of multiple correlation is equal to .70, then one can state that 49% of the variance for the dependent variable is predictable on the basis of the set of independent variables.

Because multiple regression can deal effectively with data that are nominal, ordinal, interval, and ratio in nature, it is important to note that the obtained regression coefficients cannot be compared against one another in a meaningful way. In other words, attempts to make direct comparisons of regression coefficients would be like trying to compare apples and oranges. Multiple regression deals with this issue by converting the regression coefficients into comparable units called *beta weights.* Beta weights are standardized regression coefficients (i.e., the regression coefficients that would have been obtained if each of the independent variables were equal to one another in terms of means and standard deviations) that enable direct comparisons of the relative relationship of each of the independent variables and the dependent variable. The independent variable that has the largest beta weight (regardless of whether the beta weight is positive or negative) is most strongly related to the dependent variable. Conversely, a small beta weight indicates that the associated independent variable is not strongly related to the dependent variable.

Beta weights are not necessarily better than regression coefficients or vice versa. Beta weights and regression coefficients provide different types of information. Beta weights provide information regarding the relative strength of the relationship between the independent variables and the dependent variable, whereas the regression coefficients provide information regarding the overall relationship between a set of independent variables and the dependent variable or the set of factors that predict the dependent variable. Thus, researchers will provide beta weights when they want to show the relative relationship between each set of independent variables and a dependent variable; they will provide the regression coefficients if they want to show the overall relationship between a set of independent variables and a dependent variable. Of course, researchers typically provide both the regression coefficients and beta weights because they want to show both the overall and relative relationship between a set of independent variables and a dependent variable. 

When interpreting the magnitude of regression coefficients, our discussion of interpreting correlation coefficients directly applies. As with the correlation coefficient, it might appear that a large regression coefficient might indicate that there must be some kind of causal link between independent variables and a dependent variable. Of course, this interpretation is not true. Because a set of independent variables consistently increases or decreases in unison with a dependent variable does not mean that one causes the other. This statement is true no matter how large the regression coefficients are. Additionally, although it is possible for researchers to use multiple regression to explore causal relationships, they must meet the three requirements identified by Cook and Campbell (1979) to assert that such a relationship exists.

Statistical Significance of Multiple Regression. Before proceeding with our discussion of the statistical significance of multiple regression, it is important to note that the obtained multiple correlation, regression coefficients, and beta weights are unique to the specific sample of participants. Although there is a wide range of tests of statistical significance that can be conducted with multiple regression, three tests of statistical significance are most commonly used by researchers.

The first test of statistical significance is commonly used by researchers to establish whether the multiple correlation coefficient or regression coefficients obtained differ significantly from zero.

The second test of statistical significance is commonly used by researchers to establish whether the obtained regression coefficients for each of the independent variables differ from one another. Although there will be typically an increase in the multiple correlation coefficient with the addition of each independent variable, it is of interest to determine whether the obtained increase is statistically significant. This type of statistical significance testing can be employed to not only establish the best set of independent variables that can predict the dependent variable, but to also explore potential causal relationships between variables. Recall that if an obtained correlation between two variables is unaffected by the addition of other potentially causal variables, the relationship may be causal in nature.

The final test of statistical significance used by researchers is to establish whether the obtained beta weights differ significantly from zero. The goal of this test of statistical significance is similar to testing the statistical significance of the difference in the obtained regression coefficients. If a particular independent variable is not strongly related to the dependent variable, then the beta weight for this independent variable will be close to zero. On the other hand, if a particular independent variable is strongly related to the dependent variable, then the beta weight for this independent variable will differ significantly from zero. Again, researchers employ this type of statistical significance testing when they are interested in demonstrating, with some degree of certainty, whether the beta weights are significantly different from zero in the population.

Canonical Correlation. Multiple regression is used in those cases in which researchers are interested in determining the relationship between a set of independent variables and a dependent variable. Multiple regression can be generalized to cases in which researchers are interested in determining the relationship between a set of independent variables and a set of dependent variables. The statistical technique for determining this type of relationship is canonical correlation. Canonical correlation, which was developed by Hotelling (1935), is a complex statistical procedure both in terms of calculation and interpretation. Thus, it is used infrequently by researchers. Because it is infrequently used by researchers, we will not discuss it further. It is only important for critical research consumers to know that the canonical correlation procedure is available to researchers in those cases in which they are interested in determining the relationship between a *set* of independent variables and a *set* of dependent variables.

Discriminant Function Analysis. Multiple regression is applied in situations in which the dependent variable is measured on an interval or ratio scale. Discriminant function analysis is employed in those cases in which the dependent variable is nominal in nature (i.e., group membership) rather than ordinal, interval, or ratio. For example, extending from our earlier college example, suppose a particular academic division at a university is interested in determining whether high school GPA and SAT scores predict students who will graduate within 4 years rather than predicting their college GPA. In this case, the dependent variable is dichotomous because an individual can only fall into one of two groups (those who graduate within 4 years and those who do not). There are two main types of discriminant function analyses. A two-group or simple discriminant function analysis is appropriate for nominal dependent variables with two categories; a multiple discriminant function analysis is appropriate with three or more categories.

In contrast to multiple regression in which the goal is to identify the best set of independent variables that predict a dependent variable, the goal of discriminant function analysis is to identify the best set of independent variables that maximize the correct classification of participants. The coefficients obtained are referred to as discriminant function or structure coefficients. Now return to our college example in which the goal is to identify students who graduate within 4 years. Using discriminant analysis, high school GPA, SAT scores, and absence rate would be used to predict which students will graduate within 4 years rather than their college GPA.

Interpretation of the discriminant function coefficients directly parallels the interpretation of regression coefficients. Raw discriminant function coefficients do not enable interpretation of the relative relationship between each of the independent variables and the dependent variable. Thus, standardized discriminant function coefficients, which have a mean of 0 and a standard deviation of 1, are used by researchers. Additionally, the three types of statistical significance used by researchers with regard to discriminant analysis directly parallel those used with multiple regression. The questions addressed by the tests of statistical significance include the following:

1. Does the obtained overall discriminant function coefficient differ significantly from zero?
2. Do the discriminant function coefficients differ significantly from one another?
3. Do the particular standardized discriminant function coefficients differ significantly from zero?

Factor Analysis. Factor analysis was developed by Spearman in his work on intelligence (Ferguson, 1989). Spearman argued that all functions of intelligence are encompassed within one general function or factor. The general factor was called "*g*." Spearman's work led to the extensive use of factor analysis procedures used by researchers in education and psychology. Factor analysis is a multivariate statistical method that is used to identify unobserved or latent variables regarded more commonly as factors or constructs. Examples of latent variables include self-concept, anxiety, depression, and teacher expectancy. It is clear that latent variables represent theoretical constructs that cannot be observed directly and are presumed to underlie particular observed scores on some measurement device.

Factor analysis is used by researchers in an effort to identify factors or latent variables that underlie observed scores. Factor analysis is most commonly used in the development of measurement devices in which the goal of researchers is either to confirm (confirmatory factor analysis) or identify (exploratory factor analysis) factors included within a measurement device. Factor analysis is also used to identify patterns of relations among a large number of variables in correlational research. In contrast to other correlational statistical procedures in which a distinction is made between independent and dependent variables, factor analysis does not make a distinction between independent and dependent variables. Rather, the concern is with the description and interpretation of interdependencies or interrelationships within a set of variables.

Factor analysis, which refers to a variety of methods, can be thought of as a somewhat subjective process in which a large number of items (in the case of a measurement device) or variables (in the case of identifying patterns of interrelationships among variables) are reduced to a smaller set of factors or to a single factor. A single factor (or smaller set of factors) is thought of as more basic, and causal or explanatory explanations may more easily be attributed to them. In other words, the goal of factor analysis is to reduce a large set of variables (or items) describing a complex phenomenon with the purpose of creating a better understanding of the phenomenon through simplification. For example, an individual's IQ score provides a simplified description of a wide range of extremely complex variables that underlie the construct of IQ.

The goal of factor analysis is to identify a structure or pattern within a set of variables. Consider a bivariate frequency distribution between two variables. The arrangement of the data points for the variables on a scattergram may be haphazard (random). This haphazard arrangement would be considered to be without structure. In contrast, the data points may tend to be arranged along a straight line. This arrangement of the data with respect to each other would be considered to be a linear structure. Of course, the data points may arrange themselves in any number of structures (e.g., quadratic, cubic). Thus, structure emerges from a set of variables as the arrangement of data points departs from a random state.

Identifying the structure within a set of variables is accomplished through a variety of mathematical methods that underlie factor analysis. In essence, the structure within a set of variables are identified as factors. Factors are clusters or variables that are correlated with each other. The first set of variables that cluster together is called the first factor. The first factor represents the group of variables that are most interrelated. This factor can then be represented as an individual score for each participant based on the scores from all of the variables included in the factor. The second set of variables that cluster together is called the second factor and represents the next group of variables that are most interrelated and so on. The individual coefficients for each variable are referred to as the loading of each variable on the factor.

Factor Analysis Procedures. There are a variety of factor analyses that yield different solutions or outcomes. The two most common factor analysis procedures are an orthogonal solution and an oblique solution. An orthogonal solution results in factors that are unrelated to one another. An orthogonal solution is used in those cases in which researchers are interested in obtaining a pure set of factors, each measuring a construct that does not overlap with constructs measured by other factors. An oblique solution results in factors that are related to one another. An oblique solution is used in those cases in which researchers are interested in obtaining a set of factors that measure underlying constructs of some overall general construct. For example, a factor analysis of a stress measure might yield such factors as emotional, physical, and social stress that underlie the general construct of stress.

Interpretation. Interpretation of the meaning of the factors is a somewhat subjective process. Researchers need to look at the variables included within each factor and determine the conceptual meaning of the underlying factor. Of course, the same problems regarding the meaningfulness of the variables arise with factor analysis as with any correlational research. Because it is not uncommon for variables to be related to one another, researchers must ensure that the relationship is meaningful.

Path Analysis. Path analysis, which was developed by Wright (1921), is closely related to multiple regression in computational procedures and interpretation but differs in its rationale or purpose. Like multiple regression, path analysis enables researchers to determine the amount of variance in a dependent variable that can be accounted for by a set of independent variables. In contrast to multiple regression, path analysis has the additional aim of determining whether the pattern of shared variances among the independent and dependent variables is consistent with particular causal pathways. These causal pathways must be a priori hypotheses by the researcher.

Consider a hypothetical study in which the relationship among home experiences, academic experiences, and college success is of interest. Several causal pathways are plausible. The first step in a path analysis is to diagram the causal pathways among which a choice is to be made. One plausible sequence is that home experiences affect academic experiences and that academic experiences, in turn, cause college success; see Figure 7.9(a). A second possibility is that home experiences and academic experiences both independently cause college success; see Figure 7.9(b). A third possibility is that home experiences directly affect both academic experiences and college success. In this case, the correlation between academic experiences and college success would be by both having home experiences. Although there could be a number of other possible pathways explaining college success, assume that they have been ruled out on logical grounds by the researcher based on previous research and the data collection procedures.

Path coefficients are then computed for the relationships between the dependent variable (college success) and the independent variables (home experiences and academic experiences) in the second step. A path coefficient (Þ) is the proportion of variance in the dependent variable for which the independent variable is uniquely responsible with the effects of the other independent variables partialled out. Path coefficients are regression coefficients obtained by transforming the independent and dependent variables into standard scores that have a mean of 0 and a standard deviation of 1 (beta weight), and computing the regression of the dependent variable on each independent variable in turn, with all of the other independent variables partialled out. The interpretation of path coefficients is similar to regression coefficients. The values for path coefficients can range from −1.00 to +1.00. Additionally, if all of the variance in the dependent variable is accounted for by the independent variables, the path coefficients will add up to 1.00.

Returning to our hypothetical study, suppose we find that the path coefficient for academic ex-

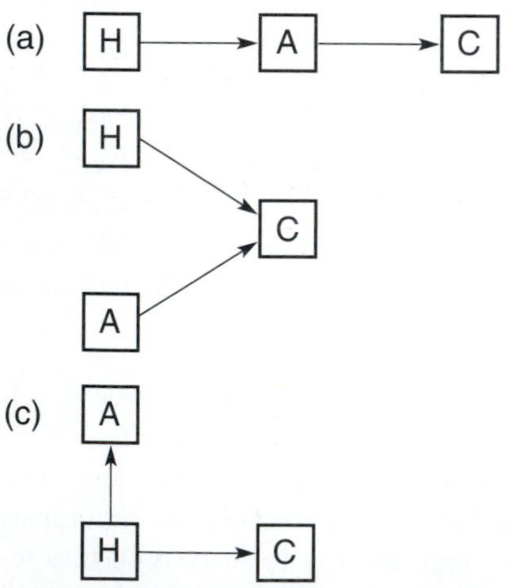

FIGURE 7.9 Three path models of determinants of college success. (*Note:* H = home experiences; A = academic experiences; and C = college success.)

periences is .40, and that the path coefficient for home experiences is .00. This statistic means that, with the effects of home experiences partialled out, academic experiences account for 40% of the variance in college success; with the affect of academic experiences partialled out, home experiences account for none of the variance in college success. The path coefficient for academic experiences and home experiences is then computed to complete the path analysis. We find that the obtained path coefficient is .50.

Figure 7.10 depicts the path diagram showing the coefficients (designated as *p*) for our hypothetical study. Inspection of the path diagram reveals that of the two independent variables, only academic experiences directly affect college success. Additionally, the diagram shows that home experiences affect college success only by affecting academic experiences.

Limitation on Causal Inferences. It is evident that there are limitations on causal inferences from path analysis. The first major limitation is that path analysis only enables researchers to choose among several competing causal explanations for a set of coefficients. In our hypothetical study, path analysis made it possible to choose one of the three causal explanations portrayed in Figure 7.9. However, the findings were also compatible with other causal explanations. For example, the coefficient between home experiences and academic learning history might result because children's access to particular academic learning histories results in particular home experiences rather than the home experiences resulting in particular academic learning histories. Although such a reversal of the hypothesized causal relationship would not invalidate the conclusion that academic experiences affect college success, it would invalidate the conclusion that home experiences affect academic experiences.

Another major limitation of path analysis is that other variables may account for more variance in the dependent variable. These other variables might be independent of the variables already identified or they might account for the apparent contribution of the identified variables themselves. For example, if socioeconomic status was included in our hypothetical study, its presence might reduce the contribution of academic experiences to college success because the obtained contribution is actually due to the effect of socioeconomic status. Thus, the effective use of path analysis requires the formulation of clear-cut and comprehensive models based on a sound theoretical base and previous research.

Structural Equation Modeling. Structural equation modeling is similar to path analysis in that it is used by researchers to test causal relationships among variables. Structural equation modeling is also called LISREL, which is the name of the computer program that researchers use (Joreskog & Sorbom, 1986) and includes methods derived from economics, psychometrics, sociometrics, and multivariate statistics (Byrne, 1994). Structural

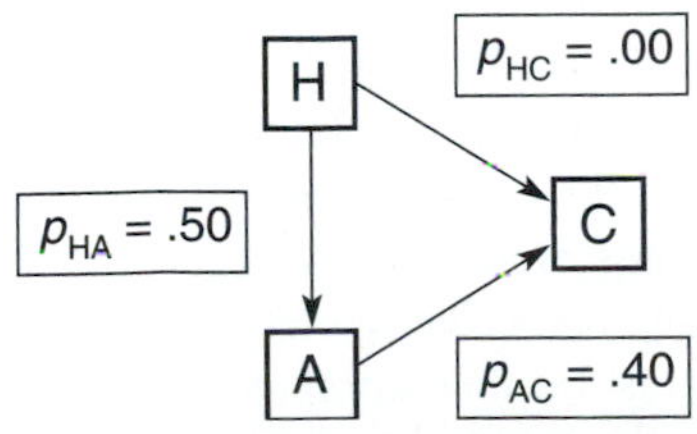

FIGURE 7.10 Diagram of path coefficients relating to college success. (*Note:* H = home experiences; A = academic experiences; and C = college success.)

equation modeling is a statistical methodology that enables researchers to take a confirmatory approach to correlational research. Like some of the other multivariate statistical procedures used by researchers to explore causal relationships, structural equation modeling includes the use of regression models to represent the causal relationships under study. These regression models are similar in nature to the regression models that we discussed previously under multiple regression and path analysis.

In contrast to other multivariate statistics used by researchers to explore causal relationships, structural equation modeling differs in two important ways (Fornell, 1982). The first aspect of structural equation modeling that sets it apart from other multivariate statistical procedures is that it takes an explicit confirmatory approach to data analysis rather than an exploratory one. Although other multivariate procedures such as path analysis may be used to explore potential causal relationships, they are typically used in a descriptive or exploratory in manner. For example, recall that path analysis only allows researchers to choose from a number of potential explanatory pathways. In contrast, structural equation modeling requires that the nature and pattern of relationship among variables be specified a priori. Structural equation modeling lends itself to inferential data analysis that enables researchers to assess small deviations from an explicit model. Significant deviations from the model would invalidate the hypothesized causal relationships among variables.

The second aspect of structural equation modeling that sets it apart from other multivariate statistical procedures is its ability to provide explicit estimates of measurement error. Providing explicit estimates enables the researcher to obtain a more accurate picture of the relationships among variables that other multivariate statistical procedures cannot provide.

Finally, structural equation modeling enables researchers to incorporate both observed and unobserved or latent variables in their models. Recall that latent variables or factors represent theoretical constructs that cannot be observed directly but are presumed to underlie observed measures.

The use of latent variables in structural equation modeling enables researchers to combine a number of measures to assess the constructs of interest. Each of the measures underlying the constructs measures a different aspect of each particular construct that is the same principle that we discussed under factor analysis (i.e., a large number of variables on a measurement device are reduced to a factor or set of factors).

Consider a hypothetical study in which the relationship among parental psychological control, parental behavioral control, quality of child care, and child social adjustment is of interest. The first step in structural equation modeling is to specify the causal relationship among each of the latent variables. In our hypothetical study, we will use three measures to assess each of the latent variables. Figure 7.11 depicts the causal relationship among parental psychological control, parental behavioral control, quality of child care, and child social adjustment. The model used in the structural equation model is similar to that used in path analysis. The latent variables are depicted by ovals and the specific measures (referred to as manifest variables) used to assess aspects of the latent variables are depicted by rectangles. Inspection of Figure 7.11 reveals that three manifest measures were used to assess each of the latent variables. The straight arrows indicate hypothesized causal relationships. The curved arrows indicate a relationship between variables.

The manifest variables are then combined in the second step through a factor analytic process. This process identifies the common variance among the manifest variables or the factor they share in common. The factor analysis process also tests whether each manifest variable correlates at a sufficiently high level with the factor used to represent the particular latent variable.

Path coefficients are then computed for each hypothesized causal relationship between latent variables in the final step of structural equation modeling. Again, a path coefficient is the proportion of variance in a dependent variable for which

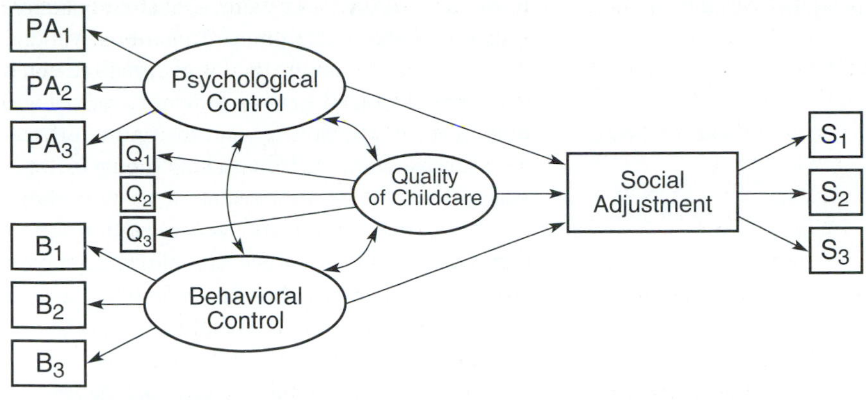

FIGURE 7.11 A figure of the causal relationship between parental psychological control, parental behavioral control, quality child care, and child social adjustment.

the independent variable is uniquely responsible, with the effects of the other independent variables partialled out. Returning to our hypothetical study, say that the obtained path coefficients are as follows: .55 for psychological control, .03 for quality of child care, and .70 for behavioral control. We would conclude that parental behavioral control and parental psychological control have more influence on child social adjustment than quality of child care because a larger path coefficient indicates a larger influence.

Structural equation modeling is a statistical procedure that is commonly used by researchers to explore causal relationships in correlational research. Although structural equation modeling is more sophisticated than path analysis, many of the same limitations we discussed with path analysis apply with structural equation modeling. The strength of structural equation modeling lies primarily in its ability to measure latent variables with maximal reliability. This ability provides a level of precision that is not available with path analysis.

Internal Validity. As with the causal-comparative research design, the threats to internal validity do not match the correlational design well. There are some obvious threats, but most of the threats discussed previously are not applicable to correlational research. Most of the threats are not applicable because the correlational research design has not traditionally been used to determine cause-and-effect relationships. However, we can say that interpreting the results of correlational research studies should be done cautiously. Critical research consumers should not assume correlational findings to be proof of cause-and-effect relationships. Researchers must ensure that all of the potential explanatory variables for the phenomenon under study can be accounted for or included in their analyses. One study cannot account for all of the potential explanatory variables even when the researcher has employed advanced statistical procedures such as path analysis or structural equation modeling that tend to meet the criteria established by Cook and Campbell (1979) for concluding that a causal relationship exists among variables.

As with experimental studies, causal relationships can only be established through multiple replications. As such, several threats to internal validity exist for correlational studies. These threats are shown in Table 7.4. As shown in the table, the major threats are instrumentation and testing. Instrumentation may be a threat if there is a concern with the reliability of the measurement device. Recall from Chapter 3, validity

TABLE 7.4 Threats to the Internal Validity of Correlational Research

THREAT	RESEARCH DESIGN CORRELATIONAL
1. Maturation	Not applicable
2. Selection	Not applicable
3. Selection by maturation interaction	Not applicable
4. Statistical regression	Not applicable
5. Mortality	Not applicable
6. Instrumentation	Possible concern
7. Testing	Possible concern
8. History	Not applicable
9. Resentful demoralization of the control group	Not applicable
10. Diffusion of treatment	Not applicable
11. Compensatory rivalry by the control group	Not applicable
12. Compensatory equalization	Not applicable

Note: This table is meant only as a general guideline. Decisions with regard to threats to internal validity must be made after the specifics of an investigation are known and understood. Thus, interpretations of internal validity threats must be made on a study-by-study basis.

is affected by reliability. Therefore, if a researcher is using a test with low reliability, the validity of the results must be in question.

Testing is an obvious problem because participants are exposed to two assessments. Exposure to the first assessment may affect the performance on the second, increasing the correlation of the two assessments. For example, if one were to test the correlation between teacher attitudes held toward students and student success in the classroom, the teacher's exposure to an attitude test may affect the way the teacher interacts with the students (e.g., provides more or less instructional support), which in turn affects the students' classroom performance. Thus, the teacher's attitudes toward students may not be the cause of student performance, but the exposure to the first assessment may have led to the change in student performance.

External Validity. As with causal-comparative research, some of the threats to external validity do not typically apply to correlational research (e.g., interaction of personological variables and treatment effects, novelty and disruption effects, pretest sensitization). However, as shown in Table 7.5, several threats are present. A primary threat to the external validity is "generalization across participants." Convenience sampling techniques are frequently used rather than random selection procedures. Therefore, the results of the study are unlikely to generalize across participants.

Other external validity threats include interaction of time of measurement and treatment effects,

TABLE 7.5 Threats to the External Validity of Correlational Research

THREAT	RESEARCH DESIGN CORRELATIONAL
1. Generalization across participants	Possible concern
2. Interaction of personological variables and treatment effects	Not applicable
3. Verification of independent variable	Not applicable
4. Multiple treatment interference	Not applicable
5. Novelty and disruption effects	Not applicable
6. Hawthorne effect	Not applicable
7. Experimenter effects	Not applicable
8. Pretest sensitization	Not applicable
9. Posttest sensitization	Not applicable
10. Interaction of time of measurement and treatment effects	Possible concern
11. Measurement of the dependent variable	Possible concern
12. Interaction of history and treatment effects	Possible concern

Note: This table is meant only as a general guideline. Decisions with regard to threats to external validity must be made after the specifics of an investigation are known and understood. Thus, interpretations of external validity threats must be made on a study-by-study basis.

measurement of the dependent variable, and interaction of history and treatment effects. Interaction of time of measurement and treatment effects is a threat since we would not expect the results to maintain for any length of time unless there was evidence to that effect. The measurement of the dependent variable is also a problem if the measurements are indirect versus direct (e.g., observation). Thus, researchers must look closely at the dependent variable to determine whether the results would generalize beyond the dependent measure used in the study. Finally, there may be an interaction of history and treatment effects if we suspect that there is some event or situation that occurred during the assessments that could have affected participants' responses to those assessments. For example, if teachers were undergoing budget cuts when their attitudes toward students were assessed, the responses to the attitude assessment may be different than if they were not going through such cuts in funding. In other words, the concern is whether there would be a similar correlation between attitudes toward students and student classroom performance if teachers in another school district were not faced with similar circumstances.

Research Examples

We have chosen two studies in which the researchers employed regression analysis procedures to explore the relationships among variables for two reasons. First, these procedures are commonly used by researchers in correlational research. Second, multiple regression is one of the most versatile multivariate statistical procedures available to researchers. Researchers use regression analysis procedures because these procedures enable them to better explore the overall relationships and interrelationships between a set of independent variables and a dependent variable. The use of regression analysis allows researchers to maximize the usefulness of the correlational research method. Indeed, there are relatively few correlational studies in which researchers explore the relationship between only two variables. In the examples, we provide a brief overview of the findings including tables depicting the key findings. We will more fully describe how to interpret the results of a multiple regression analysis in our description of the procedure that follows.

Exploring Relationships Study. An example of correlational research that is aimed at exploring relationships among variables is a study conducted by Burchinal, Roberts, Nabors, and Bryant (1996). Burchinal and colleagues used the correlational research method to explore the relationship between quality of center child care and child development. Quality of child care, whether it is delivered in homes or centers, is believed to be positively related to child development. Burchinal and colleagues were interested in studying the effects of quality of child care on child development because of the dramatic changes occurring in American society regarding the care of young children. Growing numbers of young children are spending large amounts of time in child care centers rather than in home settings. Data on the quality of child-rearing environments and infant development (i.e., mental development index, expressive language, receptive language, and communication skills) were collected on 79 African American 12-month-old children enrolled in nine different centers.

Burchinal and colleagues (1996) used four sets (models) of regression analysis procedures to explore the relationship between quality of center child care and child development. The first set of regression analysis procedures was used to explore the relationship between the process quality of child care (i.e., the environment, curriculum, teacher–child interactions, and teaching practices) and child development and whether this relationship was moderated by child or family characteristics (see Model 1 in Table 7.6). The second set of regression analysis procedures was used to study the relationships between the structural quality of child care (i.e., class size, child/adult ratio, and teacher education) and child development and whether this relationship was moderated by child and family characteristics (see Models 2, 3, and 4 in Table 7.6).

The results indicated that quality of child care was positively correlated with scores on standardized assessments of cognitive development (Bayley Scales of Infant Development), language development (Sequenced Inventory of Communication Development), and communication skills (Communication and Symbolic Behavior Scales). When the relationship between quality of care in centers and home was adjusted, the process quality of child care independently related to child cognitive development and one structural quality of care variable (i.e., child/adult ratio) related to the overall communication skills of young children. Neither child or family factors were found to moderate or affect the relationship between quality of child care and child development.

Predictive Study. An example of correlational research that is predictive in nature involves a study conducted by Kochenderfer and Ladd (1996). Kochenderfer and Ladd used the correlational research method to examine whether peer

TABLE 7.6 Regression Results: Relating Child Care Quality and Characteristics of the Family and Child to Infant Cognitive and Language Outcomes

	STANDARDIZED REGRESSION COEFFICIENT			
	MENTAL DEVELOPMENT INDEX (MDI)	EXPRESSIVE LANGUAGE (SICD-ECA)	RECEPTIVE LANGUAGE (SICD-RCA)	COMMUNICATION SKILLS (CSBS TOTAL)
Model 1				
ITERS	.32*	.12	.10	.10
Day-care-entry age	.13	.25	.10	.20
HOME	.19	.08	.37**	.20
Poverty	.15	–.16	–.11	–.19
Sex (male)	–.06	–.12	–.09	–.04
Model 2				
Infant-adult ratio	–.17	–.06	–.17	–.30*
Day-care-entry age	.19	.28**	.10	.21
HOME	.24	.11	.37**	.19
Poverty	.12	–.18	–.11	–.19
Sex (male)	–.07	–.13	–.10	–.08
Model 3				
Infant class size	–.08	–.17	–.09	–.22
Day-care-entry age	.19	.30*	.12	.22
HOME	.26*	.13	.40**	.23
Poverty	.12	–.17	–.12	–.19
Sex (male)	–.06	–.13	–.10	–.05
Model 4				
Teacher education	.05	.18	.03	.02
Day-care-entry age	.21	.25	.11	.20
HOME	.23	.09	.40**	.23
Poverty	.11	–.14	–.09	–.18
Sex (male)	–.09	–.12	–.11	–.05

Source: Adapted from Burchinal et al. (1996, Table 4, p. 615). Quality of center child care and infant cognitive and language development. *Child Development, 67,* 606–620.
*$p < .05$; **$p < .01$.

victimization is a precursor to school maladjustment. They were interested in exploring this because previous research had shown that a substantial number of children are victimized by their peers and are at risk for a variety of adjustment problems. Data on peer victimization and school maladjustment (loneliness, school liking, school avoidance, and academic achievement) were collected on two hundred 5- and 6-year-old children in the fall and spring of kindergarten. Kochenderfer and Ladd used the kindergarten year because as children enter kindergarten, they are typically placed in new peer groups and know relatively few, if any, of their classmates thereby providing a natural context for examining whether early victimization predicts school maladjustment.

Kochenderfer and Ladd (1996) used two contrasting sets of four regression analysis procedures to explore whether peer victimization is a precursor of children's school maladjustment on each set. The first set of four regression analysis procedures was used to explore whether peer victimization predicted school maladjustment, and the second set of four regression analysis procedures was used to explore whether early school maladjustment was predictive of peer victimization. Regression analysis procedures were used for each of the four measures of school adjustment (loneliness, school liking, school avoidance, and academic achievement).

Consider Table 7.7, which presents the results of the multiple regression analysis for the

TABLE 7.7 Results of a Four-Regression Analysis Procedure: Predicting Changes in School Adjustment from Early Peer Victimization

	R_2	R_2INC	β
Spring loneliness			
Fall loneliness	.16	.16***	.41
Sex	.17	.00	.07
Fall victimization	.21	.04***	.22
Sex victimization	.21***	.00	.06
Spring school liking			
Fall school liking	.28	.28***	.53
Sex	.28	.00	.01
Fall victimization	.29***	.00	–.12
Sex × victimization	.29***	.00	.13
Spring school avoidance			
Fall school avoidance	.22	.22***	.47
Sex	.23	.00	–.06
Fall victimization	.28	.06***	.25
Sex × victimization	.29***	.01	.27
Spring academic achievement			
Fall achievement	.46	.46***	.68
Sex	.46	.00	–.01
Fall victimization	.46	.00	.00
Sex × victimization	.46***	.01	–.27

Source: Adapted from Kochenderfer & Ladd (1996, Table 3, p. 1311). Peer victimization: Cause or consequence of school maladjustment? *Child Development, 67,* 1305–1317.

***$p < .001$.

study to help us understand how to interpret the results of the multiple regression analysis. The far left hand column presents the four different regression models (i.e., Spring loneliness, Spring school liking, Spring school avoidance, and Spring academic achievement) that Kochenderfer and Ladd (1996) studied using multiple regression procedures. The second column (R^2) presents the obtained overall regression coefficient associated with the addition of each independent variable. The third column (R^2inc) presents the increment increase in the overall regression coefficient with the addition of each of the predictors. For example, the introduction of sex in the second regression model (Spring school liking) did not change the overall correlation coefficient (.28). Thus, the increment change in R^2 was zero. The fourth column (ß) presents the beta weights associated with each of the independent variables. This column provides the best indicator of the relative effect of each of the independent variables on the dependent variables. Early peer victimization emerged as a significant predictor of changes in loneliness and school avoidance. Sex and sex by victimization effects failed to achieve statistical significance.

To examine the proposition that early school maladjustment is predictive of peer victimization for each regression analysis procedure, the spring peer victimization scores were entered as the dependent variable and the fall peer victimization scores were entered in Step 1. Sex was entered in Step 2 to control for possible gender differences in victimization. In each regression analysis procedure, one of the four measures of school maladjustment was entered in Step 3 followed by the corresponding sex by school maladjustment interaction term. Fall school maladjustment failed to emerge as a significant predictor of changes in peer victimization. The main term for sex and the sex by school maladjustment interaction term failed to achieve statistical significance.

Taken together, the results of these two contrasting sets of regression analysis procedures indicated that peer victimization is a precursor of school maladjustment. Of course, as with all correlational research, it is important for researchers not to draw causal conclusions based on the results of one study. Although the findings are relatively convincing because Kochenderfer and Ladd (1996) established both the temporal order and association between peer victimization and school maladjustment, a great deal of additional research would be needed to draw such conclusions. Issues associated with the interpretations of correlational research are described in more detail in what follows.

WHEN SHOULD RESEARCHERS USE THE CORRELATIONAL RESEARCH METHOD?

The correlational research method is commonly used by researchers for a number of reasons. First, as with the causal-comparative research method, the correlational research method is used in those cases in which it is difficult or next to impossible to manipulate the variable of interest experimentally or when researchers are exploring potential causal relationships among variables. Second, although education and psychology rely on an experimental paradigm in which a single presumed causal variable is manipulated while other potential variables are held constant, this paradigm may not adequately address the complexity of matters (e.g., achievement motivation, psychosis, anxiety) studied in education and psychology. The correlational research method enables researchers to manage the multiplicity of factors often associated with any given variable under study. Third, correlational statistical procedures can be used to sort out the effect of relationships among variables. In some cases, sorting out the effect of the relationships among variables may be more important than identifying the overall effect of factors associated with any given variable under study. Fourth, correlational statistical procedures such as multiple regression enable researchers to use information from various scales of measurement. Finally, correlational statistical procedures such as path analysis and structural equation modeling can be used to establish causal relationships among variables.

DISCUSSION QUESTIONS

1. Upon studying the correlational research method, a student begins to realize just how many studies reported in the media are correlational in nature. The student begins to wonder what the purpose is of all of these studies. What would you say is the purpose of correlational research?

2. Unfortunately, although correlational research is used so often, many people do not understand issues involved with their use. What are some of the critical issues that researchers should consider when designing correlational research?

3. A friend is told that it is useful to use a variance interpretation of correlation coefficients in correlational research. Why would this be so?

4. Beta weights are sometimes confusing to students when studying the correlational research method. Explain what beta weights are and describe why is it more useful to consider beta weights when interpreting multiple correlations.

5. Some researchers indicate that correlational research cannot determine cause-and-effect relationships. With the more powerful statistical procedures present today, cause-and-effect relationships can be determined statistically (although many researchers will make an argument that one needs to manipulate the independent variable directly to establish a cause-and-effect relationship). What types of correlational statistical procedures are used to establish cause-and-effect relationships between variables?

6. You learned about univariate distributions in Chapter 4. Describe what a bivariate frequency distribution is. For the following scores, graph the bivariate distribution and make a statement (i.e., low, moderate, high) about the relationship between the variables by looking at the graph (make an estimate).

Student	Variable *A*	Variable *B*
1	20	5
2	15	2
3	25	8
4	10	7
5	18	10
6	12	4
7	14	4
8	10	3
9	23	9
10	22	10

7. You are reading a correlational research article and notice that the researcher used inferential statistics to help interpret her data. You remember that inferential statistics are used to infer back to the population from the sample. Explain the logic behind the researcher's decision to use statistical significance testing with correlation coefficients.

8. A colleague is unsure of the relationship between the correlation coefficient and causality. What would you tell him?

9. The colleague asks you how many researchers can claim to determine cause-and-effect relationships from correlational data. You indicate that there are three conditions researchers must meet in order to infer a causal relationship between two variables using the correlational research method. What are these conditions?

10. Recall from Chapter 4 that there are several scales of measurement. The colleague asks you if correlational research can be done only with interval-scale data. You indicate that there are different statistical tests for different scales of measurement. Describe the correlational statistical procedures applicable for the different scales of measurement.

PEER VICTIMIZATION: CAUSE OR CONSEQUENCE OF SCHOOL MALADJUSTMENT?

BECKY J. KOCHENDERFER AND GARY W. LADD
University of Illinois at Urbana–Champaign

Kochenderfer, Becky J., and Ladd, Gary W. Peer Victimization: Cause or Consequence Of School Maladjustment? Child Development, *1996, 67, 1305–1317. Past research has shown that peer victimization and school maladjustment are related, but it is unclear whether victimization is a cause or consequence of such difficulties. This study examined whether (*a*) peer victimization is a precursor of school maladjustment, (*b*) the effects are limited to the period of victimization, and (*c*) stable peer victimization experiences compound adjustment difficulties. Toward this end, data were collected on 200 5- and 6-year-old children (105 males, 95 females) in the fall and spring of kindergarten. Findings supported the hypothesis that victimization is a precursor of children's loneliness and school avoidance. Whereas children's feelings of loneliness were more pronounced while victimization was occurring, delayed effects were found for school avoidance. Furthermore, the duration of children's victimization experiences was related to the magnitude of their school adjustment problems.*

Concern about children who are victimized by their peers has increased as a result of research conducted on childhood aggression (see Patterson, Littman, & Bricker, 1967; Perry, Kusel, & Perry, 1988) and bullying behavior (Boulton & Underwood, 1992; Olweus, 1991). However, peer victimization has not been as well defined nor as well investigated relative to its counterparts—aggressive and bullying behaviors (see Perry et al., 1988). Whereas some researchers have construed peer victimization as an outcome of bullying behaviors (i.e., a subtype of aggression that is unprovoked, occurs repeatedly and over time, and is perpetrated by a stronger child against a weaker one; see Olweus, 1991), others have framed the concept of victimization more broadly as a role or position that children occupy in aggressive encounters (i.e., the target of peers' aggressive behaviors; see Perry et al., 1988). Consistent with Perry, Kusel, and Perry, we define peer victimization more broadly, that is, as a form of peer abuse in which a child is frequently the target of peer aggression.

Recent investigations have shown that a substantial number of children are victimized by their peers at school (Boulton & Underwood, 1992; Olweus, 1991; Perry et al., 1988). Findings from these studies suggest that approximately 9%–10% of 8–16-year-olds are teased or attacked by schoolmates on a regular basis. There is also evidence to suggest that the prevalence of peer victimization is greater among younger as compared to older

Preparation of this article was supported by National Institute of Mental Health Grant MH-49223 to Gary W. Ladd. Correspondence concerning this article should be addressed to Becky Kochenderfer or Gary Ladd, University of Illinois, 183 Children's Research Center, 51 Gerty Drive, Champaign, IL 61820.

school-age populations. Olweus (1991) found that the proportion of students victimized by peers in second through sixth grade (11.6%) was twice that of students in grades 7–9 (5.4%). Kochenderfer and Ladd (in press) found even higher rates of victimization among kindergarten children; 22.6% of their sample of 5–6-year-olds reported moderate to high levels of peer victimization.

There is also growing evidence to indicate that victimized children are at risk for a variety of adjustment problems. Studies have shown that victimized children are more anxious and insecure (Olweus, 1993), have lower self-esteem (Alsaker, 1993; Bjorkqvist, Ekman, & Lagerspetz, 1982; Lagerspetz, Bjorkqvist, Berts, & King, 1982; Olweus, 1993), and are more likely to be depressed (Bjorkqvist et al., 1982; Olweus, 1992) than nonvictimized age mates. Additionally, victimized children appear to have greater difficulty adjusting to school. Compared to nonvictimized classmates, victimized children are lonelier (Boulton & Underwood, 1992; Kochenderfer & Ladd, in press; Olweus, 1993) and less happy in school (Boulton & Underwood, 1992), and display lower levels of school liking and higher levels of school avoidance (Kochenderfer & Ladd, in press).

Unfortunately, the linkage between peer victimization and children's adjustment problems has not been well investigated. Because most researchers have relied primarily on concurrent assessments to examine the relation between these constructs, it remains unclear as to whether peer victimization is a cause or a consequence of children's adjustment problems. Moreover, much of the data on the relation between peer victimization and children's adjustment has been gathered during the middle grade school years when victimization patterns have been shown to be relatively stable (see Boulton & Underwood, 1992). By this point in children's school careers, it may be difficult to disentangle the linkage between victimization and children's adjustment, as these relations may already be well established.

In order to obtain clues about the causal priority of these variables, there is a need to conduct longitudinal studies with samples of relatively unacquainted children—before aggressor/victim patterns have been established. By identifying such samples and assessing both victimization and adjustment at multiple points in time, it would be possible for investigators to determine whether it is early victimization that predicts changes in adjustment or vice versa.

Kindergarten provides a natural window for examining this question because as children enter grade school they are typically placed in new peer groups and know relatively few, if any, of their classmates (Ladd & Price, 1987). Furthermore, kindergarten is unique in that, upon entering grade school, children are faced with many new demands, such as adjusting to a novel school environment and unfamiliar personnel, gaining acceptance into a new peer group, and confronting more challenging academic demands (Ladd & Price, 1987). On one hand, it is possible that children who are victimized during this challenging period may have more difficulty adjusting to school. Being victimized early in the school year may lead some children to develop negative attitudes, feelings and perceptions toward school. On the other hand, it is plausible that children who have difficulty adjusting to school may evoke higher levels of victimization from peers. Children who exhibit negative attitudes and/or effects early during the school year may display a kind of vulnerability that may invite attacks from peers.

Hence, one objective of the present investigation was to examine more closely the link between children's victimization experiences and their school adjustment in kindergarten. Specifically, it was of interest to explore the hypothesis that early peer victimization has a negative impact on children's school adjustment and, in particular, leads to the formation of negative school attitudes, perceptions, and feelings. Toward this end, we identified a sample of kindergarten children and assessed both peer victimization and school adjustment twice during the school year (i.e., fall, spring). Several school adjustment indices (see Ladd, 1989; Ladd & Price, 1987) were assessed at each time of measurement, including (*a*) school attitudes (i.e., how much children like school), (*b*) school affect (i.e., loneliness in school), (*c*) school involvement (i.e., expressed desire to avoid school), and (*d*) academic achievement. Data produced by this longitudinal design were analyzed to determine whether early victimization experiences predicted changes in children's school adjustment or whether early adjustment difficulties forecasted changes in children's victimization status. Consistent with our hypotheses, it was anticipated that the results of these analyses would support the interpretation that peer victimization is a precursor of children's school adjustment problems.

Furthermore, the timing and duration of peer victimization may play a crucial role in the adjustment outcomes experienced by young victimized children. Although there is evidence to suggest that peer victimization is a relatively stable phenomenon as early as second grade (by 8 or 9 years of age; Boulton & Underwood, 1992; Olweus, 1992), little is known about the onset and stability of peer victimization at younger grade levels. It is conceivable that young children's exposure to peer victimization may be either an acute or chronic experience and may emerge at different times during the school year. For instance, Perry, Perry, and Boldizar (1990) have argued that, as children enter new peer groups (e.g., kindergarten), aggressive children direct negative behaviors toward a variety of targets. Then, as aggressors learn the reactions of their victims, the field of victims become increasingly narrow. Based on this contention, it was anticipated that many children would be exposed to peer aggression soon after they entered kindergarten, but only a minority of students would continue to be victimized throughout the school year.

Additionally, it is possible that other factors emerge during the school year that increase children's risk for peer victimization. Thus, children who are not initially exposed to peer aggression may become so as their characteristics (i.e., individual differences) become apparent to peers. For example, school activities, such as academics or sports, may become more salient as the year progresses, and children who perform less well in such domains may be targeted for peer victimization. Consequently, it was also expected that some children would not be exposed to victimization until later in the school year.

To date, researchers have not examined how the *duration* of children's victimization experiences may affect their adjustment. As data from concurrent assessments illustrate, peer victimization is often accompanied by adjustment difficulties (Alsaker, 1993; Boulton & Underwood, 1992; Kochenderfer, 1995). However, it is unknown whether children's difficulties abate when they are no longer victimized, nor is it known whether their difficulties are accentuated if victimization continues. It is conceivable that adjustment problems are closely associated with children's victimization experiences and persist only as long as victimization is occurring. Conversely, brief exposures to victimization may have effects that endure throughout the school year, even after the victimization has ceased. It is also possible that the magnitude or severity of children's school adjustment problems may be even greater when children experience victimization over protracted periods of time.

To investigate these potential linkages, groups of children were identified who experienced peer victimization at different times during the school year (i.e., fall vs. spring), and for different durations (i.e., only in the fall, only in the spring, or both). One group consisted of children who were exposed to victimization in the fall of kindergarten but did not report such experiences in the spring (i.e., Fall Only Victims). A second group included children who were not victimized in the fall, but were so in the spring (i.e., Spring Only Victims). Children who reported victimization at both points in time were assigned to a third group (i.e., Stable Victims). Finally, children who were classified as nonvictims constituted a fourth group (i.e., Nonvictims).

Comparisons among these groups allowed us to address the issues raised above. First, this design allowed a closer examination of the linkage between concurrently measured indices of victimization and school adjustment. Based on past evidence indicating that children's victimization experiences coincide with their adjustment difficulties (Alsaker, 1993; Boulton & Underwood, 1992; Kochenderfer, 1995), it was expected that children's reports of such problems would be greatest during periods of victimization. Specifically, we hypothesized that children who were exposed to victimization in the fall (i.e., Fall Only Victim and Stable Victim groups) would show higher levels of school adjustment difficulties in the fall compared to children in the Nonvictim group. Similarly, in the spring, it was expected that the Spring Only Victim and Stable Victim groups would display greater adjustment difficulties as compared to children not targeted for peer aggression (i.e., Nonvictims).

Second, this longitudinal, group design permitted an examination of the extent to which school adjustment problems are linked to changes in children's exposure to victimization over time. It was hypothesized that adjustment problems are limited to the time victimization is occurring. Thus, it was anticipated that adjustment problems displayed early in the school year (i.e., in the fall) by the Fall Only Victims would abate in the spring when these children were no longer victimized. Also consistent with this logic, children in the Spring Only Victim group were not expected to display adjustment problems until later in the school year when they encountered higher levels of victimization. Therefore, two specific hypotheses were tested in the present investigation: (*a*) children in the Fall Only Victim group would exhibit significant decreases in school adjustment difficulties from fall to spring, and (*b*) children in the Spring Only Victim group would evidence significant increases in school adjustment problems from fall to spring.

However, it was also possible that children in the Fall Only Victim group would continue to display adjustment problems in the spring, even though they are no longer victimized by their peers. Findings indicating that the early adjustment difficulties exhibited by the Fall Only Victim group do *not* decrease significantly would lend support to the counterargument that peer victimization has enduring effects on children's school adjustment.

The third issue examined was the possibility that stable victimization experiences compound children's school adjustment difficulties. It was anticipated that children who continued to be victimized over the school year (i.e., Stable Victims) would show significant increases in school maladjustment from fall to spring of kindergarten.

METHOD

Subjects

The sample consisted of 200 kindergarten children who were recruited from three school systems in the midwestern United States.[1] There were 105 males and 95 females whose mean age was 5.50 at the beginning of the school year. All subjects were participants in a larger 5-year longitudinal project, and informed parental consent was obtained for all children as they entered kindergarten. Only classrooms for which permission rates exceeded 80% were included in the project (n = 16). Participants came from diverse socioeconomic backgrounds: 36.8% were lower- to lower-middle income (less than $20,000); 30.6% were middle income ($21,000-$40,000); and the

---

[1]This sample of 200 5–6-year-old children was used in an earlier study (Kochenderfer & Ladd, in press) that examined the prevalence rate, manifestation, and behavioral correlates of peer victimization early in kindergarten. Further, findings from this initial investigation showed that peer victimization early in the school year (i.e., fall) was predictive of school adjustment later in kindergarten (i.e., spring). These findings raised the need for a more detailed examination of how variations in children's peer victimization experiences over the course of the school year (i.e., timing and duration) are related to *changes* in school adjustment.

remainder were upper-middle to high-income families (above $41,000). The ethnic composition of the sample was representative of that found in the participating school systems: 20.0% African American, 2.0% Latino; 73.5% Caucasian; and 4.5% mixed race and other.

Measures

Self-Reports of Peer Victimization. The Perceptions of Peer Support Scale (PPSS; see Ladd, Kochenderfer, & Coleman, 1996) was administered to children during individual interviews to obtain information about children's perceptions of classroom peers. Four of the items on this scale allowed children to self-report the extent to which they had experienced peer aggression. These items loaded on a factor that was separate from the remaining items on the scale and produced a relatively consistent pattern of responses from children (alpha of four-item subscale = .74). During interviews, the items were presented to children as follows: Does anyone in your class ever: (1) pick on you at school? (2) hit you at school? (3) say mean things to you at school? (4) say bad things about you to other kids at school? Prior to asking these questions, interviewers trained children to use a three-point response format (scale): no (1), sometimes (2), a lot (3). Victimization scores were calculated by averaging the four items (scores ranged from 1.00 to 3.00).

In order to identify a group of children who had experienced high levels of peer aggression, children were classified as victims if, across the four items, they received scores that averaged above the scale's midpoint of "sometimes" (i.e., 2.25 on the three-point scale). This criterion is consistent with the conceptualization of peer victimization as a form of abuse in which a child is frequently targeted for peer aggression. For instance, Olweus (1991) considered children to be victims if they reported being targeted for aggressive behaviors repeatedly and over time. Thus, our cut-off is an attempt to distinguish between those kindergartners who are occasionally the recipients of peers' aggressive overtures and those children who are *persistently* targeted for aggression. Furthermore, this cut-off criterion was chosen to be comparable to the "now and then, or more often" self-report criterion utilized by Olweus to identify victimized children. Moreover, the proportion of children identified using this criterion (20.5%) approximates that found in other samples of kindergarten children (18%; Kochenderfer, 1995) and Olweus's youngest sample of children (17%; second graders).

The validity of the self-report measure of peer victimization was examined with a separate sample of kindergarten children (see Kochenderfer & Ladd, 1996). Based on observational data, these investigators concluded that the self-report measure produced sufficiently reliable and valid data for identifying young victims. That is, children who were identified as victims based on self-reports were also rated by observers as experiencing significantly higher levels of peer aggression in their classrooms compared to children who were classified as nonvictims. Additionally, evidence of concurrent validity for both self-reports and observer ratings of victimization was obtained. Specifically, both victimization measures correlated positively with loneliness (see Alsaker, 1993; Boulton & Underwood, 1992) and negatively with peer acceptance (see Alsaker, 1993; Boulton & Underwood, 1992; Perry, Kusel, & Perry, 1988).

Over 75% of kindergarten children reported experiencing some level of peer aggression at each assessment period (i.e., received an average score that was greater than 1.05; Fall: $M = 1.66$, $SD = .57$; Spring: $M = 1.61$, $SD = .56$). However, as mentioned above, in order to be classified as a "victim" a child had to receive a victimization score which indicated that she or he was *frequently* targeted for peer aggression. Based on this criterion, victimization groups were created by identifying children who had scores above 2.25 only in the fall (Fall Only Victim) and only in the spring (Spring Only Victim). Children who reported this relatively high level of victimization in both fall and spring were assigned to a Stable Victim group, and children whose victimization scores fell below the cut-off criterion at both points in time were assigned to the Nonvictim group.[2]

School Liking and Avoidance. A revised version of the School Liking and Avoidance Questionnaire (Ladd & Price, 1987) was also administered to children during individual interviews to tap differences in their school attitudes (e.g., how much they like school) and involvement (i.e., expressed desire to avoid school). This 14-item scale factored into a nine-item school liking subscale (e.g., "Do you like being in school?" alpha = .91) and a five-item school avoidance subscale (e.g., "Do you wish you didn't have to come to school?" alpha = .81) Children were trained to respond to a three-point response format (scale): yes (3), sometimes (2), or no (1). Scores were obtained for each subscale by averaging children's scores across items.

Loneliness. The Cassidy and Asher (1992) Loneliness and Social Dissatisfaction Questionnaire (LSDQ) was also individually administered to children. To obtain a measure of loneliness that was distinct from social dissatisfaction, a subscale was created that included three LSDQ items (those that refer directly to loneliness) and two additional items that were added to the scale (i.e., "Is school a lonely place for you?" "Are you sad and alone at school?"). Scores were created by averaging children's yes (3), sometimes (2), or no (1) responses over these five items (alpha = .78).

Academic achievement. The Metropolitan Readiness Test (MRT; Nurss & McGauvran, 1986) was used to assess children's academic progress at two points in time. For the fall assessment, Level 1 was administered during individual interviews. A fall achievement score was calculated by averaging the verbal and language stanine scores. During the spring semester, Level 2 of the MRT was administered in groups of about 15 children. Spring achievement scores were computed by averaging the stanine scores for the verbal, language, and quantitative subtests.

Procedure. As part of the larger longitudinal study, children were individually interviewed during two 40-min sessions during both the fall and spring of the kindergarten year. With the exception of the MRT, which was group-administered in the spring, the same measures were given in both semesters and were administered in a counterbalanced order across sessions. Before each interview, children were told that their participation was voluntary and that their responses were confidential. After each session, children received colorful stickers and pencils for their participation.

RESULTS

Relations among School Adjustment Measures

Correlations among the fall and spring school adjustment indices were low to moderate in magnitude (see Table 1). The magnitude of these correlations suggests that the subscales tap different aspects of school adjustment and, consequently, all subscales were retained for the following analyses.

---

[2]A more extreme nonvictim group was also created that included only those children in the sample who received scores of 1.00 at both points in time (n = 18; 9% of the sample). MANOVAs recalculated using this group (see "Results" section) produced findings that were nearly identical to those reported for the group of 135 children with scores below the 2.25 cut-off at both assessment periods. Means for this extreme nonvictim group were as follows: fall loneliness (1.16), spring loneliness (1.11), fall school liking (2.93), spring school liking (2.84), fall avoidance (1.83), spring avoidance (1.54), fall achievement (5.06), spring achievement (5.56).

TABLE 1 Correlation among Fall and Spring School Adjustment Indices

	Fall Assessment		
	SCHOOL LIKING	**SCHOOL AVOIDANCE**	**ACADEMIC ACHIEVEMENT**
Loneliness	−.23***	.26***	−.34***
School liking	...	−.45***	.18**
School avoidance	...	...	−.21**
	Spring Assessment		
	SCHOOL LIKING	**SCHOOL AVOIDANCE**	**ACADEMIC ACHIEVEMENT**
Loneliness	−.35***	.29***	−.23***
School liking	...	−.64***	.15*
School avoidance	...	...	−.13

*$p < .05$.
**$p < .01$.
***$p < .001$.

TABLE 2 Correlations between Peer Victimization and School Adjustment Indices

	FALL VICTIMIZATION	**SPRING VICTIMIZATION**
Fall school adjustment indices:		
Loneliness	.31***	.17*
School liking	−.21**	−.17*
School avoidance	.19**	.17*
Academic Achievement	−.09	−.12
Spring school adjustment indices:		
Loneliness	.33***	.30***
School liking	−.27**	−.27***
School avoidance	.33***	.36***
Academic achievement	−.06	−.24***

*$p < .05$.
**$p < .01$.
***$p < .001$.

Prevalence and Stability of Peer Victimization

In the fall, 20.5% of the kindergartners reported being victimized, on the average, more than "sometimes" (i.e., scores above 2.25; see "Method" section above). The same proportion of victimized children was found in the spring. However, the correlation between fall and spring victimization scores was low in magnitude ($r = .24$, $p < .001$), indicating that, for many children, victimization was not a stable experience. An inspection of victimization scores showed that 8.5% of the children in this sample were persistently exposed to peer aggression (i.e., scored above 2.25 at both assessment periods).

This variability in children's exposure to peer victimization made it possible to form groups based on the timing and duration of their victimization experiences. Application of the criterion specified in the "Method" section resulted in the assignment of 24 children to each of the Fall Only Victim and Spring Only Victim groups, 17 children to the Stable Victim group, and 135 children to the Nonvictim group.

Relations between Peer Victimization and School Adjustment

Correlations between victimization scores and the school adjustment indices are presented in Table 2. In general, correlations between fall victimization and both fall and spring school adjustment were moderate in magnitude and in expected directions. The correlations obtained between spring victimization and school adjustment followed the same pattern, but the magnitude of these relations tended to be stronger with the spring school adjustment indices (concurrent measures) than with those obtained in the fall. Specifically, the correlations obtained in the spring were significantly larger for school avoidance ($t = 2.77$, $p < .01$) and achievement ($t = -2.16$, $p < .05$) and marginally so for loneliness ($t = 1.76$, $p < .08$). One notable exception was the relation between peer victimization scores and academic achievement; a significant negative correlation was found only for the spring measures of victimization and academic achievement.

Is Peer Victimization a Precursor of Children's School Maladjustment?

To explore the hypothesis that early peer victimization has a negative impact on children's school adjustment, two sets of hierarchical regression analyses were computed. The first set of equations examined the extent to which changes in school adjustment could be predicted by early peer victimization. Conversely, the second group of equations were calculated to determine if changes in peer victimization status could be predicted from early school adjustment.

Predicting Changes in School Adjustment from Early Victimization. Four regression analyses were employed to examine changes in each of the different school adjustment indices (i.e., loneliness, school liking, school avoidance, and academic achievement). For each equation, the spring school adjustment scores were entered as the dependent variable and the corresponding fall adjustment index was entered on step 1. Next, to test for the possibility of gender differences in school adjustment, sex was entered on the second step. Fall victimization scores were entered on the third step, followed by the sex × victimization interaction term.

All four of the overall regression equations were significant (all Fs > 17.8, $p < .001$). Moreover, early peer victimization emerged as a significant predictor of changes in loneliness and school avoidance (see Table 3). None of the sex and sex × victimization effects achieved significance.

Predicting Changes in Peer Victimization from Early School Adjustment. It was also of interest to determine if early school adjustment problems were predictive of changes in peer victimization. To examine this proposition, four regression equations were calculated with spring peer victimization as the dependent variable and fall peer victimization entered on step 1. Sex was entered on step 2 to control for possible gender difference in victimization. In each regression

TABLE 3 Predicting Changes in School Adjustment from Early Peer Victimization

	R_2	R_2INC	β
Spring loneliness:			
Fall loneliness	.16	.16***	.41
Sex	.17	.00	.07
Fall victimization	.21	.04***	.22
Sex × victimization	.21***	.00	.06
Spring school liking:			
Fall school liking	.28	.28***	.53
Sex	.28	.00	.01
Fall victimization	.29	.01	−.12
Sex × victimization	.29***	.00	.13
Spring school avoidance:			
Fall school avoidance	.22	.22***	.47
Sex	.23	.00	−.06
Fall victimization	.28	.06***	.25
Sex × victimization	.29***	.01	.27
Spring academic achievement:			
Fall achievement	.46	.46***	.68
Sex	.46.	.00	−.01
Fall victimization	.46	.00	.00
Sex × victimization	.46***	.01	−.27

*$p < .05$.
** $p < .01$.
***$p < .001$.

analysis, one of the four fall school adjustment indices was entered on step 3, followed by the corresponding sex × school adjustment interaction term.

Results indicated that all four of the regression equations were statistically significant (all Fs > 4.75, $p < .01$). However, in each case, the increments attributable to the fall school adjustment indices, sex, and the sex × adjustment interaction terms failed to achieve significance.

Linkages among the Timing and Duration of Children's Victimization Experiences and Their School Adjustment

Because specific hypotheses were formulated about the relation among the timing and duration of children's peer victimization experiences and their school adjustment, a priori planned comparisons were employed. Hertzog and Rovine (1985) and Rosenthal and Rosnow (1988) recommend that a priori planned comparisons be used whenever hypotheses can be constructed that are more specific than the omnibus null hypothesis. The planned comparison approach offers several advantages over omnibus tests (e.g., repeated-measures ANOVAS): (*a*) statistical tests are directly linked to the substantive hypotheses of interest, (*b*) statistical sensitivity is increased, and (*c*) mixed model assumptions are avoided.

Concurrent Victimization and School Maladjustment. The first set of a priori planned comparisons was calculated to test the hypothesis that children's reports of school maladjustment would be highest during periods of victimization. Specifically, in the fall, the Fall Only and Stable Victim groups were expected to exhibit greater adjustment difficulty compared to children who were not victimized (i.e., Nonvictims).[3] Additionally, it was anticipated that children in the Spring Only Victim group would not differ from children in the Nonvictim group, because they had not yet been exposed to high levels of peer aggression. Twelve planned comparisons were computed to compare each of the three victim groups (Fall Only, Spring Only, Stable) to the Nonvictim group on the four school adjustment indices (loneliness, school liking, school avoidance, achievement). A priori analyses for fall loneliness revealed that children in the Fall Only Victim group ($t = 3.24$, $p < .001$) and Stable Victim group ($t = 1.99$, $p < .05$) were significantly more lonely than children in the Nonvictim group. Also consistent with our hypotheses, the Spring Only victim group did not differ significantly from the Nonvictim group on any of the adjustment indices: loneliness ($t = 1.11$, N.S.); school liking ($t = -1.25$, N.S.); school avoidance ($t = 1.61$, N.S.); and achievement ($t = -.81$, N.S.). No other group differences emerged for comparisons between the Fall Only and Stable Victim groups and the Nonvictim group (see Table 4).

In the spring, it was expected that children in the Spring Only and Stable Victim groups would display higher levels of school maladjustment than children in the Nonvictim group. Further, because children in the Fall Only Victim group were no longer exposed to high levels of victimization, they were not expected to differ significantly from the Nonvictim group. To test these hypotheses, 12 planned comparisons were computed to compare each of the three victim groups (Fall Only, Spring Only, Stable) to the Nonvictim group on the four school adjustment indices (loneliness, school liking, school avoidance, achievement). As expected, children who were victimized in the spring were significantly more lonely (Spring Only: $t = 2.09$, $p < .05$; Stable: $t = 3.54$, $p < .001$), were more school avoidant (Spring Only: $t = 3.42$, $p < .00 1$; Stable: $t = 2.72$, $p < .01$), and liked school less (Spring Only: $t = -2.44$, $p < .02$; Stable: $t = -2.77$, $p < .01$) than nonvictim children. Achievement scores for the Spring Only Victim group approached levels that were significantly lower as compared to nonvictim children ($t = -1.93$, $p < .06$). Also as hypothesized, the Fall Only Victim group did not differ significantly from the Nonvictim group for contrasts calculated on three of the four adjustment measures (loneliness: $t = 1.66$, N.S.; school liking: $t = 1.34$, N.S.; achievement: $t = 1.08$, N.S.). However, children in the Fall Only Victim group reported significantly higher levels of school avoidance than did nonvictim children ($t = 2.79$, $p < .01$).

School Adjustment Difficulties of Victim Groups Over Time. The second set of a priori comparisons were utilized to address the following hypotheses: (*a*) children in the Fall Only Victim group would exhibit significant decreases in school adjustment difficulties in the spring, when they were no longer victimized; (*b*) children in the Spring Only Victim group would evidence

[3]Although the logic of this approach implies comparing *all* victimized children at a given point in time to *all* children not currently being victimized, we wanted to rely on a "stable" nonvictim group for fall and spring group comparisons, because it was unknown how the Fall Only Victim and Spring Only Victim groups' adjustment scores would change over time. However, we did run such a priori planned comparisons, and the results were similar to those presented in this article. Specifically, in the fall, planned comparison analyses were used to compare children in both the Fall Only Victim group and Stable Victim group (both currently "victimized") to children in both the Spring Only and Nonvictim group (neither group "victimized") on all four adjustment indices: Only the contrast for fall loneliness was significant ($t = 2.55$, $p < .02$). For the spring contrasts that compared both the Spring Only Victim and Stable Victim groups to both the Fall Only Victim and Nonvictim groups, all four contrasts were significant: fall loneliness ($t = 2.60$, $p < .01$), spring liking ($t = -2.48$, $p < .02$), spring avoidance ($t = 2.20$, $p < .03$), academic achievement ($t = -2.55$, $p < .02$). Of these significant findings, only the contrast for academic achievement provided information about the relation between peer victimization and school adjustment that was not revealed by the planned comparisons presented in the "Results" section.

TABLE 4 Mean Scores (Standard Deviations in Parentheses) for School Adjustment Measures for Each Victimization Group across Assessment Periods

	FALL ASSESSMENT	SPRING ASSESSMENT	CHANGE FROM FALL TO SPRING
Loneliness:			
Nonvictims	1.37 (.48)[a]	1.41 (.48)[a]	N.T.
Fall only victims	1.81 (.66)[b]	1.64 (.60)	N.S.
Spring only victims	1.54 (.54)	1.70 (.68)[b]	$p < .001$
Stable victims	1.68 (.61)[b]	1.98 (.66)[b]	$p < .05$
School liking:			
Nonvictims	2.74 (.41)	2.64 (.48)[a]	N.T.
Fall only victims	2.63 (.49)	2.47 (.53)	N.T
Spring only victims	2.57 (.55)	2.30 (.53)[b]	$p < .02$
Stable victims	2.54 (.48)	2.22 (.74)[b]	$p < .01$
School avoidance:			
Nonvictims	1.99 (.62)	1.86 (.60)[a]	N.T.
Fall only victims	2.09 (.58)	2.33 (.71)[b]	N.T.
Spring only victims	2.27 (.68)	2.39 (.64)[b]	N.S.
Stable victims	2.29 (.68)	2.39 (.76)[b]	N.S.
Academic Achievement:			
Nonvictims	5.31 (1.33)	5.50 (1.58)	N.T.
Fall only victims	5.63 (1.35)	5.94 (1.56)	N.T.
Spring only victims	4.96 (1.20)	4.69 (1.71)	N.S.
Stable victims	4.91 (1.23)	4.90 (1.49)	N.S.

Note: Means denoted with different letters differ significantly ($p < .05$); N.S. = nonsignificant; N.T. = contrast not tested.

significant increases in school adjustment problems later in the school year, as they encountered higher levels of victimization; and (*c*) children in the Stable Victim group would display significant increases in school maladjustment as exposure to victimization persisted and, thus, compounded their adjustment problems.

Because adjustment difficulties for the Fall Only Victim group were limited to loneliness in the fall, one a priori comparison was conducted to determine whether children in this group displayed significantly lower levels of loneliness in the spring. Although the mean level of loneliness declined, this contrast was nonsignificant ($t = 1.36$, N.S.).

Four a priori comparisons were computed to determine whether children in the Spring Only group displayed significantly higher levels of maladjustment later in the school year. Two of the four contrasts achieved significance; children in the Spring Only group reported significant increases in loneliness ($t = -3.75$, $p < .001$) and significant decreases in school liking ($t = 2.51$, $p < .02$).

For the Stable Victim group, the fall to spring comparisons performed on each of the adjustment measures produced significant findings for loneliness and school liking. Stably victimized children became more lonely ($t = -2.02$, $p < .05$) and liked school less ($t = 2.64$, $p < .01$) as the year progressed.

DISCUSSION

Results from the current investigation suggest that, for many children, the experience of being victimized by one's peers begins at an early age and is quite common in newly formed peer groups, such as those found in kindergarten classrooms. Our findings revealed that a substantial proportion of kindergarten children are exposed to peer victimization—fully 20.5% of our sample reported moderate to high levels of victimization in both the fall and spring of kindergarten. However, for many of these children victimization was not a stable experience; less than 9% emerged as stably victimized.

This finding, that approximately 9% of children continued to be targeted for peer aggression, is consistent with prior researchers' estimates of the prevalence of victimization among older samples of children (Boulton & Underwood, 1992; Perry et al., 1988). Thus far, prior studies indicate that children's victimization experiences are relatively stable by the time they reach 8 or 9 years old (see Boulton & Underwood, 1992). Results from the current study suggest that peer victimization may become a stable experience for some children at even earlier ages (i.e., 5 or 6 years old). In other words, for some children, kindergarten may be a time when the aggressor/victim patterns become established. Findings from this investigation are consistent with Perry et al.'s (1990) proposition that, in the early stages of group formation (i.e., entrance into new peer groups), children direct aggressive behaviors at a variety of targets; as they learn the reactions of their peers, their pool of victims becomes increasingly smaller and their choice of victims more consistent. More data are needed to determine whether or not the victimization patterns that were established in kindergarten will persist as children progress through grade school.

Consistent with the extant literature on peer victimization, findings from this investigation offer further evidence that children who were victimized by their peers experienced greater adjustment difficulties than nonvictimized age mates (Alsaker, 1993; Boulton & Underwood, 1992; Kochenderfer, 1995). Correlational analyses indicated moderate, positive relations between peer victimization and feelings of loneliness and expressed desire to avoid the school environment, and a negative, moderate relation between victimization and the degree to which children reported liking school.

Moreover, results from this study supported the argument that peer victimization is a precursor of some school adjustment problems. Findings from the regression analyses revealed that victimized children tend to become more lonely and school avoidant after they are victimized by peers. Specifically, changes in these school adjustment indices could be predicted from early peer victimization. Further, no support was found for the counterargument that school adjustment difficulties precede exposure to victimization—that is, changes in peer victimization could not be predicted from the early school adjustment indices that were examined in this study. Additionally, no significant group differences emerged indicating that children were having difficulty adjusting to school before they were victimized. In fact, examinations of group differences suggest that, except for the Fall Only and Stable Victim groups' higher fall loneliness scores, children who were victimized in the fall did not differ significantly on the school adjustment indices until later in the school year. This pattern is most evident in the results obtained for the Stable Victim group; children in this group, even though they were exposed to peer victimization in both the fall and the spring, did not exhibit significant adjustment problems (i.e., liked school less and expressed more school avoidance) until the spring.

Two additional objectives of this study were to ascertain if (*a*) children's school adjustment difficulties *abate* once they are no longer exposed to peers' aggression and (*b*) adjustment difficulties *emerge* as children are exposed to higher levels of victimization. Evidence suggests that school adjustment problems are strongly linked to (but not necessarily limited to) the period in which the victimization is occurring.

Results obtained for the Fall Only Victim group best reflect on the question of the extent to which adjustment problems dissipate once victimization has ceased, because children in this group had been victimized in the fall but were no longer so in the spring. The trend found for this group was for feelings of loneliness to decline once victimization was reduced. Specifically, we found that, compared to nonvictims, children in the Fall Only Victim group were significantly lonelier in the fall but were no longer significantly more lonely in the spring. However, though the trend was for loneliness to decline over time, the decrease from fall to spring was not significant—thus it appears that feelings of loneliness may linger even after victimization has subsided (i.e., carry-over effects).

Moreover, the data also suggest that other difficulties may emerge at later points in time (i.e., delayed effects). For instance, children in the Fall Only Victim group were found to be significantly more avoidant of school in the spring than were children in the Nonvictim group. This finding is consistent with the inference that peer victimization may result in delayed school adjustment problems (such as school avoidance). Similarly, school liking scores were lower in the spring for the Fall Only Victim group, although this difference between the Fall Only Victim and Nonvictim groups did not reach statistical significance. Still, these trends in the data offer more evidence for the argument that children begin school with relatively positive attitudes, but that, after being victimized, they develop less favorable opinions of that environment. It is conceivable that victimization experiences undermine children's sense of security, and that these feelings of vulnerability persist even after the victimization ceases.

Data obtained from the Spring Only Victim group revealed that school adjustment difficulties emerged as children's exposure to peer victimization increased. Children in this victim group did not exhibit significant adjustment difficulties in the fall but did so in the spring when they were experiencing higher levels of victimization. Specifically, these children were lonelier, liked school less, and expressed more school avoidance as compared to nonvictim children. Furthermore, the over-time contrasts for the Spring Only Victim group indicated that the increase in loneliness and the decrease in school liking were statistically significant.

Findings from the present investigation supported the hypothesis that stable victimization experiences exacerbate some forms of school maladjustment. Specifically, children who were exposed to peer victimization throughout kindergarten evidenced a significant increase in feelings of loneliness from fall to spring and a significant decrease in the extent to which they reported liking school.

It is important to note that all victimized children (i.e., Fall Only, Spring Only, and Stable Victim groups) expressed more desire to avoid the school context in the spring than children who were classified as nonvictims. This is especially noteworthy given that no group differences were found for school avoidance in the fall. This finding further supports the contention that although most children begin school without strong feelings of avoidance, those who are exposed to peers' aggressive behaviors are more likely to develop a desire to withdraw from this context.

The linkage between peer victimization and academic achievement is difficult to disentangle. Results of the analyses that were designed to shed light on the causal priority of these two variables were inconclusive; that is, peer victimization scores could not predict changes in academic achievement, but neither could academic achievement predict changes in peer victimization. These null findings need to be considered when attempting to interpret the low, but statistically significant, negative correlation which emerged between peer victimization and academic achievement in the spring. Additionally, although planned comparisons for the Spring Only Victim group and the

Stable Victim did not reveal significant group differences when they were compared to the Nonvictim group, nor when examining *changes* in achievement from fall to spring, supplemental analyses showed that children who were not experiencing peer victimization in the spring (i.e., the Nonvictim and Fall Only Victim groups) were performing significantly better academically than children who were currently targeted for peer aggression (i.e., Spring Only and Stable Victim groups; see n. 3 above).

One possible interpretation of this link between peer victimization and academic achievement is that some children begin kindergarten academically slightly behind, or ahead, of their age mates, but that their academic competencies do not become apparent until later in the school year when academic demands are more challenging. This argument suggests that as children's "poor" academic skills become more salient to peers, it may increase their risk for peer victimization. Conversely, as children's "superior" academic competencies become known to classmates, it may decrease their risk. If this interpretation were accurate, it could explain why children in the Fall Only Victim group who had the highest academic achievement scores were no longer victimized in the spring. Furthermore, it would also explain why children who were not initially exposed to peer victimization (i.e., Spring Only Victim group), yet had the lowest academic scores, experienced increased levels of peer victimization in the spring.

However, because no firm conclusions can be drawn about the direction of effect, it is also possible that peer victimization affects children's achievement. For instance, children may begin kindergarten with relatively similar levels of academic achievement (as shown by nonsignificant group differences found in the fall for academic achievement), but exposure to peer victimization may thwart their progress. It is possible that some third factor (e.g., parent or teacher support) helped children in the Fall Only Victim group cease their exposure to victimization, and once that occurred, they were able to make successful strides in their academic endeavors. Likewise, children in the Spring Only Victim group may have been making satisfactory progress in the fall when they were not being victimized; but once exposed to peer aggression, their ability to succeed in the academic domain was compromised.

One potential criticism of the current study is that self-report measures were used to assess both peer victimization and several dimensions of school adjustment, thus raising the concern that some findings may be an artifact of shared method variance. However, although some caution may be warranted in interpreting the current findings, a number of factors suggest that shared method variance was not a serious confound in the present investigation. First, there is evidence to indicate that kindergarten children's reports of their victimization experiences are reliable and valid (see "Methods" section; Kochenderfer & Ladd, 1996). Second, the longitudinal design allowed us to control for factors that contribute to shared method variance, such as verbal response bias. Specifically, in regression analyses, fall adjustment measures were partialed, thus removing some of the variability attributable to response biases. Third, the specificity of the observed differences in school adjustment that emerged across victimization groups and over time argues against the view that the obtained findings were due to children's response tendencies.

In sum, the hypothesis that children's victimization experiences affect their school adjustment received greater support from this investigation than did the contention that school maladjustment fosters peer victimization. These findings have important implications for the policies and practices that educators implement for children as they enter grade school. If exposure to peer victimization negatively affects children's school adjustment, then it will be important for educators to (*a*) be more proactive in the identification of victimized children and (*b*) devise policies and practices that not only discourage bullying but also support children who are the targets of peers' aggressive behaviors. Moreover, evidence indicating that early exposure to victimization may produce both immediate and delayed effects and that prolonged exposure may compound children's school difficulties suggests that preventive interventions should be implemented early in the school year or as soon as bully-victim problems are detected.

REFERENCES

Alsaker, F. (1993, March). *Bully/victim problems in day-care centers, measurement issues and associations with children's psychosocial health.* Paper presented at the biennial meeting of the Society for Research in Child Development, New Orleans.

Bjorkqvist, K., Ekman, K., & Lagerspetz, K. (1982). Bullies and victims: Their ego picture, ideal ego picture and normative ego picture. *Scandinavian Journal of Psychiatry, 23,* 307–313.

Boulton, M. J., & Underwood, K. (1992). Bully/victim problems among middle school children. *British Journal of Educational Psychology, 62,* 73–87.

Cassidy, J., & Asher, S. R. (1992). Loneliness and peer relations in young children. *Child Development, 63,* 350–365.

Hertzog, C., & Rovine, M. (1985). Repeated-measures analysis of variance in developmental research: Selected issues. *Child Development, 56,* 787–809.

Kochenderfer, B. J. (1995). *Peer victimization in kindergarten: Are responses to aggression predictive of changes in victimization?* Unpublished master's thesis, University of Illinois at Urbana–Champaign.

Kochenderfer, B. J., & Ladd, G. W. (1996). *Victimized children's responses to peers' aggression: Behaviors associated with reduced versus continued victimization.* Manuscript under review.

Kochenderfer, B. J., & Ladd, G. W. (in press). Peer victimization: Manifestations and relations to school adjustment in kindergarten. *Journal of School Psychology.*

Ladd, G. W. (1989). Children's social competence and social supports: Precursors of early school adjustment? In B. Schneider, G. Attili, J. Nadel, & R. Weissberg (Eds.), *Social competence in developmental perspective.* Amsterdam: Kluwer.

Ladd, G. W., Kochenderfer, B. J., & Coleman, C. (1996). Friendship quality as a predictor of young children's early school adjustment. *Child Development, 67,* 1103–1118.

Ladd, G. W., & Price, J. M. (1987). Predicting children's social and school adjustment following the transition from preschool to kindergarten. *Child Development, 58,* 1168–1189.

Lagerspetz, K., Bjorkqvist, K., Berts, M., & King, E. (1982). Group aggression among school children in three schools. *Scandinavian Journal of Psychiatry, 23,* 45–52.

Nurss, J. R., & McGauvran, M. E. (1986). *Metropolitan Readiness Tests.* New York: Harcourt Brace Jovanovich.

Olweus, D. (1991). Bully/victim problems among schoolchildren: Basic facts and effects of a school-based intervention program. In D. Pepler & K. Rubin (Eds.), *The development and treatment of childhood aggression* (pp. 411–448). Hillsdale, NJ: Erlbaum.

Olweus, D. (1992). Victimization by peers: Antecedents and long-term outcomes. In K. H. Rubin & J. B. Asendorf (Eds.), *Social withdrawal, inhibition, and shyness in childhood* (pp. 315–341). Hillsdale, NJ: Erlbaum.

Olweus, D. (1993). Bullies on the playground: The role of victimization. In C. H. Hart (Ed.), *Children on playgrounds* (pp. 85–128). Albany: State University of New York Press.

Patterson, G. R., Littman, R. A., & Bricker, W. (1967). Assertive behavior in children: A step toward a theory of aggression. *Monographs of the Society for Research in Child Development, 35*(5, Serial No. 113).

Perry, D. G., Kusel, S. J., & Perry, L. C. (1988). Victims of peer aggression. *Developmental Psychology, 24,* 807–814.

Perry, D. G., Perry, L. C., & Boldizar, J. P. (1990). Learning of aggression. In M. Lewis & S. Miller (Eds.), *Handbook of developmental psychopathology* (pp. 135–146). New York: Plenum.

Rosenthal, R., & Rosnow, R. L. (1988). *Contrast analysis: Focused comparisons in the analysis Of variance.* New York: Cambridge University Press.

FACTUAL QUESTIONS

1. What was the purpose of the study?
2. What theoretical base was the study based on?
3. Who were the participants?
4. Why did the authors include kindergarten children in the study?
5. How did the authors define peer victimization?
5. What dependent measures did the authors use?
6. What primary statistical analysis procedure was used by the authors?
7. What factors were included in the analysis procedures?
8. According to the authors, how did the results of study relate to previous research findings?
9. According to the authors, what general conclusions can be made about the results?
10. What limitations did the authors discuss?

DISCUSSION QUESTIONS

1. Are there any problems with the population validity of the study? Why?
2. Why did the authors focus on peer victimization?
3. Did authors' analysis procedures address the stated purpose of the study? Why?
4. Did the authors base the study on a strong empirical and/or theoretical base?
5. Why did the authors believe that peer victimization leads to school maladjustment?
6. What factors did the authors include in their analyses?
7. How did the authors establish that peer victimization resulted in school maladjustment?
8. How confident are you based on the findings of this study that peer victimization results in school maladjustment?
9. What are some potential threats to the internal validity of the study? Provide a justification for each threat.
10. What are some potential treats to the external validity of this study? Provide a justification for each threat.

THREATS TO INTERNAL VALIDITY

Circle the number corresponding to the likelihood of each threat to internal validity being present in the investigation and provide a justification.

1 = definitely not a threat 2 = not a likely threat 3 = somewhat likely threat
4 = likely threat 5 = definite threat NA = Not applicable for this design

Results in Differences Within or Between Individuals

1. Maturation **1 2 3 4 5 NA**

Justification ____

____

2. Selection **1 2 3 4 5 NA**

Justification ____

____

3. Selection by Maturation Interaction **1 2 3 4 5 NA**

Justification ____

____

4. Statistical Regression **1 2 3 4 5 NA**

Justification ____

____

5. Mortality **1 2 3 4 5 NA**

Justification ____

____

6. Instrumentation **1 2 3 4 5 NA**

Justification ____

____

7. Testing 1 2 3 4 5 NA

Justification ____

____

8. History 1 2 3 4 5 NA

Justification ____

____

9. Resentful Demoralization of the Control Group 1 2 3 4 5 NA

Justification ____

____

Results in Similarities Within or Between Individuals

10. Diffusion of Treatment 1 2 3 4 5 NA

Justification ____

____

11. Compensatory Rivalry by the Control Group 1 2 3 4 5 NA

Justification ____

____

12. Compensatory Equalization of Treatments 1 2 3 4 5 NA

Justification ____

____

Abstract: Write a one page abstract summarizing the overall conclusions of the authors and whether or not you feel the authors' conclusions are valid based on the internal validity of the investigation.

THREATS TO EXTERNAL VALIDITY

Circle the number corresponding to the likelihood of each threat to external validity being present in the investigation according to the following scale:

1 = definitely not a threat   2 = not a likely threat   3 = somewhat likely threat
4 = likely threat   5 = definite threat   NA = Not applicable for this design

Population

1. **Generalization Across Subjects** **1 2 3 4 5 NA**

   Justification ____________________

   ____

2. **Interaction of Personological Variables and Treatment** **1 2 3 4 5 NA**

   Justification ____________________

   ____

Ecological

3. **Verification of the Independent Variable** **1 2 3 4 5 NA**

   Justification ____________________

   ____

4. **Multiple Treatment Interference** **1 2 3 4 5 NA**

   Justification ____________________

   ____

5. **Hawthorne Effect** **1 2 3 4 5 NA**

   Justification ____________________

   ____

6. **Novelty and Disruption Effects** **1 2 3 4 5 NA**

   Justification ____________________

   ____

7. Experimenter Effects 1 2 3 4 5 NA

Justification ______________________________

____

8. Pretest Sensitization 1 2 3 4 5 NA

Justification ______________________________

____

9. Posttest Sensitization 1 2 3 4 5 NA

Justification ______________________________

____

10. Interaction of Time of Measurement and Treatment Effects 1 2 3 4 5 NA

Justification ______________________________

____

11. Measurement of the Dependent Variable 1 2 3 4 5 NA

Justification ______________________________

____

12. Interaction of History and Treatment Effects 1 2 3 4 5 NA

Justification ______________________________

____

Abstract: Write a one page abstract summarizing the overall conclusions of the authors and whether or not you feel the authors' conclusions are valid based on the external validity of the investigation.

PART FOUR

QUALITATIVE RESEARCH METHODS

CHAPTER 8 **QUALITATIVE RESEARCH: METHODS**

CHAPTER 9 **QUALITATIVE RESEARCH: DATA COLLECTION AND DESIGNS**

CHAPTER 8

QUALITATIVE RESEARCH: METHODS

OBJECTIVES

After studying this chapter you should be able to:

1. Describe the concerns of qualitative researchers.
2. Describe the characteristics of qualitative research and indicate how qualitative research differs from quantitative research.
3. Describe the phases in various qualitative research procedures.
4. Describe the different sampling procedures used in qualitative research methods.
5. Describe the ways of understanding qualitative research methods including the different forms of validity.
6. Describe the various evaluative criteria for judging the reliability and validity of qualitative research.
7. Describe what is meant by triangulation.
8. Describe the different forms of triangulation.
9. Critique a research article containing a qualitative design.

OVERVIEW

Up to this point, we have been primarily discussing quantitative research methods. As indicated in Chapter 3, qualitative researchers view reliability and validity somewhat differently than do quantitative researchers. Unfortunately, rather than viewing the merits of differing methodologies, we often attempt to discount findings generated from research methods that differ from our own. Many quantitative researchers have tried to discount findings from qualitative methods simply because the data were generated in qualitative research. Similarly, many qualitative researchers may reject findings from quantitative research saying that quantitative researchers do not take into account the process of learning or other critical phenomena occurring outside of the narrowly defined dependent variable. For example, suppose a quantitative researcher generates data to answer the question of the differential effectiveness of direct instruction and discovery learning and finds one method superior to the other. The qualitative researcher may argue that other equally important variables were not taken into account—those that cannot be operationally defined before the investigation and directly measured as outcomes such as self-esteem or preference.

Unfortunately, what often is forgotten in the debate between quantitative and qualitative methods are the types of questions answered by the different methodologies. In other words, the arguments for or against quantitative and qualitative methodologies seem to assume that both methodologies attempt to answer the same research questions or assume that both are based on the same assumptions. A better way to examine the methodologies is to view the types of questions asked and then determine if the methodology used was appropriate to answer the question (Howe & Eisenhart, 1990). This view of matching the methodology to the types of questions asked is similar to the one expressed in earlier chapters. For example, it is not appropriate to use a preexperimental design to answer a cause-and-effect question. Similarly, it is not appropriate to use an experimental design to answer questions better addressed through naturalistic inquiry (e.g., social patterns of teachers in a teacher's lounge). Therefore, this chapter is concerned with investigating the types of research questions appropriate for qualitative research. The best way to think of qualitative and quantitative research is not which is better but how they can be used to address different issues.

As described in earlier chapters, quantitative research is concerned with the reliable and valid investigation of the impact of independent variables on dependent variables or the relationships between or among variables. Quantitative researchers are concerned with the outcomes of an intervention and in measuring the dependent variable objectively. Qualitative researchers are concerned with how people feel about classroom procedures, what they believe about certain instructional methods, how they process information, and what meanings they attach to experiences. Qualitative researchers are concerned with understanding the context in which behavior occurs, not just the extent to which it occurs. The assessment may be more subjective in that the dependent variables are not necessarily defined in observable terms. In fact, qualitative researchers are not concerned with a few narrowly defined variables but are concerned with the interaction of multiple variables over a period of time.

For example, suppose one wished to know what makes an outstanding teacher. Quantitatively, we may define specific teaching behaviors that we believe are responsible for positive student outcomes. Once these behaviors are identified, we may take a sample of teachers and randomly assign teachers to one of two groups. Each group would then be provided an assessment of academic performance. Following the pretest, one group could be taught the instructional behaviors thought to be associated with student achievement and the other group provided with some form of interaction that lasts an equal amount of time as does the instructional training (providing an equal amount of time in interactions with the two groups would control for an alternative explanation of extra attention provided to the "experimental" group). A posttest would then be provided, and the groups' mean scores compared. If the students of those who received the instructional training outperformed the other students on an academic performance test, there would be support for the hypothesis that the defined teacher instructional behaviors can improve academic performance of students.

Notice how the preceding example answers a particular research question; that is, "Is a set of defined instructional behaviors related to improved student performance?" The example does not answer questions such as, "What do the teachers think about the instructional behaviors taught?" "How do the students feel about the change in how their teachers' approach instruction?" "Are there other instructional variables present that could account for improved student performance?" "Do the assessments used measure important learner traits?" "How do the instructional behaviors taught affect the process of learning rather than just the outcome?" "Do teachers see the instructional strategies as helpful?" "If so, which ones and why? If not, why?" and "What do the teachers base their answers or beliefs on?" In order to answer these types of questions, other research methodologies must be used. Qualitative methodologies are well suited to answering these questions.

For example, a qualitative researcher may visit a single classroom over time, become involved in classroom activities, and examine the nature of the activities in depth. The researcher may set up multiple sources of data gathering such as interviews with teachers, students, and parents. The investigation may continue for the academic year or even longer. The main attempt here is to get a "real world" feel for the operations of a classroom, what makes it work, how teachers and students interact, and what seems to affect student classroom performance. The data generated may be in the form of interviews, narrations, or journal entries by all of the involved parties. Once the investigation is finished, the researcher codes the data in terms of categories and begins to interpret the results. (*Note:* These examples are only meant to be illustrative of possible investigations; the examples are not representative of all possible investigations that can be conducted to answer the aforementioned research questions.)

Notice how the methodologies differ not only in format but in the nature of the questions asked and the types of answers provided. The critical point here is that quantitative research is no better nor worse than qualitative research; quantitative research is different than qualitative research in approach and purpose. That said, it does not seem fruitful to argue the superiority of one methodology over the other. A more appropriate discussion should center on when and why each should be used. Also, the two methodologies are not mutually exclusive. They can, and in many cases should, be used together. Think of the powerful information that could be gathered if the two methods were combined in the preceding examples.

For instance, there are two groups of teachers in the experimental example. Suppose we could reduce the number of teachers to two. Now we have two classrooms. The instructional behaviors are taught to one class (determined randomly). Qualitative researchers go into both classrooms as described before. Since everything is equal in both classrooms except for the instructional training, we still have good experimental control. Granted, the design is not truly experimental, but would be a nonequivalent control-group design (see Chapter 5). We would sacrifice some constraints over the participants but gain a great deal of information from the qualitative data. (*Note:* Many qualitative researchers may be more comfortable in using quantitative and qualitative methods in a complementary manner rather than mixing both approaches to develop a "new" research method.)

A way both methodologies can be complementary to one another would be by conducting an experimental design and determining the social validity of the outcomes (see Chapter 2). The methodologies can also work together but not at the same time. For example, if we wanted to determine the effective instructional behaviors necessary for increased academic performance, we could use qualitative research to generate hypotheses. In this case, the qualitative investigation would occur first. Out of the data analysis would be hypotheses generated based on the information gathered. The qualitative research would provide us with inductive information, and the experimental research would provide us with deductive information. We would most likely be much more successful in determining when to use certain instructional practices if we first learn about the context under which the participants are operating before we attempt to implement independent variables that may not fit the particular contexts.

This chapter will focus on the characteristics of qualitative research methods. Additionally, qualitative research procedures will be discussed. Finally, methods of understanding the reliability and validity of qualitative research will be provided for critique.

WHAT ARE THE CHARACTERISTICS OF QUALITATIVE RESEARCH?

Before we discuss the characteristics of qualitative research, we must point out that there is not agreement by all qualitative researchers with regard to what qualitative research is. Potter (1996) provides a detailed discussion of how qualitative research is defined by different scholars (see Table 8.1). Potter demonstrated that qualitative research definitions can range from "any kind of research that produces findings not arrived at by means of statistical procedures or other means of quantification" (Strauss & Corbin, 1990, p. 17) to Pauly's (1991) five-step process including "(a) finding a topic, (b) formulating research questions, (c) gathering the evidence, (d) interpreting the evidence, and (e) telling the researcher's story" (cited in Potter, 1996, p. 7). However, for the purposes of this chapter, it seems worthwhile to agree on some common characteristics of qualitative research definitions. Silverman (1993) attempted to do just this. He described three distinctive characteristics of qualitative research outlined by Hammersley and Atkinson (1983). Two of the characteristics seem especially relevant for our purposes. First, "field research can provide a broader version of theory than simply a relationship between variables" (Silverman, 1993, p. 27). In other words, a more general version of a theory is one that takes into consideration the mechanisms or processes that generate the relationships among the identified variables. For example, rather than simply indicating that there is a strong relationship between social status and academic performance, we may wish to discover how social status affects academic performance such as the attitudes parents from high socioeconomic backgrounds have toward school.

Second, "the flexibility of field research 'allows theory development to be pursued in a highly effective and economical manner'" (Silverman, 1993, p. 28). In this way, additional, more interesting questions can be generated by allowing the research to be flexible and possibly move in directions or observe phenomena that ordinarily would have been missed or taken for granted. For example, if we were observing a third-grade teacher using direct instruction methods and use a narrowly defined observation method (i.e., looking for specific teacher behaviors), we may not see anything remarkable about what was occurring. This finding may be due to the narrowness of our observational system. If, on the other hand, we visited the same classroom but did not have predefined behaviors to look for, we may begin to generate a structure through which to organize our observations.

Table 8.2 presents a summary of the characteristics of qualitative research according to Patton (1990). We will expand on each of these characteristics throughout the chapter.

WHAT ARE THE DIFFERENCES BETWEEN QUALITATIVE AND QUANTITATIVE RESEARCH?

Qualitative and quantitative research methods are clearly different in many regards. The obvious difference has to do with how each approaches subject matter. The following is a brief discussion of how quantitative and qualitative methodologies differ as outlined by Bogdan and Biklen (1992).

Source of Data

First, the direct source of data for qualitative research is the natural setting. Although much quantitative research may be conducted in artificial settings or under artificial contexts, qualitative researchers are concerned with "real world" or "big picture" questions. There is less concern with isolating variables in high constraint situations since those situations most likely bear little resemblance to real contexts. Along these lines, the researcher is the key data collection instrument. The assumption is that individuals are affected by their environmental situations or contexts. Therefore, the data collection must occur in those contexts to be understood. If measurement instruments are used outside of the context, a great deal of information is lost. Additionally, if a researcher uses a measurement device, the variables under study must be narrowly defined. Therefore, interviews, observations, transcripts, historical records, and so on are used to avoid the narrowness inherent in measurement instruments.

TABLE 8.1 Types of Definitions of Qualitative

A. Formal Definition: This is a dictionary type of definition where the essence of the concept is made explicit. This type of definition "centers' readers by telling them what to focus on and where the boundaries are; it provides a foundation for the reader to judge what should be included and what should not.

1. J. A. Anderson (1987): "A research paradigm which emphasizes inductive, interpretive methods applied to the everyday world which is seen as subjective and socially created" (p. 384). He also provided an oppositional definition (see Item B.1).
2. Bogdan and Taylor (1975): "Qualitative methodologies refer to research procedures which produce descriptive data: people's own written or spoken words and observable behavior." It "directs itself at settings and the individuals within those settings holistically; that is, the subject of the study, be it an organization or an individual, is not reduced to an isolated variable or to an hypothesis, but is viewed instead as part of a whole" (p. 2).
3. Lindlof (1991): "Qualitative inquiry examines *the constitution of meaning in everyday social phenomena....* Probably the fundamental touchstone for the term is methodological. Qualitative research seeks to *preserve the form, content, and context of social phenomena and analyze their qualities,* rather than separate them from historical and institutional surroundings" (italics in original; p. 24).
4. Lindlof (1995): "Qualitative researchers seek to preserve the form and content of human behavior and to analyze its qualities, rather than subject it to mathematical or other formal transformations" (p. 21).
5. Lofland (1971): "Qualitative analysis is addressed to the task of delineating forms, kinds of social phenomena; of documenting in loving detail the things that exist" (p. 13).
6. Pauly (1991): "Qualitative studies investigate meaning-making" (p. 2).

B. Contrasting Definition: Some scholars define qualitative in contrast to something else. That something else is usually quantitative, but the term quantitative is usually a synonym for something such as reductionism, radical empiricism, and so forth.

1. J. A. Anderson (1987) defined qualitative (in contrast to quantitative) as inductive (deductive), eidetic (atomistic), subjective (objective), contextual (generalizable), mundane (purified), textual (measurable), preservationistic (aggregated), interactive (independent), and interpretive (material).
2. J. A. Anderson and Meyer (1988) declared, "Qualitative research methods are distinguished from quantitative methods in that they do not rest their evidence on the logic of mathematics, the principle of numbers, or the methods of statistical analysis" (p. 247).
3. Bogdan and Taylor (1975), in their book *Introduction to Qualitative Research Methods: A Phenomenological Approach to the Social Sciences,* made a contrast on the philosophical level. They contrasted the positivism of Comte with the phenomenological approach of Weber and Deutscher: "The positivist seeks the facts or causes of social phenomena with little regard for the subjective states of individuals" (p. 2). They stated that "Durkheim advised the social scientist to consider 'social facts,' or social phenomena, as 'things' that exercise an external and coercive influence on human behavior" (p. 2). In contrast, phenomenologists are "concerned with

(continued)

TABLE 8.1 Continued

understanding human behavior from the actor's own frame of reference.... The important reality is what people imagine it to be" (p. 2). They also defined the phenomenon as "the process of interpretation" (p. 14).

4. Christians and Carey (1989) contrasted physical sciences with social sciences—a distinction such as made in Europe.
5. Jensen and Jankowski (1991): In contrasting qualitative with quantitative they asserted that qualitative is concerned with "meaning in phenomenological and contextual terms," not information "in the sense of discrete items transporting significance through mass media" (p. 4). "Qualitative analysis focuses on the *occurrence* of its analytical objects in a particular context, as opposed to the *recurrence* of formally similar elements in different contexts" (p. 4). It also requires an internal approach to looking at indivisible experience through exegesis with a focus on process "which is contextualized and inextricably integrated with wider social and cultural practices" (p. 4). They further stated that "there seems to be no way around the quantitative-qualitative distinction. Although it sometimes serves to confuse rather than clarify research issues, the distinction is a fact of research practice which has major epistemological and political implications that no scholar can afford to ignore" (p. 5).
6. Lancy (1993) provided a contrast of qualitative with quantitative focusing on the choice of topics, sampling, role of investigator, bias, context, length of study and report.
7. Lindlof and Meyer (1987) drew a distinction between what they called deterministic, functionalist, and interpretive paradigms: "The deterministic paradigm responds to the perceived need for universal probability statements regarding audience behavior that can be applied to transient social problems. Emphasis is placed on the types of attitudinal or behavioral effects that can be produced under certain optimal conditions" (p. 3). "The functionalist paradigm, on the other hand, casts the audience member as a 'free agent' media user whose goal is to assess the utility of more or less equivalent sources of social and psychological gratification" (p. 3). The interpretive paradigm focuses on the "fields of meaning" that people construct in their social lives (p. 4).
8. Schwartz and Jacobs (1979) asserted that quantitative researchers assign numbers to qualitative observations and thereby produce data by counting and measuring things. Qualitative researchers report observations in their natural language. They defined quantitative researchers in sociology as positivists. They stated that positivists are concerned with:

> the sharpening up of an otherwise fuzzy picture of "what's really going on out there." The picture is fuzzy because lay persons have their own practical ways of describing the particulars of the world they inhabit....That is, it displays inconsistency, vagueness, multiple meanings, and other characteristics that contribute to a blurred and sketchy picture. It is therefore understood that one of positivistic sociology's services to society is to provide more accurate information. A familiar procedure is to take a lay concept, such as crime or suicide, and repair it or "clean it up" by precise definition and the development of measurement procedures in the hope that it will become capable of being used in scientific theory. With its new definition and new use, the altered concept can be presented to colleagues and the society at large as contributing to a clearer, more valid picture of the world than its lay counterpart. (pp. 5–6)

TABLE 8.1 Continued

9. J. K. Smith (1983) compared qualitative and quantitative on the issues of (a) the relationship of the investigator to the phenomenon, (b) the relationship between facts and values in the process of investigation, and (c) the goal of the investigation.
10. J. K. Smith and Heshusius (1986) cited Dilthey's position of an interpretive or hermeneutical approach, which is a direct challenge to positivism. Positivism might work with physical sciences that focus on "inanimate objects that could be seen as existing outside of us (a world of external, objectively knowable facts)" (p. 5). In contrast, social science focuses on "the products of the human mind with all its subjectivity, emotions, and values" (p. 5).
11. Strauss and Corbin (1990) defined qualitative research as "any kind of research that produces findings that are not arrived at by means of statistical procedures or other means of quantification" (p. 17). They clarified this position by adding that qualitative reports may contain some numbers, such as census data, "but the analysis itself is a qualitative one" (p. 17).
12. Wimmer and Dominick (1991) saw three main differences between qualitative and quantitative. First, they asserted that qualitative believes that there is no single reality, and that each person creates a subjective reality that is holistic and not reducible to component parts. Second, qualitative believes that individuals are fundamentally different and that they cannot be categorized. And third, qualitative strives for unique explanations about particular situations and individuals.

C. Component Definition: Some scholars illuminate some components or characteristics. This gives readers a sense of the parts or concerns within the qualitative domain, but it does not provide a sense of the boundaries or limits.

1. Bogdan and Taylor (1975), who used phenomenology as a synonym for qualitative research, argued that phenomenology itself has two components: symbolic interactionism and ethnomethodology. In their view, ethnomethodology means qualitative methods, but qualitative methods does not mean ethnomethodology because there is more to qualitative research than the component of ethnomethodology.
2. Christians and Carey (1989) mentioned four subsets as follows: symbolic interactionism, ethnomethodology, humanistic sociology, and cultural hermeneutics.
3. Jacob (1988) perceived six domains: human ethology, holistic ethnography, ethnography of communication, cognitive anthropology, ecological psychology, and symbolic interactionism. However, she asserted that human ethology is based on positivist traditions and is not really a form of qualitative research. There are then five qualitative components as she presented in her earlier treatment (Jacob, 1987).
4. Jankowski and Wester (1991) presented two unique elements in their definition. First is the idea of *verstehen,* which "refers to an understanding of the meaning that people ascribe to their social situation and activities. Because people act on the basis of the meanings they attribute to themselves and others, the focus of qualitative social science is on everyday life and its significance as perceived by the participants" (pp. 44–45). The second element is role taking, which expresses the idea that people are active and their roles change across situations.

(continued)

TABLE 8.1 Continued

5. Jensen and Jankowski (1991) examined discourse analysis, textual analysis, reception analysis, ethnography, and history.
6. Lancy (1993) identified ethnography, ethnomethodology, ecological psychology, and history.
7. Lindlof and Meyer (1987) broke down their interpretive paradigm into ethnomethodology, ecological psychology, symbolic interactionism. Lindlof (1991) divided qualitative research in media audience studies into five components, each of which is composed of subcomponents. Those five components are: social-phenomenological (which includes social reality construction, ethnomethodology, symbolic interactionism, and cultural hermeneutics), communication rules (which includes rules theory, ethnography of communication, and conversational analysis), cultural studies (which appears to include discourse analysis, social-structuralism, political economy criticism, poststructuralism, and ethnography again), reception study (which includes the antecedents of literary theory and criticism), and feminist research (which "in many respects...shares the same goals and methods as cultural studies" (p. 29). His structure provides a generally neat categorization scheme, but some terms overlap (such as ethnography) into more than one superordinate area.
8. Strauss and Corbin (1990) stated that "some of the different types of qualitative research are: grounded theory, ethnography, phenomenological approach, life histories, and conversational analysis" (p. 21).

D. Procedural Definition: Qualitative can be defined in terms of a list of steps.

1. Lincoln and Guba (1985) offered two prime tenets: that "first, no manipulation on the part of the inquirer is implied, and, second, the inquirer imposes no a priori units on the outcome" (p. 8).
2. Pauly (1991) attempted to "guide the work of beginners" who want to try qualitative research by providing a "step by step explanation of how one might do qualitative research" (pp. 1–2). He presented five steps: (a) finding a topic, (b) formulating research questions, (c) gathering the evidence, (d) interpreting the evidence, and (e) telling the researcher's story.

E. Product Definition: Some theoreticians define *qualitative* in terms of the end point of a process.

1. Bogdan and Taylor (1975) asserted that "qualitative methodologies refer to research procedures which produce descriptive data: people's own written or spoken words and observable behavior." It "directs itself at settings and the individuals within those settings holistically; that is, the subject of the study, be it an organization or an individual, is not reduced to an isolated variable or to an hypothesis, but is viewed instead as part of a whole" (p. 2).
2. Lofland (1971) stated, "Qualitative analysis is addressed to the task of delineating forms, kinds of social phenomena; of documenting in loving detail the things that exist" (p. 13).

TABLE 8.2 Major Characteristics of Qualitative Research

1. Naturalistic inquiry	Studying real-world situations as they unfold naturally; non-manipulative, unobtrusive, and non-controlling; openness to whatever emerges—lack of predetermined constraints on outcomes
2. Inductive analysis	Immersion in the details and specifics of the data to discover important categories, dimensions, and interrelationships; begin by exploring genuinely open questions rather than testing theoretically derived (deductive) hypotheses
3. Holistic perspective	The *whole* phenomenon under study is understood as a complex system that is more than the sum of its parts; focus on complex interdependencies not meaningfully reduced to a few discrete variables and linear, cause-effect relationships
4. Qualitative data	Detailed, thick description; inquiry in depth; direct quotations capturing people's personal perspectives and experiences
5. Personal contact and insight	The researcher has direct contact with and gets close to the people, situation, and phenomenon under study; researcher's personal experiences and insights are an important part of the inquiry and critical to understanding the phenomenon
6. Dynamic systems	Attention to process; assumes change is constant and ongoing whether the focus is on an individual or an entire culture
7. Unique case orientation	Assumes each case is special and unique; the first level of inquiry is being true to, respecting, and capturing the details of the individual cases being studied; cross-case analysis follows from and depends on the quality of individual case studies
8. Context sensitivity	Places findings in a social, historical, and temporal context; dubious of the possibility or meaningfulness of generalizations across time and space.
9. Empathic neutrality	Complete objectivity is impossible; pure subjectivity undermines credibility; the researcher's passion is understanding the world in all its complexity—not proving something, not advocating, not advancing personal agendas, but understanding; the researcher includes personal experience and empathic insight as part of the relevant data, while taking a neutral nonjudgmental stance toward whatever content may emerge
10. Design flexibility	Open to adapting inquiry as understanding deepens and/or situations change; avoids getting locked into rigid designs that eliminate responsiveness; pursues new paths of discovery as they emerge

Source: Reprinted from Michael Quinn Patton (1990). *Qualitative evaluation and research methods,* 2nd ed. Newbury Park. CA: Sage, pp. 40–41.

Nature of Data

Second, qualitative research is descriptive in nature. Although quantitative researchers use numbers to represent the dependent variable, numbers do not represent the whole story. (*Note:* Obviously, quantitative researchers also describe events; however, the nature of the descriptions are usually numerical versus narrative.) Numbers summarize what was measured but do not necessarily represent fully what was seen. For example, suppose we wished to determine the extent to which a student improves in a reading class. We could use a standardized measurement device to determine the reading gains the student makes. However, we do not have information on other possibly important concerns such as how the student responds each day when reading assignments are required (i.e., happy and feeling excited to become engaged in reading or moping and depressed about beginning the reading assignment). Information is lacking on whether the student has made connections between what he or she is reading about and other subjects or if the topic being read about is interesting to the child. We do not have information on what the teacher thinks about the program. Does the teacher wish to make modifications or drop the program altogether? We do not have information on how others in the classroom or school feel about the program. And we do not have information from parents in terms of their satisfaction with the program. For instance, parents may report that the children are excited to go to school or that they have difficulty motivating the children to go to school. Students may make comments about how they love reading class or how they despise it. Therefore, qualitative researchers attempt to gather as much information as possible to see the entire movie rather than a few frames from the film. They insist that since what is missing from the film may be as important as what is captured in the selected frames, descriptive information allows us to see as much of the film as possible to gain more of an appreciation of the larger story.

Process of Change

Third, a consideration of a couple of the variables that impact outcomes or products may not be considered as important as the process of change. Quantitative researchers tend to look at the outcomes (i.e., through posttest assessments), whereas qualitative researchers focus on the process as well as the outcome. For example, in studying reading achievement, we could measure the reading performance of students both before and after the reading instruction. We could then determine how much the children have changed in their ability to read. On the other hand, we may wish to know not how much children have changed but why they have changed or how they have improved. The attitudes of the students may have affected the reading performance in some manner. Or, the teacher expectations may have had an impact.

The critical questions to be answered then are: "How are these attitudes or expectations translated into the daily reading activities?" "How do the interactions of the other students affect the process of reading acquisition?" and "How does the classroom climate overall affect the process of learning to read?" A more pragmatic difficulty with looking at only outcomes is that once we have a narrowly defined outcome limited by the variables observed, we have little chance of making a change to improve our instruction simply because it is too late. If we assess the process of change, we can readily see if and how the student is being affected. If the student is not progressing, we can make changes before the student fails to achieve. Studying the process of change, then, involves a descriptive and enhanced assessment of the daily changes that occur through interactions, activities, and procedures.

Type of Reasoning

Fourth, qualitative researchers use a combination of inductive and deductive reasoning in interpreting their research. Quantitative researchers tend to use a deductive approach. They tend to generate hypotheses from theories and attempt to disprove these hypotheses and/or theories. Qualitative researchers do not generate hypotheses for testing before the investigation. They generate research questions and attempt to enter into the research without any preconceived notion of possible outcomes. Once findings have been accumulated, theories may be developed. Theories such as these are called *grounded theories* (Glaser & Strauss, 1967) because they are grounded in a solid foundation of research and because the process that generated the theory cannot be separated from the theory. Within this framework, a theory is developed from the data (Krahn, Hohn, & Kime, 1995). Historically, researchers from diverse philosophical orientations also believe in the need to ground a theory in solid research data.

For example, B. F. Skinner described theory making in a similar vein. According to Zuriff (1995), Skinner indicated that a theory "evolves as additional empirical relationships are presented in a formal way, and as it develops, it integrates more facts in increasingly more economical formulations" (p. 171). Similarly, Chiesa (1994) stated the following: "Skinner clearly preferred a Machian approach to explanatory theories; a type of theory that is descriptive, relies on observation, and whose terms integrate relations among basic data" (p. 140). Finally, Skinner himself indicated that, "[A theory] has nothing to do with the presence or absence of experimental confirmation. Facts and theories do not stand in opposition to each other. The relation, rather, is this: theories are based upon facts; they are statements about organizations of facts" (Skinner, 1947/1972, p. 302). Thus, it seems that Skinner was essentially saying that theories should be grounded in the data (see Strauss & Corbin, 1990 for a through discussion of grounded theory) revealed in observed research findings.

Focus of Research

Fifth, the focus of qualitative research is the meaning individuals assign to their lives. Quantitative researchers are more concerned with "hard data" that is objective and narrowly defined. These data are usually not concerned with the "meaning" individuals attach to their experiences, but with the observable changes enacted on individuals. Perhaps, this characteristic sets quantitative research apart from qualitative research more than any of the other four characteristics. Qualitative researchers are concerned with phenomena such as values, attitudes, assumptions, and beliefs and how these phenomena affect the individuals under investigation. In other words, qualitative researchers are concerned with cognitive processes (i.e., what and how people think) as well as why they process information in some manner. These phenomena are not easily defined in operational terms that allow us to observe them directly. Thus, an alternative method of investigation must take place to study these phenomena. Qualitative research does just that. Qualitative researchers may spend a great deal of time interacting with the participants in an investigation to assess these difficult to measure phenomena. Quantitative researchers have a difficult time doing the same thing since they must attempt to maintain as much objectivity as possible. (*Note:* Many qualitative researchers may argue whether quantitative researchers are really objective and whether anyone really wants to be objective if it were possible.) Their measurement instruments also take these very complex phenomena and measure them by observing by-products of the phenomena and then summarizing and signifying what was observed with numbers. Qualitative researchers view this practice in isolation as problematic since a large chunk of data is missing; these data include an examination of more of the complexity of their lives. Table 8.3 shows some of the differences between quantitative and qualitative methods. As seen in the table, the differences do not make the two methods mutually exclusive. However, understanding these differences will aid the critical research consumer in making conclusions as to the utility and meaning of the researcher's conclusions.

WHAT ARE QUALITATIVE RESEARCH PROCEDURES?

Phases

There are several methods of conducting qualitative research. In fact, a major difference between qualitative and quantitative research methodologies is that qualitative methods are so flexible (i.e., they can change). Therefore, there are no specific steps used in the design of qualitative methods that are the same for all types of designs. However, we can list some phases that researchers typically go through before and during the qualitative research endeavor. The reason for pointing out these steps is to demonstrate how much more flexible qualitative research is than quantitative research. The ways in which researchers decide to implement each step will form the design. Realize that these steps do

TABLE 8.3 Differences between Quantitative and Qualitative Research Methods

QUANTITATIVE RESEARCH	QUALITATIVE RESEARCH
Primary purpose is to determine cause-and-effect relationships.	Primary purpose is to describe on-going processes.
Precise hypothesis is stated before the start of the investigation; theories govern the purpose of the investigation in a deductive manner.	Hypotheses are developed during the investigation; questions govern the purpose of the investigation; theories are developed inductively.
The independent variable is controlled and manipulated.	There is no specific independent variable; the concern is to study naturally occurring phenomena without interference.
Objective collection of data is a requirement.	Objective collection of data is not a requirement; data collectors may interact with the participants.
Research design is specified before the start of the investigation.	Research design is flexible and develops throughout the investigation.
Data are represented and summarized in numerical form.	Data are represented or summarized in narrative or verbal forms.
Reliability and validity determined through statistical and logical methods.	Reliability and validity determined through multiple sources of information (triangulation).
Samples are selected to represent the population.	Samples are purposefully selected or single cases are studied.
Study of behavior is in the natural or artificial setting.	Study of behavior is in the natural setting.
Use of design or statistical analyses to control for threats to internal validity.	Use of logical analyses to control or account for alternative explanations.
Use of inferential statistical procedures to demonstrate external validity (specifically, population validity).	Use of similar cases to determine the generalizability of findings (logical generalization) if at all.
Rely on research design and data gathering instruments to control for procedural bias.	Rely on the researcher to come to terms with procedural bias.
Phenomena are broken down or simplified for study.	Phenomena are studied holistically, as a complex system.
Conclusions are stated with a predetermined degree of certainty (i.e., α level).	Conclusions are tentative and subjected to ongoing examination.

not only occur before the investigation but continue throughout and do not necessarily occur in the same order as presented here. Potter (1996) identifies decisions that must be made within each step before and throughout the investigation. The first phase is to ask a research question. Obviously, the question can come from several sources such as observing the world, reading other research, or attempting to solve a problem.

The second phase is to decide on how to collect the data. Researchers should decide on whether to examine written documents, interview participants, observe participants, or a combination of these. Researchers should decide on whether to identify themselves or not, and, if so, as researchers and/or group members. Researchers should also decide if they will be active or passive observers or active participants. Finally, researchers should decide on how long the data should be collected to gather enough evidence to make firm assertions about the data.

The third phase involves deciding on a sample. It is critical to understand that the size of the sample is of concern. However, rather than being concerned about sample size to ensure the representativeness of the sample to the population, qualitative researchers are concerned with access to relevant evidence about a phenomenon (Potter, 1996). Several sampling methods are used in qualitative research and will be discussed in more detail later.

The fourth phase is data analysis. This phase also continues throughout the investigation. Researchers must decide on the type of analysis that will be conducted. This decision is based on the purpose of the investigation. Potter (1996) describes 20 of the most prevalently used techniques. These techniques were placed into four categories—orienting methods, deductive methods of construction, inductive methods of construction, and other methods of construction. A description of each of these methods is beyond the scope of this text; however, the reader is encouraged to seek out information from Potter (1996) to gain an appreciation of the complexity of data analysis in qualitative research.

The final phase of a qualitative investigation is to make conclusions or understandings based on the data. These understandings will be in the form of descriptions, interpretations, theories, assertions, generalizations, and evaluations. These understandings will be described in more detail later in the chapter.

Sampling

Although sampling procedures were discussed in Chapter 4, a discussion of qualitative sampling procedures seems appropriate. Similar to quantitative research, a sample must be taken since it is usually not possible to study the entire population. Identifying a sample is one of the first steps in designing a qualitative research study. The setting, population, and phenomena to be studied should also be decided. Under some circumstances, phenomena under study will also define the site and the population to be studied. For example, Pajak and Blase (1984) studied the reasons why teachers go to bars. Once the phenomenon was defined, the setting was determined (i.e., a local bar). The population was also defined (i.e., teachers who went to bars).

Sampling in a qualitative study may or may not be the same as convenience sampling used in other methods of research. With convenience sampling, the sample is selected because it is available and relatively easy to integrate into the research. With sampling in many qualitative research investigations, although the sample may be convenient in many cases, the purpose of selecting the sample is to address the research question specifically. In order to determine if the sample was adequate, we must address the purpose of the research and determine if the sample allows for the generation of answers to the questions posed. Thus, to answer the question of why teachers go to bars, the sample would be less adequate if a local bar was selected simply because it was local. A bar would be selected that had a large number of specific types of patrons—teachers. Thus, although the sample may be convenient in one way, the sample is selected to help answer the research questions. As stated by Schatzman and Strauss (1973) when discussing how a researcher may select his sample:

> *Certainly he could do the sampling task randomly; but again he has selected samples in mind, and probably in such density as to insure the necessary coverage of all the important or at least obvious ones. He will probably select from among the universe of people according to their functions* for his research. *(p. 42)*

The sampling method used by qualitative researchers is termed purposeful sampling by Patton (1987). Patton indicated that purposeful sampling is used to select information-rich cases for in-depth study. The samples consist of cases where a great deal can be learned about issues of central importance for the research. Patton described 10 purposeful sampling methods; however, he indicated that there are other qualitative sampling methods. It should be noted that these sampling methods are not mutually exclusive. For our purposes, the 10 sampling methods described by Patton will suffice. (*Note:* Examples used throughout the following descriptions of sampling procedures will focus on one topic—reading instruction, due to an attempt to remain consistent throughout.)

Extreme or Deviant Case Sampling. Extreme or deviant case sampling involves focusing on cases that have important information because they are unusual or special in some way. For example, if one were to study reading instruction in a public school, one may choose to study reading instruction with fourth-grade students with learning disabilities in reading. (*Note:* By the very nature of qualifying these students for special education services, these students must have a severe discrepancy between their abilities and their achievement; thus, by definition, these students' academic performance are deviant from what we would expect.) A purpose for this would be to obtain information that may be valuable for typical students involved in reading classes. In other words, if we found that a specific reading method was effective for students with learning disabilities in reading, we may be better able to teach students without learning disabilities how to read, or at least prevent students from being identified as having learning disabilities in the first place.

Maximum Variation Sampling. Maximum variation sampling involves "capturing and describing the central themes or principle outcomes that cut across a great deal of participant or program variation" (Patton, 1987, p. 53). For example, one could select students with learning disabilities in reading, gifted students, and typical students in the fourth grade to examine reading instruction. The purpose of this sampling method is to obtain high-quality and detailed descriptions of each case to document uniqueness and to determine general patterns that are shared by the heterogeneous sample.

Homogeneous Sampling. Homogeneous sampling is the opposite of maximum variation sampling in that participants similar to one another are selected to decrease the variation within the sample. For example, one could select students who are in the fourth grade who are at grade level in reading to assess reading instruction. Note that this sample is not extreme but is homogeneous in that the students selected are all in the same grade and are at a similar level in reading ability.

Typical Case Sampling. Typical case sampling involves selecting one or more typical cases. What is typical would be decided on by significant others (i.e., parents, teachers, community leaders, administrators, etc.) in the setting. For example, if one were to study reading instruction in the fourth grade, the researcher would have the fourth-grade teacher(s)determine what are typical reading levels of students and help select those students who meet the definition of typical. These students would then comprise the sample involved in the investigation. The purpose of this sampling method is to provide others who are not "familiar with the program...a qualitative profile of one or more 'typical' cases" (Patton, 1987, p. 54). Thus, the purpose of typical case sampling is to inform others about the program, not to generalize results to the population as is attempted with random sampling procedures in quantitative approaches.

Critical Case Sampling. Critical case sampling is used to identify critical cases that are particularly important for some reason. For example, suppose one were studying the reading instruction of a fourth-grade class and wished to identify a sample that would allow us to generalize to other cases. We may select students who come from high stimulating environments since we know that a high level of stimulation received in the early years (e.g., before entering into kindergarten) can have a significant impact on later reading abilities (Adams, 1992). We observe our sample and discover that most of the students in a reading class were having difficulty in reading. We would then attempt to make the conclusion that if these students were having difficulty, others from less stimulating environments placed in similar learning situations probably were also experiencing difficulties.

Snowball or Chain Sampling. Snowball or chain sampling involves asking others who would be a good choice to be involved in the sample. This sampling method is similar to looking for literature on a chosen topic. For example, suppose that one was interested in the literature base for whole-language instruction in reading (i.e., a method used to facilitate the development of reading). One could look at the reference section of one article and find what other articles were referenced (an ancestral search). This process could be repeated across subsequent articles. This process continues until a large sample of articles are identified. Once the same articles begin to show up in subsequent reference sections, these articles are considered especially important to the topic. A similar scenario would happen with snowball or chain sampling in that when asking who would be particularly adept at teaching reading, several names may be generated until the same names begin to show up repeatedly. The purpose of this sampling procedure is to identify critical individuals to include in the sample.

Criterion Sampling. Criterion sampling involves setting a criterion of performance; individuals who meet or surpass the criterion will be included in the sample. For example, one may wish to select teachers with at least 10 years of reading instruction to include in the sample since these teachers may have particular experiences with success and failure in teaching reading. The purpose of criterion sampling is to provide rich information that can be used to improve a program or system.

Confirming and Disconfirming Cases. Confirming and disconfirming cases involve the attempt to confirm what was found during the exploratory state of the investigation. In other words, once some conclusions have been drawn from the data (in field work or from other sources such as stakeholders), these conclusions should be confirmed or disconfirmed. For example, based on exploratory information, a researcher may wish to confirm that children involved in wholistic approaches to reading instruction have more positive attitudes toward reading than students involved in teacher-directed reading instruction. Thus, the interpretation is that the type of reading instruction has an impact on student attitudes toward reading. Thus, the researcher could sample students who are involved in a wholistic reading class and students in a teacher-directed reading class and determine the respected attitudes toward reading. In this manner, the cases involved in the sample will either confirm or disconfirm the earlier interpretations. As stated by Patton (1987):

> *Thinking about the challenge of finding confirmatory and disconfirming cases emphasizes the relationship between sampling and evaluation conclusions. The sample determines what the evaluator will have something to say about, thus the importance of sampling carefully and thoughtfully. (p. 57)*

Sampling Politically Important Cases. Sampling politically important cases involves a variation of the critical case strategy. Researchers will attempt to select a politically sensitive site or conduct an analysis of a politically sensitive topic. In some cases, researchers may attempt to avoid the politically sensitive site or topic. For example, in the early to late 1990's, we experienced a political "hot potato" with regard to reading instruction. For whatever reason, standardized test scores decreased over a period of several years. (*Note:* There are several possible reasons for these decreases that are beyond the scope of this example and text.) To better understand this decline, a researcher may purposefully select reading instruction for investigation in an area (e.g., district, school) that has experienced major problems with reading proficiency. The selection of this site for the study could have political consequences but could provide critical information in that political climate. One purpose of this sampling method would be to increase the usefulness and utilization of the gathered information and possibly increase the visibility and impact of the findings.

Convenience Sampling. Convenience sampling was described in Chapter 4. However, although convenience sampling is a common sampling method, it is not viewed as desirable (Patton, 1987). Patton states the following: "Purposeful, strategic sampling can yield crucial information about critical cases. Convenience sampling is neither purposeful nor strategic" (p. 58).

When reading a qualitative research article, it is important to determine how the sample was selected. Researchers must make certain that the sample was chosen to address the research question directly. The manner in which the sample was chosen goes directly to the credibility of the data. Additionally, according to Patton, there are also no rules for sample sizes; the size of the sample must be determined by taking into consideration the needs of interested parties (e.g., stakeholders, decision makers, information seekers). The sample must be large enough to add credibility to the data generated but small enough to allow for an in-depth analysis of the data. Researchers must be aware that the findings will be critiqued in some manner and must anticipate the questions that reviewers may raise. They must make sure that the reasons for the selections are stated and explicit (Patton, 1987). An attempt should be made to find these reasons to help determine the data's credibility.

WHAT IS UNDERSTANDING IN QUALITATIVE RESEARCH?

Understanding refers to the way we interpret our data and how that interpretation actually allows us to understand the phenomenon of interest. Maxwell (1992) believed that *understanding* in qualitative research is more fundamental than is validity. Maxwell stated, "I see the types of validity that I present here as derivative from the kinds of understanding gained from qualitative inquiry; my typology of validity categories is also a typology of the kinds of understanding at which qualitative research aims" (p. 281). From a qualitative perspective, validity refers to the apparent truthfulness of the collected accounts, not to the data or the methods used to gather these data. The inferences drawn from the data may or may not be valid; the data itself is neither. This is a critical point. If validity refers to the inferences or conclusions we make about our data, then the validity of our conclusions must be considered. Quantitative researchers many times look at the types of designs or the statistical methods used and make a statement of validity or invalidity based on these methods.

For example, if we used a preexperimental design, a quantitative researcher may conclude that the validity of the data and any conclusions made based on that data are hampered by an inability to control for threats to internal validity. However, qualitative researchers see the conclusions of paramount importance compared with the design. For qualitative researchers, a preexperimental design may generate valid or invalid conclusions and inferences; the same can be said about true experimental designs. The design is not the critical aspect with making valid conclusions; however, the data generated with these designs impact the validity of the conclusions. Understanding, then, is concerned with how well we come to learn about a phenomenon. Maxwell (1992) argues that there are five broad categories of understanding in qualitative research and five corresponding types of validity—descriptive, interpretive, theoretical, generalizability, and evaluative. A description of each of the validities follows.

Descriptive Validity

Descriptive validity refers to the factual accuracy of the researcher's or observer's account. The concern here is whether the data gathered are contrived or distorted. Others should be able to agree that the events or situations occurred. This agreement is similar to interobserver agreement discussed in Chapter 3. Also, descriptive validity must be viewed in terms of what was included as well as excluded in the account. For example, if we were interested in studying student reactions to child-centered teaching approaches, leaving out body and facial expressions may be a serious threat to descriptive validity. Descriptive validity, then, refers to the extent to which researchers are able to report accurate data and that the data accurately represent the phenomenon under study. The critical research consumer should take into consideration the extent to which the researcher included as well as excluded data or the extent to which others agree on the data gathered.

Interpretive Validity

Interpretive validity refers to being concerned with the subjective meanings of objects, events, and behaviors to the individuals engaged in and with the objects, events, and behaviors (Maxwell, 1992). Interpretive validity is specifically relevant to qualitative research. There is no quantitative counterpart to interpretive validity. Rather than being concerned with the physical aspects of what one observes, interpretive validity is concerned with those things that cannot be observed. For example, how one believes he or she is doing is apart from how one is actually doing. Descriptive validity would be concerned with how one is doing in a class; interpretive validity is concerned with how one believes he or she is doing in the class. Thus, the participants' perspective is the basis on which a phenomenon is studied and understood.

Interpretive validity does not only rely on what the person describes to be his or her beliefs, attitudes, cognitions, intentions, and evaluations. Interpretive validity also relies on the researcher's ability to construct the participants' meanings through observing not only what they say, but by observing their body language, past actions, and considering accounts from other sources such as other individuals also in the situation. Thus, interpretive validity is concerned with the accuracy of the interpretations made by the researcher with regard to the participants' intentions, beliefs, attitudes, evaluations, and cognitions, both consciously as well as unconsciously. The critical research consumer must be concerned with the methods used by the researcher to gain the understanding necessary to make valid interpretations such as asking the participants, asking others, describing nonverbal behaviors such as body position, and gaining information from the participants' past.

Theoretical Validity

Whereas the first two types of validity refer to the accuracy with which researchers describe or interpret data, theoretical validity is concerned with an *explanation* as well as a description and interpretation of an account (Maxwell, 1992). Theories go beyond the data in that they attempt to provide an explanation for what is observed. With descriptive validity, one is concerned with the accuracy of the description; with interpretive validity, one is concerned with the accuracy of the interpretation of the data; and with theoretical validity, one is concerned with taking these descriptions and interpretations and constructing a grounded theory to help explain the phenomenon. Maxwell indicates that there are two components to a theory. The first component involves the validity of the concepts that developed the validity, and the second is concerned with the relationships among the concepts. For example, Maxwell (1992) points out that

> *one could label the student's throwing of the eraser as an act of resistance, and connect this act to the repressive behavior or values of the teacher, the social structure of the school, and class relationships in U.S. society. The identification of the throwing as "resistance" constitutes the application of a theoretical construct to the descriptive and interpretive understanding of the action; the connection of this to other aspects of the participants, the school, or the community constitutes the postulation of theoretical relationships among these constructs. (p. 291)*

Notice that the first aspect of theoretical validity is similar to the construct validity explained in Chapter 3. The second aspect of theoretical validity is concerned with what we called internal validity in Chapter 2. However, rather than attempting to deal with specific threats to internal validity through a predetermined design, theoretical validity depends more on the community's interpretation and acceptance of the theoretical account. Thus, qualitatively, theoretical or internal validity is a logical and subjective determination rather than an objective one. (*Note:* Many qualitative researchers do not believe that true objectivity exists.) Therefore, even in quantitative research, the determination of internal validity is subjective since the determination is dependent on the researcher's theoretical framework, beliefs, purposes, and perspective. The critical research consumer should look at how the theory was constructed, the agreement among others that the theory is solid, whether the descriptions and interpretations that built the theory are accurate or not, and how the concepts derived from the data were put together. A determination should be made about whether the construction of the theory fits within the overall general framework of what is known about the phenomenon from an accumulation of research studies rather than one isolated study.

Generalizability

Generalizability is similar to the external validity described in Chapter 2 (*Note:* Many qualitative researchers reject the concept of generalization. Generalization requires at least some orderliness of phenomena that, according to many qualitative researchers, is not possible when dealing with such a complex subject matter of human behavior that is context-specific); however, there is a major difference. As with external validity, generalizability refers to the ability to extend the results of an investigation to other persons, settings, or times. The difference lies in the manner in which this extension is accomplished. Recall from earlier chapters, external validity, and specifically population validity, can be enhanced through randomly selecting participants from the population. The assumption is that if the sample mirrors the population, the results found with the sample will most likely hold true for others in the population. However, in qualitative research, random selection of participants is not usually accomplished. As indicated previously, sampling in qualitative research is usually purposeful rather than random. Thus, qualitative researchers must have other ways of generalizing or extending their findings to a broader population.

One method is called logical generalization. An inference may be made to others with the same or similar characteristic, as the participants involved in the investigation. A second method is by generating a theory that is not only valid (or seemingly so) for the participants or situations studied (i.e., makes sense of what they do), but also shows how different results may be obtained in different situations or conditions (Maxwell, 1992) and how similar results may be obtained in similar situations or conditions. Generalizability, then, is more of a logical or subjective endeavor rather than an objective or statistical one. The critical research consumer must determine if the theory makes sense for those in the investigation and determine if the theory would likely hold up in other situations, conditions, or with other individuals.

Maxwell (1992) makes a discrimination between two types of generalizability. The first type is called internal generalizability. Internal generalizability refers to the ability to generalize within the community or group being investigated to those not directly involved in the investigation. For example, in the study by Pajak and Blase (1984), all teachers in the bar were not interviewed. The researchers interviewed and interacted with many of the teachers, but many simply did not have the opportunity to share their opinions on why they go to the bar. The researchers attempted to generalize the results to all of the teachers frequenting the particular bar where the study took place.

The second type of generalizability is generalizing to other communities or groups and is called external generalizability. Pajak and Blase generalized the results to teachers in general and made conclusions about the teaching profession. They did this by placing the results within a specific theory (i.e., self theory). According to Maxwell (1992), internal generalizability is more important to qualitative researchers. Qualitative researchers rarely make explicit claims of external generalizability. Some qualitative researchers may in fact insist on a lack of external generalizability in special situations such as studying extreme or ideal cases. The critical research consumer should be aware of the type of generalization being attempted by researchers and determine if the theory makes sense in the other situations or conditions. Overall, generalizability is not a central concern of qualitative researchers; descriptive, interpretive, and theoretical validity are more important concerns for qualitative researchers.

Evaluative Validity

Similar to generalizability, evaluative validity is not of central concern for qualitative researchers (Maxwell, 1992). Evaluative validity is essentially the ability to make valid right or wrong statements. For example, for the teachers in the bar study, Pajak and Blase (1984) make an evaluative statement that indicates that it is incorrect for schools to restrict authentic contacts between students and teachers—the authors indicated that this practice is troublesome. The evaluative validity of this statement from the perspective of the critical research consumer will be based on their own beliefs of right and wrong. Thus, evaluative validity refers to whether a researcher's evaluation of the situation fits with his or her public's. Another example would involve the use of corporal punishment in the public schools. A researcher's evaluation that corporal punishment is not best practice and should be stopped due to the impact of the punishment on students' self-esteem may be valid for some but not for others due to differences in the beliefs of correct and incorrect child management techniques.

WHAT ARE THE EVALUATIVE CRITERIA FOR JUDGING THE RELIABILITY AND VALIDITY OF QUALITATIVE RESEARCH?

Franklin and Jordan (1995) provide several evaluative criteria for judging the reliability and validity of qualitative data or as qualitative researchers may say, the apparent truthfulness of a study. They indicate the following:

> *Validity and reliability of qualitative assessment data rest on the credibility, thoroughness, completeness, and consistency of the information interpreted within a narrative assessment report and the logical inferences the clinician uses to draw conclusions from this information about the client. Although accuracy of the clinician's report is difficult to ascertain, the validity and reliability of the interpretations made by the clinician may be evaluated by using the criteria listed below. (p. 291)*

Following is a description of each of the evaluative criteria for judging qualitative research (i.e., completeness of information; adequacy of interpretation; determination of inconsistencies in data; adequacy of metaphors, pictures, or diagrams; collaboration with participants; and multiple methods to gather data).

It is important to note that qualitative researchers such as Howe and Eisenhart (1990) have indicated, "Except at a very high level of abstraction, it is fruitless to try to set standards for qualitative research per se. Even when the focus within qualitative research is significantly restricted, the issue associated with standards are quite complex and extensive" (p. 4). However, Howe and Eisenhart presented standards for evaluating educational research including: (a) the fit between research questions and data collection analysis techniques, (b) the effective application of specific data collection and analysis techniques, (c) alertness to and coherence of background assumptions (i.e., existing knowledge), (d) overall warrant (i.e., applying knowledge from outside a particular perspective), and (e) value constraints (i.e., external—worth of research for educators and internal—research ethics). Thus, standards or criteria should be viewed as general guidelines so as to avoid restrictive interpretations of qualitative research.

Criterion 1: Completeness of Information

The first criterion is concerned with the completeness of the information presented. There should be a limited amount of gaps in the information, and the data should be coherent enough to make a clear connection with the researcher's conclusions. For example, suppose a researcher wishes to conduct a case study on a particular student in a seventh-grade classroom. The researcher reports complete information for the first semester, but a gap of 2 weeks during the second semester is present. The student may have been ill during this time or some other reason was present to prevent the collection of data; however, the researcher should explain this gap.

Criterion 2: Adequacy of Interpretation

The second criterion is concerned with the adequacy of the researcher's interpretations. For example, if the researcher suggests that the student has a developmental disability, but there is missing information about the diagnosis, a concern should be raised.

Criterion 3: Determination of Inconsistencies in Data

The third criterion involves determining whether there are inconsistencies in the data. For example, if a researcher indicated that a student being observed in the classroom was well behaved, but then later stated that the child had to be disciplined for a class infraction, an apparent inconsistency has occurred and should be explained.

Criterion 4: Adequacy of Metaphors, Pictures, or Diagrams

The fourth criterion is concerned with the adequacy of metaphors, pictures, or diagrams. The use of these techniques should allow for the understanding of information being presented more fully. For example, a sample of a picture drawn by the student should allow for a more complete understanding of the student and his or her environment.

Criterion 5: Collaboration with Participants

The fifth criterion involves the collaboration with the participant(s) by the researcher. The participants' views should be fully reported and integrated throughout the report. These views add credibility to the researcher's conclusions. For example, if the researcher concluded that a student prefers to be placed in an integrated classroom rather than a resource room (students spend part of the day for extra aid in a subject area), it would be beneficial to have statements from the student that back up this conclusion.

Criterion 6: Multiple Methods to Gather Data

The sixth criterion involves the use of multiple methods to gather the data. This question is a critical one. Qualitative research methods must have some method of ensuring the reliability and validity of the data collected. One of the most desirable ways to strengthen an investigation's reliability and validity is through triangulation (Silverman, 1993), which is one of the most important methods one can use to document and describe what is going on in the research setting (Fetterman, 1991). According to Patton (1990), triangulation is the use of "several kinds of methods or data, including using both quantitative and qualitative approaches" (p. 187). The logic behind triangulation is that all data collection methods have strengths and weaknesses. It is to the advantage of researchers to use a combination of data collection methods (such as observation, interview, and document analyses) so that the strength of one method can compensate for a weakness of another method. (*Note:* Observation, interview, and document analysis methods will be discussed in more detail in the following chapter.)

Observations. According to Patton (1990), observations have several strengths. First, observations provide a picture of what is occurring in the context. What is being observed is occurring at that very point in time in that context. Second, the ability to obtain firsthand experience allows researchers to be more open and discovery-oriented; they can access unexpected information. Finally, observations also allow researchers to view things that may have been missed if observers were not present.

Observational methods have a number of potential weaknesses (Patton, 1990). First, there may be observer bias in that what the observer views is not reflected in what he or she documents. Second, there may be reactivity in the observations. Consider what your reaction may be if someone was watching everything you did and taking notes. Third, only external behaviors are recorded. Internal behaviors such as beliefs and attitudes are not directly observed. Finally, there is only a limited sample of the total time period that can be observed. Consider if you were observed for 4 hours during the day. The concern would be if the observed 4 hours are an adequate representation of the entire day's activities and behaviors.

Interviews. Interviews can overcome these observation weaknesses in several ways. First, the data are solicited from the participants rather than from an observer. Second, there can be a check on the observer's accuracy in that if an observer reported one thing occurring and through an interview a participant also indicated something occurred, the event's likelihood is increased. For example, suppose that an observer reported that a participant seemed to have fun with a reading activity. The participant can be asked what his or her reaction to the reading activity was. If the participant indicates that he or she had fun or enjoyed the reading activity, our confidence in the accuracy of the observation is increased. Third, internal behaviors can be measured, albeit indirectly. For example, an observer reporting that a teacher used a certain curriculum in her classroom is documented through watching the teacher's classroom behavior. However, the observer cannot directly report on whether the teacher likes the curriculum; the observer would have to make an inference through behaviors such as body position, facial expressions, and tone of voice. Through an interview, the interviewer could ask the teacher to comment on the curriculum. The teacher's attitude toward the curriculum is then examined when it could not be directly examined through observation. Finally, an interviewer can attempt to sample a much wider range of program activities and situations than one could through an observation. An interviewer could ask what occurred during the nonobservational period or last year or 10 years ago. The point here is that information can be gained through interviews that cannot be gained through observations because doing so is impossible or impractical.

Although interviews can overcome or compensate for problems with observations, they do have weaknesses. First, there may be a distortion in the perceptions or perspectives of the interviewee due to the researcher's state of mind. Statements that reflect anger, bias, or lack of awareness could distort the information the researcher provides in an interview. If, for example, we asked about the job performance of someone we did not like, we may be more apt to provide inaccurate information either by downplaying achievements or highlighting failures or weaknesses. Second, there may be a lack of recall during the interview. Based on much memory research, we know that people have a tendency to put in fictitious information where there are gaps in memory. Thus, the reliability and validity of information obtained from interviews may be suspect in certain circumstances, especially where information on obscure events or events that occurred some time ago is needed. Finally, interviews are problematic when there is reactivity to the interviewer. This reactivity may include an interviewee telling the interviewer what he or she thinks the interviewer wants to hear, or an interviewee exaggerating an event to make himself or herself look better or downplaying an event for the same purposes. Obviously, observations can help overcome the problems with interviews. Observations can help verify information provided by interviewees.

Document Analysis. Another data collection method is document analysis. Document analyses are popular methods of data collection for qualitative researchers where the data are presented as a permanent product. Document analyses may include incident reports in a school, number and types of arrests on school grounds, or test scores and other information on student achievement.

Document analyses have several advantages over observations and interviews for some types of information. First, document analyses are permanent products. That is, they can be studied by several individuals at different times. Second, there is no reactivity on the part of participants. Finally, information that may not be available anywhere else may be available in documents. Thus, document analyses can fill in for gaps in observational or interview data and provide a check for that information. For example, suppose that a school administrator was concerned with the level of truancy in her school. The administrator indicates that the problem is severe and steps should be taken to correct for the problem. However, based on records kept in the office, the truancy problem is about half of that of other local schools. In this case, although truancy may be a problem, the administrator's perception of the severity of the problem may be questioned due to data in the official records.

However, document analyses have weaknesses. First, the information found in the documents may be incomplete. Second, the information in the documents may be inaccurate. Just because information is in an official document, the accuracy is not assured. Any number of variables could make the information inaccurate such as biased reporting by the person entering the information. Third, the information in documents may highlight only the positive and leave out the negative. Finally, documents are usually variable in the quality of information they contain and the specificity of that information. Again, combining other sources of data collection with document analysis will improve the believability of the data. Observations and interviews can verify the information obtained through documents.

Criterion 7: Disqualification of Interpretations

The final criterion has to do with the attempt made by the researcher to disqualify his or her own interpretations of the data. In other words, the concern that should come to mind as one reads a qualitative investigation is whether researchers have put forth other explanations for the obtained data. Rationalism is a central concept to science. When researchers are attempting to explain their results in a number of ways, they are practicing rationalism. For example, suppose a researcher is attempting to find out why students tend to drop out of school. The researcher visits a school with a high level of dropouts and interviews the teachers and students. The researcher also makes contact with other students who have dropped out of school within the past 2 years and interviews them. After analyzing the data, the researcher concludes the reason why most of the students drop out of school is a lack of understanding of the material being taught, which in turn, made them outcasts. The teachers indicate that the students most prone to drop out have difficulties keeping up in class. The students currently in school indicate that of those students who dropped out, most were not in the "in crowd." The students who dropped out indicated that school was not enjoyable and difficult. Alternative explanations the researcher tried to support included a problem with parental support, the need for outside income for the family, and being in a large school environment. These other explanations were not supported by the data, and the researcher's explanation seemed to have the greatest support from the data.

WHAT ARE THE TYPES OF TRIANGULATION METHODS?

When reviewing a qualitative investigation, triangulation methods should be one of the first concerns the critical research consumer has. As stated by Pitman and Maxwell (1992),

> *Acknowledging that qualitative research allows more scope for researchers to see what they choose and, thus, greater chance for the intentional neglect of evidence contrary to one's values or interests, Eisner argues that, "it is especially important not only to use multiple sources of data, but also to consider disaffirming evidence and contrary interpretations or appraisals when one presents one's own conclusions [emphasis in original]" (Eisner, 1991:111). (p. 748)*

As indicated in the previous discussion, combining data sources have the advantage of overcoming the weaknesses of using a single data source. However, combining several data sources is not the only method of triangulation. Patton (1990) indicates that there are four types of triangulation: (a) data sources, (b) analyst, (c) theory/perspective, and (d) methods.

Data Sources Triangulation

Triangulation of data sources means:

> *(1) comparing observational data with interview data; (2) comparing what people say in public with what they say in private; (3) checking for the consistency of what people say about the same thing over time; and (4) comparing the perspectives of people from other points of view—staff views, client views, funder views, and views expressed by people outside the program. (Patton, 1990, p. 467)*

The main purpose of triangulation of data sources is to provide validation information obtained from one source by gathering information from another source. For example, if we wanted to discover how satisfied secondary teachers in a large metropolitan area are, we could interview the teachers and find out that their job satisfaction is fairly low. We could also observe the teachers and see that they are not excited on arriving to work and leave the school building as soon as the last class has ended. The two sources of very different data seem to correspond. However, the information gathered from two or more sources may not be congruent. In other words, there are times when the information from multiple sources do not support one another. Suppose that we interviewed the teachers in regard to job satisfaction and also interviewed administrators. We may find that the teachers indicate that they have low job satisfaction, but the administrators perceive the job satisfaction of teachers as high. In this case, there would be incongruence. However, a lack of correspondence is not all bad. The reason for the lack of consistent findings present a new research question. It would be important, for example, to find out why the teacher and supervisor perceptions are so different. Ultimately, the critical research consumer will have to judge if conclusions based on inconsistent information from multiple data sources are compromised.

Analyst Triangulation

Analyst triangulation refers to the use of multiple analysts such as multiple interviewers or observers (Patton, 1990). The importance of multiple analysts is that there is an accuracy check for the information obtained. When there is a single person collecting all of the data, the chance for bias is relatively strong. When multiple analysts are involved, this bias should be reduced. For example, suppose that a researcher is observing the social interactions of students in cooperative learning situations. Also suppose that the researcher was a major advocate of cooperative learning. If the researcher was the only observer, bias in the observations is a possibility. On the other hand, if there were one or more observers apart from the researcher, and the information obtained from these other observers was consistent with the researcher's, the researcher's data would be more believable. Patton also recognized another form of multiple analysts. Besides using more than one observer or interviewer, two or more individuals may assess existing data and compare their conclusions. The purpose of this type of triangulation is to verify the conclusions of the researchers. However, it is unlikely that everyone will reach agreement in their conclusions. This disagreement can be, in fact, healthy. Since we all have different experiences, it is unlikely that we will all interpret the same thing in a similar manner. Therefore, the reasons for the differences in the interpretations can also lead to new research questions.

Theory/Perspective Triangulation

Patton (1990) suggests that triangulation can be achieved through interpreting data from different theoretical perspectives. For example, one could conduct research on teaching students how to become more independent via learning how to solve problems. Problem solving has a long research history by investigators from several theoretical positions. The data on problem solving can be gathered and interpreted from a cognitive and a behavioral viewpoint, for example. A cognitive interpretation may center on how the cognitions were changed in some manner that aided the individual to process information differently. The change in the processing of information allowed the individual to solve encountered problems. The behavioral interpretation may center on how the environment was changed to allow for specific or novel responses to be emitted to stimuli present in the environment. Patton indicates that the purpose of theory triangulation is to "understand how findings are affected by different assumptions and fundamental premises" (p. 470). Again, it is unlikely that the interpretations will be in agreement. This disagreement is not viewed as problematic. The assumptions that led to the disagreement can become the focus of research in future investigations.

Methods Triangulation

Methods triangulation involves comparing the data generated from two or more methodologies such as qualitative and quantitative methods (Patton, 1990). The difficulty with methods triangulation is that any two methodologies are not always appropriate to use for the same research question. However, the point with methods triangulation is that if researchers can come to the same conclusion using different methods, the conclusions are more likely to be accurate.

For example, suppose that a researcher wished to study the effects of a compensatory reading program. The researcher may implement the reading program in one class but not in a comparable class. Pretests are taken for both classes, and the pretest average reading abilities are similar. A posttest is then provided to both classes after the reading program is concluded for the first class. The class receiving the compensatory reading program outperforms the other class. This scenario illustrates an example of a quantitative design. We could also send in observers to each class and collect observational data on how the students behave within the context of the classroom. We could observe, for example, how the students approach the reading assignments, how they discuss the reading program with one another, and how they behave once the reading program is over for the day. We could also observe the teacher's behavior. Are the teachers happy and excited about the reading program? How do they treat the students? What are the teacher's nonverbal behaviors like? The information gained from the qualitative observations may indicate that there is great excitement about the program, the teachers are willing to use the program, and the students are willing to put forth effort during the program. If the researcher concluded that the reading program was more effective than the traditional program, the conclusion would be more believable with the qualitative data indicating that the classroom staff and students were excited about and willing to use the compensatory program. However, this agreement of the methodologies may not occur often. In fact, it would be possible that the quantitative data suggested that the compensatory reading program was effective, and the qualitative data suggested that the teachers and students seemed to be restricted in their creativity by a focused and structured program.

SUMMARY

Qualitative research is designed to answer certain research questions that may not be appropriate for quantitative research methods. However, qualitative and quantitative methods are not diametrically opposed to one another. The different research methods can complement each other or each can be used to answer research questions that can only be answered by the appropriate method. The critical research consumer must understand that it is not a question of always using one over the other but when each should be used. It is up to researchers to use the most appropriate research methodology to answer their research questions; it is up to critical research consumers to determine if the correct methodology was used.

In order to make this determination, critical research consumers must have at least a basic understanding of the issues in several areas. First, the characteristics of qualitative research should be known. Qualitative research can be differentiated from quantitative research in several areas including the source of data, process of measured change, type of reasoning, and the focus of the research. An appreciation must also be gained of the procedures used by qualitative researchers especially in the phases of the research process and sampling methods. Additionally, qualitative researchers strive for understanding of phenomena. This understanding involves several types of validities that can be used to evaluate and interpret qualitative research (i.e., descriptive, interpretive, theoretical, generalizability, and evaluative). Another area that must be considered is the criteria one can use to judge the reliability and validity of qualitative research (i.e., completeness of information; adequacy of interpretation; determination of inconsistencies in data; adequacy of metaphors, pictures, or diagrams; collaboration with participants; and multiple methods to gather data). These criteria can aid critical research consumers in the examination of qualitative research. Finally, triangulation methods should be seen as an important aspect of data gathering in qualitative research. Triangulation methods allow for an increase in the believability of the obtained data as well as the conclusions and inferences made.

Once these issues are understood, it is important to become aware of the issues involved in the collection and analysis of data as well as the different designs used in qualitative research. The following chapter will provide greater detail in qualitative research methods including data collection and analysis and designs.

DISCUSSION QUESTIONS

1. A psychology student friend comes up to you and indicates that qualitative research methods are not scientific. How would you respond?
2. The friend also criticizes qualitative methods saying that they are not as valid as quantitative methods. Is he correct or not?
3. The friend indicates that a major problem with qualitative methods is that random sampling rarely takes place. Is the lack of random sampling a weakness of qualitative research methods? Why or why not?
4. Another student in your research class is unclear of the differences between qualitative

and quantitative research methods. What would you tell the student?

5. You notice a critique of qualitative research in a journal. The author indicates that qualitative methods lack not only internal and external validity, but do not seem to have any obvious form of validity whatsoever. Is the author correct? Why or why not?

6. A debate that has raged for some time between quantitative and qualitative researchers is the use of quantitative research evaluation methods with qualitative designs (e.g., trying to determine if the research demonstrated internal or external validity, searching for the reliability and validity of a measurement device). What is the problem with judging qualitative research methods from a quantitative viewpoint?

7. You are part of a research team and are asked to help with the determination of reliability and validity of your methods. What evaluative criteria do Franklin and Jordan (1995) suggest you use? Provide a novel example for each criterion.

8. A friend of yours who is studying qualitative research methods asks you to explain what is meant by triangulation. Explain what triangulation is, and describe the different forms of triangulation.

9. Your friend also asks you to explain the purpose of triangulation. She is not sure how triangulation allows one to be more confident of the findings. Explain to your friend how triangulation helps increase the reliability and validity of the conclusions made based on the collected data.

10. After studying quantitative and qualitative methods, you are interested in conducting an investigation using both qualitative and quantitative research methods. What are some of the difficulties you will have to overcome to integrate the two methods?

CHAPTER 9

QUALITATIVE RESEARCH
DATA COLLECTION AND DESIGNS

OBJECTIVES

After studying this chapter you should be able to:

1. Describe case study research.
2. Describe observation studies.
3. Discriminate between participant and nonparticipant observation methods.
4. Describe problems of, and solutions to, observer effects and observer bias.
5. Describe what field notes are and discriminate between good and poor field notes.
6. Describe naturalistic observation studies and simulations.
7. Describe interview studies.
8. Describe the continuum of interview types.
9. Describe the types of interview questions.
10. Describe ethnographic research.
11. Describe what is meant by document analysis, and explain why document analyses are conducted.
12. Explain how qualitative data are analyzed including internal and external validity concerns.
13. Describe when it would be appropriate to use the different designs in research.
14. Critique a research article containing a qualitative design.

OVERVIEW

As discussed in the previous chapter, qualitative research is a methodology that has different purposes than does quantitative research. In addition, validity and reliability issues are interpreted differently than in quantitative research by many qualitative researchers. Finally, the actual methods used are different from those used by quantitative researchers. Quantitative researchers have specific designs that are rigid and defined before the collection of data. Qualitative research designs evolve as a result of the collection of data throughout the investigation. The methods (i.e., designs) are not as easily defined as those methods used in quantitative research. Qualitative research methods are tied to the method of data collection. For example, interview or observation studies are defined by the methods used in collecting a type of data. Quantitative research designs are independent of the data collection methods (e.g., quantitative research studies are not defined as, for example, a standardized test study).

Since qualitative research and data collection methods are so closely related, this chapter describes data collection methods in conjunction with research methods. The methods discussed in this chapter are representative of the most frequently used qualitative research methods. However, a comprehensive discussion of all qualitative research methods is beyond the scope of this chapter. At the end of the chapter, an example of a qualitative investigation is presented for critique.

WHAT ARE FIELD-ORIENTED STUDIES?

Case Study

Essentially, all of the designs in this chapter can be considered case study designs in that each involves an intense study of the phenomenon of interest (Wolcott, 1992). Case study research is useful for an in-depth study of problems to understand processes or situations in context (Gilgun, 1994). A great deal of information can be learned in this way. Case study research does not always involve one participant. It identifies one participant, one setting, one situation, or one event. The term case study, then, comes from the in-depth analysis of a single case such as one school or one school district. For example, say one were to study a particular elementary school due to its unusual test scores (e.g., the average for the school is in the upper 95% of the nation), we could visit the school and assess how the students were taught. We could use any number of data collection methods such as document analysis of the average parental income and educational levels in the area; interview techniques aimed at teachers, parents, children, and administrators; and/or observational techniques such as participant observations of classrooms where we become involved in the instruction or nonparticipant observation where we observe from afar.

What makes case studies different from other methods is the focus on a single case and an in-depth analysis of that case. Once we have collected and analyzed our data from the elementary school, interpretations of the data will begin. One possible interpretation may be that the students have more hands-on learning opportunities or students are taught in skill-intensive classrooms. The parents may come from a higher socioeconomic status than the average family or there is more parental involvement in their children's schooling. The administration may give more autonomy to the teachers with regard to curriculum decisions, or specific curricula are required. The information gained from case study research can help develop hypotheses and theories for later studies. Finally, a case narrative is written to present a holistic portrayal of the case.

The critical research consumer must have at least two general concerns when judging the adequacy of a case study. First, the information for each case must be as complete as possible. If the researcher left out critical facts or made claims that are not substantiated by the data gathered in the case study, the validity of those claims must be considered carefully. Second, the critical research consumer should expect that the description of the case be logical and easy to follow. If the readability of the case study is not adequate, it will be more difficult to understand and to interpret the results of the investigation.

Observation Studies

An observation study is a form of a case study. It is helpful to think of observations on a continuum from complete participant to complete observer (Bogdan & Biklen, 1992; Gold, 1969).

Complete Participant. With complete participation, observers become involved with the participants as if the observers were part of the group. The participants usually do not know they are being observed. For example, if one were interested in seeing what it was like to be a high school student today as opposed to 10 years ago, one could enter the school as a student (if one looked young enough). The researcher would spend the year in the school and take classes with all of the other students. Thus, the researcher would get firsthand information on what it was like to be in high school today. There are several examples of complete participation in other occupations. For example, police officials routinely use complete participation in undercover operations (albeit for a different purpose). There are cases in which police officers have enrolled in high schools to determine the level of drug use. Similarly, psychologists have entered into psychiatric wards to determine what it is like in those settings.

The difficulty with complete participation is with the secrecy of the technique. There may be ethical problems observing people when they are not aware they are being observed. Typically, if complete participation is used, some form of debriefing must be used to inform the participants that they were observed. An advantage of complete participation is that the reactivity of the observation is reduced or possibly eliminated. Also, observers are able to get firsthand information about what occurs in the context.

Complete Observer. At the other end of the spectrum is complete observer. The complete observer method is similar to the types of observations used in single-case (not to be confused with case study) research (see Chapters 10 to 12). When one is a complete observer, there is an attempt to remain separated from the subject matter. For example, if one wished to see what it was like to be a high school student today, one could visit a high school and make observations over a period of time. The participants may or may not be aware that they are being observed. Again, if the participants do not know they are being observed, ethical concerns may be raised. An obvious advantage of the complete observer is that the observer is able to remain separate and distinct from the group, which may decrease the participants' reaction (i.e., participants may behave differently than they normally would otherwise) to a new person interacting with them in their environment. A disadvantage is that observers will not be able to pick up on other critical information such as what goes on when they are not present or on other nonobservable information such as the participants' thoughts, feelings, attitudes, or beliefs.

Participant-as-Observer and Observer-as-Participant. Between complete participant and complete observer are participant-as-observer and observer-as-participant approaches. Participant-as-observer involves observers engaging with the participants, but also informing the participants of their intent to observe them. Observer-as-participant involves the observers remaining separate from the participants, but the participants are informed that they will be observed. These methods of observation overcome the ethical problem of complete observation. However, observers also risk reactivity on the part of the participants as a result of being aware that they are being observed.

The two methods (i.e., participant-as-observer and observer-as-participant) are similar in that both involve informing the participants of the researcher's purpose; however, they differ in that observers do not become involved with the participants in the observer-as-participant method. For example, a researcher studying what it is like to be a high school student today using the observer-as-participant method will inform the participants of his or her purpose but will remove himself or herself from the participants' activities and watch them. The researcher may interview and interact with the participants, but does not attempt to become part of the group. The disadvantages involve a lack of information that could have been gained by becoming a member of the participant group and the reactivity associated with informing the participants they were to be observed. If the researcher wanted to overcome this problem, he or she could use the participant-as-observer in which the observer interacts with the students.

Determining the Observation Method to Use. The type of observation method used in qualitative research methods will depend on the purpose of the investigation. If, for example, the purpose is to find out how students process information when doing math problems, complete observations most likely will not be appropriate. If the purpose of an investigation is to determine how students interact with one another while in the classroom, becoming a participant may not be beneficial. The critical research consumer must determine what the purpose of the investigation was and assess if the observation method used was appropriate (i.e., was able to generate the data necessary to answer the research question).

Determining the Method Used to Analyze Observational Data. Researchers must also determine the method used to analyze observational data. According to Patton (1990), researchers should determine how best to present the findings to an audience. Researchers must determine how to get the information across so that the audience will understand what occurred during the investigation. Providing this information is especially useful when attempting to critique or replicate what was done during the investigation. Patton lists six options available to qualitative researchers conducting analyses on observational data. The first option is to report the chronology of what was observed over time. Essentially, the observer tells a story from beginning to end. The second option is to report key events. The reporting of key events need not be in order of occurrence but in order of importance. Reporting various settings is the third option. Here the researcher describes the various settings involved in the research and then analyzes any patterns in the data across settings. The fourth option involves reporting case studies of people involved in the investigation. Here the unit of analysis is each individual involved in the study. A fifth option is the description of processes such as methods of communication observed throughout the investigation. The reporting of key issues such as reporting how the participants were affected by something occurring in the setting is the sixth option. Once the researcher has decided on the best method of presenting the data, he or she can then collect the data, paying especially close attention to those variables on which he or she will report. The important point here is that if a researcher decides on how he or she will present the data, the analysis of the subsequent data is somewhat simplified.

Observer Effects. A potential problem with conducting observations in field settings is affecting the behavior of the participant or participants; this is especially true with complete participation. According to Bogdan and Biklen (1992), observer effects can be minimized when working with a larger group of participants in which the observer can blend into the crowd. When working with a small number of participants or one participant, observer effects become more likely. A method researchers could use to decrease observer effects is to allow for the participants to become used to the observer's presence. For example, the observer could be in the setting with the participants for a period of time without actually gathering data, allowing any effects brought on by the observer to subside. Observer effects must always be a concern since the researcher's conclusions could be seriously compromised by these effects. Critical research consumers should attempt to find out if and how researchers attempted to reduce observer effects throughout the investigation.

Another strategy a researcher could use would be to integrate the observer effects into the investigation. For example, if observer effects were seen or suspected, the observer could document how the participant's behavior was changed by his or her presence. Data could come from the observations themselves (i.e., the participant nervously looks at the observer when the participant is teaching) or interviews with the participant. Another method of checking on observer effects would be through the use of multiple sources of information. Data sources from other individuals familiar with the participant's behavior or documents relating to similar information could be used (triangulation). Thus, observer effects could be a rich source of data.

Observer Bias. Observer bias is a concern whenever direct observations are conducted. Observer bias refers to recording what was seen inaccurately because of a preexisting attitude or experience. For example, if one were studying how a child interacts with other children, the observer may code interactions differently, depending on how well the child is liked. Subjectivity is typically seen as a strength of qualitative research since it is a basis for an observer's distinctive contribution; the data are joined with personal interpretations in collecting and analyzing the data (Peshkin, 1988). However, subjectivity in observations can also be seen as a weakness in that the observer's recordings may not be a true reflection of what really occurred.

Qualitative observations are usually more subjective than quantitative forms of data collection; therefore, researchers should be aware of the possibility of observer bias. According to Bogdan and Biklen (1992), one way to handle observer bias is for the observer to document what he or she was feeling during the observations. Such data can be important when interpreting the data. Another method of preventing bias or determining if it occurs is to obtain information from a variety of sources such as through interviews and documents.

The critical research consumer must also be aware of the possibility of bias. Researchers should provide information on the resulting bias that occurred during the observations or document the methods used to prevent bias.

Participant Observation Study

One purpose of observing without becoming involved with the participants is not to have an effect on the participants. Yet, only those things that are directly observable are recorded when observers distance themselves from the participants. However, qualitative researchers "make the assumption that behavior is purposeful and expressive of deeper beliefs and values" (Potter, 1996, p. 99). Therefore, the one method that allows for the consideration of these deeper beliefs and values is to become personally acquainted with the participants. Researchers interact with the participants in an attempt to see if they say what they believe and believe what they say. In other words, there is a concern with the correspondence between what an individual says about a topic and how he or she actually views the topic. For example, think of someone you know really well. You may be able to pick up on some behaviors that tell you that the person is feeling troubled about something. You go up to the person and ask if anything is wrong and the person says that everything is great. If you stopped there, you would conclude that there was nothing wrong. However, since you know the individual well, you can pick up on other signs that tell you the person is not telling you how he or she really feels. Qualitative researchers attempt to do the same thing. They try to get to know the participants well enough to pick up on these other signs. An added advantage is that once the participants get to know the researchers on an individual basis, they may begin to open up more than they would have during a nonparticipant observation.

Field Notes. Participant observations are usually recorded as *field notes*. Potter (1996) indicates that these notes usually are on two levels. The first level (surface) contains the facts or direct descriptions of what was seen and or overheard (this can also be in the form of audio recordings). The second level involves observers writing down their thoughts about the events and interviews. The purpose for this second level is to provide a context for the facts observed on the surface level and to add what the researcher thinks the facts mean. As stated by Patton (1987), the purpose of participant observation is not only to see what is going on, but to feel what it is like to be part of the group.

Field notes are a critical part of qualitative research. Field notes aid researchers in collecting and remembering information from observational sessions. According to Potter (1996), notes can come in many forms such as audiotapes, videotapes, and photographs. However, when the notes are written out by the observer, they must be complete. One would need to include information such as who was present, what the students were doing, what the teachers were doing, what materials were present, how long each activity lasted, the interruptions that occurred, the arrangement of the classroom, and the reactions of the students to the teachers and the teachers to the students. In other words, field notes must include not only what was going on in a setting, but must also include details about the physical setting and the reactions of the individuals present to the event that did occur. The recordings are very difficult to do well since the ability to attend to several details at one time is required. Additionally, the mass of the written material can become overwhelming.

The amount of written material poses an additional problem. The analysis of the notes is a must in qualitative research. Observers must set up the criteria for categorizing or coding and begin to make sense of the data. Observers must weave together the facts from the data in a narrative story of the events observed. The difficulty of the task is represented by Potter (1996):

> *When dealing with the facet of people, the qualitative researcher must develop a composite picture about how people think about things. Each person's belief may be different because people focus their attention on different things and interpret the same things differently. Also, their beliefs change over time. The researcher must make sense out of all of this seemingly conflicting information. The researcher must try to examine why there are differences in meanings. (p. 123)*

Thus, there must be a good level of detail from the field notes. Patton (1990) provides several examples of detailed field notes. He also shows how these detailed field notes can be written in a manner that loses critical information. The following is an example from Patton that shows a vague note.

> *The new client was uneasy waiting for her intake interview. (p. 240)*

Now, compare this note with the detailed one:

> *At first the new client sat very stiffly on the chair next to the receptionist's desk. She picked up a magazine and let the pages flutter through her fingers very quickly without really looking at any of the pages. She set the magazine down, looked at her watch, pulled her skirt down, and picked up the magazine again. This time she didn't look at the magazine. She set it back down, took out a cigarette, and began smoking. She would watch the receptionist out of the corner of her eye, and then look down at the magazine, and back up at the two or three other people waiting in the room. Her eyes moved from the people to the magazine to the cigarette to the people to the magazine in rapid succession. She avoided eye contact. When her name was finally called she jumped like she was startled. (p. 24)*

The point here is that field notes must be detailed. They must tell a story. They must not leave out important information, but also must not go overboard in the description where unimportant information is included.

Field notes are also a reflection of how the observer sees the events. Therefore, field notes include the observer's interpretations of the events. Potter (1996) indicates that some professionals believe field notes should be written after a period of time so the observers can reflect on what was observed. Other professionals believe field notes should include almost every detail possible and should be written during or as soon after the event as possible. The critical research consumer should consider the level of detail provided by researchers in the investigation and consider if there is enough information to justify conclusions made by the researchers. Researchers should indicate if the notes are descriptions of what occurred or if the notes are interpretations or judgments of what was observed. Researchers should also include their own thoughts, feelings, and experiences throughout the investigation. Researchers should provide other evidence of the events as well in the form of triangulation to help verify the notes taken (e.g., interviews, notes from others, documents). Direct quotes can also be used to help verify some of the notes taken. Finally, the critical research consumer should attempt to ascertain how researchers were able to synthesize the information. The synthesis provides the basis for conclusions drawn and is, therefore, critical in judging the adequacy of those conclusions.

Nonparticipant Observation Study

The difference between participant and nonparticipant studies has to do with the extent to which observers become involved with the participants. It is important to note that the degree to which observers are separated from the participants varies from study to study. In the purest sense, nonparticipant observations would occur in a covert manner. In this way, the observer's presence is unknown to the participants. The advantage of this method of observation is clear—the reactivity associated with observations is all but eliminated. However, there are serious ethical concerns if one were to conduct covert observations. Another difficulty is that the ability to interact with the participants and to find out more about them on a personal level is limited. Only those things that are observed are recorded. Other important information that can only be obtained by interacting with the participant is not considered.

Nonparticipant observations can also be where the participants are aware of the observer's presence, but there is no or limited interaction with the participants. There is a chance of reactivity, but the threat is reduced since there is an effort on the part of observers to not interfere with the participants' activities. With this type of observation, there may be a time period before actual data are collected but the observer is present. The purpose of this time period is to allow the participants to become used to the observer's presence. Once the observer is present for some time period, data collection begins. A check for observer bias may be obtained by having a second observer present to also record the behaviors. An advantage of nonparticipant observations is the lower observer effects present. However, a problem again stems from the type of information desired. If one wanted to learn about what the participants felt, believed, or valued, nonparticipant observations are wanting. Thus, it is important to ascertain what the purpose of the investigation was. If conclusions are made based on the beliefs of the participants, some form of interaction must have taken place between the observer and the participant. Nonparticipant observations will not likely allow for such conclusions to be based on valid information.

Naturalistic Observation Study

Naturalistic observation studies involve observing participants in their natural settings. There is no attempt to manipulate what goes on in the setting and the observations are unobtrusive (Patton, 1990). The observations are typically nonparticipant, although they can be participant. For example, Jean Piaget interacted with the participants in his studies to a certain extent. He set up situations and observed how children responded to those situations. There was no attempt to "teach" the children how to respond to the situations, but he also did not sit back and observe children without manipulating the environment in some fashion. On the other hand, Diane Fossey studied gorillas and made no attempt to interact with them in the beginning. She simply watched from afar. Later, she began to interact with the gorillas and, thus, changed the environment in some manner. In fact, there really is no true unobtrusive observation method unless the participants are totally unaware of the observer's presence. Whenever an observation occurs and the participants are aware of the observer's presence, some manipulation of the environment has taken place. However, the question of what happens when no one is present is somewhat like the question of whether the falling tree makes a sound in the forest when no one is there. Thus, the critical research consumer must determine if the obtrusiveness of the observation may have changed the situations to such an extent that the "normal" behavior patterns of the participants were disrupted. Obviously, in Piaget's and Fossey's studies, this was not the case. If one is going to use naturalistic observation methods, one must use the most unobtrusive methods available (i.e., nonparticipant methods).

Simulations

There are times when researchers wish to obtain information on certain phenomena, but the ability to collect such information is compromised because the event does not occur frequently enough or it would be unethical to allow an event to occur. In such cases, simulations may be used. Simulations involve the creation or re-creation of a situation to see how the participants will react under such circumstances. For example, airline pilots go through simulation training before being allowed to fly; astronauts go through simulations before embarking into space; teachers may teach in front of their peers before going out "in the real world"; and children may be approached by confederates (i.e., research staff not known to the participants) during abduction training. Simulations have been used in the assessment of safety skills. As stated by Gast, Wellons, and Collins (1994), "the initial teaching of safety skills may need to occur in a simulated, rather than a natural, environment" (p. 16). Therefore, researchers unable to observe the participants in the natural environment may be forced to set up simulations. These simulations can involve either individuals or groups of individuals. The critical concern is that the simulation be as close to the natural environment as possible. In order to generalize to the natural environment, the simulations must have most, if not all, of the same properties. The extent to which the simulation approached situations encountered in the natural environment must be determined.

Interview Studies

According to Patton (1990), "the purpose of interviewing is to find out what is in and on someone else's mind" (p. 278). Interviewing is an alternative to and a compatible method of gathering information with observations. The advantage of interviewing over observing is that not everything can be observed, either because it would be impractical (e.g., following each participant through his or her life) or impossible to do so (e.g., finding out what someone is thinking). However, interviewing is a difficult thing to do well. Interviewers must have the skill of bringing out information from the interviewee in such a way that the interviewer is allowed to understand the interviewee's world. As stated by Patton, "*The quality of the information obtained during an interview is largely dependent on the interviewer*" (p. 279).

Patton (1990) describes three types of interviewing—the informal conversational interview, the general interview guide approach, and the standardized open-ended interview. Notice that the closed, fixed-response interview is not included. According to Bogdan and Bilken (1992), qualitative interviewers should avoid closed-ended items such as "yes" or "no" questions. The problem with closed or fixed-response interviews is that details and particulars will be lost when the interviewees are not allowed to expand on their responses. Therefore, the purpose of qualitative interviewing is not met (i.e., to get inside of the interviewees' world to understand more fully what those individuals are experiencing). As Patton points out:

> *The purpose of qualitative interviewing in evaluation is to understand how program staff and participants view the program, to learn* their *terminology and judgments, and to capture the complexities of* their *individual perceptions and experiences. This is what distinguishes qualitative interviewing from the closed interview, questionnaire, or test typically used in quantitative evaluations. Such closed instruments force program participants to fit their knowledge, experiences, and feelings into the evaluator's categories. The fundamental principle of qualitative interviewing is to provide a framework within which respondents can express* their *own understandings in their own terms. (p. 290)*

Informal Conversational Interview. The informal conversational interview usually occurs with the participant observation in the field and is the most open-ended interviewing method. The interview proceeds as a conversation in which interviewers ask spontaneous questions. There is no structured format, although interviewers should have some notion of the type of information they desire. In some instances, those being interviewed may be unaware of the interview. In these cases, interviewers will not take notes during the interview, but will take notes after they have left the situation. At other times, participants may be aware of the interview; during these situations, interviewers will usually take notes during the interview and may use a tape recorder. The disadvantage of allowing participants to know that an interview is occurring is the reactivity of the knowledge. On the other hand, there may be ethical concerns with not informing participants that seemingly casual conversation is really an interview.

As the name implies, the interview format is like that of a normal conversation. Thus, interviewers must be quick on their feet since questions must be generated spontaneously throughout the interview. A difficulty with this type of interview is that it may take several sessions to get the information desired. This difficulty is due to the inefficient nature of the interview. The indirect approach of the interview makes it much more difficult to steer the interview in the direction required to gain the needed information. On the other hand, the spontaneity of the interview allows researchers to go in any number of directions. Researchers can probe new areas that were not thought of before the interview began. New and interesting information can be generated with the informal conversational interview.

The data analysis involved with the informal conversational interview is very difficult. Since there are no general guidelines for researchers to follow, categories must be developed. The knowledge of the subject area must be in depth and researchers must know what they are looking for since some information must be dropped during the analysis. If important information is left out of the analysis, the validity of the conclusions must be in question.

General Interview Guide Approach. The general interview guide approach essentially involves having an outline of topics to be covered during the interview; however, the order in which the topics is addressed is not set. The questions are not formulated beforehand. The purpose of outlines or guides is to aid interviewers in addressing each of the topics. The main purpose of the guides is to ensure that the same topics are covered for each of the participants. The main difference with the informal conversational interview is that the topics are determined beforehand. Thus, the general interview guide approach is more structured than the informal conversational interview.

This difference is also an advantage in that interviewers can be sure to cover the needed topics for each participant. The questions are still generated spontaneously but within specific topics. Another difference is that whereas the informal conversational interview is more suited to individualized interviews due to the changes in coverage from session to session, the general interview guide is well suited for groups where the same or similar information must be collected. A disadvantage with the general interview guide is that the interviews are not as free flowing as the informal conversational interview. Interviewers in the informal conversational interview can cover a much wider topical area than can interviewers in the general interview guide.

The analysis of the data is slightly easier than with the general interview guide since topics were preselected. However, the information gained within each topic must be coded in some manner. Researchers must integrate the information in some manner to make conclusions about the data. Researchers may use examples of statements from the participants, create categories of statements made within each topic, tally the number of and type of statements made, or develop assertions that summarize the statements in some way. It must be pointed out that however researchers decide to analyze the data, some information will be lost or omitted.

Standardized Open-Ended Interview. The standardized open-ended interview is perhaps the most familiar. This method involves set topics similar to the general interview guide but also has predeveloped questions that researchers ask throughout the interview. Each participant is exposed to the same topics and questions in the same order. The purpose for this method is to help researchers become more efficient in obtaining needed information and to help reduce any interviewer effects. In other words, two interviewers would ask the same questions in the same order with the standardized open-ended interview, but would likely ask different questions with the general interview guide. The questions are worded in an open-ended format with interviewers avoiding "yes" or "no" questions and fixed responses. The participants are free to provide any answer to the questions and expand on their responses.

There are a number of strengths to the standardized open-ended interview. First, since the questions are set prior to the interview and are provided in the same order, the interview instrument can be inspected by others. Second, the variability in the manner in which interviewers ask questions can be minimized; thus, the interviews are standardized. Third, unlike the informal conversational interview, the interview is focused so that a great deal of information is gained within a limited amount of time. Finally, the scoring of the standardized open-ended interview is simplified since researchers already have the categories for scoring determined in advance.

The weaknesses involve the limiting of information that is obtained in two ways. First, since the interview is standardized, the questions are not tailored to each participant and situation. Information is lost because interviewers cannot probe for reasons of particular responses or perspectives. Second, the naturalness of asking the questions is lost. In the informal conversational interview, the interview is more free flowing; with the standardized open-ended interview, the interview is more formal and less spontaneous. This structure may weaken or lessen the explanations provided by participants. Also, since the questions are less natural and are not individualized for each participant, some of the questions may lose their relevance. This irrelevance frequently happens when interview questions are developed beforehand, but the researchers realize during the interview that the questions are not evoking the anticipated types of responses from the participants. Researchers will then say something like, "I wish I would have asked her...."

As with the method of observation used, the type of interview format depends on the type of research question and the type of information sought. The critical research consumer should make a determination of the research question and assess whether or not researchers use an appropriate interview technique.

Types of Interview Questions. Patton (1990) indicates that a number of decisions must be made by researchers when developing an interview. First, researchers must determine the type of interview to use. Second, researchers must decide on the location of the interview. Many interviews are conducted in the field during participant observations. Third, researchers must decide on the length of the interview. Finally, researchers must decide at minimum what type of information needs to be collected and at the most what type of questions to ask.

Patton (1990) discusses six kinds of questions that are asked of participants. These question types can be asked in any of the interview methods and about any topic. They can also be stated in past (e.g. "What did you...?"), present (e.g., "What are you...?"), or future tense (e.g., "What will you...?") and are considered by Patton as *time-frame questions.* The question types include (a) experience/behavior, (b) opinion/values, (c) feeling, (d) knowledge, (e) sensory, (f) and background/demographic.

Experience/Behavior Questions. Experience/behavior questions refer to what one has done in the past or what one is presently doing. The purpose for experience/behavior questions is to gather information one would have had access to if one had been able to observe the individual. The purpose for these questions is not to obtain information about phenomena that are impossible to observe (e.g., feelings, thoughts), but to obtain information that is not presently available (i.e., what has already passed). An example of an experience/behavior question would be, "If I had been in the teacher's lounge with you, what would I have seen you do?"

Opinion/Values Questions. Opinion/values questions seek to find out information about phenomena that are impossible to observe. One cannot directly observe the opinions or values of others; however, one can ask about a person's opinions or values. Thus, although the information may be available, it is not possible to document it directly. An example of an opinion/values question would be, "Tell me what you think is the best method of teaching reading and why?"

Feeling Questions. Feeling questions are aimed at finding out the emotional state of others or how they respond emotionally to experiences and thoughts. As with opinion/values questions, the information may be available, but it is not accessible directly. A feeling question may be as follows, "To what extent do the increasing illiteracy rates among our school-age population make you feel anxious about the future of our country?" Notice the question was not stated as, "What do you think of the increasing illiteracy rates among our school-age population?" or "What do you think is the cause of the growing numbers of school-age children who are illiterate?" Patton (1990) makes it clear that feeling questions must not be confused with opinion/ values questions. The purpose of feeling questions is to find out how people feel about something, not what they think about something.

Knowledge Questions. Knowledge questions are ones that are aimed at gathering factual information. They attempt to find out what people know, not what they think or feel about something. The information may be available from other sources such as asking individuals to perform a task that demonstrates knowledge, but it is more efficient to ask the participants what they know about something. These questions should not be confused with feeling or opinion/values questions. An example of a knowledge question is, "How many students do you have in your school who are below grade level in reading?" These questions are aimed at finding out what individuals understand to be correct.

Sensory Questions. Sensory questions involve the experiences participants have with their senses. These questions are aimed at finding out what the participants have seen, smelled, felt (tactile, not emotionally), tasted, or heard. The information here is available but not accessible directly by observers. The purpose of these questions is to find out the type of experiences/behaviors in which the participants' senses were exposed. An example of a sensory question is, "When you entered into the school building, what did you hear?"

Background/Demographic Questions. Background /demographic questions are aimed at obtaining personal information about the participants. Information such as the participants' age, educational level, occupation, and living situations are important to determine how each participant fits within the sample of participants. This information is critical for determining logical generalization (see Chapter 8). A background/demographic question may be, "Where do you live?" This information is available from other sources, but the purpose of these questions is to gather the information in an efficient manner.

Ethnography

Everything discussed up to this point can be combined to form a special type of qualitative research method. Ethnography essentially combines observational methods and in-depth interview methods to investigate a phenomenon from a cultural perspective (Patton, 1990). It must be pointed out that in this chapter, ethnography refers to a particular method of gathering data. Ethnography can also refer to a philosophical paradigm to which one is committed (Atkinson & Hammersley, 1994). What distinguishes ethnography from the other methods described (e.g., observation and interview studies) is the combination of several data gathering methods as well as the intensity and degree to which the data are gathered. The focus is more holistic in ethnography than in either observation or interview studies, and the involvement in the field is long-term (Potter, 1996). As stated by Fetterman (1989):

> *Ethnography is the art and science of describing a group or culture. The description may be of a small tribal group in some exotic land or a classroom in middle-class suburbia. The task is much like the one taken on by an investigative reporter, who interviews relevant people, reviews records, weighs the credibility of one person's opinions against another's, looks for ties to special interests and organizations, and writes the story for a concerned public as well as for professional colleagues. A key difference between the investigative reporter and the ethnographer, however, is that where the journalist seeks out the unusual—the murder, the plane crash, the bank robbery—the ethnographer writes*

about the routine, daily lives of people. The more predictable patterns of human thought and behavior are the focus of inquiry. (p. 11)

As with much of the qualitative research previously described, ethnographic researchers enter into the field or research situation without any preconceived notion of what they will find. There are usually no specific or precise hypotheses as there are when conducting quantitative research. The conclusions drawn from the research develop over time as the researcher becomes a part of the culture. In ethnographic research, the culture can be defined somewhat more liberally in that a classroom may be considered a culture, as can a workplace. Thus, when one studies a culture, one studies all of the variables that may be affecting the participant(s) while in a certain context.

For example, suppose that a researcher was interested in studying the question, "What is the school environment like in an urban high school located in a low socioeconomic area?" The researcher would make arrangements to visit the school to get a "feel" for the place. She would begin to talk to the students and staff. She would possibly take over some teaching duties to understand the school from a teacher's perspective. She would interact with other teachers and administrators and take field notes. She would conduct formal and informal interviews with the questions becoming more specific the longer she stays in the school. The researcher begins to notice that there are "cliques" that develop among the students and staff. The groups seem to be organized along racial lines. Black students seem to sit alongside black students more and white students tend to associate more with other white students. The researcher documents these and other observations. The researcher observes how the staff interacts with the students. She notices that male students are asked different types of questions than are female students. The researcher observes the students and faculty in as many situations as possible. She interviews students and staff on an ongoing basis. The researcher audiotapes many of the interviews, especially from those individuals who provide her with the richest information. The researcher also videotapes the interactions in classrooms that tend to represent the school climate as a whole. The researcher continues the study for an entire school year. It would not be enough to conduct the investigation for a day, a week, or a month. The data that are desirable cannot be obtained in a short time period.

Once the researcher has collected all of her field notes, interviews, audiotapes, and videotapes, she is ready to interpret her data. According to Fetterman (1989), analysis of ethnographic data may involve several components including thinking (i.e., attempting to find where each piece of data fits into the big picture), triangulation (i.e., obtaining and comparing multiple sources of data), patterns (i.e., finding when thoughts and behaviors begin to be repeated), key events (i.e., determining a representative event to act as a focal point in understanding the culture), maps (i.e., developing visual representations of the culture), flow charts (i.e., determining how activities and information flow through the system), organizational charts (i.e., laying out the hierarchy of the organization from top to bottom), matrices (i.e., establishing a picture of behavior or thought categories), content analysis (i.e., analyzing written and electronic data), statistics (i.e., using nonparametric statistics such as nominal and ordinal scales), and crystalization (i.e., everything finally falls into place).

For example, our researcher determines that there are certain kinds of interactions that occur in the high school. She attempts to find out how these interactions affect the overall operation of the school (thinking). She finds that most of the negative interactions between students occurs outside the school (patterns). She remembers that one event that typified the school climate was an assembly later in the year when the students were widely excited about the success of the football team (key event). She was able to show a flow chart of how information about other students (rumors) moved through the school. She was also able to determine a hierarchy among staff and students in the school. She found that the athletes were put on a higher social level by both students and staff.

The researcher also found that much of the publicity about the school was about the sports teams (content analysis). She obtained information from several sources such as faculty, students, parents, and newspapers (triangulation). She used nominal scale data to show the school breakdown of ethnic groups. After all of the data analysis, the information was finally crystalized. The researcher determined that the school culture centered around sports. She found that the students were likely to segregate themselves during nonsports-related situations, but when sports were involved, the students were joined together. She also found that the sports "stars" were more respected and admired by teachers and students regardless of ethnicity. However, if a student was not involved in sports, both student and teacher responses to them were different based on ethnicity (such as seating arrangements during lunch) and during instruction (such as the types of questions asked of males and females).

The final step for the researcher is to provide a written account of what she found. The written account should essentially tell a story. The reader should be able to visualize what the school was like. The description should be alive and rich with information. Metaphorical language should reveal degrees of understanding about the school, and the reader should obtain a holistic view of the situation.

Features. As with other qualitative research, ethnography is an inductive versus deductive approach to inquiry. Additionally, the data are open to many interpretations depending on the person making the interpretations (Potter, 1996). As such, the adequacy of the conclusions can be suspect in cases when researchers do not communicate their personal biases to the readers. These personal biases are not necessarily seen as a disadvantage of ethnography but as an advantage, assuming they are revealed and analyzed by the researchers. If the researchers have communicated their personal perspectives, the reader is allowed to take these biases into consideration.

According to qualitative researchers, we all interpret our world from our own unique perspective, even quantitative researchers. The difference is that qualitative researchers are aware of their biases and integrate these into the investigation. Potter (1996) also suggests that data "are not collected in a closed set of analytical categories" (p. 51). In other words, the investigation is holistic (i.e., the investigation is not constrained by predetermined categories). Additionally, the investigation is based on a small number of cases. In the example provided earlier, the high school was looked at as a single case. There was not an investigation of each individual student or staff member. The school was looked at as a single entity. The advantage of the intensive study of a small number of cases is that an in-depth analysis can be made. Potter also indicates that the analysis of the data "is an explicit interpretation of meanings of language and human actions" (p. 51). Thus, researchers describe interpretations in a manner that is direct and clear to the reader.

However, as with all research methods, the strengths can also lead to weaknesses. For example, since a small number of cases is involved, the ability to generalize findings to other cases is limited or nonexistent. From a qualitative perspective, this point may not be a weakness since the investigation informed us about the particular case and there was no interest in generalizing. However, from another perspective, community members may ask, "What do these results mean to me?" A second problem is the subjectivity of the process. There is no way to identify if there was any reliability of the data collection methods. In fact, qualitative researchers understand this not to be a particular problem since attempting to take away subjectivity may constrain the collection of data. However, if there is a lack of reliability, there is also a lack of validity. Thus, it is critical for researchers to demonstrate triangulation. The critical research consumer should determine if triangulation was present and whether the researchers communicated the biases they held throughout the investigation.

Document Analysis

Although document analysis may not be a research design per se, it is a method of obtaining information and making conclusions about a phenomenon. Document analysis involves obtaining data from any number of written or visual sources such as diaries, novels, incident reports, pictures, advertisements, speeches, official documents, files, films, audiotapes, books, newspapers, and so on. According to Potter (1996), document analysis is especially important to historians (see Chapter 13) investigating trends in the past when there may not be anyone alive to provide information or the information that exists is too limiting. Document analysis is also used in situations where researchers want to obtain information unobtrusively or when the information cannot be obtained in a more efficient or valid manner such as an observation.

For example, it may be interesting to investigate the attitude in the United States during the 1960s. If one wished to do this, one could look at magazines, newspapers, art, and speeches by politicians to get a handle on the country's attitudes. In several studies conducted by one of the authors of this text, the level of disruption in schools was investigated. A primary data source were records kept by school staff on the number of students sent to the office for discipline problems. Incident reports in the school could also show the level of disruptions (i.e., the severity of the disruptive behaviors) as well as the teacher's response to the disruptions. Another example is the use of student files for programming reasons. Students with disabilities will have files documenting difficulties in the classroom in terms of behavior and academic problems. One could review these documents to obtain critical information on the students to help with educational program developments.

The difficulty with document analysis is that researchers should have some idea of what they are looking for, even if in general terms. The point here is that the critical research consumer must glean from the research report information as to what researchers were looking for, the categories used in the analysis, what was included and what was ignored, and the results found. A major advantage of document analysis is that it allows for extensions or continuations of the research by other researchers.

Analysis of Data

Qualitative researchers have their own data analysis procedures. In many regards, the data analysis involved with qualitative research methods is much more difficult to complete than in quantitative research. Think of it this way. Suppose we wanted to identify how study guides for a social studies class affected the students in a classroom. We could use either quantitative or qualitative approaches (a combination of the two would likely be beneficial). If we selected quantitative, we may proceed as follows: develop the study guides, define the student behaviors we wish to measure such as academic performance (i.e., test scores), distribute study guides for each unit, give a unit test, determine each student's score, and get an average test score for the class. (*Note:* We are using a repeated measures design.) We also have a second social studies class but do not provide study guides. At the end of the study, we see if the class receiving study guides outperformed the class that did not receive the study guides.

If we selected a qualitative design, we would most likely study one classroom. We attempt to gather data from several sources (i.e., triangulation of data) to aid in the validation of the data collection. The data gathered are in the form of narration through journal entries. The teacher, researcher, and students are each independently writing reactions, beliefs, attitudes, expectations, interpretations, and evaluations of the study guides. Throughout the study, we continuously review the data and decide on some method of synthesizing the data. Also throughout the study, we are analyzing how the data are collected and the type of information produced. At the end of the investigation, there are mounds of journal entries. We have a coding system and begin to code the data. We look for "significant classes of things, persons and events and the properties which characterize them" (Schatzman & Strauss, 1973, p. 110).

For instance, we may find that the teachers frequently report that they are anxious when instructing since they want to cover all of the material contained in the study guide. We may find that many of the students report that they do not like the study guides because they take too long to complete. We also may find that many of the teachers do not think the study guides are helping the students gain information outside of what is listed on the study guide. Here, we have themes emerging such as the length of the study guides, the type of information contained on the study guides, and the restrictiveness of the study guides. Once these themes or categories emerge, some tentative conclusions and questions can be generated such as the study guides were too long and should be shortened. However, if we shorten them, how do we include more relevant information? Teachers should not feel constrained by the study guides when preparing their instruction; but should the information contained in the instruction be represented on the study guide? The difficulty is to make sure the coding system contains all of the important information. Once the data have been coded, conclusions are made. We may wish to use numbers to help in the process of interpretation such as the number of students who thought the journal entries were worthwhile; however, the main data source are words.

As can be seen, there can be difficulty with qualitative data analysis. The analysis of qualitative data is not nearly as straightforward as quantitative data and requires a great deal more thought and effort to do well. Strauss and Corbin (1990) indicate that judgments must be made on three areas of qualitative research—the reliability, validity, and credibility of the data; the adequacy of the research process, and the empirical grounding of the research process. The critical research consumer should consider each of the three areas to evaluate a qualitative investigation. This method of evaluation is different than the one used by quantitative researchers in that when looking at threats to internal and external validity, the design is paramount in the evaluation. With qualitative research, the whole process of the study is paramount, not simply the design.

In what follows, we describe how to interpret qualitative research. It is probably not useful to interpret a qualitative study using quantitative evaluation methods (Maxwell, 1992; Silverman, 1993) Qualitative and quantitative methods rest on different assumptions and have different purposes. However, since we have considered threats to internal and external validity in previous chapters, we will do the same in this chapter. We will also add new validity categories for analyzing the data in qualitative research.

Internal Validity. Qualitative research serves many purposes. Qualitative research is not specifically designed to answer cause-and-effect questions. In other words, researchers in qualitative research do not actively attempt to manipulate an independent variable. However, the question of internal validity is, from a qualitative perspective, a desirable one for many researchers (Maxwell, 1992). On the other hand, Mishler (1990) has argued that to extend the concept of validity from quantitative methods to qualitative research is misguided. He indicated that validity is dependent on researchers' judgments rather than dependent on following certain procedures. Thus, the concept of internal validity is different from a qualitative viewpoint.

Internal validity is a quantitative concept that relies on a set of certain assumptions about how to find cause-and-effect associations. The use of specific designs and other set procedures such as measurement, manipulation of the independent variable, and participant assignments are critical in demonstrating internal validity for quantitative designs. On the other hand, qualitative designs rely on the understanding of the context under which the participants perform and on the theory that explains why something occurs. The manner in which qualitative researchers demonstrate internal validity is one of logic and subjective reasoning rather than of assessing the research methods objectively. The problem with viewing qualitative research from a quantitative viewpoint in terms of internal validity is that qualitative research almost never meets the criteria for being internally valid.

External Validity. External validity is viewed similarly by qualitative and quantitative researchers

(Bogdan & Biklen, 1992). Qualitative and quantitative researchers view external validity as an attempt to generalize results of an investigation to other individuals, in other settings, and across time. However, the role of external validity is different for different forms of research. Quantitative studies many times will use sampling methods (i.e., random selection) to allow for external validity claims to be made.

Qualitative research is not usually designed to allow for systematic generalizations to other individuals. Qualitative researchers may use logical generalizations; they may also utilize extensions or continuations to help demonstrate generalizability of their results. Another method qualitative researchers may use to establish external validity is to develop a theory from the data that can be used in other situations or with different people. However, there are no statistical methods that can be used to achieve external validity in a qualitative investigation. Additionally, claims of external validity in qualitative research may be made by critical research consumers rather than researchers (Eisner, 1991). Qualitative researchers are usually more cautious in their claims and rely on the research consumers to decide whether the results would benefit them, their students, or their setting. As with internal validity, the demonstration is more one of logical interpretations of the data than statistical manipulations of the data or special quantitative research designs aimed at these two validity types.

Analyzing Qualitative Research. Potter (1996) provides a template for analyzing these issues. Table 9.1 shows that there are four categories for analysis. The first category is *expectations.* Potter indicated that there are three ways in which expectations guide research—deductive, inductive, and a mixed approach. With deduction, researchers enter into the investigation with a priori expectations. In other words, they have determined before the investigation begins what is expected to be found and design the collection and analysis of data around the expectations. Induction refers to beginning the investigation with some observations, attempting to rule out nothing from analysis. After the investigation is finished, researchers attempt to interpret the data. In other words, there are no expectations guiding the investigation. With the mixed approach, researchers formulate the topic such as a research question. Most, if not all, researchers have some initial formulation before an investigation. Potter (1996) indicates that it is probably impossible for researchers to have little or no formulation as in an inductive process. Once the investigation begins, researchers make conclusions and then test these conclusions on an ongoing basis.

The second category involves the *process* of analysis. The six criteria developed by Franklin and Jordan (1995) (see Chapter 8) fit within this category. Process analysis refers to the extent to which researchers explain or describe the methods used in the investigation to construct their arguments and/or findings. Maxwell (1992) described this in terms of descriptive validity. The accuracy of the data collection and analysis is critical in the process.

The third category involves the *conceptual leverage* used in the analysis of the data. Potter (1996) describes three levels of conceptual leverage. First, *concrete description* refers to a lack of inference made on the data. The data are described as observed. There is no attempt to infer to motives, beliefs, interests, or theories. The second level involves *low-level interference* in that inferences are made in regard to those things not directly observed. This level is similar to Maxwell's (1992) interpretive validity where the concern is with mental rather than physical understanding. The final level involves *high-level inference* in which a connection is made between the data and some theory or construction. There may be an attempt to determine cause-and-effect relationships through high-level inference. However, Potter (1996) indicates that few qualitative researchers view this type of inference as desirable.

Many qualitative researchers reject the concept of causality altogether based on philosophical grounds. Thus, most qualitative researchers use low-level inference. This type of inference is similar to Maxwell's (1992) theoretical validity where there is an attempt to explain why something occurred rather than simply to describe what occurred. High-level inference is also similar to Maxwell's evaluative validity where there is

TABLE 9.1 Template for Analysis Issues

Issue 1: Expectations
Key Question: To what extent do expectations for findings guide the selection of evidence? **Alternative Answers:** 1. A Priori Expectations: The researchers have set out a very clear goal for what data they need. With social science, theory and hypotheses are a clear guide. Also, ideologies serve as a priori guides. 2. Emerging Expectations: No beginning expectations, but as researchers gather data, they become more focused on searching for certain data and ignoring other data.
Issue 2: Process of Analysis
Key Question: To what extent does the researcher illuminate the process of using the evidence to construct arguments/findings for the written report? **Alternative Answers:** 1. Authors describe the steps taken in analyzing the data, that is, the step between data gathering and presenting the report. 2. Authors do *not* describe the steps used in analyzing their data.
Issue 3: Conceptual Leverage
Key Question: To what extent does the researcher extend his or her arguments/findings beyond reporting on the elements of evidence into a general conceptual level? **Alternative Answers:** 1. None: No attempt to move beyond describing literal events in the data. The reporting is limited to description of the actual data themselves. 2. Low Level: The researcher constructs patterns (through his or her own processes of inference) to make sense of the literal data. 3. High Level: Inferring a connection to an a priori construction such as a theory or ideology.
Issue 4: Generalizability
Key Question: To what extent does the researcher attempt to use his or her evidence to generalize? **Alternative Answers:** 1. No Generalizations: Researchers only present data or patterns about their observed subjects during the times and places they were observed. 2. Generalization: Researchers exhibit a large move from data to conclusion. The largeness in the degree can be due to the very small size of the sample or the very broad nature of the conclusions.

an attempt to make evaluative statements from an ideological framework.

The final category involves generalizability. Potter (1996) indicates that generalizability refers to the attempt made by researchers to extend the results of investigations to other individuals or situations. Potter suggests that many qualitative researchers do not believe that generalization is a possibility for a number of reasons (e.g., true objectivity is not possible and each situation is unique to itself; random sampling is not possible). Other researchers indicate that generalization is possible in the form of grounded theory and through induction. Potter states that most researchers take the middle ground in that there are a number of definitions of generalization. Potter's generalizability is similar to the generalizability described by Maxwell (1992).

The critical point in judging qualitative research is determining the conclusions/claims made by researchers and investigating if the data support the conclusions/claims. The subject of cause-and-effect relationships and generalizability will likely always be controversial in qualitative research. As stated by Potter (1996):

> *Like with the issue of conceptual leverage, the key to appreciating generalizability is in looking for correspondence between evidence and conclusions. Whether generalization should be permissible or not within the qualitative approach is a debate that will not likely be resolved given the strongly held beliefs of the scholars on each side. So it is best to accept the range of beliefs. However, once a scholar establishes his or her position, we as readers can check to make sure that their beliefs as reflected in their design support the level of generalization in their research. (p. 133)*

Research Examples

Case Study. Tse (1996) conducted a case study to determine the effects of a reading program on an adult English-language learner. The participant was a 36-year-old Indonesian woman enrolled in an intensive English-language program at an American university. The course was 15 weeks in length and was considered the foundation course for the program. The course ran 1.5 hours per day, 5 days per week. Students were encouraged to read material quickly and to guess the meanings of unknown words rather than to interrupt their reading by looking up words in the dictionary. If they were unable to guess the word, they were encouraged to skip it and continue reading. The students in the class read four books, two selected by the instructor and two selected by the students. The students read during part of the class, but the majority of class time was spent discussing the reading. Students were also asked to read 15 to 25 pages per night and were asked questions about language they encountered or about content. The researcher took participant observations and conducted interviews throughout the investigation. Data were collected across three categories: opinion and value, feeling, and knowledge. The author found that the student believed that her opinion of reading had changed positively, she felt more confident about reading, and she gained more knowledge about the American culture and about herself. The researcher concluded that a reading orientation should take place when developing a second language curriculum.

Observation Study. Martella, Marchand-Martella, Macfarlane, and Young (1993) conducted an investigation to demonstrate how paraprofessional training could improve the classroom behavior of a student with Down syndrome. The investigation essentially had two parts. The first part was a descriptive analysis (i.e., nonparticipant observation study), and the second part was an intervention study. The description here is only on the descriptive investigation.

The student was a 14-year-old male enrolled in a self-contained classroom in a rural high school. He was mainstreamed in physical education and received community-based instruction. The student was on the verge of being referred for residential services due to his high level of aggressive and destructive behaviors. The researchers conducted a nonparticipant investigation to determine the possible causes of the student's unwanted behaviors. Two observers entered the classroom and sat away from the students. The observers sat apart and were in the classroom for a period of three weeks before the observations began. After the three weeks, the students in the classroom did not attend to the observers. Thus, the possibility of observer effects was minimized as much as possible. The two observers also independently took narrative data to compare at a later time and to decrease the possibility of observer bias. The observers wrote down key events that took place in the classroom such as what the task was, who was providing the instruction, the type of instruction, the number of other students present, the location of the other students, and the time of day. Over the course of five weeks, the observers had a substantial amount of data gathered.

The data analysis was conducted as follows. The researchers separated the data into three categories. The first category included all of the events that occurred before the student displayed unwanted behaviors (e.g., the teacher individually working with the student on a reading task in the morning with other students sitting away from the student). The second category included the behaviors that the student was exhibiting (e.g., swearing). The final category included the events that came after the student's behaviors (e.g., reprimands, ignoring the student). Next, the researchers looked for some pattern in the data. What was found was that when a particular individual worked with the student, that individual would provide instruction that most would consider to be less than acceptable. The student would misbehave during this instruction and the instructor would reprimand the student. Finally, the researchers developed hypotheses of possible causes for the student's misbehavior. These hypotheses were later tested in the second study.

Interview Study. Martella and Marchand-Martella (1995) conducted an interview study to investigate the importance of safety skills instruction for persons enrolled in vocational training situations. The researchers interviewed individuals who were key stakeholders for individuals receiving job training. These individuals included a consumer of the job training, a business manager who hires trainees, an insurance agent who was responsible for insuring business that hire trainees, and a vocational counselor who was responsible for training the consumers. The interview was open-ended and standardized. The types of questions were largely opinion/values questions. The purpose of the interview was to find out what stakeholders viewed as being critical skills for individuals in job training situations to learn. The goal of this information was to make conclusions as to the most appropriate types of skills to teach trainees and whether to include a safety skills component in job training programs.

The researchers found that the stakeholders agreed on the types of skills needed by trainees including safety skills training. The responses made by the stakeholders were categorized by question, and similarities and differences in responses were noted. General conclusions were made based on stakeholder responses, and these conclusions were interpreted based on previous research findings in the area of vocational skill development. Finally, recommendations for future vocational training programs were made based on the stakeholders' responses.

Ethnography. Goto (1996) conducted an investigation to help determine why Asian students do poorly in school even though they may come from advantaged homes and from a culture that values education. An enthographic design was used to help answer the research question. The investigation was conducted at an urban high school over two semesters in which interviews with students and observations were conducted. The high school served primarily low- and middle-income students as well as some affluent students. Goto focused on eight middle-class Chinese American and Taiwanese American students to see how they saw themselves as learners and group members.

He attempted to determine specifically the students' concerns about peers. He illustrated the findings with the data gathered from one 16-year-old student. The family/culture theory (i.e., "the family is the primary mechanism for conveying cultural values," p. 75) was discussed, but Goto indicated that the theory was inadequate for explaining why students such as the example case were minimally invested in academic achievement. He also placed the research findings into context with other research findings such as the "hidden curriculum" in which researchers argue that "academic achievement is measured by one's well-roundedness, as well as one's grades" (p. 75). Goto indicated that the example student seemed to believe the same thing (i.e., "education is based on 'life experience,'" p. 75). However, he believed that the family/culture theory and the hidden curriculum theory underestimated the influence of extrafamilial factors such as peers on students' perspectives about education. He indicated that the students in the study were worried about being outcasts for academic success. The students seemed to be motivated to fit into the predominant student culture which did not value academic success.

The interesting finding of the investigation was that the Asian American students had to resolve a conflict between the two cultures to which they belonged (i.e., student and family). Therefore, decisions made by the students have certain consequences. For example, if they wish to obtain good grades, they may have to endure ridicule from peers but receive praise from teachers and parents. If they do not obtain good grades, they will fit in with the "in crowd" but disappoint teachers and parents. Goto suggests that the student culture is a critical component in understanding the influences over the academic success of Asian students.

Document Analysis. Nelson, Martella, and Galand (1997) utilized document analyses to determine the levels of rule violations (i.e., late from recess/assembly, running, misuse of ground/equipment, throwing items/spitting, gum/candy/food, inappropriate items, and interruption of learning environment) and rights violations (i.e., harming/threatening others, verbal abuse/inappropriate language, disobedience/disrespect, destroying property/stealing, fighting/pushing, and harassment) in an elementary school located in a medium-sized city in the Pacific Northwest. The documents analyzed were formal office disciplinary referrals. The archival data were obtained over a period of four years. The researchers learned that the level of rule and rights violations in the school was fairly high across six grade levels until a formal disciplinary procedure was implemented along with a school-wide organizational program in which ecological arrangements were made, behavioral guidelines set, and closer supervision of students was activated.

WHEN SHOULD RESEARCHERS USE EACH QUALITATIVE RESEARCH DESIGN?

Qualitative research has many uses. Integrating qualitative and quantitative methods should never be seen as a right–wrong proposition. Qualitative research is very useful for generating hypotheses to be tested later, for generating grounded theories, for disproving a theory, and for describing a phenomenon in the natural world. Quantitative research has its uses and contributions to our understanding. Quantitative methods are more specific and methodology driven, whereas qualitative methods are more general and, as Howe and Eisenhart (1990) indicate, question- and analysis-driven. However, they can provide answers to different questions and provide valuable information to complement each other. For example, the investigation described previously with regard to the use of study guides in a social studies class was one that actually occurred. The interesting point of the investigation was that qualitative and quantitative researchers combined forces to conduct the investigation. Data were generated with regard to student test performance and teacher, student, and observer beliefs, attitudes, expectations, and preferences of study guides. The investigators gained an appreciation for the type of information each methodology could generate.

If one decided to use a qualitative design, the decision of what type of design to use must be made. Case studies are used when researchers wish to study an individual or a "case" in depth. Researchers attempt to gain a deep understanding of a particular phenomenon under study, and an in-depth examination of several individuals or cases is not practical. Researchers use an observation study when the phenomenon of interest can be investigated by assessing observable behavior. Additionally, observations allow researchers to investigate the phenomenon in context. This is to say that researchers will collect data while the participants are interacting with the natural environment. When information is needed that cannot be obtained through observations such as in cases where it is impossible (e.g., thinking, feelings) or improbable (e.g., observing every minute of every day), interview methods will be utilized.

Interviews have an advantage over observations in that they allow for the collection of data that cannot be obtained through observations; however, the weakness with interview data is that the reliability and validity of that data are questionable. The use of ethnography allows researchers to combine several data gathering techniques to investigate a phenomenon. In ethnography, researchers conduct in-depth interviewing and participant and nonparticipant observational techniques to obtain a holistic picture of the phenomena. The investigation occurs over an extended period of time. Researchers will use ethnographies to allow for the in-depth study of a culture, be it a classroom or a workplace. Finally, the use of document analyses is needed when researchers wish to further verify data collected from other sources or when the data cannot be found in any other form such as through observations. Document analysis has the advantage of being unobtrusive in that the data are available without having to observe or interview participants.

DISCUSSION QUESTIONS

1. A colleague wishes to conduct a case study of a local elementary classroom to determine how the use of instructional methods impact student interest in the topic. Describe to your colleague the phases she should go through to conduct such a study.
2. Another student tells you that he is unsure of the difference between participant and nonparticipant observations. Describe to him the difference. In your response, describe if observer effects is a problem with one or both of the observation types.
3. After you tell the student the difference between participant and nonparticipant observations, the student asks you if you see an ethical problem in participant observations, specifically, complete participation. How would you respond?
4. After your conversation with the student, you begin to wonder about the effects of observer bias on an investigation. If you were conducting an observation study, how would you control for observer bias?
5. During class one day, your professor asks the students to describe briefly the different types of interviews. You believe that you know the different types. Briefly describe each of the types of interview formats.
6. Once you finish answering the professor's question, she asks you to tell the class the strengths and weaknesses of each format. What would you say?
7. After your class, the other students think that you are the expert on qualitative research. One student comes up to you and asks why you would select an interview method of data collection over an observation method or an observation method over an interview method. What would you tell the student?
8. You are part of a research team and are ready to begin an investigation on the experiences of teachers working in an inner city high school. The team decides to use ethnography to study the inner-city school experiences of teachers. Describe the phases one would go through during the ethnographic investigation.
9. When contemplating whether to use ethnography or not, you were asked by members of the research team for your input. You were asked specifically about what you see as the advantages and disadvantages of ethnographic research in general and the advantages and disadvantages of ethnographic research conducted in the inner-city school specifically. How would you address the questions?

10. After your explanation of the advantages and disadvantages of ethnographic research, one member of the research team asked you if acquiring data through other means along with observations and interviews was possible. You indicated that document analyses can be conducted. For an investigation looking at teacher experiences in an inner-city high school, what types of documents could give you insight into teacher experience?

SUCCESSFUL MAINSTREAMING IN ELEMENTARY SCIENCE CLASSES: A QUALITATIVE STUDY OF THREE REPUTATIONAL CASES

THOMAS E. SCRUGGS

MARGO A. MASTROPIERI
Purdue University

The overall purpose of this investigation was to identify variables meaningfully associated with mainstreaming success in science classes, across grade levels, and across categories of disability. Subsequent to 2 years' collaborative work with teachers, we studied, over a school year, three science classes in which students with disabilities were successfully included. Associated building and district-level practices were also examined. Evidence gathered included observational field notes, student and teacher products, videotaped records, curriculum materials, and interviews with students, teachers, and administrators. Seven variables were identified that were common to all settings and independent of grade level or disability category. Most of these served also to enhance the shared experience of all students in the science classes. Implications for mainstreaming and for science education are discussed.

Recent and contemporary thinking in special education has tended to emphasize the value of inclusion, to the greatest extent possible, of students with disabilities into the mainstream school environment (e.g., Kauffman, 1993). Debate on this issue, which has at times become contentious (e.g., Fuchs & Fuchs, 1988a, 1988b, 1994; Reynolds, Wang, & Walberg, 1987; Wang & Walberg, 1988), has nevertheless focused on the extent to which students with disabilities should be included and has generally taken for granted the notion that mainstreaming is often, or even frequently, a positive intervention for nondisabled students as well as for students with special needs. With few exceptions (e.g., Gartner & Lipsky, 1987; Singer & But-

Thomas E. Scruggs is a Professor in the Department of Educational Studies at Purdue University, LAEB, 5th Floor, West Lafayette, IN 47907. His specializations are learning and memory, special education, and science.

Margo A. Mastropieri is a Professor in the Department of Educational Studies at Purdue University, LAEB, 5th Floor, West Lafayette, IN 47907. Her specializations are teacher effectiveness, special education, and mainstreaming.

ler, 1987), however, dialogue regarding the merits of mainstreaming or full inclusion of students with disabilities has typically occurred in the special education literature, while the actual effects of intensified inclusiveness have been likely to impact greatly on the "regular" classroom.

Experimental evidence concerning the effects of mainstreaming has been equivocal (e.g., Carlberg & Kavale, 1980; Kauffman, 1993). This suggests that inclusion, by itself, may lead to differential outcomes, depending on the degree of success of specific, presently unspecified classroom implementation variables. One potentially important variable, which has only recently received attention, is the interaction of the characteristics of students with disabilities with the characteristics of mainstream classroom curriculum. Scruggs and Mastropieri (1992) recently compared the characteristics of students with disabilities with the characteristics of different science education curriculum approaches and concluded that curriculum characteristics may play an important role in mainstreaming success. For example, most school-identified students with disabilities exhibit difficulties in areas related to language and literacy, and prior knowledge (Hallahan & Kauffman, 1994; Scruggs & Mastropieri, 1992); in such cases, curriculum approaches which emphasize concrete, meaningful experiences and de-emphasize vocabulary acquisition and textbook learning appear likely to be facilitative of mainstreaming success. Such approaches are also endorsed strongly by professional science organizations (e.g., Rutherford & Ahlgren, 1990).

Further, science may be a particularly important area of study for students with disabilities (Mastropieri & Scruggs, 1992). It has been pointed out that many students with special learning needs can potentially benefit greatly from the experiential, systematic study of the universe, as well as the promotion of scientific reasoning via the process skills (e.g., observing, classifying, predicting) that are frequently part of the science curriculum (e.g., Esler, Midgett, & Bird, 1977; Patton, 1993). Finally, science is often identified by teachers as an important subject for mainstreaming (Atwood & Oldham, 1985), because of the nature of the subject and the fact that mainstream settings typically are staffed with trained science teachers and contain curriculum materials that are much less likely to be available in special education settings.

A recent comprehensive literature search of science education for students with disabilities (Mastropieri & Scruggs, 1992) yielded 66 reports, which provided much important information on how students with disabilities learn science. However, few investigations have involved students with disabilities in mainstream science classes. MacDougall, Schnur, Berger, and Vernon (1981) found that students with learning disabilities, behavioral disorders, or mental handicaps behaved and interacted more positively with peers when hands-on science activities were employed than when more traditional school activities were being undertaken. Linn, Hadary, Rosenberg, and Haushalter (1979) observed similar progress of hearing impaired students in special and mainstream science classes, although the special education classes tended more to emphasize language acquisition through science activities. Morocco, Dalton, and Tivnan (1990) documented the mainstreaming of students with learning disabilities into science classes and noted some specific challenges, such as behavior management. Bay, Staver, Bryan, and Hale (1992) evaluated the performance of students with learning disabilities and behavioral disorders in science classes using either an activities approach or a textbook approach. They concluded that the students with disabilities in the activities approach performed better on delayed tests and generalization tests than their counterparts using the textbook approach. Finally, Putnam, Rynders, Johnson, and Johnson (1989) included students with moderate and severe disabilities in science activities with nondisabled students and reported that nondisabled students instructed in collaborative skills interacted more with students with disabilities than did control students.

These studies, taken as a whole, provide important information regarding the processes and outcomes associated with mainstreaming students with disabilities into science classes. However, many questions remain to be addressed. Pertinent to the present investigation, we were concerned with variables associated with successful mainstreaming in science that appeared to be robust across grade levels and specific categories of disability. Although much research has been conducted on the consequences of mainstreaming, we were primarily concerned in this investigation with the processes of mainstreaming—that is, how successful mainstreaming is accomplished.

In order to gather information on this issue, we identified a school district that was nationally acknowledged for excellence in science education and highly regarded for its special education programs. We identified three classrooms in which exemplary mainstreaming practices were said to be undertaken and gathered evidence that we felt would lead us to some general conclusions about mainstreaming success in science using a design similar to the multiple case study designs described by Yin (1989).

METHOD

Participants

All participants were from a relatively large (about 50,000 students), middle SES school district in a western metropolitan area. This district was one of four with whom we collaborated as part of a larger project to study science and disability. We interviewed district science education administrative personnel, building level administrators, teachers, and special education personnel in that district to identify reputational cases (LeCompte & Preissle, 1993) of mainstreaming success in science (2/18/1–2/22/1; 3/7/2–3/12/2).[1] During these periods, we also observed in identified classrooms. Three classrooms, in three different schools, were identified. During the first and second project years, we worked with these and other district teachers and specialists (along with those of the three other school districts) to develop and refine guidelines for including students with disabilities in science classes. We presented them with draft versions of our guidelines, developed from information from previous literature and previously published guidelines (e.g., Hadary & Cohen, 1978; Hofman & Ricker, 1979), and we solicited and received written feedback. We revised the guidelines based on their feedback on two separate occasions throughout the 2-year period. The final product (Mastropieri & Scruggs, 1994b) contained information on characteristics of specific disability categories, general mainstreaming strategies applied to science classes, and strategies for adapting specific science activities (e.g., electricity units) for students with disabilities. Copies were distributed to all cooperating teachers and administrators. Teachers in the three targeted classrooms were asked to refer to the guidelines when needed, but they were under no obligation to do so. Nevertheless, all teachers reported informally that they had referred to the guidelines frequently. Following is a description of each of these classrooms.

Classroom A. Classroom A was a third grade classroom of 25 students in a regular elementary school containing kindergarten through grade 6 students. The school in which Classroom A was located had enrolled 72 students with hearing impairments and contained special education teachers with specialized training in teaching students with hearing impairments, as well as specialized facilities for students with hearing impairments (e.g., fire alarms that also produced flashing lights). Classroom A included two Caucasian students with hearing impairments in science class. One was a boy with a nearly complete hearing loss, who was provided a sign language interpreter to assist in communication. The other student had a partial hearing loss, and she benefited greatly from an FM phonic ear system. In addition to the two students with hearing impairments, four students with learning disabilities, two students receiving supplementary services for low SES students (Chapter 1), and two students for whom English was a second language were also enrolled. All students who had been classified as learning disabled in these three classrooms were 2 or more years below grade level in reading. In addition, the boy with a severe hearing loss read at an early first grade level, while the girl with the partial hearing loss read at about a second grade level. The teacher, Ms. A, had about 5 years' teaching experience and held no certification in special education.

Students were seated at desks in rows, with adjacent desks touching or nearly touching one another, facing toward the teacher's desk. A wide aisle divided the class laterally into two halves, and the teacher made frequent use of this aisle in moving freely about the classroom. Desks were moved when classroom activities required it. The two students with hearing impairments were seated in the row nearest the teacher, on opposite sides of the room.

Classroom B. Classroom B was a fourth grade class located in a regular elementary school that had enrolled 17 students with visual impairments of varying severity. This school had a special education teacher who was specially trained in teaching students with visual impairments. One Caucasian girl with a nearly total visual impairment was included in this class, in addition to three students with learning disabilities. Although reading achievement is difficult to assess using traditional standardized measures with students who read braille, the girl in this classroom did read more slowly, and at a somewhat lower level, than most of her classmates. The teacher, Ms. B, had about 7 years' teaching experience and held no special education certification.

The classroom was arranged with desks in groups of four that faced one another. The visually impaired student was given additional space to accommodate a braille typewriter (brailler) and braille materials, and her desk was located in a group with two other students near the outside door, at the back of the classroom.

Classroom C. Classroom C was a fifth grade class located in a regular elementary school that had enrolled a number of students with physical disabilities and that included special education teachers who were specially trained in teaching students with physical disabilities. This school was well equipped with wheelchair ramps, adaptable classrooms, and even a playground that could accommodate students in wheelchairs. Classroom C had three Caucasian students with physical disabilities in science class. Two female students, affected by cerebral palsy, employed motorized wheelchairs to assist mobility and also exhibited significant difficulties with motor and speech activities. As a consequence, traditional academic achievement in basic skills areas was very difficult to determine. However, both students exhibited adequate listening comprehension. The third student with physical disabilities was a boy who was affected by arthritis and moved with the aid of arm braces and a motorized walker. He could accomplish, with effort, general pincer-grasp movements. His reading ability was at about grade level, but manual writing presented greater difficulties. Two students with learning disabilities also attended the science class. The teacher, Mr. C., had about 9 years' teaching experience and held no special education certification.

Classroom C was located in a small building near the other school buildings and near the special education classrooms, and it had the most unconventional interior arrangement. Teacher C had asked his students to decide the seating arrangement, and they had elected to place their desks in clusters of three or four, spread around the classroom, facing all different directions (interview, 11/14/3). Sufficient space was allocated for wheelchairs to pass throughout the classroom. One of the physically handicapped students had elected to have his desk located on the opposite side of the room from the outside door. The outside door was connected to the outside sidewalk by a wheelchair ramp, which all students used to enter and exit the classroom. The teacher's desk and teaching materials were located in a back corner of the room, and Teacher C was never observed seated at this desk during class time.

Curriculum

The cooperating district has a very positive reputation for excellence in science education, and in fact is one of a relatively small number of districts listed by the National Science Resource Center in Washington, DC, as "exemplary." This district has created its own science curriculum materials, which are housed in a district distribution center. From this center, science kits for individual units are created, stored, inventoried, and delivered to teacher's classrooms throughout the district on request. Four specific units are targeted for each academic year in the elementary grades, and teachers may elect to request other age-appropriate units. According to personnel from the National Science Resource Center, such a distribution system is strongly associated with the success over time of hands-on science programs in individual school districts (Deputy Director S. G. Shuler, personal communication, 2/1/1).

The curriculum had been based originally on the Elementary Science Study (ESS) and other materials from the 1960s but had been revised on a continuous, ongoing basis, in response to teacher feedback; district needs; local cultural, geographical, and meteorological conditions; and contemporary trends in science education (interview with district science specialist, 2/18/1). The most recent revisions had included integration with other curriculum areas, such as social studies, and included reading passages of differing levels of difficulty to help accommodate diverse reading abilities. District teachers were actively involved in revising these materials on an ongoing basis. Guidelines for accommodating students with disabilities are not specifically included in these materials (they very rarely are in any science curriculum materials, e.g., Parmar & Cawley, 1993), but the materials themselves—focusing on experiential, conceptual learning and de-emphasizing textbook learning—are thought to be potentially accommodating to the needs of students with disabilities (Scruggs & Mastropieri, 1992).

The district materials have a broad, wide scope, covering areas of ecology and life sciences, earth sciences, physical sciences, and scientific method, and are distributed throughout the elementary grades. All include relevant materials for completing activities, and teacher and student editions of activity books that include brief reading passages and recording sheets for relevant activities. For example, one unit entitled "Chemistry" was developed for use in the fifth grade. During this unit, students examine and classify the physical properties of matter; manipulate and observe material changes in a clod of dirt; examine the interactions with solids and liquids in solutions, including food coloring, butyl stearate, ice, and water; measure changes in volume when alcohol and salt are combined with water; observe and measure chemical changes associated with different kinds of oxidation; combine ammonia, water, vinegar, and bromothymol blue in various solutions and record observations; combine vinegar with baking soda or salt and observe reactions; test for acids and bases with litmus paper; and study home safety with chemicals.

Another unit, entitled "Fin and Feather, Tooth and Tail," was developed for use in third grade classrooms. During this unit, students learn about and discuss adaptation; study opposable thumbs; observe and describe which teeth they use to bite and chew various foods; determine eating habits based on pictures of animal skulls; experiment with nonverbal communication and study animal warning signs; act out various types of animal locomotion and identify animals by studying their feet; simulate animal camouflage using different kinds of wallpaper, potatoes, and various art supplies; study and describe adaptation in different vertebrates; study the concept of *home range* and map out their own home ranges; study animal characteristics using jigsaw activities; and create poster presentations for an animal of their own choice.

RESEARCHER BACKGROUND, DATA COLLECTION, AND ANALYSIS

Researcher Background

We entered this project with extensive backgrounds in special education research and practice (particularly involving students with mild disabilities) but with little experience with, or knowledge of, mainstream science curriculum. If anything, the behavioral influences on the field of special education, and our knowledge of the characteristics of special education students, had made us cautious of *discovery* or inquiry-based approaches, for fear that students with disabilities might be excluded or fall behind peers who pursued learning more actively and independently. Our special education methods textbook (Mastropieri & Scruggs, 1987, 1994a), based on instructional research relevant to students with special needs, recommends an approach to teaching that is more structured and teacher directed, particularly in its first edition, than the methods often proposed by science educators (e.g., Abruscato, 1992). Our previous research in science education focused on mnemonic enhancement of science facts, classifications, vocabulary, and verbal concepts with students with learning disabilities and mild mental retardation (e.g., Mastropieri & Scruggs, 1989; Scruggs, Mastropieri, Levin, & Gaffney, 1985). We have made, and have defended, several assumptions relevant to the field of special education—for example, that disabilities are conditions individuals sometimes have (although these conditions can be partly socially determined), that special education practice often can be helpful for such individuals, and that improvement in practice can be influenced by research (Scruggs, 1993; for a critique of such assumptions, see Skrtic, 1991).

During the earlier stages of this project, we first reviewed all available literature on science and students with disabilities (Mastropieri & Scruggs, 1992) and critically examined relevant science curriculum from four school districts across the nation (Mastropieri & Scruggs, 1994c). Our work in this area led us to appreciate the value of hands-on science in providing concrete and meaningful experiences to students who may experience difficulty in deriving meaning from more abstract text presentations or who may have had more limited background experience (Mastropieri & Scruggs, in press; Scruggs & Mastropieri, 1992). As we consulted literature and the expert opinion of teachers, curriculum developers, and national science organizations in developing our guidelines, we began to feel that hands-on science instruction, appropriately implemented, could be highly complementary to the special needs of students with disabilities. We had collected recommendations for adapting science curriculum for students with various disabilities. We were also aware that several other factors might be of critical importance in enhancing mainstreaming. However, we had not systematically preconceptualized all factors that might be necessary for a successful mainstream experience in science.

Data Collection

During the first and second project years, we met with district and building level administrators and collaborated with special education and regular class teachers, including the target teachers, while compiling our guidelines for facilitating mainstreaming. During the third project year, we observed and videotaped in the three science classrooms described previously over a 5-week period in the fall semester and during an additional 3-week period in the spring semester. We also interviewed students, teachers, and administrators and collected examples of student and teacher products. We made follow-up contact during the fourth project year. Overall, we collected data from a number of sources, including observational field notes, videotape and audiotape records, student and teacher products, curriculum materials, and interviews of students, classroom teachers, special education teachers, and building and district-level administrators.

Observations were made during approximately 35 class meetings during the fall semester and approximately 15 class meetings during the spring semester. Two observers were present at least twice in every classroom, so that observers would have familiarity with all settings. We videotaped at least two classes in each of the three settings and took field notes during all classes observed. Additionally, we interviewed the targeted students and peers, the three teachers and cooperating special education teachers, building principals, and district-level personnel in science education and special education. Dialogue with teachers continued throughout the investigation, as the need arose. However, all teachers were asked at least the following questions: (a) What things happen to make mainstreaming successful, and how would you define success in this context? (b) What would you say about [district name] science curriculum versus textbook-based science curriculum? (c) What specific adaptations do you make in science class for students with disabilities? And, (d) do you think administrative support, building or district level, is helpful? These interviews were recorded on audiotape. As described earlier, initial contacts with target teachers began nearly 2 years prior to our classroom observations and included follow-up contact during the year subsequent to our classroom observations.

Data Analysis

After several weeks of interviews and site visits during the third project year, we considered all sources of information collected to date. We then analyzed all data for consistencies and inconsistencies, using analytic induction and the constant comparative method (LeCompte & Preissle, 1993). Divergent cases or instances were also investigated. We then developed a preliminary list of five variables that appeared to be highly relevant to the issue of successful mainstreaming in science. This preliminary list became the basis for future analyses and was revised several times as additional information became available.

At the end of the third year of the project, the list of variables was again reconsidered with respect to all information that had been gathered throughout the project. This analysis yielded a final list of seven variables, which appeared to be consistent and robust with respect to all data sources across the three different classrooms. These variables also were supported by previous research literature, including both convergent and divergent instances. Finally, all final conclusions were re-examined to ensure that they were directly supported by evidence gathered in this investigation, a feature sometimes missing in qualitative research on learning and behavioral disorders (Scruggs & Mastropieri, in press-b).

Although it may have been less appropriate to address concerns of "reliability" and "validity," at least in the more traditional quantitative sense, in this investigation, we nevertheless wished to ensure that our data collection had been accurate and systematic and that our conclusions logically proceeded from the interactions of those data sources with our personal perspectives. We addressed these issues by obtaining multiple sources of evidence in support of each of our conclusions and by planning and implementing extended interaction with the participants. We also addressed the issue of consistency by confirming that all conclusions were supported by evidence from each classroom, considered independently.

RESULTS AND DISCUSSION

Our first consideration was: Were the three science classrooms successful in mainstreaming students with visual, physical, auditory, and learning disabilities? Our conclusion, based on all available evidence, was that these classrooms had been successful. Teachers (interviews, 2/5/3; 2/10/3) stated that mainstreaming efforts were successful and that they defined success in this context as meaningful participation, throughout the school year, in classroom science activities and classroom discussion and as completion of (possibly adapted) classroom assignments. Administrators generally concurred with these statements (e.g., 11/13/3).

Our analysis of field notes and videotapes suggested that all students did in fact participate meaningfully in science activities and class discussion and that they completed relevant classroom assignments. For example, the girl with a mild hearing impairment in Classroom A led the class in a data collection and recording activity (videotape record, 11/20/3); the student with a visual impairment in Classroom B took her regular turn in a "Simon Says" communication activity (videotape record 2/10/3), and children with physical and learning disabilities participated fully in an activity involving testing for the presence of chemical acids and bases in Classroom C (field notes, 11/16/3; 11/20/3). Teacher B reported that her student with a visual impairment completed assignments throughout the year, using the brailler and/or peer recorders, although sometimes additional prompting was needed to ensure task completion (interview, 2/10/3).

We did observe a negative instance of successful mainstreaming, using the same definition, in a school in a small village in northern Italy, in which inclusive practices were being undertaken as part of Italy's national education policy (Organisation for Economic Co-Operation and Development, 1985). In one such classroom, we observed one student with disabilities independently coloring a coloring book while all other students were participating in class discussion and relevant activities (videotape record, 3/15/4). Such practices would not be considered to be successful mainstreaming by the standards employed in this investigation, because the student was simply physically present in the classroom, without actively participating in relevant classroom activities.

Analysis of all data collected for this investigation revealed seven variables which appeared to be meaningfully associated with observed mainstreaming success, across categories of disability and grade level. These seven variables included administrative support; support from special education personnel; an accepting, positive classroom atmosphere; appropriate curriculum; effective general teaching skills; peer assistance; and disability-specific teaching skills. Each is now described in detail.

Variable 1: Administrative Support

All classrooms clearly benefited from administrative support for the mainstreaming effort, provided both at the district and the building level. Interviews with science education and special education district personnel confirmed that integration of students with disabilities had a high priority in the district and that an active, problem-solving approach was used to facilitate such mainstreaming efforts. In interviews, all building administrators also voiced strong support for mainstreaming efforts and were well informed about mainstreaming activities being undertaken in their buildings. Further, all administrators took apparent pride in mainstreaming successes at their schools. The principal of School C, for example, openly praised Teacher C for his work on developing the mainstreaming guidelines and his work with physically handicapped children (field notes, teacher meeting, School C, 11/12/3). Principals of all three schools could readily identify by name the teachers who were most facilitative in mainstreaming (interviews with principals, 2/18/1–2/20/1; 11/12/2; 11/13/2; 11/13/3). In turn, teachers in interviews in this investigation spoke positively of their administrative support and administrative arrangements and underlined the importance of this variable. Research literature has also underlined the importance of administrative support in promoting mainstreaming (e.g., Center, Ward, Parmenter, & Nash, 1985).

District and local administration had also provided excellent physical facilities for meeting the needs of students with disabilities. All buildings were single story and provided very easy access between classrooms. More specifically, School A included fire alarms with flashing lights and distributed FM systems when needed to all teachers interacting with students with hearing impairments. School B offered braillers, closed-circuit televisions, and adapted computer systems. School C had single-story construction and ramps whenever needed (e.g., to make portable buildings accessible), in addition to a wheelchair-accessible playground.

Variable 2: Support from Special Education Personnel

The direct assistance of special education teachers and staff was very much in evidence in all three classrooms. Teacher A communicated regularly with special education teachers about her students with hearing impairments and learning disabilities (Teacher A interview, 2/5/3); a licensed sign language interpreter provided a necessary communication link. Teacher B relied on the special education teacher and aide to provide braille curriculum materials and interlining (writing in between braille lines), braillers, and methods and materials for reducing stereotypic behaviors and other special problems (Teacher B interview, 2/10/3). Teacher C received regular assistance and support from special education teachers regarding the needs of his students with physical disabilities. In addition, a special education undergraduate student from a local university was employed to assist students with physical disabilities in the classroom (Teacher C interview, 2/5/3).

All teachers acknowledged the necessary assistance of special education staff in interviews, and observational records and interviews with principals supported the critical role played by special education personnel. These teachers and staff were seen to assume responsibility in several critical areas, including assisting students with disabilities to and from class, monitoring and adjusting class procedures and assignments, preparing regular education students for students with disabilities prior to mainstreaming, conferring with classroom teachers, recommending teaching strategies, and providing social support for their mainstreaming efforts. These roles follow very closely those identified in a major mainstreaming text (Wood, 1993, p. 51).

Overall, the ongoing support of special education personnel appeared to play a critical role in the continued presence of students with disabilities in regular classrooms. Teacher B, for example, commented,

> *[Special education teacher] is really great to work with. I know she's busy, but she's always got a moment for me when I need to talk to her about [name], or if I am having a problem, or if I am not sure of something. She is always there for me, which I think is very important. (Interview, 2/10/3)*

Similarly, Teacher C commented,

> *[Special education teacher] came in and talked specifically about my children and my classroom. She was very supportive. She wanted to know exactly what we were doing and how we were doing it—how we were making it so this child could be mainstreamed into my classroom. I just felt like whatever I asked for they [special education staff] were going to see if it's feasible and work with me to get it that way. I feel like they trust me, too. (Interview, 2/5/3)*

Investigations by others have also underlined the important role of special education personnel in supporting mainstreaming efforts. Glang, Gersten, and Morvant (in press), for example, described the critical role of special education personnel working in a consultant capacity in improving basic skills functioning of students with disabilities in the regular education classroom.

Variable 3: Accepting, Positive Classroom Atmosphere

All teachers not only accepted the idea of diverse learning needs in their classrooms but voiced opinions that all students benefited from the atmosphere created by such diversity. Teacher A remarked to her class (videotape record, 2/10/3),

> *We're all different in some ways. Even [name] wears glasses. And the twins, they were different, weren't they? You have to expect that kind of difference; it's sometimes fun and happy to work with someone who is a little bit different. You don't always want to work with the same kinds of people, do you? It makes life more exciting to work with different kinds of people.*

Teacher B commented, "I think it is something I have set up. Everybody belongs here. . . . I work very hard to make all my kids feel accepted" (interview, 2/10/3). Teacher C concurred, "I think if a teacher puts some effort into it, everything can be adapted so that [students with disabilities] can do it" (interview, 2/5/3).

Evidence for positive classroom atmosphere was also obtained in observations of all classrooms. All three teachers were seen to be very accepting of divergent answers and other unexpected responses from all students. This open environment was also perceived by students with and without disabilities as positive and accommodating, as expressed in student interviews. For example, when asked how it feels to come to science class, the boy with hearing impairments in Classroom A signed, "Fine, I like to come to Room #—" (field notes, 2/10/3).

One specific way in which this open classroom atmosphere was expressed across classrooms was in teacher responses to incorrect answers or statements. Each of the three teachers responded positively to both correct and incorrect statements, reinforcing correct answers and following incorrect statements with further questioning, and expressing approval for the student volunteering a response (field notes, all classes). For another example, all three teachers took a very personal view of the teaching process, knew all their students well, and interacted with them in a friendly, positive manner. Interviews with students suggested that students were aware of, and appreciative of, this personal approach to teaching.

In contrast, a negative or hostile atmosphere can hinder mainstreaming efforts. Centra (1990) described the accounts of several students with learning disabilities who had encountered a lack of acceptance in mainstream environments and the resulting negative effects. For instance, one female student reported,

> *I was put in Mr. Sheldon's class to see if I could do the work. He found out that I was having a hard time. I was supposed to go to resource to take tests and all that. He would always say, "You can't go." You know, he was always sticking his nose up at me. He never said anything to me; he would just be failing me.... He was like—he wanted nothing to do with me whatsoever. It hurt really bad. I finally went down to guidance and told them I couldn't take it any more. (p. 151)*

Variable 4: Appropriate Curriculum

Scruggs and Mastropieri (1992) argued that science curriculum that de-emphasized textbook and vocabulary learning and emphasized active exploration of scientific phenomena would be likely to be associated with mainstreaming success. This hypothesis was partially supported by previous research—such as, that of Bay et al. (1992), MacDougall et al. (1981), Linn et al. (1979), Putnam et al. (1989), and Morocco et al. (1990)—all of which demonstrated to some extent the facilitative effects of activities-oriented curricula on mainstreaming outcomes. Further support is evidenced by an experiment by Scruggs, Mastropieri, Bakken, and Brigham (1993), who demonstrated that students with learning disabilities in self-contained classes learned and applied more science information from activities-oriented lessons than from textbook/lecture lessons. More recent research has supported the value of more inquiry-based teaching methods in promoting science learning of students with learning disabilities and mild mental retardation (Scruggs, Mastropieri, and Sullivan, 1994).

In the present investigation, students with disabilities were typically performing markedly below grade level in reading and writing skills. Further, many of them lacked experiences or prior knowledge relevant to the areas being studied. In this context, activities-oriented lessons allowed all students to experience, explore, and investigate new phenomena for themselves, without reliance on literacy skills. Finally, the nature of the curriculum allowed them to interact freely with peers, who could lend assistance or support when needed. All the teachers expressed appreciation for the facilitative effects of the science curriculum. For example, Teacher C remarked,

> *Science curriculum is easily adaptable if you work with cooperative groups.... I am not a textbook person. I think it makes it easier if they have a hands-on experience; they can actually see what's going on. That's not just for handicapped children, but for every child.... Some of these kids that have come from [classrooms for students with physical disabilities] to a regular classroom have never seen things like this before [science materials]. If you explain it they have no concept, no idea, of what's going on. When you actually go ahead and show them, they're just as fascinated [as nondisabled students] and they can come up with their own ideas of "Why did it happen?" and "How did it happen?" and so forth. (Interview, 2/5/3)*

Teacher A expressed a similar opinion:

> *[Students are successful] because science is so hands-on, and that's exactly what our special needs children need. They need the hands-on activities to*

> *help them understand and learn.... There's no way that these kids can't learn something because they don't have to sit and read a book. They might not catch on to...one part of our activity that day, but there are so many activities.... I think each and every one of them learns something. (Interview, 2/5/3)*

Teacher B also agreed, "The hands-on science is nice...the kids have a good time using it..." (interview, 2/10/3).

Interviews with classroom teachers revealed that all appreciated the value of concreteness and meaningfulness in teaching science to students with disabilities. These two variables have been considered extremely important in special education methods textbooks (e.g., Mastropieri & Scruggs, 1994a).

Teachers also remarked positively about the role of the district administration in making hands-on science activities easily available to teachers, thus ensuring that such activities are more likely to take place. Teacher B commented,

> *Most of the [materials] are included in the kit, which makes it very nice, and very easy to use, and the kids...have a good time using it too, because we can do all the experiments and we don't have to worry about if we've got enough of this. They've experimented to make sure they have enough of everything. (2/10/3)*

Variable 5: Effective General Teaching Skills

Teachers in all classrooms employed many, if not most, of the effective teaching skills described by—for example, Brophy and Good (1986) and Rosenshine and Stevens (1986). Mastropieri and Scruggs (1994a) summarized many of these as the *SCREAM* variables: structure, clarity, redundancy, enthusiasm, appropriate pace, and maximized student engagement. Structure and clarity were employed in shaping the purpose and focus of overall lessons, but they were not used to stifle or suppress student divergent thinking. Redundancy was applied as needed, typically in summarizing or reinforcing lesson content. Enthusiasm was expressed by all teachers toward the content of each lesson, in order to focus attention and model positive attitudes toward science. Finally, appropriate pace and maximized student engagement were employed to maintain a positive learning atmosphere (all field notes).

In addition, all teachers employed well-established and systematic behavior management programs, although the structure appeared more concrete in the lower grades and less so in the higher grades. For example, all elementary teachers posted class rules; the third grade teacher also posted possible rewards and penalties. Teacher A used a number of tangible rewards and prizes to keep her third grade class attentive and appropriately engaged; Teacher B used goldfish crackers to reinforce task engagement, but she discontinued this during the year and later relied more on direct appeals for cooperation.

> *First, I would do it just on behavior. If they were working together well, then they would get the goldfish. And then I slowly progressed into looking at the outcomes...then I wean them off of it, because I want it to become more intrinsic, instead of extrinsic and always wanting that food reward. (Interview, 2/10/3)*

Teacher C used more abstract cues, such as "E.O.M." (for "Eyes on me"), when he felt the need to refocus his fifth grade students' attention. He also used longer term rewards (e.g., class party, field notes, 11/19/3) for cooperation and task engagement. Nevertheless, all teachers effectively enlisted the cooperation and task engagement of their respective classes. Finally, all teachers were seen to use the positive, personal relations they had established with students to engage their support and cooperation with classroom activities.

These effective teaching procedures did not appear to serve as an inhibiting effect on students' efforts to construct scientific knowledge; on the contrary, these procedures appeared to create an atmosphere that was conducive to, and respectful for, scientific learning (see also Scruggs & Mastropieri, in press-a; Mastropieri, Scruggs & Bohs, 1994). In all classes, the overall structure of the lessons was maintained, while students were encouraged to express divergent thoughts regarding particular lessons. The open acceptance of different ideas appeared to be related to the open acceptance of diversity in the classrooms, described previously.

Overall, the structure and order of the classrooms, within the context of free inquiry, served to establish and maintain an overall environment that was safe, predictable, and facilitative of the needs of students with disabilities, who appeared to benefit greatly from these environments. Such environments also appeared to be facilitative of peers' appropriate interaction with students with disabilities. The present observations are further supported by one of the few teacher effectiveness studies to include mainstreamed handicapped students (Larrivee, 1985). Teacher behaviors said to be facilitative of mainstreaming included positive feedback, ensuring a positive success rate, using time efficiently, and reducing off-task behavior.

Variable 6: Peer Assistance

In all classrooms, nondisabled student peers were also employed to assist students with disabilities. For instance, Teacher A employed students to provide social and communicative support for the hearing impaired children; Teacher B employed student peers to assist the blind girl's movements through the classroom, and Teacher C employed peers to assist and encourage physically handicapped students with science activities. All teachers employed peer assistance for students with learning disabilities (field notes, videotape records, interviews with teachers).

Classroom observations and interviews suggested that nondisabled peers generally felt positively about lending assistance to students with disabilities and felt that they learned from the interactions. Questioned by Teacher A about working with "extra special" people in the room (field notes, 2/10/3), students replied, "helpful," "great," "I feel happy and fun and different," "I'm surprised at how I learned to make signs like that." One student reported that working with students with disabilities was "frustrating," a response which was also openly accepted by Teacher A.

In the present investigation, peer assistance, commonly described as an important mainstreaming strategy in the literature (e.g., Lewis & Doorlag, 1991; Wood, 1993), seemed clearly necessary. These three classrooms, while not excessive in class size, were nevertheless large enough to render it impossible for the teacher to provide all necessary individual assistance. The use of small groups for many of the classroom activities provided opportunities for classroom peers to provide necessary support for students with special needs. Typically, students enjoyed helping other students, as evidenced by interviews and observational records, and appeared to gain additional insight and focus on relevant tasks as a consequence of lending assistance. Teacher B commented,

> *The kids are real good with her...but I'm not sure if that's because they are just used to having blind kids on campus. [name] has always been in their classroom, so she is just one of the persons there.... They really try to help her. In fact, to the point they are sometimes too helpful, and I have to stop them.... They do too much for her. (Interview, 2/10/3)*

Teacher C, referring to a student with physical disabilities, commented (interview, 2/5/3), "She's put with kids who'll work with her. They work directly with her all the time...." Referring to students with learning disabilities, Teacher C commented,

> *There's a lot of peer tutoring that goes on with those children. They have to be with kids who grab the concepts. [They can] explain it to them in terms they can understand. I usually put my LD children with somebody that is a higher achiever. They usually are successful that way. (Interview, 2/5/3)*

These teacher observations have been supported to some extent by neo-Piagetian researchers (e.g., Perret-Clermont, 1980), who have suggested that higher functioning students can be helpful in leading lower functioning students in constructing scientific knowledge.

Interestingly, the idea of students helping other students as a normal class function appears to have been accepted by students with disabilities. One student with hearing impairments remarked, "[I'm] sort of happy [to come to the mainstream class] because I get to help other people out" (field notes, 2/10/3). This supports the results of a previous meta-analysis, which found that students with disabilities could serve as tutors and that they benefited socially and academically when they did so (Cook, Scruggs, Mastropieri, & Casto, 1985–1986).

Variable 7: Disability-Specific Teaching Skills

Although all three teachers lacked formal special education certification, all exhibited skill in adapting their instruction to the special needs of specific disability areas. These skills went beyond the general teacher effectiveness skills and were acquired through previous experience with students with similar disabilities, interaction with the special education teachers, and consultation with the guidelines for mainstreaming in science (Mastropieri & Scruggs, 1994b), which we provided to all participating teachers. As Teacher A commented, "When you work with these children, you learn that if you explain something to them and they don't understand it, you have to take another route" (interview, 2/10/3).

These diverse skills impacted directly on the disability areas of the students being mainstreamed. For example, Teacher A moved her students with hearing impairments to the front row; used a clear direct speaking voice; did not stand in front of light sources; used pantomime when necessary; and carefully repeated important information. Periodically, she checked for understanding and comprehension (field notes and videotape records). Such procedures also appeared to be helpful for others in the class, including her normative English speaking students. When relevant, she openly discussed the special needs of her students. In a communication activity ("Telephone"), she allowed classroom peers to hold hands in a circle and send a tactual, rather than a vocal, message around the group (field notes, 11/12/3). At another time, she allowed classroom peers to use her own microphone to communicate with the hearing impaired girl. She then used this example to discuss diverse communication needs (field notes, 11/16/3). In a lesson on opposable thumbs of primates, she adapted an activity which involved taping students' thumbs, so that manual signing would not be inhibited (field notes, 11/9/3).

Similar to the activities of special education teachers in the Linn, Hadary, Rosenberg, and Haushalter (1979) study, Teacher A promoted the acquisition of language in her science teaching:

> *Lots of visual—Any new words, we draw pictures of the new words, we put them on the board, the kids interact with those new words, act out new words, to learn vocabulary. With the kind of kids I work with, it's really the main focus, because they don't know vocabulary, they don't hear it like other kids hear it, and [vocabulary enhancement] reinforces [their learning]. (Interview, 2/10/3)*

Such enhancement was also thought to be helpful for her students served by Chapter 1, normative English-speaking students, and students with learning disabilities—which suggests that even *disability-specific* interventions can have positive applications with other students. Teacher A also carefully monitored data recording tasks with her students with learning disabilities who appeared to exhibit literacy problems, blackboard copying problems, or other perceptual-motor problems (videotape record, 11/20/3).

Teacher B also adapted her instruction for the special needs of her visually impaired student, as shown throughout in field notes, videotape records, and interview data. She used careful, concrete descriptions, avoiding vague referents, and was careful to note when more visually-oriented tasks were being employed:

> *There are more concrete models I have to provide.... If she can feel it, she'll understand it better that way... [if she doesn't understand the vocabulary] she says, "Let me see it," and that is her way of seeing it—holding it and touching it. (Interview, 2/10/3)*

Teacher B trained classroom peers to offer an arm to the visually impaired girl, rather than push or pull her into position. Teacher B provided additional space and furniture for a brailler and braille reading materials. Teacher B also implemented a self-monitoring strategy to control stereotypic head movements:

> *We just put a bean bag on top of her head. [Special education teacher] did it for walking back and forth to her classroom, because we have to improve her posture, because she has a gait to her walk and she has nothing physically wrong. It is just not being able to see what she is doing and get reinforcement by watching how other kids walk.... So I saw her walk into the classroom one day with it on, and she put it on her desk, and her head started moving around as soon as she took it off and set it down. And I said, "[name], put that bean bag back on your head." And the kids are real accepting—which really helps. And when we start something new like that—wearing a bean bag is not your ordinary, normal, everyday thing. And I could see [other students] weren't going to say anything, but...it is different from the rest. [So I said], "Boy, [name], this is really going to improve your posture. And, that is what models do to improve their posture." So the rest of the kids kind of think it is neat, too. (interview, 2/10/3)*

Teacher B also noted when the student's disability appeared to impact positively in classroom activities. For instance, in a "Simon Says" activity used as part of a communication unit, she told the class that the student appeared to have an advantage in not being distracted by irrelevant or contradictory visual cues (videotape record and field notes, 2/10/3).

Teacher C also used several specific techniques for accommodating students with physical disabilities. He consulted his class about their preferences for seating arrangements and, using their input, arranged his classroom in clusters of desks that left larger open spaces to facilitate the movement of wheelchairs. He used Velcro bindings to help one student keep his braces attached to his desk, yet easily disengage them manually when needed. He also arranged for this student to have a lower desk than other students and for the other two students with physical disabilities to have large desks to accommodate their wheelchairs (interview, Teacher C, 2/5/3). When engaged in lessons that involved a good deal of fine motor control—for example, mixing chemicals and solutions—peers provided necessary assistance (field notes, 11/16/3). When conducting a reaction time experiment, in which all students were to be tested individually, he adapted relevant apparatus to be engaged manually rather than with the feet for one student who was unable to use her feet for this purpose (videotape record, 2/14/3). When introducing reaction time, he used as an example his own reaction time in avoiding the path of an electrically driven wheelchair. When working in cooperative groups, students were periodically required to be the group "getter," which meant collecting/obtaining relevant materials from a centrally designated space. Students with physical disabilities also played the role of getter when it was their turn, and Teacher C signaled them when it was easiest to acquire group materials and provided assistance as needed (e.g., field notes, 2/14/3). Overall, disability-specific teaching skills appeared to play an essential role in the successful inclusion of students with disabilities in all three science classes.

In contrast, inappropriate adaptations can result in learning failures. Centra (1990), for example, cited a student's recollections of inappropriate learning adaptations: "When the rest of the class did their reading work, the teachers took me and a few others who had trouble reading and had us do puzzles in the corner. I didn't learn anything!" (p. 147). Although such an example seems extreme, Parmar and Cawley (1993) reported that many currently available science textbooks recommend "adaptations" that are not far removed from this example.

GENERAL DISCUSSION

In the present investigation, success in mainstreaming was first identified by teacher and administrator consensus. Direct observation and analysis of classroom activities, student products, student responses to teacher questioning, and interviews with teachers and students provided further evidence that students with disabilities were indeed successfully participating in all aspects of the science curriculum in the three classrooms.

Seven variables were observed consistently in the three classrooms which appeared to be meaningfully associated with this successful mainstreaming. These variables included administrative support, support from special education personnel, accepting classroom atmosphere, appropriate curriculum, effective teaching skills, peer assistance, and disability-specific teaching skills. Although the importance of most or all of these variables has been previously emphasized when studied in isolation, the present investigation is the first known instance in which all variables have been identified and considered simultaneously in mainstream science environments across grade levels and diverse disability areas.

Far from impeding the progress of the nondisabled students, these variables appeared to provide either a neutral or a facilitative effect on learning for the classroom as a whole. For example, the curriculum employed seemed particularly well suited to facilitating mainstreaming, yet it also was compatible with the reform efforts promoted by national science organizations (Mastropieri & Scruggs, 1992; Rutherford & Ahlgren, 1990). This observation suggests that accommodating students with disabilities may also help accommodate contemporary school reform efforts (Scruggs, 1993).

It is possible that, to an unknown extent, participant teachers reacted to the presence of observers in this investigation. That is, although they tended to demonstrate or explicate how they thought a successful mainstreaming class should function, their actual unobserved beliefs and practices may have been different from this. LeCompte and Preissle have stated that, "the ethnographer's chief source of data, participant observation, is more fraught with problems of reactivity than any other mode of data collection" (1993, p. 344). However, we doubt that such reactivity was a significant problem in this investigation, for the following reasons: (a) All conclusions were supported with multiple sources of information across three schools; (b) teachers' stated beliefs and practices were confirmed by their observed behavior; (c) teacher practices generally conformed to principals' and special education teachers' prior descriptions of those practices; and (d) our extended interaction with the participants could be expected to have reduced some artificial reactions (LeCompte & Preissle, 1993). Finally, students' behavior, when we observed, was indicative of students who are quite familiar with the classroom atmosphere and the classroom routines we were observing.

It could also be argued that the present findings provide little new information, beyond the rather self-evident point that, when instruction is good and educational environments are supportive, all students benefit. Yet, the present observations appear to suggest that there is much more to successful mainstreaming than this. For example, "good," supportive instruction certainly appears to be critical to mainstreaming success. And yet, without administrative support, even good teachers are subject to stress and attrition (e.g., Brissie, Hoover-Demsey, & Bassler, 1988; Natale, 1993). Without assistance from special educators and classroom peers, good teachers are unlikely to have sufficient time to devote to special needs of individual students (Putnam et al., 1989). Without appropriate curriculum, students with special needs may find it difficult or impossible to succeed (Mastropieri & Scruggs, in press). Finally, many good and supportive teachers may be simply uninformed regarding optimal practices for interacting with students with special needs (Salvia & Munson, 1986). On the other hand, without concerned and highly skilled teachers, any one of the other variables taken independently seems unlikely to facilitate mainstreaming.

The results of the present investigation can be placed within a rational context of mainstreaming success and therefore can be said to possess analytical generalization (Yin, 1989). Further, a measure of external validity can be argued by virtue of the fact that a previous investigation, conducted in a single classroom in a different state, in which a student with emotional handicaps was being mainstreamed in science, revealed essentially the same variables associated with mainstreaming success (Mastropieri, Scruggs, & Bohs, 1994). In that investigation, however, support from special education personnel appeared to play a less prominent role. This may have been due, in part, to the fact that that particular classroom teacher had a master's degree in special education and had worked previously as a special education teacher.

Examination of student records, interviews, and observational records suggested to us that students with disabilities in the present investigation were representative of students with similar disabilities in schools around the nation. Consistent with previous research on the characteristics of students with disabilities (e.g., Hallahan & Kauffman, 1994), the students with disabilities in the present investigation often exhibited problems with language and literacy; cognitive skills, including prior knowledge; and sensory/physical functioning.

It should be noted that students characterized as mentally handicapped or mentally retarded were not included in these exemplary classrooms and that, in fact, such students are typically less likely to be included in mainstream classes (Hallahan & Kauffman, 1994). Further, students with emotional/behavioral disabilities as a primary classification also were not in evidence, although some emotional response to specific handicapping conditions was sometimes apparent. Such students typically are among the most difficult to mainstream, and surveys of regular class teachers suggest that students with emotional/behavioral problems are the least well tolerated of any handicapping condition (Lloyd, Kauffman, & Kupersmidt, 1990). In a previous study of the mainstreaming of an emotionally disturbed boy in a fifth grade science class (Mastropieri, Scruggs, & Bohs, 1994), it was noted that the boy was characterized as more socially withdrawn than socially aggressive, and, indeed, such characteristics may lend themselves more readily to mainstreaming success (Lloyd et al., 1990).

Overall, then, the students with disabilities in this investigation appeared to be generally representative of many students with disabilities in other schools, with the exception that significant intellectual or behavioral problems were not noted. However, as with the Mastropieri, Scruggs, and Bohs (1994) investigation, it is more difficult to characterize the teachers and schools as generally representative. The district itself was a rapidly growing district in a western metropolitan area, well supported by the community and noted for many innovations in public education. The science programs are nationally recognized and receive many in-state and out-of-state visitors interested in replicating the district model of science education. Similarly, the special education programs are highly regarded throughout the state in which the district is located, and they also engage in educational innovations.

All three classroom teachers promoted student-centered approaches to learning and appeared to take a very personal interest in the welfare of all their students. They all regarded diversity in their classrooms as an asset, rather than a burden, and remained open to new suggestions or ideas for improving their practices. The special education teachers in these schools also appeared very highly skilled. Further, communication between special and regular education teachers was open, continuous, and dynamic, a condition often lacking in schools (Wood, 1993).

In contrast, survey results suggest that many teachers may not tolerate many of the behaviors exhibited by students with disabilities (Kauffman, Lloyd, & McGee, 1989); many teachers are not aware of possible reaching modifications (Salvia & Munson, 1986), and many regular classroom teachers may not have been, through teacher education or in-service programs, well prepared to implement effective mainstreaming strategies (Bender & Ukeje, 1989). Because many university teacher education programs, including those at our own university, do not require course work in special education or mainstreaming, this situation appears unlikely to change in the near future. Further, Good (1987) summarized classroom observation research and concluded that teachers frequently employ fewer *teacher effectiveness* variables (e.g., are less positive, less accepting, and provide less feedback) for lower achieving students. Although some recent progress has been made, survey research in mainstreaming suggests that a large percentage of general education teachers still feel unable or unwilling to accommodate students with disabilities in their classrooms (Wood, 1993). Therefore, although the present investigation uncovered variables that appeared to be meaningfully associated with mainstreaming success, whether or not such variables are generally present in today's schools appears far less likely at present (e.g., Baker & Zigmond, 1990).

Although observations, teacher records, and student reports suggested that students with disabilities were successfully learning, none of the three teachers engaged in systematic, objective assessment of student progress toward specific goals and objectives (e.g., Fuchs, Fuchs, & Fernstrom, 1993). Because this was the case, it is more difficult to state that students were progressing optimally in meeting curriculum objectives, that all objectives were being met, or that students retained acquired concepts over more extended time intervals. Direct, objective measurement may have been helpful in ensuring that all relevant objectives were being met or in determining whether further modifications were warranted. Further, performance assessment techniques (e.g., Baron, 1990), which allow students to demonstrate their understanding of scientific concepts using scientific materials, rather than paper-and-pencil tasks, may have been particularly valid for assessing the progress of students with disabilities, for whom traditional or informal assessment procedures may be less useful. What also is unknown from the present investigation is whether the extent of academic and social learning that occurred in these mainstream contexts was greater or less than that which may have been obtained in special education settings, given that appropriate methods and materials were available in those settings.

Unfortunately, when ongoing, objective measurement of student academic progress has been conducted in regular class settings, students with disabilities, particularly those with learning disabilities, have not always fared well (e.g., Baker & Zigmond, 1990; Fuchs, Fuchs, & Fernstrom, 1993; Marston, 1987–1988; Zigmond & Baker, 1994; Zigmond et al., in press). However, these investigations have examined progress in basic skills areas such as reading fluency and math. On the other hand, many students with disabilities may find themselves able to progress adequately in hands-on science classes in which basic skills functioning is de-emphasized or for which they may obtain peer assistance. For example, a mainstreamed student with learning disabilities in the Zigmond and Baker (1994) study could read the grade-level reading text at a rate of only about 20 words per minute, a rate well below that of other students, and obviously had difficulty participating on grade level reading tasks. However, students with learning disabilities in the present investigation were able to participate in the study of grade-level science content, when less emphasis was placed on reading and writing.

The present investigation provides important evidence regarding how students with disabilities are, or can be, included in science classes. Future research can address the similarity or differences of variables associated with mainstreaming success under other circumstances, the validity of these seven variables in promoting successful mainstreaming, and the degree to which such variables can be implemented in schools that are less successful in accommodating learner diversity.

NOTES

Preparation of this manuscript was funded in part from a cooperative agreement from the U.S. Department of Education, Special Education Programs, No. H023DO010. We offer special thanks to Dr. Tom Hanley, USDOE, Special Education Programs, and the students, teachers, and administrators who worked with us on this project. Although we cannot name these participants specifically, their generous cooperation was nonetheless essential to our project and was greatly appreciated.

[1]In order to protect the anonymity of the students in these classes, dates provide a contact year rather than a calendar year. That is, 11/5/3, refers to November 5th, in the third academic year of contact with this district, which is not necessarily coincident with the third year of the larger funded project. Finally, teachers' years of experience are given as approximate, so that a specific year cannot be identified.

REFERENCES

Abruscato, J. (1992). *Teaching children science* (3rd ed.). Boston: Allyn & Bacon.

Atwood, R. K., & Oldham, B. R. (1985). Teachers' perceptions of mainstreaming in an inquiry-oriented elementary science program. *Science Education, 69,* 619–624.

Baker, J. M., & Zigmond, N. (1990). Are regular education classes equipped to accommodate students with learning disabilities? *Exceptional Children, 56,* 515–526.

Baron, J. B. (1990). Performance assessment: Blurring the edges among assessment, curriculum, and instruction. In A. B. Champagne, B. E. Lovitts, & B. J. Calinger (Eds.), *Assessment in the service of instruction* (pp. 127–148). Washington, DC: American Association for the Advancement of Science.

Bay, M., Staver, J. R., Bryan, T., & Hale, J. B. (1992). Science instruction for the mildly handicapped: Direct instruction versus discovery teaching. *Journal of Research in Science Teaching, 29,* 555–570.

Bender, W. N., & Ukeje, I. C. (1989). Instructional strategies in mainstream classrooms: Prediction of the strategies teachers select. *Remedial and Special Education, 10* (2), 23–30.

Brissie, J. S., Hoover-Demsey, K. V., & Bassler, O. C. (1988). Individual, situational contributors to teacher burnout. *Journal of Educational Research, 82,* 106–112.

Brophy, J., & Good, T. (1986). Teacher behavior and student achievement. In M. C. Wittrock (Ed.), *Handbook of research on teaching* (3rd ed., pp. 328–375). New York: Macmillan.

Carlberg, C.,& Kavale, K. (1980). The efficacy of special versus regular class placement for exceptional children: A meta-analysis. *Journal of Special Education, 14,* 295–309.

Center, Y., Ward, J., Parmenter, T., & Nash, R. (1985). Principals' attitudes toward the integration of disabled children into regular schools. *The Exceptional Child, 32,* 149–161.

Centra, N. H. (1990). *A qualitative study of high school students in a resource program.* Unpublished doctoral dissertation, Syracuse University.

Cook, S., Scruggs, T. E., Mastropieri, M. A., & Casto, G. (1985–1986). Handicapped students as tutors. *Journal of Special Education, 19,* 483–492.

Esler, W. K., Midgett, J., & Bird, R. C. (1977). Elementary science materials and the exceptional child. *Science Education, 61,* 181–184.

Fuchs, D., & Fuchs, L. S. (1988a). Evaluation of the adaptive learning environments model. *Exceptional Children, 55,* 115–127.

Fuchs, D., & Fuchs, L. S. (1988b). Response to Wang and Walberg. *Exceptional Children, 55,* 138–146.

Fuchs, D., & Fuchs, L. S. (1994). Inclusive schools movement and the radicalization of special education reform. *Exceptional Children, 60,* 294–309.

Fuchs, D., Fuchs, L. S., & Fernstrom, D. (1993). A conservative approach to special education reform: Mainstreaming through transenvironmental programming and curriculum-based measurement. *American Educational Research Journal, 30,* 149–177.

Gartner, A., & Lipsky, D. K. (1987). Beyond special education: Toward a quality system for all students. *Harvard Educational Review, 57,* 367–395.

Glang, A., Gersten, R., & Morvant, M. (in press). A directive approach toward the consultation process: A case study. *Learning Disabilities Research & Practice.*

Good, T. L. (1987). Two decades of research on teacher expectations: Findings and future directions. *Journal of Teacher Education, 38* (4), 32–47.

Hadary, D. E., & Cohen, S. H. (1978). *Laboratory science and art for blind, deaf, and emotionally disturbed children: A mainstreaming approach.* Baltimore, MD: University Park Press.

Hallahan, D. P., & Kauffman, J. (1994). *Exceptional children: Introduction to special education* (6th ed.). Boston: Allyn & Bacon.

Hofman, H. H., & Ricker, K. S. (1979). *Science education and the physically handicapped.* Washington, DC: National Science Teachers Association.

Kauffman, J. M. (1993). How we might achieve the radical reform of special education. *Exceptional Children, 60,* 6–16.

Kauffman, J. M., Lloyd, J. W., & McGee, K. A. (1989). Adaptive and maladaptive behavior: Teachers' attitudes and their technical assistance needs. *Journal of Special Education, 23,* 185–200.

Larrivee, B. (1985). *Effective teaching for successful mainstreaming.* New York: Longman.

LeCompte, M. D., & Preissle, J. (1993). *Ethnography and qualitative design in educational research.* New York: Academic Press.

Lewis, R. B., & Doorlag, D. H. (1991). *Teaching special students in the mainstream* (3rd ed.). Columbus, OH: Merrill.

Linn, M. C., Hadary, D., Rosenberg, R., & Haushalter, R. (1979). Science education for the deaf: Comparison of ideal resource and mainstream settings. *Journal of Research in Science Teaching, 10,* 83–90.

Lloyd, J. W., Kauffman, J. M., & Kupersmidt, J. B. (1990). Integration of students with behavior disorders in regular education environments. In K. Gadow (Ed.), *Advances in learning and behavioral disabilities* (Vol. 6, pp. 225–264). Greenwich, CT: JAI.

MacDougall, A., Schnur, R., Berger, C., & Vernon, D. (1981). The use of activity centered science activities to facilitate the mainstreaming of elementary school children with special needs. *Science Education, 65,* 467–475.

Marston, D. (1987–1988). The effectiveness of special education: A time series analysis of reading performance in regular and special education settings. *Journal of Special Education, 21,* 13–26.

Mastropieri,M. A., & Scruggs, T. E. (1987). *Effective instruction for special education.* Boston: College Hill.

Mastropieri, M. A., & Scruggs, T. E. (1989). Constructing more meaningful relationships: Mnemonic instruction for special populations. *Educational Psychology Review, 1,* 83–111.

Mastropieri, M. A., & Scruggs, T. E. (1992). Science and students with disabilities. *Review of Educational Research, 62,* 377–411.

Mastropieri, M. A., & Scruggs, T. E. (1994a). *Effective instruction for special education* (2nd ed.). Austin, TX: Pro-Ed.

Mastropieri, M. A., & Scruggs, T. E. (1994b). *A practical guide for teaching science to students with special needs in inclusive settings.* Austin, TX: Pro-Ed.

Mastropieri, M. A., & Scruggs, T. E. (1994c). Text-based versus activities-oriented science curriculum: Implications for students with disabilities. *Remedial and Special Education, 15,* 72–85.

Mastropieri, M. A., & Scruggs, T. E. (in press). Trends in science education: Implications for special education. In C. Warger & M. Pugach (Eds.), *What's worth knowing: How curriculum trends will affect special education.* New York: Teachers College Press.

Mastropieri, M. A., Scruggs, T. E., & Bohs, K. (1994). Mainstreaming an emotionally handicapped student in science: A qualitative investigation. In T. E. Scruggs & M. A. Mastropieri (Eds.), *Advances in learning and behavioral disabilities* (Vol. 8, pp. 131–146). Greenwich, CT: JAI.

Morocco, C. C., Dalton, B., & Tivnan, T. (1990). *Interim report: Problem solving science project.* Newton, MA: Education Development Center.

Natale, J. A. (1993). Why teachers leave. *Executive Educator, 15*(7), 14–18.

Organisation for Economic Co-Operation and Development. (1985). *Educational reforms in Italy.* Washington, DC: Author.

Parmar, R. S., & Cawley, J. F. (1993). Analysis of science textbook recommendations provided for students with disabilities. *Exceptional Children, 59,* 518–531.

Patton, J. R. (1993). Individualizing for science and social studies. In J. Wood (Ed.), *Mainstreaming: A practical approach for teachers* (2nd ed., pp. 301–351). Columbus, OH: Merrill.

Perret-Clermont, A. N. (1980). *Social interaction and cognitive development in children.* New York: Academic Press.

Putnam, J. P., Rynders, J. E., Johnson, R. T., & Johnson, D. W. (1989). Collaborative skill instruction for promoting positive interactions between mentally handicapped and nonhandicapped children. *Exceptional Children, 55,* 550–557.

Reynolds, M. C., Wang, M. C., & Walberg, H. J. (1987). The necessary restructuring of special and general education. *Exceptional Children, 53,* 391–398.

Rosenshine, B., & Stevens, R. (1986). Teaching functions. In M. C. Wittrock (Ed.), *Handbook of research on teaching* (3rd ed., pp. 376–391). New York: Macmillan.

Rutherford, F. J., & Ahlgren, A. (1990). *Science for all Americans.* New York: Oxford University Press.

Salvia, J., & Munson, S. (1986). Attitudes of regular education teachers toward mainstreaming mildly handicapped students. In C. J. Meisel (Ed.), *Mainstreaming handicapped children: Outcomes, controversies, and new directions* (pp. 111–128). Hillsdale, NJ: Erlbaum.

Scruggs, T. E. (1993). Special education and the problems of schooling. *Educational Theory, 43,* 433–447.

Scruggs, T. E., & Mastropieri, M. A. (1992). Current approaches to science education: Implications for mainstream instruction of students with disabilities. *Remedial and Special Education, 14* (1), 15–24.

Scruggs, T. E., & Mastropieri, M. A. (in press-a). The construction of scientific knowledge by students with mild disabilities. *Journal of Special Education.*

Scruggs, T. E., & Mastropieri, M. A. (in press-b). Qualitative research methodology in the study of learning and behavioral disabilities: An analysis of recent research. In T. E. Scruggs & M. A. Mastropieri (Eds.), *Advances in learning and behavioral disabilities* (Vol. 9). Greenwich, CT: JAI.

Scruggs, T. E., Mastropieri, M. A., Bakken, J. P., & Brigham, F. J. (1993). Reading versus doing: The relative effects of textbook-based and inquiry-oriented approaches to science learning in special education classrooms. *Journal of Special Education, 27,* 1–15.

Scruggs, T. E., Mastropieri, M. A., Levin, J. R., & Gaffney, J. S. (1985). Facilitating the acquisition of science facts in learning disabled students. *American Educational Research Journal, 22,* 575–586.

Scruggs, T. E., Mastropieri, M. A., & Sullivan, G. S. (1994). Promoting relational thinking skills: Elaborative interrogation for mildly handicapped students. *Exceptional Children, 60,* 450–457.

Singer, J. D., & Butler, J. A. (1987). The Education for All Handicapped Children Act: Schools as agents of social reform. *Harvard Educational Review, 57,* 125–152.

Skrtic, T. (1991). *Behind special education.* Denver: Love.

Wang, M. C., & Walberg, H. J. (1988). Four fallacies of segregationism. *Exceptional Children, 55,* 128–137.

Wood, J. (1993). *Mainstreaming: A practical approach for teachers* (2nd ed.). Columbus, OH: Merrill.

Yin, R. K. (1989). *Case study research: Design and methods.* Newbury Park, CA: Sage.

Zigmond, N., & Baker, J. M. (1994). Is the mainstream a more appropriate educational setting for Randy? A case study of one student with learning disabilities. *Learning Disabilities Research & Practice, 9,* 108–117.

Zigmond, N., Jenkins, J., Fuchs, L., Deno, S., Fuchs, D., Baker, J. N., Jenkins, L., & Coutinho, M. (in press). Special education in restructured schools: Findings from three multi-year studies. *Phi Delta Kappan.*

Manuscript received November 1, 1993
Revision received June 13, 1994
Accepted June 13, 1994

FACTUAL QUESTIONS

1. What was the overall purpose of the investigation?
2. Who were the participants?
3. What were the characteristics of the curriculum?
4. What were the backgrounds of the researchers? What previous work had they conducted that supports the current investigation?
5. How were the data collected?
6. How and when did the researchers analyze the data?
7. What was the first consideration of the researchers? What did they conclude?
8. There were seven meaningful variables. What were they, and what was the general conclusion made for each variable?
9. The authors indicated that the results of the investigation can be placed within a rational context and possess a certain type of generalization. What was the context and the type of generalization?
10. What type of qualitative design was used?

DISCUSSION QUESTIONS

1. Why do curriculum characteristics play an important role in mainstreaming success?
2. Why do you think students with disabilities have not been typically involved in studies in science education?
3. Why do you think the researchers selected the school district acknowledged for excellence in science education? What does this do to external validity claims, if anything?
4. What do you think are some critical aspects of the curriculum used in the classrooms? Why?
5. Could an interview only study have attained the same type of information or were observations necessary?
6. How did the authors attempt to address reliability and validity of their data collection? Do you think what they did was adequate?

7. Are the examples provided as support for conclusions adequate? Do they help you come to the same conclusions?
8. Did the researchers fit their results within the framework of past research and/or theories?
9. Could there have been a problem with reactivity on the part of the teachers? What could have been tried to avoid this?
10. Did the investigation provide evidence of a cause-and-effect relationship between mainstreaming in a science class and improved academic ability in science? Is this a problem?

QUALITATIVE RESEARCH EXAMINATION

Circle the number corresponding to the extent to which the researcher(s) demonstrated the five analysis issues.

1 = High extent	2 = Moderate extent	3 = Small extent
4 = Minimal extent	5 = Nonexistent	NA = Not applicable for this design

Expectations

a. a priori	**1**	**2**	**3**	**4**	**5**	**NA**
b. emerging	**1**	**2**	**3**	**4**	**5**	**NA**

Justification ____

____.

Process of Analysis	**1**	**2**	**3**	**4**	**5**	**NA**

Justification ____

____.

Conceptual Leverage

a. low level	**1**	**2**	**3**	**4**	**5**	**NA**
b. high level	**1**	**2**	**3**	**4**	**5**	**NA**

Justification ____

____.

Generalizability	**1**	**2**	**3**	**4**	**5**	**NA**

Justification ____

____.

Abstract: Write a one-page abstract summarizing the overall conclusions of the authors and whether you feel the authors' conclusions are valid based on the analysis you conducted on the investigation.

PART FIVE

SINGLE-CASE RESEARCH METHODS

CHAPTER 10 **WITHDRAWAL AND ASSOCIATED DESIGNS**

CHAPTER 11 **MULTIPLE-BASELINE DESIGNS**

CHAPTER 12 **ADDITIONAL SINGLE-CASE DESIGNS**

CHAPTER 10

WITHDRAWAL AND ASSOCIATED DESIGNS

OBJECTIVES

After studying this chapter you should be able to:

1. Explain how single-case methods are similar to and different than quantitative and qualitative research methods.
2. Explain what a baseline is and why it is used.
3. Explain what an A-B design is.
4. Explain what a withdrawal (A-B-A) design is.
5. Explain what an A-B-A-B design is.
6. Explain what a B-A-B design is.
7. Explain what an A-B-C-B design is.
8. Describe internal validity issues surrounding the use of these designs.
9. Describe external validity issues surrounding the use of these designs.
10. Describe when one would choose a particular design.
11. Critique a research article containing an A-B-BC design.

OVERVIEW

Throughout this chapter, you will learn about several types of single-case designs. Single-case designs may be considered a combination of quantitative and qualitative research designs. (See Table 10.1 for a summary of the similarities and differences between single-case and quantitative research methods and Table 10.2 for a summary of the similarities and differences between single-case and qualitative research methods.) Recall from the previous chapter that there are five features of qualitative research—the natural setting is the direct source of data and the researcher is the key measurement instrument, the research is descriptive, the concern is on the process rather than with outcomes or products, the data tend to be analyzed inductively, and the meaning of the data is of essential concern (Bogdan & Biklen, 1992). Single-case research is similar in three aspects. First, single-case researchers who operate in the applied arena usually conduct research in natural settings and the researcher/observer is the key measurement instrument. Second, single-case researchers are concerned with the "process" of skill acquisition versus a final outcome of an intervention. Finally, single-case researchers do not work off of hypotheses as do quantitative researchers. Instead, single-case researchers ask research questions and consider the process to be inductive in nature. Additionally, single-case designs develop during the investigation; thus, single-case designs

TABLE 10.1 Similarities and Differences between Single-Case and Quantitative Research Methods

SINGLE-CASE RESEARCH	QUANTITATIVE RESEARCH
Primary purpose is to determine cause-and-effect relationships	*Primary purpose is to determine cause-and-effect relationships*
Hypotheses are developed during the investigation; questions govern the purpose of the investigation; theories are developed inductively	Precise hypothesis is stated before the start of the investigation; theories govern the purpose of the investigation in a deductive manner
The independent variable is controlled and manipulated	*The independent variable is controlled and manipulated*
Objective collection of data is a requirement	*Objective collection of data is a requirement*
Research design is flexible and develops throughout the investigation	Research design is specified before the start of the investigation
Data are represented and summarized in numerical or graphical form	*Data are represented and summarized in numerical form*
Reliability and validity are determined through multiple sources of information (interobserver agreement)	Reliability and validity are determined through statistical and logical methods
Samples are purposefully selected or single cases are studied	Samples are selected to represent the population
Study of behavior is usually in the natural setting	Study of behavior is in the natural or artificial setting
Use of design controls for threats to internal validity	*Use of design or statistical analyses controls for threats to internal validity*
Use of similar cases to determine the generalizability of findings (logical generalization)	Use of inferential statistical procedures to demonstrate external validity (specifically, population validity)
Rely on the researcher to control for procedural bias	Rely on research design and data gathering instruments to control for procedural bias
Phenomena are broken down or simplified for study	*Phenomena are broken down or simplified for study*
Conclusions are tentative and subjected to ongoing examination (replications)	Conclusions are stated with a predetermined degree of certainty (i.e., α level)

Note: Descriptions in *italics* indicate similarities or commonalities between the methodologies.

are flexible. This attribute is similar to qualitative designs in that the specific design is not predetermined; a research design develops throughout the investigation.

One major difference between the single-case and qualitative methodologies is that single-case researchers attempt to minimize subjectivity in their collection of data (see Chapter 3 for interobserver agreement methods) and the data are quantified. In other words, single-case researchers report their data in numerical form. However, there is a rich history of single-case researchers using descriptive analyses in the formulation of research questions and in the development of hypotheses for further study (see Iwata, Vollmer, & Zarcone, 1990, for examples of one use for such analyses). A second major difference is that most single-case researchers try to avoid making inferences of internal cognitive processes and report on observable and measurable behaviors. Thus, meaning for most single-case re-

TABLE 10.2 Similarities and Differences between Single-Case and Qualitative Research Methods

SINGLE-CASE RESEARCH	QUALITATIVE RESEARCH
Primary purpose is to determine cause-and-effect relationships	Primary purpose is to describe ongoing processes
Hypotheses are developed during the investigation; questions govern the purpose of the investigation; theories are developed inductively	*Hypotheses are developed during the investigation; questions govern the purpose of the investigation; theories are developed inductively*
The independent variable is controlled and manipulated	There is no specific independent variable; the concern is to study naturally occurring phenomena without interference
Objective collection of data is a requirement	Objective collection of data is not a requirement; data collectors may interact with the participants
Research design is flexible and develops throughout the investigation	*Research design is flexible and develops throughout the investigation*
Data are represented and summarized in numerical or graphical form	Data are represented and summarized in narrative or verbal forms.
Reliability and validity determined through multiple sources of information (interobserver agreement)	*Reliability and validity determined through multiple sources of information (triangulation)*
Samples are purposefully selected or single cases are studied	*Samples are purposefully selected or single cases are studied*
Study of behavior is usually in the natural setting	*Study of behavior is in the natural setting*
Use of design controls for threats to internal validity	Use of logical analyses controls or accounts for alternative explanations
Use of similar cases to determine the generalizability of findings (logical generalization)	*Use of similar cases to determine the generalizability of findings (logical generalization) if at all*
Rely on the researcher to control for procedural bias	*Rely on the researcher to come to terms with procedural bias*
Phenomena are broken down or simplified for study	Phenomena are studied holistically, as a complex system
Conclusions are tentative and subjected to ongoing examination (replications)	*Conclusions are tentative and subjected to ongoing examination*

Note: Descriptions in *italics* indicate similarities or commonalities between the methodologies.

searchers is on the interaction of observed environmental variables (both before and after the observed behavior) and the individual.

Single-case research is also similar to other quantitative research methods in that the data are quantified and researchers attempt to remain objective during data collection. However, single-case designs have an advantage over the quantitative group designs previously discussed; that is, single-case designs do not require several participants (see Table 10.1). Single-case designs require at least one participant. However, there have been investigations involving thousands and even millions of participants in single-case experiments (Kazdin, 1982). Thus, the flexibility of single-case designs is a positive attribute. This flexibility allows for the use of single-case designs in applied settings such as the classroom or clinic (Tripodi, 1994). In fact, the use of single-case experiments has increased over a period of years and continues to the present.

Single-case designs are considered experimental since they can control for threats to internal validity and can be readily applied in settings in which group designs are difficult to implement. Thus, they have advantages over other methodologies. Teachers and practitioners should be clear about how to implement single-case designs in their classrooms/settings when they wish to determine the effects of instruction or management techniques. Thus, single-case designs are designs that can be easily incorporated into ongoing activities in the form of *action research* (see Chapter 15). That is, teachers and practitioners can begin to generate their own data to guide their teaching/intervention methods rather than solely relying on the research community to supply them with answers. In a sense, single-case designs allow individuals to become scientists/practitioners. Additionally, as with other designs, critical consumers of research must be able to understand what researchers do and why before they can read, understand, and apply what is read from the research literature. The designs discussed in this chapter include the A-B, A-B-A, A-B-A-B, B-A-B, and A-B-C-B designs. (*Note:* Withdrawal design and A-B-A design are used interchangeably.)

This chapter focuses on several issues surrounding the withdrawal and associated designs. First, graphing issues are highlighted. Since a visual analysis is critical in withdrawal and associated designs, a high skill level in interpreting graphs is critical. Second, the withdrawal design is described along with the following associated designs: A-B, A-B-A-B, B-A-B, and A-B-C-B designs. The methods of analyzing the data follow the discussion of the different designs. Finally, research examples highlighting the different designs are presented throughout the chapter and an illustrative investigation is included at the end of the chapter for critique. (*Note:* You should attempt to analyze the graphs presented from the research examples.)

WHAT ARE GRAPHING METHODS IN WITHDRAWAL DESIGNS?

Since this is the introductory chapter in single-case methodology, it is appropriate to discuss briefly the information contained in a graph. Single-case researchers primarily use graphs to demonstrate treatment effects. Thus, understanding how graphs are constructed is critical. Figure 10.1 provides a line graph. The line graph is the most commonly used system to display data. The vertical axis (also called the *y* axis, or ordinate) provides a brief description of the dependent measure. The dependent measure is an indication of how we measured the dependent variable. For example, if we were teaching reading, reading comprehension may be the dependent variable. Percentage of questions answered correctly on a passage read would be the dependent measure. If you are studying this book for class, the dependent variable is probably knowledge gained on research methods. The dependent measure would possibly be scores on tests over the material read.

The horizontal axis (also called the *x* axis, or abscissa) indicates some measure of time. For example, sessions, days, months, or trials can be measures of time passed. Sessions is the most frequently used time measure in single-case research. A rule of thumb to use when constructing a graph is to use a ratio of the vertical to the horizontal axis of 1/1.6 to 1/2.2 (Tufte, 1983). In other words, if the horizontal axis is 4 inches in length, the vertical axis should be somewhere between 1.8 to 2.52 inches in length. According to Tufte, the horizontal axis should be the focus, not the vertical axis. If the vertical axis is as long or longer than the horizontal one, the attention of the reader may be focused on the wrong axis. Another reason for the ratios is that one should visually represent the data in such a manner that the data have good spacing and do not appear to be crowded (Tawney & Gast, 1984).

Located just above the graph are condition identifications. For example, the first condition may be "baseline" (described later) followed by the intervention. The intervention is called the independent variable. In your research methods class, the instruction you receive is the independent variable. Conditions are separated by condition lines. These lines indicate when the condition has changed. Notice on the figure that the data points are not connected across the condition

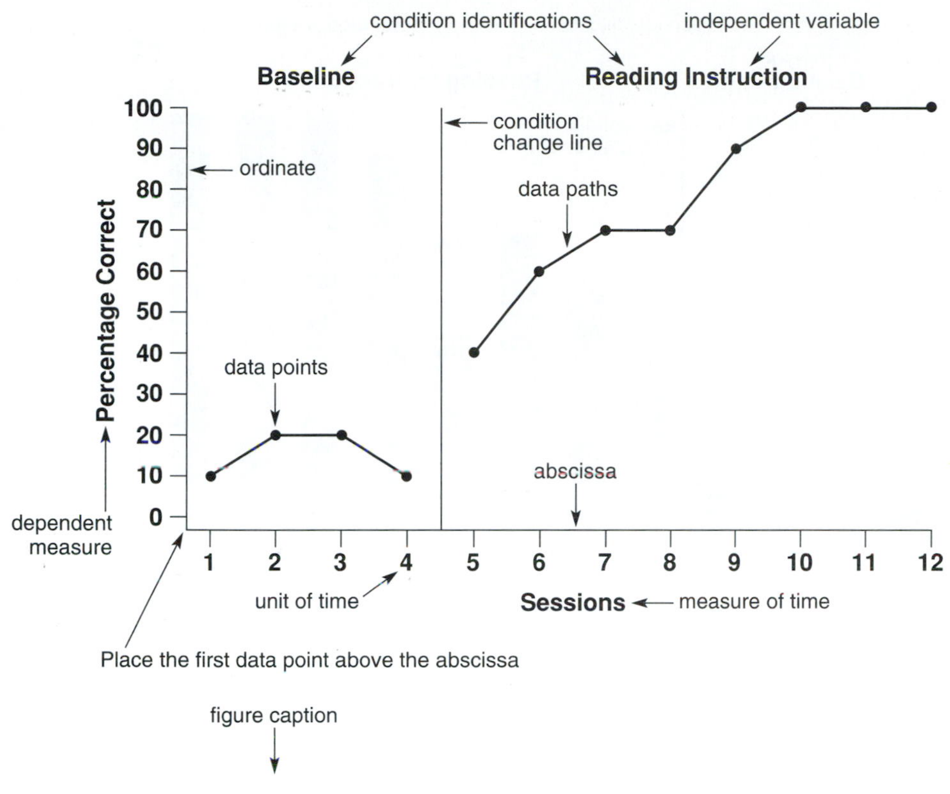

FIGURE 10.1 The percentage of questions answered correctly across baseline and reading instruction conditions.

lines. The round points on the graph are the data points. These are placed on the graph by finding the time at which the data point was collected (such as Session 5) and the results of the measure (such as 50%). Data points are connected by data paths. Data paths help with the visual analysis of the data; trends are much easier to see if the points are connected. Finally, there is usually a figure caption located under the graph. The figure caption is a summary of the figure and oftentimes lists the dependent measure and the independent variable.

Another frequently used graph is the bar graph, or histogram. Figure 10.2 shows a bar graph with the same data as shown in Figure 10.1. The method of displaying the data is different across the two graphs.

WHAT ARE WITHDRAWAL AND ASSOCIATED DESIGNS?

A-B Design

When understanding single-case designs, one must know the meaning of symbols. In single-case designs, "A" refers to baseline. A baseline is the repeated measurement of a behavior under natural conditions. The baseline indicates the level at which the participant performs a behavior without the intervention. The baseline is of critical importance when considering single-case designs since it is the best estimate of what would have occurred if the intervention were not applied. The baseline, then, provides a comparison to the intervention condition ("B"). The "B," or intervention condition, is the time that the independent variable is in

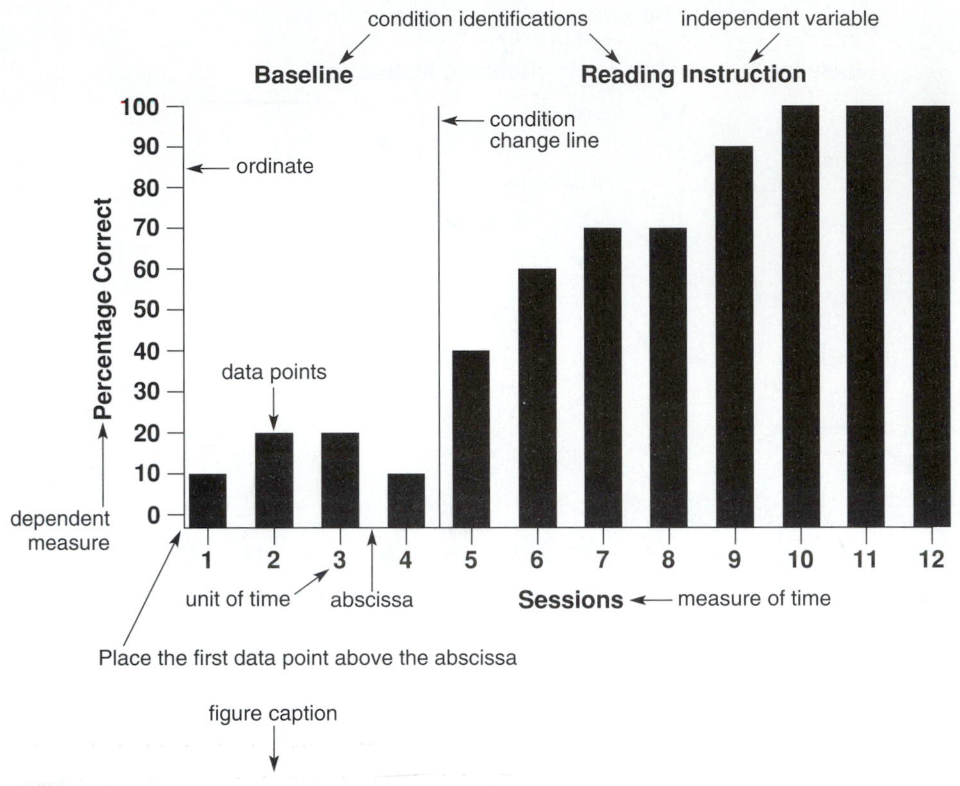

FIGURE 10.2 The percentage of questions answered correctly across baseline and reading instruction conditions.

effect. Typically, the "B" condition is used in isolation (Tawney & Gast, 1984). In other words, a skill is usually taught and measured over a period of time. However, a "B" design is especially problematic since it is not possible to indicate where the participant was before the intervention. In order to solve for this difficulty, several assessments could be provided before the intervention to determine where the participants are at present. Also, it is important to make sure that participants are not improving on their own since the intervention may not be warranted. Therefore, the A-B design combines the baseline or preintervention measurements with a "B" condition to determine the effectiveness of an intervention.

Figure 10.3 shows an A-B design. As can be seen, several assessments occur before the intervention and several more occur during the intervention. Looking at the data in Figure 10.3, one can see that the intervention seemed to be effective. However, there is a major problem with A-B designs. The problem with this type of design is that it fails to control for several threats to internal validity. For example, history is a critical concern since something may have occurred during the intervention that improved the participant's performance. For this reason, the A-B design is considered to be a quasi-experimental design (Campbell & Stanley, 1963) in that the design does not permit a complete examination of the effects of the independent variable on the dependent variable while ruling out the effects of extraneous variables. Thus, Risley and Wolf (1972) called for an elaboration of the A-B design to improve the ability of the design to control or

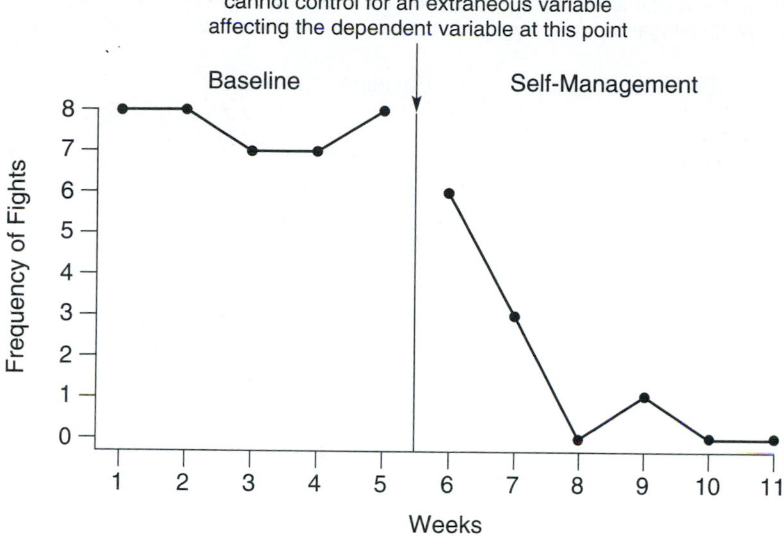

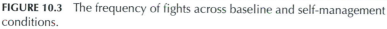

FIGURE 10.3 The frequency of fights across baseline and self-management conditions.

to rule out the effects of extraneous variables or threats to the internal validity of the investigation.

Withdrawal Design

The elaboration of the A-B design that Risley and Wolf (1972) called for was the withdrawal (A-B-A) design. The A-B-A design has been called a withdrawal design and a reversal design (Barlow & Hersen, 1984). However, technically, it is probably more appropriate to label the design a withdrawal rather than a reversal (i.e., the reversal design may signify an active attempt on the part of the researcher to change the level of participant behavior during the "B" condition such as reinforcing the behavior opposite of the desired one rather than simply removing the intervention [Barlow & Hersen, 1984]; see Chapter 12 for a discussion of how a reversal design can be combined with a changing criterion design to increase experimental control).

The withdrawal design is a methodologically powerful tool in allowing for the control of threats to internal validity (Kazdin, 1982). In the withdrawal design, the baseline is the first condition, followed by the intervention, and ends on a return to baseline. The logic behind the withdrawal design is that if a behavior changed during the "B" condition and then returned to the first baseline level during the second baseline condition, the intervention would have been shown to be effective. In this way, a functional relationship between the intervention and the behavior can be shown. Figure 10.4 provides data indicating a functional relationship using a withdrawal design; remember that a functional relationship means that when a change is produced (intervention) it is reliably followed by changes in the dependent variable. Of course, if the behavior did not return to baseline levels on the implementation of the second baseline, a functional relationship would not have been demonstrated.

If data were gathered as shown in Figure 10.4, the threats to internal validity would be at a minimum because it is unlikely that something occurred at the precise time of the presentation of the intervention to cause an increase in the behavior and at the precise instance of the removal of the intervention to cause a decrease in the behavior.

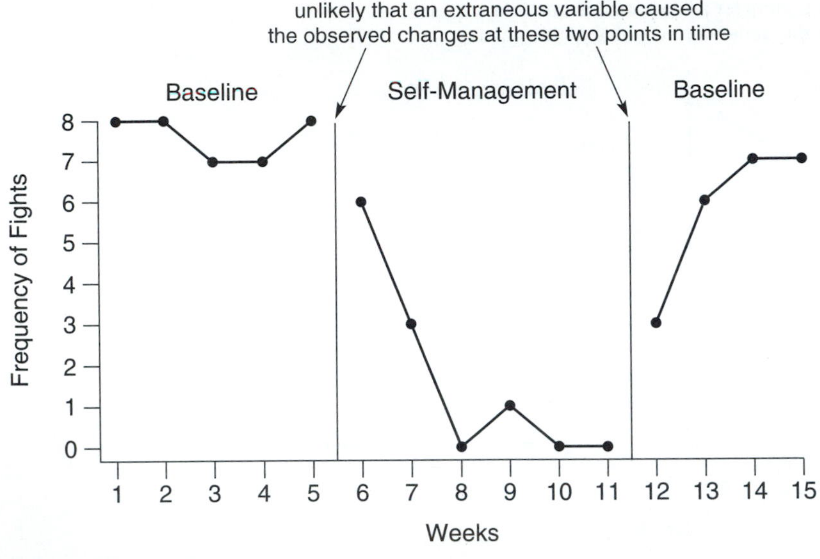

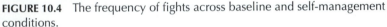

FIGURE 10.4 The frequency of fights across baseline and self-management conditions.

However, according to Tawney and Gast (1984), the introduction and withdrawal of the intervention may coincide with natural cyclical variations of the dependent variable. This possibility is probably remote and can be controlled by changing the length of time a participant is in the "B" condition and/or the second "A" condition.

The withdrawal design can be used to test the effects of interventions aimed at increasing or decreasing behaviors. As can be seen, the withdrawal design has a great deal of flexibility over a group design in that a smaller number of participants are required, ongoing data collection is involved, and the design can be used readily in applied settings. However, the withdrawal design has a serious weakness with regard to the ethicality of leaving participants in the "A" condition. It is unlikely that researchers would be allowed to end the study without some final improvement shown. Thus, an extension of the withdrawal design is frequently applied.

A-B-A-B Design

The A-B-A-B design is similar to the withdrawal design in that the first three conditions (i.e., A-B-A) refer to the same activities on the part of the researcher. In fact, the A-B-A-B design may be called a withdrawal design by researchers. The difference is the final "B" condition in the A-B-A-B design. Researchers in this design end with an intervention rather than ending with a withdrawal of treatment. The advantage of doing this is evident—the ethical problem of leaving the participant(s) without an intervention is avoided. Figure 10.5 shows data for an A-B-A-B design. Again, as in Figure 10.4, a functional relationship between the intervention and the behavior is demonstrated.

B-A-B Design

One potential problem with the withdrawal and A-B-A-B designs is that the initial sessions of data collection occur during a time when no intervention is present. There may be times when a participant's behavior is so severe that researchers cannot wait until enough data have been gathered to complete a baseline (Kazdin, 1982). Additionally, a B-A-B design may be utilized if there is an obvious lack of behavior since the participant

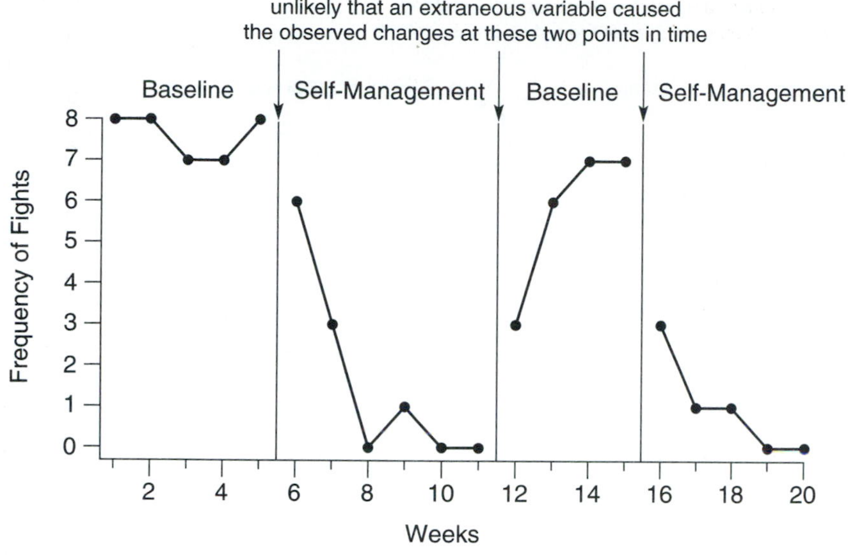

FIGURE 10.5 The frequency of fights across baseline and self-management conditions.

may have never exhibited the behavior in the past and, thus, a preintervention baseline would be essentially obvious and serve no useful purpose (Kazdin, 1982). Finally, a B-A-B design may be used in applied situations where an intervention is already ongoing and researchers wish to establish a functional relationship between the intervention and the dependent variable.

The B-A-B design has been used by several researchers with much success. As with the previous designs discussed, the "B" condition refers to an intervention and the "A" condition refers to a removal of the intervention. Figure 10.6 provides data for a B-A-B design.

A-B-C-B Design

The A-B-C-B design is a further modification of the withdrawal design. The "A" and "B" symbols are the same as in the previous designs. The "C" symbol is an addition. The "C" in this design refers to an additional intervention (i.e., one that is a variation of the first intervention in the "B" condition). In the first two conditions, the baseline and intervention data are collected. During the "C" condition, the intervention is changed to allow for the control of extra attention a participant may have received during the "B" condition. For example, if a researcher were testing the effects of contingent reinforcement (i.e., reinforcement that is applied only when a participant responds in a certain manner), a control for the attention may be warranted. One could safely argue that the contingent reinforcement may not be responsible for the measured effects but the attention received via the contingent reinforcement was. An analogous example to this problem is seen in drug studies in which there is a placebo concern. Was the drug responsible for the measured effects, or were the effects due to the reception of a pill and the expectation of results? Thus, the "C" condition serves as a type of placebo. In the example of contingent reinforcement ("B" condition), the "C" condition could be noncontingent reinforcement (i.e., reinforcement that is applied regardless of how the participant responds). Thus, if data are gathered as shown in Figure 10.7, a conclusion can be made that contingent praise is critical for improved performance as compared to mere increases in praise provided to the student.

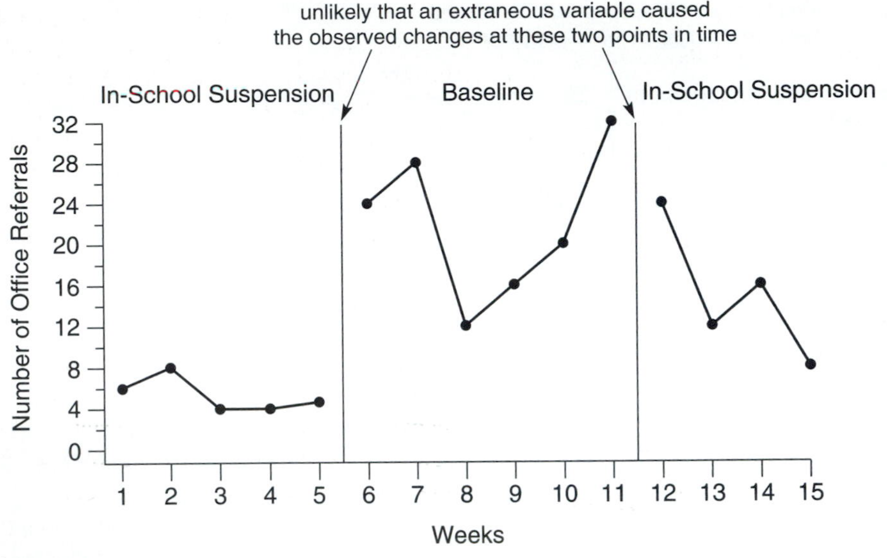

FIGURE 10.6 The number of office referrals across in-school suspension and baseline conditions.

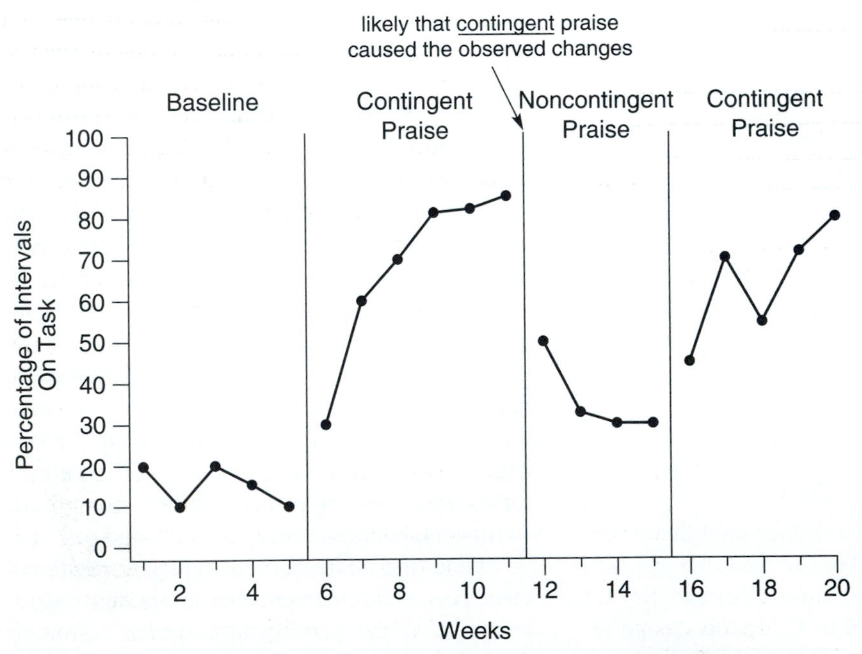

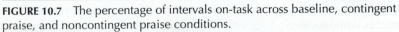

FIGURE 10.7 The percentage of intervals on-task across baseline, contingent praise, and noncontingent praise conditions.

Analysis of Data

Possibly the most important part of understanding withdrawal and associated designs is to understand how to analyze the data. The design, data, and presentation of those data help control for threats to the internal validity of the investigation. Withdrawal designs present data in such a manner that a visual analysis of the data can help the critical research consumer determine whether these threats are present. In order to understand how to analyze the data of withdrawal and associated designs, it is critical to understand appropriate ways of displaying the data. (*Note:* There are advanced statistical techniques that can be used to aid in the analysis of data; however, visual inspection is the primary method of analyzing data in withdrawal and associated designs. A description of the use of statistics is beyond the scope of this text; however, the reader is encouraged to refer to Barlow and Hersen (1984) or Kazdin (1982) for information on the issue.) Additionally, two critical concerns are present when analyzing the data—one must consider the internal validity and the external validity of the investigation.

Internal Validity. When assessing the internal validity of the withdrawal and associated designs, several concerns must be taken into consideration. These concerns involve the condition length (including the trend of the data), changing one variable at a time, the level and rapidity of change, and whether the behavior returns to baseline levels. Table 10.3 summarizes the major threats to internal validity of the designs discussed in this chapter.

Condition Length. The condition length refers to how long a condition is in effect. The condition length is essentially the number of data points gathered during a condition. This number will depend on a critical factor called variability. In general, researchers should see at least three stable data points or three data points moving in a counter therapeutic direction (i.e., movement in the opposite direction of what is ultimately desired). Three is the minimum number of data points needed to indicate a trend. Thus, if researchers were to have three stable data points at the start of baseline, three data points would be all that is required. However, the more variability in the data or if the data are moving in the ultimate desired direction, the more data points needed. As shown in Figure 10.8(a), the data are relatively stable. There are three data points all within a narrow range. Figure 10.8(b) shows data moving in a countertherapeutic direction, which would indicate that the condition length is suitable. Figure 10.8(c) demonstrates how variable data could lengthen the condition. At the most, there are two data points moving in a countertherapeutic direction. However, the requirement is a minimum of three data points; thus, researchers must stay in the condition for a longer period of time. Figure 10.8(d) shows data moving in a therapeutic direction. If the condition was ended and intervention started, a conclusion as to the effects of the intervention could not be made.

Of course, in the applied world, it may be difficult to achieve three stable data points or three data points moving in a countertherapeutic trend. There may be practical problems such as a need to get on with the intervention due to a shortage of time or an ethical problem such as dangerous behavior present. When reading and analyzing a study, critical research consumers must always be aware of the difficulties associated with applied research. The ultimate decision as to whether or not the lack of stability in the data damages the integrity of the study is a decision that must ultimately rest with critical research consumers. They must decide if the researchers took the lack of stability into consideration when making claims and conclusions based on the data.

Change One Variable at a Time. One of the most critical rules in single-case research is to change only one variable at a time when moving from one condition to the other. For example, suppose that a researcher wanted to measure the effects of a study strategy for high school students. The researcher collects several data points and then introduces the students to the study strategy. After students learn how to use the strategy, the researcher removes

TABLE 10.3 Threats to Internal Validity for Each of the Withdrawal and Associated Designs

RESEARCH DESIGN THREAT	A-B DESIGN	A-B-A DESIGN	A-B-A-B DESIGN	B-A-B DESIGN	A-B-C-B DESIGN
1. Maturation	Possible concern	Controlled	Controlled	Controlled	Controlled
2. Selection	Not applicable	Not applicable	Not applicable	Not applicable	Not applicable
3. Selection by maturation interaction	Not applicable	Not applicable	Not applicable	Not applicable	Not applicable
4. Statistical regression	Possible concern	Controlled	Controlled	Controlled	Controlled
5. Mortality	Controlled	Controlled	Controlled	Controlled	Controlled
6. Instrumentation	Controlled	Controlled	Controlled	Controlled	Controlled
7. Testing	Controlled	Controlled	Controlled	Controlled	Controlled
8. History	Possible Concern	Controlled	Controlled	Controlled	Controlled
9. Resentful demoralization of the control group	Not applicable	Not applicable	Not applicable	Not applicable	Not applicable
10. Diffusion of treatment	Not applicable	Controlled	Controlled	Controlled	Controlled
11. Compensatory rivalry by the control group	Not applicable	Not applicable	Not applicable	Not applicable	Not applicable
12. Compensatory equalization	Not applicable	Not applicable	Not applicable	Not applicable	Not applicable

Note: This table is meant only as a general guideline. Decisions with regard to threats to internal validity must be made after the specifics of an investigation are known and understood. Thus, interpretations of internal validity threats must be made on a study-by-study basis.

the intervention and requests that the students go back to their old ways of studying. In this case, the researcher is studying the effects of an intervention package (i.e., reading and note-taking strategies) against no intervention. The researcher is clearly using a withdrawal design. The researcher has also changed one variable at a time—present the intervention then remove the intervention. This example does not pose any problems. An assessment of the intervention package can be made.

Now suppose that the researcher wanted to continue this line of research and decided to assess the combination of both procedures—reading strategies, or "B," and note-taking strategies, or "C," compared to reading strategies ("B") in isolation. First, a baseline is conducted followed by the intervention package (now referred to as "BC" signifying the two procedures). After the "BC" condition, a return to baseline is conducted. Next, the researcher implements the reading strategy ("B") in isolation. Essentially, the researcher has developed an A-BC-A-B design. The "B" condition provides us with some information. Unfortunately, the only thing the researcher can conclude in this experiment is that the "BC" condition together was or was not effective (depending on the data). Note, the "BC" condition is surrounded by "A" conditions. Thus, this is the only comparison that can be made. The "B" condition is not surrounded by any-

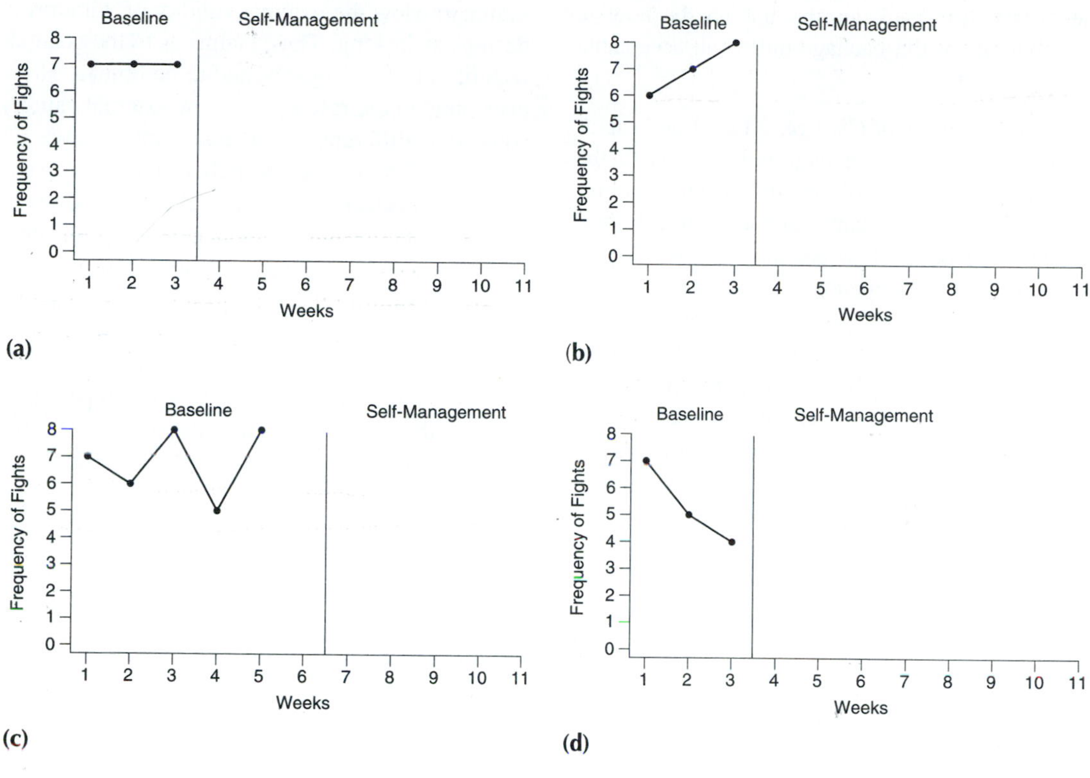

FIGURE 10.8 (a) Stable baseline; may begin instruction. (b) Data moving in a counter-therapeutic direction; may begin instruction. (c) Variable data; should not begin instruction. (d) Data moving in therapeutic direction; should not begin instruction.

thing; essentially what the researcher has is an A-B design, with previous exposure to the treatment package confounding any conclusions. The second "A" condition is surrounded by the "BC" and "B" conditions, which is meaningless. Thus, the researcher put a great deal of time and effort into the study and ended up not answering the research question.

If the researcher wished to answer the question as to the contributions of each component of the intervention package as compared to reading strategies in isolation, a variation of the withdrawal design would be required. Pay particular attention to the following design and notice how only one variable is changed—A-BC-A-BC-B-BC. Looking at the first example, the effects of the "BC" condition can be analyzed since it is surrounded by the "A" conditions. The effects of the "B" condition can be analyzed as to its contribution to the packet since it is surrounded by the "BC" conditions. Notice that the A-BC-B portion of the design does not provide the researcher with any meaningful information since two variables were changed from the second "A" and "BC" conditions to the "B" condition.

Thus, when analyzing a withdrawal design or many of its variants, it is critical to determine if only one variable has been changed at a time. If this is not the case, the researcher's conclusions are most likely erroneous. Finally, be aware that the question asked by the researcher is of critical concern. If the question only deals with the intervention package, the conclusion must be based on only the intervention package and not on the relative contributions of the package unless an acceptable design is used.

Level and Rapidity of Change. Level and rapidity of change refers to the magnitude with which the data change at the time of the implementation or removal of the independent variable. Figure 10.9(a) indicates that the baseline has stability. Upon implementation of the independent variable, the participant's level of fighting does not change for a period of four sessions. This is not a great demonstration of experimental control. If the independent variable were effective, one would assume that the participant's behavior would change in a more timely fashion. Of course, the independent variable may have been effective but not of sufficient strength to cause an immediate change. The behavior may have been resistant to change as well. Whatever the explanation, the demonstration of experimental control is seriously weakened. Figure 10.9(b) indicates that there was a change in the dependent variable, but the initial change was of small magnitude. Figure 10.9(c) indicates that there was a large magnitude change when the independent variable was implemented. This demonstration is much stronger than the other two. We would be more inclined to accept an argument of the effectiveness of the independent variable in this case than in the other two.

Return to Baseline Levels. When returning to baseline in Figure 10.9(d), we see that there was not a rapid change. This lack of immediate return to baseline levels hurts the experimental control of the investigation. Essentially, we have an A-B design since something may have occurred at the time the self-monitoring intervention was applied. The fact that the behavior did not return to baseline levels makes it probable that an extraneous variable caused the observed effects. On the other hand, Figure 10.9(e) indicates that the change was abrupt with a return to near baseline levels. This demonstration indicates that the independent variable was likely responsible for the changes in the dependent variable.

External Validity. A major concern of withdrawal designs is external validity. Many quantitative researchers view the external validity of withdrawal designs as lacking. Thus, claims as to the generalizability of the designs is said to be limited. However, single-case researchers view external validity somewhat differently than many quantitative researchers. Single-case researchers agree that external validity is lacking with a single study; however, isolated data are meaningless in science. In other words, *any* study, whether withdrawal or quantitative designs are used, has a lack of external validity. This lack of validity can be viewed in degrees. Isolated data should never be thought of as valid; it is the combining of data that takes on importance. Thus, withdrawal designs in isolation have external validity problems as do quantitative designs.

Single-case researchers attempt to increase the external validity of withdrawal designs by completing replications of the study (discussed in Chapter 1). Withdrawal designs do have a lack of external validity; however, the lack of external validity is due to isolated data versus the number of participants in the experiment. Single-case researchers view external validity as including more than generalization across participants. Being able to generalize across settings or ecological validity is also critical. Table 10.4 summarizes the major threats to external validity of the designs discussed in this chapter.

Research Examples

A-B Design. Martella, Marchand-Martella, Young, and Macfarlane (1995) investigated the collateral effects of peer tutor training on the classroom behaviors of a student with severe disabilities. The student (Dan) was a 14-year-old male with Down syndrome. He was enrolled in a self-contained classroom at an area high school. The classroom curriculum focused on academic skills and community-based teaching. Several peer tutors worked with the student. Unfortunately, these peer tutors spent less time tutoring the student in academic areas and more time responding to behavioral outbursts (e.g., time-out, physical restraints). Two peer tutors were taught effective instructional behaviors including appropriate instructional commands, specific praise statements, and appropriate

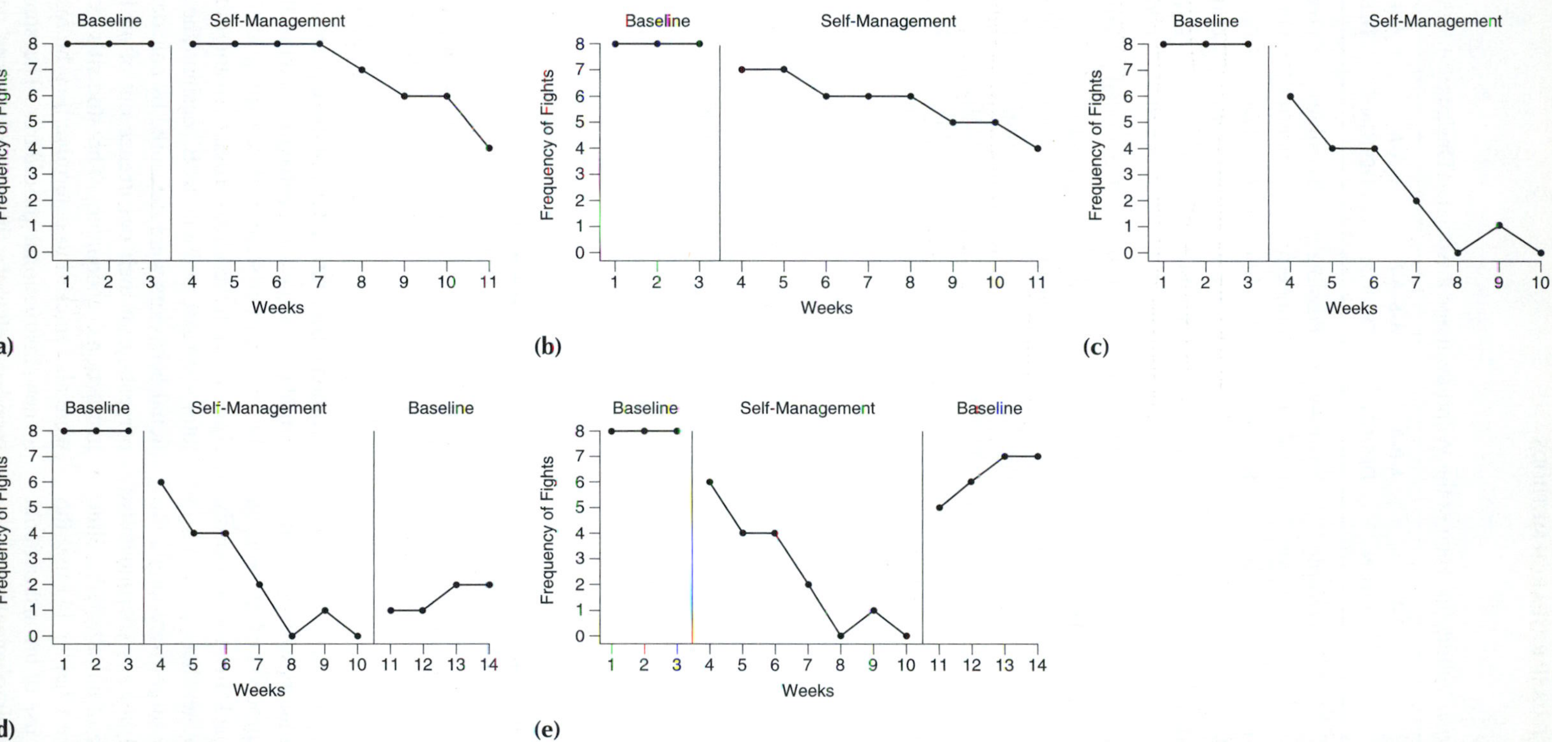

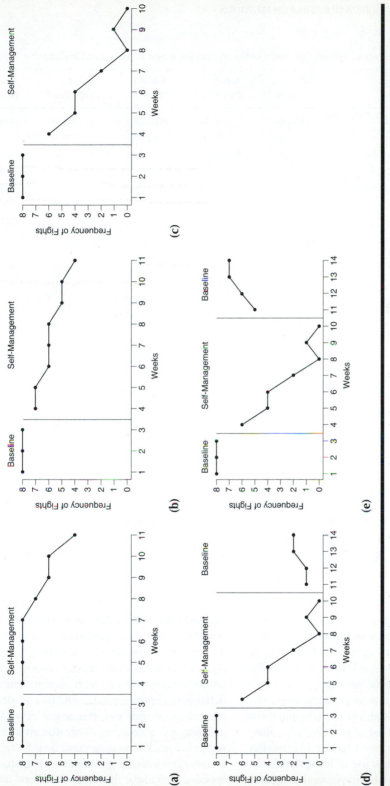

FIGURE 10.9 (a) Lack of immediate change; weak experimental control. (b) Small immediate change; better experimental control, but still weak. (c) Large immediate change; stronger experimental control. (d) Immediate change; stronger experimental control. However, there was a lack of return to near baseline levels weakening the experimental control. (e) Immediate change; stronger experimental control. Additionally, there was a return to near the baseline level adding to the experimental control.

TABLE 10.4 Threats to External Validity for Each of the Withdrawal and Associated Designs

RESEARCH DESIGN THREAT	A-B DESIGN	A-B-A DESIGN	A-B-A-B DESIGN	B-A-B DESIGN	A-B-C-B DESIGN
1. Generalization across participants	Possible concern	Possible concern	Possible concern	Possible concern	Possible concern
2. Interaction of personological variables and treatment effects	Possible concern	Possible concern	Possible concern	Possible concern	Possible concern
3. Verification of independent variable	Possible concern	Possible concern	Possible concern	Possible concern	Possible concern
4. Multiple treatment interference	Controlled	Controlled	Controlled	Controlled	Controlled
5. Novelty and disruption effects	Possible concern	Possible concern	Possible concern	Possible concern	Possible concern
6. Hawthorne effect	Possible concern	Possible concern	Possible concern	Possible concern	Possible concern
7. Experimenter effects	Possible concern	Possible concern	Possible concern	Possible concern	Possible concern
8. Pretest sensitization	Not applicable	Not applicable	Not applicable	Not applicable	Not applicable
9. Posttest sensitization	Not applicable	Not applicable	Not applicable	Not applicable	Not applicable
10. Interaction of time of measurement and treatment effects	Possible concern	Possible concern	Possible concern	Possible concern	Possible concern
11. Measurement of the dependent variable	Possible concern	Possible concern	Possible concern	Possible concern	Possible concern
12. Interaction of history and treatment effects	Possible concern	Possible concern	Possible concern	Possible concern	Possible concern

Note: This table is meant only as a general guideline. Decisions with regard to threats to external validity must be made after the specifics of an investigation are known and understood. Thus, interpretations of external validity threats must be made on a study-by-study basis.

error correction procedures. The intervention consisted of providing the peer tutors written descriptions of the instructional procedures as well as frequent and specific feedback from a previously trained instructional aide and teacher.

After the first two peer tutors were taught the instructional behaviors and it was experimentally determined (through the use of a multiple-baseline design across behaviors; see Chapter 11) that the intervention improved their use of the instructional behaviors, case studies were implemented on two additional peer tutors. One of these peer tutors was taught the instructional behaviors and the effects of the intervention were assessed using an A-B design. The intervention's effects on the other peer tutor were assessed with a "B" design. The instructional behaviors were measured by calculating the percentage of their occurrence out of all possible instructional encounters. The student's behaviors were also tracked to determine how he responded to new instructional procedures. The student responded well to the first two peer tutors' use of the instructional behaviors showing far fewer instances of unwanted behaviors (i.e., noncompliance, feet stomping, inappropriate verbalizations).

Table 10.5 shows the average percentages of instructional behaviors and the student's classroom behaviors. There was an improvement in the use of instructional behaviors and a corresponding improvement in the student's classroom behaviors. Figure 10.10 shows the graphed data for the peer tutors. Again, there is an improvement in the peer tutor's and student's behaviors.

Withdrawal Design. Tan, Moore, Dixon, and Nicholson (1994) used a withdrawal design to study the effects of rapid decoding training on reading comprehension with English as a second language (ESL) adults who were immigrants to New Zealand. The independent variable was providing the participants drill and practice on 25 difficult words in isolation. The participants were required to read all of the words in 1.5 seconds or less.

The dependent variable was the reading ability of the participants. This reading ability was measured four ways: (a) the average number of seconds taken to read the 25 words, (b) the average time taken to read all words in an assigned passage, (c) the accuracy of reading words from the word list, and (d) the accuracy of correctly answered questions from a 12-item comprehension test.

TABLE 10.5 Average Percentages and Rates of John's and Carey's Teaching Behaviors and Dan's Classroom Behaviors Across Conditions

	BASELINE	TRAINING	POSTCHECKS
John			
Specific praise	12.6%	65.8%	90.7%
(Rate per minute)	2.14	2.66	2.88
Appropriate commands	4.6%	73.6%	90.5%
(Rate per minute)	4.67	4.94	4.69
Negative statements	38.4%	9.9%	1.2%
(Rate per minute)	1.40	.02	.04
Dan			
Compliance	37.4%	46.6%	67.2%
Inappropriate verbalizations	.25	.01	.10
Foot stomps	.39	.17	.08

	Training		
	ROLE PLAY	PEER TUTORING	POSTCHECKS
Carey			
Specific praise	59.8%	83.7%	94.0%
(Rate per minute)	—	2.58	4.00
Appropriate commands	83.8%	84.7%	87.5%
(Rate per minute)	—	6.07	5.40
Negative statements	14.6%	0%	0%
(Rate per minute)	—	.00	.00
Dan			
Compliance	—	69.7%	76.5%
Inappropriate verbalizations	—	.00	.00
Foot stomps	—	.00	.08

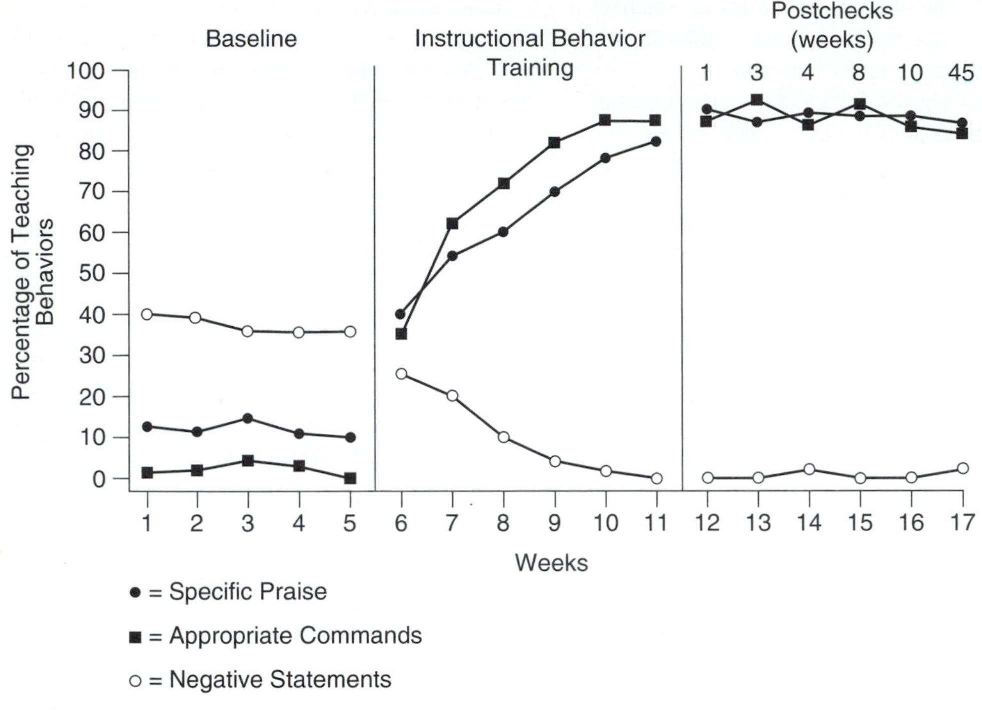

FIGURE 10.10 The percentage of teaching behaviors across baseline, instructional behavior training, and postcheck conditions.

The authors concluded that decoding training on an isolated word list was associated with increases in, among other things, improvements in comprehension. Figure 10.11 shows one of the sets of graphs. (*Note:* Other data were left out of this summary.) The three participants demonstrated improved performance on the comprehension test after they were exposed to the decoding training. Interobserver agreement was at 100% for all responses to comprehension questions.

A-B-A-B Design. Stewart and McLaughlin (1992) evaluated the effects of a self-recording intervention on the off-task behavior of a 15-year-old high school student with the label of attention deficit disorder with hyperactivity. The independent variable included an explanation of the purpose of the intervention in which on-task and off-task behaviors were defined. The student also had the self-recording system modeled to him. In addition to the self-recording system, good behavior points were recorded for on-task behavior and sent home with each weekly report card.

The dependent variable was off-task behavior; the dependent measure was the percentage of five-minute intervals off-task. According to the authors, the results indicated that the self-recording intervention package had an effect on off-task behavior (see Figure 10.12). The interobserver agreement percentages across 25% of the sessions ranged from 70 to 100%, with an average of 82%.

B-A-B Design. Kamps, Leonard, Dugen, Boland, and Greenwood (1991) investigated the use of ecobehavioral assessment to identify effective procedures occurring naturally in classrooms serving students with autism and other developmental disabilities. Kamps and colleagues described two stud-

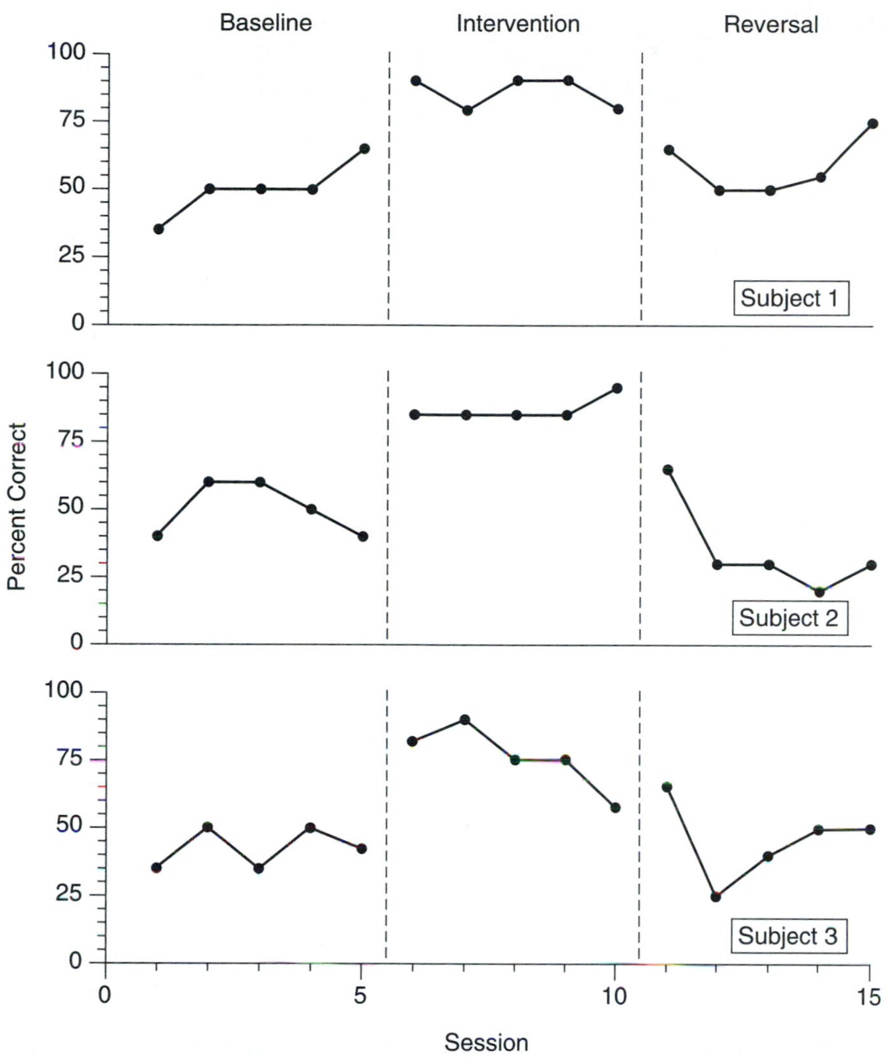

FIGURE 10.11 Mean percent correct in daily comprehension tests across experimental phases.

ies. Study 1 contained 24 participants ranging in age from 5 to 11 years from six different classrooms. An ecobehavioral analysis model was used in which systematic observations were implemented to measure environmental effects on student performance. Data-based and qualitative descriptions of naturally occurring classroom procedures and events were gathered. Study 2 (the focus of this summary) was undertaken to determine the functional relationships between the identified effective procedures from Study 1 and the levels of student academic performance. Twenty-one participants from five of the classrooms participated in the study.

Several research designs were used in Study 2—A-B-A, B-A-B, A-B-A-B, and A-B-A-C-A-C. The intervention in two of the classrooms (i.e.,

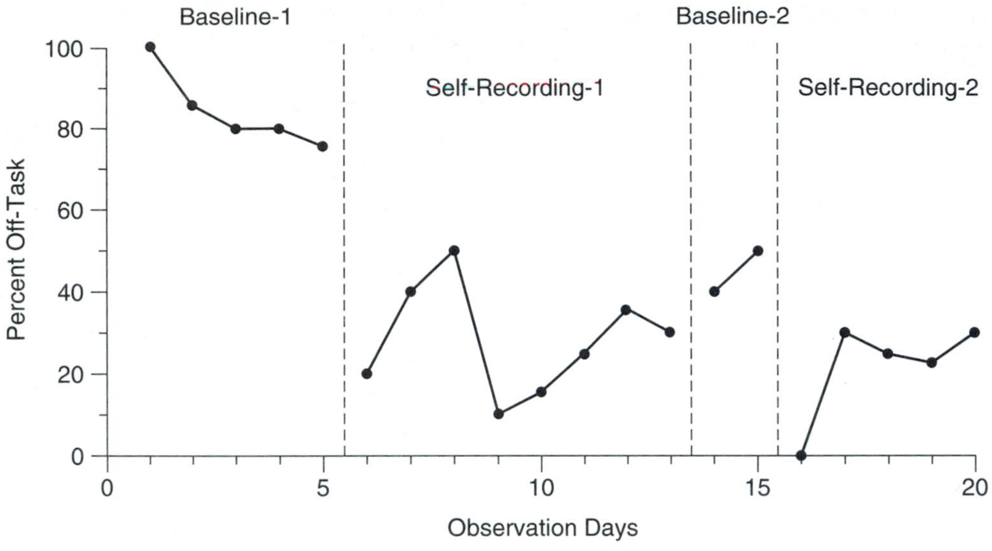

FIGURE 10.12 Percent of five-minute intervals scored as off-task for the participant.

Classroom 1, Group 2 and Classroom 3) was assessed using a B-A-B design. The independent variable was selected based on the results from Study 1. In other words, the interventions were designed to "best fit" the areas (e.g., discussion format, whole-class instruction) in need of improvement in each classroom. The following were required to determine the "best fit": low academic responding by students; nonfunctional instructional sessions (e.g., overuse of worksheets) to teach concepts; high rates of discussion with few or no media materials present; overuse of one-on-one instruction with extended wait periods for other students; and slower-paced noninteractive groups. The interventions were designed to match these instructional difficulties. For example, increasing the use of media materials would "best fit" high rates of discussion with few or no media materials present. The authors reported that they measured treatment fidelity (i.e., verification of the independent variable). The percentages for accurate implementation of the independent variable ranged from 80 to 98% across classrooms. Other measures were utilized as well, indicating that the independent variables were implemented as described.

The dependent variable was academic performance and was measured by recording academic responding (e.g., task participation, reading aloud) and criterion-referenced assessments. The instructional situation was recorded using a computer-based recording system entitled the MainStream Version of the Code for Instructional Structure and Student Academic Response (MS-CISSAR). Reliability ranged from 79 to 100% across all measured areas (i.e., activity, task, physical arrangement, instructional arrangement, teacher definition, teacher behavior, approval/disapproval, teacher focus, teacher position, academic responding, task management, and competing responding). Criterion-referenced assessments included 15 to 20 questions that were probed twice a week and were based on the content taught during the session. However, the authors indicated that formal reliability was not recorded on student learning measures (i.e., criterion-referenced assessments). Informal observations by the classroom teachers served as a validity check to the assessment items and student responses.

Although several designs were used for our purposes, only the two B-A-B designs will be discussed. The results indicated that the interventions had an impact on student performance as measured by the criterion-referenced assessments; see Figures 10.13(a) and (b). Figure 10.13(a) indicates that the performance improved for students in Classroom 1, Group 2. The students in Classroom 3—Figure 10.13b—also demonstrated improved performance when the intervention was implemented.

A-B-C-B Design. There are several modifications of the A-B-C-B design. Examples include the A-B-BC-B and A-BC-B-BC designs. Lazarus (1993) used an A-BC-B-BC design to measure the effects of guided notes for five students with learning disabilities ($n = 4$) or behavior disorders ($n = 1$) during the first of two investigations. Investigation 1 was conducted in an urban high school with a middle-class population and included five of the eight students (four with learning disabilities and one with a behavior disorder). Two classes were included in the investigation. The majority of students in each class did not have disabilities (22 out of 25 students in Class 1 and 24 out of 26 in Class 2). Baseline consisted of the students recording notes independently while they listened to the lecture, were asked questions, were involved in discussions, and wrote words or phrases on the chalkboard or on transparencies. The students were measured on their percentage of correct responses out of 20 to 30 multiple-choice questions on teacher-made tests on each chapter. During the "BC" condition, teachers and students were taught how to use guided notes with a review. During the "B" condition, guided notes alone were in effect. The interobserver agreement for Investigation 1 was at least 94%. Figure 10.14 shows the results of three of the five students in the investigation.

As can be seen, the performance of all students improved during the guided notes condition. The authors concluded that the guided notes strategy with a review was effective in improving the test performance of students with learning disabilities or behavior disorders over guided notes alone.

WHEN SHOULD RESEARCHERS USE EACH WITHDRAWAL AND ASSOCIATED DESIGN?

Researchers must always consider what the research question is and how best to answer it. The type of research design selected is critical in the decision-making process. Researchers must consider several options before a study is started. For example, the first concern is whether a qualitative design is best to use or if a single-case design is more appropriate. If, after considering the options, the researcher selects a single-case design, the type of single-case design must be considered. The A-B design is usually most appropriate for practitioners not necessarily concerned with scientific rigor. However, researchers may consider the A-B design if they wish to cast doubt on theoretical assumptions, refine techniques, or provide clinical and applied examples (Tawney & Gast, 1984).

The A-B design should not be selected if researchers wish to demonstrate a functional relationship between the independent variable and the dependent variable rather than a correlational one. In other words, the A-B design does not control for threats to internal validity. If researchers wish to control for internal validity threats, the A-B design is not a suitable choice. However, many times researchers may not have much of an option. For example, suppose that a researcher planned to use a withdrawal design and the participant was unable or unwilling to continue in the study after the "B" condition. The researcher would then have to settle for an A-B design.

If researchers wished to control for the internal validity threats, the withdrawal design would be appropriate. However, according to Tawney and Gast (1984), researchers rarely select the withdrawal design before beginning a study. One reason for this is that practitioners may not allow for the withdrawal of the intervention. Consider for a moment dealing with a severely disruptive student in the classroom. A researcher enters and takes baseline data and then implements a management program. You notice the student's behavior improving when the researcher informs you that the intervention will be pulled with the

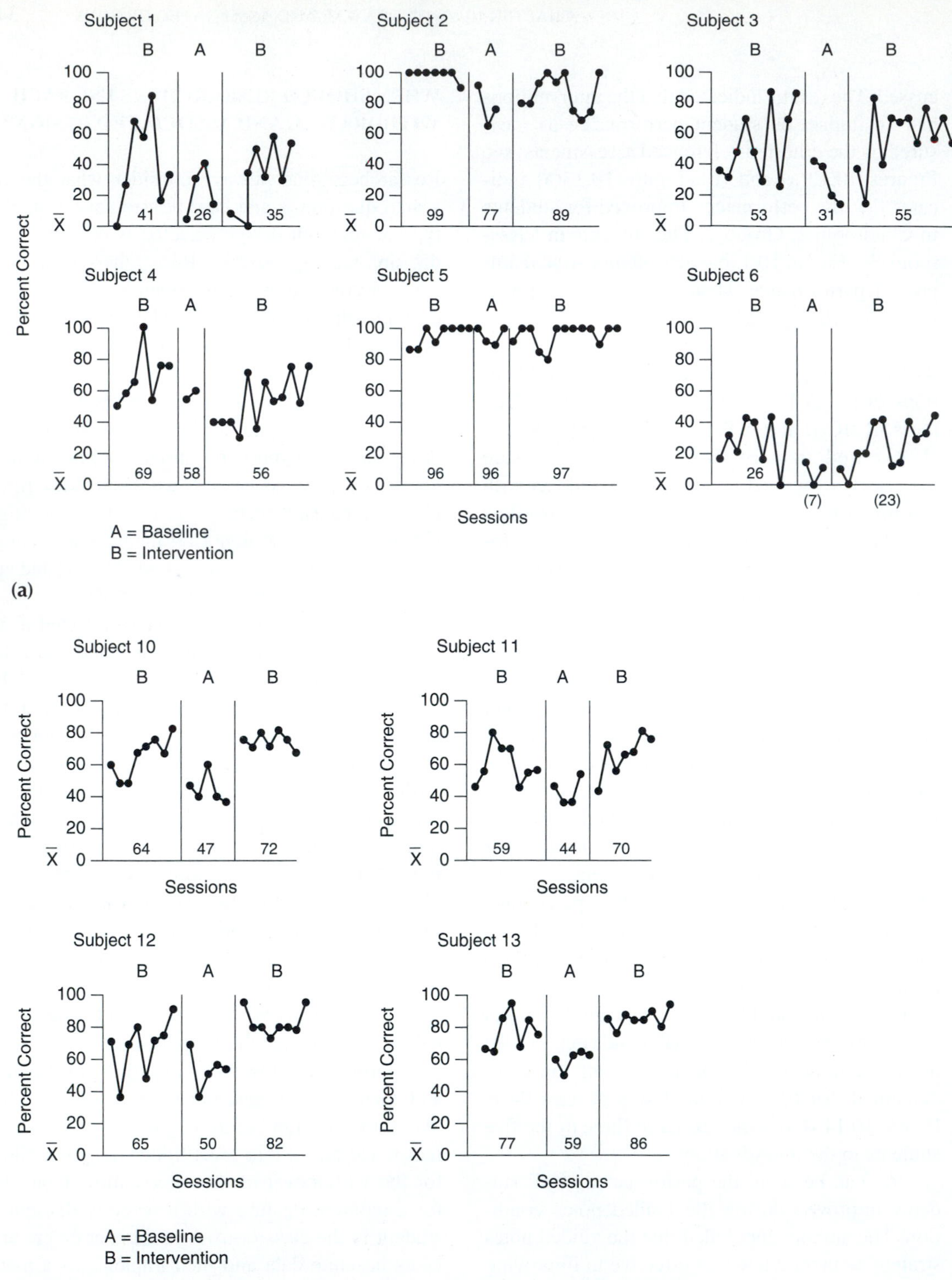

FIGURE 10.13 (a) Criterion-referenced assessments for Classroom 1, group 2. (b) Criterion-referenced assessments for Classroom 3.

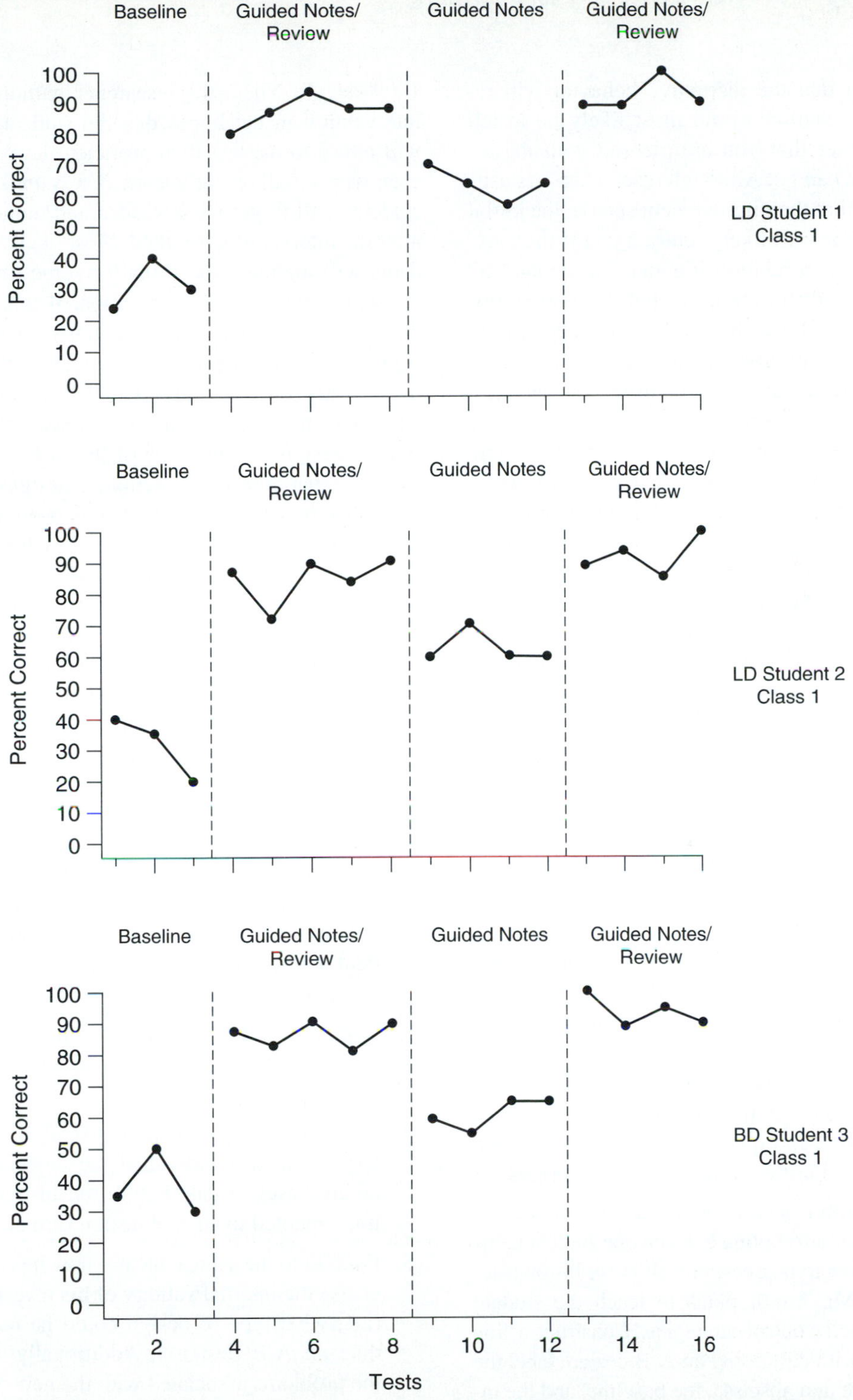

FIGURE 10.14 Percentage of correct responses earned on chapter tests by Class 1 Students 1, 2, and 3 during Study 1.

expectation that the disruptive behavior will return. Your reaction would most likely be to tell the researcher that you are pleased with the results and he can go. Although researchers are usually aware that the improvement seen in the initial "B" condition will likely return again if there exists a functional relationship and if a second "B" condition is added, reality is that many practitioners are wary of a withdrawal of the intervention. Researchers may propose the A-B-A-B design to avoid ending on the "A" condition, but again, a return to baseline is required.

A second problem is that the withdrawal and associated design (i.e., A-B-A-B and B-A-B designs) require a return to baseline levels. Thus, if one were working with a skill acquisition program, a return to baseline would not be expected (at least not initially). For example, suppose that a researcher was teaching students a math problem-solving technique. During baseline, the students were less than proficient in performing the required operations. During the intervention, the students' problem-solving abilities improve to near 100% levels. Then, the researcher withdraws the intervention in the hopes that the students' skills will return to the less than proficient levels. However, with a skill recently learned, it is unlikely that students will forget what was learned immediately after the intervention is pulled. Most likely, the students will maintain the skills for some time after the withdrawal of the intervention. If this occurs, the researcher is left with essentially an A-B design. There would be numerous threats to the internal validity of the study. Thus, if a researcher wished to study a skill acquisition intervention, the A-B-A design or variations of the A-B-A design would be inappropriate. Alternative designs will be presented in Chapter 12 that will overcome the problem of an inability to return to baseline levels.

As stated previously, the A-B-C-B design can be used when there is a concern about the effects of the independent variable being due to the intended intervention or due to some intended side effect of the intervention such as increased attention. However, researchers run the same risks associated with the withdrawal and associated designs.

DISCUSSION QUESTIONS

1. You hear a discussion between two fellow students about the differences and similarities of qualitative and quantitative research methods. One of the students states that a combination of the two methods would be worthwhile in some instances. However, she indicates that there are no such research designs. You interject by telling the students how single-case research methods have things in common with qualitative and quantitative methods. Explain these similarities as well as the differences.
2. Mr. Smith is a classroom teacher of first graders. He is attempting to teach one student in his class how to take responsibility for his own actions. Mr. Smith plans to teach the student some self-control strategies. Construct a line graph with data using an A-B design, label the ordinate and abscissa, the baseline, and the independent variable. Construct the graph in such a manner that the self-control instruction seemed to have an effect. Then, interpret the data based on threats to internal and external validity and indicate to Mr. Smith how confident he should be as to the effectiveness of his self-control instruction.
3. Regraph the data in Question 2 in a bar graph. How does the type of graph affect your interpretations, if at all?
4. Another educator wishes to use a "B" design. Explain to this individual the advantages of taking baseline data before the instruction is implemented in an A-B design format.
5. Explain to the same educator how he could increase the internal validity of his investigation (i.e., what type of design could he use other than an A-B design?). Additionally, explain the problems associated with the new design.
6. Describe the purpose of an A-B-A-B design. How would this design help the aforemen-

tioned educator in solving one of the problems of the design in Question 4.

7. Describe a problem encountered with external validity when using A-B-A designs and indicate a solution to this problem.

8. Another design that can be used in research is the B-A-B design. Why would a researcher select this design over another design such as an A-B-A design?

9. What is a purpose of the A-B-C-B design? Additionally, how does this design control for threats to internal validity?

10. Explain the concerns surrounding the following:
(a) condition length
(b) change one variable at a time
(c) level and rapidity of change
(d) return to baseline levels

REDUCING NEGATIVE COMMENTS THROUGH SELF-MONITORING AND CONTINGENCY CONTRACTING

PAMELA S. COURSON-KRAUSE
The University of Montana

NANCY MARCHAND-MARTELLA, RONALD C. MARTELLA
Eastern Washington University

BRENDA SCHMITT
Hellgate High School, Missoula, Montana

ABSTRACT

We examined the effects of a self-monitoring and a self-monitoring with contingency contracting program on reducing the frequency of negative comments of an adolescent student with developmental disabilities who was enrolled in a supportive services classroom at a local high school. The results showed that a decrease in the number of negative comments occurred at the beginning of self-monitoring instruction. Negative statements decreased further after contingency contracting was added to the self-monitoring program. Maintenance data collected 5 weeks after the termination of training indicated that the student maintained zero levels of negative comments.

REDUCING NEGATIVE COMMENTS THROUGH SELF-MONITORING AND CONTINGENCY CONTRACTING

Self-monitoring includes the process in which participants independently record their own behavior without an external cue. Dunlap, Dunlap, Koegel, and Koegel (1991) noted that self-monitoring programs are relatively simple to implement, require little supervision time, and can be effective in helping students become more successful and independent in their classroom and daily lives. Martella, Leonard, Marchand-Martella, and Agran (1992) taught a student with mild mental retardation to reduce negative statements via self-monitoring. Decreases in the target behavior were noted. Additionally, Seabaugh and Schumaker (1994) reported the success of a self-regulation training program that involved self-monitoring. In this study, four secondary-level students with a history of school failure substantially increased their rate of lesson completion. Also included in this self-regulation training program was contingency contracting.

Contingency contracting involves a document that specifies a contingent relationship between completion of a targeted behavior and delivery of a specified reward (Cooper, Heron, & Heward, 1987). According to Downing (1990), contingency contracts are beneficial components of programs where student self-esteem and accountability need to be further promoted. Cooper et al. (1987) indicated that contingency contracts are especially effective in reducing unwanted classroom behaviors when combined with self-management procedures.

Although self-monitoring and contingency contracting have been shown to be effective when used in isolation and together, there is a paucity of research which demonstrates the efficacy of adding contingency contracting to an already established self-monitoring program. In other words, researchers have not attempted to determine the influences of a self-management component (i.e., self-monitoring) alone and then in combination with another self-management component (i.e., contingency contracting).

The purpose of this study was to assess the effects of a program that included self-monitoring alone and then in combination with contingency contracting on the frequency of negative comments displayed by an adolescent student with developmental disabilities. However, the purpose of the study was not to demonstrate a functional relationship. The study was an attempt to demonstrate in a classroom environment the advantages of adding a contingency to an existing self-monitoring program. Interobserver agreement between the student and an instructor on the student's recording accuracy was assessed. Additionally, maintenance data up to 5 weeks posttraining were collected.

Method

Participant and Setting. Amy was a 14-year-old ninth grade student with developmental disabilities. Her verbal, performance, and full scale WISC-R scores were 65, 68, and 64, respectively. Special education services were provided in a supportive services classroom at a local high school in the areas of math, reading and language arts, communication, and written language. Amy attended regular education classes for physical education and computer keyboarding.

Amy emitted frequent negative comments directed toward herself, others, objects, and tasks throughout her school day, which resulted in exclusion from peers and classroom teachers. Also, Amy's parents were increasingly concerned with her negative comments in the home environment. A personal/social skills class was recommended as part of Amy's Individualized Education Program (I. E. P.) to improve her social skills and to eliminate negative comments toward others.

This study was conducted during a personal/social skills class for students with developmental disabilities and emotional disorders. Three students were enrolled in the class. Instruction was provided by a special education teacher and a student teacher. The class lasted 50 minutes and included instruction in self-care and personal and social skills.

Materials. A curriculum was designed to improve Amy's ability to interact with peers in a high school setting and to teach her suitable social mannerisms, appropriate decision making, and assertive statements. Additionally, the curriculum included personal care issues such as appearance, proper posture, and positive self-image. The class curriculum consisted of a text and workbook: *Choices: A Teen Woman's Journal for Self-Awareness and Personal Planning* (Bingham, Edmondson, & Stryker, 1994). Supplemental materials included packets about self-esteem, body care, setting goals, values/beliefs, assertive behavior, and peer pressure. Cooperative group activities consisted of a "slip game" to promote personal sharing, to explore appropriate attitudes about drugs and alcohol, and to build peer support. In the "slip game," each student was allowed to pick prepared question slips from a bag (e.g., "What makes you happy?" or "What is your favorite place and why?") and give his or her answer to the group (Gibbs, 1987). Feedback on student responses was provided by the classroom teacher and student teacher. Additionally, other students were allowed to provide additional information to answer the question after the original student was finished with his or her response.

Additional materials included self-monitoring forms, posted charts, and contingency contracts. The self-monitoring form was 9.8 cm × 7.2 cm and included the heading, *Negative Comments.* This form had 45 boxes in which Amy could record each occurrence of the target behavior. Examples of the target behavior were provided on a bulletin board and work table. A form was given to Amy at the beginning of each daily session.

A standard piece of graph paper was used for a visual chart of Amy's progress. The vertical axis indicated the number of negative comments emitted; the horizontal axis specified the daily sessions. The student teacher kept the chart in a folder in the classroom.

The contingency contract explained the purpose of the program and specified the target behavior, a criterion of 3 consecutive sessions of meeting a daily goal *and* being within 80% agreement with the instructor on a specified number of negative comments emitted in order to earn "small" reinforcers (e.g., candy, pop), and a criterion of 10 consecutive sessions of zero negative comments in order to earn a "large" reinforcer (i.e., audiotape). The teachers and student signed the contract before the study began. Signing the contract indicated that Amy understood the contract and agreed to participate in the program to reduce her negative comments.

Dependent Variable. Negative comments were targeted and assessed to ascertain the effects of instruction. The operational definition for negative comments was as follows: derogatory single word utterances or statements separated by a break in speech that are directed toward self/others/objects/tasks (e.g., "I'm no good," "I'll get my brothers to kick your butt," "This — machine can't do anything right," "I can't do math, it's too hard"). Interruptions (emitting comments while another person is talking) were also included in the definition of negative comments.

Observation and Recording Procedures. An undergraduate student teacher, working on an elementary degree and endorsement in special education, was the instructor and primary rater and recorded data during baseline and training conditions. The secondary rater was a special education teacher with a B. A. in elementary education, endorsement in special education, and 3 years public school experience. She gathered data for purposes of interobserver agreement. The instructor/primary rater and the secondary rater recorded the frequency (the time of each occurrence was recorded) of negative comments using a data collection form that included a column for negative comments.

Interobserver Agreement. Point-by-point interobserver agreement was scored during 30% of the baseline and self-monitoring instructional sessions and 10% of the self-monitoring with contingency contracting sessions. The agreement percentages were calculated as follows: First, the primary and secondary raters synchronized their watches. Second, they recorded the time (rounded to the nearest minute) for each occurrence of negative comments. Finally, an agreement was scored if the times recorded by the raters were the same. Interobserver agreement was calculated by dividing the number of agreements by the number of agreements plus disagreements and multiplying by 100. Interobserver agreement for negative comments averaged 96% (range 95–100%) across all sessions.

Procedures

Baseline. Ongoing personal/social skills class instructional procedures (i.e., the *Choices* curriculum, supplementary curriculum materials, and the "slip game") continued during baseline. The teachers praised Amy for personal behaviors in class such as proper back posture, wearing her glasses, and emitting positive statements. Amy's negative comments were ignored when she was completing individualized seat work. If Amy interrupted others she was asked to raise her hand.

Self-Monitoring Instruction. Self-monitoring instruction involved teaching Amy to self-monitor negative comments. During each class she was given a self-monitoring sheet to record negative comments. For the first two self-monitoring instructional sessions, the instructor stated 12 examples of negative and positive statements (six each) in a random order. Amy was asked to indicate what type of statement it was. If she responded incorrectly, the correct response was modeled and Amy was requested to provide the correct response. Additionally, the instructor demonstrated the recording of negative comments. Amy was praised for identifying negative and positive comments, including raising her hand to speak. During group lecture, a pencil was used to define the speaker (i.e., "If you have the pencil you can speak, and if you want the pencil you have to raise your hand and politely ask for the'speaker's marker'. If you do not have the pencil, you are not allowed to speak"). In the third and fourth self-monitoring instructional sessions, Amy was given a verbal test that included eight novel negative and positive comments (four of each; randomly) and was asked to indicate the type of statement. In the fifth self-monitoring instructional session Amy was allowed to monitor the instructor's negative and positive comments. The instructor "role-played" the student and periodically emitted these comments. The sixth day of self-monitoring instruction was similar to the third and fourth session, except Amy was asked to give 10 examples of negative and positive statements (five each). On the last day of self-monitoring instruction, the "speaker marker" was eliminated. Self-monitoring instruction lasted 6 days.

Self-Monitoring with Contingency Contracting. Based on the baseline conditions, an average frequency of negative comments was calculated. This average was used to establish the first criterion level. The total frequency of Amy's negative comments had to be at or below the criterion for three consecutive sessions in order for the next criterion level to be implemented. Criterion levels following each successive level were established by decreasing the previous criterion by two (e.g., the frequency of the first criterion level was 10, the next criterion level was 8, and so on).

Before each class, the instructor would advise Amy of the maximum number of negative comments she could emit during the period by highlighting the number of boxes on the self-monitoring form that matched the criterion level. Amy would put a mark in the box whenever she expressed a negative comment. If the frequency data recorded by Amy were in agreement with the instructor (i.e., 80% or higher), and the number of negative comments was at or below the criterion level for three consecutive sessions, she received a piece of candy. Amy charted the frequency of her negative comments by putting an "x" on the graph.

Generalization. The instructor observed Amy during a math class and collected data for 30 minutes on frequency of negative comments. Amy did not self-monitor during math. A student teacher gave math lectures from Sessions 31–46.

Maintenance. All components of the intervention were withdrawn with the exception of the self-monitoring form. The criterion level was not highlighted on the form. Follow-up data were collected up to 5 weeks after self-monitoring instruction had ended.

Results

Baseline, Self-Monitoring Instruction, and Self-Monitoring and Contingency Contracting. As shown in Figure 1, Amy's negative comments decreased throughout the intervention. The average number of negative comments across baseline sessions was 8.8. This average decreased across the self-monitoring instructional sessions to 2.7. Finally, Amy's average number of negative comments further decreased across the self-monitoring with

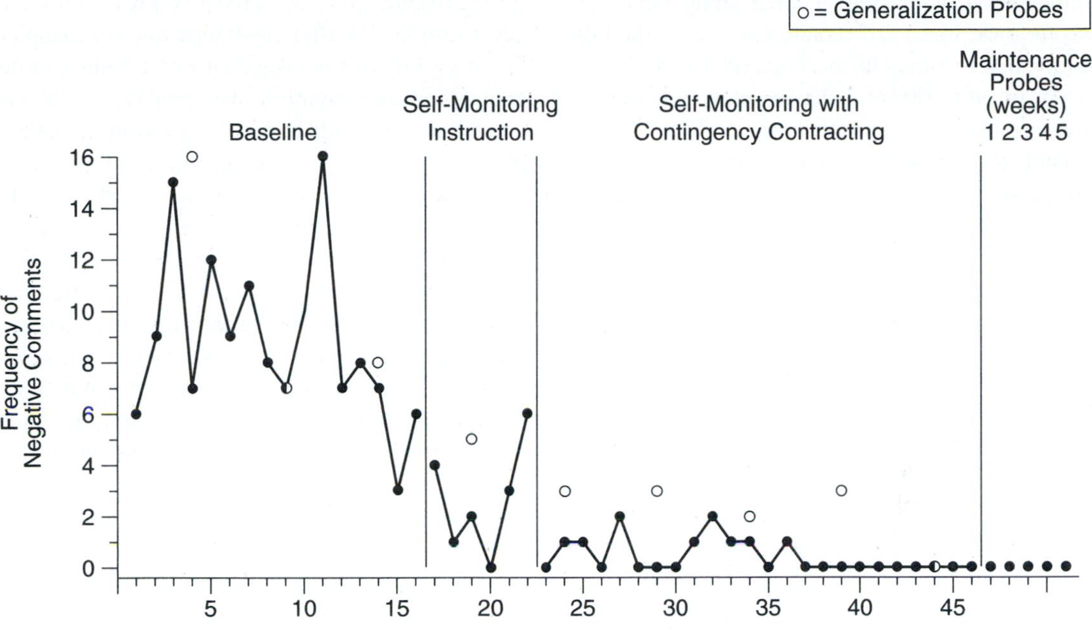

FIGURE 1 Frequency of negative comments across baseline, self-monitoring, and self-monitoring with contingency contracting sessions; and maintenance and generalization probes.

contingency contracting condition to an average of .42. She had no instances of negative comments throughout the final 10 instructional sessions.

Generalization and Maintenance. Figure 1 shows that Amy's negative comments decreased during math. The baseline average for negative comments was 10.3; she had five negative comments during self-monitoring instruction; during the self-monitoring with contingency contracting condition, Amy had an average of only 2.8 negative comments during math. More importantly, Amy had an average of only 2.5 negative comments during math when a new teacher was present.

Amy's negative comments maintained at zero instances 5 weeks after self-monitoring with contingency contracting condition ended.

Accuracy Data. Amy's accuracy of recording her frequency of negative comments was consistent with the instructor averaging 95% (range 97–100%) across instructional sessions.

Discussion

The results of this investigation reveal that the implementation of the self-monitoring program was correlated with an initial reduction of Amy's negative comments. Additionally, Amy's negative comments began to increase after the fourth session of the self-monitoring intervention. The last three data points indicate a steep incline in her negative statements. When contingency contracting was added to the self-monitoring training program, further decreases in negative comments were noted. Amy's reduction of negative comments maintained at zero instances for 5 consecutive weeks after training had ended.

The initial decrease, then increase in Amy's negative comments during self-monitoring instruction is consistent with what one might expect by the implementation of the instructional components for two reasons. First, self-monitoring is a method of observation that may be reactive (Schloss & Smith, 1994). In other words, behavior may change as a direct result of the observation (Kazdin, 1982). Second, even though Amy was provided instruction on self-monitoring and demonstrated that she could self-monitor, there were no contingencies in place to ensure that she would continue to emit low levels of negative comments. Therefore, we would expect that the self-monitoring would result in initial decreases due to its reactivity and a lack of maintenance in the observed changes due to a lack of consequences for the behavior change.

Once the contingency contracting was added to the self-monitoring program, Amy's negative comments decreased quickly and stayed at a level below the average of the self-monitoring condition. These results suggest that simply implementing a self-monitoring program is not sufficient to maintain the behavior change. What is also needed is some method of consequating the behavior change. One such method is contingency contracting.

An added benefit of the study was a verification of Downing's (1990) claim that contingency contracts are beneficial components of programs where student self-esteem and accountability need to be promoted. Amy was given the *Coopersmith Self-Esteem Inventories* (1981) before baseline commenced and during the fifth week of the maintenance probes. The results indicated that Amy's scores on the four subscales (i.e., General Self, Social Self-Peers, Home-Parents, School-Academics) improved. Her "Total Self" score also showed an improvement. Additionally, Amy showed an improvement on the "Lie Scale" which measures the veracity of her responses. Therefore, it seems as if Amy's self-esteem and truthfulness improved from prebaseline to the fifth week of maintenance.

In addition to the positive instructional results, Amy also exhibited fewer negative comments during math class (generalization site). Interestingly, unsolicited responses were given by other teachers indicating that Amy demonstrated marked improvement in different settings. Amy's math, English, and keyboarding teachers commented that Amy exhibited positive behaviors toward staff and peers during and after the intervention. Examples of Amy's improvements with positive behaviors included common courtesy statements (e.g., "thank you," "please," and "hello" or "good-bye"). Other positive behavior changes such as an increase in assisting other students, a reduction of placing objects in her mouth, and a consistency with correct body posture were noticed anecdotally.

A final positive result of this investigation was the accuracy data obtained. According to Martella et al. (1993), there is a lack of information with regard to the ability of individuals with developmental disabilities to self-monitor and then record their own behavior independent of an external cue. Amy was able to record the frequency of her negative comments very accurately. Therefore, the accuracy information adds to the literature indicating that individuals with developmental disabilities are able to monitor and record the occurrence of their own behaviors independent of external cues.

Although several positive results were seen throughout the investigation, several caveats are worth noting. First, as indicated in the purpose statement, there was a lack of experimental control. Therefore, a functional analysis was not conducted and cause-and-effect statements could not be made.

Second, the present design does not permit a comparison of the efficacy of self-monitoring alone and self-monitoring with contingency contracting. Therefore, only a weak conclusion can be made as to the internal validity of self-monitoring with contingency contracting as compared to self-monitoring alone.

Third, there was a lack of interobserver agreement during generalization probes. Since observations were being made in another teacher's classroom, it was not possible to place a second observer in this site to gather agreement data. Therefore, the reliability of the generalization data may be in question. However, since the teacher in the math class was not aware of when each experimental condition was in place, we may be more confident that a change did take place since large changes in Amy's behavior did not occur until after the intervention was implemented.

Finally, since there was a decreasing trend in baseline, experimental control is diminished. However, when the self-monitoring with contingency contracting condition began, Amy's negative comments were increasing. Therefore, if one were to view the self-monitoring condition as a training baseline, a small amount of experimental control is gained.

Based on the results, a few conclusions may be made. First, we would expect some reactivity due to self-monitoring instruction. Second, a self-monitoring program by itself is not sufficient for the maintenance of behavioral gains. Some type of contingency system should be in place. Contingency contracting is an ideal combination with self-monitoring. Contingency contracting set by external agents can be faded out and self-contracting faded in (Cooper et al., 1987). This promotes an ability to self-manage one's own behavior. Third, generalization of self-monitoring instruction may occur once an individual is able to identify his or her own behavior. Finally, self-monitoring and contingency contracting are relatively easy and effective procedures for reducing behavior problems that classroom personnel can implement without special training.

REFERENCES

Bingham, M., Edmondson, J., & Stryker, S. (1994). *Choices: A teen woman's journal for self-awareness and personal planning.* Santa Barbara, CA: Advocacy Press.

Cooper, J. O., Heron, T. E., & Heward, W. L. (1987). *Applied behavior analysis.* Columbus, OH: Merrill.

Coopersmith, S., (1981). *Coopersmith Self-esteem Inventories.* Palo Alto, CA: Consulting Psychologists Press.

Downing, J. A. (1990). Contingency contracts: A step-by-step format. *Intervention in School and Clinic, 26,* 111–113.

Dunlap, L., Dunlap, G., Koegel, L., & Koegel, R. (1991). Using self-monitoring to increase independence. *Teaching Exceptional Children, 23,* 17–22.

Gibbs, J. (1987). *Tribes.* Santa Rosa, CA: Center Source.

Kazdin, A. E. (1982). *Single-case research designs: Methods for clinical and applied settings.* New York: Oxford University Press.

Martella, R. C., Leonard, I., Marchand-Martella, N. E., & Agran, M. (1993). Self-monitoring negative statements. *Journal of Behavioral Education, 3,* 77–86.

Seabaugh, G. O., & Schumaker, J. B. (1994). The effects of self-regulation training on the academic productivity of secondary students with learning problems. *Journal of Behavioral Education, 4,* 109–133.

Schloss, P. J., & Smith, M. A. (1994). *Applied behavior analysis in the classroom.* Boston: Allyn & Bacon.

FACTUAL QUESTIONS

1. What was the purpose of the investigation?
2. Who was the participant? Where was the setting?
3. What were the materials used?
4. What were the dependent and independent variables, and how was the dependent variable measured?
5. Who were the primary and secondary raters? What were their responsibilities?
6. How was interobserver agreement calculated? Was it adequate?
7. What type of design was used? What occurred during each of the conditions?
8. Why was the contingency contract condition added?
9. What happened when the self-monitoring condition was added? How did the addition of the contingency contracting condition help the student's behavior?
10. What occurred in the generalization setting? Did the student's behavior change or maintain?

DISCUSSION QUESTIONS

1. Why did the authors indicate that the purpose of the investigation was not to demonstrate a functional relationship?
2. What are the effects on external validity using this one student? To what type of student could we confidently generalize these results? What would you do to improve population validity?
3. Is there a problem with the instructor also being the primary rater? If so, suggest an alternative.
4. What was the purpose of adding the contingency contracting condition?
5. How do the generalization and maintenance results aid the external validity? Or do they?
6. What is the significance of the accuracy data?
7. Are the authors correct in suggesting that the implementation of the self-monitoring program was correlated with an initial reduction in negative comments?
8. What are the weaknesses with this design? Why do you think the authors used such a design? What type of single-case design would have been more appropriate and why?
9. Why would the authors also provide a measure of self-esteem? What effect could this have on external validity?
10. The authors listed four difficulties with the investigation. What were these and how do these difficulties affect the internal and external validity of the investigation?

THREATS TO INTERNAL VALIDITY

Circle the number corresponding to the likelihood of each threat to internal validity being present in the investigation and provide a justification.

1 = definitely not a threat   2 = not a likely threat   3 = somewhat likely threat
4 = likely threat   5 = definite threat   NA = Not applicable for this design

Results in Differences within or between Individuals

1. Maturation **1 2 3 4 5 NA**

Justification ______________________________

____

2. Selection **1 2 3 4 5 NA**

Justification ______________________________

____

3. Selection by Maturation Interaction **1 2 3 4 5 NA**

Justification ______________________________

____

4. Statistical Regression **1 2 3 4 5 NA**

Justification ______________________________

____

5. Mortality **1 2 3 4 5 NA**

Justification ______________________________

____

6. Instrumentation **1 2 3 4 5 NA**

Justification ______________________________

____

7. Testing **1 2 3 4 5 NA**

Justification ____________________

____

8. History **1 2 3 4 5 NA**

Justification ____________________

____

9. Resentful Demoralization of the Control Group **1 2 3 4 5 NA**

Justification ____________________

____

Results in Similarities within or between Individuals

10. Diffusion of Treatment **1 2 3 4 5 NA**

Justification ____________________

____

11. Compensatory Rivalry by the Control Group **1 2 3 4 5 NA**

Justification ____________________

____

12. Compensatory Equalization of Treatments **1 2 3 4 5 NA**

Justification ____________________

____

Abstract: Write a one-page abstract summarizing the overall conclusions of the authors and whether you feel the authors' conclusions are valid based on the internal validity of the investigation.

THREATS TO EXTERNAL VALIDITY

Circle the number corresponding to the likelihood of each threat to external validity being present in the investigation according to the following scale:

1 = definitely not a threat	2 = not a likely threat	3 = somewhat likely threat
4 = likely threat	5 = definite threat	NA = Not applicable for this design

Also, provide a justification for each rating.

Population

1. **Generalization across Subjects** 1 2 3 4 5 NA

Justification ______________________________

____

2. **Interaction of Personological Variables and Treatment** 1 2 3 4 5 NA

Justification ______________________________

____

Ecological

3. **Verification of the Independent Variable** 1 2 3 4 5 NA

Justification ______________________________

____

4. **Multiple Treatment Interference** 1 2 3 4 5 NA

Justification ______________________________

____

5. **Hawthorne Effect** 1 2 3 4 5 NA

Justification ______________________________

____

6. **Novelty and Disruption Effects** 1 2 3 4 5 NA

Justification ______________________________

____

7. Experimenter Effects 1 2 3 4 5 NA

Justification ____

____

8. Pretest Sensitization 1 2 3 4 5 NA

Justification ____

____

9. Posttest Sensitization 1 2 3 4 5 NA

Justification ____

____

10. Interaction of Time of Measurement and Treatment Effects 1 2 3 4 5 NA

Justification ____

____

11. Measurement of the Dependent Variable 1 2 3 4 5 NA

Justification ____

____

12. Interaction of History and Treatment Effects 1 2 3 4 5 NA

Justification ____

____

Abstract: Write a one page abstract summarizing the overall conclusions of the authors and whether you feel the authors' conclusions are valid based on the external validity of the investigation.

CHAPTER 11

MULTIPLE-BASELINE DESIGNS

OBJECTIVES

After studying this chapter you should be able to:

1. Define multiple baseline designs. Describe their advantages and disadvantages.
2. Explain what a multiple-baseline design across behaviors is.
3. Explain what a multiple-baseline design across participants is.
4. Explain what a multiple-baseline design across settings is.
5. Explain what a multiple-probe design is.
6. Describe various issues related to the analysis of graphically displayed data in the multiple-baseline design.
7. Describe internal validity issues surrounding the use of these designs.
8. Describe the external validity issues surrounding the use of these designs.
9. Describe when one would use a particular multiple-baseline design.
10. Critique a research article containing a multiple-baseline design.

OVERVIEW

The use of the withdrawal and associated designs have decreased in recent years. Although these designs can control for threats to internal validity, they have several disadvantages. First, when teaching a skill such as reading, it is unlikely that the participant's behavior will return to baseline levels when the intervention is removed. For example, suppose that we teach a student how to decode words. At the end of the intervention ("B") condition, we return to baseline. However, we just taught a skill. We would expect the skill to maintain for some time after we remove the independent variable. We would not expect to see a return to baseline levels. We probably could not tell the student to forget what was learned. Thus, we would essentially have an A-B design.

There would be several threats to the internal validity of this investigation. Withdrawal designs are appropriate for instances when there is a motivational problem or when we are attempting to remove an unwanted behavior. If the lack of performance is motivational in nature, we could implement a motivational system to improve the student's performance. Upon removal of the motivational system, we would expect a return to baseline levels since the student would no longer have the same motivation to perform the task. In this case, there would be a higher level of internal validity.

A second problem with withdrawal designs has to do with ethical concerns. For example, suppose that we are attempting to control the aggressive responses of a youth with behavior disorders. We implement a management program and see a decrease in the student's aggressive behavior. Then, we decide to remove the management program in the "hopes" (from a scientific perspective anyway) that the behavior will worsen. There is a major ethical concern here. Many staff would not wish to return to baseline levels. We may argue that if we really wanted to know the scientific merits of the management program as the "cause" of the behavior change, we must remove the program and see if the behavior returns. Staff may say, "no thanks." They may indicate that they do not really care what the cause of the behavior change was; they only care that something happened to change the student's behavior. Of course, from a practical standpoint, it is critical to determine why the student's behavior changed if for no other reason than to determine what to do in the future if the behavior returns or if other students have similar behavior problems. However, the ethical concern is one that must be taken into consideration when one conducts research.

A third problem deals with staff cooperation. This problem relates to the previous problem and involves ethical considerations. Staff may simply refuse to allow or be involved in the withdrawal of the intervention. Even if the behavior is not destructive or dangerous but simply annoying, staff may not be willing to allow the behavior to return. If staff have objections to the use of a particular method used in research, alternatives must be found.

This chapter focuses on several issues surrounding the multiple-baseline design. First, graphing issues are highlighted. Second, three types of multiple-baseline designs are discussed. The three types are multiple-baseline designs across behaviors, participants, and settings. A fourth design is also described. This design (i.e., multiple-probe) is a modification of the multiple-baseline design. The methods of analyzing the data follow the discussion of design types. Third, research examples highlighting the different designs are presented. (*Note:* You should attempt to analyze the graphs presented from the research examples.) Finally, an illustrative investigation is included at the end of the chapter for critique.

WHAT ARE GRAPHING METHODS IN MULTIPLE-BASELINE DESIGNS?

The visual display of data in multiple-baseline designs is similar to the withdrawal and associated designs in that the placement of descriptors (i.e., dependent measure, baseline, independent variable, time measurement, data points, data paths, condition change lines, and figure captions) are all displayed in the same manner. However, instead of having one graph, the multiple-baseline display involves placing individual graphs on top of each other. Figure 11.1 demonstrates a typical multiple-baseline graph. Notice how the graphs are aligned. Additional descriptors are also placed on the figure. For instance, the display in Figure 11.1 shows a multiple-baseline design across settings. If this graph displayed a multiple-baseline design across behaviors, the type of behaviors would be indicated. Likewise, if this were a multiple-baseline across participants, the descriptors of "Participant 1, Participant 2," or the names of the participants or some other form of identification would be included. Additionally, the condition change lines are drawn down to the second (third and so on) baseline to show how the conditions overlap. In Figure 11.1, the intervention took place on Session 5 in the first setting and on Session 8 in the second setting.

WHAT ARE MULTIPLE-BASELINE DESIGNS?

An alternative to the withdrawal design is the multiple-baseline design. Multiple-baseline designs could be thought of as a series of A-B designs (Barlow & Hersen, 1984). In this way, multiple-baseline designs have several advantages over withdrawal designs. For example, in a multiple-baseline design, there is not a requirement to remove or withdraw the intervention. Along these lines, there is not a need to return to baseline levels in the future. Thus, multiple-baseline designs are appropriate for investigations of skill acquisitions as well as motivational

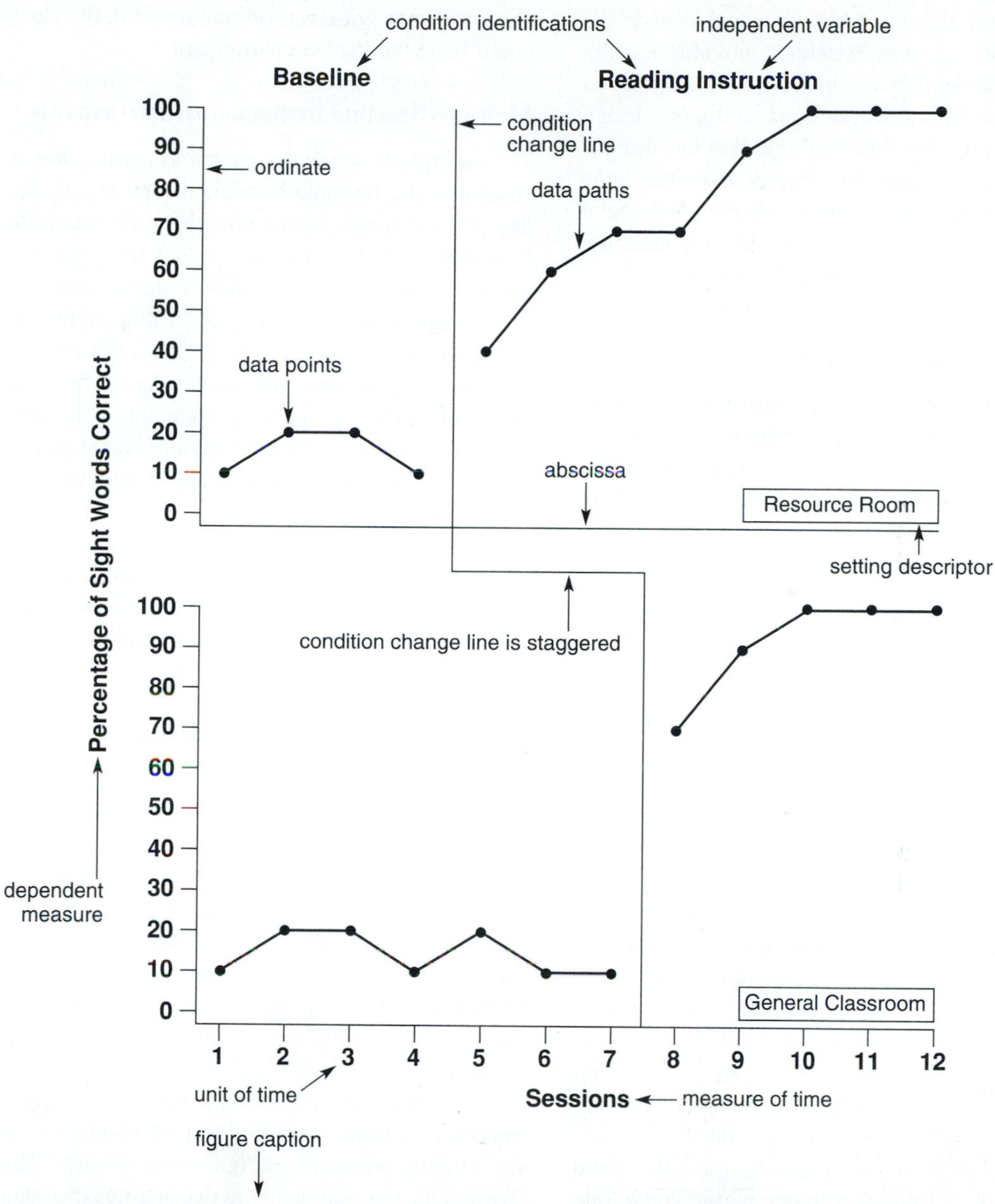

FIGURE 11.1 The percentage of sight words answered correctly across baseline and reading instruction conditions across resource room and general education settings.

problems and the reduction of unwanted behaviors. Multiple-baseline designs are in many ways more versatile than withdrawal designs. Additionally, multiple-baseline designs allow for the replication of interventions effects across behaviors, participants, and/or settings (discussed later).

However, multiple-baseline designs have several weaknesses. These weaknesses will be discussed throughout the chapter and include the need for two or more baselines, possible lengthy baselines for some participants, less experimental control than withdrawal designs, and more design considerations. Since the multiple-baseline designs discussed throughout this chapter have the same design considerations for gaining experimental control, a discussion will take place later on design considerations for all multiple-baselines.

Multiple-Baseline Design across Behaviors

The multiple-baseline design across behaviors requires at least two separate behaviors that are independent of one another. In other words, if a researcher applies an intervention to one behavior, there should not be a corresponding change in the other behavior (called covariation). Once these behaviors are targeted and a measurement system is put into place, baseline data should be collected for each behavior. Suppose that a researcher has two behaviors she is interested in investigating. The researcher begins taking baseline measurements for both of these behaviors simultaneously. Then, the first behavior receives the intervention and the second remains in baseline. Keeping the second behavior in baseline is critical. If the researcher implemented the intervention with both behaviors at the same time, she would have two simultaneous A-B designs. Figure 11.2 demonstrates this problem. All of the disadvantages of using an A-B design would come into play. It would not be possible to explain away extraneous variables such as history. The resulting improvement in both behaviors may have resulted from some history effect.

The critical aspect of this design is that there are multiple behaviors with one participant or one unit of analysis in one setting. A unit of analysis is how a researcher views the participant or the makeup of the group of participants (Gall, Borg, & Gall, 1996). In other words, even if a researcher had several participants involved in a study, he could treat the "group" as a single participant. For example, if a researcher was investigating the effects of a reading program on a single class of fourth graders (nonrandomized), the class could be treated as one participant.

Multiple-Baseline Design across Participants

The multiple-baseline design across participants is similar to the multiple-baseline design across behaviors in that two or more baselines are required. However, there is a need for two or more participants. The researcher then takes frequent measures of the targeted behavior for each participant during and after baseline. Figure 11.3 shows a multiple-baseline design across participants. As can be seen, the graphs indicate who the participants were. Notice also how the researcher kept the second participant in baseline while the first participant received the intervention.

There are several important aspects of this design. First, the design must include multiple participants or several groups of participants such as two or more classrooms. Additionally, there is one behavior measured as opposed to several in the multiple-baseline design across behaviors. Finally, there is a single setting that is the same as the multiple-baseline design across behaviors.

Multiple-Baseline Design across Settings

The multiple-baseline design across settings is similar to the previous two designs except that the researcher selects two or more settings. The researcher then measures the participant's behavior in each of these settings. She takes baseline measures in each setting and then introduces the intervention in only the first setting. The participant's behavior in the second setting is not exposed to the intervention until later. Figure 11.1 displays data for a multiple-baseline design across settings. The figure indicates that there are two settings included in the investigation.

There are several important aspects of this design. First, there should be several settings as opposed to one setting with the multiple-baseline design across behaviors or participants. There is also one behavior measured that is the same as with the multiple-baseline design across participants. Recall that there are several behaviors in the multiple-

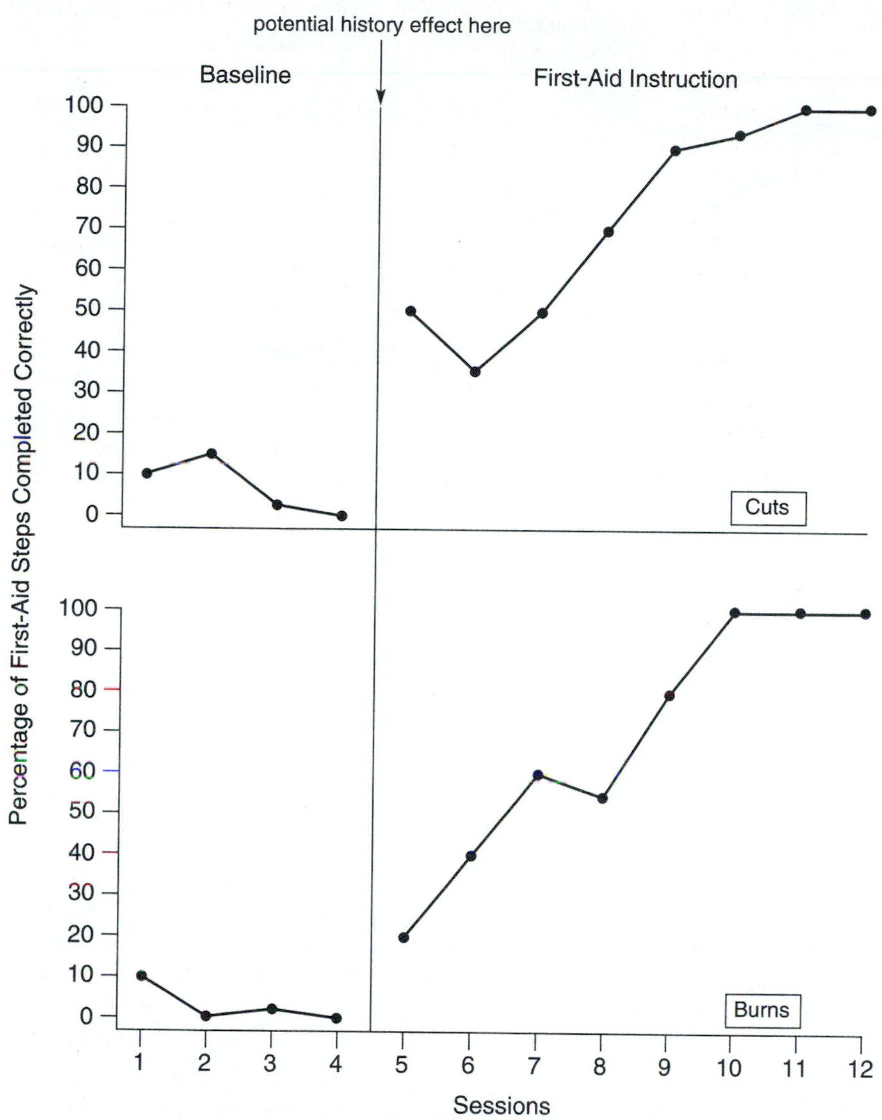

FIGURE 11.2 The percentage of first-aid steps completed correctly across baseline and first-aid instruction conditions for cuts and burns.

baseline design across behaviors. Finally, there is a single participant or a single group of participants treated as a single participant as in the multiple-baseline design across behaviors; this is different from the multiple-baseline design across participants that requires more than one participant or group.

Multiple-Probe Design

One potential problem with multiple-baseline designs is the need for repeated measurements. At times, repeated measurements may result in reactivity during baseline (a testing problem or a change in

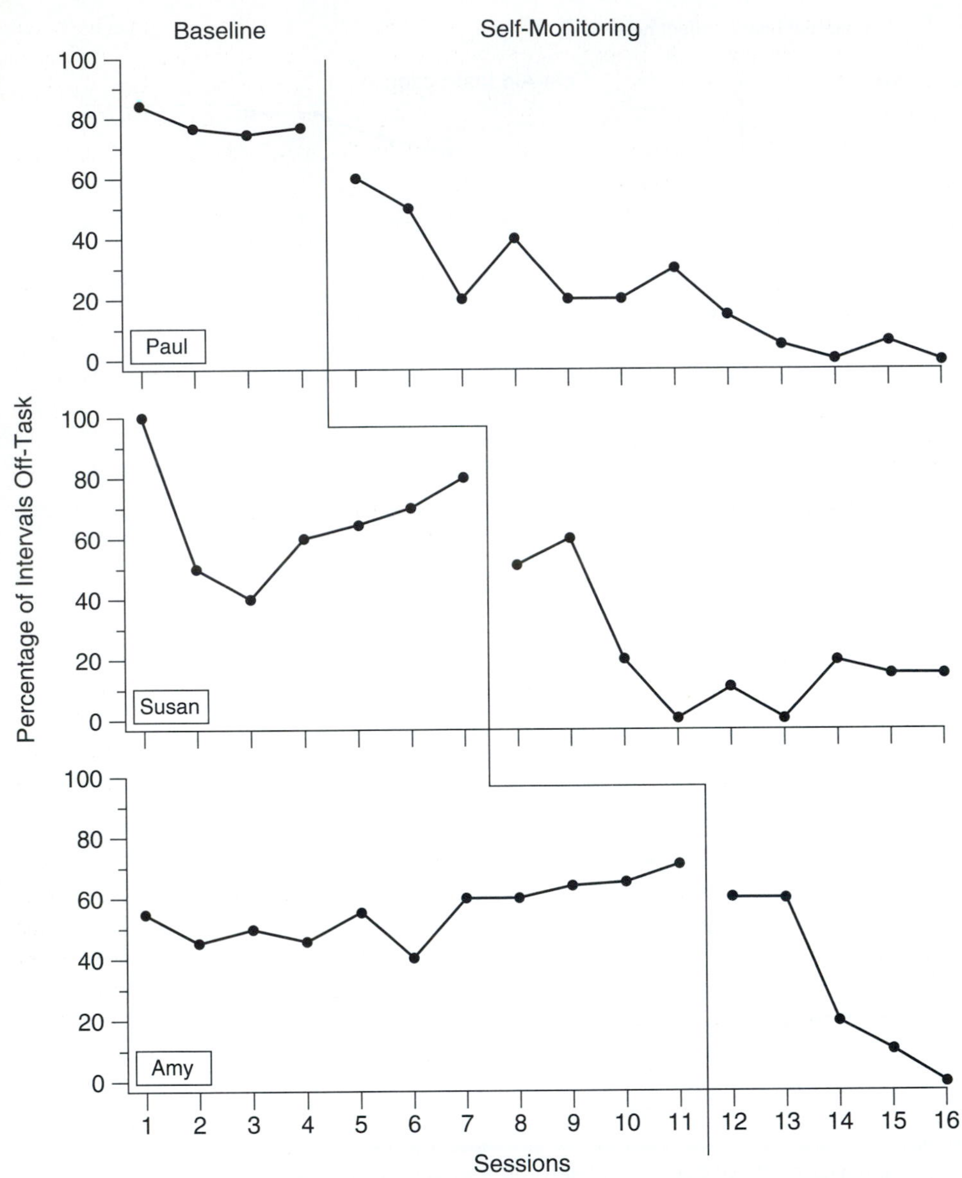

FIGURE 11.3 Percentage of intervals of off-task across baseline and self-monitoring conditions for Paul, Susan, and Amy.

the behavior due to repetition of assessment) (Horner & Baer, 1978). There are other times that frequent assessments may not be feasible and alternative assessment methods must be used. For example, we would probably not wish to provide frequent intelligence testing (i.e., once per day) over a long period of time. First, providing such a standardized test most likely would lead to reactivity. Second, frequent intelligence testing may be too costly and time-consuming. An alternative to frequent or repeated measurements is to "probe" the behavior every so often (e.g., once per week) during the baseline condition.

A further concern surrounding repeated measures involves the frequency with which researchers measure the behavior during the intervention condition. According to Barlow and Hersen (1984), if reactivity of measurement is the reason the multiple-probe technique is used, probes should also continue in the intervention condition. Barlow and Hersen also indicate that if the problem is the feasibility of providing frequent measures during baseline, or if researchers have reason to believe that the baseline would have been stable had frequent measures taken place, frequent measurements may be applied during the intervention condition.

Additionally, Kazdin (1982) indicated that probes may be used in situations where behaviors were not the target for intervention as in the case of assessing generalization/transfer or maintenance of intervention effects. Finally, a combination of multiple-baseline and multiple-probe designs may be used in situations where frequent measurements are applied to behaviors that are targeted for change and probes are conducted to assess generalization/transfer.

Multiple-probe designs are essentially multiple-baseline designs where the measurements are not conducted on a frequent basis. Figure 11.4 demonstrates a multiple-probe design across participants. Notice that there are fewer data points during baseline and intervention sessions. Obviously, a potential problem is a lack of data points to show stability or a trend. Generally, three data points are required for such a demonstration. In the figure, only Susan and Amy had three baseline data points. However, the advantage of having fewer data points to avoid reactivity is probably greater than the disadvantage of having too few data points.

Analysis of Data

As with withdrawal designs, critical research consumers must understand how to analyze the graphically displayed data. (*Note:* As with withdrawal and associated designs, statistics have been developed to aid in the interpretation of multiple-baseline designs; however, visual inspection is the primary method of analyzing data in multiple-baseline designs.) Additionally, critical research consumers must consider the internal and the external validity of the investigation.

Internal Validity. When assessing the internal validity of multiple-baseline designs, several concerns must be taken into consideration. These concerns involve the condition length; independence of behaviors; the amount of overlap of the data; the number of baselines; independence of the behaviors, participants, or settings; and the level and rapidity of change. Table 11.1 summarizes the major threats to internal validity of the designs discussed in this chapter.

Condition Length. The condition length of multiple-baseline designs is the same as in withdrawal and associated designs. There must be at least three stable data points or a countertherapeutic trend. However, the number of data points increases as the number of baselines increases (see the amount of data overlap).

Independence of Behaviors. Possibly the most critical rule in multiple-baseline designs is the independence of behaviors. Consider a multiple-baseline design across behaviors. Suppose that a researcher was conducting research on investigating different methods of math instruction. The researcher defined two separate behaviors that she was going to measure. The behaviors included adding two to other numbers (e.g., 2 plus 1, 2 plus 2, 2 plus three, etc., up to 2 plus 9) and adding three to other numbers (e.g., 3 plus 1, 3 plus 2, 3 plus 3, etc., up to 3 plus 9). The researcher took baseline data on each of the skills and implemented the intervention on adding 2 to numbers 1 to 9. Adding 3 to numbers 1 to 9 continued in baseline. The intervention involved using blocks or manipulatives to solve the problems. The skill of adding 2 to other numbers improved quickly and substantially. However, adding 3 to other numbers also improved. It is quite apparent that the skills were not independent. In fact, since the skills were

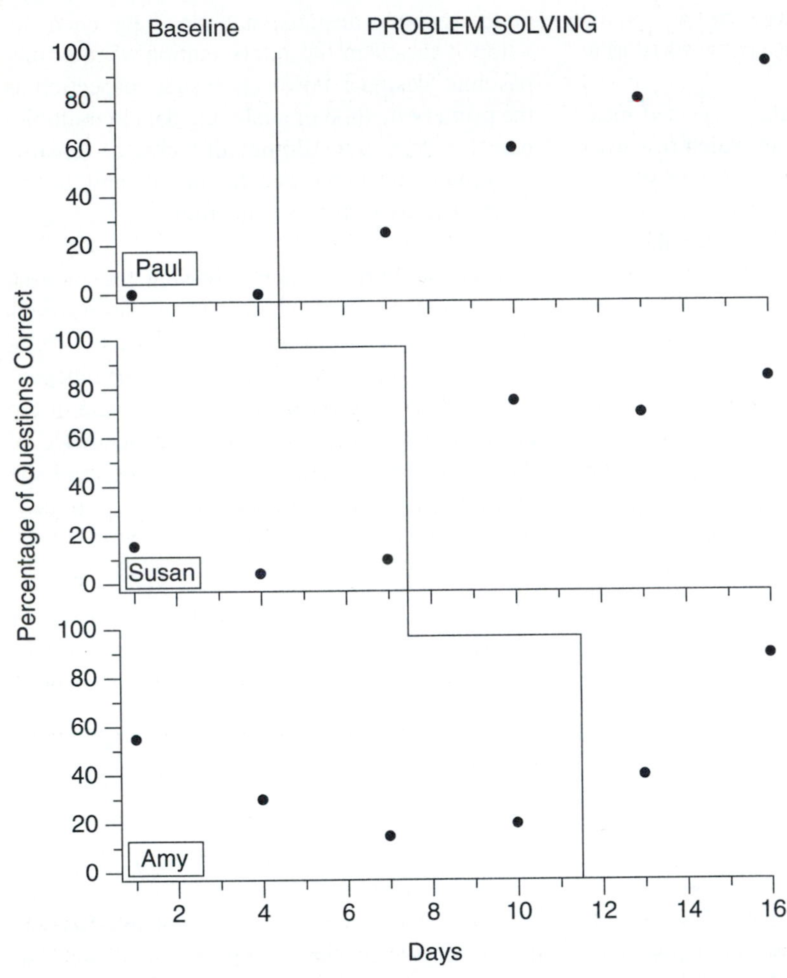

FIGURE 11.4 Percentage of math problems answered correctly across baseline and problem-solving conditions for Paul, Susan, and Amy.

dependent on the same underlying math operation, the two skills improved together. The experimental control was thus weakened.

Many times, the behaviors being measured do not look the same such as taking care of a burn and an abrasion. The end product should look different and many of the steps leading up to the first aid of the injury are different. However, as Marchand-Martella and Martella (1990) have shown, the behaviors may be in the same response class. That is, taking care of burns has some things in common with taking care of abrasions. When participants are taught how to care for one injury, improvements in other injuries may also be seen. The internal validity threat for this is likely diffusion of treatment. In other words, the independent variable had unintended effects on the behavior that was in baseline. Researchers must take care to ensure that behaviors are independent.

When researchers are using a multiple-baseline design across participants, a similar thing can happen. That is, the improvements seen in the

TABLE 11.1 Threats to Internal Validity for Each of the Designs Described in Chapter 11

	Multiple-Baseline Design across			
RESEARCH DESIGN THREAT	**BEHAVIORS**	**PARTICIPANTS**	**SETTINGS**	**MULTIPLE-PROBE DESIGN**
1. Maturation	Controlled	Controlled	Controlled	Controlled
2. Selection	Not applicable	Not applicable	Not applicable	Not applicable
3. Selection by maturation interaction	Not applicable	Not applicable	Not applicable	Not applicable
4. Statistical regression	Possible concern	Controlled	Controlled	Controlled
5. Mortality	Controlled	Controlled	Controlled	Controlled
6. Instrumentation	Controlled	Controlled	Controlled	Controlled
7. Testing	Controlled	Controlled	Controlled	Controlled
8. History	Controlled	Controlled	Controlled	Controlled
9. Resentful demoralization of the control group	Not applicable	Not applicable	Not applicable	Not applicable
10. Diffusion of treatment	Controlled	Controlled	Controlled	Controlled
11. Compensatory rivalry by the control group	Not applicable	Not applicable	Not applicable	Not applicable
12. Compensatory equalization	Not applicable	Not applicable	Not applicable	Not applicable

Note: This table is meant only as a general guideline. Decisions with regard to threats to internal validity must be made after the specifics of an investigation are known and understood. Thus, interpretations of internal validity threats must be made on a study-by-study basis.

behavior of one participant may also be seen in other participants. This improvement may occur if a participant sees another participant displaying the skill and imitates the model or the participants talk to one another. Consider teaching a particular skill such as problem solving to a class of second graders. The students are taught math strategies to use during story problems. The students display an improved ability to do math story problems that correspond to their problem-solving training. The second graders go to recess on a daily basis. On the same playground is another second-grade class that is still in baseline. The students from the first class talk to the students from the second class and tell them the great things they are leaning from their teacher. They tell the other students that they are learning problem-solving strategies to help with difficult math problems, and they are doing better as a result. The class still in baseline has been exposed to some part of the intervention. It is possible, although remote, that the class in baseline learned enough to affect their ability to problem solve and, in turn, exhibited an improved ability to solve math story problems. Again, we have a problem here with diffusion of treatment since the participants were not independent. Researchers must attempt to ensure that their participants have as little contact with others or remain as independent as possible.

Researchers must also ensure independence of behaviors when using a multiple-baseline design across settings. There are more potential problems with this design. There may be diffusion of treatment since the participant fails to discriminate the conditions in place in one classroom from another. For example, suppose that a researcher is investigating the effects of a management program for a seventh-grade student displaying aggressive outbursts. The student is taught relaxation exercises to use when he gets angry. The researcher hopes that getting the student to concentrate on doing something else besides the aggressive act when angry will help decrease the frequency of aggressive episodes. The researcher implements the intervention in Period 1 while keeping the behavior in baseline in Period 2. During the relaxation training, the student's aggressive behavior begins to decrease. The aggressive episodes also begin to decrease in Period 2. From a practical standpoint, what has happened is great. The student is behaving more acceptably in Period 2 without being exposed to the intervention. However, from an experimental perspective, the student's improved behavior is a problem. The behavior in Period 1 is not independent of the behavior in Period 2.

Generalization or transfer of treatment effects in this case harm the internal validity of the investigation. Again, we have diffusion of treatment. The intervention effects "leaked" into Period 2. Essentially, the researcher has an A-B design with all of its problems (see Figure 11.5). Researchers must make sure that the settings are substantially different from one another so that independence is achieved or aid the participant in discriminating when the intervention is in effect and when it is not in effect such as telling the student or posting this information.

Amount of Data Overlap. The amount of data overlap is important in multiple-baseline designs. As with a baseline in a withdrawal design, there should be a minimum of three stable data points or three data points moving in a countertherapeutic direction to show a trend. This is also true with the baseline in a multiple-baseline design. However, there is one additional feature with multiple baselines that adds to the complexity of condition length. The successive baselines (e.g., each one after the initial baseline) should have at least three data points during the intervention of the previous behavior. In other words, there is a minimum of three overlapping data points for the first baseline and a minimum of three for the second baseline plus three additional data points of overlap during the intervention of the first behavior. In all, there is a minimum of six data points for the second baseline.

Figure 11.6(a) shows a multiple-baseline design across participants where there is only one data point of overlap. This demonstration can hinder the experimental demonstration of the effects of the independent variable. The reason for this is that one should project the condition line straight down from the previous behavior. The control comes from demonstrating that the previous behavior would not have changed if the intervention was not implemented. This demonstration comes from the other behavior(s) remaining stable. The least amount of data needed to detect a trend is three. Thus, the way researchers can demonstrate stability or a countertherapeutic trend is to generate three data points. Thus, an argument that can be made about the data in Figure 11.6(a) is that one data point is not enough to demonstrate that the first behavior would not have changed if the intervention was not provided.

Figure 11.6(b) shows the overlap of three data points. This overlap is clearly a better demonstration of experimental control since a therapeutic trend is not detected in the following behavior. Thus, when interpreting the data of a multiple-baseline design, critical research consumers must look at the amount of data overlap as well as the trend in the data for the behavior(s) that follows.

Number of Baselines. In order to have a multiple-baseline design, researchers must have at least two baselines. However, the question to ask is whether two baselines are sufficient to demonstrate experimental control. In order to answer this question, we must first look at how experimental control comes from the multiple-baseline design. As stated in the previous section, we must project the data down from the previous behavior(s); see Figure 11.6(b). Notice that we must infer whether the behavior would have remained at baseline levels if the intervention had not taken place. On the other hand, in the withdrawal design, the participant serves as his or her own control. We can claim that the behavior would have stayed the same or had little change

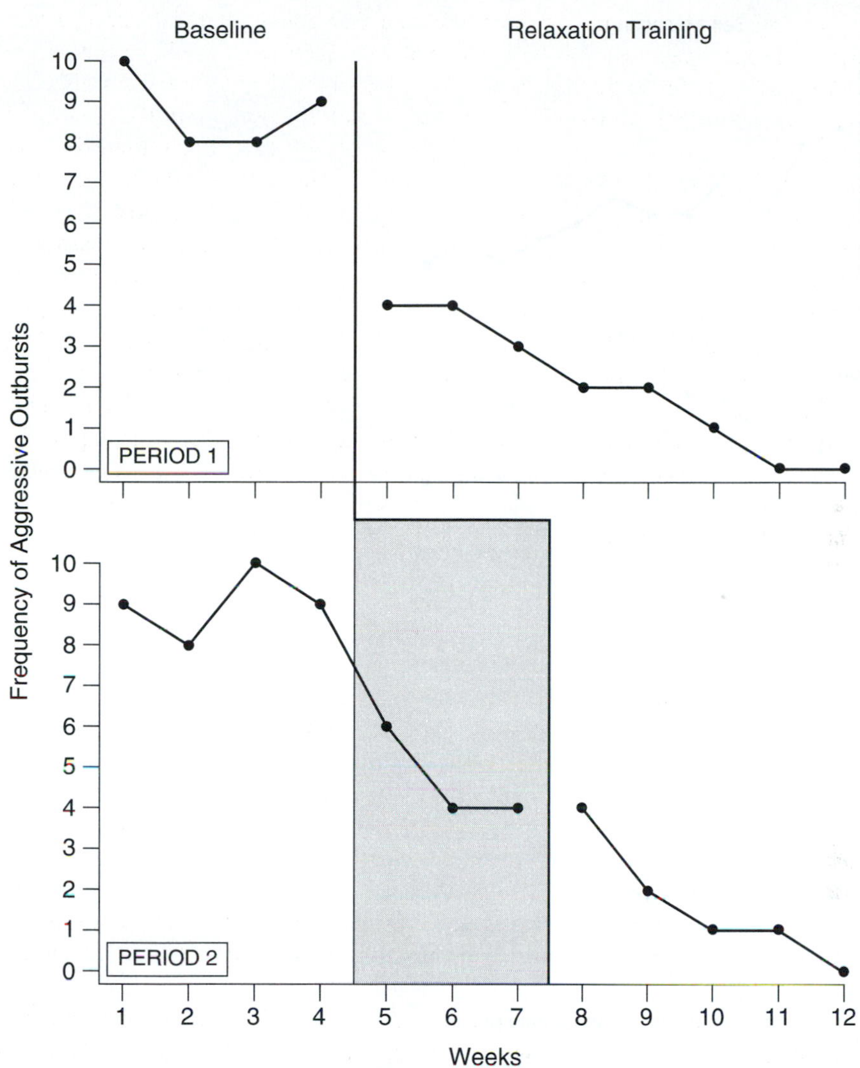

FIGURE 11.5 The frequency of aggressive outbursts across baseline and relaxation training conditions across Periods 1 and 2.

since the behavior returns to near baseline levels. The amount of inference is considerably less with the withdrawal design than with the multiple-baseline design. For this reason, the withdrawal design is considered to have a higher level of internal validity than the multiple-baseline design (Barlow & Hersen, 1984). Multiple-baseline designs are weaker because the participant does not serve as his or her own control; different behaviors, participants, or settings that follow the initial graph serve as the control.

Recall that a multiple-baseline design is simply a series of A-B designs. The experimental control of an A-B design is not considered to be especially strong (see Chapter 10). However, when a multiple-baseline design is implemented, the A-B

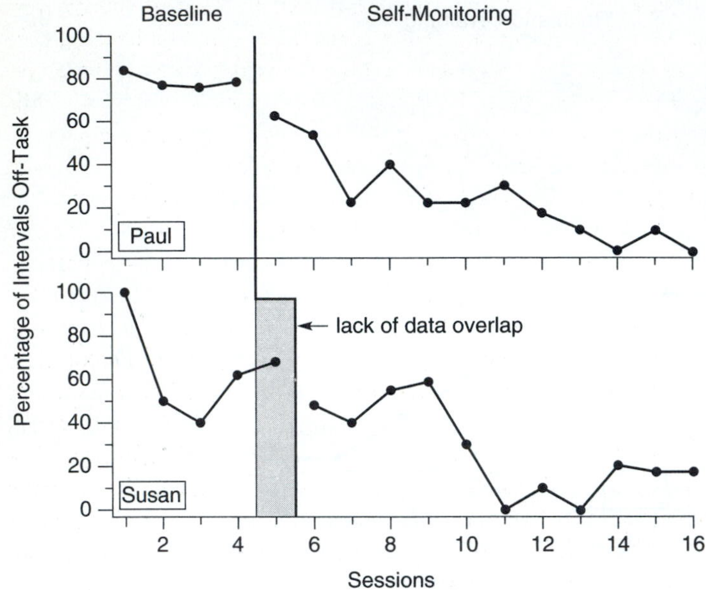

(a)

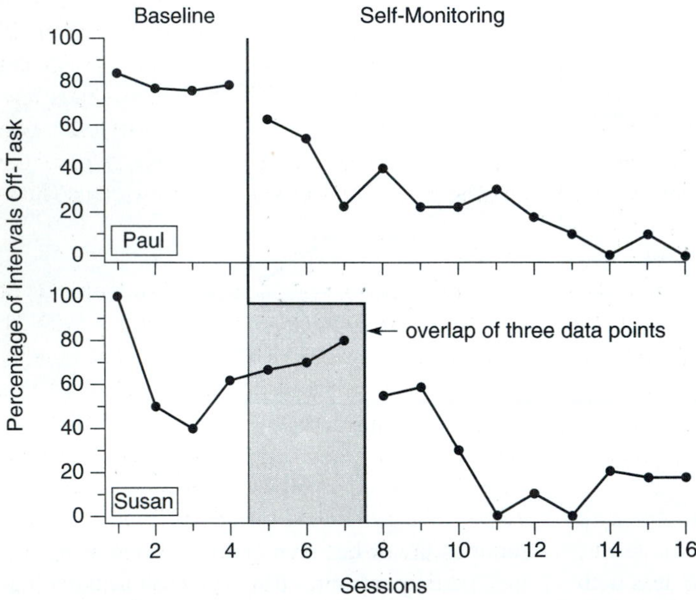

(b)

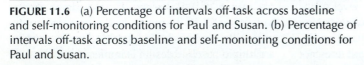

FIGURE 11.6 (a) Percentage of intervals off-task across baseline and self-monitoring conditions for Paul and Susan. (b) Percentage of intervals off-task across baseline and self-monitoring conditions for Paul and Susan.

designs are combined where the baselines begin at the same time but the interventions occur at different times. Thus, the number of baselines is critical for the demonstration of experimental control. The chances that history or some other extraneous variable caused the change in the independent variable is fairly high with the A-B design; see Figure 11.7(a). The chances that an extraneous variable caused the results with a multiple-baseline design across two behaviors, participants, or settings is lessened since it is less likely that the same extraneous event caused the observed changes for both behaviors/participants/settings at different points in time; see Figure11.7(b). The chances that an extraneous event caused the changes in a multiple-baseline design across three behaviors, participants, or settings is even less; see Figure 11.7(c). Finally, the chances that an extraneous variable caused the changes in a multiple-baseline design across four behaviors, participants, or settings, is much lower; see Figure 11.7(d).

In summary, the larger the number of baselines, the higher the level of experimental control simply because the probability that an extraneous variable caused the observed changes in each of the behaviors becomes less likely the more behaviors, participants, or settings we have. Barlow and Hersen (1984) and Wolf and Risley (1971) recommend that there be a minimum of three to four baselines, and Kazdin (1982) recommends more than three baselines to clarify the effects of the independent variable.

Thus, it would seem that four or more baselines should be the goal of researchers. However, there is a major problem with a higher number of baselines. That is, the more baselines, the longer the later behaviors remain in baseline or are kept from receiving the intervention. For example, if we go with the three data point overlap rule, the first behavior is in baseline for at least three sessions; the second for six sessions; the third for nine sessions; the fourth for 12 sessions. Thus, there are a minimum of 12 sessions for the fourth baseline. If there is any variability or if a behavior is moving in a therapeutic direction, the number of sessions will increase from there. Thus, there are times when less than three data points of overlap are used or when fewer than four baselines are included. The critical research consumer may remember the following general guidelines: the fewer baselines, the weaker the experimental control; the fewer the number of data points with overlap, the weaker the experimental control.

A further advantage of more baselines is that if we have, say, five baselines and the intervention does not work as intended for one of these or if the behavior begins to improve before the intervention, there are still four more baselines to demonstrate experimental control (see the data in Figure 11.8 for Amy). Of course, the experimental control demonstration is weakened in such a situation. The more "failures" in the multiple-baseline design (e.g., two or more behaviors failing to improve or improving too soon), the weaker the control. Consider if a researcher had only two baselines and the second behavior did not respond to intervention or improved before the intervention. The experimental control is weak since the researcher is left with an A-B design. On one hand, there are advantages to many baselines; on the other hand, the amount of time needed to run several baselines may be prohibitive. However, if researchers use only two baselines, the levels and rapidity of change and the stability of the data must be especially clear (Kazdin, 1982).

Level and Rapidity of Change. The concept of level and rapidity of change is the same as with the withdrawal design. However, the level and rapidity of change are critical for all of the behaviors in a multiple-baseline design. For example, Figure 11.9 shows a multiple-baseline design across participants. The first participant showed rapid and significant improvements in the ability to read. The second participant had difficulty obtaining the skill, and acquisition was slower and not as pronounced at first. The third student had a similar response as the first participant. The behavior change was rapid and substantial. Notice that if the researcher only had two baselines, the experimental control would have been much weaker. Essentially, with two baselines and the data presented in

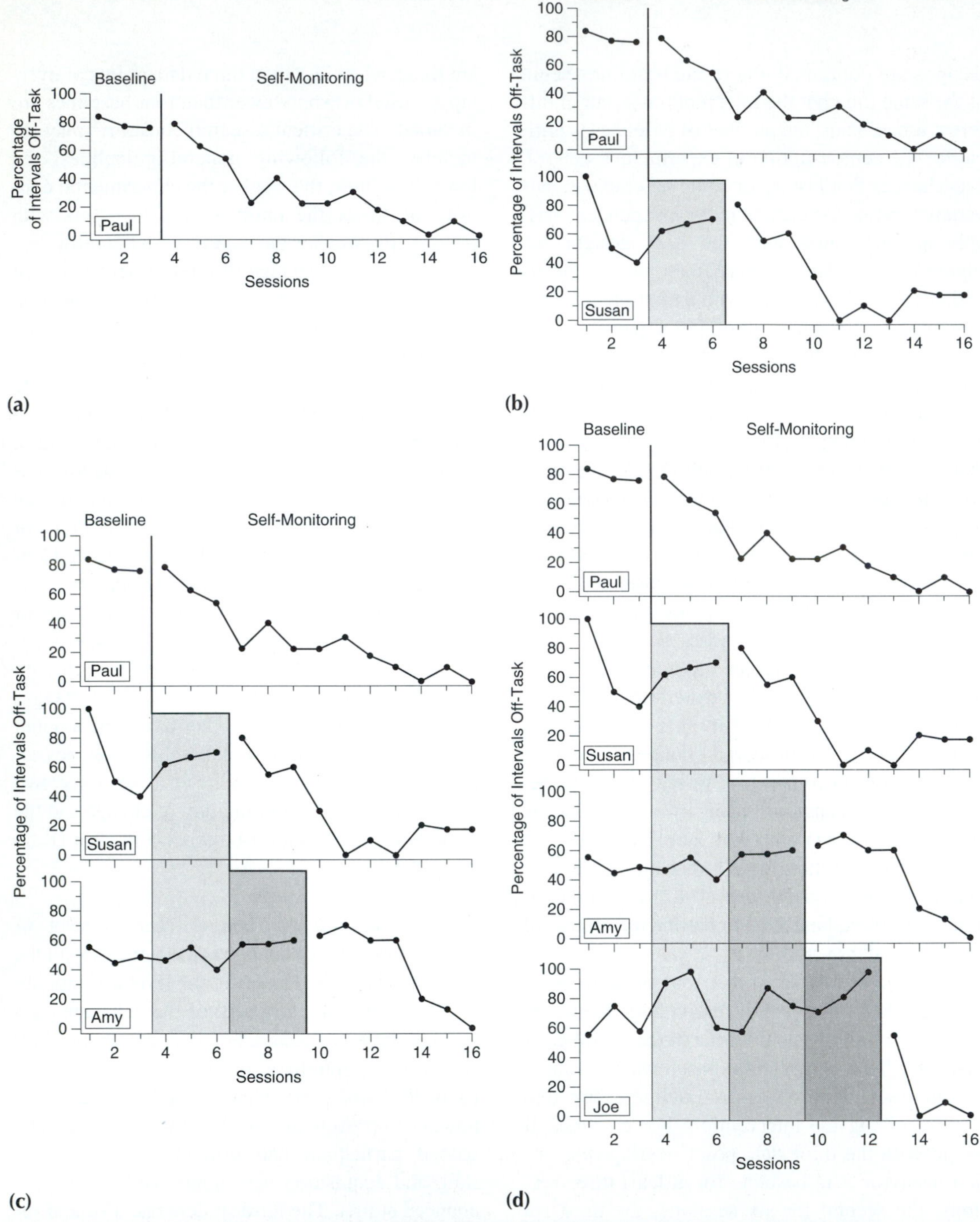

FIGURE 11.7 (a) Percentage of intervals off-task across baseline and self-monitoring conditions. (b) Percentage of intervals off-task across baseline and self-monitoring conditions for Paul and Susan. (c) Percentage of intervals off-task across baseline and self-monitoring conditions for Paul, Susan, and Amy. (d) Percentage of intervals off-task across baseline and self-monitoring conditions for Paul, Susan, Amy, and Joe.

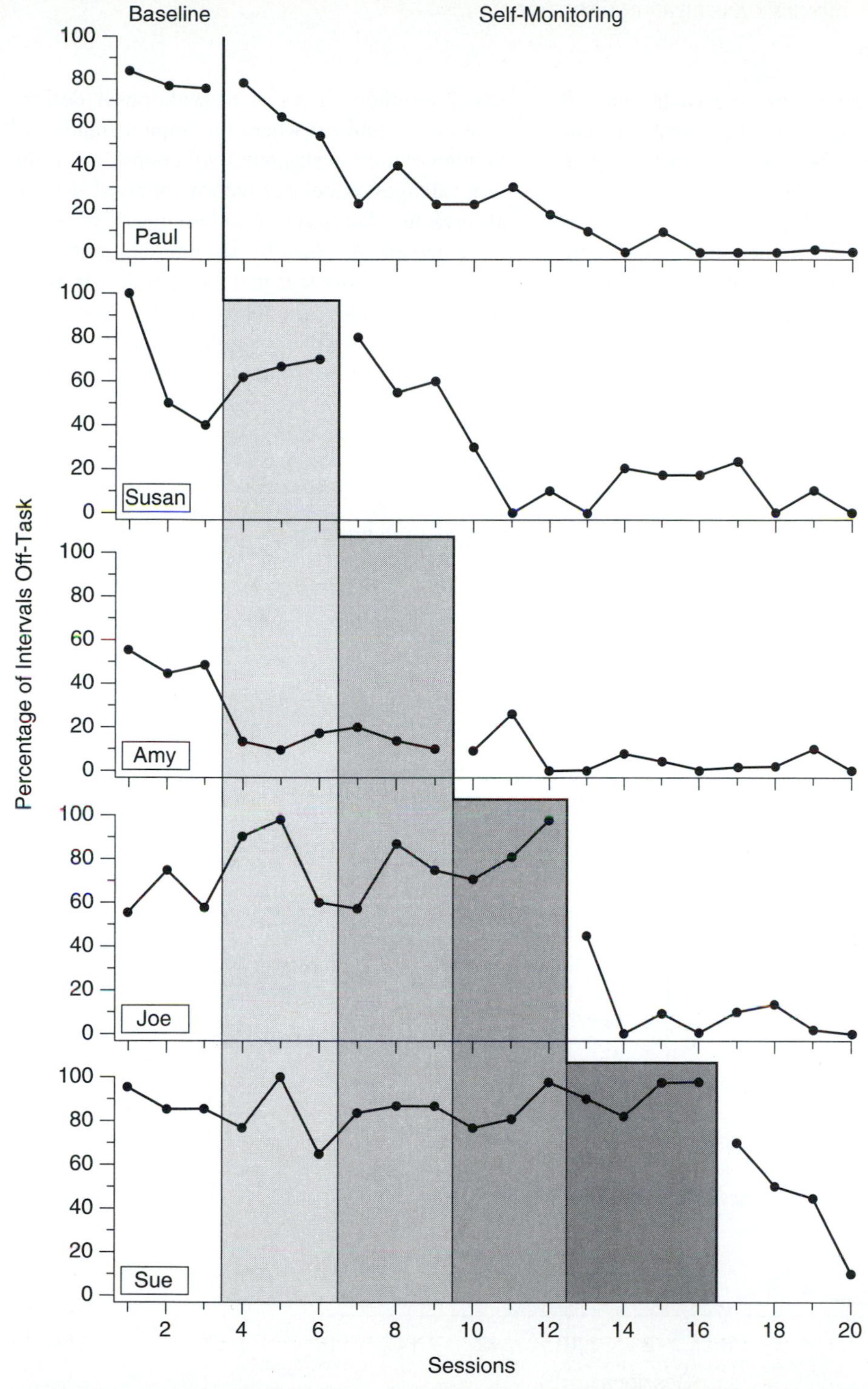

FIGURE 11.8 Percentage of intervals off-task across baseline and self-monitoring conditions for Paul, Susan, Amy, Joe, and Sue.

Figure 11.9, the researcher would have had an A-B design. Thus, the change should be substantial and rapid for each of the behaviors if strong experimental control is to be achieved.

Withdrawal. One method that one can use to increase the internal validity of multiple-baseline designs is to withdraw the intervention from each of the behaviors/participants/settings. In other words, one would return to the baseline condition after an effect has been seen during the intervention condition. Essentially, a series of withdrawal designs would be combined where the implementation of the intervention is staggered. Of course, all of the disadvantages associated with withdrawal designs are present when a return-to-baseline condition is implemented. A return to baseline may not occur for skill acquisitions; it may be unethical in some instances to remove the intervention; or it may not be ethically defensible to end on a baseline condition (of course, this problem is easily rectified with an additional "B" condition). A primary reason re-

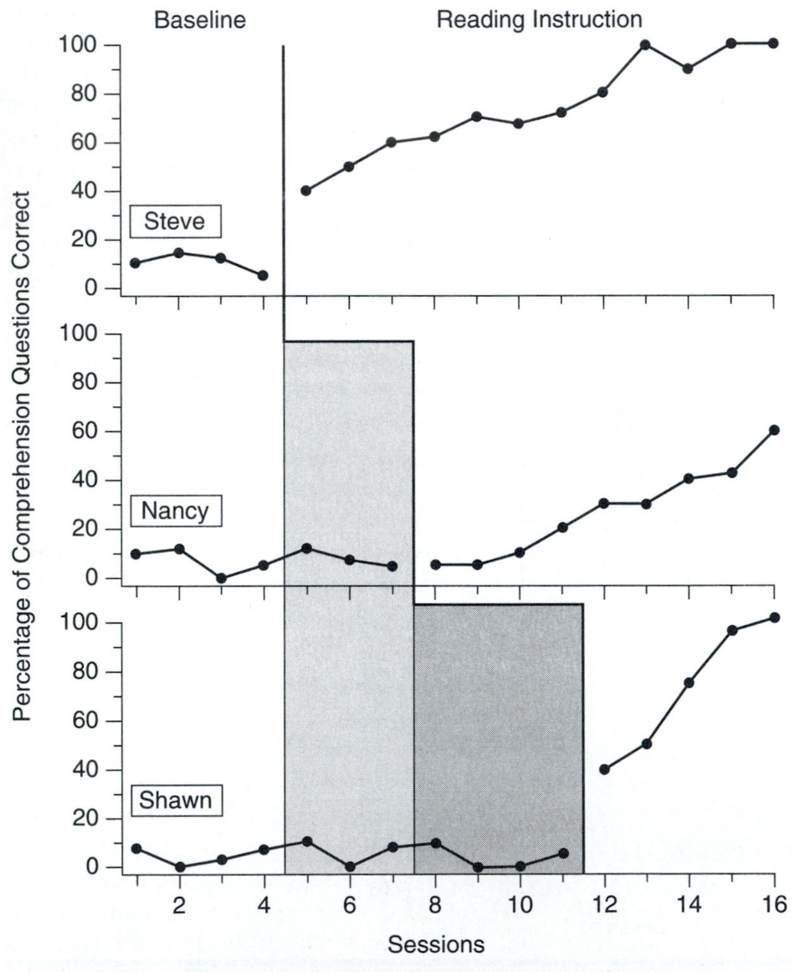

FIGURE 11.9 Percentage of reading comprehension questions correct across baseline and reading instruction conditions for Steve, Nancy, and Shawn.

searchers would opt for a multiple-baseline design over a withdrawal design is due to the difficulties associated with the withdrawal design.

External Validity. The external validity of multiple-baseline designs can best be assessed by reviewing what is meant by external validity. External validity is essentially the generalization of the treatment effects to other people (population validity) or different situations (ecological validity). There is no standard that suggests how many participants researchers must have (Researchers frequently determine the number of participants required to increase power; however, this is an internal validity concern, not specifically an external one), or how many settings or measures researchers must have to make a claim of external validity.

Recall the primary problem with the withdrawal design—there is typically one participant in one setting with one behavior of concern. Of course, as indicated previously, single-case studies are not limited to one participant. However, the withdrawal design generally has a lack of external validity. The primary advantage that multiple-baseline designs have over the withdrawal design is that they represent the real world more closely. We can have several participants at one time as in a multiple-baseline design across participants; we can have several settings available as in a multiple-baseline design across settings; we can have several behaviors under investigation at one time as in a multiple-baseline design across behaviors; or we can have behaviors not under explicit investigation (i.e., not a primary dependent variable) assessed for carryover or generalization effects as in a multiple-probe design (Kazdin, 1982).

Thus, the external validity of multiple-baseline designs (including the multiple-probe design) is stronger than the withdrawal design. However, the primary purpose of multiple-baseline designs is to control for threats to internal validity, not external validity. We should view multiple-baseline designs as alternatives to withdrawal designs in determining the effects of the independent variable on the dependent variable, not as a method of demonstrating the generalizability of treatment effects. Single-case researchers attempt to determine the generalization of treatment effects through replications (see Chapter 1). Table 11.2 summarizes the major threats to external validity of the designs discussed in this chapter.

Research Examples

Multiple-Baseline Design across Behaviors. Martella, Marchand-Martella, Young, and Macfarlane (1995) used a multiple-baseline design across behaviors to measure the effects of teaching peer tutors three effective instructional behaviors: specific praise statements, effective error correction procedures to decrease negative statements made to the student, and appropriate instructions. The peer tutors, who were high school seniors without disabilities, had two months of peer tutoring experience working with a 14-year-old male student with Down syndrome who was placed in a self-contained special education classroom. The problem encountered by the peer tutors was that the student would become agitated during instruction and engage in destructive and aggressive acts. Upon conducting an analysis of the situation, the authors concluded that the instructional behaviors displayed by the peer tutors left a great deal to be desired and decided to teach basic effective instructional skills. Training involved providing the peer tutors with definitions and examples of acceptable instructional methods and providing specific and immediate verbal and written feedback to the peer tutors after an instructional session with the student. The intervention included instruction for praise statements, followed by error corrections, and ended with appropriate instructional commands.

The dependent measures included the percentage of specific praise statements (the goal was 50% of all praise statements being specific), percentage of negative statements (the goal was less than 20% of all statements), and percentage of appropriate instructional commands (the goal was 80%). (*Note:* The term commands or instructional commands was common when the investigation took place. A more appropriate term is simply

TABLE 11.2 Threats to External Validity for Each of the Designs Described in Chapter 11

	Multiple-Baseline Design across			
RESEARCH DESIGN THREAT	**BEHAVIORS**	**PARTICIPANTS**	**SETTINGS**	**MULTIPLE-PROBE DESIGN**
1. Generalization across participants	Possible concern	Possible concern[1]	Possible concern	Possible concern
2. Interaction of personological variables and treatment effects	Possible concern	Possible concern[1]	Possible concern	Possible concern
3. Verification of independent variable possible concern	Possible concern	Possible concern	Possible concern	Possible concern
4. Multiple treatment interference	Controlled	Controlled	Controlled	Controlled
5. Novelty and disruption effects	Possible concern	Possible concern	Possible concern	Possible concern
6. Hawthorne effect	Possible concern	Possible concern	Possible concern	Possible concern
7. Experimenter effects	Possible concern	Possible concern	Possible concern	Possible concern
8. Pretest sensitization	Not applicable	Not applicable	Not applicable	Not applicable
9. Posttest sensitization	Not applicable	Not applicable	Not applicable	Not applicable
10. Interaction of time of measurement and treatment effects	Possible concern	Possible concern	Possible concern	Possible concern
11. Measurement of the dependent variable	Possible concern[2]	Possible concern	Possible concern	Possible concern
12. Interaction of history and treatment effects	Possible concern	Possible concern	Possible concern	Possible concern

[1]Could be stronger than other single-case designs depending on the number of participants; however, most likely, the participants are not representative of the general population.

[2]Could be stronger since there are multiple behaviors being measured.

Note: This table is meant only as a general guideline. Decisions with regard to threats to external validity must be made after the specifics of an investigation are known and understood. Thus, interpretations of external validity threats must be made on a study-by-study basis.

instructions.) The results (shown in the graph in Figure 11.10) indicate that the training package was effective in improving the instructional behaviors of the peer tutors. Additionally, the student's behavior greatly improved, and this improvement was correlated with the implementation of the training program.

Multiple-Baseline Design across Participants. Marchand-Martella, Martella, Agran, and Young (1991) assessed the effects of an intervention package on the first-aid skills of elementary-aged children. There were six children involved in the investigation ranging in age from six to eight years. All six children attended a local elementary school.

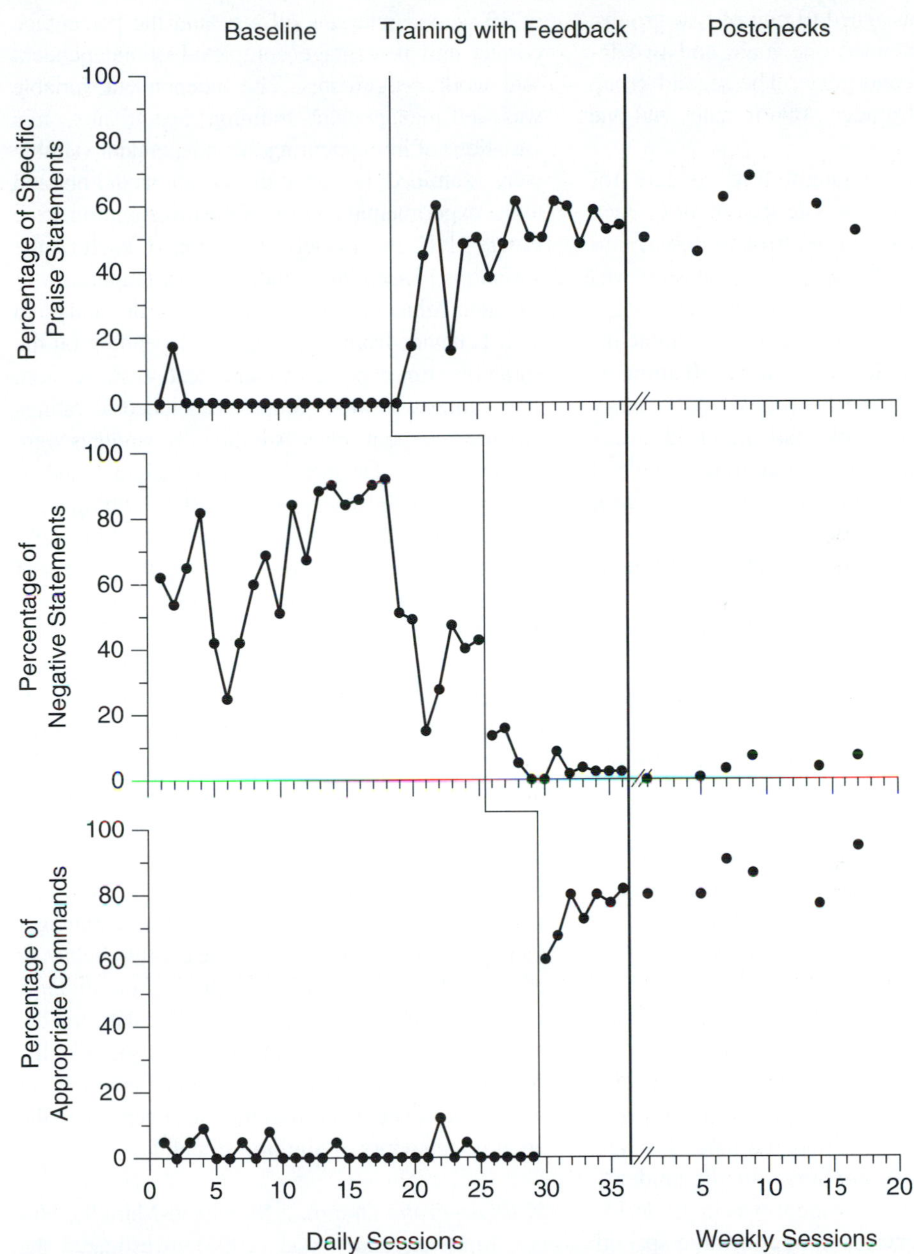

FIGURE 11.10 The percentages of Darrin's and Keith's appropriate commands, negative statements, and specific praise statements while instructing Dan during baseline, training, and postcheck sessions.

The children were assigned to one of two groups. The first group contained one male and two females, all in the second grade. The second group contained three first graders, two females and one male.

The children were taught how to care for burns, abrasions, and cuts. The treatment of each injury was task-analyzed (i.e., broken down) into several small steps. The dependent measure was the average percentage of task-analyzed steps completed correctly. The independent variable involved group instruction that lasted 20 minutes per session. The first-aid instructor read a story out of a first-aid storybook, had the children repeat the story of how to care for an injury, and had the children role-play first-aid treatment with puppets represented in the storybook. The instructor provided praise for correct first-aid treatment and corrected mistakes.

As shown in Figure 11.11, the two groups improved when instruction was implemented. The baseline data for all three injuries were relatively stable for each group, and there was an immediate and rapid improvement in each group's performance.

Multiple-Baseline Design across Settings. Smith, Nelson, Young, and West (1992) used a multiple-baseline design across settings to measure the effects of a self-management procedure on the off-task behavior and the academic work of eight students with mild disabilities (i.e., behavior disorders [n = 4] or learning disabilities [n = 4]). Students spent part of the school day in a special education setting and the other part of the day in a general education setting. Students ranged in age between 12 and 16 years. Seven of the students were in grade 10 and one student was in grade 11. Students received services in one of three special education classrooms. All eight students were in the same general education classroom.

The dependent variables included off-task behavior (i.e., failing to use academic materials appropriately) and academic behavior (i.e., correct and complete seat work assignments). The dependent variables were measured by recording the percentage of 10-second intervals off-task and the percentage correct and percentage completed of independent seat work assignments. The independent variable was self-management training. Specifically, five variations of implementing the independent variable were examined; however, the variations did not add to the experimental control of the investigation. (See Figure 11.12 for a brief description of each of the variations.) Essentially, students were taught how to rate their behaviors against classroom rules and rated their behavior from one to three (depending on the variation) times per 30-minute seat work session. This rating was then compared/matched to ratings provided by the teacher. Additionally, students were taught how to set academic goals, which included labeling assignments, sequencing tasks, dividing work equally across the number of days, and setting daily academic completion goals indicating the amount of work that would be completed during the independent seat work period.

The variations throughout the investigation included adding academic goal setting and matching student with teacher ratings from one to three times during the 30-minute session, presenting the matchings alone three times during the 30-minute session, and presenting the matchings alone one or three times with a peer versus a teacher (general education classroom only).

As shown in Figure 11.12, the self-management program had an effect on the off-task behavior of the students. (*Note:* Data for three of the students are presented in this description. The data for the other five students are not presented graphically. Additionally, the data for academic behavior is not presented.) There was an immediate decrease in the off-task behaviors of all three students.

Multiple-Probe Design. Marchand-Martella, Huber, Martella, and Wood (1996) investigated the long-term maintenance of abduction prevention skills by preschoolers. The authors taught two preschool-age children to prevent the opportunity for abduction by exhibiting a proper vocalization (i.e., "No, I have to go ask my teacher") and a proper motor response (i.e., moving toward the school building for a minimum of 20 feet within three seconds after their vocalization or an abduction lure from a confederate [unfamiliar person who was part of the research team]). The participants' responses were measured for three types of abduction lures: simple (e.g., "How would you like to go with me?"), authority (e.g., "Come with me. Your teacher said you could"), or incentive (e.g., "Would you like to come see the surprise in my car?"). During baseline and training sessions, confederates approached the children while they were on the playground or away from the school grounds and attempted to lure the children away. The type of lure was determined randomly. Pretraining consisted of rehearsals by research assistants while each student watched, followed by rehearsals with the student. Correct responses were praised. During training, the teacher provided praise for correct responses to the confederate's lure. Incorrect

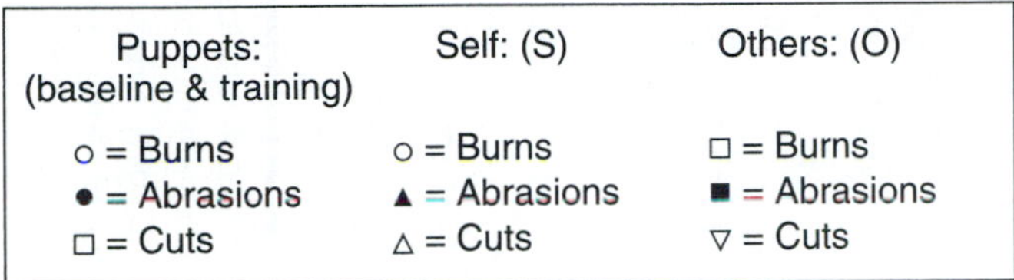

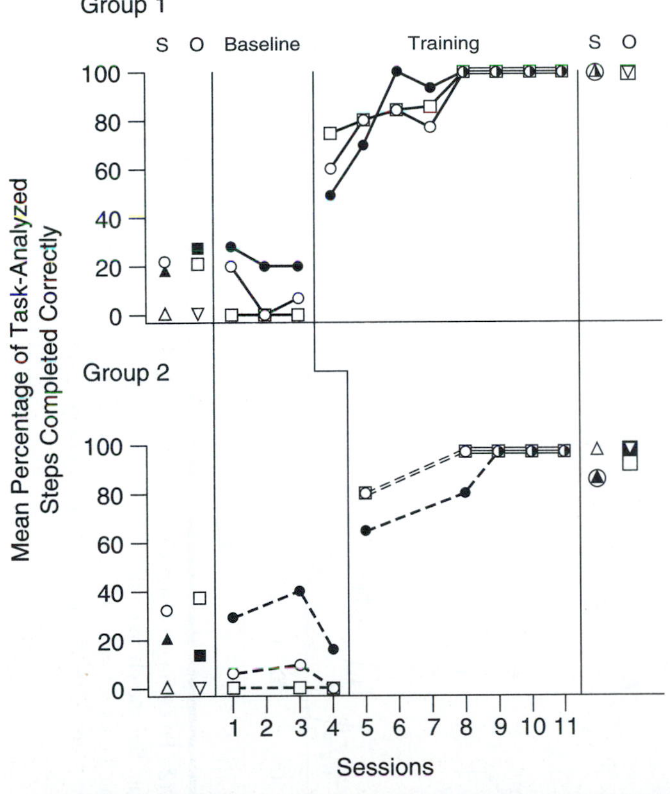

FIGURE 11.11 Mean percentage of task-analyzed steps completed correctly across two groups of three elementary-aged children.

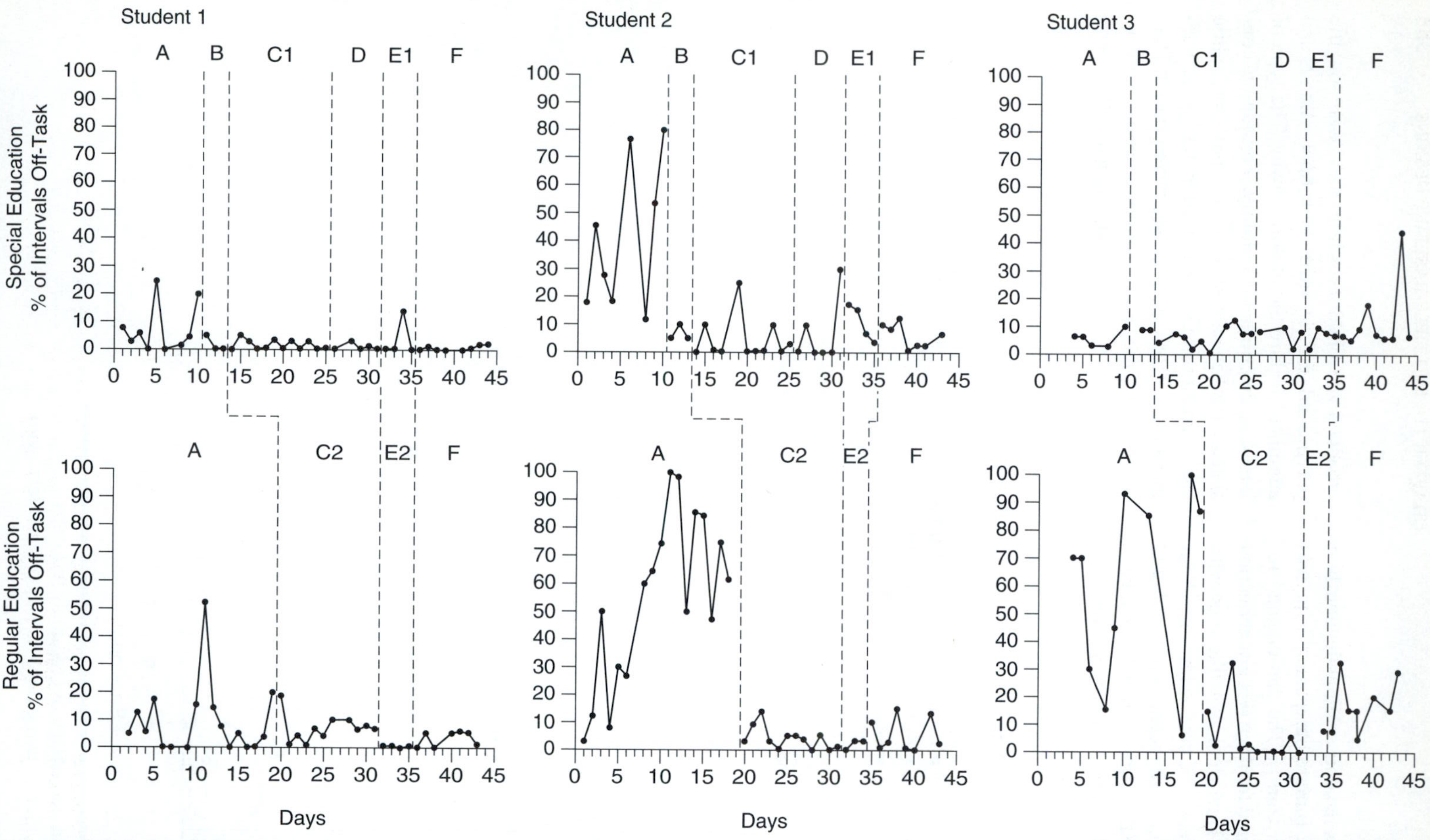

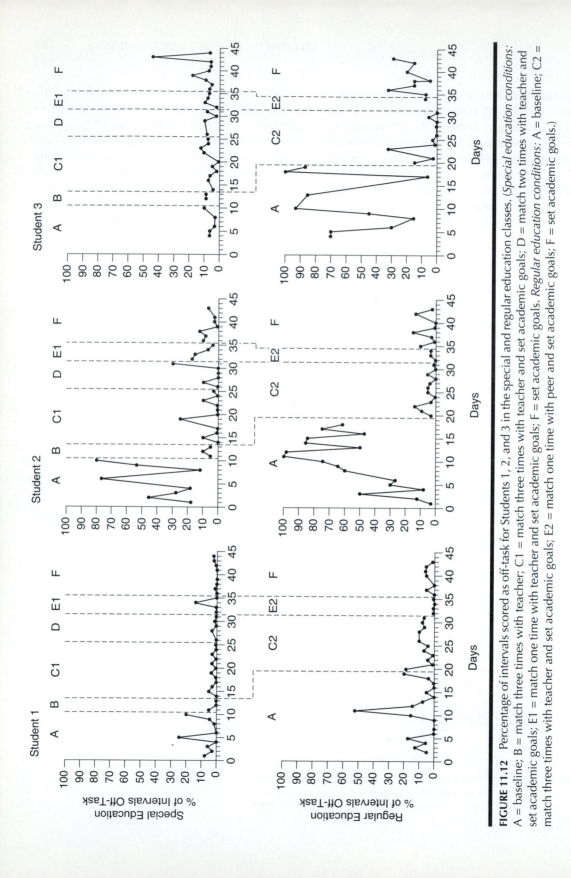

FIGURE 11.12 Percentage of intervals scored as off-task for Students 1, 2, and 3 in the special and regular education classes. (*Special education conditions:* A = baseline; B = match three times with teacher; C1 = match three times with teacher and set academic goals; D = match two times with teacher and set academic goals; E1 = match one time with teacher and set academic goals; F = set academic goals. *Regular education conditions:* A = baseline; C2 = match three times with teacher and set academic goals; E2 = match one time with peer and set academic goals; F = set academic goals.)

responses to lures were corrected by having each student rehearse or practice the correct responses with the teacher.

The dependent measure was the level of appropriateness of abduction prevention responses based on safety ratings of student responses. A multiple-probe design across participants was used to isolate the effects of the independent variable. Figure 11.13 shows the results of the program. As shown, the program improved the abduction prevention responses for the two students.

WHEN SHOULD RESEARCHERS USE EACH MULTIPLE-BASELINE DESIGN?

It should be apparent that there are several options that one can choose from when conducting single-case research. To determine the type of design one should use, one must determine the research question. For example, suppose that we were interested in investigating the effects of a behavior management program with an individual with autism. The procedure that we wished to use

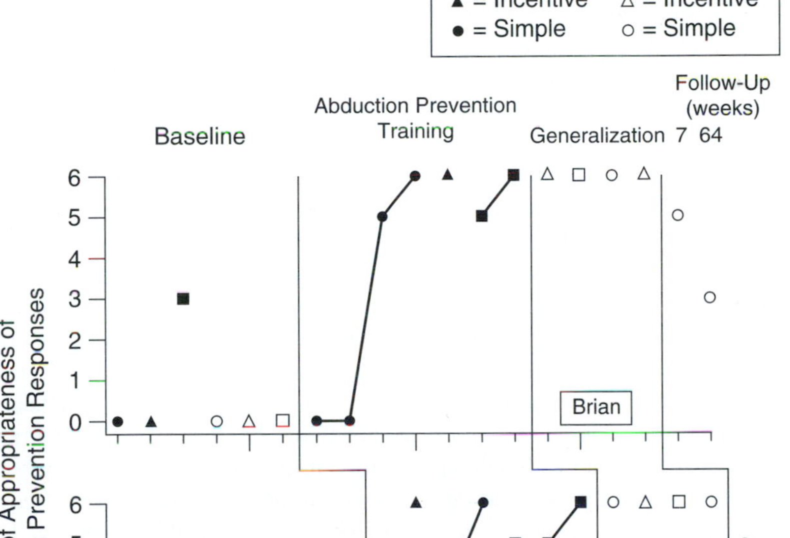

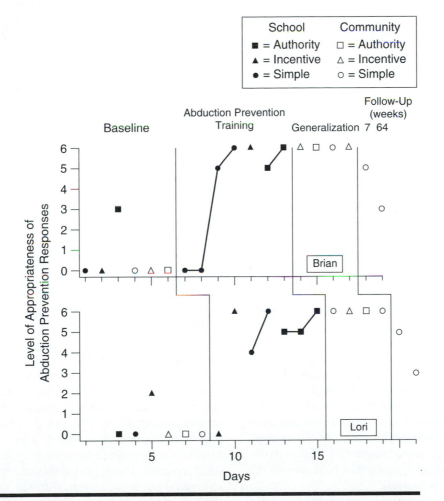

FIGURE 11.13 The level of appropriateness of abduction prevention responses across days for baseline and training conditions and generalization and follow-up observations for Brian and Lori.

was to allow the individual to engage in self-stimulatory behavior (e.g., rocking back and forth) if he sits still for 30 seconds. In this way, we would make rocking dependent on sitting still. In this case, we are only concerned with one particular individual and one behavior. Suppose that we were also concerned with the treatment effects across several settings such as school and home. Also suppose that teachers and parents were concerned with the return to baseline that would likely result in a withdrawal design. The most appropriate design would clearly be the multiple-baseline design across settings.

Now suppose that we were interested in teaching self-instructional skills to individuals in a mathematics class. We hypothesized that the self-instructions would help students solve problems since they would acquire a meta-cognitive technique that would aid in the prompting of appropriate math calculations. We are interested at this point in only the mathematics skill and in only one setting. We have three classrooms at the same level of mathematics instruction. Thus, the most appropriate single-case design would be the multiple-baseline design across participants. We would conduct baseline measures in all three classrooms and implement the self-instructional training in a staggered fashion.

Consider a situation where we are concerned with the teacher's behavior on the in-class performance of students. We are concerned with one set of students, one teacher, and only one setting. However, teachers display several behaviors that can effect the behavior of students. For example, the type of instructions provided, the error corrections used, and the frequency and type of praise can all influence student behavior. Thus, we define three instructional behaviors of interest—appropriate instructions, effective error correction methods, and meaningful praise. In this example the most appropriate single-case design is the multiple-baseline design across behaviors (in this case, teacher behaviors).

Finally, assume that a researcher was interested in measuring the effects of learning letter-sound combinations on the comprehension of young children (aged five to six years). Several children were involved in the investigation from different classrooms. The researcher was interested in only one primary dependent variable (i.e., letter-sound combinations) in only one setting (i.e., a public elementary school). However, the generalization of learning letter-sound combinations was of concern. Thus, the researcher decided to use a multiple-probe design (actually, the design would be a combination of a multiple-baseline design across participants and a multiple-probe design) with the probes conducted on comprehension skills. The researcher did not wish to intervene on comprehension directly, but wished to see if learning letter-sound combinations aided in the comprehension of reading material. Thus, as conceived by the researcher, comprehension may be affected by, or be a generalized skill of, letter-sound combinations. The researcher did not wish to conduct frequent and consistent measurements of comprehension on comprehension passages because he was concerned with practice effects. Therefore, the multiple-probe design would be most appropriate for the researcher.

As shown in the previous scenarios, the questions posed by the researchers are critical in determining the most appropriate single-case design to use. Additionally, ethical or practical concerns, the availability of other behaviors, participants, or settings, the possibility of carryover effects, or the likelihood of practice effects due to frequent measures will help determine the best design. For example, if there are ethical or practical concerns, a withdrawal design should not be used and a multiple-baseline design should be considered. If only one participant is available, a multiple-baseline design across participants is not appropriate. If there are several participants available but in only one setting, a multiple-baseline design across settings would not be possible. If there was only one behavior of concern, a multiple-baseline across behaviors would not be of interest. If it was likely that there would be carryover effects or diffusion of treatment due to participants' communication with one another, a likelihood of generalization of behavior change across settings, or nonindependence of behaviors, multiple-baseline designs are probably not appropriate. Finally, if there is a likelihood of practice effects, a multiple-probe design is appropriate. Ultimately, the decision as to which design to use lies with the researcher; however, the decision must not be made lightly. The decision could increase or decrease internal validity.

DISCUSSION QUESTIONS

1. Ms. Jones teaches eleventh-grade social studies. She wishes to examine the effectiveness of using study guides. She decides to use her unit tests as the dependent measure of student knowledge in social studies. Ms. Jones plans on teaching the students how to study from study guides and develops a study guide for each unit. Indicate situations that would allow Ms. Jones to use each of three types of multiple-baseline designs (i.e., across behaviors, participants, settings).
2. For each of the multiple-baseline designs in Question 1, draw a graph with fictitious data showing that study guides are effective.
3. A fellow teacher wishes to learn more about alternative research methods. He asks you if a withdrawal design is the only single-case design that allows for a demonstration of experimental control. After you answer that multiple-baseline designs are alternatives to withdrawal designs, he asks why one would use a multiple-baseline design rather than a withdrawal design and if there are any disadvantages of multiple-baseline designs. How would you answer his questions?
4. After you answer, the same teacher indicates that he understands how to utilize a multiple-baseline design but is unsure how experimental control is achieved. Explain how experimental control is achieved with a multiple-baseline design.
5. Another educator overhears your discussion in the previous questions. The educator states that there is a lack of external validity with multiple-baseline designs. She even goes so far as to state that multiple-baseline designs have no external validity at all. How would you respond?
6. You hear from a friend that although multiple-baseline designs are good alternatives to withdrawal designs, they are not as strong in controlling threats to internal validity as are withdrawal designs. Do you agree with your friend? Why or why not?
7. You are concerned with the number of exposures to the measurement used in a multiple-baseline design across behaviors. You believe that there will be some reactivity to being exposed to the same measurement several times during baseline. What alternative do you have? Describe how the alternative you indicated solves the difficulty with reactivity to repeated assessments and graph (using fictitious data) how the alternative would look.
8. You are aware of the possible weaknesses of multiple-baseline designs—carryover effects or diffusion of treatment, inference of no change in the behavior from other behaviors, participants, settings. How could you increase the interval validity of multiple-baseline designs to make the level of control the same as withdrawal designs? What are some problems with doing this?
9. Explain the concerns surrounding the following:
   (a) condition length
   (b) independence of behaviors
   (c) the amount of overlap of the data
   (d) the number of baselines
   (e) independence of the behaviors, participants, or settings
   (f) the level and rapidity of change
10. For the six concerns listed in Question 9, construct a graph (you may use any type of multiple-baseline design) showing one example and one nonexample of each.

GENERALIZED EFFECTS OF A PEER-DELIVERED FIRST AID PROGRAM FOR STUDENTS WITH MODERATE INTELLECTUAL DISABILITIES

NANCY E. MARCHAND-MARTELLA AND RONALD C. MARTELLA
Drake University

MARTIN AGRAN, CHARLES L. SALZBERG, K. RICHARD YOUNG, AND DANIEL MORGAN
Utah State University

Peers with mild intellectual disabilities taught first aid skills to 4 students with moderate intellectual disabilities. A multiple probe design across participants was used to examine the effects of the peer teaching program during an acquisition and a partial sequential withdrawal phase. Generalization assessments were conducted in the participants' homes using novel, randomized simulated injuries. Results suggested that the peer teaching program resulted in acquisition of first aid skills, and the participants' skills generalized to the home, to novel simulated-injury locations, and to new trainers. Additionally, a more detailed analysis of the generalized responding suggested that when given a choice among first aid materials, participants treated burns using large adhesive bandages rather than the materials used in training. Participants also successfully treated injuries when novel instructional cues were used. The findings are discussed with respect to training issues, generalization and maintenance of the acquired skills, and the use of peer tutors with disabilities.

DESCRIPTORS: *first aid, generalized responding, error analysis, injury treatment, peer tutors, maintenance, simulation*

First aid training is an important community survival skill (Collins, Wolery, & Gast, 1991) necessary for persons with disabilities to live independently. Foege (1988) reported that "injury is the principal public health problem in America today; . . . it will touch one of every three Americans this year" (p. 1). One person in 11 incurred a home injury requiring medical attention or resulting in one half-day or more of restricted activity (National Safety Council, 1988). One percent of the population suffers burn injuries each year (Tarnowski, Rasnake, & Drabman, 1987).

This research was directed by Nancy E. Marchand-Martella in partial fulfillment of the requirements for a Ph.D. in Behavior Analysis in Special Education at Utah State University. The authors gratefully acknowledge Pat Barton at Summit Elementary School for allowing us to conduct this project in her classroom, and Ann and Brant Christensen for serving as data collectors. Additionally, we thank Benjamin Lignugaris/Kraft for his suggestion on the use of novel instructional cues and the Journal Breeding Group at Utah State University for their editorial comments on an earlier version of this manuscript. This project was supported by a student-initiated grant from the U.S. Department of Education, Office of Special Education and Rehabilitative Services.

Requests for reprints should be sent to Nancy E. Marchand-Martella, Drake University, Department of Psychology, 318 Olin Hall, Des Moines, Iowa 50311.

First aid studies that used individuals with or without disabilities (e.g., Marchand-Martella & Martella, 1990; Peterson, 1984; Spooner, Stem, & Test, 1989) have not included an analysis of generalized responding if generalization was assessed. Stokes and Osnes (1988) indicated that this information is essential to the development of mature technologies that are effective in community settings.

Several aspects of the first aid literature regarding generalized responding are in need of study. First, most first aid investigations (e.g., Marchand-Martella & Martella, 1990; Peterson, 1984) included a limited number of injury locations during training (e.g., hands) without assessing the participants' ability to treat injuries on novel body locations. These assessments are critical because one often incurs injuries on a variety of body locations that require different treatment procedures (e.g., bandaging an injured finger compared to an injured knee). Second, most first aid investigations did not include assessments of the participants' ability to treat injuries in their own homes. For example, Spooner et al. (1989) and Marchand-Martella, Martella, Agran, and Young (1991) included first aid assessments only in public school settings. In-home assessments are necessary because children are more likely to be injured at home (National Safety Council, 1988). Third, in the first aid investigations that involved the treatment of three injuries (i.e., Marchand-Martella & Martella, 1990; Marchand-Martella et al., 1991; Marchand-Martella, Martella, Christensen, Agran, & Young, in press), none assessed the treatment of injuries using instructional cues that were different from those used in training. Because it is unlikely that an individual will always receive the same instructional cues when injured, it is important to assess whether or not participants can discriminate among injuries when a descriptor such as "burned" or "cut" is missing. Fourth, no previous first aid investigations have included error analyses. These analyses provide important information on which injuries and steps in treating those injuries produce difficulties. Finally, no previous first aid investigations have included measures of functionally equivalent treatment methods. Given that participants may have access to a variety of first aid materials, it is important to assess whether participants use certain materials (e.g., adhesive bandage) more than others (e.g., sterile pad, gauze, or tape).

This study investigated the effects of a first aid training program delivered by elementary-aged peer tutors with mild disabilities to students in the same grade with moderate disabilities. Students' acquisition of three first aid skills (treating abrasions, second-degree burns, and severe cuts) and generalization of these skills to their homes were assessed. In addition, the students' generalized responding was analyzed to determine patterns of errors, use of functionally equivalent procedures, and differences between treating themselves and others.

METHOD

Participants and Peer Tutors

Four students with moderate intellectual disabilities enrolled in a self-contained classroom in a regular public school were participants in this study. None had previously received first aid training. Two students with mild intellectual disabilities served as peer tutors. Each peer tutor taught 2 participants. Table 1 displays the characteristics of the participants and the peer tutors.

Settings

All baseline and training sessions were conducted in a kitchen area of a building near the public school. This kitchen area contained a sink, refrigerator, stove, counter, and two chairs. All generalization assessments were conducted in the kitchen or bathroom of the participants' homes, depending on where the parents most often treated injuries and where they kept the first aid kit provided by project staff.

Materials

Simulated Injuries. The simulated injuries used for training were manufactured by Simulaids.

TABLE 1 Participant and Peer Tutor Characteristics

PARTICIPANT/ PEER TUTOR	AGE	GENDER	TEST AND SCORES	ADDITIONAL INFORMATION
Allen	7	M	Leiter = 59; Slosson Intelligence Test = 48	Visual impairment due to congenital glaucoma; limited receptive (3.25 years) and expressive (2.5 years) language skills as indicated on the Preschool Language Scale.
Carrie	9	F	Vineland = 53; Stanford Binet = 44	Difficulties in language as indicated by Goldman-Fristoe Test of Articulation; medication taken including Depakote ®, 125 mg (3/day) and phenobarbital, 30 mg (2/day); medication did not affect alertness.
Melissa	11	F	Vineland = 62; Lieter = 52	Delayed expressive and receptive skills (e.g., echolalic speech) as indicated on the Expressive One-word Picture Vocabulary Test (functioned at 3.5 years).
Lance	11	M	Vineland = 57; Leiter = 42	Limited receptive language skills (3.2 years) as indicated on Test for Auditory Comprehension of Language–Revised; nonverbal with limited signing; aggressive, destructive, and noncompliant behaviors.
Steve	8	M	Vineland = 61; Leiter = 82	Assigned to work with Carrie and Lance; no previous peer tutor training; mainstreamed part of the school day.
Amy	10	F	Vineland = 70; Kaufman Assessment Battery = 71	Assigned to work with Allen and Melissa; no previous peer tutor training; mainstreamed part of the school day.

(Simulated injuries can be purchased from Simulaids, Inc., P.O. Box 807/Dixon Avenue, Woodstock, New York 12498.) Two-way tape was used to attach the simulated injuries to the skin. Simulated blood was used on severe cuts, dirt was placed on abrasions, and embalmer's wax was applied to burns to simulate blisters.

Abrasions were defined as a scraping of cell tissue from the outer layers of the body that produces limited bleeding (American National Red Cross, 1988). Second-degree burns were defined as a redness of the skin, blisters with swelling, and a wet appearance as a result of the skin touching something hot (American National Red Cross, 1988). Severe cuts were defined as incised wounds that occur when body tissue is cut by knives, rough edges, broken glass, or other sharp objects; bleeding may be rapid and heavy (American National Red Cross, 1988).

Injury sizes and locations were determined by asking a first aid instructor to identify the most common sizes and locations of actual abrasions, second-degree burns, and severe cuts on children. The instructor reported that abrasions are approximately 5.08 cm, burns are approximately 3.81 cm, and severe cuts are usually 1.27 cm in length (D. McArthur, Logan Regional Hospital, personal communication, February 1, 1990). Therefore, all simulated injuries were trimmed to fit these measurements. Four locations were identified for abrasions: the left and right elbows and knees. Twenty-six locations were identified for burns and cuts: all fingers (top and bottom, left and right), palm (left and right), hand (top, left and right), and forearm (top, left and right).

First Aid Kit. The investigators supplied participants with a first aid kit for their homes that consisted of soap, paper tape, 5.08-cm square sterile pads, rolled cling gauze, clean cloth or paper towels, child-safe scissors, and adhesive bandage strips (5.08 cm by 11.43 cm). These materials were contained in a plastic box with a handle and with the words "first aid" and a red cross on the lid. These materials were also used in all baseline and training sessions.

Data Collection and Dependent Measure

A trial-based procedure was used to collect data on the participants' treatment of each of the three injuries (abrasions, burns, and cuts) by a trainer (first author) during baseline and training conditions. An observer collected data on the participants' treatment of each of the three injuries during generalization assessments. Treatment of each injury was divided into a sequence of steps based on task analyses adapted from the American National Red Cross (1988). This adaptation involved adding a requirement that the participant tell an adult "I'm hurt" or "I scraped (burned) (cut) myself" either verbally or by signing before, during, or after treating an abrasion or burn and after caring for a severe cut. The correct or incorrect completion or noncompletion of each step of the task analyses was recorded. The percentage of each of the three injuries treated accurately was calculated and served as the primary dependent measure. The task analyses for the three injuries are shown in Table 2.

Another adaptation was added to include functionally equivalent alternate responses for the steps of the task analyses for burns and abrasions. These alternate responses were putting a sterile pad, gauze, or tape on an abrasion instead of an adhesive bandage and placing an adhesive bandage on a burn instead of using a sterile pad, gauze, or tape.

TABLE 2 Task Analyses of First Aid Skills

Abrasions

1. Wash wound under cool running water with soap.
2. Blot dry with sterile gauze or clean dry cloth.
3. Peel off adhesive plastic protectors without touching sterile pad.
 * Place sterile nonstick pad over injuries.
4. Place bandage pad over wound so that it covers the wound completely.
 * Wrap with gauze to secure pad.
5. Press adhesive strips so that they adhere to undamaged skin.
 * Tape gauze to secure pad.
6. Show or tell an adult.

Second Degree Burns

1. Immerse in cold water.
2. Blot dry with sterile gauze or clean dry cloth.
3. Place sterile nonstick pad over injuries.
 * Peel off adhesive plastic protectors without touching sterile pad.
4. Wrap with gauze to secure pad.
 * Place bandage pad over wound so that it covers the wound completely.
5. Tape gauze to secure pad.
 * Press adhesive strips so that they adhere to undamaged skin.
6. Show or tell an adult.

Severe Cuts

1. Cover wound with cloth or sterile gauze pad.
2. Apply pressure to wound.
3. Continue applying pressure and elevate injury above the heart.
4. Continue with Steps 1–3 and show or tell an adult.

*Functionally equivalent step.

Experimental Design

A multiple probe design across 4 participants was used to assess the effects of the intervention (Barlow & Hersen, 1984). The experimental conditions included baseline, training with two phases, and generalization assessments.

Procedure

Pretraining. Both tutors had participated previously in a first aid investigation (Marchand-Martella et al., in press), and had learned to treat abrasions, burns, and cuts on puppets. The peer tutors were taught to provide instructional cues, to correct errors, and to praise correct completion of steps.

Assessment of Novel Injuries Prior to Baseline. This assessment was conducted in the participant's home while the peer tutor was not present. A simulated injury was placed on the participant or his or her sibling, and an observer pointed out the injury and cued the participant to apply first aid (e.g., for abrasions, "You (he) scraped yourself (himself). Show me how to take care of it"). Therefore, each participant was assessed with six simulated injuries (i.e., abrasions, burns, and cuts on self and others). The injury locations were randomly selected from the total number of abrasion, burn, and cut locations. After the session, the participant and his or her sibling were praised for their hard work (i.e., contingent on the absence of noncompliant, aggressive, or disruptive behavior) and were given stickers or small school supplies for participation.

Baseline. A simulated injury was placed on the participant, and the peer tutor pointed out the injury and cued him or her to take care of it (e.g., "You cut yourself. Show me how to take care of it"). The simulated wounds were placed on the back of the participants' hands and were alternated between the left and right hands. The type of injury was counterbalanced across sessions (e.g., abrasions, burns, and cuts for Session 1 were followed by burns, cuts, and abrasions for Session 2 and cuts, abrasions, and burns for Session 3). No modeling or feedback was provided by either the peer tutor or the trainer. Following the session, the participant and tutor were praised for working hard and received praise, stickers, or small school supplies for participation.

Assessment of Novel Injuries after Baseline. All conditions remained the same as in the assessment prior to baseline.

Peer Instruction. Peer instruction of participants consisted of three components—modeling, participant practice with corrective feedback and praise, and a retest. First, the tutor told the participant that he or she was injured and was going to take care of it (e.g., "I scraped myself. I will show you how to take care of it"). The peer tutor modeled each treatment step on his or her own injury. Next, the tutor provided the instructional care (e.g., "You scraped yourself. Show me how to take care of it") and the participant practiced the skill with his or her own injury. The tutor provided corrective feedback for incorrect responses and praised correct responses. Finally, the participant practiced again without tutor feedback (retest). The three-component procedure was repeated each session for all three injuries. Again, the simulated wounds were placed on the back of the participant's hands and were alternated between the left and right hands. Criterion for completing this phase of training was completion of 100% of the steps correctly for each of the three injuries for three consecutive sessions.

Feedback Only. This phase of training included the removal of two training components (i.e., modeling and participant practice) from the intervention. Thus, the tutor cued the participant to respond and, after the participant had treated the injury, provided corrective feedback or praised correct responses. This procedure was repeated each session for all three injuries. Criterion for completing this phase of training was completion of 100% of the steps correctly for each of the three injuries for three consecutive sessions.

Assessment of Novel Injuries after Feedback Only. All conditions remained the same as in the previous two assessments.

Booster Training and School Assessment. Each participant who did not complete 100% of the steps correctly for each injury during the assessment following the feedback-only phase was given additional training tailored to the injuries for which errors occurred. Training consisted of practice with feedback followed by a retest as previously conducted in the peer instruction phase. Peer modeling was not conducted. After the participant reached 100% correct performance for three retests in booster training, a school assessment was conducted.

During the school assessment, an observer assessed the participant's response to the injuries practiced in booster training. If 100% performance was not achieved, booster training was reinstated followed by an additional school assessment. No feedback was given during these school assessments. However, the participant was praised for working hard and received a small reward for participation.

Assessment of Novel Injuries after Booster Training and School Assessment. After completing 100% of the steps correctly for the injuries in the school assessment, each participant treated six novel injuries at home. After completing this assessment, booster training was provided if the participant achieved less than 100% correct on any injury treatment.

Assessment of Novel Injuries (1, 2, and 3 Months) and Novel Instructional Cue Assessment (3 Months). All conditions remained the same as those described in the assessment following booster training and school assessment. However, before the 3-month assessment, an assessment with novel instructional cues was conducted. In this assessment, participants were asked to treat six injuries on themselves and others when novel instructional cues were delivered (for abrasions, "You (he) fell down and look what happened. Show me how to take care of it"; for burns, "You (she) touched a hot pan and look what happened. Show me how to take care of it"; and for cuts, "You (he) were slicing vegetables with a knife and look what happened. Show me how to take care of it"). Two participants, Melissa and Lance, did not receive rewarding or corrective feedback on their performance before, during, or after the novel instructional cue assessment. However, the observer mistakenly conducted booster training with Allen and Carrie after the six injuries were treated.

After the novel instructional cue assessment and before the 3 -month assessment, parents were taught how to treat each injury by an additional observer who modeled and explained treatment procedures and demonstrated appropriate and inappropriate procedures. After the parents reached 100% agreement with this observer, they were asked to take data during the 3-month assessment.

Generalized Responding

An error analysis of the generalization assessments following the feedback-only phase was conducted to determine patterns of errors for treating abrasions, burns, and cuts. An error was scored for any step missed or performed incorrectly. In addition, a comparison of treatments for each injury on self versus others and the use of functionally equivalent procedures were examined (see Results).

Interobserver Agreement

Two observers received training in first aid skills that included demonstrations and explanations of appropriate and inappropriate skill performance for each injury and practice recording. One observer served as the secondary observer for all baseline and training sessions and as the primary observer for all generalization assessments (including the novel instructional cue assessment) in the parents' homes and the assessments after booster training conducted in the school. The trainer (senior author) served as the primary observer for training and booster training. The second observer conducted the generalization assessments in the parents' homes and in the school. This observer also trained the parents.

Interobserver agreement was calculated for occurrence, nonoccurrence, and total agreement by dividing agreements for each step of the task analyses by agreements plus disagreements and multiplying by 100. Interobserver agreement was calculated on 41% of baseline sessions, 20% of peer instruction and feedback-only sessions, 17% of school assessments, and 82% of generalization assessments.

Agreement was examined separately for baseline, peer instruction, and feedback-only conditions, school assessments, and generalization assessments. The average for occurrence, nonoccurrence, and total interobserver agreement for treatment of injuries for all conditions was 98.3% (range, 67.7% to 100%), 97.9% (range, 83.3% to 100%), and 98.9% (range, 83.3% to 100%), respectively. Interobserver agreement during the 3-month assessment averaged 100% between the first and second observers and 100% between the first observer and parents. Agreement was not taken during the novel instructional cue assessment because the second observer was training the parents at this time.

RESULTS

Assessment of Novel Injuries Prior to, During, and after Baseline

Figures 1 and 2 display the percentages of steps completed correctly for treating injuries by Allen, Carrie, Melissa, and Lance. Prior to base-

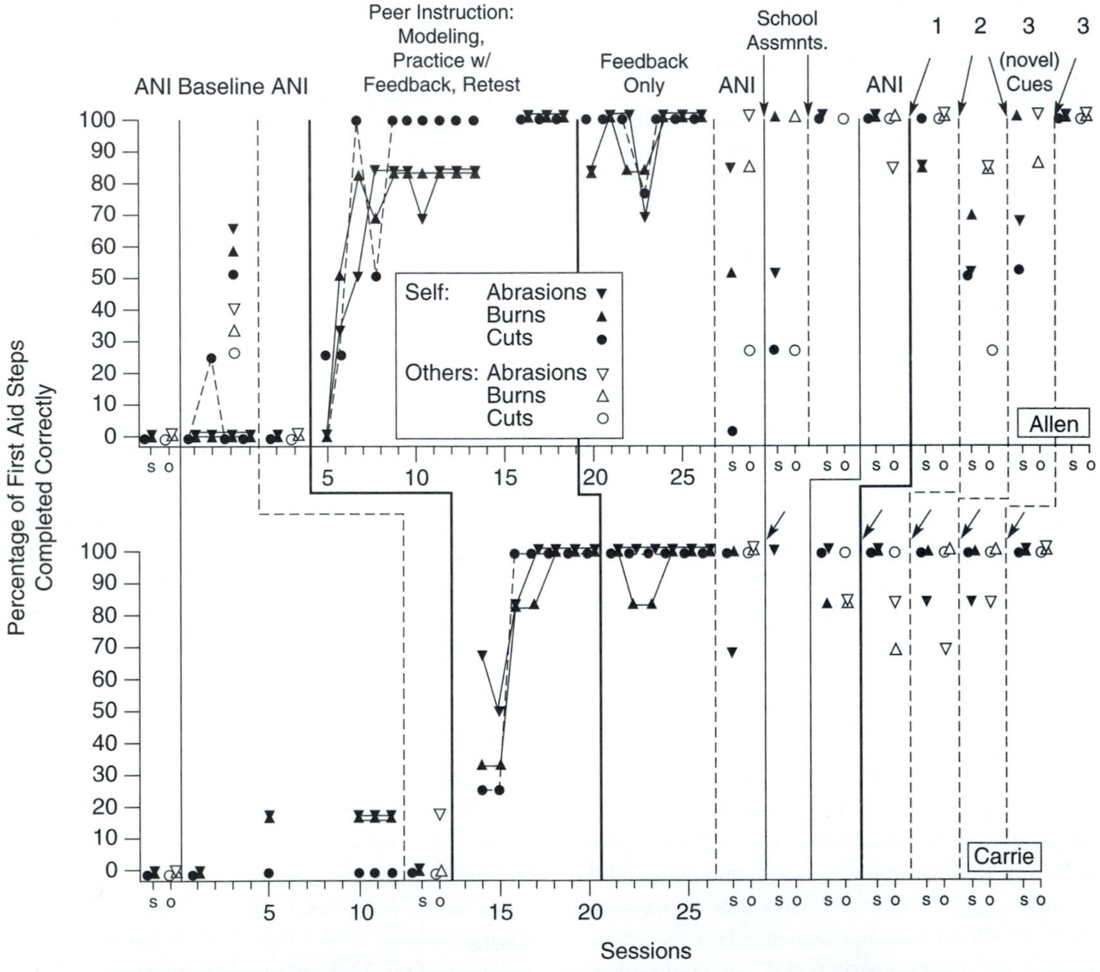

FIGURE 1 Percentage for treating abrasions, burns, and cuts for Allen and Carrie. Arrows indicate when booster training occurred. ANI = assessment of novel injuries. The numbers above the last four phases refer to the 1-, 2-, and 3-month assessment of novel injuries and the 3-month assessment of novel instructional cues.

line, none of the participants performed any of the steps correctly for treating abrasions, burns, and cuts. During baseline, participants completed 25% or less of the steps for cuts and 16.7% or less of the steps for abrasions and burns. During the assessment after baseline, Allen, Melissa, and Lance again failed to complete any of the steps correctly, whereas Carrie completed one step correctly when caring for an abrasion on others.

Peer Instruction and Feedback Only

During the peer instruction phase, participants quickly acquired the three first aid skills. Participants completed more steps correctly when treating cuts than when treating abrasions or burns. During the feedback-only phase, participant scores across injury treatments were all above 66.7%.

Assessment of Novel Injuries after Feedback Only

Participants completed 100% of the steps correctly for at least one injury (Allen, one; Carrie, five; Melissa, two; Lance, three) at their homes.

Booster Training and School Assessment

During the first school assessment, Carrie and Lance completed 100% of the steps correctly for

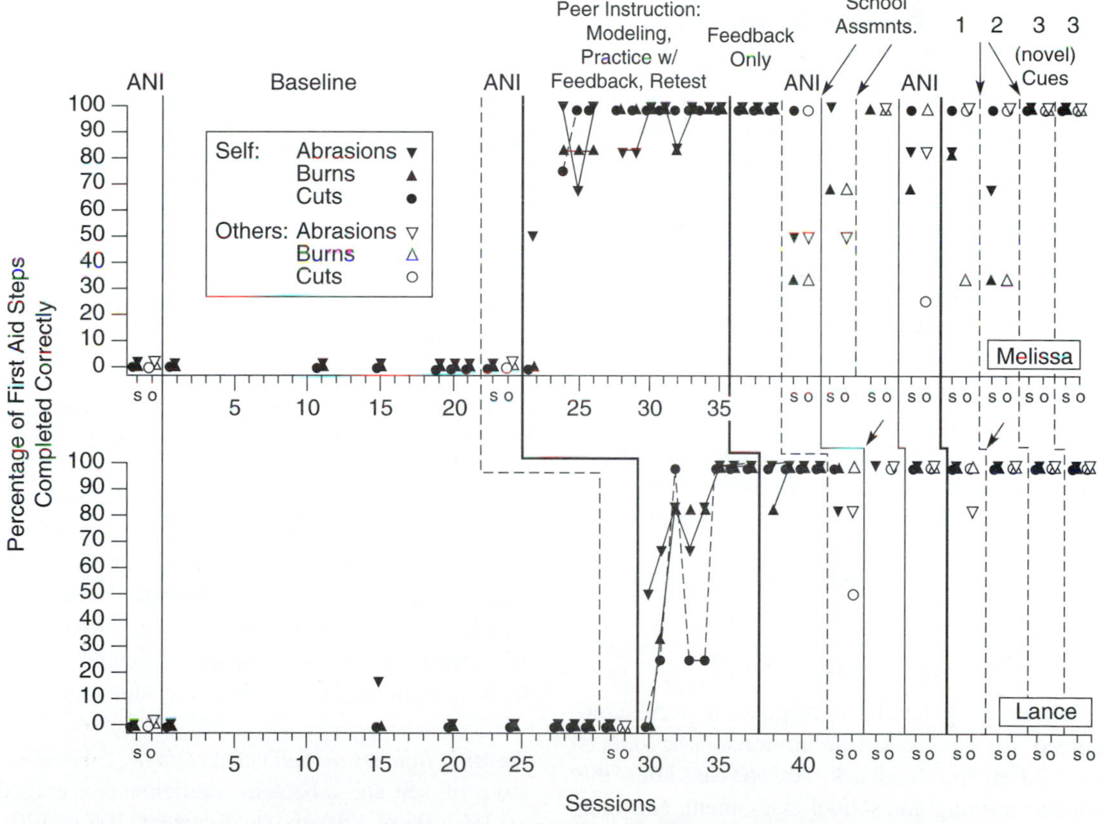

FIGURE 2 Percentage for treating abrasions, burns, and cuts for Melissa and Lance. Arrows indicate when booster training occurred. ANI = assessment of novel injuries. The numbers above the last four phases refer to the 1-, 2-, and 3-month assessment of novel injuries and the 3-month assessment of novel instructional cues.

the injuries in which they had received booster training. Because Allen and Melissa scored less than 100% during the first school assessment, additional booster training was conducted, followed by a second school assessment. Allen and Melissa performed 100% of the steps correctly on the second school assessment.

Assessment of Novel Injuries after Booster Training and School Assessment

Lance achieved 100% correct on treating all injuries; Allen, Carrie, and Melissa scored less than 100% on one or more injuries and, therefore, required booster training.

Assessment of Novel Injuries (1, 2, and 3 Months) and Novel Instructional Cue Assessment

After the 1-month assessment, Lance required booster training on only one injury. Carrie and Allen required booster training on two injuries, and Melissa required booster training on three injuries. After the 2-month assessment, Lance did not require booster training, Carrie required booster training on two injuries, Melissa required booster training on three injuries, and Allen required booster training on all six injuries. Finally, after the 3-month assessment, none of the participants required booster training.

For the novel instructional cue assessment, Melissa and Lance completed 100% of the steps correctly for all six injuries; Carrie completed at least 83.3% of the steps correctly; Allen completed at least 50% of steps correctly for all injuries.

Generalized Responding

Analyses of generalized responding were conducted for the following in-home assessments (i.e., after the feedback-only phase, after the booster training and school assessment, and 1, 2, and 3 months after booster training and school assessments).

Error Analysis. The errors noted for each participant on each step of the task analyses are presented in Table 3. For abrasions on knees and elbows, 28 errors occurred. Step 1 (washing the injury) produced the most frequent errors (11). Eight of these 11 errors were due to using water without soap (Carrie and Melissa) and three were due to the failure to use soap and water (Allen). Ten of these 11 errors occurred when taking care of abrasions on knees. The second most frequently occurring error was Step 4 (placing bandage over wound, wrap with gauze to secure pad), for which seven errors were noted. Again, more errors occurred on knee injuries than on elbow injuries (five of the seven errors). All of these errors occurred because the bandage pad did not cover the wound completely and occurred when participants treated knee injuries on themselves.

There were 35 errors for burns on the palm, forearm, and fingers. Step 5 (taping the gauze, press adhesive strips of bandage) was performed incorrectly nine times. These errors were due to the participants' failure to put on a sterile pad, which led to a failure to secure the pad with tape or to press down adhesive parts of bandage so as to adhere the bandage to the undamaged skin around the wound. Steps 1 (immerse in cold water), 2 (blot dry), and 4 (wrap with gauze, place bandage pad over wound) were completed incorrectly seven times each. These errors were due to the use of soap (Step 1), failure to blot dry (Step 2), and failure to secure sterile pad with gauze or to cover wound completely with adhesive bandage (Step 4).

Treating cuts on the forearms and fingers resulted in 17 errors. Most errors occurred on Steps 3 (continue with pressure and elevate above heart) and 4 (continue with Steps 1 through 3 and show an adult), with six errors for each step. These errors occurred most often because the participants failed to elevate and apply pressure at the same time.

Treating Injuries on Self versus Others. For abrasions on self and others, the participants averaged 86.7% (104 of 120) and 90% correct (108 of 120), respectively. For burns on self, the participants averaged 85% correct (102 of 120); for burns on others, the participants averaged 86.7% correct (104 of 120). Finally, for cuts on self, the average was

TABLE 3 Number of Errors per Step for Each Participant during In-Home Assessments of Novel Injuries Following the Feedback-Only Phase

	Participants				
TASK ANALYSES (STEPS)	**ALLEN**	**CARRIE**	**MELISSA**	**LANCE**	**TOTAL**
Abrasions					
1	3	4	4	0	11
2	1	0	0	1	2
3	1	0	0	0	1
4	1	2	3	1	7
5	0	1	4	0	5
6	1	0	0	1	2
Total	7	7	11	3	28
Burns					
1	0	0	7	0	7
2	3	1	3	0	7
3	1	0	3	0	4
4	1	1	5	0	7
5	2	2	5	0	9
6	1	0	0	0	1
Total	8	4	23	0	35
Cuts					
1	1	0	0	0	1
2	3	0	1	0	4
3	4	0	1	1	6
4	4	0	1	1	6
Total	12	0	3	2	17

92.5% correct (74 of 80) versus 88.8% correct (71 of 80) for cuts on others.

Functionally Equivalent Procedures. For abrasions, the original training procedure was used 38 out of 40 times (95%). Of these 38 procedures, 23 were completed correctly (60.5%). Functionally equivalent procedures were used two out of 40 times (5%) with one completed correctly (50%). For burns, the original procedure was used 13 out of 40 times (32.5%). Of these 13 procedures, six were completed correctly (46.2%). Functionally equivalent procedures were used 27 out of 40 times (67.5%) for burns, with 19 completed correctly (70.4%).

DISCUSSION

Four elementary-aged students with moderate disabilities learned to treat abrasions, burns, and severe cuts in a training program implemented by peer tutors with mild disabilities. The participants acquired these skills in a relatively short period of time; more importantly, the newly learned skills generalized across settings, trainers, and injury locations. After learning to treat abrasions, burns, and cuts on themselves (back of hands), the participants required little or no additional training to treat injuries on novel body locations on themselves or others. This generalized skill is important in first aid because a variety of injuries may occur on numerous body locations, and children may frequently be in a position to help an injured friend or sibling. One parent (Allen's mother) collected data on the percentage of steps completed correctly by her son when he treated his knee after falling off his bicycle. Allen completed 100% of the steps correctly and independently. This finding is consistent with generalization data reported by Marchand-Martella and Martella (1990) and Spooner et al. (1989).

Assessing maintenance of performance is critical for skills not practiced regularly (Homer, Williams, & Knobbe, 1985). During training, participants in this study practiced first aid treatments daily; however, during maintenance, when participants practiced treatment of injuries once per month, performance deteriorated somewhat. Therefore, it seems that at least for these individuals, frequent opportunities to practice first aid skills are essential. Spooner et al. (1989) indicated that individuals without disabilities also need to review first aid skills periodically.

Discrimination training may be related to generalization and maintenance of skills (Spooner et al., 1989). In the feedback-only phase, when tutor modeling and practice with feedback were withdrawn, the participants' ability to discriminate among injuries became evident. In this phase, the participants had to care for an injury based on its physical characteristics rather than on specific instructions (e.g., modeling and feedback) provided by the trainer. To be sure that characteristics of the injury rather than verbal cues were controlling responding, novel cues were used during the 3-month assessment. Results indicated that the participants discriminated among injuries based on appearance, not on the instructional cues used in training. Previous investigations of first aid did not include instructional cues different from those used in training; therefore, participants' ability to select treatment procedures based on the characteristics of the injury was not examined.

The error analyses of the generalization assessment data yielded some interesting findings. First, participants had difficulty washing abrasions on knees with soap and water. This difficulty may have arisen because the participants had been taught to wash injuries under running water in the sink. Therefore, in the generalization assessments, the participants often had to improvise (e.g., Lance washed his knee in the bathtub; Carrie used a wet paper towel with soap on it to wash her knee). Participants also had difficulty putting the bandages on their own knees. They had less difficulty placing an adhesive bandage on someone else's knee. One can stand or sit upright when treating someone else's knee and the injury is in full view. In contrast, treating one's own knee requires some physically awkward positioning.

Another possible explanation for some of the failures to provide appropriate first aid may have been due to differences in settings. For example, the first observer indicated that she almost always had to interrupt the participants when they were engaged in preferred activities at home (e.g., playing outside, playing Nintendo®). By contrast, the trainer almost always interrupted classroom instruction. Therefore, it seemed as though the participants tried to rush through the assessments conducted at home in order to return to playing outside, but were less anxious to return to the classroom.

The findings concerning the participants' use of functionally equivalent procedures were informative. The participants used alternate procedures more often when caring for burns than abrasions. This probably occurred because it is easier to put an adhesive bandage on an injury than it is to place a sterile pad on an injury, wrap it with gauze, and tape it to secure the pad.

The findings concerning functionally equivalent procedures as well as the error analyses have important implications for training. First, the children were more likely to use adhesive bandages than sterile pads, gauze, and tape and were more successful that way. Adhesive bandages also cost 67% less than sterile pads, gauze, tape, and child-safe scissors. Thus, we suggest adhesive bandages be used in lieu of the other materials in training. Second, participants make more errors treating knees than other injuries because the procedures used in training (running water over the injury in the sink) are often not possible when real injuries occur. Therefore, it seems appropriate to add a training component to teach children what to do when they cannot run the injury under water in the sink.

This investigation also used peers as instructors, which is a new method in the literature on first aid instruction. Although the purpose of the present study was not to demonstrate the effects of peer instruction on the instructors themselves, it should be noted that the first aid skills of the two instructors were maintained at higher mean levels for up to 12 weeks after training compared to the other participants with similar disabilities (i.e., 85.8% vs. 70.2% for abrasions, 88.3% vs. 75.6% for burns, and 92.5% vs. 51.8% for cuts) in the investigation of Marchand-Martella et al. (in press). This finding is consistent with the findings of other researchers on the learning benefit of peer instruction (e.g., Parson & Heward, 1979). An important future consideration is an efficiency and cost–benefit analysis for the use of peer instructors.

The findings suggest that first aid treatment generalized across settings and injury locations; however, several caveats are in order. First, participants were not taught to discriminate among injuries requiring immediate outside help and those they could treat themselves. Future programs should teach this discrimination depending on the type, severity, and location of the injury. Second, in this study, booster training prevented atrophy of skills over time. Future research is needed to determine the optimal frequency for maintenance assessments and booster training. Third, when injuries were treated following novel instructional cues, feedback was provided to Allen and Carrie. Further, the same injury locations were used in the 3-month assessment, which followed shortly after the novel instructional cue assessment. Therefore, it is not certain that participants would have completed 100% of the steps correctly during the 3-month assessment if they had not received this additional training. Finally, a pretest was not conducted with the novel instructional cues used during the 3-month assessment. Thus, although it seems unlikely, it is possible that participants might have responded to these instructions before intervention.

In summary, this study presents a promising program to teach children with moderate disabilities basic first aid skills that generalize to their homes and to novel injury locations. More important, procedures used in this study appear to promote efficient learning because the participants exhibited generalized responding to novel injuries on different body locations.

REFERENCES

American National Red Cross. (1988). *Standard first aid and personal safety* (3rd ed.). Washington, DC: Author.

Barlow, D. H., & Hersen, M. (1984). *Single case experimental designs: Strategies for studying behavior change* (2nd ed.). New York: Pergamon Press.

Collins, B. C., Wolery, M., & Gast, D. L. (1991). A survey of safety concerns for students with special needs. *Education and Training in Mental Retardation, 26,* 305–318.

Foege, W. H. (1988, November). *Newsletter of the Family Health Services Division Utah Department of Health.* (Available from Stephen McDonald, 288 North 1460 West, Salt Lake City, Utah 84116–0650)

Horner, R. H., Williams, J. A., & Knobbe, C. A. (1985). The effect of "opportunity to perform" on the maintenance of skills learned by high school students with severe handicaps. *Journal of the Association for Persons with Severe Handicaps, 10,* 172–175.

Marchand-Martella, N. E., & Martella, R. C. (1990). The acquisition, generalization, and maintenance of first-aid skills by youth with handicaps. *Behavioral Residential Treatment, 5,* 221–237.

Marchand-Martella, N. E., Martella, R. C., Agran, M., & Young, K. R. (1991). Assessing the acquisition of first aid treatments by elementary-aged children. *Child & Family Behavior Therapy, 13*(4), 29–43.

Marchand-Martella, N. E., Martella, R. C., Christensen, A. M., Agran, M., & Young, K. R. (in press). Assessing the duration of first-aid treatments by elementary-aged students with disabilities. *Child & Family Behavior Therapy.*

National Safety Council. (1988). *Accident facts.* Chicago: Author.

Parson, L. R., & Heward, W. L. (1979). Training peers to tutor: Evaluation of a tutor training package for primary learning disabled students. *Journal of Applied Behavior Analysis, 12,* 309–310.

Peterson, L. (1984). Teaching home safety and survival skills to latch-key children: A comparison of two manuals and methods. *Journal of Applied Behavior Analysis, 17,* 279–293.

Spooner, F., Stem, B., & Test, D. W. (1989). Teaching first aid skills to adolescents who are moderately mentally handicapped. *Education and Training in Mental Retardation, 24,* 341–351.

Stokes, T. F., & Osnes, P. G. (1988). The developing applied technology of generalization and maintenance. In R. H. Horner, G. Dunlap, & R. L. Koegel (Eds.), *Generalization and maintenance: Life-style changes in applied settings* (pp. 5–19). Baltimore: Paul H. Brookes.

Tarnowski, K. J., Rasnake, L. K., & Drabman, R. S. (1987). Behavioral assessment and treatment of pediatric burn injuries: A review. *Behavior Therapy, 18,* 417–441.

Received June 24, 1991
Initial editorial decision September 4, 1991
Revisions received December 26, 1991; March 12, 1992; April 27, 1992
Final acceptance June 30, 1992
Action Editor, F. Charles Mace

FACTUAL QUESTIONS

1. What was the purpose of the study?
2. Who were the participants (students and peer tutors)? What were the settings?
3. What were the materials used?
4. How were the data collected, what was the dependent variable, and how was the dependent variable measured?
5. Describe how the independent variable was presented.
6. What were the conditions and what was the type of design used?
7. What occurred during the error analysis of the generalization assessments and what was found?
8. Why was booster training initiated?
9. What did the assessment of observer agreement reveal?
10. What were the results for each participant during each condition? Did the learned first-aid skills maintain? Did the skills generalize? If so, explain the generalized responding results.

DISCUSSION QUESTIONS

1. Based on the characteristics of the students and the peer tutors, to whom could you generalize these results?
2. Why would generalization assessments occur in the homes? Why do you think the training occurred in a building near the school versus in the home?
3. Why would it be important to conduct an error analysis?
4. Why were peers used to teach the first-aid skills rather than an adult?
5. Why were varying percentages correct occurring during the generalization and maintenance conditions across injuries?
6. What was the purpose of assessing generalization before the baseline condition?
7. Why did the investigators choose not to conduct consecutive baseline sessions for Carrie, Melissa, and Lance?
8. Is there a possible testing effect for the generalization assessments? Explain.
9. Why did the authors consider the findings concerning functionally equivalent procedures to be important? What do you think?
10. What were the caveats suggested by the authors and why are they potential problems?

THREATS TO INTERNAL VALIDITY

Circle the number corresponding to the likelihood of each threat to internal validity being present in the investigation and provide a justification.

1 = definitely not a threat	2 = not a likely threat	3 = somewhat likely threat
4 = likely threat	5 = definite threat	NA = Not applicable for this design

Results in Differences within or between Individuals

1. **Maturation** **1 2 3 4 5 NA**

   Justification ______________________________

   ____

2. **Selection** **1 2 3 4 5 NA**

   Justification ______________________________

   ____

3. **Selection by Maturation Interaction** **1 2 3 4 5 NA**

   Justification ______________________________

   ____

4. **Statistical Regression** **1 2 3 4 5 NA**

   Justification ______________________________

   ____

5. **Mortality** **1 2 3 4 5 NA**

   Justification ______________________________

   ____

6. **Instrumentation** **1 2 3 4 5 NA**

   Justification ______________________________

   ____

7. Testing 1 2 3 4 5 NA

Justification ____

____

8. History 1 2 3 4 5 NA

Justification ____

____

9. Resentful Demoralization of the Control Group 1 2 3 4 5 NA

Justification ____

____

Results in Similarities within or between Individuals

10. Diffusion of Treatment 1 2 3 4 5 NA

Justification ____

____

11. Compensatory Rivalry by the Control Group 1 2 3 4 5 NA

Justification ____

____

12. Compensatory Equalization of Treatments 1 2 3 4 5 NA

Justification ____

____

Abstract: Write a one-page abstract summarizing the overall conclusions of the authors and whether you feel the authors' conclusions are valid based on the internal validity of the investigation.

THREATS TO EXTERNAL VALIDITY

Circle the number corresponding to the likelihood of each threat to external validity being present in the investigation according to the following scale:

1 = definitely not a threat	2 = not a likely threat	3 = somewhat likely threat
4 = likely threat	5 = definite threat	NA = Not applicable for this design

Also, provide a justification for each rating.

Population

1. **Generalization across Subjects** 1 2 3 4 5 NA

Justification ____________________

____

2. **Interaction of Personological Variables and Treatment** 1 2 3 4 5 NA

Justification ____________________

____

Ecological

3. **Verification of the Independent Variable** 1 2 3 4 5 NA

Justification ____________________

____

4. **Multiple Treatment Interference** 1 2 3 4 5 NA

Justification ____________________

____

5. **Hawthorne Effect** 1 2 3 4 5 NA

Justification ____________________

____

6. **Novelty and Disruption Effects** 1 2 3 4 5 NA

Justification ____________________

____

7. Experimenter Effects 1 2 3 4 5 NA

Justification ______________________________

____

8. Pretest Sensitization 1 2 3 4 5 NA

Justification ______________________________

____

9. Posttest Sensitization 1 2 3 4 5 NA

Justification ______________________________

____

10. Interaction of Time of Measurement and Treatment Effects 1 2 3 4 5 NA

Justification ______________________________

____

11. Measurement of the Dependent Variable 1 2 3 4 5 NA

Justification ______________________________

____

12. Interaction of History and Treatment Effects 1 2 3 4 5 NA

Justification ______________________________

____

Abstract: Write a one-page abstract summarizing the overall conclusions of the authors and whether you feel the authors' conclusions are valid based on the external validity of the investigation.

Chapter 12

ADDITIONAL SINGLE-CASE DESIGNS

OBJECTIVES

After studying this chapter you should be able to:

1. Describe the design features of the changing-criterion design.
2. Describe the design features of the multitreatment design.
3. Describe the design features of the alternating treatments design.
4. Describe the different combinations of single-case designs.
5. Describe internal validity issues surrounding the use of these designs.
6. Describe external validity issues surrounding the use of these designs.
7. Describe when one would choose a particular design.
8. Critique a research article containing a combination design.

OVERVIEW

Although the mainstays of single-case research are the withdrawal and multiple-baseline designs, other designs are used as well. These designs are used based on the behavior to be changed, the type of research question asked (e.g., what is the most effective method of teaching reading?), or the constraints present (e.g., ethical issues surrounding the use of withdrawal designs, lack of multiple behaviors, participants, or settings).

This chapter focuses on additional single-case designs. The changing-criterion design, multitreatment design, alternating treatments design, and combination designs are described in detail. Concerns with the analysis of data are described within each design. Research examples demonstrating each design are highlighted throughout the chapter. (*Note:* You should attempt to analyze the graphs presented from the research examples.) Finally, an illustrative investigation is included at the end of the chapter for critique.

WHAT IS A CHANGING-CRITERION DESIGN?

The changing-criterion design has not been a popular design used in research (Barlow & Hersen, 1984; Tawney & Gast, 1984). Researchers have used alternative designs to demonstrate experimental control. However, the changing-criterion design is an important design researchers can use under the appropriate circumstances (Hartman & Hall, 1976). Figure 12.1 shows a fictional changing-criterion design. As seen in the figure, a baseline condition is conducted followed by the intervention condition. Essentially, without the "phase" lines (i.e., changes within the intervention condition), the design looks the same as an A-B design. The difference between a changing-criterion design and an A-B design is the use of a criterion within each phase. As shown in the figure, the horizontal lines between phase lines depict the criteria. Think of a changing-criterion design as an attempt to reduce or increase some dependent variable in a stepwise manner. In fact,

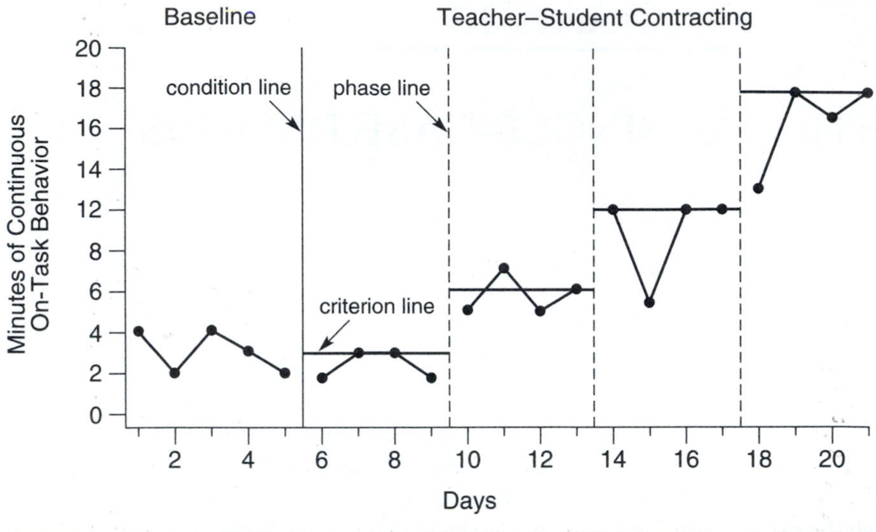

FIGURE 12.1 Minutes of continuous on-task behavior across baseline and teacher–student contracting conditions.

this is what the design is intended to do—to increase or decrease a dependent variable gradually. Thus, the changing-criterion design is useful for dealing with addictive behaviors such as caffeine consumption or smoking. In many smoking cessation programs, one attempts to fade out the use of nicotine. The changing-criterion design is specially suited for such an attempt. Additionally, the changing-criterion design may be useful in monitoring other dependent variables (Hartman & Hall, 1976) such as classroom management problems or academic difficulties.

The method of implementing a changing-criterion design is a combination of planning and good guessing. What is meant by this is that researchers should plan investigations as they would other investigations. The independent and dependent variables must be well defined, the method of data collection must be determined, and the participant(s) must be prepared to become involved in the investigation. Researchers need to rely on good guessing in that they must determine the level of criterion changes throughout the investigation and hope that the steps are not too large or too small. To implement a changing-criterion design, researchers must do the following. First, they must collect baseline data. Second, the first criterion level should be set around the average of the baseline (Hall & Fox, 1977). Third, once the participant meets some predetermined level such as three data points at or below (in cases where the behavior is to decrease) or above (in cases where the behavior is to increase) the criterion, the criterion should be changed to a new level.

The difficulty with this final step is determining how large the change should be. For example, if the change is too large, the participant may not be able to meet the new level. Consider attempting to decrease the number of cigarettes one smokes per day. Suppose that an individual smoked an average of 40 cigarettes per day. The first criterion is then set at 40 cigarettes. Once the participant smokes 40 or less cigarettes per day for five consecutive days, we move to 10 cigarettes per day. The step may be too much. The researcher is doomed to fail by requiring the behavior to be decreased too rapidly. Figure 12.2 demonstrates when a criterion is changed too fast. As can be

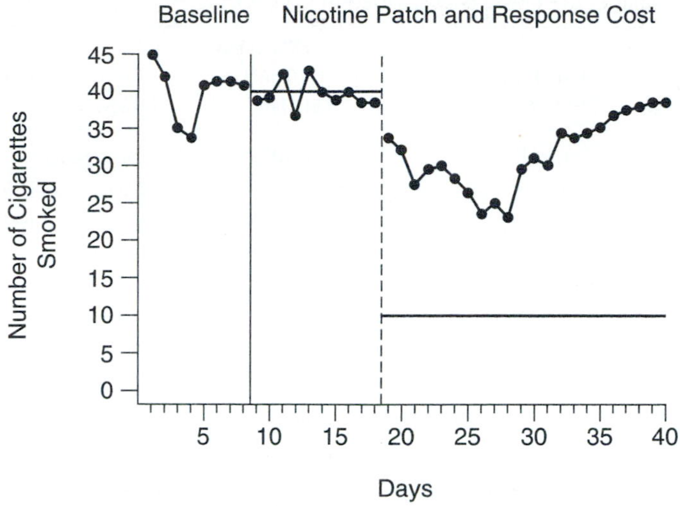

FIGURE 12.2 Number of cigarettes smoked across baseline and nicotine patch and response cost conditions.

seen, the participant cannot meet the required criterion. On the other hand, if the researcher decided to go from 40 to 39 cigarettes after five consecutive days, the move may be too small. It will take too long to get down to zero cigarettes per day. Thus, researchers must determine how quickly to reduce or increase the dependent variable. This determination is a difficult one to make since experimental control depends on it.

Analysis of Data

Internal Validity. When assessing the internal validity of the changing-criterion design, several concerns must be taken into consideration. These concerns involve the condition length (including the trend of the data), whether the behavior stays near the criterion level, the stability of baseline data and immediacy of change, the number of criterion levels, and other control procedures. Table 12.1 summarizes the major threats to internal validity of the changing-criterion design.

Condition Length. The consideration of condition length for a changing-criterion design is similar to the withdrawal and multiple-baseline designs. During the baseline condition, there should be at least three data points demonstrating stability or showing the behavior moving in a countertherapeutic direction. If there are less than three data points or the data are moving in a therapeutic direction, experimental control is weakened considerably.

After the intervention is implemented, the critical concern is whether or not the data are clustered around the criterion line. Researchers will generally set a criterion that must be met before the participant moves to the next phase (i.e., before the criterion line is changed). The critical demonstration in each phase is controlling the behavior at the criterion line for at least three consecutive sessions. Thus, the three data points rule holds here as well. Researchers may require more than three data points at each phase before changing the criterion. For example, Martella, Leonard, Marchand-Martella, and Agran (1993) required four data points at or under the criterion line for a behavioral excess (i.e., a behavior that occurs too often). As shown in Figure 12.3, there are three consecutive data points in baseline showing stable performance; however, in the second phase of the intervention, there were not three consecutive data points clustered around

TABLE 12.1 Threats to Internal Validity for Each of the Designs Described in Chapter 12

RESEARCH DESIGN THREAT	CHANGING-CRITERION DESIGN	MULTITREATMENT DESIGN	ALTERNATING TREATMENTS DESIGN	COMBINATION DESIGNS
1. Maturation	Controlled	Controlled	Controlled	Controlled
2. Selection	Not applicable	Not applicable	Not applicable	Not applicable
3. Selection by maturation interaction	Not applicable	Not applicable	Not applicable	Not applicable
4. Statistical regression	Controlled	Controlled	Controlled	Controlled
5. Mortality	Controlled	Controlled	Controlled	Controlled
6. Instrumentation	Controlled	Controlled	Controlled	Controlled
7. Testing	Controlled	Controlled	Controlled	Controlled
8. History	Controlled	Controlled	Controlled	Controlled
9. Resentful demoralization of the control group	Not applicable	Not applicable	Not applicable	Not applicable
10. Diffusion of treatment	Controlled	Possible concern	Possible concern	Controlled
11. Compensatory rivalry by the control group	Not applicable	Not applicable	Not applicable	Not applicable
12. Compensatory equalization	Not applicable	Not applicable	Not applicable	Not applicable

Note: This table is meant only as a general guideline. Decisions with regard to threats to internal validity must be made after the specifics of an investigation are known and understood. Thus, interpretations of internal validity threats must be made on a study-by-study basis.

the criterion line. This demonstration makes the claim of internal validity more difficult to make. If there were three consecutive data points clustered around the criterion line, the experimental demonstration would have been greater.

Criterion Level. Initially, the criterion level should be set at a level that is attainable. This level may be set at the mean level of baseline or just below or above this level (depending if one were to decrease or increase a behavior). Once the participant has met the criterion at this initial criterion level, there should be a change in the next criterion. The difficulty here is that the level change should not be so small as to "overreinforce" the participant at a previous level nor so large that the participant is unable to meet this level. In these cases, the participant's behavior of meeting the level and/or his or her effort in doing so may extinguish or cease. Thus, researchers must be especially cautious when changing the levels of criteria throughout the investigation. Although a given intervention may be effective, a mistake in the level of criterion change could lead to a conclusion that the intervention is inadequate.

Stability and Immediacy. A critical concern with changing-criterion designs is the stability and immediacy of change. Experimental control comes from demonstrating that the participant's behavior

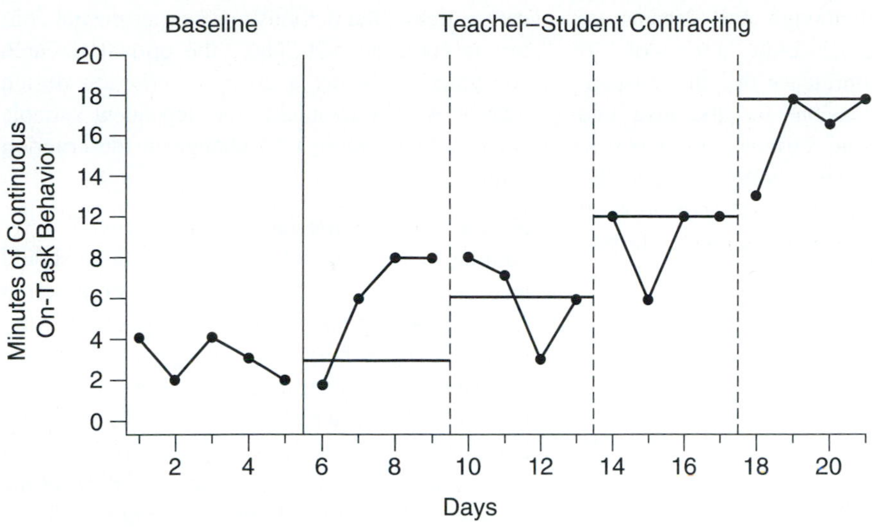

FIGURE 12.3 Minutes of continuous on-task behavior across baseline and teacher–student contracting conditions.

is held at a certain level. If the behavior is held at each criterion level as in Figure 12.1, one could conclude that the researcher had experimental control over the behavior. However, suppose that the data looked like those in Figure 12.4. The problem here is that the researcher essentially has an A-B design with all of its associated weaknesses..

One way to think of a changing-criterion design is as a series of A-B designs. Essentially, the logic of the changing-criterion design is a series of

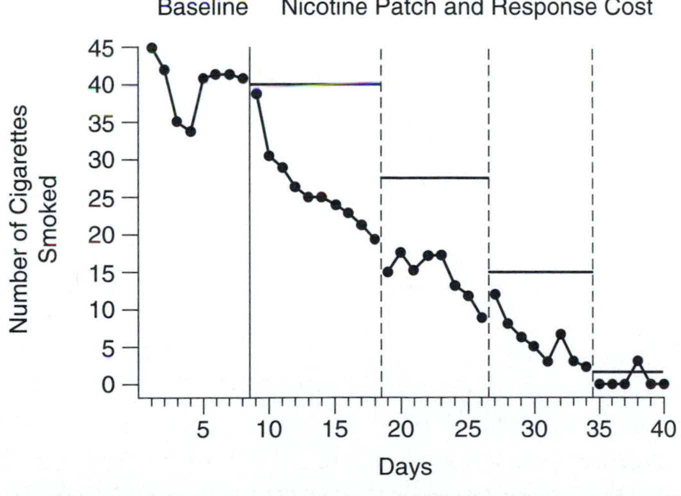

FIGURE 12.4 Number of cigarettes smoked across baseline and nicotine patch and response cost conditions.

A-B replications. Even though A-B designs are considered weak in internal validity, a series of A-B designs increase the confidence that the independent variable is responsible for the measured changes in the dependent variable. As shown in Figure 12.5, each phase acts as both an "A" and "B" condition; that is, each phase is an "A" condition for the following phase and a "B" condition for the previous phase. If there is an inability to keep the dependent variable at the criterion level in one or more of the criterion phases, the internal validity is weakened. The extent of the threat to internal validity is dependent on how far the data venture from the criterion line as well as the number of phases where there was an inability to control the behavior.

Another concern has to do with the immediacy of change. When a criterion is changed, there should be an immediate change in the level of the dependent variable. The longer it takes for the data to cluster around the criterion level, the more likely it is that there is a potential threat to the internal validity of the investigation. Again, the purpose of the changing-criterion design is to demonstrate that there is control over the dependent variable. Whenever there is an inability to control the dependent variable, the demonstrated experimental control is compromised. Thus, the critical research consumer analyzing a changing-criterion design must look at how quickly the dependent variable changes in response to a change in the criterion level.

Number of Criterion Levels (Replications). According to Tawney and Gast (1984), there should be a minimum of four replications or criterion phases. The purpose of this is to replicate the behavior changes frequently enough to show that changes did not occur by chance. The rule is similar to the rule stated by Kazdin (1982) for multiple-baseline designs; that is, four A-B replications at minimum are required to replicate the effects of the independent variable on the dependent variable to make a determination of the internal validity of the investigation. Thus, if there were fewer than four criterion change phases in an experiment, the internal validity of the investigation is weakened much as it is with a multiple-baseline design.

Other Control Procedures. Overall, the changing-criterion design is not considered one of the stronger designs since this design is simply a series of

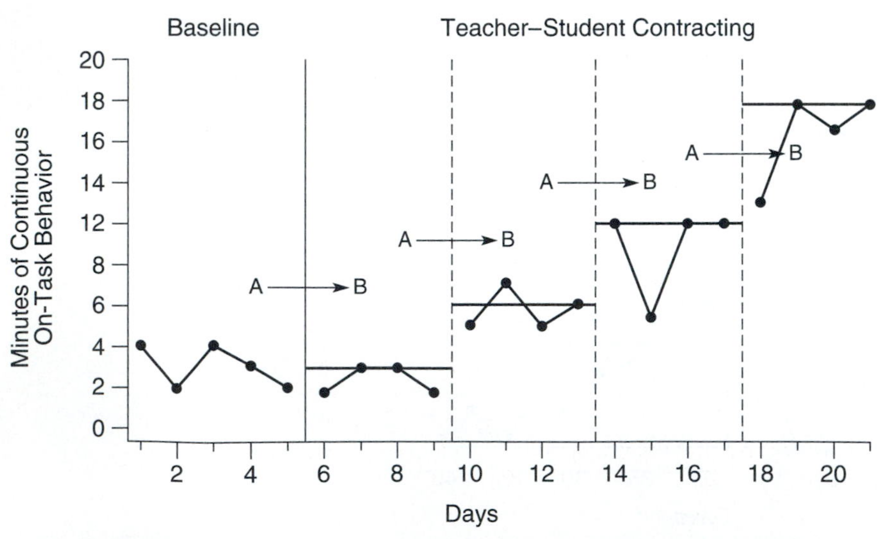

FIGURE 12.5 Minutes of continuous on-task behavior across baseline and teacher–student contracting conditions.

A-B designs. The inference of experimental control is greater with the changing-criterion design than it is with other single-case designs. Researchers must infer that the control is coming from the independent variable; however, some of the control certainly comes from the criterion level. Additionally, the control may come from a history factor, for example, in combination with the criterion level. The independent variable may have very little to do with the observed changes if the intervention is separated from the changing-criterion levels. In other words, there is no direct investigation of the independent variable's effects on the dependent variable.

Threats to internal validity are difficult to rule out with this design. However, there are steps researchers can take to improve the internal validity of the changing-criterion design. The first technique is to vary the level of changes in the criterion level. For example, the researcher could decrease or increase (depending on the dependent variable to be changed) the criterion level by 25% in the first phase, 10% in the second, and 50% in the third phase. Varying the level of changes aids in the demonstration of the control over the dependent variable. Along these lines, researchers could also vary the length of each criterion phase. Rather than requiring four consecutive data points at or near the criterion line, five or six consecutive data points may be required.

A more rigorous demonstration that directly measures the effects of the independent variable over the dependent variable is to reverse the criterion. Recall that history is difficult to rule out with a changing-criterion design. Suppose that the researcher has three phases of decreasing criteria, as shown in Figure 12.6. Then, the researcher reverses the dependent variable by increasing the criterion in the fourth phase. Then, the fifth phase shows a decrease in the criterion. Notice that what was done was to combine two designs—a changing-criterion design and a reversal (not a withdrawal) design. The strength of the reversal design is combined with the changing-criterion design to produce a powerful demonstration of experimental control.

External Validity. Clearly, the external validity of the changing-criterion design is fairly weak. There is typically one participant in one setting

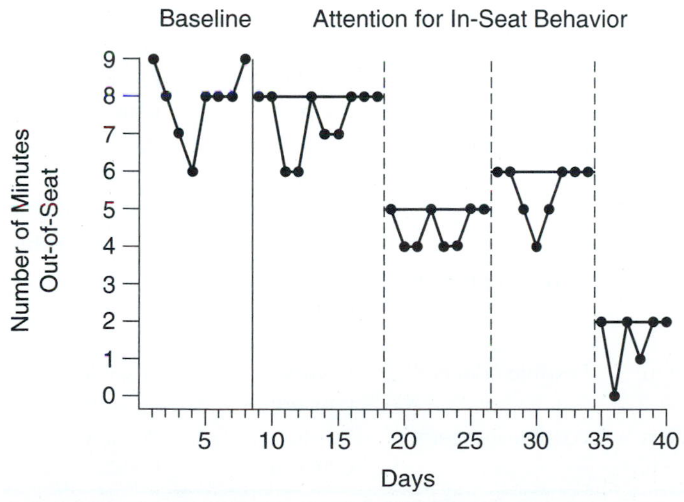

FIGURE 12.6 Number of minutes out-of-seat across baseline and attention for in-seat behavior conditions.

with one measure of the dependent variable. There is also a difficulty with the method of changing the dependent variable. It is probably not too common to decrease or increase behaviors in such a stepwise manner. This is not to say that it is not ineffective to do so, only that it doesn't occur frequently in many applied settings such as a classroom. As explained before, single-case researchers look to replications to demonstrate external validity in a systematic manner. Many researchers do not see how a single investigation can demonstrate external validity. Table 12.2 summarizes the major threats to external validity of the changing-criterion design.

Research Example

Allen and Kramer (1990) used a changing-criterion design to investigate the efficacy of contingency contracting when integrated within a behavioral

TABLE 12.2 Threats to External Validity for Each of the Designs Described in Chapter 12

RESEARCH DESIGN THREAT	CHANGING-CRITERION DESIGN	MULTITREATMENT DESIGN	ALTERNATING TREATMENTS DESIGN	COMBINATION DESIGNS
1. Generalization across participants	Possible concern	Possible concern	Possible concern	Possible concern
2. Interaction of personological variables and treatment effects	Possible concern	Possible concern	Possible concern	Possible concern
3. Verification of independent variable	Possible concern	Possible concern	Possible concern	Possible concern
4. Multiple treatment interference	Controlled	Possible concern	Possible concern	Controlled
5. Novelty and disruption effects	Possible concern	Possible concern	Possible concern	Possible concern
6. Hawthorne effect	Possible concern	Possible concern	Possible concern	Possible concern
7. Experimenter effects	Possible concern	Possible concern	Possible concern	Possible concern
8. Pretest sensitization	Not applicable	Not applicable	Not applicable	Not applicable
9. Posttest sensitization	Not applicable	Not applicable	Not applicable	Not applicable
10. Interaction of time of measurement and treatment effects	Possible concern	Possible concern	Possible concern	Possible concern
11. Measurement of the dependent variable	Possible concern	Possible concern	Possible concern	Possible concern
12. Interaction of history and treatment effects	Possible concern	Possible concern	Possible concern	Possible concern

Note: This table is meant only as a general guideline. Decisions with regard to threats to external validity must be made after the specifics of an investigation are known and understood. Thus, interpretations of external validity threats must be made on a study-by-study basis.

consultation model used by school psychologists. The participant was a 12-year-old male who was enrolled in a cross-categorical resource room that included fifth- and sixth-grade students. He was referred to a psychologist in training because of poor personal hygiene and grooming needs.

The independent variable consisted of contingency contracting. Six behaviors were identified that the participant was expected to display (i.e., having combed hair upon arrival at school, having clean hair, wearing pants different from the ones worn the previous day, wearing a shirt different from the one worn the previous day, wearing clean articles of clothing, and having clean face and hands upon arrival at school). Tokens were distributed to the participant as part of an in-class token economy program. At the end of each week, the tokens were exchanged for privileges outlined in the contract. Two phases of the intervention were implemented. The first phase involved providing the participant 15 minutes of free time with a person of the participant's choice as a bonus for obtaining 13 or more tokens per week. Phase II involved requiring 20 or more tokens per week in exchange for an additional 2 minutes of free time. Procedural checks consisted of the psychologist in training contacting the teacher each week to ensure that the intervention was being implemented as planned. The psychologist did not directly observe the program but did review daily grooming assessment data.

The dependent variable was personal hygiene and grooming skills. These skills were measured by the teacher at the beginning of the school day by marking whether each (e.g., clean hair) was observed. Thus, the maximum number of skills that could be displayed per day was six. A total of 30 tokens (six skills multiplied by five days) were available per week. Additionally, social validation measures were implemented to obtain feedback from the participant's reading, vocal music, media, and computer science teachers as well as paraprofessionals from the participant's classroom and health office. The six hygiene and grooming problem areas were listed as well as three decoy items. The respondents were asked to indicate if they noticed the problems as well as the degree of change. No interobserver agreement percentages were listed for the scoring of hygiene and grooming skills.

The results indicated that the participant's hygiene and grooming skills improved (see Figure 12.7). Additionally, the survey revealed that the majority of respondents noticed the hygiene and grooming problems and improvements in these skills. The respondents also were able to discriminate between actual hygiene and grooming problems and the decoy items.

WHAT IS A MULTITREATMENT DESIGN?

The multitreatment design is an associated design of the withdrawal design discussed in Chapter 10. The multitreatment design is planned in such a way as to allow for the comparison of two or more interventions or the additive components of an intervention. This design is an alternative to group designs that allow for the same type of comparisons to be made. Several variations of the withdrawal design are possible that demonstrate the effects of several interventions or components of an intervention. For example, if two interventions were to be compared, an A-B-A-C-A design could be used. In this case, it is possible to determine which intervention is more successful at changing the dependent variable in comparison to the baseline condition. What is critical to understand here is that this design is consistent with the "change one variable at a time rule." As shown in Figure 12.8, the token economy system was more effective in reducing talkouts in comparison to baseline than was the warning condition. The difficulty with this design is that interpreting the relative effectiveness of "B" and "C" is a problem. Conditions "B" and "C" are never directly compared. A related problem is the possibility of sequencing effects. In other words, was the "C" condition more or less effective than the "B" condition because the "B" condition preceded it?

Another variation of the withdrawal design is one in which interaction effects of intervention components are compared. For example, the A-B-A-B-BC-B-BC design compares the "B" intervention with the addition of the "C" intervention. The advantage of this design is obvious. That is, additive

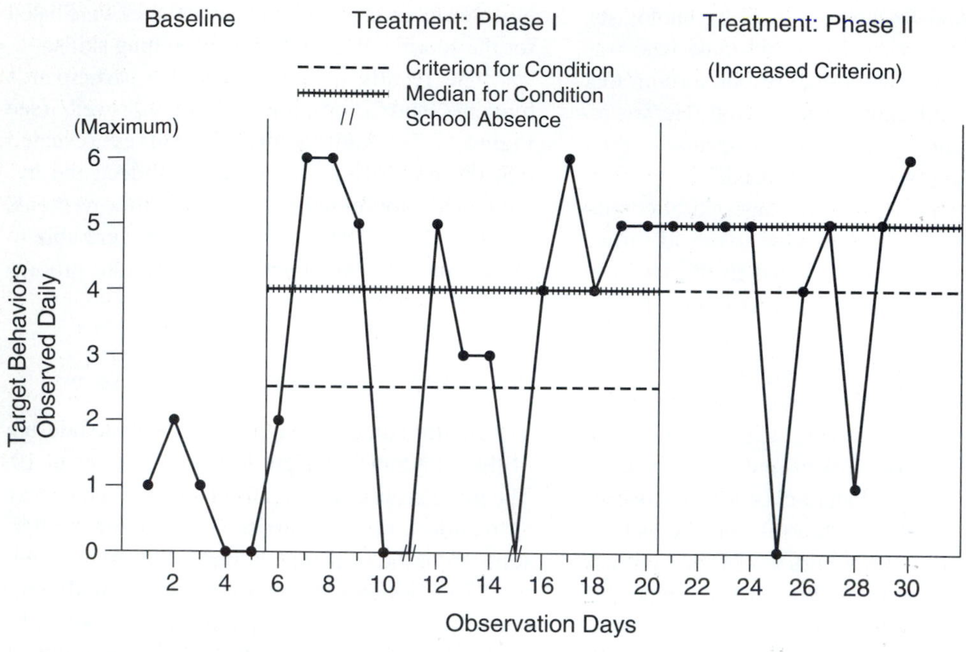

FIGURE 12.7 Median incidents of target behaviors based on daily observations.

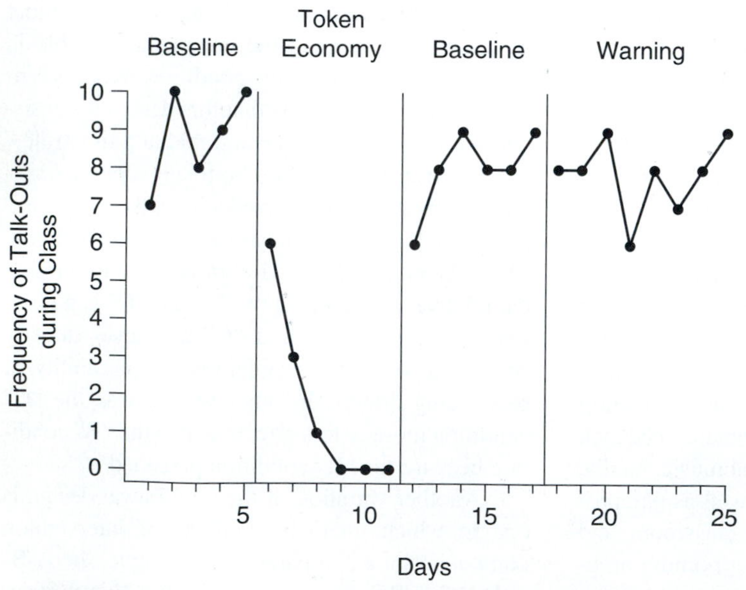

FIGURE 12.8 The frequency of talk-outs during class across baseline, token-economy, and warning conditions.

effects of interventions are important to test since rarely is one variable in effect in isolation in applied settings. The comparisons come from "BC" being surrounded by "B" and "B" being surrounded by "BC."

A similar design is the case when a researcher wishes to compare the addition of different components in an intervention. For example, suppose that she wanted to use a self-management program containing two separate variables ("B" and "C") with a student who has difficulty staying in his seat. Most self-management programs contain several components such as self-reinforcement, self-monitoring, and self-evaluation. Now suppose that the self-management program contained two instructional components (i.e., self-monitoring and self-instructions). The researcher implements the self-management program and finds that the dependent variable decreases immediately after the implementation of the independent variable. The question of the contributions of the components to the package is raised. Thus, the researcher implements the self-management package without the self-instructions (C). She also implements the package without self-monitoring (B). Thus, an A-BC-A-B-A-C-A design could be used. If the relative effectiveness were to be compared, the researcher could do the following: A-BC-A-BC-B-BC-C-BC-B-C-B. Several combinations are compared in this example—the comparisons of "BC" with baseline, "B" with "BC," "C" with "BC," and "C" with "B." An example investigation is shown in Figure 12.9. As the figure indicates, the combination of the two components is effective at increasing in-seat behavior. The relative effectiveness of the self-instructions is also apparent. The self-monitoring alone is almost as effective as the combination intervention; the self-instruction condition alone is clearly less effective

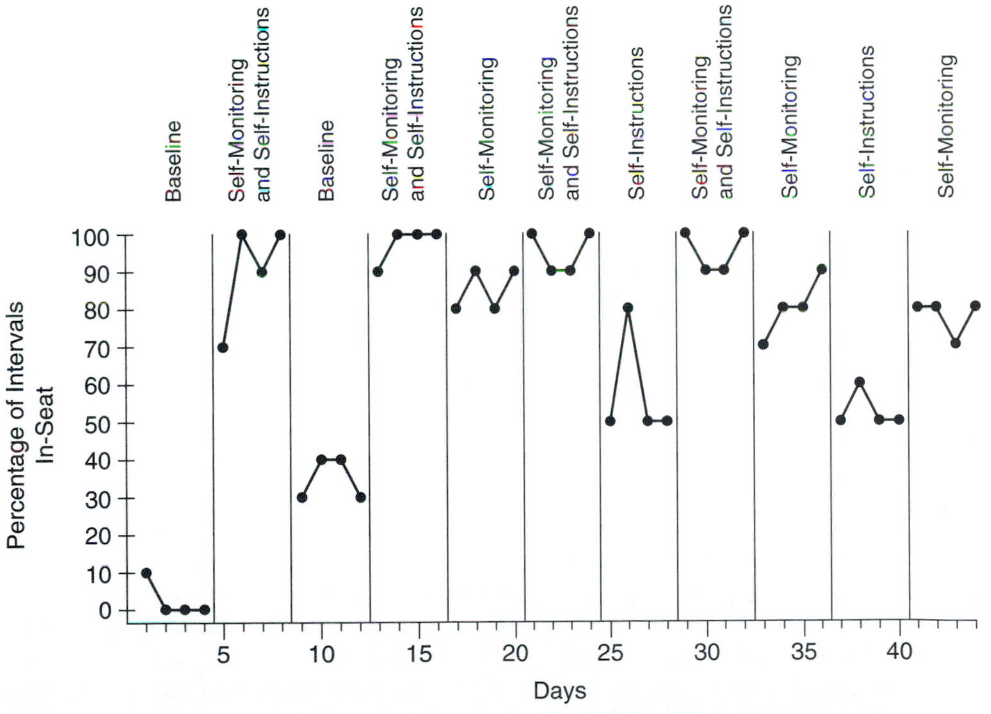

FIGURE 12.9 Percentage of intervals in-seat across baseline, self-monitoring and self-instruction, self-monitoring alone, and self-instruction alone conditions.

than the self-monitoring. Thus, the self-instruction component adds little to the effectiveness of the self-management program.

Analysis of Data

Internal Validity. The threats to internal validity of the multitreatment design are similar to other designs discussed thus far. The threats especially critical to control are history and maturation. The following all have an impact on the control of threats to internal validity: condition length, changing one variable at a time, level and rapidity of change, return to baseline levels, and time of implementation. Table 12.1 summarizes the major threats to internal validity of the multitreatment design.

Condition Length. The condition length criterion is the same as the other designs discussed thus far. There must be a minimum of three consecutive stable data points or three consecutive data points moving in a countertherapeutic direction.

Change One Variable at a Time. As indicated in Chapter 10, there must be a change in one variable at a time to demonstrate the effectiveness of each intervention compared to the baseline condition or to determine the relative effectiveness of multiple interventions. Additionally, a design such as an A-BC-B-A-B-BC design does not demonstrate experimental control. The reason for this lack of control is that no comparisons are being made. Notice that the two "BC" conditions are not surrounded by an "A" or a "B" condition. Likewise, the "B" conditions are not surrounded by an "A" or a "BC" condition.

In order to demonstrate the effectiveness of the interventions as compared to the baseline, an A-BC-A-B-A design would be appropriate. To compare the relative effectiveness of the interventions together versus one intervention in isolation, an A-BC-A-BC-B-BC-B design could be used. In the last example, the critical comparisons are as follows: A-BC-A, BC-A-BC, BC-B-BC, and B-BC-B. Unfortunately, researchers may make a mistake with the "change one variable at a time rule." If this occurs, some experimental control is lost, and conclusions made should be viewed as the conclusion drawn when using an A-B design.

Level and Rapidity of Change. The level and rapidity of change is the same as explained in previous chapters. The change in level of the dependent variable should be fairly substantial and should occur as soon as possible once the condition change occurs. If there is a lack of change or a very small one, the demonstration of experimental control is weakened. Likewise, the demonstration of experimental control is compromised if there is a delay in the change of the dependent variable.

Return to Baseline Levels. An inability to return to baseline levels is also referred to as a problem with reversibility. As with the withdrawal design, if the dependent variable does not return to baseline levels in a design such as the A-BC-A-B-A design, the experimental control is compromised. There must be a return to baseline or near baseline levels for firm conclusions to be made on the effects of the independent variable on the dependent variable.

When a design is used that allows for direct comparisons to be made between or among multiple interventions, the rule is changed somewhat. For example, in an A-B-A-B-BC-B-BC design, there should be a return to baseline levels in the two baseline conditions; however, what is required for the adjacent "B" and "BC" conditions is a difference in the levels of performance. If there are no changes occurring in the dependent variable when conditions are changed, the conclusion as to the differential effectiveness of the "B" and "BC" conditions becomes more difficult.

Suppose that there were little or no changes between the conditions, as shown in Figure 12.10. In this case, the self-instructions with self-reinforcement showed no advantages over the self-instructional intervention alone. However, what can be concluded? We can conclude that the addition of self-reinforcement adds little to nothing to the overall effects of the self-instructional intervention. However, we cannot conclude that the self-instructional component (B) is more effective

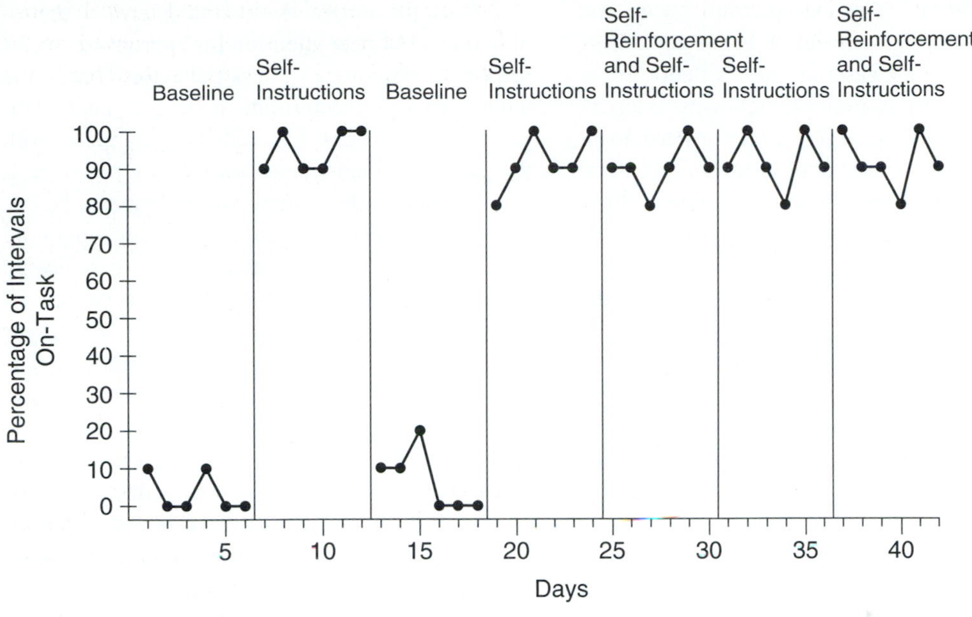

FIGURE 12.10 Percentage of intervals on-task across baseline, self-instruction and self-reinforcement, and self-instruction alone conditions.

than the self-reinforcement component (C). In order to make this comparison, we would have to add something like the following to the design: B-C-B-C. Now a direct comparison is being made. In the earlier design, the "B" and "C" components are not directly compared. Although the self-reinforcement component adds nothing to the overall impact of the intervention, the self-instruction component may actually suppress the effects of the self-reinforcement component. In other words, when combined with self-instructions, self-reinforcement loses its effectiveness, but when viewed alone, it is more effective than self-instructions alone. Again, researchers must be careful in the conclusions made, and critical research consumers must also be careful in interpreting the results of investigations, especially the conclusions made based on those investigations.

Time of Implementation. A final concern is the amount of time it takes to implement a multitreatment design (Gast & Wolery, 1988). Consider an A-B-A-C-A design. There are five conditions. Thus, a minimum of 15 data points must be gathered (three consecutive stable data points or data points moving in a countertherapeutic direction per condition). Now consider the A-B-A-BC-B-BC-B design. There are seven conditions for a minimum of 21 data points. What if three interventions were to be compared? Suppose that we compare the relative effectiveness of extrinsic reinforcement (B), intrinsic reinforcement (C), and a combination of the two (BC) on the motivation of school children. We would use a design such as: A-B-A-B-C-B-C-BC-C-BC-B-BC-B. We can compare the following: A-B-A, B-A-B, B-C-B, C-B-C, C-BC-C, BC-C-BC, BC-B-BC, and B-BC-B. There are 13 conditions with a minimum of 39 data points. Not only is the multitreatment design cumbersome, but it also takes a great deal of time to implement. The problem with taking such a long time to implement a design is that the potential for history and maturation to have an effect is increased.

External Validity. The external validity of the multitreatment design is weak. It is not any different from other single-case designs. A major threat to external validity is multiple-treatment interference (Gast & Wolery, 1988). Since a participant will be exposed to a number of interventions, there is concern that if others outside of the investigation are not exposed to the interventions in the same order, the generalizability of the results are suspect. For example, if the "B" condition comes before the "BC" condition in the investigation, will it also need to occur before a combination intervention outside of the investigation? Suppose we again implemented a self-management procedure. The "B" condition was self-instructions and the "C" condition was self-reinforcement. The question that should be addressed is whether or not the self-instructions must come before the combination of both interventions to make the combination more effective. What if a teacher attempted to use the combination without implementing self-instructions alone first? Would her results be different than those reported by the researchers? Table 12.2 summarizes the major threats to external validity of the multitreatment design.

All of the other threats to external validity are present in this design. As with other single-case designs, replications must be conducted to increase our confidence in the generalizability of the results.

Research Example

Lewis and Sugai (1996) used an A-B-C-D-C-D design to assess the effectiveness of an assessment-based intervention with a 6-year-old first-grade student without disabilities. The classroom contained 25 students. The student displayed high rates of inappropriate interactions with peers (e.g., hitting, calling names, making noises) during academic and free-play times. The dependent variable was on-task behavior during the reading period, and the dependent measure was the percentage of six-second intervals on-task. The authors conducted several assessments and determined that the student was engaging in the inappropriate responses due to peer attention.

Thus, the authors decided to determine the required level of peer attention for appropriate social responses to improve on-task behavior. That is, the authors wished to determine the level of peer attention for on-task behavior needed to "compete" with the peer attention received for off-task behavior. It was hoped that the student would begin to be on-task to gain peer attention rather than remaining off-task. The authors planned a research design that consisted of four conditions: (A) baseline, (B) peer attention for on-task behavior only [Peer DRI], (C) peer attention for on-task behavior plus the opportunity to earn free time for being on-task [Peer DRI+], and (D) assigning a peer tutor to the student to help with reading [Peer Tutor].

Figure 12.11 shows the results of the investigation. There was a low level of on-task behavior during the baseline condition. When the peers provided attention to the student for on-task behavior, the student's on-task behavior did not improve. There was a slight improvement when the peers provided attention for on-task behavior and the student earned free time. The major improvement came when a peer tutor began working with the student. The on-task improvement was reversed in the subsequent condition and returned back to the previous high level when the peer tutor began working with the student once again.

The authors concluded that there was a need to provide constant peer attention to the student in the form of peer tutoring to reduce the student's need to gain attention through inappropriate classroom responses. In addition, the attention provided by peers for on-task behavior was not constant enough to override the student's need to gain attention.

WHAT IS AN ALTERNATING TREATMENTS DESIGN?

Although the multitreatment design is adequate for making comparisons of components of intervention packages or comparisons of interventions, the disadvantages are difficult to overcome. An alternative to the use of multitreatment designs is the alternating treatments design (ATD) also called the multielement design (Sidman,

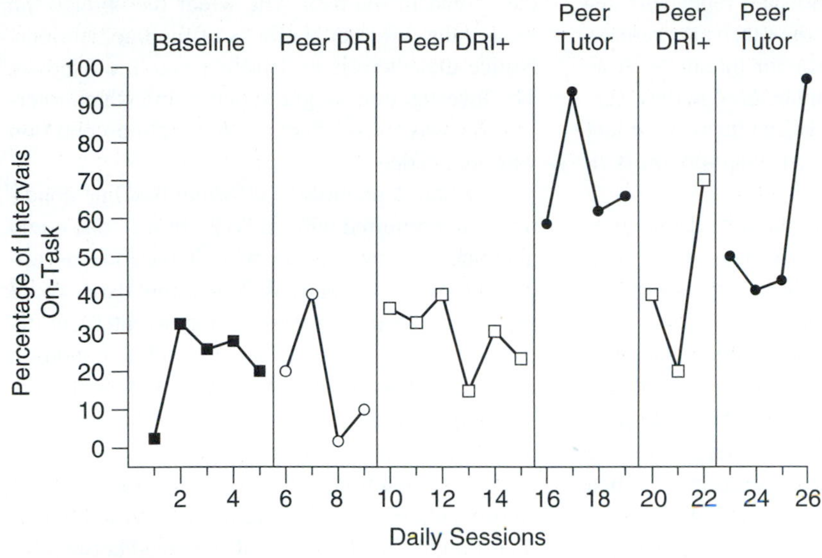

FIGURE 12.11 Percentage of intervals on-task across baseline and assessment-based intervention conditions.

1960; Ulman & Sulzer-Azaroff, 1975). According to Gast and Wolery (1988), many researchers choose the ATD over the multitreatment design due to the aforementioned concerns.

The main purpose of the ATD is to make comparisons between or among two or more conditions or interventions such as baseline and intervention(s) or multiple interventions. A secondary function is to determine experimental control. The other single-case designs discussed thus far (with the possible exception of the multitreatment design) are planned to control only for the threats to internal validity. On the other hand, the ATD attempts to demonstrate the superiority of one intervention over the other. Thus, for most purposes, the ATD is used to compare two or more conditions or interventions as well as to control for the threats to internal validity.

The ATD is the single-case alternative to the factorial design used in group research. The experimental control achieved through this design can be quite extensive since one way to increase one's statistical power is by eliminating intersubject variability or unsystematic variance. Essentially, the ATD splits the participant into equal parts and provides the different interventions to each part. Thus, if a participant is exposed to a historical situation such as difficulty at home, the history will affect all of the interventions equally (Barlow & Hersen, 1984). Any differences seen between or among the conditions or interventions would be the differential effects of the interventions.

The ATD achieves this ability to overcome threats to internal validity and to make equal comparisons between or among conditions or interventions by alternating the presentation of each condition or intervention. For example, suppose we wished to compare two methods of classroom management such as in-class time-out and reprimands. We alternate the interventions to see the relative effects of each on the classroom behavior of the students. The manner in which we alternate the interventions can vary. For example, we could split the day in half and run one intervention in the morning and the other in the afternoon. We could also run one on Monday, Wednesday, and Friday during the first week, Tuesday and Thursday during the second week, and then repeat the sequence. We would then run the other intervention on the other days. To control for threats such as maturation (e.g., students may be tired in the afternoon, which leads to more difficulties), we must randomly determine when each intervention is in effect.

Suppose that we elect to alternate days rather than time of day. We randomly determine when each intervention is in effect. Researchers may set a rule on the number of consecutive times the same intervention can occur. Due to the chance factor, it would be possible to have an entire week with the same intervention. Thus, a rule may be made such as a maximum of two consecutive days with the same intervention. Once it is determined when each intervention will be implemented, data can be collected on the effects of each intervention. Figure 12.12 shows an example of the ATD. In the figure, no more than two consecutive days of the same intervention are allowed. The interventions are alternated on a daily basis. Conclusions can be drawn based on the data in Figure 12.12. It seems as though the time-out was more effective than the reprimands. We can determine this by looking at the spread in the data. The wider the spread, the greater the differential effects of the interventions. Notice that there is no baseline condition shown. The investigation sought to determine which intervention was most effective. A baseline condition was not needed.

As stated previously, a formal baseline condition is not required with an ATD. In fact, one could alternate an intervention with a baseline as opposed to two interventions. The comparison would then be between intervention and no intervention. However, many times a formal baseline condition is initiated. Figure 12.13 shows an ATD with such a baseline condition. The figure also shows a comparison between two interventions.

On completion of the comparison between or among conditions or interventions, a visual analysis is conducted. The amount of spread between or among the conditions or interventions indicates the level of differential effectiveness. For example, in Figure 12.13, a token system was clearly found to be superior to the time-out condition, which was more effective than contingency contracting. If there were a lack of spread between or among the data, the conclusion would be that there were few

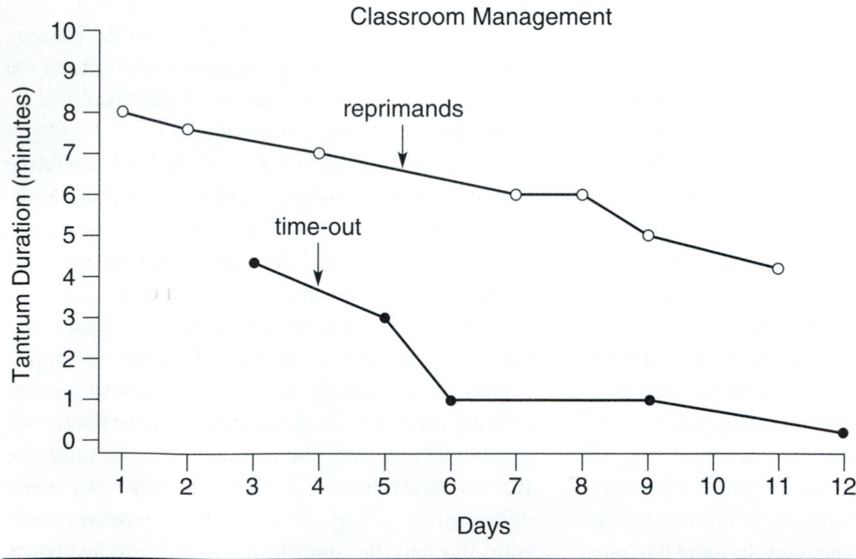

FIGURE 12.12 The daily duration of tantrums across time-out and reprimand conditions.

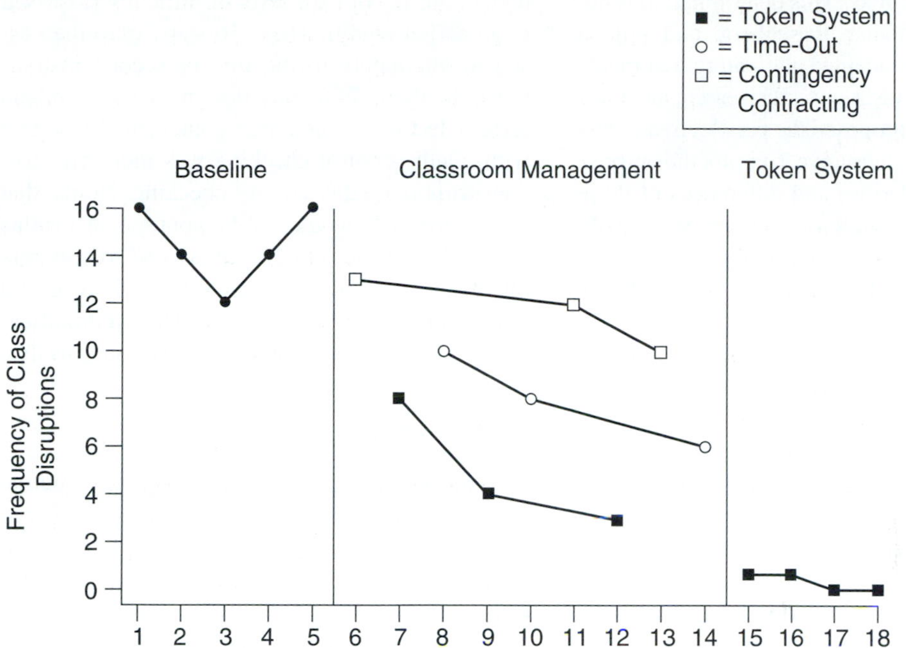

FIGURE 12.13 The frequency of class disruptions across baseline, token system, time-out, and contingency contracting conditions.

or no differences between or among the conditions or interventions.

Once a determination has been made with regard to the relative effectiveness of the conditions or interventions, a final condition may be added to the design (Kazdin & Hartman, 1978). Figure 12.13 demonstrates this added condition. Many times, researchers will implement the condition or intervention singularly. The most effective condition or intervention would be implemented at all times such as every day rather than alternating days. This final condition demonstrates that the condition or intervention can sustain the dependent variable change across other times or situations.

Skill Acquisition Programs. Recall a major problem with the withdrawal design is that the dependent variable must be reversible. That is, the dependent variable must return to baseline levels when the intervention is removed. Acquiring skills is an example of a nonreversible dependent variable. If researchers were to teach problem-solving skills, they probably could not tell the participant to forget everything he or she has learned. The multiple-baseline design corrects for this problem by not requiring the dependent variable to revert to baseline levels. A problem with the multiple-baseline design is that direct comparisons between or among several independent variables cannot be made. The multitreatment design and the ATD allow for such a comparison. The multitreatment design requires the dependent variable to be reversible; however, the ATD does not require this (Gast & Wolery, 1988). Unfortunately, the ATD allows for only one dependent variable. This fact raises a problem with skill acquisition programs. How could a researcher teach problem solving using two separate teaching techniques and still determine the relative contributions of each teaching method? This determination is not possible. Thus, Sindelar, Rosenberg, and Wilson (1985) proposed the adapted alternating treatments design (AATD) for instructional research, and Gast and Wolery (1988) proposed the parallel treatments design (PTD) as an alternative. (It is not the purpose to explain the similarities and differences of these two designs; they are similar in most respects but do have some differences. For our purposes, an overall general discussion of the key points made by Sindelar and colleagues and Gast and Wolery will suffice.)

Essentially, the AATD and PTD are modifications of the ATD. These designs help solve the problem of investigating the relative effectiveness of different instructional methods on skill acquisition dependent variables. The AATD and PTD require that two or more "sets" of dependent variables or behaviors be developed. These dependent variables or behaviors should be similar in difficulty and effort to perform. For example, suppose that a researcher is teaching reading skills. She would take two aspects of reading that are equal in difficulty and randomly assign these aspects to the different instructional methods. The difficulty here is that the sets must be independent. If one method of instruction is effective in teaching some aspect of reading, there should be no carryover to the other behaviors or aspects involved in reading. Researchers may attempt to find two parallel dependent variables or behaviors or take a set of behaviors and randomly assign these to the instructional methods. When two sets of dependent variables are used in this manner, the difficulty seen with the ATD with regard to identifying the more effective instructional method for skill acquisition is overcome.

Likins, Salzberg, Stowitschek, Lignugaris/Kraft, and Curl (1989) used a PTD to investigate relative effectiveness of coincidental teaching with quality-control checking versus without quality-control checking when teaching students with mild or moderate mental retardation to make a salad. The salad-making task was broken into 19 steps. Then, three steps were omitted in the instructional condition since the participants could already perform these skills. The remaining 16 steps were ordered in terms of their level of difficulty (assessed in an earlier study). These 16 steps were then assigned alternately to the first or second instructional method. With this design, the researchers were able to determine that coincidental teaching with quality-control checking was more effective than without quality-control checking. Notice that a standard ATD would not be appropriate for this study. If all 16 steps to making a salad were taught one of two ways on alternating days, there would most likely be carryover effects. Thus, a modification of the ATD is appropriate in cases such as this.

Analysis of Data

Internal Validity. When assessing the internal validity of the ATD and its variations, several concerns must be taken into consideration. These concerns involve condition length and carryover effects (i.e., diffusion or treatment). Table 12.1 summarizes the major threats to internal validity of the ATD.

Condition Length. As with all of the other designs discussed in Chapters 10, 11, and 12, the length of the baseline condition should be at least three consecutive stable data points or three consecutive data points moving in a countertherapeutic direction. This concern is valid when there is a formal baseline condition. For the intervention condition, there should be at least two data points per condition or intervention (Barlow & Hersen, 1984); however, the larger the number of data points collected, the better. Obviously, this is a major advantage of the ATD; it takes only a minimum of four sessions to compare two conditions or interventions. If a study has fewer than two data points per condition or intervention, the experimental control is seriously weakened. A trend must be demonstrated in single-case research, and fewer than two data points per condition or intervention cannot establish a trend when using the ATD.

Carryover Effects. One major threat comes from carryover problems. If an intervention has an effect on the other intervention irrespective of how the interventions were sequenced, the differences between the interventions may be minimal or nonexistent or may be greater than would occur otherwise. This result would not be because the interventions are equal in effectiveness or that one intervention was clearly less effective than the other but because the effectiveness of one intervention improved or harmed the performance of the other intervention. The conclusion that one intervention is not superior to another or that one intervention may be superior to the other may be incorrect due to this threat. This was the justification for proposing the AATD and PTD. Carryover effects are expected to be present under some conditions such as when teaching a skill.

There are two types of carryover effects—positive and negative (Barlow & Hersen, 1984). Positive carryover effects occur when the effects of one intervention are enhanced when alternated with the other intervention. Negative carryover effects occur when one intervention is less effective when alternated with the other intervention. Both carryover effects compromise the ability to make adequate conclusions with regard to the effects of each independent variable on the dependent variable. To prevent carryover effects, researchers should do the following: (a) Counterbalance the order of interventions (i.e., ensure that there is an equal number of instances where the first intervention comes before and after the second intervention). (b) Separate interventions with a time interval. This interval aids the participant in discriminating when one intervention is in effect as opposed to the other one. The participant must be able to tell when one intervention is in effect since an inability to do so will result in a lack of differential responding to the different interventions. (c) Be careful that the speed of alterations is not too rapid. For example, if interventions are rotated every hour, the participant may again have difficulty in discriminating when each intervention is in effect.

If the critical research consumer suspects carryover effects, the conclusions made by the researcher may be suspect. These threats may lead to erroneous conclusions about the internal validity of the investigation.

External Validity. The ATD has the same difficulties as other single-case designs with regard to external validity. An added threat to external validity is multiple-treatment interference. However, participants in applied research rarely go without experiencing some multiple-treatment interference. If an intervention is used in an applied setting, it may have to compete against or with other factors such as history, maturation, and so on. Thus, when looking at several conditions or interventions, one can determine the effects of the intervention when the participant is also exposed to other conditions or interventions.

Specifically, a threat associated with multiple-treatment interference is sequential confounding. Sequential confounding occurs when one intervention may be more or less effective since it always follows the other intervention. Thus, the reason for randomly alternating the interventions is to prevent such a result. This is a threat to the external validity of the investigation since the conclusion of the generalizability of an intervention's effectiveness may be incorrect if it is tied to how that intervention was ordered.

When considering the external validity of the ATD, one must realize that the external validity can be improved with replications of the investigation's results. The researcher should report enough information in sufficient detail to allow for replications and logical generalization. Table 12.2 summarizes the major threats to external validity of the ATD.

Research Example

Nelson, Johnson, and Marchand-Martella (1996) investigated the differential effects of direct instruction, cooperative learning, and independent learning practices on the classroom behavior of students with behavioral disorders. There were four male students ranging in age from 8 years, 4 months, to 9 years, 10 months. They were enrolled in a self-contained classroom for students with behavior disorders. These students were integrated into an experimental classroom with 8 to 12 third-grade students who were randomly selected from two general education classrooms. The independent variables were the three aforementioned instructional techniques, and the dependent variables were the on-task and disruptive behaviors of the students. An ATD was used to determine the relative effectiveness of the three instructional methods. The dependent measure was the percentage of 10-second intervals the students were on-task and/or disruptive.

Figure 12.14(a)–12.14(d) demonstrates the relative effectiveness of the three interventions. The direct instruction method resulted in better on-task percentages and lower levels of disruptive behavior. This result was replicated across the four students. The authors concluded that the direct instruction method resulted in a better educational climate, whereas the independent learning approach resulted in higher levels of disruptive behavior.

WHAT ARE COMBINATION DESIGNS?

One advantage of single-case designs is the ability to combine two or more designs readily. As was mentioned in Chapter 11, multiple-probe designs can be combined with multiple-baseline designs to assess the generalizability of the dependent variable. Other combination designs that have appeared in the literature include changing-criterion within a multiple baseline, alternating treatments within a multiple baseline, withdrawal within a multiple baseline and within a changing-criterion, and a multiple-baseline design across participants within a multiple-baseline across behaviors.

The advantage of combination designs is that they can improve the internal validity of the investigation. For example, suppose that we were working with a single participant who had difficulty reading and doing math. We could implement a study strategy that we hope would help her reading and math abilities. We implement the intervention in a staggered fashion (i.e., a multiple-baseline design across behaviors). However, there is a weakness with a multiple-baseline design across two behaviors. Thus, we could combine the design with another such as a withdrawal design in such a way that the intervention is removed (i.e., the participant is no longer supplied with the materials necessary for study strategy behavior). If the behavior (e.g., reading) maintains after the intervention is removed, we still have a multiple-baseline design across two behaviors. On the other hand, if the behavior (e.g., reading) decreases to baseline levels, we have a strong demonstration of experimental control.

Another example involves the difficulty of having only two participants in one setting. We could use a multiple-baseline design across two participants; however, we still have a weakness. Suppose that we wanted to test the effects of compliance instruction in the classroom for the two participants. We could use the multiple-baseline design across participants but also test the intervention in other settings as shown in Figure 12.15. Notice how the combination of the designs increases the internal validity of the investigation. The addition of one more setting improved the research design substantially.

Combination designs can also add information to designs that may not have been set up to probe for such additional information. Recall the primary purpose of the ATD is to compare two or more conditions or interventions. Suppose that we wanted to compare one instructional method of teaching problem solving to another. The first method involved a standard problem-solving format such that a participant was taught to recognize the problem, define the problem, generate solutions, compare each solution to the predicted consequences, apply the solution, and assess the results. The second method involved a new method that added self-instructions such that each participant was required to talk him- or herself through the problem to reach a solution. We decided to use an ATD in which two sets of different, but comparable (in terms of difficulty level), problem situations were developed. In addition to measuring the relative effects of the interventions, we became interested in seeing if the same results would hold true for others. Thus, we could combine the ATD with a multiple-baseline design across participants. Figure 12.16 demonstrates the case where the self-instruction problem-solving format was superior to the standard format for all four participants. This

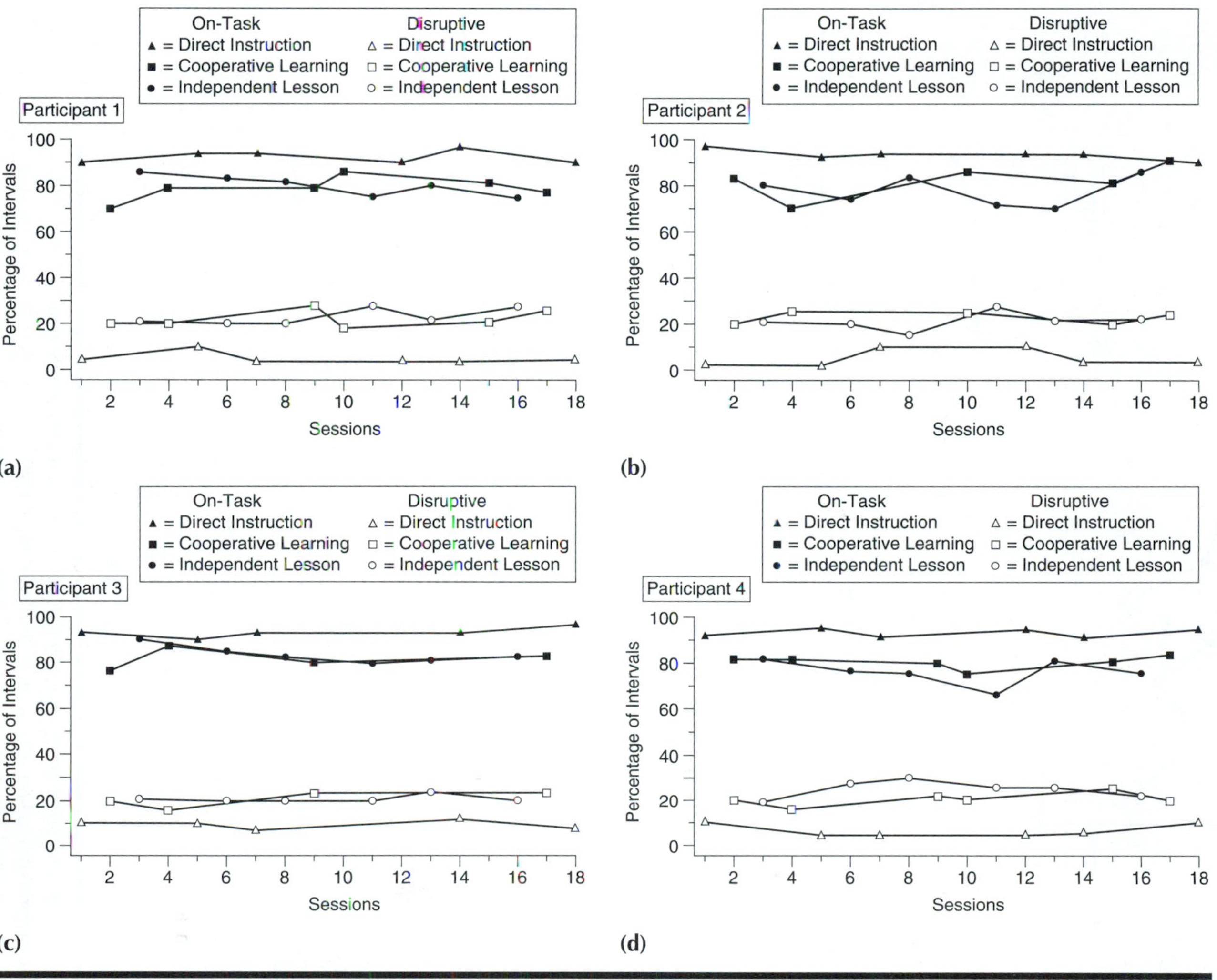

FIGURE 12.14 Percentage of intervals scored as on-task and disruptive behavior for (a) Participant 1, (b) Participant 2, (c) Participant 3, and (d) Participant 4.

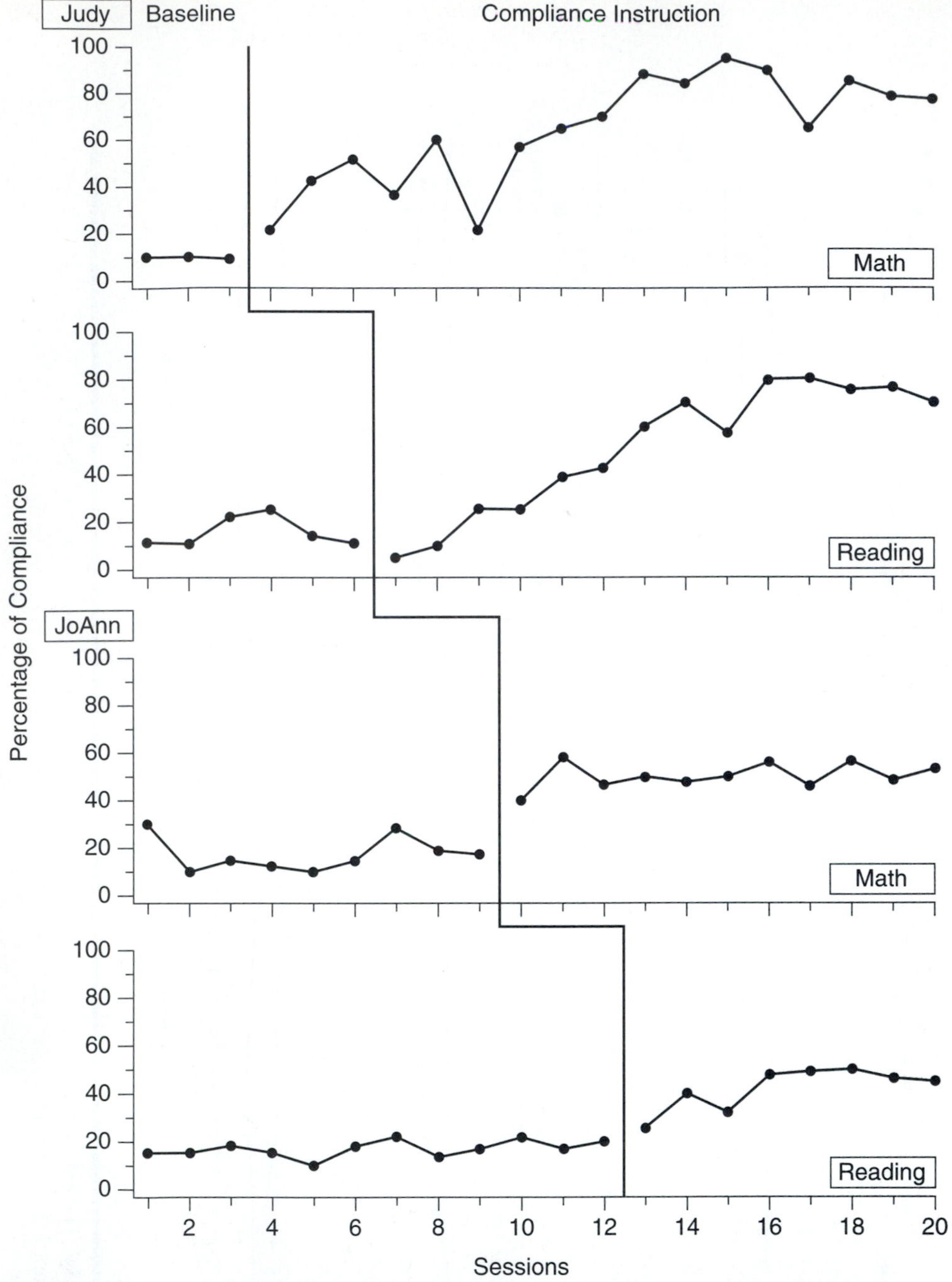

FIGURE 12.15 Percentage of compliance across baseline and compliance instruction conditions for Judy and JoAnn across math and reading classes.

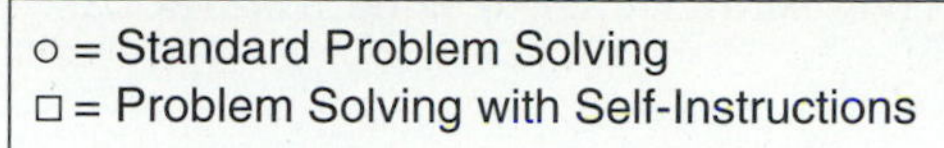

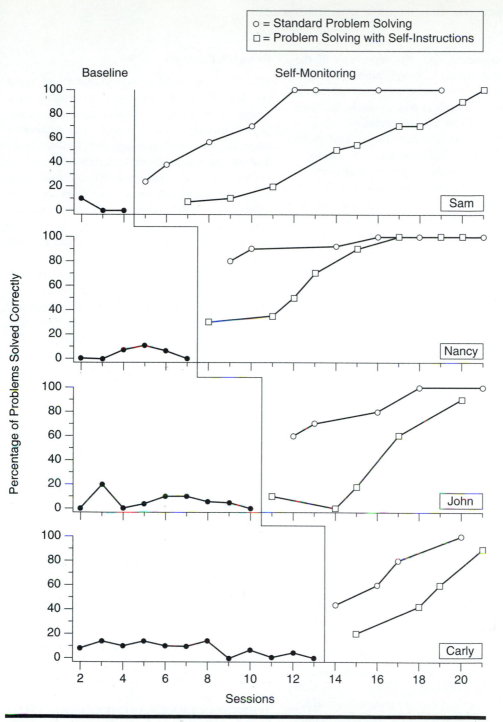

FIGURE 12.16 Percentage of problems solved correctly across baseline, standard problem solving, and problem solving with self-instruction conditions for Sam, Nancy, John, and Carly.

finding is important since the superiority of the self-instruction format was replicated across four individuals. This replication increases our confidence in the superiority of adding self-instructions to a standard problem-solving format.

Combination designs can also be used to increase the internal validity of single-case designs that are initially considered to be weaker from the start such as the changing-criterion design. As previously described, a withdrawal design can be added to a changing-criterion design, and a changing-criterion design can be placed within a multiple-baseline design.

Analysis of Data

Internal Validity. As mentioned, the combination of single-case designs may improve the internal validity of the investigation and/or gather additional information. When conducted appropriately, the combination of two or more designs can increase the internal validity of the investigation. The control issues (e.g., level of change, return to baseline, carryover or sequential confounding effects) discussed in Chapters 10 and 11 and the present one are all in effect here.

External Validity. The threats to external validity are always a problem with single-case designs when considering isolated investigations. However, the combinations of designs can improve the external validity in some ways. For example, the combination of single-case designs within multiple-baseline designs could increase the external validity across behaviors, participants, and settings. The combination of other single-case designs with an ATD could increase the external validity across multiple treatments (more like real life where many extraneous variables are constantly present). The combination of multiple-probe designs with other single-case designs can increase external validity across response measures. Thus, the combination of several single-case designs can have important advantages over isolated single-case designs in terms of external validity.

Research Example

Martella, Leonard, Marchand-Martella, and Agran (1993) used a combination of a changing-criterion design within a multiple-baseline design across settings to investigate the effects of a self-monitoring program on a student's negative verbalizations. The student was a 12-year-old male with mild retardation. He was served in a self-contained classroom. His verbal behaviors (derogatory to self or others) were so disruptive in the classroom that educational staff considered removing the student and placing him in a classroom for youth with behavior disorders.

The independent variable consisted of self-monitoring, self-charting, and reinforcement for reaching daily goals (i.e., criteria). The dependent variable was negative statements. Positive statements were also measured to determine the collateral effects of the intervention. The dependent measures were the rates of negative and positive statements in two different periods. During the baseline condition, pretraining on how to self-monitor took place to ensure the changes were not due to the student learning how to self-monitor, but due to the contingencies set in place for his self-monitoring.

As shown in Figure 12.17, the student's negative statements decreased when the intervention program was implemented. The negative statements were reduced in a stepwise fashion. The teacher in the classroom did not believe the student's negative verbalizations would be reduced over the long run unless they were reduced gradually. The student's negative statements decreased to a final level of zero and maintained at that level over 8 weeks of follow-up. The positive statements increased to a level of approximately .5 statement per minute in Period 2 and one statement per minute in Period 1.

WHEN SHOULD RESEARCHERS USE EACH OF THE ADDITIONAL SINGLE-CASE DESIGNS?

As with the designs in Chapters 10 and 11, the designs discussed in the present chapter serve special

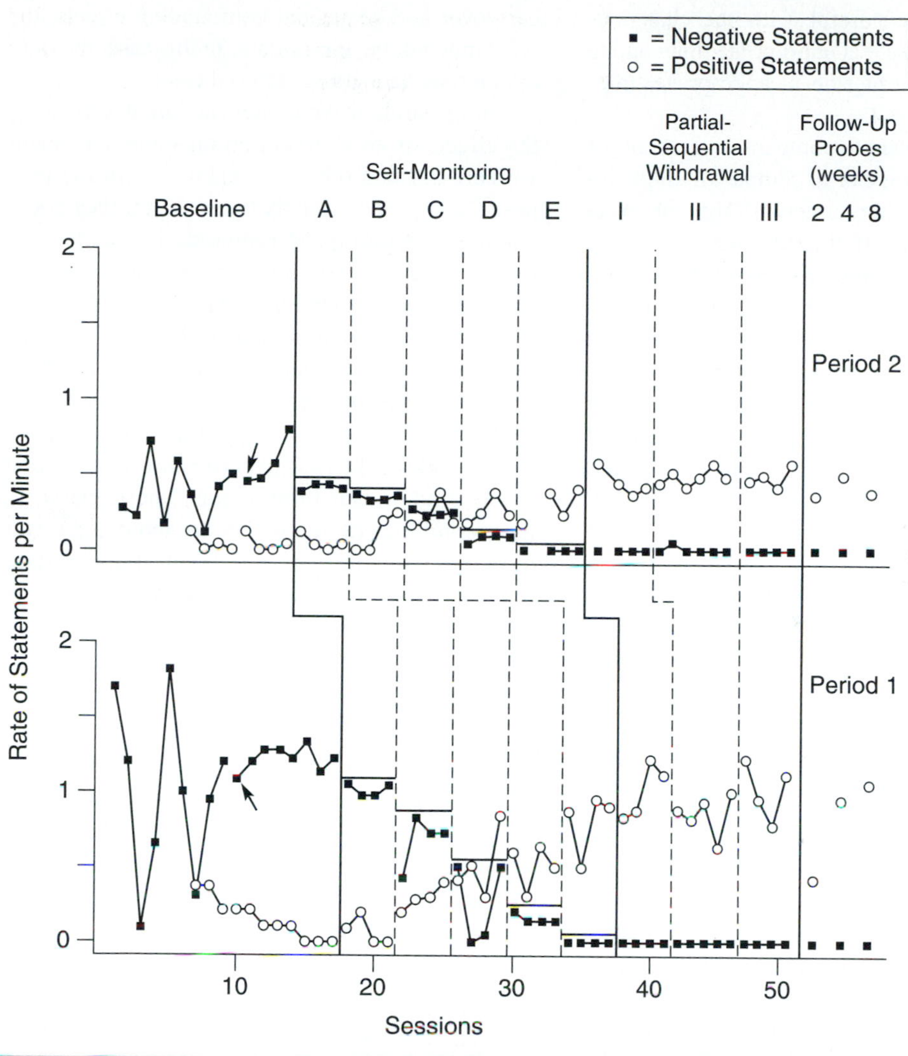

FIGURE 12.17 The rate of negative and positive statements per minute for an adolescent student with mild mental retardation across Periods 2 and 1. The arrows indicate when pretraining began.

purposes in research. Depending on the research question, one design may be more appropriate than the others. For example, if a researcher was attempting to reduce an addictive behavior, one that is resistant to quick changes, the changing-criterion design would be appropriate. Similarly, if a researcher were to teach a skill that is best acquired in stages, the changing-criterion design would be appropriate. However, the experimental control exerted by a changing-criterion design is more difficult to demonstrate. The dependent variable must cluster around the criterion level during each change in the criterion phase. If not, the experimental control is seriously weakened. Thus, researchers must be careful with the changing-criterion design to use it at appropriate times and to set and change the criterion at appropriate times and at appropriate levels.

If researchers want to compare components of an intervention package or to compare multiple interventions, the multitreatment design or ATD would be acceptable. If they decided to use the multitreatment design, the problem of irreversibility must be taken into account. If it would not be possible to reverse the dependent variable or it would be unethical to do so, the multitreatment design should not be used. Additionally, carryover or sequential confounding effects are also problems with the multitreatment design, which may preclude its use. Finally, since the multitreatment design is cumbersome and can take a great deal of time to complete, it would be unwise to use the design when simplicity or timely decision making is desired. In this case, researchers would select the ATD. However, if researchers are worried about carryover and sequential confounding effects, the ATD may not be appropriate. In this case, the only option may be a group factorial design.

If researchers were interested in investigating the effects of an intervention on some dependent variable but had obvious weaknesses in the proposed design such as only two settings, they could combine the multiple-baseline design across settings with another design. If researchers were interested in generalization issues, a multiple-probe design could be combined with other designs. The use of combined single-case designs is not always the result of overcoming the weaknesses of another stand-alone design, but the combinations can provide additional experimental control and produce additional information. The decision to use a combined design will come about as a result of the research question and the most appropriate method to answer that research question, as is true with the other designs.

DISCUSSION QUESTIONS

1. Mr. Simpson, an eighth-grade teacher, has a difficult student in his class. The student frequently interrupts instruction by blurting out answers to questions and making comments. Mr. Simpson does not believe that the student can stop doing this all at once since the student has been allowed to do the same thing in other classes for several years. He believes that the disruptive comments could be reduced gradually but does not know how to do this, or how to determine the effectiveness of a management program he may implement. Describe the type of design Mr. Simpson can use to meet his needs.
2. For each of the designs in Question 1, draw a graph with fictitious data showing that a self-control procedure was effective when implemented by Mr. Simpson.
3. You read a research report in which the researcher utilizes a multiple-baseline design across two behaviors. However, the researcher uses two separate interventions (one per behavior). She then makes a determination of the most effective intervention by comparing the data (i.e., viewing the intervention that increases the dependent variable the fastest). Is this an appropriate use of the multiple-baseline design? If not, what would have been an appropriate design for the researcher to use?
4. You notice in a research report that a researcher uses a changing-criterion design. However, each of the criterion changes were the same. How could the researcher have improved his experimental control using the same design?
5. You are asked by a colleague about how one could judge the most efficient instructional method for teaching spelling. The colleague does not want to use a group design due to a number of factors. Explain how your colleague could judge the most efficient instruc-

tional method, and explain concerns for which she should be mindful.

6. You are aware of the weaknesses of the multitreatment design. Explain an alternative design and indicate why this design is a better alternative.
7. You have learned why one should use three or more baselines in a multiple-baseline design. Indicate how one could use a combined design to increase the experimental control of a multiple-baseline design across two subjects.
8. When one wishes to judge the generalizability of an intervention, a multiple-probe technique can be used. Explain how a multiple-probe design and a multiple-baseline design across behaviors can be combined to assess generalization.
9. Explain the internal validity concerns with the following research designs:
   (a) changing-criterion
   (b) multitreatment
   (c) alternating treatments
10. Take two single-case designs and combine them to form a new design in order to answer the following research question: What is the most effective instructional procedure to use when teaching basic math facts to students in the general education classroom and to those located in a resource room?

PROBLEM SOLVING TO PREVENT WORK INJURIES IN SUPPORTED EMPLOYMENT

RONALD C. MARTELLA
Drake University

MARTIN AGRAN
Utah State University

NANCY E. MARCHAND-MARTELLA
Drake University

A problem-solving strategy was used to teach three groups of 3 individuals in supported employment how to prevent work-related injuries. The problem-solving strategy was taught in two training phases. The first training phase involved the use of cue cards, and the second involved the withdrawal of the cue cards. Interviews and staged generalization assessments in the participants' natural work environments were conducted before, during, and up to 12 weeks after training. In these assessments, situations were presented that were either similar or dissimilar to situations presented in training. Results of both the interviews and staged assessments indicated that the participants' newly acquired problem-solving skills generalized to similar and dissimilar situations.

DESCRIPTORS: problem solving, injury prevention, supported employment, injuries, staged situations, generalization, maintenance, safety skills

---

Acquisition of safety skills by individuals with disabilities is important because it increases independence and promotes employability (Martin, Rusch, & Heal, 1982). For example, Mueller, Wilgosh, and Dennis (1989) found that employers in competitive industries in Alberta, Canada, rated safe work behavior and safety awareness as most important for job survival for all employees (i.e., with or without disabilities).

One safety skill area largely ignored in the vocational research literature is work safety. According to the U.S. Department of Commerce (1990), 10,600 workers were killed and 1,800,000 were disabled due to work-related injuries in 1988. The National Safety Council (1991) reported that 60,000 workers received permanent impairments and approximately 1,700,000 received temporary disabilities as a result of an injury sustained while at work in 1990. In addition, the National Safety Council reported that there were 35 million work days lost as a result of work injuries. Finally, work-related injuries cost $63.8 billion; each worker in the United States must produce $540 of goods and services to offset the cost of work injuries. Clearly, these statistics indicate a critical need for safety skills training.

One approach to teaching safety skills in the workplace is problem solving (Hale & Holt, 1986). Problem solving provides a means for individuals to generate solutions across a variety of problem situations. A potentially successful method of teaching problem solving to persons with disabilities was developed by Foxx, Martella, and Marchand-Martella (1989). With this method, individuals are taught to solve problems by generating initial and alternative solutions considered appropriate by persons who are important in a trainee's environment (e.g., employers, vocational specialists, rehabilitation counselors) (Foxx & Faw, 1990).

The key to any successful training program is to teach skills that generalize and maintain over time. A number of safety skills and problem-solving programs have assessed generalization; however, generalization probes usually included a verbal cue to prompt the behavior (e.g., Edelstein, Couture, Cray, Dickens, & Lusebrink, 1980; Marchand-Martella & Martella, 1990; O'Reilly, Green, & Braunling-McMorrow, 1990; Tisdelle & St. Lawrence, 1988). For example, during generalization assessments, O'Reilly et al. (1990) used the verbal cue, "Let's see how well you can find and fix potential hazards in this room. When you have finished leave the room and tell me that you have finished" (p. 438). Although generalized responding was demonstrated, it is unknown how participants would have responded without the verbal cue.

The present investigation had two objectives. The first was to assess the effects of a problem-solving safety skills program in which participants were taught to prevent work-related injuries. The second objective was to conduct two types of generalization assessments, an interview assessment and a staged assessment. The interview measured the participants' verbal ability to solve problem situations; staged assessments measured the participants' ability to respond appropriately to problem situations without any verbal prompts.

METHOD

Participants and Settings

Nine individuals involved in supported employment services, affiliated with an area vocational training center, participated in this investigation. They were selected by job coaches who indicated

---

This work was conducted by Ronald C. Martella in partial fulfillment of the requirements for a Ph.D. in Behavior Analysis in Special Education at Utah State University. We thank Cache Industries, Logan, Utah, for allowing us to conduct this program at their facility. Special thanks are extended to Sharon Allen and Sheri Alsop for serving as data collectors. Additionally, we thank Richard Young, Charles Salzberg, and Daniel Morgan and the "Journal Breeding" Group at Utah State University for their comments on an early draft of this manuscript. This project was supported by an innovation grant from the National Institute on Disability and Rehabilitation Research.

Reprints can be obtained by writing to Ronald C. Martella, Department of Psychology, Drake University, 318 Olin Hall, Des Moines, Iowa 50311.

that the participants could benefit from such training. Table 1 displays characteristics of the participants.

All baseline, training, and interview assessment sessions were conducted in a small classroom at the vocational training center. This classroom contained a large rectangular table with six chairs and a blackboard. Staged assessments were conducted at the following employment sites: parks (public restrooms), department stores (restrooms and hallways), campgrounds (in and around public restrooms), and the cafeteria (dish room and dining room).

Materials

A list of 24 problem-solving situations were developed through a search of the work-safety literature. These 24 problem situations were sent to six employers and two job coaches who had experience working with individuals with disabilities. The employers and job coaches were asked to provide solutions for each of the 24 problem situations, which they did. These situations were later divided into four criterion components used to score the participants' responses. The four components were: (a) how could an accident happen? (*how*); (b) when would an accident be prevented? (*when*); (c) who would you talk to? (*who*); and (d) what would you do or say? (*what*).

Twelve of the 24 problem situations were used for training; 12 were reserved for interview assessments. In addition, six of these situations were modified in order to use them in the staged assessments conducted in natural settings outside the classroom (see Table 2). Thus, a total of 30 problems formed the training and assessment pool. Half of the interview and staged situations were similar to the training situations and half were dissimilar.

Each training and interview situation was printed on an index card. Each participant received a cue card listing the four problem-solving components and a scoring sheet including nine boxes (labeled from one to nine) on which to record correct solutions.

Data Collection

Data were collected on participant solutions to problem situations, four to five times per week, in sessions lasting from 40 to 60 min. These solutions were compared to the ones provided by the employers and job coaches for scoring.

Measurement of the Dependent Variable. The dependent measure was the percentage of criterion components present in a problem situation.

TABLE 1 Characteristics of Participants

			WAIS-R[1]				
GROUP	NAME	AGE	V	P	FS	RESIDENTIAL PLACEMENT	EMPLOYMENT SETTING
1	Mark	28	79	82	79	Independent	Parks Service
	Ann	36	71	70	69	Independent	Parks Service
	Dan	32	71	71	70	Independent	Department store
2	John	56	79	73	75	Supervised	Forest Service
	Tammy	62	71	76	73	Group Home	Forest Service
	Rob	26	99	80	89	Group Home	Forest Service
3	Larry	41	57	59	54	Family	Cafeteria
	Bob	28	71	67	67	Family	Cafeteria
	Sandy	35	53	62	54	Family	Cafeteria

[1]V = Verbal; P = Performance; FS = Full Scale.

TABLE 2 List of Problems Used for Training, Interviews, and Staged Probes

TRAINING	INTERVIEW	STAGED
	Similar	*Similar*
Box lying in the middle of the aisle	Metal lying on the floor of the aisle	Box in the aisle (path) in the work area
		Piece of twine on the floor (ground)
Water on the floor	Grease on the floor	Ice on the ground
Can of paint near a heat source	Can of spray paint near an open flame	
Exposed electrical wires	Bare electrical wires	
Broken glass on the floor	Nails in the aisle	
Sharp object protruding from a tabletop	Nail sticking out from table	
	Dissimilar	*Dissimilar*
Patch of slippery ice on a sidewalk	A hot pan just taken from the oven	Recently extinguished match in the work area
Paper lying on a heater	Power line on the ground	Unlabeled cleaning fluid in the work area
Frayed appliance cord	Smell of gasoline	Empty can with a sharp lid sticking upward
Smoking appliance	Shelf holding heavy objects is about to fall	
Spilled ice on the floor	Disposal of a hot match	
Water dripping from the ceiling onto electrical equipment	Unlabeled cleaning fluid in the work area	

Criterion components were specific responses required in each solution (i.e., *how, when, who,* and *what*). There were two categories of participant responses—initial and alternative. An initial response was the first solution to a problem provided by 1 participant. An alternative response was provided by the other 2 participants after the initial response. An alternative response needed to include different responses to the *who* and *what* components than were provided in the other response(s) (i.e., during the initial response and during a previous alternative response if one had been emitted by the 2nd participant).

During training sessions, the trainer recorded on a precoded data sheet whether or not each of the components were present and appropriate in each solution. The interviewer followed the same procedures for interview assessments. Two raters also followed the same procedures; however, the raters' recordings were made at a later time from audiotapes recorded during the training sessions and interview assessments. Some responses were scored as correct without the third (*who*) component if participants correctly stated what they would do. (Scoring rules may be obtained by written request to the first author.)

During the staged assessments, a job coach wrote a description of the participant's response to each problem situation. This description was later categorized into the components by the job coach and two raters. Responses to staged assessments were scored in the same manner as previously described in training sessions and interview assessments. However, the participant's response to the problem situation was observed in the natural environment, and the required response was the response that prevented a work injury, which could range from the single response of moving the hazard (*what*), to several responses, which could include speaking with the supervisor (*who*), identifying the hazard (*how*), identifying what should be done about the hazard (*when*), and removing the hazard (*what*).

The percentages of criterion components completed correctly for training and probe sessions were obtained by dividing the number of correct criterion components by the total number of criterion components possible and multiplying by 100.

Manipulation Check. Two components of the independent variable, praise and correction, were assessed by the secondary rater. Appropriate praise was scored when the trainer said "good, you included the ___ component," after the participant independently included a component that was correct in his or her response. The definition of appropriate correction required two components: (a) praise of the attempt or component(s) present and appropriate in a response (e.g., "good, you included the ___ component"), and (b) indication of which component(s) were incorrect or omitted, a request to the participant to provide a solution including the component(s), and provision of the correct response(s) if the participant was unable to do so. Scoring was completed from audiotapes recorded during 25% of the sessions for both training phases.

Experimental Design

To assess the effects of the intervention, a multiple-baseline design across the three groups was used (Barlow & Hersen, 1984). Participants in each group were exposed to a baseline condition and two training phases (i.e., training with cue and training with no cue). In addition, generalization probes were conducted throughout the investigation.

Baseline. Training was conducted in groups of 3 participants. The trainer presented 9 of the 12 problem situations per session. These nine situations were selected on a rotating basis (e.g., Session I included Situations 1 through 9, Session 2 included Situations 4 through 12, Session 3 included Situations 7 through 12 and 1 through 3, and Session 4 included Situations 10 through 12 and 1 through 6). Situations were rotated to prevent exposure to the same 12 problems every session and to decrease the chances of stimulus satiation. Participants were told to listen to every problem situation and think of an alternative solution. After 1 participant provided an initial solution, the trainer asked the other participants to generate alternative solutions. Thus, each participant generated three initial solutions and six alternative solutions. The trainer did not solve any of the problem situations and did not provide feedback. After the session, participants received monetary compensation for attendance based on their hourly pay rate.

Training with Cue. All conditions were the same as in baseline, with the following additions. Participants were given the cue card and scoring sheet. They were instructed to refer to the cue card when formulating a response to a problem situation.

During training, if a correct response was given, the trainer stated, "good answer, you included all of the components." A 50% coupon for food or drink at a local restaurant was given to participants when they met or surpassed their own individualized performance criterion. This individualized criterion was based on the number of correct solutions provided by each participant. Initially, the criterion was one correct solution, after which it increased by 33% when a participant met the criterion (e.g., if a participant correctly responded to six situations, the criterion was set at eight in the next session). To help the participants remember their individualized criterion, the number was circled on their scorecards.

If a response was incorrect, the trainer indicated to the participant which component was incorrect or omitted and prompted the correct use of the component. The trainer provided the correct response(s) only when a participant did not. Training terminated after all participants achieved 100% of the criterion components correctly for four consecutive sessions.

Training with No Cue. All training conditions remained the same except the cue cards were removed. Again, prompting a correct response was continued if a participant's response was incorrect. Training terminated after all participants achieved 100% of the criterion components correctly for four consecutive sessions.

Generalization and Maintenance Probes. Generalization probes were conducted before baseline (PP), after baseline (P-1), after training with cue (P-2), after training with no cue (P-3), and 2, 6, and 12 weeks (maintenance) after training ended. These probes included interview and staged assessments of situations that were either similar or dissimilar to those used in training. Similar situations required the same response as the parallel training situation. Dissimilar situations required a different response than the one in the training situation.

During the interview assessments, 12 situations (six similar and six dissimilar) were presented verbally to each participant by an interviewer. Following the presentation of each problem situation, an instructional cue ("What should you do or say?") was delivered by the interviewer. During the staged assessments, six situations (three similar and three dissimilar) were staged in each participant's work environment. The three similar situations were subsets of the training and interview situations, and the three dissimilar situations were situations distinct from those used in the interview assessments. During these assessments, a job coach told each participant to complete a task that did not involve the staged situation (e.g., "clean the sink," when there was glass on the floor, as opposed to "sweep the floor"). The participant's response to the staged situation (broken glass) then was assessed. No cue or feedback was provided during or after these situations.

Social Validation. The 9 participants and their job coaches rated their satisfaction with the training program on five items after the training program ended. Ratings based on a 5-point Likert-type scale ranged from 1 (strongly agree) to 5 (strongly disagree). The rating forms were distributed by a vocational specialist.

Interobserver Agreement. One rater served as a secondary rater and independently scored the training sessions from audiotapes. An additional rater, naive to the design and intent of the study, scored the training sessions from audiotapes. The naive rater was provided a scoring matrix used by the trainer, observers, and secondary rater. This scoring matrix included all of the problem situations and a sample of correct responses to the criterion components.

Generalization probes were scored by the interviewer (interview assessments) or the job coach (staged assessments), as well as the secondary and naive raters. During interviews, participants' responses were audiotaped and scored by the secondary and naive raters. During the staged assessments, written records were scored by the secondary and naive raters.

Interobserver agreement was calculated during approximately 25% of the baseline and training sessions and 100% of the interview and staged generalization assessments. Interobserver agreement was calculated by dividing the number of agreements of criterion components correct by the number of agreements plus disagreements of criterion components correct and multiplying by 100 (Hall, 1983). The range of mean interobserver agreement scores for correct and incorrect responses across participants, groups, and sessions during baseline, training with cue, and training with no cue exceeded 90%. The mean interobserver agreement scores across all interview assessments across all staged assessments likewise exceeded 90%.

RESULTS

Baseline and Training

Figure 1 shows group averages for initial and alternative responses. During baseline, Groups 1, 2, and 3 averaged 15% to 28% and 4% to 13% for initial and alternative responses, respectively. When the training with cues was implemented,

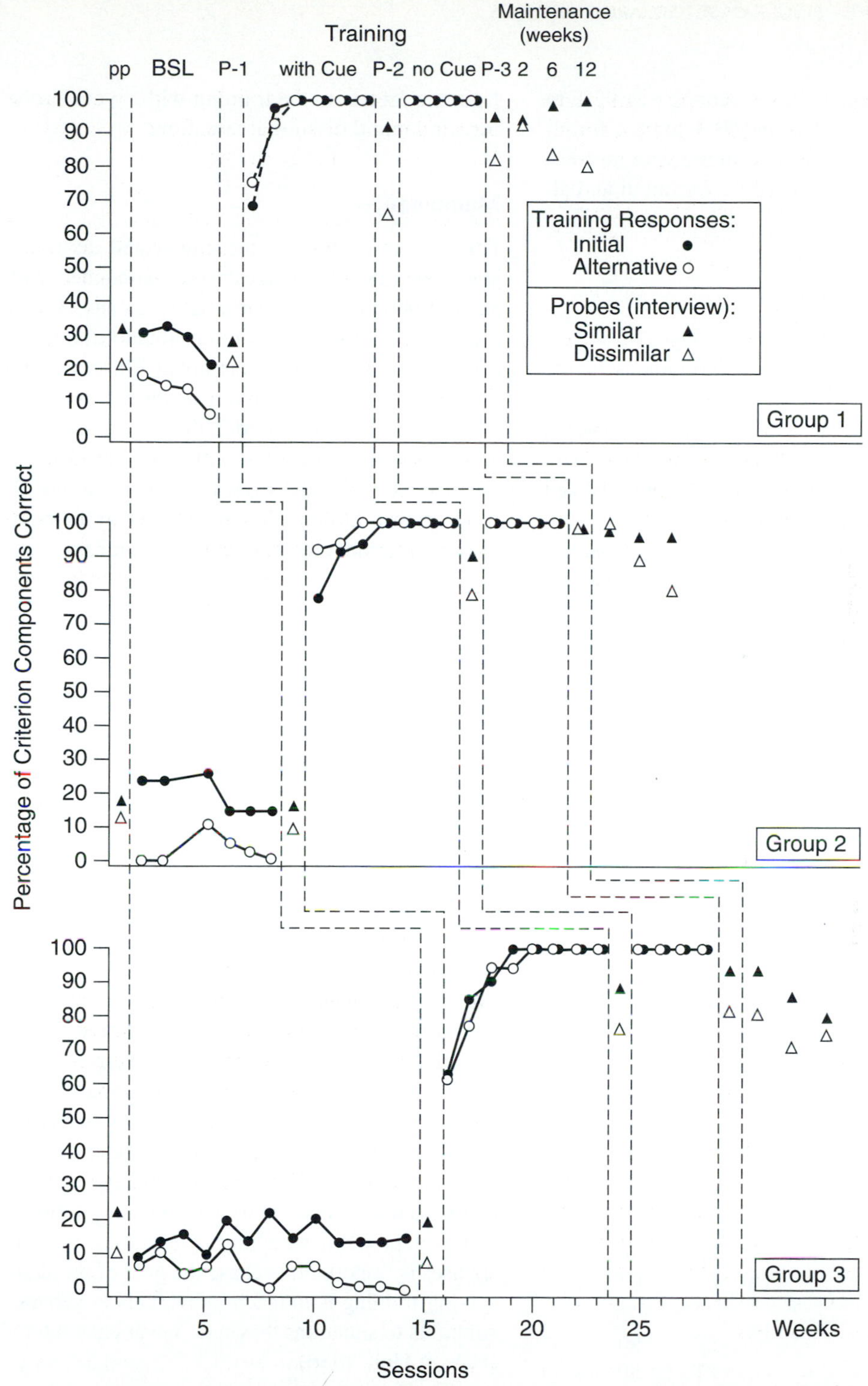

FIGURE 1 Percentage of criterion components correct across baseline, training, and generalization and maintenance probe sessions for groups 1, 2, and 3. PP represents the pretest probe, and P-1, P-2, and P-3 represent probes conducted after each phase.

the mean range for the three groups was 92% to 95% for initial responses and 91% to 98% for alternative responses. During training with no cues, all three groups averaged 100% for initial and alternative responses.

Generalization Probes

As shown in Figure 1, the percentages of correct criterion components for the participants in the three groups increased across the interview assessments for similar and dissimilar situations from the pretest probe (PP) to the training with no cue probe (P-3). All group responses generalized to similar and dissimilar situations.

As shown in Table 3, all three groups had improved percentages in the staged assessments from the pretest to the training with no cue probe for similar and dissimilar situations.

TABLE 3 Group Performance During Staged Assessments for Similar and Dissimilar Situations

	Groups		
	1	**2**	**3**
Pretest			
Similar	0	0	0
Dissimilar	20	8	0
Baseline Probe (P-1)			
Similar	0	0	0
Dissimilar	20	0	0
Training with cue probe (P-2)			
Similar	29	64	88
Dissimilar	33	0	40
Training no-cue probe (P-3)			
Similar	91	78	89
Dissimilar	82	86	33
Maintenance (2 weeks)			
Similar	78	56	67
Dissimilar	67	67	50
Maintenance (6 weeks)			
Similar	89	90	67
Dissimilar	71	50	50
Maintenance (12 weeks)			
Similar	50	67	67
Dissimilar	75	67	50

Maintenance

For the interview covering similar and dissimilar situations, the percentages were maintained with small fluctuations for Groups 1, 2, and 3 (see Figure 1). For the staged similar situations, fluctuations for Groups 1 and 2 were noted. The largest decrease for Group 1 occurred from the 6-week to the 12-week probe. For Group 2, the largest decreases were noted from the training with no cue probe to the 2-week probe and from the 6-week to the 12-week probe. Group 3's percentages were maintained throughout the maintenance condition.

Manipulation Check

The mean percentage for the appropriate delivery of praise across groups was 99% (range, 87% to 100%). The mean percentage for the appropriate delivery of corrections across groups was 92% (range, 88% to 100%).

DISCUSSION

The results indicated that the training program increased the problem-solving skills of all groups when they used cue cards. Furthermore, these skills were maintained when the cue cards were eliminated. In addition to the acquisition of skills, several findings from the interview assessments are worth noting. First, participants' performances improved not only for situations similar to those used in training but also to situations dissimilar to those used in training. Therefore, the findings suggest that participants learned to generate new solutions to novel problem situations. Generating new responses is important, because the goal of problem-solving training is to teach individuals to generate solutions to situations they have never encountered (Hale & Holt, 1986).

The most important aspect of any program is determining whether the participants can respond appropriately in natural environments (Spooner, Stem, & Test, 1989). According to Foxx and Faw

(1990), a more rigorous assessment of generalization than the use of verbal cues involves assessing if participants taught to solve problems verbally could do so in the absence of verbal cues. In the present investigation, additional generalization assessments (i.e., staged) were conducted to measure the extent to which training in verbal problem solving affected responses to potential-injury causing situations in work environments. In this investigation, skill performance generalized to staged situations in various work environments. Generally, the participants' responses to situations similar to those used in training improved. More important, all participants showed improvement in staged situations dissimilar to the training situations. Therefore, the results suggest that a problem-solving strategy taught to persons in supported employment in a classroom setting can produce generalized responding in natural work environments.

An important finding was that the performance of all groups was maintained above pretest and baseline probe levels in both interview and staged assessments for up to 12 weeks following training. However, at times, performance levels in maintenance probes decreased somewhat from the peak levels reached in training. One reason for this decrease over time may be simply that there were no consequences to maintain the behavior. Unless an employer provides contingencies to prevent work injuries, optimal maintenance may not be achieved. Considering the lack of supporting contingencies in the present investigation, the maintenance performance was surprisingly robust.

The social validity reported in this investigation was an additional desirable finding. The solutions to the problem situations were developed by employers and job coaches. In addition, feedback from the job coaches and participants showed that they were satisfied with the program and believed it to be worthwhile.

Although there were a number of important findings in this investigation, some caveats and areas for future research are noteworthy. First, the number of staged situations was limited and, thus, conclusions based on their results must be made with caution. Second, although performance in the staged assessments was robust, a staff member was involved in these assessments. Thus, participant performance may not have been as desirable if no overlap in personnel between training and generalization probe settings occurred. Third, repeated exposure to staged situations led to improved performance in probes. Therefore, the effects of training on performance in generalization probes may be confounded with repeated exposures. Future research should attempt to control for the possibility of learning by incorporating more probes throughout the baseline condition and measuring the changes that occur. Finally, during the staged assessments, interobserver agreement on the actual occurrence of responses was not obtained. Instead, interobserver agreement assessments were conducted on the responses as described by the job coach. Future research should attempt to conduct assessments for purposes of interobserver agreement directly on responses rather than on a description of those responses.

In summary, the present investigation demonstrated that individuals in supported employment can be taught a problem-solving strategy to prevent work-related injuries. More important, the participants applied this strategy to similar and dissimilar situations in interview assessments and staged (workplace) assessments. In addition, the participants' performance was maintained and continued to improve up to 12 weeks after training ended. This investigation is especially timely, given the paucity of such training programs in the research literature and the importance of injury-prevention skills to both employees and employers in the work environment.

REFERENCES

Barlow, D. H., & Hersen, M. (1984). *Single case experimental designs: Strategies for studying behavior change* (2nd ed.). New York: Pergamon Press.

Edelstein, B. A., Couture, E., Cray, M., Dickens, P., & Lusebrink, N. (1980). Group training of problem-solving with psychiatric patients. In D. Upper &

S. M. Ross (Eds.), *Behavioral group therapy, 1980: An annual review* (pp. 85–102). Champaign, IL: Research Press.

Foxx, R. M., & Faw, G. D. (1990). Problem-solving skills training for psychiatric inpatients: An analysis of generalization. *Behavioral Residential Treatment, 5,* 159–176.

Foxx, R. M., Martella, R. C., & Marchand-Martella, N. E. (1989). The acquisition, maintenance, and generalization of problem-solving skills by closed head-injured adults. *Behavior Therapy, 20,* 61–76.

Hale, A., & Holt, A. S. (1986). Behavioural science. In J. Ridley (Ed.), *Safety at work* (2nd ed., pp. 229–318). London: Butterworths.

Hall, R. V. (1983). *Behavior modification: The measurement of behavior* (rev. ed.). Austin, TX: Pro-Ed.

Marchand-Martella, N. E., & Martella, R. C. (1990). The acquisition, maintenance, and generalization of first aid skills by youths with handicaps. *Behavioral Residential Treatment, 5,* 121–237.

Martin, J. E., Rusch, F. R., & Heal, L. W. (1982). Teaching community survival skills to mentally retarded adults: A review and analysis. *Journal of Special Education, 16,* 243–267.

Mueller, H. H., Wilgosh, L., & Dennis, S. (1989). Employment survival skills for entry-level occupations, *Canadian Journal of Rehabilitation, 2,* 203–221.

National Safety Council. (1991). *Accident facts.* Chicago: Author.

O'Reilly, M. F., Green, G., & Braunling-McMorrow, D. (1990). Self-administered prompts to teach home accident prevention skills to adults with brain injuries. *Journal of Applied Behavior Analysis, 23,* 431–446.

Spooner, F., Stem, B., & Test, D. W. (1989). Teaching first aid skills to adolescents who are mentally retarded. *Education and Training in Mental Retardation, 24,* 341–351.

Tisdelle, D. A., & St. Lawrence, J. S. (1988). Interpersonal problem-solving competency: Review and critique of the literature. *Clinical Psychology Review, 6,* 337–356.

U.S. Department of Commerce. (1990). *Statistical abstract of the United States: The national data book* (110th ed.). Washington, DC: Author.

Received May 10, 1991
Initial editorial decision July 1 7, 1991
Revisions received September 16, 1991; January 13, 1992;
February 17, 1992
Final acceptance May 19, 1992
Action Editor, Susan Fowler

FACTUAL QUESTIONS

1. What were the objectives of the investigation?
2. Who were the participants in the investigation? What were the settings?
3. What were the materials used before, during, and after training?
4. What was the dependent variable and how was it measured?
5. What was the independent variable? What were the conditions and the type of design used?
6. What were the four types of generalization probes used?
7. How was social validity measured?
8. How many observers (raters) were involved in the investigation? What was the level of interobserver agreement?
9. What were the results for baseline and training?
10. What were the results for the generalization and maintenance assessments?

DISCUSSION QUESTIONS

1. To what type of individual(s) would you be willing to generalize the results?
2. How were the groups formed? Is there a problem with this type of grouping?
3. What was the purpose of having four categories of generalization assessments? How could one come closer to approximating the "real-life" circumstances these individuals may encounter?

4. How could this design also be considered a combination of a multiple-baseline design across three subjects and a multiple-probe design?
5. What was the purpose of assessing social validity?
6. Why was a naive rater used? What was the purpose of audiotaping the sessions?
7. Why were the authors concerned with how the data were scored in the generalization sessions?
8. How could there be a possible testing threat for the generalization probes?
9. Why do you think the number of staged situations was so limited? Is there a way around this problem?
10. Is there a problem with having an overlap of staff in the training and generalization settings? If so, why was there such an overlap?

THREATS TO INTERNAL VALIDITY

Circle the number corresponding to the likelihood of each threat to internal validity being present in the investigation and provide a justification.

1 = definitely not a threat 2 = not a likely threat 3 = somewhat likely threat
4 = likely threat 5 = definite threat NA = Not applicable for this design

Results in Differences within or between Individuals

1. **Maturation** **1 2 3 4 5 NA**

Justification ____

____

2. **Selection** **1 2 3 4 5 NA**

Justification ____

____

3. **Selection by Maturation Interaction** **1 2 3 4 5 NA**

Justification ____

____

4. **Statistical Regression** **1 2 3 4 5 NA**

Justification ____

____

5. **Mortality** **1 2 3 4 5 NA**

Justification ____

____

6. **Instrumentation** **1 2 3 4 5 NA**

Justification ____

____

7. Testing 1 2 3 4 5 NA

Justification ______________________________

____

8. History 1 2 3 4 5 NA

Justification ______________________________

____

9. Resentful Demoralization of the Control Group 1 2 3 4 5 NA

Justification ______________________________

____

Results in Similarities within or between Individuals

10. Diffusion of Treatment 1 2 3 4 5 NA

Justification ______________________________

____

11. Compensatory Rivalry by the Control Group 1 2 3 4 5 NA

Justification ______________________________

____

12. Compensatory Equalization of Treatments 1 2 3 4 5 NA

Justification ______________________________

____

Abstract: Write a one-page abstract summarizing the overall conclusions of the authors and whether you feel the authors' conclusions are valid based on the internal validity of the investigation.

THREATS TO EXTERNAL VALIDITY

Circle the number corresponding to the likelihood of each threat to external validity being present in the investigation according to the following scale:

1 = definitely not a threat	2 = not a likely threat	3 = somewhat likely threat
4 = likely threat	5 = definite threat	NA = Not applicable for this design

Also, provide a justification for each rating.

Population

1. **Generalization across Subjects** 1 2 3 4 5 NA

Justification ____________________

____

2. **Interaction of Personological Variables and Treatment** 1 2 3 4 5 NA

Justification ____________________

____

Ecological

3. **Verification of the Independent Variable** 1 2 3 4 5 NA

Justification ____________________

____

4. **Multiple Treatment Interference** 1 2 3 4 5 NA

Justification ____________________

____

5. **Hawthorne Effect** 1 2 3 4 5 NA

Justification ____________________

____

6. **Novelty and Disruption Effects** 1 2 3 4 5 NA

Justification ____________________

____

7. Experimenter Effects **1 2 3 4 5 NA**

Justification ______________________________

____

8. Pretest Sensitization **1 2 3 4 5 NA**

Justification ______________________________

____

9. Posttest Sensitization **1 2 3 4 5 NA**

Justification ______________________________

____

10. Interaction of Time of Measurement and Treatment Effects **1 2 3 4 5 NA**

Justification ______________________________

____

11. Measurement of the Dependent Variable **1 2 3 4 5 NA**

Justification ______________________________

____

12. Interaction of History and Treatment Effects **1 2 3 4 5 NA**

Justification ______________________________

____

Abstract: Write a one-page abstract summarizing the overall conclusions of the authors and whether you feel the authors' conclusions are valid based on the external validity of the investigation.

PART SIX

ADDITIONAL RESEARCH METHODS

CHAPTER 13 SURVEY, HISTORICAL, AND PROGRAM EVALUATION RESEARCH METHODS

CHAPTER 14 CONDUCTING RESEARCH SYNTHESES

CHAPTER 13

SURVEY, HISTORICAL, AND PROGRAM EVALUATION RESEARCH METHODS

This chapter is somewhat different from the previous ones. It contains three separate research methodologies—survey, historical, and program evaluation. The reason we placed these methods together is that much of the information in each section has been covered elsewhere. For example, aspects of survey research methods were covered in Chapters 3, 4, 8, and 9; aspects of historical research methods were covered in Chapters 8 and 9; and aspects of program evaluations were covered in Chapters 4 through 12. However, it is important to describe these methods separately from the methods discussed thus far since these methods are distinct from those previously described and are used by researchers in education and psychology.

SECTION 1: SURVEY RESEARCH

OBJECTIVES

After studying this section you should be able to:

1. Describe the purposes of survey research.
2. Describe the types of surveys.
3. Describe the factors in choosing a survey method.
4. Describe the importance of sampling frames when conducting survey research.
5. Describe the importance of response rate to survey research.
6. Describe the process used to design and pilot-test surveys.
7. Describe internal and external validity concerns in survey research.
8. Describe when one would use survey research.
9. Critique a survey research article.

OVERVIEW

Survey research is the most widely used research method within and outside of the social sciences. Surveys are used to identify how people feel, think, act, and vote. Rarely a day goes by without some survey of opinions, election predictions, or consumer marketing receiving prominent play in the popular press. Researchers use a variety of surveys that differ in purpose, length, scope, structure, and content. This survey research can be useful for collecting information from relatively large numbers of dispersed groups of people rather than a small number as in the case of other research methods.

The use of questions to measure the phenomenon of interest is another essential part of survey research. High-quality survey research requires researchers to construct effective questions and to pose them to respondents in a systematic way. This systematic process is especially important in those cases in which researchers are attempting to measure phenomena that cannot be directly observed such as attitudes, feelings, and cognitions. Although most surveys have respondents answer self-administered questions, interviewers sometimes ask respondents questions and record their responses. It is critical that the interviewer not influence the answers given by respondents, and that questions are posed in a standardized fashion across respondents.

The development and refinement of survey research methods have occurred in three prominent areas. First, the work of the Census Bureau has played a key role in the sampling and questioning techniques used in survey research. Although the Census Bureau is best known for its decennial inventory of the population, the Census Bureau devotes a tremendous effort to ongoing series of sample surveys aimed at providing up-to-date demographic and economic data. Second, commercial polling and marketing firms such as those organized by Gallup and Harris have contributed both funds and expertise to the development and refinement of survey research methods. This contribution is particularly reflected in the areas of political polling and consumer marketing. Finally, researchers have played a key role in the development and refinement of survey research methods. Many universities support centers that are devoted specifically to the development, refinement, and use of survey research.

The remainder of this section on survey research begins with a discussion of the varying goals and objectives of survey research. This discussion is followed by a description of the types of surveys used by researchers. Next, a description of the process used to develop surveys is discussed. This section ends with a description of data analysis concerns of survey research and instances when surveys should be used. Research examples highlighting the different designs are presented throughout the chapter, and an illustrative investigation is included at the end of the chapter for critique.

WHAT ARE THE PURPOSES OF SURVEY RESEARCH?

There are as many reasons for conducting surveys as there are surveys. Researchers conduct surveys to explore relationships between and among variables. Business people conduct surveys to determine the demand for their products. Politicians conduct surveys to identify the views of their constituents on key issues that are under consideration. A government agency may conduct surveys to aid in the design of a new set of services. Although the reasons for conducting surveys are numerous, the purpose for conducting surveys can be categorized into three general areas: description, explanation, and exploration. Of course, the purpose of a survey may encompass two or more of these areas.

Description

Surveys are commonly conducted for the purpose of describing some population. The primary goal is to identify the distribution of characteristics, traits, or attributes of an identified group of people. In other words, researchers are primarily interested in describing the distribution of characteristics rather than why the observed distribution exists. Although researchers often describe subsamples and make comparisons among them in addition to describing the total sample, the primary purpose of descriptive surveys is to describe the distribution of characteristics, traits, or attributes of interest. The decennial report of the Census Bureau is an example of a survey in which the primary purpose is to describe the distribution of demographic characteristics of America.

Explanation

Another purpose of survey research is to explain a phenomenon of interest. The primary goal is to explain how different variables are related. Survey research that is explanatory in nature typically requires the use of multivariate analysis techniques that enable researchers to examine the relationship between two or more variables. For example, a child's academic performance in elementary school might be explained by variables such as level of parent education, gender, and socioeconomic status. Researchers would examine the relationship between academic performance and these potential explanatory variables in an attempt to "explain" the academic achievement of children.

Exploration

Researchers also use survey research in an exploratory fashion when they are investigating phenomena not previously studied. For example, researchers wanting to explore the sources of racism on a university campus may want to survey a group of students with different backgrounds using an in-depth interview or questionnaire to ensure that critical factors were not missed. Researchers could then construct a full-scale probability sample survey, which includes the factors most strongly associated with racism to identify the sources of racism on the university campus.

WHAT ARE THE DIFFERENT TYPES OF SURVEYS?

One of the most difficult decisions researchers conducting survey research make is determining the type of survey or the way in which the data will be collected. The primary types of surveys include (a) face-to-face interviewing; (b) telephone interviewing; (c) interviewer- and group-administered surveys; (d) self-administered surveys; and (e) mail surveys. Although most surveys utilize only one of these data collection methods, a combination of methods may be used. For example, researchers exploring some personal issues such as drug use as a part of a larger effort to determine the health and well being of individuals might have respondents answer a self-administered survey on their past and present use of drugs. Table 13.1 summarizes the advantages and disadvantages associated with each type of survey.

WHAT ARE THE FACTORS IN CHOOSING A SURVEY METHOD?

There are a number of primary factors that researchers should consider when choosing a survey method. These factors include (a) sampling procedures, (b) sampling population, (c) question format, (d) content of questions, (e) response rate, and (f) time and money.

Sampling Procedures

One factor that researchers should consider centers on their sampling procedures. The sampling procedures used by researchers can make it easy or difficult to use a particular type of survey method. For example, the type and accuracy of the information gathered are important if the sampling procedures used by researchers depend on a list. If the list lacks mailing addresses, using a self-administered mail survey is not an option. Another issue focuses on whether there is a designated respondent. If the sampling procedures are based on a list of individuals, any survey method is possible. In contrast, if respondents are not specifically designated and the survey is sent to a household or organization, researchers have little control over who actually completes the survey. In such cases, researchers may want to consider using a telephone survey or personal interview to ensure that respondents possess the specific characteristics of interest.

Sampling Population

A second factor that researchers should consider when selecting a survey method focuses on the sampling population. The reading and writing skills of the sampling population as well as its motivation to participate are key considerations when selecting a survey method. Self-administered surveys require more from respondents than do those that rely on interviewers. Self-administered surveys also require respondents to be more interested in the subject matter under study than do those that rely on interviewers. Thus, researchers should use self-administered surveys only when the sample

TABLE 13.1 Advantages and Disadvantages Associated with Each Type of Survey

METHOD	ADVANTAGES	DISADVANTAGES
Face-to-face interviewing	• Enhanced cooperation for completing current interview • Enhanced cooperation for follow-up interview • Address respondent questions • Probe for fuller understanding of responses from respondents • Facilitate the use of more complex instructions or question sequences • Sustain longer interviews • Address personal or sensitive issues • Quality control on responses	• More costly • Requires trained interviewers • Limited supervision of interviewers • Limited to easily accessible sample • Extended data collection period
Telephone interviewing	• Cost-efficient • Supervision of interviewers • Easy to access sample • Short data collection period • Quality control on responses	• Limited to those with telephones • Lower response rate • Limited question formats
Self-administered survey	• Cost-efficient • Use of multiple questions for an area • Address personal or sensitive issues • Efficient data collection, management, and analysis	• Extensive time needed to develop survey • Limited to closed questions • Limited to relatively well-educated and motivated sample • Lack of quality control on responses • Limited to easily accessible sample
Mail survey	• Cost-efficient • Use of multiple questions for an area • Address personal or sensitive issues • Efficient data collection, management, and analysis • Use of widely dispersed sample • More time to complete	• Extensive time needed to develop survey • Limited to closed questions • Limited to relatively well-educated and motivated sample • Lack of quality control on responses

population is relatively well-educated and interested in the subject matter under study.

Question Format

A third factor that researchers should consider when selecting a survey method centers on the question format. Self-administered surveys rely on close-ended questions in which the respondent checks a box or circles a response from a set of options. Self-administered surveys might include some open-ended questions as well. However, researchers usually treat such information as anecdotal material because such questions tend to produce data that are incomplete and not comparable across respondents. Additionally, in contrast to open-ended questions, close-ended question formats enable researchers to collect information on a large number of items or to break down complex questions into a set of simpler questions.

Content of Questions

A fourth factor that researchers should consider focuses on the content of the questions. Although generally the answers of respondents have been found to be unaffected by the type of survey (Cannell, Groves, Magilary, Mathiowetz, & Miller, 1987; Mangione, Hingson, & Barret, 1982), there are some sensitive or embarrassing issues that may be affected by the survey method used by researchers. In the case of such issues (e.g., drug use, sexual preferences), self-administered forms of data collection are preferable because interviewer-based methods tend to produce socially desirable responses. Additionally, researchers should consider the difficulty of the reporting task. In those cases in which researchers are interested in events or behaviors that extend over a period of time (e.g., physical symptoms of stress), self-administered surveys allow the respondent more time for thought and consultation with family, friends, or records.

Response Rate

The fifth factor that researchers should consider centers on the importance of the response rate. The problem of nonresponse is central to survey research because researchers have no substantive way to assess fully the extent to which the characteristics of nonrespondents differ from those of respondents. Survey methods that rely on group administration produce the highest response rates. Additionally, telephone surveys and interviewer administered surveys tend to produce higher response rates than do self-administered surveys.

Time and Money

The final factor that researchers should consider when selecting a survey method focuses on costs in terms of time and money. Some of the issues that should be considered by researchers include the amount of time required to develop the survey, the length of the survey, the geographic diffusion of the sample, the education level and interest of the sample, and the availability of trained staff to administer the survey. Survey methods that rely on face-to-face interviews with respondents are more costly than those that do not such as telephone or self-administered surveys.

HOW IS SURVEY RESEARCH DESIGNED?

Although survey research involves all of the different aspects (e.g., articulating a clear and concise research question) associated with any research method, sampling and question construction are the key elements underlying the design of surveys. Before discussing issues associated with sampling and question construction, there are two important points that researchers should consider. First, researchers should thoroughly explore the potential for gathering the information they want from the literature or from other sources. Although surveys appear to be a simple solution to try and learn about some phenomena of interest, researchers should only undertake surveys after they are certain that the information cannot be obtained in other ways. As mentioned earlier, a plethora of survey research is conducted in a variety of areas. It would not be surprising to find several studies that have addressed the phenomenon of interest.

Second, researchers should explore whether there are previously developed reliable and valid measures that they can use to address the phenomenon they are studying. There are reference materials such as *The Mental Measurements Yearbook* (Mitchell, 1985) and *Tests in Print* (Mitchell, 1983) that provide information on all of the measures including surveys used in the social sciences.

Sampling

The same sampling techniques described in Chapter 4 are used by researchers conducting survey research; thus, readers are encouraged to review Chapter 4 on sampling techniques. In this section, we present a brief review of some key sampling principles with which to judge the sample or respondents surveyed by researchers.

Although survey research uses the same research methods as all research (i.e., research conceptualization, ethical treatment of participants, sampling, measurement, data collection and analysis, and interpretation), the use of high-quality sampling techniques is critical to survey research. As with any research study, the key to good survey research is using sampling procedures that give all population members the same (or known) chance of being sampled. In other words, surveys are rarely done for the purpose of describing the particular sample under study. Rather, surveys are conducted for the purpose of understanding the larger population from which the sample was initially selected. Additionally, analyses of survey research are typically aimed at the development of generalized propositions of the phenomena under study. Thus, researchers must define their *sampling frame.*

Sampling Frames. The sampling frame is the set of people (it is always people in the case of survey research) that has the chance to be selected, given the sampling procedure(s) used by researchers. The sampling frame is the population or defined list from which the sample will be drawn. It is important that the sampling frame corresponds to the population that researchers want to describe. The sampling frame and sample selection procedures, including the size and the specific procedures used for selecting individuals to survey, will directly influence the precision of the sample estimates. In other words, researchers must determine how closely the characteristics of the sample approximate those of the population. There are three general classes of sampling frames—exhaustive, convenience, and cluster.

Exhaustive Sampling Frames. The first class of sampling frames involves those cases in which the sampling is done from a more or less complete list of individuals of the population to be studied. This typically occurs when the population is small or clearly defined, and the list is used by researchers to select a sample. For example, the members of the senior class at a regional university might be used as the sampling frame for selecting a sample to assess student satisfaction with a required capstone experience. Sampling frames such as this are referred to as "exhaustive sampling frames" because they contain an exhaustive inventory of the members of the population.

Convenience Sampling Frames. The second class of sampling frames entails those cases in which the sampling is done from a set of individuals who do something or go somewhere that enables researchers to administer a survey to them. This class of sampling frames differs from the preceeding class in that there is not an advanced list from which researchers can sample. Rather, the creation of the list or inventory of the members of the population and sampling occurs simultaneously. For example, researchers might survey every tenth individual coming through the turnstiles at a home game for a professional football team regarding the need for a new stadium.

Cluster Sampling Frames. The final class of sampling frames involves those cases in which the sampling is done in two or more stages (i.e., cluster sampling). In the first stage(s), researchers sample something other than the individuals to be surveyed. In one or more stages, these primary units are sampled from which a final sample is selected. For example, to assess the publics' perception of quality of education provided by the local public school district, researchers might randomly select houses from a neighborhood from which they would identify homes with school-age children. Researchers might then survey a random sample of the adults living in the identified homes regarding their perception of the quality of education provided by the local public school district.

Evaluating Sampling Frames. In addition to determining the characteristics of the sampling frames, there are three general characteristics we should consider when evaluating the sampling frame used in survey research—comprehensiveness of the sample, probability of being selected, and response rate.

Comprehensiveness of Sample. The first characteristic centers on the comprehensiveness of the sample. A sample can only be representative of the sampling frame. Few approaches to sampling are based on a truly "exhaustive sampling frame" in which every member of the population is known. Further, seemingly comprehensive lists such as individuals listed in telephone directories omit major segments of some populations. Thus, a key part of evaluating the sample surveyed by researchers is looking at the percentage of the study population that had a chance of being selected and the extent to which those excluded are distinctive. For example, if researchers intend to sample from a population included on a list (e.g., members of the American Educational Research Association), it is important that they examine in detail how the list was compiled. This examination should focus on the number and characteristics of people not likely to be included on the list.

Probability of Being Selected. The second characteristic focuses on the probability of being selected by researchers to complete the survey. Ideally, researchers should know the probability of each individual being selected to make reasonably accurate estimates of the relationship between the sample statistics and the population from which it was drawn. Researchers are unable to make reasonably accurate estimates of the relationship between the sample statistics and the population from which it was drawn if they do not know the probability of selection. As noted earlier, calculation of the probability of each individual being selected occurs at sample selection or at the time of data collection depending on the sampling frame or approach used by researchers.

Response Rate. The final characteristic focuses on the response rate. The response rate is a basic parameter for evaluating data collection efforts in survey research. Response rates are usually reported as the percentage of a selected sample from which data were collected. The response rate is simply the number of people surveyed (or interviewed) divided by the number of individuals sampled multiplied by 100. The numerator includes all the individuals who were selected and did respond. The denominator includes all the individuals who were selected but did not respond for whatever reason. Although there is no agreed-upon standard for a minimum response rate, generally, the lower the response rate the higher the potential for bias associated with nonrespondents. A response rate of 50% is adequate for analysis and reporting, 60% is good, and 75% or higher is considered very good. Additionally, ensuring reasonable response rates and avoiding procedures that systematically produce substantial differences between respondents and nonrespondents should play a key role in any survey research.

The nature of bias associated with nonresponse differs somewhat across survey methods that rely on personal contact between researchers and respondents (i.e., face-to-face, interviewer- and group-administered surveys) and those methods that do not (i.e., telephone, self-administered, and mail surveys). In the case of telephone surveys, availability is the most important source of nonresponse (Fowler, 1993). For example, the people who will be available to be surveyed will be distinctive if data collection is conducted during working hours Mondays through Fridays. Such a survey would likely yield high proportions of parents with small children, in-home childcare professionals, unemployed individuals, and retired persons.

Accessibility is the major form of nonresponse associated with personal interview surveys. Accessibility is more common in personal interview surveys conducted in central cities than in suburbs or rural areas because it is difficult to access individuals who live in apartments (Cannell et. al., 1987). The omission of groups of individuals is another form of nonresponse associated with personal interview surveys. This omission is common when the interview is conducted in areas in which there are large groups of individuals who do not speak English (Fowler, 1993).

The nature of nonresponse associated with mail surveys differs from those conducted by telephone or through personal interviews. Individuals who have an interest in the subject matter are more likely to return mail surveys than those who are less interested. Thus, the results of mail surveys with low response rates may be biased in ways that are directly related to the purpose of the research (Jobber, 1984). Another form of nonresponse that is common in mail surveys is that better-educated individuals are more likely to return mail questionnaires than those with less education (Filion, 1975). This form of bias is more likely to be evident when the subject matter is related (even tangential) to the education level of respondents.

Developing the Survey Instrument

Using well-designed questions is critical in survey research because the answer to a question is only valuable to the extent to which it is has a predictable relationship to facts or the phenomenon of interest. Good questions maximize the relationship between what researchers are trying to measure and the answers of respondents. One goal of survey research is to ensure question reliability (i.e., respondents answer the question in the same way). Another goal is to ensure question validity (i.e., correspondence between the answers of respondents and what is purported to being measured). Thus, all of the issues discussed in Chapter 3 regarding reliability and validity play a critical role in the development of surveys. Because issues associated with reliability and validity have already been discussed in Chapter 3, the focus in this section is on the process used by researchers to develop questions for surveys. The process of developing the survey instrument includes: (a) identifying key factors (i.e., attributes, characteristics, or behaviors) associated with the phenomena under study, (b) developing questions or statements, (c) formatting and sequencing questions, and (d) pilot testing the survey.

Identifying Key Factors. Identifying the key factors associated with the phenomenon under study is critical to developing an effective survey. The aim at this point in the process of survey design is to identify all of the potential factors associated with the phenomena under study. Although researchers might be tempted to rely on brainstorming to identify the factors, they should review the literature and other sources (e.g., experts in the field) to ensure that they identify all of the key factors associated with the phenomena under study. Of course, it is important to assess the quality of the questions used by researchers who have done previous work on the phenomena under study.

At this point, researchers may begin to prioritize the factors they are interested in exploring because there may be many possible factors associated with the phenomena under study. Again, researchers should look closely at the literature to identify those factors that have been found to be associated most strongly with the phenomena under study. Identifying factors that have been found to be related to these phenomena enable researchers to construct high-quality surveys.

Developing Questions or Statements

Response Format. In the construction of questions or statements for a survey, researchers must first consider the response format they want to use. (Although researchers use both questions and statements in survey research, we refer only to questions throughout the remainder of this section.) Although there are a number of variations, researchers have two categories of options: open- and close-ended questions.

Open-Ended Questions. In the case of open-ended questions, the respondents are asked to provide their own answers to the questions. For example, respondents might be asked, "What do you think is the most important issue facing public schools today?" and be provided with a space to write in their answers or report them verbally to interviewers. The primary shortcoming of open-ended questions is the lack of uniformity of responses because respondents can respond in a variety of fashions. This lack of uniformity tends to reduce the reliability and validity of the survey.

Close-Ended Questions. In the case of close-ended questions, respondents are asked to select their answers from among those provided by the researchers. Using the preceding example, respondents might be asked to choose the most important issue facing public schools today from a list of possible issues provided by researchers (e.g., funding, violence, substance abuse, availability of well-trained teachers). Additionally, researchers use a variety of scales (e.g., Likert, Thurstone, and Guttman Scaling) with open-ended questions. Likert scales are the most commonly used by researchers. In the case of Likert-type scales, respondents are presented with a question and are asked to indicate whether they "strongly agree," "agree," are "undecided," "disagree," or "strongly disagree." Multiple modifications of the wording of the response (e.g., "approve") are used by researchers. The primary shortcoming of close-ended questions lies in how researchers have chosen and structured the possible responses.

Reviewing Questions Used in Other Surveys. After a response format has been chosen, researchers use the list of key factors to be measured to develop a set of questions to be included on the survey. Again, researchers should review questions used by researchers who have conducted similar surveys. Keep in mind that there is no guarantee the questions used by researchers conducting similar surveys are good questions or are appropriate for a particular survey. Many poor questions are asked over and over again simply because researchers do not critically evaluate whether the question content is appropriate for the population, context, and goals of a particular study.

Ensuring the Reliability and Validity of Questions. All questions should be tested to ensure that they are reliable and valid measures for the population, context, and goals of a particular study. Demographic and background information questions should yield accurate and needed information. These questions are standard to most surveys. Researchers can review other survey instruments to identify common demographic and background questions. General guidelines for constructing reliable and valid questions include (a) use clear and unambiguous wording; (b) avoid double-barreled questions (e.g., "Should America eliminate foreign aid and spend the money on family-friendly program?"); (c) avoid negative items; and (d) avoid biased items or terms.

Understanding of Questions. Prior to formatting and sequencing the survey, researchers should explore whether the draft questions are consistently understood and answered by respondents before conducting a more formal pilot test of the survey instrument. To evaluate whether the questions are consistently understood and answered by respondents, researchers typically identify a small group of respondents who are willing to help in the understanding of how the questions work. Researchers ask respondents to not only respond to the draft questions but also to complete an interview process regarding the question content and reasons for the responses. The goal is to assess whether respondents' comprehension and responses are consistent with the population, context, and goals of a particular study.

Formatting and Sequencing Questions. Once the questions have been developed and reviewed by a group of respondents for feedback purposes, researchers then format and sequence the questions. Regardless of the type of survey (e.g., interview, self-administered), the primary goal is to format and sequence questions to minimize the work of respondents and, in some cases, to reduce biasing effects associated with the order of the questions. Six general guidelines for formatting questions follow:

1. The layout of survey instrument should be attractive, clear, and uncluttered. Reduction strategies designed to include more questions on the survey should be avoided.

2. Instructions for completing the survey should be self-explanatory (this is especially critical for self-administered surveys). Enough information to ensure that respondents can complete the survey as intended should be provided.

3. Consistent question forms and response formats should be used. The more the same types of questions and response formats are used, the more reliable the information obtained and the easier the task will be for respondents.

4. The length of time required to complete the survey should be less than 30 minutes. The length of the survey should be adjusted to align with the ability and willingness of respondents to complete the survey.

5. "Skip patterns" should be kept to a minimum (e.g., Please skip to Question 10 if your answer is NO).

6. The presentation of questions in those cases in which the appearance of questions may affect the answers given by respondents to subsequent ones should be randomized.

Pilot-Testing the Survey. Conducting a pilot test of the survey is the final step in developing a survey instrument. The purpose of a pilot test is to find out how the survey instrument works under realistic conditions. Researchers typically identify 20 to 50 respondents drawn from a population the same as, or similar to, the population to be surveyed. The administration procedures should be the same as those used in the actual study. Researchers then use information gained from the pilot test to examine the reliability and validity of the survey. Researchers may also ask respondents questions regarding the survey to ensure respondents are responding to the questions as intended. For example, researchers may ask respondents to complete a rating form to evaluate whether (a) the questions are easy to read and (b) respondents consistently understand and accurately answer the questions.

Critical research consumers should consider whether the survey was pilot-tested. If the survey was pilot-tested, two questions should be answered. First, did the authors indicate that modifications were made based on the pilot-test results? The primary reason for piloting the survey is to determine if the questions are appropriate to obtain the desired information; researchers will usually modify the survey format and/or questions based on the feedback. Second, it is critical to determine who the pilot participants were. They should be representative of the respondents in the investigation. If the pilot participants are similar to the respondents, it is likely that the feedback obtained in the pilot survey was valid in providing feedback on how to modify the survey to obtain important information. If the pilot participants are not similar to the respondents, there should be a question about the adequacy of the modifications made to the survey, if any were made.

Once it has been determined that the survey is adequate to carry out the required information, the critical research consumer should consider whether cause-and-effect statements can be made based on the results. Since an independent variable is not being directly manipulated in the same way that one would be in an experimental investigation, the determination of a cause-and-effect relationship is not possible. However, through multivariate analysis techniques, it is possible to determine relationships and the strengths of those relationships among variables. Thus, the researcher could indicate that a relationship exists. Whether the relationship is causal in nature would then depend on further experimental investigations.

Analysis of Data

Internal Validity. Sampling methods are important in determining the internal validity of a survey. However, the importance has more to do with the sample of items included in the survey than with the sample of the population. How the questions are phrased and the order they are placed are critical in determining if the information received by the researchers is what the researchers wanted or expected to obtain. Thus, critical research consumers should attempt to determine if the questions provided to the respondents were adequate in obtaining the information received by the researchers.

External Validity. The ability to generalize the results of a survey to individuals not included in the survey sample depends on the nature of the sample used (i.e., was it representative?). Additionally, the description of respondent characteristics is also a critical part of the ability to make generalization claims. Although sampling errors are not the only source of bias in the findings from survey research, they represent a potential source of error.

The sampling process can affect the findings from surveys in several different ways. First, the findings will be biased if the sample frame excludes some individuals with whom we want to collect information. The magnitude of the bias will depend on the extent to which the omitted individuals differ from the respondents. Second, if the sampling approach used by researchers is not probabilistic, the relationship between the sampled population and those sampled is a problem. This is not to say that all nonprobalistic sampling approaches produce unrepresentative samples. Rather, researchers have no statistical basis for assessing the extent to which a sample is representative of the sampled population. Finally, chance errors will occur because of collecting data from only a sample of a population.

Research Example

Agran, Salzberg, and Martella (1991) conducted a survey to determine whether persons working with employees with mental retardation responded differentially to surveys as compared to individuals without previous experience working with individuals with mental retardation. The surveys were sent by mail. The survey was described in an earlier investigation by Salzberg, Agran, and Lignugaris/Kraft (1986) to determine the critical social behaviors that were associated with job success.

The more recent survey was slightly modified so that four categories of surveys resulted—(a) those sent to supervisors with experience working with persons with mental retardation; (b) those sent to supervisors without experience working with persons with mental retardation; (c) surveys that referenced persons with mental retardation in the cover letter (i.e., the information to be obtained from the survey will be used to identify critical social-vocational skills for employees with mental retardation); and (d) surveys that did not reference persons with mental retardation (i.e., the information to be obtained from the survey will be used to identify critical social-vocational skills for employees).

The sample was selected from a pool of potential businesses from each of nine job categories. These businesses were selected at random from each of the job categories. A total of 160 surveys were sent to employers (40 in each survey category) (i.e., 40 were sent with reference to individuals with mental retardation to employers with experience supervising individuals with mental retardation; 40 were sent without reference to individuals with mental retardation to employers with experience supervising individuals with mental retardation; 40 were sent with reference to individuals with mental retardation to employers without experience supervising individuals with mental retardation; and 40 were sent without reference to individuals with mental retardation to employers without experience supervising individuals with mental retardation). In all, 86% of the surveys were returned.

The results indicated that prior experience with persons with mental retardation did not affect ratings of critical social-vocational skills. However, there were differences in the frequency with which employers rated the number of specific behaviors occurring, but there were no differences in the ratings of importance of social behaviors. The survey's results provided important information on the extent to which differences in experience with persons with mental retardation and the reference to persons with mental retardation affected the responses of supervisors.

WHEN SHOULD RESEARCHERS USE SURVEY RESEARCH?

Survey research is appropriate for the study of a wide range of phenomena in education and psychology. However, survey research should be conducted when other methods are not possible or appropriate to use. If the number of individuals with whom researchers are interested in obtaining information is so large that another methodology is not possible, survey research should be used. Likewise, if the individuals with whom we wish to obtain information are dispersed across a large area for example, we may not be able to conduct another form of research. In such a case, a survey method would be most appropriate. Finally, some research questions may simply require a survey method such as when asking school psychologists to indicate their support or nonsupport for categorical labeling of special education students (e.g., learning disabled, behavior disordered, mentally retarded).

SECTION 2: HISTORICAL RESEARCH

OBJECTIVES

After studying this section you should be able to:

1. Describe four similarities of historical research with other methodologies.
2. Describe the characteristics and purposes of historical research.
3. Describe the steps in the historical research process.
4. Describe how to analyze historical data including external and internal criticism and synthesis.
5. Describe when one would conduct historical research.

OVERVIEW

Historical research can be regarded as quantitative or qualitative (Potter, 1996); however, it is not easy to categorize historical research into any one category, mainly because historical research does not have highly developed methodology around which there is a consensus (Kaestle, 1992). Historical research is geared to describe relations, correct inaccurate conclusions from other historical reports, or to explain what has occurred in the past.

Historical research involves a systematic process of researching for data from the past that can help us understand what is going on now and what may occur in the future. The systematic nature of historical research makes it a scientific process. Edson (1986) described four similarities of historical research with other methodologies. First, historical research is concerned with the context under which events took place. This concern for the context of the investigation is congruent with that of qualitative and single-case researchers, for example. Second, historical researchers are concerned with the "wholeness" of the situation under investigation. In other words, historical researchers are concerned with all of the contextual factors surrounding an historical event or events. Third, historical researchers study their subject matter in the natural surroundings rather than in contrived or theoretical settings. The emphasis, then, is what occurred under actual situations, not during artificially derived situations. Finally, historical researchers are focused on the centrality of the interpretation in the research process. In other words, historical researchers are focused on making the interpretation of their data the focus of their research versus focusing on the events themselves. Historical researchers may also use quantitative data in their research to help interpret certain events. Therefore, historical research shares several characteristics with both qualitative research methods as well as quantitative and single-case research methods.

The remainder of this section on historical research begins with a description of the characteristics and purposes of historical research. This discussion is followed by a description of how historical research is designed. The next section includes a discussion on how to analyze historical data. Additionally, a description of an historical research investigation is described. Finally, we describe when historical research should be conducted.

WHAT ARE THE CHARACTERISTICS AND PURPOSES OF HISTORICAL RESEARCH?

Characteristics

Historical research has several defining characteristics (Potter, 1996). First, historical research emphasizes what occurred in the past. Other methods deal with the present. Second, historical research is empirical in that there is an attempt to obtain information from a variety of sources. Recall that empiricism is critical for the development of a science. Empiricism involves gaining information from our senses. When conducting historical research, we make observations of past events through historical sources. Finally, historical research involves the attempt to make meaning out of the subject matter.

Purposes

Historical research can serve a number of purposes. First, historical research can answer factual questions about the past (Connors, 1992). For example, if we were to question how educators approached the instruction of students 100 years ago, we could analyze written accounts from the period, talk with individuals who had firsthand or secondhand information about the period, or analyze photos from the era.

Second, historical research may, under certain circumstances, aid us in determining what has worked in the past (or what has failed) to help us in the future (Mason, McKenny, & Copeland, 1997). For example, suppose we wanted to determine what disciplinary methods were used 25 years ago and how effective these practices were. If we found out what worked several years ago, we could attempt to use those methods today to solve some of our disciplinary problems. This is, in fact, what some people propose on a much more informal level. Many people will tell you that "when I was growing up, the teacher would paddle us for misbehaving. We rarely had behavior problems in our classroom." However, the type of information available to substantiate this claim is usually not present since the question is one of cause-and-effect. It is probably not possible to determine the variables that caused something to occur or not occur in the past. Mason and colleagues (1997) noted that "cause-and-effect relationships, are, of course, established precariously and with great caution in nonexperimental situations because an induction can never be proven in any formal logical system" (p. 315). (*Note:* The ability of historical research to establish cause-and-effect relationships is a philosophical argument similar to the ability of qualitative research to determine such relationships.)

In our example of disciplinary methods, suppose a researcher determined that corporal punishment seemed to keep disciplinary problems down in urban schools 25 years ago. She determined this by talking to former teachers and students, examining disciplinary records from several schools, and reviewing the concern for behavior problems in the media or in publications. The difficulty results when one considers that other variables may have been in effect at the same time such as the type of instruction typically used in the classroom, the makeup of the students, the level of violence seen in the media, and the familial support present. Being able to make definitive conclusions based on such historical accounts is difficult to do. Connors (1992) states this difficulty as follows:

> *Historical research cannot tell us what we should and should not do in any given set of circumstances. It cannot give us the plausible "certainties" provided by statistical analysis. History is always*

written from probabilistic, and therefore rhetorical, points of view. All it can do is tell us stories, stories that may move us to actions but that in themselves cannot guide our actions according to any system. If history were, or could be, systematic, things might be different. But history is not, and never has been, systematic or scientific. Any attempt to make history predictive would have to assume that there are dependable recurring circumstances, which is simply not the case. In fact, history is narrative, and every attempt to create a system to give that narrative a predictive meaning is fraught with peril. (p. 31)

Third, historical research can aid us in the understanding of how we came to this point in time (Mason et al., 1997). For example, we may wonder how we came to teach mathematics in some manner. Historical research can aid us in answering this question. We may find that the use of manipulatives became more prevalent in the 1960s when educators began to consider Piaget's theory of development and its educational implications. Or, we may find that the use of manipulatives began earlier due to other factors. We may also, for example, find that the authentic literature movement in reading instruction took hold in the 1980s when New Zealand began to disseminate results of reading achievement in that country where a literature-based or whole-language approach was used.

Fourth, historical research can aid us in seeing trends or patterns (Mason et al., 1997). For example, if a researcher were to investigate the educational methods used during much of the 1960s, he would find that many of the techniques are being used today. There seem to be trends in education where one instructional technique comes into vogue and falls out of favor only to come back at a later time. One educational trend seen today is the back-to-basics movement that began in California and elsewhere. This movement is similar to what occurred in the 1960s and 1970s. The basics took a back seat to more progressive methods in the 1980s and early 1990s. However, a concern for teaching the basics is being seen in more communities today.

Finally, historical research can serve as a basis for later interview or observation studies (Marshall & Rossman, 1995) or in the development of new hypotheses/research questions (Mason et al., 1997). For example, suppose that we are interested in investigating how public schools have changed over the last 100 years. We could conduct historical research to determine the characteristics of schools of the past and then conduct an observational study in a present-day school to see if those characteristics determined by the historical research are still present.

HOW IS HISTORICAL RESEARCH DESIGNED?

Researchers conducting historical research have several steps they must complete in order to turn out a research report. However, the steps in conducting historical research are not necessarily completed in a linear fashion. Several of the steps are conducted at the same time, and researchers may go back and add to the information gained in a previous step.

Research Question or Hypothesis

The first step in the process of historical research is the generation of a research question or hypothesis. This first step involves essentially the same process as used by other researchers. Research questions or hypotheses can be generated by a desire to solve a current problem, to add to our information about the past, to satisfy a source of confusion, or to satisfy curiosity. However, a major difference with historical research and other forms of research is that much of the data may already be in existence in some form, or if not available, lost forever. In other forms of research, researchers go out and generate the data. Historical researchers attempt to find the data that are already generated or may attempt to generate the data through other means such as interviewing individuals from the era under study. For example, if a researcher wished to investigate the extent to which multicultural practices were taught in schools in the 1950s, the researcher would need to find information related to the question. She may search professional journals, curricular materials, books, and newspaper articles. The researcher may also interview teachers from the era to gather information on educational practices.

Data Collection

The second step in the research process involves a search for relevant sources. These sources can be placed into one of two categories—primary and secondary (Marshall & Rossman, 1995; Mason et al., 1997).

Primary Sources. The first category, primary sources, includes oral testimony of individuals who were present at the time, documents, records, and relics. The obvious advantage of primary sources is that the data come from sources who were present when the events took place. These sources are considered to be primary since the information came from sources present or developed during the time period under investigation. These sources are usually considered as being the most reliable type of information. The reason these primary sources are considered more reliable than other sources is that as we go farther from the original source of information, the information tends to change. For example, a typical exercise in introduction to psychology classes is to begin a story at one side of the room. A professor may tell one student that "research is an important endeavor because we can learn about ourselves." The first student tells a second student the same thing as accurately as possible. This continues until we reach the last student in the class. Finally, the professor asks the last student what she was told, and the original statement is stated as, "Research is the most important thing students can do because research can help to prevent educational learning problems that we may encounter in our careers." As we go farther from the original student and what he stated, we get more and more changes. Thus, if we want to know what the original statement was, we should get as close to the first student or the original source as possible.

Secondary Sources. The second category of data includes secondary sources. These sources may include reports from individuals who relay information from people who were present during the historical period, reports from individuals who have read information from the past, and books about the period under question such as history books and encyclopedias. These sources are secondary since the information did not come directly from individuals or documents from the specified historical period. The information obtained from secondary sources may not be as reliable or accurate as the data from primary sources. A critical concern is whether the researcher is able to show that other sources also reveal the same information (i.e., reliable findings) (Firby, 1993). If several sources, even if they are secondary, are shown to contain the same or similar information, the reliability of the information is enhanced.

Interviews. Interviewing methods have been discussed in Chapter 9. It is important to point out that interviews are important sources of data in historical research. The interviews can be from either primary or secondary sources. For example, an early educational reform advocate (Fred Keller) was interviewed just before he passed away. The information he provided during this interview included educational reform attempts and early research on alternative educational practices. These interviews were videotaped to preserve the information from a primary source.

Document Analysis. Document analyses are also used in historical analyses and were discussed in Chapter 9. Document analyses may be used to obtain information from either primary or secondary sources and exist in some written or printed form. Documents can contain important information that does not exist elsewhere or can contain several perspectives. For example, a few years ago, one of the authors completed a document analysis of a court case involving the treatment of individuals with disabilities. This case involved a social service office suing a facility that treated individuals with severe behavior problems. The state attempted to revoke the license of the facility because a resident at the facility died while undergoing a behavior intervention. The state ultimately lost the case. In order to determine why the case was lost, the author contacted all newspapers in the area, the social service office, the facility, and others who had access to court documents. All newspaper articles published on the case were obtained as well as court documents and documents from the social service office and facility. Once the author analyzed all of the documents, it became apparent that the case was won by the facility primarily due to the support of the parents of the residents. Thus, the use of documents allowed the author to make conclusions in terms of why the case was decided as it was.

Other forms of data analysis which are similar to document analysis involve the analysis of pictures or other visual materials. Although we defined document analysis as information contained in written form, we can also consider information obtained in the form of pictures as a form of a document. Thus, we can get historical information from pictures, films, or drawings.

Analysis of Data

The third step in historical research involves the analysis of data. The analysis of historical data is unlike other forms of research since the subject matter (i.e., past) is different from other subject matter (i.e., present). Data analysis is based on three concerns—external criticism, internal criticism, and synthesis of information (Connors, 1992). Before a description of the two criticisms of historical research is presented, it should be pointed out that internal and external criticism cannot be separated completely. Variables affecting one may also, and frequently do, impact the other. (*Note:* Because the sample article at the end of the chapter is a survey investigation, an example of a historical rating form is located in Table 13.2.)

External Criticism. External criticism refers to the authenticity of the information obtained. In other words, external criticism has to do with the choice of sources historical researchers will read (Connors, 1992). This choice of sources leads to a concern in many debates such as the authenticity of the Dead Sea Scrolls. When historical evidence is found, researchers must be cautious to determine if the evidence is indeed authentic. In order to make this determination, researchers should ask several questions (Gall, Borg, & Gall, 1996).

First, researchers must ask, "Where was this document written?" Is it possible that the person writing this document would have obtained the information in a particular location? For example, suppose that a researcher found a document regarding a method of teaching reading in the east during the mid-1950s; this document may be viewed with caution if the author of the document was from the south. The researcher would have to determine if the author made trips to the east, or determine how the individual obtained the information. It is possible for the individual to be an authority on the subject even if he or she lived in another part of the country; however, the individual must have some way of obtaining the information firsthand.

The second question refers to when the document was written. If the document in the preceding example were dated 1952, the document would be viewed with some suspicion. How could one write about a decade of instruction when the document only covers the first two years of the period? Similarly, if the document were dated 1990, suspicion is again aroused since the passage of 40 years could make one question the authenticity of the information. (Obviously, this example also would make one question the accuracy of the information as well.)

Third, researchers should ask, "Who wrote the document?" Historical researchers are concerned with whether the documents are authentic or are forgeries. Forgeries are documents written by someone other than the listed author. For example, suppose that a historical researcher located a document written by John Dewey. The document described the implications of approaching instruction from a more progressive manner. However, the signature on the document does not match others with Dewey's signature. The historical researcher will review the document much more closely to determine its authenticity by looking at variables such as sentence structure across other documents

TABLE 13.2 Historical Research Rating Form.

THREATS TO HISTORICAL VALIDITY

External Criticism

1. **Is it possible that the person writing this document would have obtained the information in the particular location?** **YES NO ?**

   Justification ____

   ____.

2. **Was the document written at the time the historical event occurred?** **YES NO ?**

   Justification ____

   ____.

3. **Could authentic information have been obtained at that time?** **YES NO ?**

   Justification ____

   ____.

4. **Who wrote the document? Did it seem authentic?** **YES NO ?**

   Justification ____

   ____.

5. **Could the author have written an authentic document under the prevailing conditions?** **YES NO ?**

   Justification ____

   ____.

6. **Is the document an original?** **YES NO ?**

   Justification ____

   ____.

7. **Overall, does the obtained information seem authentic?** **YES NO ?**

   Justification ____

   ____.

(continued)

TABLE 13.2 Continued

Internal Criticism

1. **Does the author seem to be without a particular bias?** **YES NO ?**

   Justification ____

   ____.

2. **Were the individuals cited able to remember what occurred at a particular point in time?** **YES NO ?**

   Justification ____

   ____.

3. **Was the source a primary one?** **YES NO ?**

   Justification ____

   ____.

4. **Did the person providing the information have expertise in the area?** **YES NO ?**

   Justification ____

   ____.

5. **Overall, does the obtained information seem accurate?** **YES NO ?**

   Justification ____

   ____.

Synthesis

1. **Can generalization claims be made?** **YES NO ?**

   Justification ____

   ____.

Abstract: Write a one-page abstract summarizing the overall conclusions of the authors and whether you feel the authors' conclusions are valid based on the external and internal criticism of the investigation.

prepared by Dewey. It may be found that the writing style and signature do not match other Dewey documents, and thus, the document is likely a forgery.

A fourth question is, "Under what conditions was the document written?" For example, suppose that in the early 1960s a nontenured college faculty member was asked by her dean to prepare a document to describe effective instructional methods. The nontenured faculty member may present information based on what she perceived the dean and other tenured faculty to value. The document may not reflect what the author sees as effective teaching techniques, but what the author thinks others view as effective. The historical researcher must try to determine if the document was an authentic representation of the faculty member's views.

The final question asks, "Is this the original document or a copy of the original?" If the document is original, the authenticity of it is easier to determine. If the document is a copy and, thus, other versions exist, the authenticity is more difficult to determine. A concern of the historical researcher is whether the document has been altered. Given today's technology, it is difficult to determine if a document has been altered in some manner. Thus, it is important to determine if the document is an original.

The critical research consumer should attempt to answer these questions while considering the author's conclusions. The more evidence researchers can present that shows the authenticity of the documents, the more likely the conclusions drawn from those documents are considered to be valid.

Internal Criticism. Internal criticism refers to the accuracy of the information obtained; the documents are examined with the intent of making sure they are judged correctly (Connors, 1992). Determining the accuracy of the information is more difficult than determining the authenticity of the document. Further, the determination of the accuracy of the information cannot occur until the authenticity of the document has been shown and comparisons are made with claims in other documents.

There are several possible reasons why an authentic document may not be accurate. For example, some individuals may have particular biases that prevent them from documenting how things actually were. Suppose a school psychologist with a particular philosophical bent documented the effectiveness of a counseling method that he was opposed to on philosophical grounds. The counselor may have actually seen improvements in the students' attitude toward school, but she documents that the students did not show any improved attitudes. In this case, the philosophical orientation of the counselor interferes with her ability to provide an accurate portrayal of what actually occurred.

Another difficulty with the accuracy of the information is the extent to which individuals can remember what occurred at a particular point in time. An example of this is the uncertainty of eyewitness testimony. Two people can see the same thing occur but report different and sometimes conflicting information. The differences may have also been due to whether the individuals were participants or observers of the event. Persons who are observers may be able to provide more detailed or objective documentation of an event than a participant can.

A third problem has to do with whether the source was a primary or secondary one. If the person reporting the information is a secondary source, the historical researcher must be cautious about the accuracy of the information obtained. For example, suppose a person documented the advantages and disadvantages of the one-room schoolhouse. If the individual taught in such a school, the information would be primary. However, if the author documented what she was told by former teachers in such schools or her own grandparents who experienced this firsthand, the information would be secondary. Thus, the historical researcher must be concerned with the accuracy of the original information.

A final concern is the expertise of the person reporting. Say a person with no background in pedagogy observes several classrooms and documents what was seen. The concern is whether the observer has the background to understand the sometimes subtle complexities of the classroom environment. If the observer is not capable of understanding the pedagogy, the accuracy of the information is of concern.

The critical research consumer should be concerned with the internal criticism of documents reported by researchers. Simply demonstrating that documents are authentic is not sufficient. It is up to researchers to also demonstrate that the information obtained is accurate. If the information is not accurate, the researchers' conclusions will be suspect.

Synthesis of Information. The synthesis of the information involves organizing the information, making conclusions, and, finally, making generalizations. Synthesis can also be thought of as a final step in historical research (Mason et al., 1997). This step is similar in all of the research methodologies discussed throughout this text.

However, the critical research consumer should be cautious of generalization claims. The ability of historical research to make generalized statements is limited. The problem lies with the nature of the research. Entire populations are not likely to be investigated nor are all of the potential variables that may have accounted for the historical events analyzed.

This problem is not limited only to historical research. Some researchers may mistakenly indicate that the problem with historical research is the fact that too few samples are selected for study. For example, if we studied 100 one-room schools versus 10, we can make a stronger case for generalization. However, the number is not the critical variable nor is the number of participants. What is critical are the characteristics of the schoolhouses examined. For example, their location, size, ages of the students, and so on are important factors. The conclusions are logical rather than statistical; therefore, the claims of generalization are also logical. Logical generalization suggests that we can generalize to other cases that have similar characteristics to the one used in the investigation. Thus, the size of the sample is not necessarily a major obstacle in generalizing conclusions to other cases.

What is a difficulty in making generalization claims is the validity of the inferences made during the investigation and in the conclusions drawn. Since it is not possible to determine a causal variable because it cannot be manipulated or changed, it is not possible to make general statements to other cases. These general statements cannot be made because the other cases may have the influence of variables different from the original investigation.

Research Example

Hart and Pavlovic (1991) described an historical investigation considering children's rights in education. The researchers traced "the major themes of the children's rights movement and educational progress" (p. 345). Two lines were considered including: "(a) the development of the idea and political reality of human rights, and (b) the development of the modern concept of (prolonged) childhood, established by the introduction of formalized compulsory schooling" (p. 345). The information came mostly from secondary sources such as books describing what occurred in the past.

The researchers traced children's rights from the fifteenth to the twentieth century. They also described the origins of children's rights by discussing different theories such as, "the development of rights is influenced by the ongoing struggle of the oppressed for the redistribution of power in society" (p. 347). The progress toward person status was also described. The importance of self-determination was mentioned in the discussion.

The major historical themes and the education toward person status were described with regard to the formalization of special class treatment. The different school movements such as progressive education were discussed. The current direction of education was described as having shown a convergence of cognitive and humanistic branches of education and psychology.

The researchers also examined the children's rights benchmark, which they indicated was the United Nations Convention of the Child. They discussed the relevance of the Convention to education. The source for this primary information was from the Articles of the Convention. The researchers recognized the importance the Convention gave toward autonomy for education. They cited specific pages in several articles that supported their claims.

Finally, the researchers described the desired advances in the relationships between the children's rights movements and educational improvements. Essentially, the researchers made conclusions about future needs and directions from their historical information and described how different professionals can aid in the development of these relationships.

WHEN SHOULD RESEARCHERS USE HISTORICAL RESEARCH?

Historical research is important in our research endeavors. It allows us to develop a critical database that can serve several purposes. First, historical research should be conducted when we wish to know about past events and how these past events may have affected current practices. Second, historical research aids us in predicting what may occur in the future. Finally, and possibly most importantly, historical research should be conducted when we want to avoid making the same or similar mistakes. It does no one any good, especially our students, if we continue to regurgitate ineffective practices that have been tried and have failed in the past. Therefore, a solid understanding of historical events in fields like education and psycholog

However, if we wished to determine the exact causes of current events, we may be more hard pressed to find these causal relations through historical research. The conclusions made with regard to causal events should be made with caution since a manipulation of an independent variable has not taken place. However, historical research can direct us to possible causal events and point us to future research concerns.

Although historical research can have a great impact on current practices, historical research cannot tell us what we should and should not do in any given circumstance (Connors, 1992). This is a critical point. The determination of what we should or should not do must be made on current events and contexts. Historical research may help us reach a conclusion with regard to what we should or should not do, but other information is needed to help us answer this question. Information from the other types of research methodologies will also be critical in helping us determine a direction for the future.

SECTION 3: PROGRAM EVALUATION

OBJECTIVES

After studying this section you should be able to:

1. Discuss the history of program evaluation.
2. Discuss the different approaches to program evaluation.
3. Discuss the goal and objectives of program evaluation.
4. Describe the types of program evaluations.
5. Discuss the difference between formative and summative evaluations.
6. Describe the general framework used to conduct a program evaluation.
7. Describe when one would use program evaluation.

OVERVIEW

Evaluation is a part of everyday life. Athletes continually evaluate their performance to decide where they need to make improvements. Teachers assess whether their students acquire various academic skills. Similarly, social service and education programs use evaluations to not only improve services, but to document the effectiveness of the provided services. Although social service and education programs have been in existence for many years, the field of program evaluation is relatively young and is continually evolving. This field has evolved based on the particular needs of society.

In the late 1960s and early 1970s, program evaluations emphasized experimental methods, standardized data collection, large samples, and provision of scientific data. It was believed that experimental methods would not only yield unequivocal evidence of the effectiveness of programs, but also provide a sound rationale for social service programs. This type of information was critical at the time because policy makers believed that social service programs could be used to eliminate most problems facing society. However, experimental methods began to be considered unresponsive to the unique characteristics of local programs; thus, evaluations began to focus on the unique characteristics and processes within local settings and issues perceived to be important to stakeholders (i.e., program participants, staff, site administrators, governing board, and community members). Such evaluations were designed on the premise that social service programs are often complex and that they vary significantly from one community to another. These responsive program evaluations stress the importance of using qualitative methods for understanding how a program is run and its effects on program participants.

Although the preceding discussion has briefly detailed the trend in program evaluations, there are a number of models or approaches used by program evaluators. Table 13.3 presents some of the more common evaluation models used by program evaluators. As you look over the table, it is important to note that these program evaluation models are not mutually exclusive. That is, the methods employed under each of the models are similar. We do not discuss any particular program evaluation model or approach in the remainder of this section because we have drawn, at least in part, from all of the models.

This section begins with a discussion of the varying goals and objectives of program evaluations. This discussion is followed by a description of the types of program evaluations used by evaluators and others. The remainder of this section includes a description of the general process used to conduct a program evaluation, to evaluate program evaluation data, and to decide when program evaluations are to be conducted.

TABLE 13.3 Program Evaluation Models

Participant-Oriented

- Focus is on program processes and the perspectives of stakeholders

Objectives-Oriented

- Focus is on the extent to which a program meets its established objectives

Management-Oriented

- Focus is on providing program managers information to aid decision making

Expertise-Oriented

- Focus is on the judgment of an expert

Adversary-Oriented

- Focus is on incorporating negative and positive views in the evaluation

WHAT ARE THE GOAL AND OBJECTIVES OF PROGRAM EVALUATION?

Goal

The overall goal of program evaluation is to provide feedback to those professionals who decide which social services are to be offered, design new programs, or make changes in existing approaches (Posavac & Carey, 1997). Feedback, as with any activity, is critical to the success of social service and education programs and practices. As noted before, the practice of evaluating one's own efforts is commonplace.

Objectives

Within the overall goal of providing feedback, there are five general objectives of program evaluation—

meet existing needs, provide services, determine effectiveness of services, determine relative effectiveness of programs, and maintain and improve programs.

Meet Existing Needs. The first objective is to ensure that social service and education programs meet existing needs. Social service and education programs must be designed and targeted at the most critical of these existing needs. Although it may seem obvious to direct social service and education programs to meet the most critical existing needs, it is not uncommon for programs to be developed with little thought given to whether they will truly meet an existing need, much less a critical one. Thus, it is important that program evaluations be used to establish social service and education programs that meet a specified existing need.

Provide Services. The second objective of program evaluations is to verify that planned programs do provide services. Once social service and education programs are developed, it is crucial to check if they were implemented as prescribed. Consequently, program evaluations should be conducted to monitor whether social service and education programs have been implemented as specified. Although it may appear unnecessary for program evaluations to be concerned with the monitoring of programs, programs must be implemented if results are to be obtained and assessed.

Determine Effectiveness of Programs. The third objective of program evaluation is to determine whether a social service and education program is effective. Although many program managers believe that providing services is equivalent to rendering quality services, program evaluations must be conducted to determine whether a program leads to improved outcomes for the program participants. Additionally, program evaluations aimed at assessing the effectiveness of social service and education programs should also determine whether such programs have any unplanned side effects. For example, social service programs aimed at moving people off welfare may result in greater demands being placed on other social service agencies such as churches and food banks.

Determine Relative Effectiveness of Programs. The fourth objective of program evaluation is to determine which particular program produces the best outcomes. Social service and education programs designed to meet a specified need often can be constructed in a number of ways. For example, a tutoring program for students at risk for school failure might be provided one-on-one or in a small group format. Program evaluations enable social service and education providers to choose among potential programs.

Maintain and Improve Programs. The final objective of program evaluation is to provide information to maintain and improve social service and education programs. The focus here is not necessarily on determining whether a social service or education program works (see the preceding third objective). Rather, the goal is to provide information with which to seek improvements in the services offered. Such program evaluations are especially important in those cases in which the social service and education program is mandated (e.g., bilingual and special education).

WHAT ARE THE TYPES OF PROGRAM EVALUATIONS?

Program evaluation efforts help organizations focus on important needs, develop effective programs, and assess and monitor the quality of programs. The four major types of program evaluations include needs assessments, process evaluations, outcome evaluations, and efficiency evaluations. Although program evaluations may utilize only one of these types of evaluation methods, a combination of methods may be used. For example, program evaluators exploring the effectiveness of an after-school academic and social program for students at risk for school failure might assess the quality of the program and any existing needs within the program. Figure 13.1 depicts the relationship among the four major types of program evaluations that

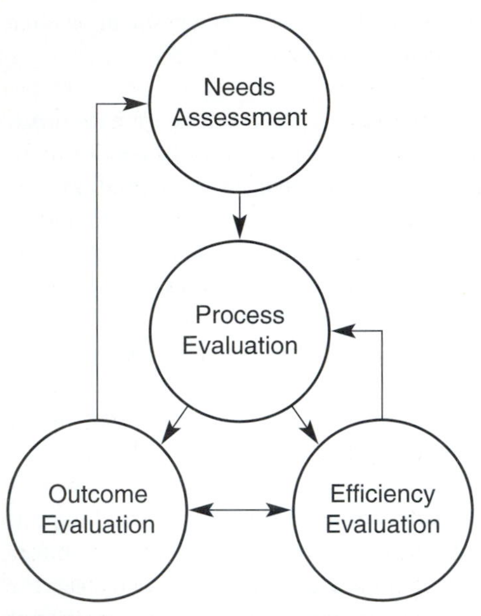

FIGURE 13.1 Relationship among the major types of program evaluations conducted throughout the life of a program.

would be conducted throughout the life of a program.

Before describing the four types of program evaluations, it is important to note that program evaluations are often categorized as either formative or summative evaluations depending on the goal of the evaluation. The goal of formative evaluations is to lead to the implementation of a new social service or education program or to changes in an existing one. On the other hand, the goal of summative evaluations is to describe the implementation of a program and its effects on program participants. Although we have chosen not to categorize program evaluations as formative or summative, you might consider these categories as you read our descriptions of the different types of program evaluations.

Needs Assessments

Social service and education programs are developed to serve a need. The goal of needs assessments is to identify the level of existing needs within an organization or program. In other words, the goal is to look for potential, but unavailable, services for an identified population of individuals. An important part of conducting needs assessments entails defining what is meant by "needs." Needs will differ depending on the organization or program. Needs can be defined as discrepancies between an actual state and a (a) normative, (b) minimum, or (c) desired or expected state. For example, needs assessments for programs for students at risk for school failure are often based on discrepancies from a norm. Scriven and Roth (1990) provide a general definition of needs that do not rely on any given procedure or one source of data to develop a valid needs assessment. A need refers to something (X) that people must have to be in a satisfactory state. Without X, they would be in an unsatisfactory state; with X, they achieve but do not exceed a satisfactory state. This definition of need provides a useful framework for structuring needs assessments.

Additionally, it is important to distinguish between the incidence and the prevalence of an existing need or problem. Incidence refers to the number of people experiencing a problem during a specified time period, whereas prevalence refers to the number of people who have a problem at a given time. Making a distinction between the incidence and the prevalence of a problem is important because a program designed to address a widespread temporary problem will differ from one designed to address a less widespread long lasting problem. For example, attempts to help children who experience a traumatic life event (e.g., death of a parent) will differ from those who help children who experience ongoing life events (e.g., low socioeconomic status).

Once the needs are defined for a given population, program evaluators should identify what resources are currently available to these individuals as part of their efforts to assess existing needs. Program evaluators conducting needs assessments typically study a wide range of need-relevant information. This information might include objective data about the social and economic conditions of the population (e.g., school dropout rates, crime, levels of physical illness), and the opinions of members of the population as well as experts obtained through surveys and focus groups.

Finally, needs assessments should lead to program planning. Needs assessments are of little use if they are not used to develop or restructure a program or organization. Consistent with the definition of need, program evaluators use the information gained from a needs assessment to develop a program to help members of the population obtain a satisfactory state. Program evaluators typically begin the program development or restructuring process by defining outcome goals (e.g., desired or normative state). Next, evaluators develop a series of intermediate and long-term goals that need to be achieved to reach the outcome goals. Program evaluators use a variety of strategies to develop programs that meet the needs of members of the population. What does not change dramatically is the process of working in a backward direction throughout the planning process. That is, program evaluators first identify the existing need prior to developing a program to meet it.

Process Evaluations

After a social service or education program has been developed or restructured, program evaluators should assess the extent to which the program has been implemented, serves the identified population, and operates as expected. Process evaluations are as important to program evaluation as is assessing treatment fidelity in research studies. The outcomes of a program evaluation, like a research study, are meaningful only to the extent one understands a program's activities, how it works, and the population it serves. There is little reason to assess the outcomes associated with a program if the program has not been implemented as planned.

When conducting a process evaluation, evaluators must discriminate between the program description and the program as administered. Making this discrimination is critical because the actual services provided by a social service or education program may differ substantially from its description. For example, as part of an effort to evaluate parent education programs provided by a variety of social service agencies, the authors visited the programs during periods when the parent education programs were officially scheduled, only to find that the program was not being offered due to a lack of participation. If we had based our evaluation on the program descriptions, we would have concluded that parent education programs were being offered as planned.

Information collected for a process evaluation is often available from a program's information system. Of course, the information may be recorded in a way that is hard to use. For example, information on program participants is often not summarized, and records of services received may not be recorded. Thus, it may be necessary for program evaluators to work with program managers to develop an information tracking system that is easy to use and provides critical information with which to conduct a process evaluation.

Although the information collected through a process evaluation varies depending on the particular social service or education program, there are two general types of information that are generally considered. The first type of information centers on the program participants. Social service and education programs are generally designed to meet the existing needs of a specific population. As a result, the population to be served should have been well defined during the conception of the program. Information describing the program participants actually served should be examined to assess the degree to which they match the original description of the population.

The second type of information focuses on the program itself. As noted before, programs are designed to achieve a desired or expected outcome. Thus, program evaluators must establish whether the program is being carried out as conceived. Program evaluators typically have the greatest difficulty assessing the degree to which a program is being implemented because program managers often do not collect information on implementation.

A common strategy used by evaluators is called "following the course of services." That is, tracking forms are developed to document the types and intensity of services provided to program participants. For example, a therapist working in a program that provides mental health services to students with behavioral problems might document her total case load, including active and inactive cases, the average number of sessions provided to participants, a description of the focus of the sessions, and ratings of the functional status of students when they exit the program. Information collected with the tracking forms are then compared to descriptions of how the services were originally conceived.

Outcome Evaluations

Outcome evaluations are the most common type of evaluation. Outcome evaluations are often referred to as summative evaluations because the primary goal is to develop summary statements and judgments about the program and its value. Furthermore, outcome evaluations can take on several levels of complexity. At the first level, an outcome evaluation might be designed only to determine whether program participants have improved. At the second level, an outcome evaluation may be designed to determine whether the program participants have improved relative to a similar group not receiving services. At the third level, an outcome evaluation might be designed to determine whether there is a cause-and-effect relationship between program services and the outcomes of program participants. Finally, an outcome evaluation might be designed to determine whether the program effects generalize across agencies, time, and other conditions.

Efficiency Evaluations

Although programs might be shown to help program participants, they often must show that they do so in a cost-effective way. Efficiency evaluations are conducted to deal with questions of cost. Even programs that produce significant improvements in the lives of program participants may be judged negatively if the costs necessary to achieve the improvements exceed what communities are willing to pay. Such programs might also be judged negatively if alternative approaches can be implemented that are less costly. In today's climate of dwindling resources, examining the cost-effectiveness of programs is becoming more important.

Efficiency evaluations commonly place costs into categories to identify what is needed to run or support a program (Popham, 1988). For example, one way of looking at costs is to categorize them into fixed and variable costs. Fixed costs (e.g., rent, lights, telephones, and secretarial support) are those that are necessary to open the doors to the first program participant. Such costs are fixed because they do not change regardless of whether one individual accesses the program or the maximum number of individuals do. On the other hand, there will be some costs that will vary depending on the level of program activity or number of program participants. These costs are considered variable costs and include costs such as staff salaries and supplies.

Once the costs associated with running a program have been established, several levels of analysis can be conducted. On one level, evaluators might compare program outcomes to costs. The question is, "Are the program outcomes worth the costs?" This level of analysis requires the evaluator to consider what the outcome would be if the program had not been implemented. For example, say we develop a program to increase the vocational success of students with behavioral disorders transitioning from school to the world of work. Prior to the implementation of the program, approximately 30% of the students were employed one year after graduation and their median income was $8,500. Following the implementation of the program with 50 students at a total cost of $200,000 (includes both fixed and variable costs), we find that 40% of the students were employed one year after graduation and their median income was $8,500. The question in an efficiency evaluation is, "Are the program outcomes worth the costs?" In this case, we are spending $200,000 to improve the vocational outcomes of five students. The results of this efficiency analysis might lead one to judge the program negatively even though it has increased the vocational outcomes achieved by students with behavioral disorders.

HOW IS A PROGRAM EVALUATION CONDUCTED?

The process of conducting a program evaluation, like a research study, can be quite complex. Program evaluations are often emotionally sensitive processes in which many obstacles may (will) be encountered. It is important to keep in mind that many of the key stakeholders may not fully understand the evaluation process and many may be threatened by it. Thus, program evaluators must work closely with the key stakeholders throughout the evaluation process.

Program evaluations typically include four phases: (a) establishing the boundaries of the evaluation; (b) selecting the evaluation methods; (c) collecting and analyzing information; and (d) reporting the findings (Herman, Morris, & Fitz-Gibson, 1987).

Establishing Boundaries

Establishing the boundaries of the evaluation involves determining the purpose of the evaluation (e.g., outcome evaluation) and focusing the evaluation. The program evaluator begins by meeting with key stakeholders to determine what type of evaluation needs to be conducted. This step is crucial because it is not uncommon for the key stakeholders to be unclear about the type of evaluation needed. Once the type of evaluation has been established, the program evaluator must focus the evaluation. Focusing an evaluation involves a number of wide-ranging tasks such as learning about the program through program descriptions and talking with staff and program participants. Focusing an evaluation also involves determining what tasks need to be accomplished, establishing specific objectives for the evaluation, and identifying any potential barriers to conducting the program evaluation (e.g., lack of a control group in an outcome evaluation).

Selecting Evaluation Methods

The next step involves selecting the evaluation methods. This step is much like laying out a research study. Depending on the type of program evaluation, the program evaluator must select the data collection procedures, develop a sampling strategy, and establish how the data will be analyzed. Like a research study, the selection of the evaluation methods is not only dependent on the objectives of the program evaluation but also on constraints associated with the program itself (e.g., monies available to conduct the program evaluation, access to a control group, and organizational arrangements). The program evaluator must be adept at weighing all of the issues and selecting appropriate evaluation methods.

The research methods discussed throughout this text may be useful evaluation methods. Outcome evaluations that are focused only on determining whether program participants improved may rely on preexperimental (e.g., one-shot case study) and qualitative designs. In contrast, outcome evaluations that are centered on determining whether the program participants improved relative to a group of individuals who did not receive services may rely on quasi- (e.g., nonequivalent control group design) and true-experimental (e.g., pretest and posttest control group design) designs. The particular research design used in an outcome evaluation, like in a research study, is dependent on the question being addressed.

Although experimental designs have traditionally been used in outcome evaluations, qualitative methods should not be overlooked. In qualitative program evaluations, the evaluator strives to describe and understand the program or particular aspects of its whole. The evaluator tries to understand the meaning of the program and its outcomes from the participants' perspectives. The emphasis is on detailed descriptions and on in-depth understanding as it emerges from direct contact and experience with the program and its participants. Qualitative outcome evaluations rely on observations, interviews, case studies, and other fieldwork techniques.

Collecting and Analyzing Data

After the evaluation methods have been selected, the program evaluator collects and analyzes the data. The key to efficient data collection and analyses is to establish a time frame for collecting and analyzing the data that is both clear and reasonable. The time frame for data collection must be clear so that program staff and program participants can structure the data collection into their busy days. The time frame for data collection must be reasonable because program staff and participants involved in the evaluation tend to be very busy. Again, the program evaluator must be adept at weighing all of the issues and choosing an appropriate time frame for data collection and analysis.

Reporting of Findings

Finally, the program evaluator must report the findings. Although one might assume that reporting the findings of a program evaluation would be straightforward, this often is not the case. The program evaluator begins by considering the different audiences that will view the findings and deciding what presentation mode is most appropriate (e.g., oral or written and formal or informal). Program evaluators often have to prepare several reports because the findings have to be reported to several different audiences.

Analysis of Data

The analysis of data in program evaluations is the same as the evaluation of data in the other research methods discussed throughout the text. The first step is to determine the type of research method used in the evaluation. Was the method quantitative or qualitative? If the evaluation was quantitative, was the design experimental, quasi-experimental, preexperimental, causal-comparative, or correlational? If the method was qualitative, was the design ethnographic, observation, questionnaire, or case study? Did the evaluation use document analyses? Were surveys used? Once the answers to these questions have been made, critical research consumers should determine the most appropriate method of considering the *internal validity* (if appropriate) and *external validity* (if appropriate). The review forms presented throughout this text can aid in the analysis of a program evaluation.

Evaluation Example

Nelson (1996c) evaluated a violence prevention program for rural K–12 schools. The program evaluation, conducted over a two-year period, included a needs assessment, process evaluation, and outcome evaluation. The program evaluation began with a needs assessment of 59 schools served by a large educational service district (service districts typically provide a range of support and staff development services to schools). The objective of the needs assessment was to identify the types of services that educators had in place, those in need of improvement, and services that needed to be developed. A survey instrument designed to assess service needs was developed and administered to all school staff at each of the 59 schools served by the educational service district. The results of the survey revealed that respondents believed that there was a need for school-based programs to enhance the social problem-solving skills of students and the involvement of their parents.

Based on the results of the needs assessment, a violence prevention program was developed by the educational service district. The program incorporated three components: schoolwide teaching of conflict resolution skills, enhanced social problem-solving sessions for at-risk clusters (students not responding to the schoolwide teaching of conflict resolution skills), and a parent involvement program. These three components were implemented and evaluated over the academic year. Process and outcome evaluations were conducted.

The overall goal of the process and outcome evaluations was to refine the violence prevention program. That is, the evaluations were formative in nature, providing information with which to refine the program. The primary goal of the process evaluation was to identify potential barriers to the implementation of each of the components. The primary goal of the outcome evaluation was to assess whether the program had positive effects on the social behaviors of students.

The results of the process evaluation revealed that scheduling conflicts made it difficult to establish the at-risk clusters. The results of the process evaluation also revealed that the parent involvement program was not attracting a wide range of parents. Consistent with the results of the process evaluation, the outcome evaluation showed that the program was having a limited effect on the social behavior of students.

WHEN SHOULD PROGRAM EVALUATIONS BE CONDUCTED?

Program evaluations will continue to be used and most likely will become more important in the current context of dwindling resources. Such activities are undertaken to help plan and refine programs, to assess their effectiveness, and to make changes in ongoing services. Unlike other research methods that may develop from a researcher's interest in a phenomenon, program evaluations usually result from a specific need of a program. For example, federal granting agencies require an evaluation section that describes how the project will be evaluated. Universities and programs within universities have evaluations of their programs. You will most likely be involved in one of these evaluations either during your studies at your university/college or once you graduate. Therefore, program evaluations will result out of a need to determine the effectiveness of a program. They serve a specific purpose and are used to help meet the current and future needs of those receiving services from programs.

DISCUSSION QUESTIONS

1. You are talking with your parents and they tell you that they read about a survey that indicated that college students get drunk about once per week during their first two years in school. They tell you that they are concerned about your drinking habits since you likely were drinking too much. How would you respond based on what you know about how surveys are constructed, administered, and interpreted?
2. After you respond to your parents in Question 1, they become more interested in the types of surveys. Describe the types of surveys one can use along with the advantages and disadvantages of each.
3. You are in a cooperative learning group for a research laboratory and your group's goal is to develop and administer a survey to first-year college students. Describe what your sampling frame is going to be.
4. From Question 3, how would you go about developing questions?
5. You read an editorial in your local paper that says that the world would be much better off if people knew more about the past. The author claimed that history can guide us in the future. Based on what you know in terms of the purposes of historical research, is the author correct? Why or why not?
6. Another student tells you that she would like to conduct research on how reading instruction has changed over the past 40 years. She tells you that she is unsure of how to gather the needed data. Explain to the student the different data collection methods.
7. You overhear two students from an education class discussing an article they had to read for class. The article was an historical one examining the development of multicultural education in the United States. The students were unsure of how to determine the believability of the author's conclusions. Describe to the students how they can analyze historical data to make this determination.
8. You are working for an early childhood program that has not been evaluated. Your supervisor, knowing that you are studying research

methods, asks you if you believe that the program should be evaluated. Indicate to the supervisor the objectives of program evaluations.

9. When you finish telling your supervisor in Question 8 the objectives of program evaluations, he asks you how program evaluations are done. Briefly explain to the supervisor the types of program evaluations.

10. Finally, the supervisor asks you how one conducts a program evaluation. Describe to your supervisor the steps to conducting a program evaluation.

FACULTY WILLINGNESS TO ACCOMMODATE STUDENTS WITH LEARNING DISABILITIES: A COMPARISON AMONG ACADEMIC DIVISIONS

J. RON NELSON, JOHN M. DODD, AND DEBORAH J. SMITH

One hundred seven faculty members at a northwestern college responded to a questionnaire devised to assess faculty willingness to provide students with learning disabilities instructional, assignment, examination, and special assistance accommodations. Faculty responses to the questionnaire were analyzed to determine if differences existed among faculty in the colleges of Education, Business, and Arts and Sciences. Results indicate that, in general, faculty were willing to provide students with learning disabilities accommodations, but that differences exist among the three academic divisions as to faculty willingness to provide students accommodations. The implications of these results for colleges and universities and future research are discussed.

Some students with learning disabilities (LD) pursue postsecondary education in traditional 4-year higher education institutions (ACLD Vocational Committee, 1982; Barbaro, 1982; Bireley & Maneley, 1980; Cordoni, 1978; Miller, McKinley, & Ryan, 1979; Siegel, 1979). For example, in a university learning disabilities program, Miller et al. (1979) identified 2 graduate students and 1 undergraduate student with learning disabilities; Bireley and Maneley (1980) identified 3 students with learning disabilities; and Barbaro (1982) identified 22 students with learning disabilities who had enrolled in a special 3-week diagnostic session prior to their enrollment in college. In a survey of adults with learning disabilities conducted by the Association for Children and Adults with Learning Disabilities (ACLD) Adult Vocational Committee (1982), 14% reported they had tried college and dropped out, 32% were currently attending college, and another 9% reported that they had completed their bachelor's degree.

College officials have developed an increasing number of support programs in response to the influx of students with learning disabilities on college campuses (Mangrum & Strichart, 1983). Mangrum and Strichart (1984) suggested that there are four factors associated with the increasing number of support services. First, the development of services at the college level is a logical outgrowth from the services provided to students with learning disabilities in elementary schools and, later, in junior and senior high schools. Second, the Adult Committee of ACLD and other national and local organizations have campaigned actively to convince college and university personnel to develop programs to assist these students on college campuses. Such lobbying efforts, combined with the students' interest in attending college, has brought pressure on colleges to develop programs for students with learning disabilities. Finally, many colleges face declining student enrollment, and students with learning disabilities, with the potential for college success, represent a source of new enrollments.

Experts in the field of learning disabilities have recommended that postsecondary programs for students with LD should include (a) personal or social, academic or program, or career or vocational counseling; (b) instructional accommodations provided by the institution or by individual faculty; and (c) administrative accommodations (Cordoni, 1982; Decker, Polloway, & Decker, 1985; Mangrum & Strichart, 1983; Vogel, 1982). For example, Decker et al. (1985) proposed that a comprehensive program to accommodate students with learning disabilities should include: (a) assessment procedures to identify and evaluate the individual needs of the student, (b) special admission policies, (c) a variety of support services, and (d) faculty that are trained and informed about the needs of students with LD.

In one survey, college and university officials at 121 postsecondary institutions reported that they provided services to students with learning disabilities (Cordoni, 1980). However, Cordoni reported that college officials at 14 of the 121 institutions surveyed provided students little beyond basic tutorial services. In addition to the reported lack of comprehensive programs for students with LD, there is little evidence that faculty are modifying their instructional practices to accommodate them (Barbaro, 1982).

Experts in the field of learning disabilities have suggested instructional alternatives that faculty may use to accommodate students with learning disabilities in their classes (Blackburn & Iovacchini, 1982; Brown, 1981; Hoy & Gregg, 1986; Ingram & Dettenmaier, 1987; Michael, 1987; Patton & Polloway, 1982; Vandivier & Vandivier, 1978; Vogel, 1982; Vogel & Sattler, 1981; Wiig, 1972; Yanok, 1987). For example, Vogel and Sattler (1981) suggested that faculty provide students the following 12 accommodations: (1) untimed tests; (2) readers for objective exams; (3) essay exams instead of objective exams; (4) taking exams in a separate room with a proctor; (5) allowing students to clarify questions and rephrase them in their own words as a comprehension check before answering exam questions; (6) oral, taped, or typed responses to exams instead of written responses; (7) allowing alternative methods of demonstrating mastery of course objectives; (8) avoiding double negatives, unduly complex sentence structure, and questions embedded within questions; (9) providing students alternatives to computer-scored answer sheets; (10) providing adequate paper (e.g., lined paper) to aid students with poor handwriting skills; (11) analyzing the process as well as the final solution (e.g., math computations); and (12) allowing students to use a multiplication table, calculator, and desk references for their examinations.

Critical to the types of instructional accommodations provided is the willingness of faculty to provide the accommodations in their classroom. This is a crucial factor, since individual faculty members control whether or not students are provided instructional accommodations. Authors of only one study have investigated faculty willingness to provide students with learning disabilities instructional accommodations. Matthew, Anderson, and Skolnick (1987) surveyed all the faculty at a northeastern public university to identify the accommodations that faculty were willing to provide to students. With 100 (64%) of the faculty responding, Matthew et al. (1987) found that a majority of faculty were willing to provide students with LD instructional accommodations (e.g., tape-recorded lectures, copies of lecture notes), assignment and examination accommodations (e.g., alternative assignments and testing procedures), and special assistance (e.g., proofreaders and notetakers). However, Matthew et al. did not investigate if there were differences among academic divisions in faculty willingness to provide students with instructional accommodations.

The purpose of this study was to investigate if there were differences among academic divisions in faculty willingness to provide students with learning disabilities instructional accommodations in traditional 4-year institutions.

METHOD

Respondents

Questionnaires were sent to each of the 141 teaching faculty in the academic divisions of Arts and Sciences, Education, and Business at a northwestern college. The respondents included faculty from the schools of Arts and Sciences (57, representing a return of 69%), Education (27, representing a return of 69.2%), and Business (19, representing a return of 85%), and an additional 4 faculty who had removed all identifying information regarding their academic division.

Questionnaire

The 23-item questionnaire used in this study was adapted from one used in prior research by Matthew et al. (1987) to assess faculty's willingness to provide students with learning disabilities both instructional accommodations and procedural accommodations in higher education.

Only those questions that pertained to faculty's willingness to provide students instructional accommodations were retained. The 18 questions were divided into the following four categories: (a) instructional modifications, (b) assignment modifications, (c) examination modifications, and (d) special assistance (see Table 1). For each question, respondents indicated whether they "would" or "would not" provide students with learning disabilities the designated accommodation. In addition, respondents were provided the opportunity to provide comments.

Procedure

Each respondent was sent a questionnaire with a cover letter that explained that their responses would be kept on file in the campus Student Opportunity Office so that office staff could advise students with learning disabilities regarding the types of instructional accommodations that individual faculty were willing to make in their classrooms. In addition, the letter indicated that faculty's names would be removed and only their responses would be used in the present study. Respondents were allowed 2 weeks to complete and return the questionnaire. If questionnaires were not returned, a second letter and a copy of the first mailing were sent to the faculty who had not responded. The second letter indicated that a majority of the faculty members had responded and said that another questionnaire was included, in case they had overlooked or misplaced the original.

When the questionnaires were returned, the office staff of the Student Opportunity Office recorded each faculty's responses. Next, faculty names were removed and their responses were tallied by schools. When there were qualifying notes, the responses were considered positive as long as they indicated willingness to provide students with learning disabilities the particular accommodation.

Methods of Analysis

A descriptive item analysis was conducted regarding the frequency of positive responses (see Table 1). Next, a one-way analysis of variance (ANOVA) was conducted among academic divisions. The independent variables consisted of the academic divisions (Group 1, College of Education; Group 2, College of Business; Group 3, College of Arts and Sciences). Accommodations were measured by a dichotomous variable: would make accommodations (a score of 1), and would not make accommodations (a score of 0). Furthermore, items were collapsed into the following four categories for analysis: (a) instructional accommodations (Items 1 to 2), (b) assignment accommodations (Items 3 to 7), (c) examination accommodations (Items 8 to 15), and (d) special assistance (Items 16 to 18). In addition, *t* tests were computed between the means for each of the individual colleges. A correlation ratio (ETA squared) was computed for each of the

TABLE 1 Questionnaire and Frequency of Positive Responses

This questionnaire is attempting to identify educational accommodations faculty are willing to make for learning disabled students in their classrooms. How would you respond to a student in your class if they requested any of the following educational accommodations? Place an "X" in the first column for each accommodation you would make and in the second column if you would not make the accommodation.

Note: All scores are expressed as percentages.

	EDUCATION (*n* = 19)	BUSINESS (*n* = 27)	ARTS AND SCIENCES (*n* = 57)	TOTAL (*N* = 107)
Instructional Accommodations				
1. Allow the student to tape-record classroom lectures.	100.0	100.0	94.6	98.66
2. Provide the student with copies of instructor's lecture notes after they attend the lecture.	67.9	57.9	42.9	56.23
Assignment Accommodations				
3. Extend deadlines for completion of class projects, papers, etc.	89.3	15.8	58.9	71.70
4. Allow the student to complete alternative assignments.	85.7	15.8	58.9	50.13
5. Allow the student to do extra credit assignments when this option is not available to other students.	39.3	26.3	32.1	32.56
6. Provide the student with a detailed syllabus to give ample time to complete reading and writing assignments.	85.7	78.9	80.4	81.66
7. Allow the student to give oral presentations or tape-record assignments rather than complete written projects.	75.0	57.9	69.6	67.50
Examination Accommodations				
8. Allow the student to take an alternative form of your exams. (For example, some students have trouble taking tests using computer-scored answer sheets. Others might do better on multiple choice tests than on essay tests.)	57.1	47.4	57.1	53.80
9. Allow a proctor to rephrase test questions that are not clear to the student. (For example, a double negative may need to be clarified.)	75.0	62.6	67.9	65.16
10. Allow the student extra time to complete tests.	96.4	78.9	80.4	85.23
11. Allow the student to dictate answers to a proctor.	92.9	84.2	82.1	86.40
12. Allow the student to respond orally to essay questions.	85.7	73.7	76.8	78.70
13. Analyze the process as well as the final solution. (For example, giving the student partial credit if the correct mathematical computation was used although the final answer was wrong.)	60.7	78.9	80.4	73.33

(continued)

TABLE 1 Continued

	EDUCATION (*n* = 19)	BUSINESS (*n* = 27)	ARTS AND SCIENCES (*n* = 57)	TOTAL (*N* = 107)
Examination Accommodations continued				
14. Allow the student to use basic calculators during tests.	82.1	84.2	64.3	76.86
15. Allow misspellings, incorrect punctuation, and poor grammar, without penalizing the student.	74.1	21.1	48.2	46.90
Special Assistance				
16. Allow the use of proofreaders to assist in the correction of grammar and punctuation.	100.0	78.9	75.0	94.63
17. Allow the use of proofreaders to assist in the reconstruction of the student's first draft of a written assignment.	96.4	84.2	71.4	83.93
18. Allow the use of a proofreader to assist the student in the substitution of higher level vocabulary for the original wording.	82.1	68.4	51.8	67.45

four types of instructional accommodations, to provide a measure of the strength of the association (effect size) between the dependent variable (faculty responses on the questionnaire) and independent variables (academic divisions) (Cohen & Cohen, 1983). All computations were conducted using the Statistical Package for the Social Sciences (Nie, Hull, Jenkins, Steinbrenner, & Brent, 1975).

RESULTS

The frequency of positive responses for all 18 survey items is presented in Table 1. The accommodations that faculty were willing to provide to students with learning disabilities were organized into four categories. The first category (Items 1 to 2) included instructional accommodations, the second category (Items 3 to 7) included assignment accommodations, the third category (Items 8 to 15) included examination accommodations, and the last category (Items 16 to 18) included special assistance accommodations.

Of the 141 faculty surveyed, 107 responded, representing a return of 75.8%. At least 50% of the faculty responding would provide students 16 (88%) of the 18 accommodations, while less than 50% of the faculty would provide students the two remaining accommodations (Items 5 and 15). However, of the 16 accommodations, there were accommodations that fewer faculty were willing to provide students. For example, 50.1% of the faculty responding were willing to allow students alternative assignments (Item 4), 56.2% were willing to provide students copies of their lecture notes (Item 2), 67.5% would allow students to turn in tape-recorded assignments rather than complete written assignments (Item 7), and 67.4% would allow students the use of a proofreader (Item 10). Inspection of the results suggests that, overall, faculty were willing to provide accommodations to students with learning disabilities. Furthermore, these results support those reported in prior research (Matthew et al., 1987) (see Table 1).

The College of Education faculty responded more positively to all items, as compared to the faculty of the colleges of Business and Arts and Sciences. There was also a general consistency within colleges across items. However, some items did vary across academic divisions. For example, 85.7% of Education faculty were willing to provide students assignments in advance (Item 6), while only 15.8% of Business faculty were willing to provide students the same accommodation. In addition, 71.4% of Education faculty reported that they were willing to allow misspellings, incorrect punctuation, and poor grammar on examinations (Item 15), as compared to 21.5% of Business faculty and 40.2% of the Arts and Sciences faculty. The result of the ANOVA, college by instructional accommodations (Items 1 to 2), was statistically significant $F(2, 100) = 3.154$, $p < .05$. In addition, comparison of means for the colleges of Education and Arts and Sciences was significant, $t(76) = 2.285$, $p < .05$. However, comparisons between means for the colleges of Education and Business and the colleges of Business and Arts and Sciences were not significant. Furthermore, the effect size computed, ETA squared, was .059.

The result of the ANOVA, college by assignment accommodations (Items 3 to 7), was statistically significant, $F(2, 100) = 12.915$, $p < .05$. The difference between the means for the colleges of Education and Business was significant, $t(44) = 5.601$, $p < .05$. Similarly, the difference between the means for the colleges of Education and Arts and Sciences was significant, $t(76) = 2{,}952$, $p < .05$. Furthermore, the difference between means for the colleges of Business and Arts and Sciences was significant, $t(82) = 3.437$, $p < .05$. In addition, ETA squared was .205.

Similarly, the ANOVA, college by examination accommodations (Items 8 to 15), was statistically significant $F(2, 100) = 3.973$, $p < .05$. Furthermore, comparisons between the means for the colleges of Education and Business, $t(44) = 3.437$, $p < .05$, and the colleges of Education and Arts and Sciences, $t(82) = 2.312$, $p < .05$, were significant, while the comparison of the means between the colleges of Business and Arts and Sciences was not significant. Additionally, the computed effect size, ETA squared, was .074.

The result of the ANOVA, college by special assistance (Items 16 to 18), was statistically significant, $F(2, 100) = 11.264$, $p < .05$. Comparison between the means for the colleges of Education and Business was significant, $t(44) = 3.218$, $p < .05$. Similarly, the comparison between the means for the colleges of Education and Arts and Sciences was significant, $t(74) = 5.35$, $p < .05$. However, the difference between the means for the colleges of Business and Arts and Sciences was not significant. The effect size, ETA squared, was .184.

DISCUSSION

Generally, it would appear that faculty are willing to accommodate students with learning disabilities in higher education, although close examination of the ratings suggests that there are certain accommodations that faculty are not as willing to provide to students. For example, faculty were less willing to provide students exclusive extra credit assignments, alternative assignments, and copies of lecture notes. In addition, faculty reported that they were not as willing to allow students to turn in tape-recorded assignments rather than written assignments, or to allow students the use of a proofreader. These results confirm previous research reported by Matthew et al. (1987).

The comments section of the questionnaire provided a variety of responses (87% of the respondents included comments). First, although faculty were willing to accommodate students with learning disabilities, they were concerned about maintaining academic integrity. For instance, several faculty members indicated that they would be willing to make accommodations for students with LD only if they could be assured that it would not lower academic standards. Second, a number of faculty indicated that they would be interested in learning new methods to help them meet the needs of students with LD, while still maintaining academic excellence. Third, some faculty commented that each student's case would have to be treated on an individual basis. Finally, faculty indicated that the student's attitude would influence whether or not they would provide him or her accommodations.

There appears to be little research reported in the literature regarding faculty willingness to provide accommodations in higher education to students with learning disabilities. The present study confirms and extends prior research by Matthew et al. (1987), who also found that faculty were willing to provide students accommodations. However, there appear to be differences among faculty across different academic divisions in their willingness to provide accommodations to students with LD. In all four categories of accommodations (instructional, assignment, examination, and special assistance) there were significant differences among the colleges of Education, Business, and Arts and Sciences. In addition, effect sizes were computed to provide an estimate of the magnitude of the relationship (effect size) between academic division (independent variable) and the responses on the questionnaire (dependent variable). These results ranged from .059 to .209 and indicate that, although they are moderate, there are differences among colleges.

Of course, these results must be viewed tentatively. Neither the validity nor the reliability of the questionnaire was assessed. Also, due to the confidentiality issue, demographic data were not available for the sample. As a result, inferences beyond this sample must be made cautiously.

Based on the results of this study, there is a need to replicate faculty attitudes on a nationwide basis with a variety of public and private higher education institutions. Faculty attitude regarding students with learning disabilities in higher education will influence future research in this area. In addition, researchers must begin to address the types of accommodations that will help students with learning disabilities access higher education while still maintaining academic excellence. Furthermore, college officials must provide coordinated services to students with LD to facilitate their success in higher education. Finally, college administrators must provide faculty training regarding the capabilities and special needs of students with learning disabilities.

ABOUT THE AUTHORS

J. Ron Nelson is a doctoral candidate, Department of Special Education, Utah State University. His current interests include programming for the needs of adolescents and adults with learning disabilities. John M. Dodd, Ed.D., is associate professor, Institute for Habilitative Services, Eastern Montana College. His current interests include programming for Hispanics and adults with learning disabilities. Deborah J. Smith, Ph.D., is visiting assistant professor, Department of Education, Special Education Section, Purdue University. Her current interests include self-management training for students with handicaps. Address: J. Ron Nelson, Department of Special Education, Utah State University, Logan, UT 84321.

AUTHORS' NOTE

We gratefully acknowledge Ester Peralz for her assistance in the data collection and Ben Lignugaris/Kraft and three anonymous reviewers for comments on a draft of this article.

REFERENCES

ACLD Vocational Committee. (1982). Preliminary report of the ACLD Vocational Committee survey of LD adults. *ACLD Newsbriefs, 145,* 20–23.

Barbaro, F. (1982). The learning disabled college student: Some consideration in setting objectives. *Journal of Learning Disabilities, 15,* 599–603.

Bireley, M., & Maneley, E. (1980). The learning disabled student in a college environment: A report of Wright State University's program. *Journal of Learning Disabilities, 13,* 12–15.

Blackburn, J. C., & Iovacchini, E. V. (1982). Student service responsibilities of institutions to learning disabled students. *College and University, 52,* 208–217.

Brown, D. (1981). *Counseling and accommodating the student with learning disabilities.* (Report No. ED 141556). Washington, DC: President's Committee on Employment of the Handicapped. (ERIC Document Reproduction Service No. ED 214 338)

Cohen, J., & Cohen, P. (1983). *Applied multiple regression/correlation analysis for the behavioral sciences* (2nd ed.). London: Erlbaum.

Cordoni, B. (1978). Assisting dyslexic college students. An experimental program design at a university. *Bulletin of the Orton Society, 29,* 263–268.

Cordoni, B. K. (1980). Learning disabilities: An audio journal of continuing education. In M. Gottlieb &

J. Bradford (Eds)., *College options for the learning disabled.* New York: Grune & Stratton.

Cordoni, B. K. (1982). Secondary education: Where do we go from here? *Journal of Learning Disabilities, 15,* 265–266.

Decker, T., Polloway, E., & Decker, B. (1985). Help for the LD college student. *Academic Therapy, 20,* 339–345.

Hoy, C, & Gregg, N. (1986, Summer). Learning disabled students: An emerging population on college campuses. *The Journal of Admissions,* 10–14.

Ingram, G. F., & Dettenmaier, L. (1987). LD college students and reading problems. *Academic Therapy, 22,* 513–519.

Mangrum, C. T., & Strichart, S. S. (1983). College possibilities for the learning disabled: Part two. *Learning Disabilities Focus, 2,* 69–81.

Mangrum, C. T., & Strichart, S. S. (1984). *College and the learning disabled student: A guide to program selection, development, and implementation.* Orlando, FL: Grune & Stratton.

Matthew, P., Anderson, D., & Skolnick, B. (1987). Faculty attitude toward accommodations for college students with learning disabilities. *Learning Disabilities Focus, 3,* 46–52.

Michael, R. J. (1987). Evaluating the college of choice. *Academic Therapy, 22,* 485–488.

Miller, C. D., McKinley, D. L., & Ryan, M. (1979). College students: Learning disabilities and services. *The Personnel and Guidance Journal, 58,* 154–158.

Nie, N. H., Hull, C. H., Jenkins, J. G., Steinbrenner, K., & Brent, D. H. (1975). *Statistical package for the social sciences* (2nd ed.). New York: McGraw-Hill.

Patton, J. R., & Polloway, E. A. (1982). The learning disabled: The adult years. *Learning Disability Quarterly, 2,* 5–16.

Siegel, D. (1979). Help for learning disabled college students. *American Education, 15,* 17–21.

Vandivier, P. L., & Vandivier, S. S. (1978). The latent learning in college. *Improving College and University Teaching, 26,* 211–212.

Vogel, S. A. (1982). On developing LD college programs. *Journal of Learning Disabilities, 15,* 518–528.

Vogel, S. A., & Sattler, J. L. (1981). *The college student with a learning disability: A handbook for college and university admissions officers, faculty, and administration.* DeKalb: Illinois Council for Learning Disabilities.

Wiig, E. (1972). The emerging LD crisis. *Journal of Rehabilitation, 38,* 15–17.

Yanok, J. (1987). Transforming developmental education for learning disabled students. *College and University, 63,* 70–79.

FACTUAL QUESTIONS

1. What was the purpose of the study?
2. Who were the respondents?
3. What was the rate of return?
4. How were respondents surveyed (specific procedures)?
5. What types of questions were included in the survey?
6. What response format was used?
7. What type of data analysis techniques were used?
8. What were the findings?
9. What conclusions did the authors make?
10. What did the study add to the literature?

DISCUSSION QUESTIONS

1. How did this study add to the literature on faculty willingness to accommodate college students with learning disabilities?
2. Of what population was the sample of respondents representative?
3. What type of sampling procedures would you use to obtain a representative sample of faculty members?
4. Did the authors provide enough information with which to judge the quality of the questionnaire? Why?
5. Do you think information on the quality of the questionnaire is critical to accepting the results of the study? Why?
6. Was the rate of return acceptable? Why?

7. Did the analysis procedures used by the authors address the purpose of the research?
8. Why did the authors compute effect sizes (presented in the discussion section)?
9. Were the conclusions of the authors consistent with the results?
10. Did the authors address all of the limitations to the study? What other limitations would you include?

THREATS TO SURVEY VALIDITY

Internal Validity

1. **Were the survey questions adequate in obtaining the information needed by the researchers?** **YES NO ?**

   Justification ____

   ____.

2. **Was the survey pilot-tested?** **YES NO ?**

   Justification ____

   ____.

3. **Did the authors indicate that modifications were made based on the pilot results?** **YES NO ?**

   Justification ____

   ____.

4. **Did the pilot participants represent the respondents?** **YES NO ?**

   Justification ____

   ____.

5. **Were there alternative explanations for the results?** **YES NO ?**

   Justification ____

   ____.

Abstract: Write a one-page abstract summarizing the overall conclusions of the authors and whether you feel the authors' conclusions are valid based on the internal validity of the investigation.

External Validity

1. **What type of sampling frame was used? Exhaustive? Convenience? Cluster?**

2. **Was the sampling approach used by researchers probabilistic? YES NO ?**

   Justification ____

   ____.

3. **Were the respondents described? YES NO ?**

   Justification ____

   ____.

4. **Was the sample representative of the target population? YES NO ?**

   Justification ____

   ____.

Abstract: Write a one-page abstract summarizing the overall conclusions of the authors and whether you feel the authors' conclusions are valid based on the external validity of the investigation.

Chapter 14

CONDUCTING RESEARCH SYNTHESES

OBJECTIVES

After studying this chapter you should be able to:

1. Describe the two key roles research syntheses play in research.
2. Describe the four primary purposes of research syntheses.
3. Describe the difference between unsystematic and systematic research syntheses.
4. Describe the considerations for conducting research syntheses.
5. Describe how to formulate precise research questions to guide research syntheses.
6. Describe how to define the critical terms used in research syntheses.
7. Describe how to formulate a literature search framework.
8. Describe how to search the literature.
9. Describe how to code study characteristics.
10. Describe procedures to determine the magnitude of intervention outcomes.
11. Describe how to relate study characteristics to intervention outcomes.
12. Describe how to report the results of research syntheses.
13. Describe factors that affect the validity of research syntheses.
14. Describe when one would conduct a research synthesis.
15. Critique a research article containing a research synthesis.

OVERVIEW

We have described the procedures for conducting qualitative and quantitative research throughout this book. These research methods are designed to derive new facts and findings regarding phenomena of interest. In contrast, a research synthesis is a process in which previous facts and findings are analyzed, sifted, classified, simplified, and synthesized to draw conclusions (Educational Resources Information Center, 1982). Research synthesis plays a key role in the process of designing any new study. Although the details of research synthesis may vary across experimental methodologies, all new investigations should build on existing knowledge. The underlying assumption of all research is that new studies will incorporate and improve on the findings of earlier work. Research synthesis helps ensure that new research is a cumulative process rather than simply an exploratory one.

Another key role of research synthesis is to enable researchers and other professionals such as policy makers to survey the literature to understand some phenomena more fully. Questions such as,

"What is known about a problem or issue? What attempts have been made to rectify it? How effective were these attempts? What factors influenced the effectiveness of the attempts? Should new promising attempts be made? Should different outcome measures, research designs, and analysis procedures be used?" require a thorough review of the literature or research synthesis. We focus on the research synthesis aspect of reviewing research in this chapter. An illustrative investigation is included at the end of the chapter for critique.

WHAT ARE THE PURPOSES OF RESEARCH SYNTHESES?

Research syntheses involve pulling together the facts and findings from a group of related studies that are based on different (a) theoretical frameworks, (b) independent variables, (c) dependent measures, (d) research designs, and (e) data analysis procedures. The role that research syntheses play in the accumulation of knowledge is important, particularly as the number of specialties in the social sciences increases. Research syntheses involve a broad array of procedures to identify the consistencies and inconsistencies in a group of related research studies. These syntheses integrate research findings for the following four purposes: (a) establishing cause-and-effect relationships; (b) determining the degree of relationship between two variables; (c) developing theories; and (d) assessing the external validity of findings. Each of these purposes will be described in more detail.

Establishing Cause-and-Effect Relationships

The first purpose of research syntheses is to establish cause-and-effect relationships between variables. Research syntheses can also be used to identify causal relationships between variables. If most of the research studies included in the research synthesis have high internal validity, researchers can confidently address whether there is a causal relationship between variables. On the other hand, if most of the research studies included in the research synthesis have low internal validity, researchers are unable to address whether there is a causal relationship between variables with confidence. One of the problems researchers have in conducting a research synthesis is that the degree of confidence that can be placed in a causal inference is dependent on the characteristics of the reviewed studies. In other words, the extent to which we can establish a causal relationship between variables with a research synthesis is established by the underlying research studies. For example, Rosenshine and Meister (1994) conducted a research synthesis to determine whether reciprocal teaching enhanced the comprehension of students. Reciprocal teaching is an instructional procedure that relies on dialogue between the teacher and student to teach students cognitive strategies such as summarization, question generation, clarification, and prediction. The results indicated that reciprocal teaching appears to be an effective instructional approach that teachers can use to improve the comprehension of students.

Determining the Degree of Relationship between Two Variables

The second purpose of research syntheses is to determine the degree of relationship between two variables. Recall that much research in education and psychology is based on research methods that are aimed at identifying relationships between two variables. A research synthesis can be used to bring together all of the studies that have been conducted and to identify the degree of relationship between two variables. Hattie and Marsh (1996) conducted a research synthesis to determine the degree of relationship between research and teaching in universities. The analysis of 58 studies revealed that the relationship between research and teaching was zero, meaning that faculty who do research are not necessarily good teachers and faculty who do not do research are not necessarily poor teachers.

Developing Theories

The third purpose for research syntheses is to develop and confirm theories. Research syntheses can aggregate findings from a number of studies to test theoretical relationships that could be rarely tested with a primary research study. Research syntheses can bring together and test a variety of alternative hypotheses, providing a broader basis from which to develop or confirm theoretical frameworks. Alexander, Kulikowich, and Jetton (1996) conducted a research synthesis of 66 studies to examine the role of subject-matter knowledge and interest in the processing of linear and nonlinear information. It is believed that subject-matter knowledge differentially influences the processing of linear and nonlinear information. That is, linear and nonlinear processing are specific to a particular subject of study. Although Alexander and colleagues (1996) did not identify a clear theoretical model, they provided six theoretical premises for researchers to explore in future research.

Assessing the External Validity of Findings

The final purpose for research syntheses is to assess the extent to which the findings from research can be generalized to a larger set of participants, experimental procedures, and situations beyond those of the original research studies. Research syntheses can address the extent to which the results can be generalized much better than any one individual study. Research syntheses can also provide a sense of the external validity of some effect by analyzing the findings from a number of studies. All research syntheses by design are used to explore the generalization of findings.

WHAT ARE SYSTEMATIC AND UNSYSTEMATIC RESEARCH SYNTHESES?

Research syntheses can be organized into two categories: unsystematic and systematic.

Unsystematic Research Syntheses

Traditionally, research syntheses have been unsystematic and subjective in nature. Few, if any, formal procedures and practices were used by researchers to review the literature. Often, the research synthesis raised more issues than it resolved. Unsystematic research syntheses tend to be less scientifically oriented because no formal guidelines are used to guide the review. They are typically based on a restrictive sample of studies, including the use of somewhat haphazard strategies for reviewing the research. Further, researchers tend to rely heavily on their own judgment to guide the review. In short, unsystematic research syntheses tend to be inefficient for integrating the findings of a group of related research studies that may differ greatly with regard to participants, independent and dependent variables, and experimental situations. Often, such reviews are not conducted to create research generalizations but to articulate an author's particular position on an issue.

Systematic Research Syntheses

In contrast, systematic research syntheses parallel the methodologies used in original research studies in that researchers conducting research syntheses use a set of standard procedures to guide their efforts. In this way, the procedures used are much more systematic in nature. Indeed, the research synthesis process has taken a quantum leap forward since the 1970s when Glass (1976) not only coined the term "meta-analysis" (i.e., statistical analysis and integration of the findings from an exhaustive collection of the results from primary research studies), but also established procedures for conducting systematic research syntheses. Since that time there have been several detailed conceptualizations of how to conduct systematic research syntheses (e.g., Cooper, 1989; Glass, McGaw, & Smith, 1981; Hedges & Olkin, 1985; Light & Pillemer, 1984; Rosenthal, 1984).

Systematic research syntheses differ from unsystematic ones in that researchers use a set of agreed-upon procedures and practices to review the literature. Although the procedures may vary (e.g., narrative rather than quantitative), systematic research syntheses essentially include the (a) formulation of a research question or questions; (b) specification of the procedures used to select the research studies; (c) enumeration of the study characteristics examined (e.g., research design, participants, independent variables); (d) description of the procedures used to analyze the results of the research studies; and (e) neutral representation of the results.

Comparison of Unsystematic and Systematic Research Syntheses

Although one may assume that systematic research syntheses are quantitative in nature whereas unsystematic research syntheses are qualitative in nature, this is not necessarily the case. Rather, systematic research syntheses simply involve the use of specified procedures and practices for conducting the research synthesis. The use of statistical analysis procedures only represents a particular methodology (i.e., meta-analysis) for integrating the results of research studies. Table 14.1 summarizes the similarities and differences between unsystematic and systematic research syntheses. The first column represents some of the key characteristics of the two types of research syntheses; the second and third columns depict the similarities and differences between the two.

Further inspection of Table 14.1 shows that unsystematic and systematic research syntheses typically differ on only two characteristics. The coverage of the research studies is the first characteristic where differences are noted. Systematic research syntheses tend to be exhaustive in the coverage of the research literature or, if they are not, they clearly specify the procedures for including and excluding research studies. In contrast, unsystematic research syntheses are not exhaustive and may not specify the selection procedures. The second characteristic where differences are noted between the two approaches is the stance taken by the researchers. Researchers conducting systematic research syntheses tend to take a nonjudgmental stance, whereas those conducting unsystematic research syntheses tend to take a particular position.

TABLE 14.1 Comparison of Unsystematic and Systematic Research Syntheses

CHARACTERISTIC	UNSYSTEMATIC	SYSTEMATIC
Focus	Identification of results Identification of methods Identification of practices Identification of theories	Identification of results Identification of methods Identification of practices Identification of theories
Goal	Integration of results Generalization of results Resolution of conflicts Identification of central issues	Integration of results Generalization of results Resolution of conflicts Identification of central issues
Perspective	Judgmental	Nonjudgmental
Coverage	Selected	Exhaustive Selected with identified criteria Representative
Organization	Historical Conceptual Methodological Practices	Historical Conceptual Methodological Practices
Audience	Area-related scholars General scholars Practitioners Policy makers General public	Area-related scholars General scholars Practitioners Policy makers General public

WHAT ARE THE CONSIDERATIONS FOR CONDUCTING RESEARCH SYNTHESES?

Planning and carrying out research syntheses require several considerations. These include (a) identifying primary sources, (b) identifying secondary sources, (c) overcoming selection biases, and (d) focusing the literature search.

Identifying Primary Sources

Research may be found in primary sources. Primary sources are what typically come to mind when one thinks about conducting a research synthesis and include descriptions of actual studies that are published in professional journals. Dissertations and theses as well as government reports, foundation reports, and papers from scholarly meetings or conferences are also considered primary sources. "Fugitive" literature (i.e., reports of research not published in professionally recognized journals) is also regarded as a primary source. Table 14.2 presents the types of fugitive literature and associated descriptions. Although researchers conducting a research synthesis primarily use secondary sources (described in what follows) to identify studies, the references of primary sources can be used to identify other relevant studies to include in the paper (often called an ancestral search).

Identifying Secondary Sources

Research may also be found in secondary sources. Secondary sources cite, review, and organize the material from primary studies; that is, secondary sources are "once removed" from the actual research investigations. Secondary sources are used by researchers to find primary sources. Secondary sources include (a) review journals (e.g., *Review of Educational Research, Sociology Review,* and *Psychological Bulletin*); (b) periodical reviews (e.g., *Encyclopedia of Educational Research*); and (c) bibliographic services or abstract and citation archives (e.g., *Child Development Abstracts and Bibliography, Current Index to Journals in Education, Research in Education,* and *Psychological Abstracts*). These bibliographic services are computerized and enable researchers to conduct efficient syntheses. The use of technology has greatly improved the efficiency of searching the literature; it was not long ago that researchers would have to conduct searches of the literature by hand.

TABLE 14.2 Types of Fugitive Literature

TYPE	DESCRIPTION
Dissertations, theses, and course papers	• Includes doctoral dissertations, master's theses, honors theses, and research studies completed for a course.
Paper presentations	• Includes papers presented at international, national, state, and local professional meetings and conventions. Also includes invited conferences and colloquia.
Technical reports	• Includes unpublished technical reports prepared for research funded by the government or private agencies.
Interim reports	• Includes unpublished progress reports submitted at regular intervals during ongoing research funded by the government or private agencies.
Rejected manuscripts	• Includes completed studies that have been rejected for publication.
Uncompleted research manuscripts or reports	• Includes studies that are completed but not yet formally presented or submitted for publication.

Overcoming Selection Biases

Identifying studies to be included in research syntheses is the point in time at which the most serious form of bias can occur. Selection bias is a problem because it is difficult to know exactly whether all of the relevant studies have been identified and included in the research synthesis. Although it is virtually impossible to identify every relevant study on a particular topic to be included in a research synthesis, it is critical that researchers provide a complete description of the procedures used to locate the studies included in the review. A complete description of these procedures helps the critical research consumer to assess the representativeness and completeness of the research synthesis. This description will also enable the critical research consumer to assess the generality of the results. Nelson and Lignugaris/Kraft (1989) provide an example of the procedures used to locate the studies included in a research synthesis regarding services available to postsecondary students with learning disabilities:

> *The literature examined was identified through a computer search of the* Exceptional Child Education Resources Abstracts, Dissertation Abstracts, *and* Psychological Abstracts. *Descriptors included learning disabled, dyslexia, disabilities, academic failure, learning programs, post-secondary education, adult education, higher education, and continuing education. In addition, an ancestral search was conducted from the identified articles. Articles reviewed referred specifically to programs for learning disabled students (or other commonly used classification labels, such as dyslexia) at community colleges or traditional 4-year higher education settings and were published following the enactment of Section 504 of the Rehabilitation Act of 1973. Articles not included in this review were those that examined specific characteristics (e.g., written language) of college learning disabled students or referred to post-secondary settings other than community colleges or traditional 4-year higher education institutions (e.g., vocational technical schools). (p. 247)*

Focusing the Literature Search

Carefully focusing a literature search is important if researchers are to achieve a research synthesis that accurately reflects the accumulated knowledge underlying the phenomenon of interest. Failure to plan and execute a literature search carefully may result in one or more problematic outcomes. First, the literature search may be too broad, requiring researchers to review and reject a large number of unrelated studies. Reviewing a large number of studies is not only time-consuming but frustrating. Second, the literature search may be poorly focused, either neglecting important sources or attempting to accomplish too much. Thus, carefully planning and executing a literature search eliminates wasted time, excessive costs, and irrelevant or missed primary studies.

HOW DO RESEARCHERS PLAN AND EXECUTE RESEARCH SYNTHESES?

Figure 14.1 depicts the eight steps for planning and executing a research synthesis: (a) formulating a precise research question; (b) defining critical terms; (c) formulating a literature search framework; (d) searching the literature; (e) coding study characteristics; (f) determining the magnitude of intervention outcomes; (g) relating study characteristics to intervention outcomes, and (h) reporting the results.

Formulating a Precise Research Question

The first step in planning and executing a research synthesis is to formulate a precise research question. A precise research question provides structure and guides the planning and execution of the literature search. Failure to formulate a precise research question often leads to a weak or unfocused attempt to search the literature. A wide range of questions can be used to guide the literature search. Some common questions asked by researchers are as follows:

1. What is the average effect of the independent variable?
2. With whom is the independent variable effective?
3. Are particular versions of the independent variable effective?

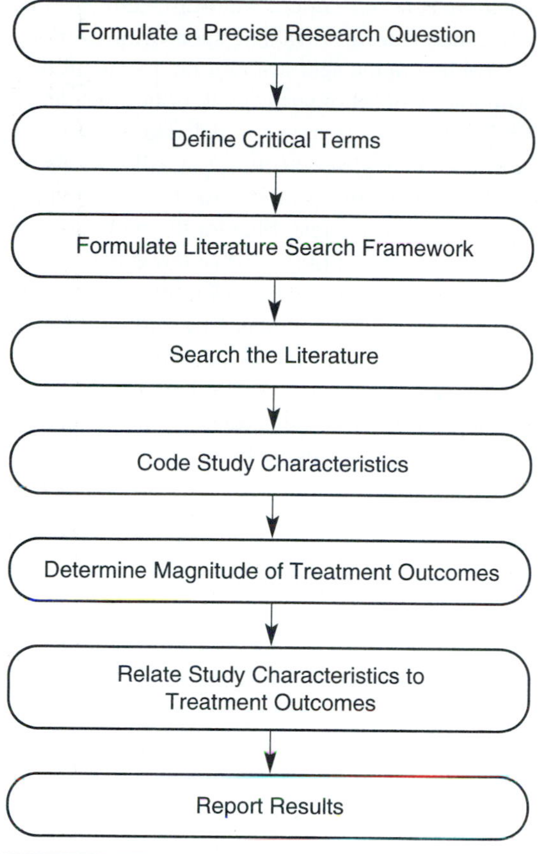

FIGURE 14.1 Steps in planning and executing a review of the literature.

4. Are particular versions of the independent variable more acceptable to key stakeholders?
5. What combination of independent variable and individuals is more effective?
6. Under what conditions is the independent variable effective?
7. How should the independent variable be implemented to ensure its effectiveness in a particular situation?
8. What is the degree of relationship between the independent and dependent variable?
9. What theoretical model is most predictive?
10. What is the relationship between study characteristics and intervention outcomes?

In addition to formulating a precise research question, it is important for researchers to determine whether the goal of the research synthesis is to test a specific hypothesis or to explore available information (Light & Pillemer, 1984). As with hypothesis testing in primary studies, researchers assert a particular outcome before searching the literature. They select and review only those primary studies that explore the particular hypothesis of interest.

In contrast, some researchers do *not* state a hypothesis before searching the literature in an exploratory literature search; they examine the empirical evidence in the literature and then work backwards to draw a conclusion. Researchers select a wide range of primary studies that explore the phenomenon under study. They cast a wide net when searching for primary studies to include in the literature search and then synthesize the primary studies to draw conclusions.

An example to illustrate hypothesis-testing and exploratory research questions when examining the relationship between teacher expectations and academic achievement of elementary-aged children follows. "Is there is a positive relationship between teacher expectations and the academic achievement of elementary-aged children?" is an example of a hypothesis-testing research question. In this case, researchers would select and review primary research studies that have specifically explored the relationship between teacher expectation and the academic achievement of elementary-aged children.

"What is the relationship between teacher expectations and the academic achievement of elementary-aged children?" is an example of an exploratory research question. In this case, researchers would select and review all of the primary research studies that have explored the effects of teacher expectations on the academic achievement of elementary-aged children.

Defining Critical Terms

Once researchers have formulated a precise research question, the next step is to identify the critical terms or features that are descriptive of the phenomenon under study. This description of terms will enable researchers to identify the relevant primary studies that have focused on the phenomenon of interest. Defining these terms will improve the precision in which relevant primary studies are identified.

Researchers begin by identifying each of the key conceptual terms involving the phenomenon of interest and their synonyms (related terms that have the same or nearly the same meaning). Using the example of the relationship between teacher expectations and the academic achievement of elementary-aged children, three primary concepts can be identified: teacher expectations, academic achievement, and elementary-aged children. Once these key conceptual terms have been identified, researchers must look carefully at the terms used by other researchers and bibliographic services to describe each of these concepts. Table 14.3 presents the relevant terms that researchers and bibliographic services (i.e., *Psychological Abstracts, ERIC,* and *Sociological Abstracts*) have used to describe teacher expectations, academic achievement, and elementary-aged children. Bibliographic services produce machine-readable files of information on a wide range of documents (e.g., primary research studies, conference proceedings, general papers, and position papers). These services can be searched using a variety of search fields such as descriptor, keyword, author, title, publication date, abstract, and sponsoring agency.

Bibliographic services rely on a standardized terminology or set of terms to describe concepts in the literature. If a term is not included in the set of terms used to describe a concept, it will not help researchers to identify primary studies exploring the phenomenon of interest. Each of the bibliographic services rely on a different set of terms to describe the same concept. Thus, a set of terms used for one bibliographic service will yield a different set of primary studies than the set of terms for another service. Because each of the bibliographic services do not use the same standardized terms and cover the same journals, researchers must refer to the thesaurus of each service (e.g., *Thesaurus of Psychological Index Terms, Thesaurus of ERIC Descriptors,* and the *Thesaurus of Sociological Indexing*). Table 14.4 presents examples of descriptors used in *Psychological Abstracts, ERIC,* and *Sociological Abstracts* for teacher expectations, one of the concepts in our example.

In addition, key terms can be identified and verified by using a number of primary studies within the literature exploring the phenomenon of interest. Researchers can examine these primary studies to identify the standardized terms that have

TABLE 14.3 Relevant Terms for Teacher Expectations, Academic Achievement, and Elementary-Aged Children

TEACHER EXPECTATIONS	ACADEMIC ACHIEVEMENT	ELEMENTARY-AGED CHILDREN
• Teacher expectations • Self-fulfilling prophecy • Teacher attitudes • Teacher characteristics • Teacher influence • Teacher response • Teacher–student relationships	• Educational attainment • Student promotion • Academic ability • Academic aptitude • Academic standards • Academic achievement • Academic failure • Achievement rating • Achievement gains • Grades/grading • Report cards • Student characteristics	• Children • Elementary education • Elementary schools

TABLE 14.4 Descriptors used in Psychological Abstracts, ERIC, and Sociological Abstracts for Teacher Expectations

PSYCHOLOGICAL ABSTRACTS	SOCIOLOGICAL ABSTRACTS	ERIC
• Teacher expectations • Teacher attitudes • Teacher characteristics • Teacher–student interaction	• Teacher expectations • Effective schooling • Student resistance • Teacher–student opinions/ expectations	• Teacher expectations • Self-fulfilling prophecy • Teacher attitudes • Teacher characteristics • Teacher influence • Teacher response • Teacher–student relationships

been used by the bibliographic services to index the studies. A comparison of the standardized terms used across a number of primary studies will provide a solid list of key terms to use in the literature search. Additionally, key terms can be identified by conducting a free-text search of the literature exploring the phenomenon of interest. Free-text searching allows researchers to search the entire literature base and identify if a term appears anywhere within the given abstract of a study. Free-text searching will identify any primary study that included the term in the title or abstract.

Formulating a Literature Search Framework

After key terms have been identified and verified, researchers must develop a strategy for linking these key terms. Although services differ somewhat with regard to how searches are constructed, they all use Boolean rules or logical operators for linking key terms. The logical operators and associated descriptions used by bibliographic services are depicted in Table 14.5.

Inspection of Table 14.5 reveals that how we use Boolean rules or logical operators in a search strategy greatly affects the particular primary studies identified. For example, using OR in educational attainment OR academic ability OR academic aptitude OR academic achievement in a search would identify primary studies indexed using either of the terms or any combination of the terms. In contrast, using AND in educational attainment AND academic ability AND academic aptitude AND academic achievement in a search would identify only those primary studies indexed using all four of the terms. It is clear that the researchers must carefully plan how they will use the logical operators to link terms together. Each of the bibliographic services provides guides to their services. Additionally, many libraries provide technical assistance to help researchers to formulate and conduct a search strategy.

Figure 14.2 depicts a search strategy for our example on the effects of teacher expectations on the academic achievement of elementary-aged children. The alternative terms associated with each of the key concepts (i.e., teacher expectations, academic achievement, and elementary-aged children) are linked with OR to allow the use of each of the alternative terms. Additionally, we linked the three key concepts with AND (symbolized by the arrows) to identify primary studies that have addressed all three of the key concepts.

Searching the Literature

Once a search strategy has been formulated, a literature search is conducted. Indeed, formulating a search strategy and searching the literature are directly connected to one another. Researchers may have to reformulate their search strategy many times once they begin to search the literature because it is difficult to identify all of the relevant research studies. Nevertheless, the goal of researchers is to achieve an accurate and impartial description

TABLE 14.5 Boolean Rules or Logical Operators Used by Bibliographic Services

OPERATOR	USE IN SEARCH	EFFECT ON SEARCH	EXAMPLE
AND	• Use AND to search for documents that include all terms linked by AND.	• Using AND to combine terms reduces the number of documents identified. AND is used to combine terms that have different meanings and narrows the search.	• A search on terms teacher expectations AND academic achievement AND elementary students would identify documents in which all of the terms appeared in each document.
OR	• Use OR to search for documents that are about any of the terms being linked by OR.	• Using OR to combine terms increases the number of documents identified. OR is used to combine terms that have similar meaning and broadens the search.	• A search on terms teacher expectations OR teacher attitudes OR teacher student relationship would identify documents in which at least one of the terms appeared in each document.
NOT	• Use NOT to eliminate documents containing a specific term.	• Using NOT to combine terms reduces the number of documents identified. NOT is used to eliminate terms that have similar meaning to the term(s) of interest and narrows the search.	• A search on terms teacher expectations NOT teacher attitudes NOT teacher student relationship would identify documents in which no mention was made of the terms teacher attitudes and teacher–student relationships.

of the study findings. Conducting such a review of the literature can be done in two ways. The first way is to conduct an exhaustive literature search. This search involves an attempt to identify every primary and fugitive source exploring the phenomenon of interest. Conducting an exhaustive literature search is especially appropriate when researchers are interested in conducting an exploratory research synthesis. Including a wide range of primary and fugitive sources can enhance the degree of confidence one would have in the findings.

The second way to conduct a literature search is to select a subsample of studies exploring the phenomenon of interest. Selecting this subsample is appropriate when researchers face an enormous number of studies; it is appropriate for conducting both hypothesis-testing and exploratory literature searches. Of course, it is critical that the process used to select a subsample of studies does not introduce any bias into the search. Although it is difficult to assess the potential bias introduced into such a literature search, researchers, at a minimum, must fully describe the selection criteria used to include as well as exclude studies in the review.

Researchers typically employ a number of approaches to select a subsample of studies. A common approach in selecting a subsample of studies is to stratify them on a number of key categories (e.g., type of experimental design and geographic location) that must be represented in the study. Researchers then select studies from each category to include in the literature search. Selecting studies from each category is especially useful when key study characteristics are related in some fashion to outcomes. For example, it might be useful to categorize studies into primary

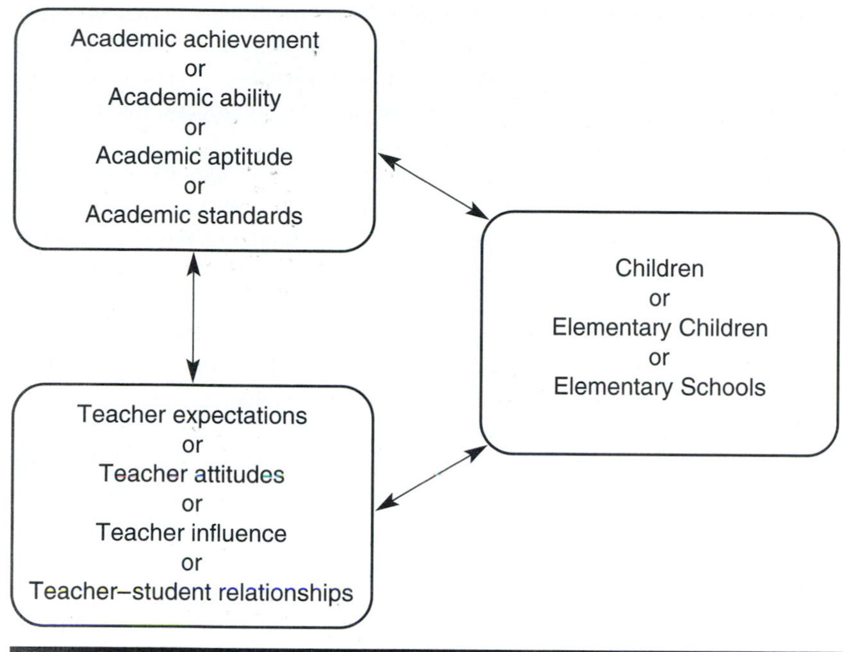

FIGURE 14.2 Example of a search strategy using logical operators.

(K–3rd grades) and intermediate (4–6 grades) in our example of the effects of teacher expectations on the academic achievement of elementary-aged children and then select a sample of representative studies from each of the categories.

Another approach to select a subsample of studies is to use only published studies, eliminating from review any fugitive studies. Including only published investigations has some advantages. First, the search process is simplified since such studies are much easier to find. Second, selected studies tend to be more technically sound because the studies have undergone a peer review process. On the other hand, including only published studies may introduce publication bias (Glass et al., 1981). Publication bias centers on the reality that statistically significant findings are more likely to be submitted and accepted for publication as compared to statistically nonsignificant findings (Greenwald, 1975). Thus, literature searches that include only published studies may overestimate the effects of the independent variable.

A final approach for selecting a subsample of studies recommended by Light and Pillemer (1984) is to use a panel of experts. Researchers and other specialists with expertise in the phenomenon of interest are either polled to identify the studies or asked to critique the studies included in the literature search. The advantage of using a panel of experts is that they have knowledge of the strengths and weaknesses of different types of studies. For example, using our example on the effects of teacher expectations on the academic achievement of elementary-aged children, a panel of experts on teacher expectations would be able not only to identify the relevant studies, but also to provide information on the study characteristics that might influence the outcomes. Of course, it is important that the panel include a range of professionals to help reduce the potential biases of expert judgment.

It should be clear by now that there are no set guidelines for searching the literature. The goal, depending on the purpose of the review of the literature, is to identify both primary and fugitive sources of studies exploring the phenomenon of interest. The first step is to begin at an academic library that can provide the traditional sources for conducting a review of the literature. These sources include the library subject catalog, abstracts, and indexes; the references in reviews of the literature; and bibliographic series. Researchers use these traditional sources to identify relevant studies from both primary and fugitive sources. Researchers then retrieve the studies and search the references found in the first set of studies to identify additional studies. Next, researchers retrieve the identified studies and repeat the retrieval process until the same studies are identified again and again. This process will lead to a relatively complete list of studies exploring the phenomenon of interest.

Coding Study Characteristics

Researchers conducting a research synthesis must choose the study characteristics they are interested in and develop methods for ensuring that the information is reliably obtained from each primary study. A well-designed method for identifying study characteristics is an important step in the search process. Although there is not one set of prescribed guidelines for determining which study characteristics to include in a research synthesis, researchers typically code key study characteristics such as (a) study identification (e.g., author, year, and source of publication); (b) setting (e.g., scope of sampling; population characteristics such as minorities, special populations, and SES level of the community or school; ecological characteristics such as school setting); (c) participants (i.e., specific characteristics of the sample(s) and/or subsample(s) including demographic characteristics such as SES level, education, age, and gender); (d) methodology (e.g., research design, attrition, experimental procedures); (e) independent variable or intervention (e.g., theoretical framework, description of experimental conditions both for the experimental and control groups, duration of independent variable, who delivered the independent variable, verification of the independent variable); (f) research quality (i.e., threats to internal and external validity); (g) dependent variable (e.g., relevance, reliability and validity, time frame); and (h) outcomes (e.g., effect size, statistically significant findings, author's conclusions).

Although each of the categories of key study characteristics should be considered when conducting a review of the literature, it is not necessary to use all of them. The particular categories and factors within categories should be selected on the basis of the research domain for the particular phenomenon of interest. The process of identifying study characteristics is ongoing, and researchers should make changes when necessary. It is not uncommon to make several adjustments in the study characteristics extracted from the primary studies.

Study characteristics to be extracted from the primary studies are then coded on a coding form. Taking the time to construct a coding form and training the coders is not only important to the quality of the research synthesis, but is necessary to manage the large amount of generated information effectively. The coding of study characteristics is more accurate if the coding forms are clear and organized to facilitate coding. Paper and pencil coding forms can be used. However, computer database programs are more desirable because they allow researchers to rearrange and organize the information to facilitate interpretation of the studies. Table 14.6 presents an example of a coding form for a research synthesis on the use of self-management procedures with students with behavioral disorders conducted by Nelson, Smith, Young, and Dodd (1991). The form depicts the major study characteristics extracted from each of the studies included in the literature search.

Training Coders. Researchers conducting a research synthesis must train the individuals who will be coding the information extracted from each of the studies. The goal of the training is to teach coders how to use the coding forms and procedures (e.g., identification of threats to internal validity) in the same way. The procedure for training coders parallels the procedure for training observers in single-case research. Stock (1994) recommends the following 10 steps for training coders.

TABLE 14.6 Example of Coding Form

Study Identification Number: ________

Publication Form: __Journal ___Book ___Thesis ___Paper Presentation __Other

Citation: ____

____

Participants

Age of Participants: ______________ Major Diagnosis:______________

Other Characteristics of Participants (e.g., SES, IQ): ______________

Setting

Setting: ___General Education Classroom ___Special Education Classroom __ Both

Design

Type

___Group: ______________________

___Single-subject: ______________________

___Other: ______________________

Selection of Subjects

___Random: ______________________

___Intact groups: ______________________

___Convenience: ______________________

___Other nonrandom: ______________________

Independent Variable(s)

Description: ______________________

____

Duration: __________ Implemented by Experimenter: __Yes ___No ___Unknown

Dependent Variable(s)

Description: ______________________

____

Reliability/Interobserver Agreement: ______________________

Threats to Internal and External Validity

___Internal Validity: ______________________

___External Validity:______________________

Outcome

___Statistical Analysis:______________________

___Visual Analysis:______________________

Comments

---

1. An overview of the review of the literature is given by the principal investigator.
2. Each item on a coding form and its associated description is read and discussed.
3. The process for using the coding forms is described.
4. A sample of five to ten studies is chosen to test the coders and coding forms.

5. A study is coded independently on the coding forms by everyone.
6. Coded forms are compared, and discrepancies are identified and resolved.
7. The coding form is revised as necessary.
8. Another group of studies is coded and reviewed and so on. Steps 4 through 8 are repeated until consensus is achieved.
9. Reliability of the coders is then checked throughout the review process. (Intercoder reliability is established in the same way as interobserver agreement.)
10. Frequent meetings are conducted with coders to discuss progress and any problems.

Determining the Magnitude of Intervention Outcomes

Although not all research syntheses are concerned with determining the magnitude of intervention outcomes, a majority are initiated to determine the effectiveness of an independent variable or the degree of relationship between two variables. Thus, it is not surprising that most advances in conducting research syntheses have centered on the use of quantitative procedures to determine the magnitude of intervention outcomes to aid in the integration of studies. The development of quantitative procedures is not surprising given the level of debate that occurs when research syntheses are based on the professional judgment of researchers regarding the magnitude of the intervention (e.g., see the debate between Graham [1995] and Cooper and Dorr [1995a, 1995b] regarding narrative versus meta-analytic reviews of race differences in motivation). This is not to say that professional judgment is useless in considering the magnitude of intervention effects. Rather, the limitation of such an approach rests on the sheer magnitude of the task. It is difficult at best for researchers to absorb and transmit the findings from a large number of primary research studies without some reliance on statistical methods.

Researchers conducting research syntheses using experimental studies typically have access to a least one of three types of information that they can use to determine the efficacy of the independent variable. These three types include information (a) that can be used to compute effect size estimates (e.g., means, standard deviations, proportions, correlations, and test statistics); (b) about whether the findings were statistically significant (i.e., p values); and (c) regarding the direction of the effects of the independent variable (i.e., positive effect, negative effect, and no effect). These types of information can be rank-ordered on the degree of precision they provide researchers regarding the effectiveness of the independent variable. If the first type of information is available, then researchers should compute effect-size estimates. The use of statistical significance is appropriate for the second and third types of information. Additionally, the proportion of overlapping data is a measure for statistically determining the effectiveness of an independent variable in the case of single-case studies. In the remainder of this section, we describe each of these measures.

Statistical Significance. Experimental research methods and statistical analysis procedures in education and psychology rely heavily on statistical significance testing. If the findings are statistically significant, researchers typically conclude that the independent variable was effective (produced effects) or that the two variables are related.

Examining the obtained p value provides a way of interpreting effectiveness of the independent variable or degree of relationship. Researchers almost always report the decision yielded by the test of statistical significance; that is, whether the test statistic did or did not exceed a conventional critical value (i.e., point at which the null hypothesis is rejected) such as $p < .05$, $p < .01$, or $p < .001$, or in the form of an actual p value. Regardless of the form, researchers conducting research syntheses identify whether the findings were statistically significant at some established critical value such as $p < .05$. Thus, these researchers can generally conclude that an independent variable is effective or that two variables are related if a study yields a test statistic that exceeds the established critical value in a positive direction (or negative direction in the case of relationship studies). Researchers can use the information obtained from statistical significance testing to synthesize the research literature in several ways. We will discuss two possible methods—vote counting and combining significance tests.

Vote Counting. In this case, researchers can then use a vote-counting procedure to integrate the studies in a review. The vote-counting procedure involves the following steps:

1. Studies that provide information on the results of statistical significance testing are examined.

2. Three possible outcomes with regard to the relationship between the independent and dependent variables are noted: (a) the relationship is statistically significantly positive; (b) the relationship is statistically significantly negative; (c) there is no discernible relationship.

3. The number of studies falling into each of these categories is tallied.

4. If a majority of studies fall into any one of these three categories, this category is declared the winner. The category with the majority of studies is declared the winner because it is assumed that it provides the best estimate of the direction of the true relationship between the independent and dependent variables.

It is important to note that a research synthesis using a vote-counting procedure is limited in several respects. First, vote-counting procedures do not incorporate sample size into the vote (Light & Smith, 1971). Recall that the probability of obtaining a statistically significant finding increases as the sample size increases. Thus, studies with large samples are more likely to result in the conclusion that there is a statistically significant relationship between the independent and dependent variables when in fact there is not. Second, the vote-counting procedure does not provide any indication of whether an intervention "wins by a nose or in a walk-away" (Glass et al., 1981, p. 95). In other words, although the vote-counting procedure provides information regarding which of the three possible outcomes is the winner, it does not provide information regarding the magnitude of that outcome. Third, the vote-counting procedure tends to have low power (i.e., ability to detect intervention effects) for the range of sample sizes and intervention effects most common in the social sciences (Hedges & Olkin, 1980). The vote-counting procedure often fails to detect intervention effects when they are small to medium. Finally, the power of the vote-counting procedure tends to be near zero as the number of studies to be integrated in the literature search increases (Hedges & Olkin, 1980).

Combining Significance Tests. Combining significance tests is another procedure for using the results of tests of statistical significance to determine whether an intervention is effective. Procedures for combining significance tests effectively deal with the previously identified problems of the vote-counting procedure. However, the use of these procedures requires that researchers report the actual obtained p value rather than general information regarding whether the test of statistical significance met a conventional critical value of $p < .05$, $p < .01$, or $p < .001$. The use of these procedures also requires knowing the sample size (this was not the case with the vote-counting procedure).

There are numerous methods for combining each study's test of statistical significance into an overall pooled test. For example, Rosenthal (1978) describes nine ways to combine statistical significance. One method for combining tests of statistical significance is adding Z scores. The Z scores from each individual study are added up across studies. The obtained sum is then divided by the square root of the number of studies. The probability level associated with combined Z scores provides an estimate of the overall level of significance for all of the studies included in the research synthesis. The probability level associated with the combined Z scores can be obtained by looking at a table of normal deviations that contains the critical values associated with Z scores.

As with the vote-counting procedure, there are a number of potential problems associated with procedures for combining tests of statistical significance. First, although these procedures provide an overall estimate of the intervention effect, they do not enable researchers to examine the distribution of the findings across study characteristics. This understanding enables researchers to examine under what conditions the independent variable is effective or the relationship between two variables exists.

Second, errors in the interpretation of the overall combined test of statistical significance are never known. For example, researchers conducting a research synthesis might conclude that the effect of the independent variable is greater than zero or that there is a relationship between two variables because the null hypothesis was rejected, when in fact it should have been accepted (Type I error). Alternatively, researchers may incorrectly conclude that the intervention had *no* effect or that there was *no* relationship between two variables because the null hypothesis was accepted (Type II error). Finally, the potential of publication bias is increased when researchers use procedures for combining tests of statistical significance since there is a tendency for studies that achieve statistical significance to be published, whereas statistically nonsignificant studies are not (Rosenthal, 1979).

An example provided by Rosenthal (1978) is provided to help understand how the method of adding Z scores compares to the vote-counting procedure described earlier. The reported p values of .12, .01, .72, .07, and .17 and associated Z scores of 1.17, –.2.33, –.58, 1.48, and .95 were obtained for five studies. Using the vote-counting procedure, we would conclude that there is no intervention effect because only one of the p values is statistically significant at the $p < .05$ level (i.e., .01). In contrast, computing the combined Z scores for the obtained studies using the method of adding Z scores (sum of the Z scores divided by the square root of the number of studies) yields a combined Z score of 2.39, $p = .009$. We would conclude that the intervention was effective. This example illustrates how the conclusions drawn by researchers are dependent on the particular procedures they use to determine whether an independent variable was in effect or that there was a relationship between two variables.

Effect Size. The effect size is currently the most common measure used by researchers conducting reviews of the literature. It provides much more information than does statistical significance. Tests of statistical significance only provide information regarding the probability that the obtained differences between the experimental and control groups are due to sampling and measurement error. The effect size goes beyond statistical significance by providing information regarding the *magnitude* of the differences between the experimental and control groups or the degree of relationship between two variables. This distinction is important because tests of statistical significance are heavily influenced by sample sizes. Extremely small differences in very large experimental and control samples can be statistically significant even though they may not be socially significant (i.e., how valuable an intervention is). Statistical significance and effect size are related to each other in the following way: Statistical significance = effect size × sample size. This direct relationship shows that any nonzero effect size will reach statistical significance given a sufficiently large sample size.

The effect size is a standardized measure of the difference between the experimental and control groups. The most common use of the effect size is to compare the mean scores of the experimental and control groups. The estimate of the effect size is then the difference between the two groups' means divided by the control group's standard deviation. The control group's standard deviation is used because it is believed to provide the best estimate of the variance in the population. This measure of effect size (ES) is known as Glass's Δ (see Table 14.7). The formula is as follows:

$$\Delta = \frac{M_1 - M_2}{SD_c}$$

where M_1 = mean of the experimental group
M_2 = mean of the control group
SD_c = standard deviation of the control group

It is important to note that some researchers suggest making a number of adjustments in the computation of effect sizes to provide estimates of the standard deviation in the population and to control for sample size. For example, many computations of effect sizes use a pooled standard deviation rather than the control group's standard deviation because they believe that it provides a better estimate of the standard deviation in the population (e.g., Hunter, Schmidt, & Jackson, 1982). The computational formula for obtaining a pooled sample standard deviation is as follows (Hedges & Olkin, 1985):

$$SD = \sqrt{\frac{(n_e - 1)(SD_e)^2 + (n_c - 1)(SD_c)^2}{n_e + n_c - 2}}$$

where SD = pooled standard deviation
n_e = sample size for the experimental group
n_c = sample size for the control group
SD_e = standard deviation for the experimental group
SD_c = standard deviation for the control group

Parametric Effect Sizes. There are parametric effect sizes available to researchers conducting research syntheses. There are two families of parametric effect sizes: *r* and *d* (Rosenthal, 1994a). These two families of effect sizes directly align with the purpose of the studies being included in the research synthesis. The *r* family of effect sizes is used in those cases in which the goal of the synthesis is to determine the magnitude of a relationship between two variables. The *d* family of effect sizes is used in those cases in which the goal of the synthesis is to determine the magnitude of the difference between the means of experimental and control conditions, for example. However, researchers often encounter situations in which there is a mixture of *r* and *d* effect sizes. This mixture is not a problem because there are procedures for converting these effect sizes into one particular effect size. Table 14.7 presents some of the most common *r* and *d* effect sizes used by researchers to conduct reviews of the literature. See Cooper and Hedges (1994), Glass et al. (1981), and Hedges and Olkin (1985) for in-depth discussions of effect sizes.

Meaning of Effect Sizes. The meaning of effect sizes can be translated into notions of overlapping distributions of scores and comparable percentiles (Glass et al., 1981). For example, say the obtained effect size for a hypothetical study on the effects of

TABLE 14.7 Common *r*-Type and *d*-Type Effect Sizes and Associated Formulas and Parameters Estimated

EFFECT SIZE	TYPE	FORMULA	PARAMETER ESTIMATED
r	r	$\frac{\Sigma Z_x Z_y}{N}$	Population correlation between variables x and y
Z_r	r	$1/2 \log_e \left[\frac{1+r}{1-r}\right]$	Population Fisher Z_r transformations of population correlations
Cohen's q	r	$Z_{r1} - Z_{r2}$	Difference between Fisher Z_r transformations of population correlations
Glass's Δ	d	$\frac{M_1 - M_2}{SD \text{ control group}}$	Difference between population means divided by the standard deviation of the population control group
Hedges g	d	$\frac{M_1 - M_2}{SD \text{ pooled}}$	Difference between population means divided by average population standard deviation
d'	d	$p_1 - p_2$	Difference between population proportions

a Direct Instruction reading program on improving the phonemic awareness of young children versus a literature-based reading program was 1.00. This positive effect size indicates that the average child in the Direct Instruction condition shows phonemic awareness one standard deviation above that of the average child in the literature-based reading condition. A negative effect size would indicate that the average child in the literature-based reading condition is one standard deviation below the average Direct Instruction child. In this example, the phonemic awareness of only 16% of the children in the Direct Instruction reading condition is worse than the average child in the literature-based reading condition. Figure 14.3 depicts the outcomes for this hypothetical study. Additionally, effect sizes that approach or are equal to zero may also occur; in this case, Direct Instruction and literature-based reading produced comparable student outcomes.

Effect sizes may also be meaningful without comparison to a control group. One approach is to compare the relative effect sizes for different treatments or for different study characteristics. For example, Rosenshine and Meister (1994) compared the effect sizes obtained with reciprocal teaching interventions across a number of study characteristics. They compared the obtained effect sizes for type of student by outcome measure in an attempt to examine whether certain students improved in comprehension by type of comprehension measure used (i.e., standardized or experimenter-developed tests: see Table 14.8). (Rosenshine and Meister made a number of comparisons in their research syntheses.) These comparisons enable the critical research consumer to examine the relative effects of these factors.

Problems Associated with Effect Sizes. Finally, it is important to mention a number of problems associated with the use of effect sizes. The first problem centers on the fact that researchers conducting primary research studies use a number of different dependent measures. Calculating and combining effect sizes are easiest when the same dependent measure is used by researchers. Researchers calculating effect sizes must consider whether it is reasonable to combine effect sizes across different dependent measures.

Related to this issue, the second problem focuses on the fact that researchers conducting pri-

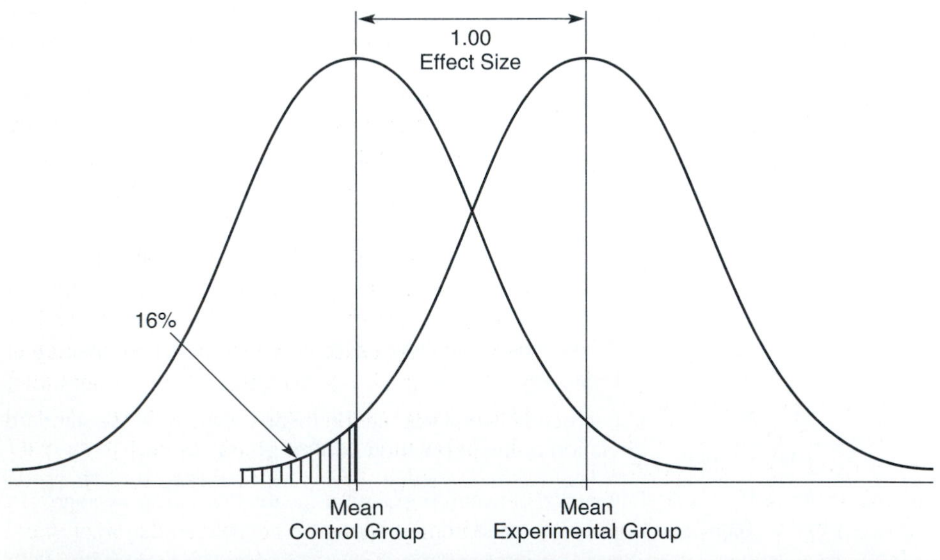

FIGURE 14.3 Illustrative example for interpreting effect sizes.

TABLE 14.8 Median Effect Sizes for Type of Student by Type of Test

TYPE OF STUDENT	STANDARDIZED TESTS	EXPERIMENTER-DEVELOPED TESTS
All students	.32 (4)	.85 (5)
Good–poor students	.29 (2)	.88 (3)
Below-average students	.08 (4)	1.15 (2)

Note: Numbers in parentheses refer to the number of studies used to compute median effect sizes.

Source: Rosenshine, B., & Meister, C. (1994). Reciprocal teaching: A review of the research. *Review of Educational Research, 64,* 479–530.

mary research studies use a number of dependent measures within a study. That is, one study yields multiple effect sizes. One approach to this problem is to compute separate effect sizes within a study. Although such an approach uses all of the information available from a study, it may weight the results of the study more heavily than studies that have used one or two dependent measures. The common approach to this problem is to treat each study as a unit of analysis and compute an average effect size across the dependent measures.

The final problem centers on the fact that a number of primary research studies will not provide all of the information necessary to compute an effect size. These studies cannot be included in the research synthesis. Of course, this may eliminate studies that might provide valuable information and is why some authors suggest that researchers conducting reviews of the literature combine narrative and quantitative approaches (e.g., Light & Pillemer, 1984).

Proportion of Nonoverlapping Data. In contrast to quantitative experimental studies, researchers have not fully developed indices with which to measure the magnitude of the intervention effects and how to combine studies using single-case designs. One measure that has been used and that is widely debated is the proportion of nonoverlapping data (PND; Scruggs, Mastropieri, & Casto, 1987; Scruggs, Mastropieri, Cook, & Escabar, 1985). The PND has not been used as extensively to integrate single-subject research as have effect sizes because of some potential theoretical problems. Nevertheless, researchers have used PND to provide an index of the magnitude of the intervention in reviews of research using single-case research (e.g., Nelson et al., 1991).

PND is defined as the number of data points that exceed the highest baseline data point in the expected direction divided by the total number of intervention data points in the intervention phase (Scruggs et al., 1985, 1987). For example, if a specific intervention phase consisted of 20 data points in the expected direction, 15 of which exceed baseline data, the resulting PND would be computed as 15 divided by 20 multiplied by 100 = 75%. The following two coding conventions are recommended for computing the PND for a study.

1. When conditions are duplicated, as in an A-B-A-B design, measures of overlap are combined by dividing the total number of nonoverlapping intervention data points by the total number of intervention data points in the two conditions.
2. In order to discriminate between appropriate and inappropriate calculations of overlapping data in the presence of floor or ceiling effects, the following rule is used: A measure of data overlap is not calculated if no more than three nor less than 33% of zero baseline data points overlap.
3. PND scores are calculated for each participant and the median PND score for each study is used.

Although there are not set standards for interpreting PND scores, previous comparisons of PND scores with visual analysis have suggested that scores of 90% and higher represent highly effective outcomes. Scores of 70 to 90% represent fair outcomes. Scores of 50 to 70% represent questionable effects. Scores below 50% represent unreliable interventions.

Look at an illustrative example to help understand how PND scores are computed. Figure 14.4 presents the results from a hypothetical study using an A-B design to study the effectiveness of a reading instruction strategy. Using the computation procedures outlined before, there are eight data points in the expected direction, six of which exceed baseline data. The resulting PND for this hypothetical study would be computed as 6 divided by 8 multiplied by 100 = 75%. By using the earlier interpretation guidelines, the obtained PND suggests that the reading instruction strategy was fairly powerful.

Relating Study Characteristics to Intervention Outcomes

One of the most important steps in conducting a research synthesis is to examine whether particular study characteristics are related to intervention outcomes. This step directly builds on the fifth step in the review process: coding study characteristics. It should be clear by now that relatively few research syntheses yield orderly outcomes or are conducted to construct an average summary of the intervention effects (i.e., emphasize a treatment's average impact without concern of how study characteristics are related to intervention outcomes). Indeed, studying conflicting findings provides researchers an opportunity to better understand those factors that influence the effects of the independent variable or the relationship between two variables. Questions such as, "Does the effectiveness of a new instructional approach depend on the level of training or duration of the instruction provided?" are critical to better understanding the effectivenèss of the intervention.

Variation of an Intervention. We will examine why there are variations in the effectiveness of an intervention before looking at some procedures for relating study characteristics to intervention outcomes. Although there are explainable variations

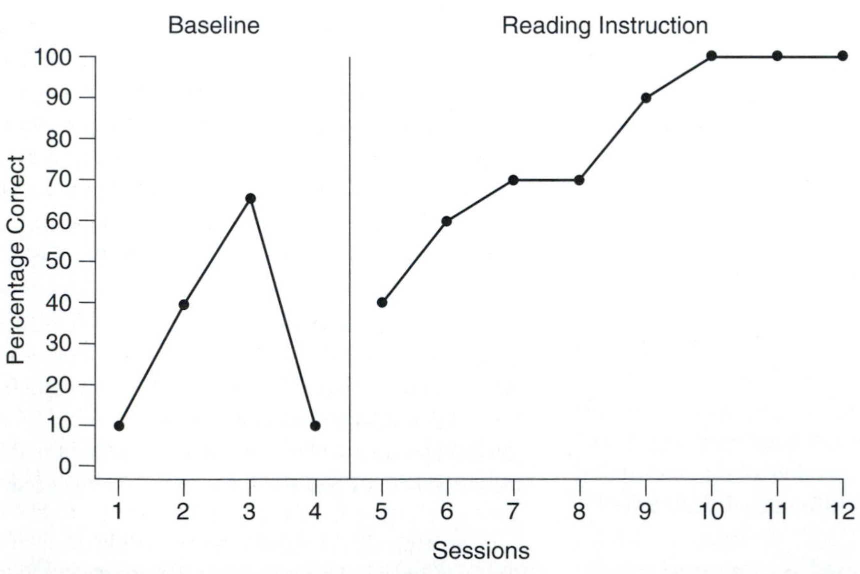

FIGURE 14.4 Illustrative example for computing PND.

in the level of participants in primary research studies, the main interest of researchers conducting a research synthesis is in those contextual variables at the study level that may influence the findings. Contextual variables (i.e., characteristics of the intervention and research methodology) such as the duration of the intervention, who implemented the intervention (e.g., experimenter vs. practitioner), level of training, and type of experimental design or dependent variable may affect the findings. This examination of contextual variables is why a research synthesis may be more useful than even the most carefully conducted primary research study. It is virtually impossible for one primary study to incorporate all of the potential contextual variables into the design. In contrast, a research synthesis enables researchers to look at which contextual variables explain differences in the effectiveness of a particular intervention.

Approaches to Relate Study Characteristics to Intervention Outcomes. As with estimating the magnitude of the effects of the intervention or degree of relationship between two variables, there are a number of approaches that researchers can use to relate study characteristics to intervention outcomes. Regardless of the approach, the goal is to assess whether variations in intervention outcomes across investigations are a function of sampling fluctuation or due to specific effects of independent variables or components of independent variables.

Professional Judgment. The first approach to relating study characteristics to intervention outcomes centers on the professional judgment of researchers. As with estimating the magnitude of the intervention effects, researchers conducting the research synthesis examine how study characteristics are related to differences in the intervention effects. It is difficult at best for researchers to absorb and relate study characteristics on the magnitude of the intervention effects from a large number of primary research studies without some reliance on statistical methods.

Statistical and Graphic Methods. When indices of intervention effects (e.g., effect sizes, correlations) have been computed for each of the primary studies, all of the standard descriptive statistical methods such as averages, measures of variability, and frequency distributions can be used to help relate study characteristics to intervention outcomes. In addition, graphic representation of the indices of the magnitude of intervention effects is one approach used by researchers to relate study characteristics to intervention effects. Researchers using this approach construct a graphic representation of the effect size obtained for each of the primary studies. A common approach is to construct frequency distributions of the obtained effect sizes. If the frequency distribution of effect sizes is normally distributed, one may assume that there is a single intervention outcome that is representative of the population of studies (see Figure 14.5). If the frequency distribution of effect sizes is not normally distributed (e.g., bimodal distribution), one may assume that there are distinct clusters of outcomes.

Figure 14.6 presents an illustrative example in which there appear to be three distinct clusters of effect sizes. These graphs highlight how a simple graphic display of obtained effect sizes can clarify whether there may be some study characteristics related to these distinct clusters of intervention outcomes. Researchers would then attempt to identify differences in study characteristics associated with each of the distinct clusters of intervention outcomes. Of course, it is important to keep in mind these frequency distributions of effect sizes are only descriptive in nature. They do not provide a statistical test of the distribution of the population. Rather, they provide information that suggests that some study characteristics are related to intervention outcomes.

Box and whiskers (Tukey, 1977) is another graphical presentation approach that can be used to explore the relationship between study characteristics and intervention outcomes more fully. A box and whiskers display uses a schematic box plot with some auxiliary features to depict the distribution of effect sizes. Figure 14.7 presents an illustrative example of a box and whiskers display depicting the relationship between some key study characteristics and intervention outcomes. The central box

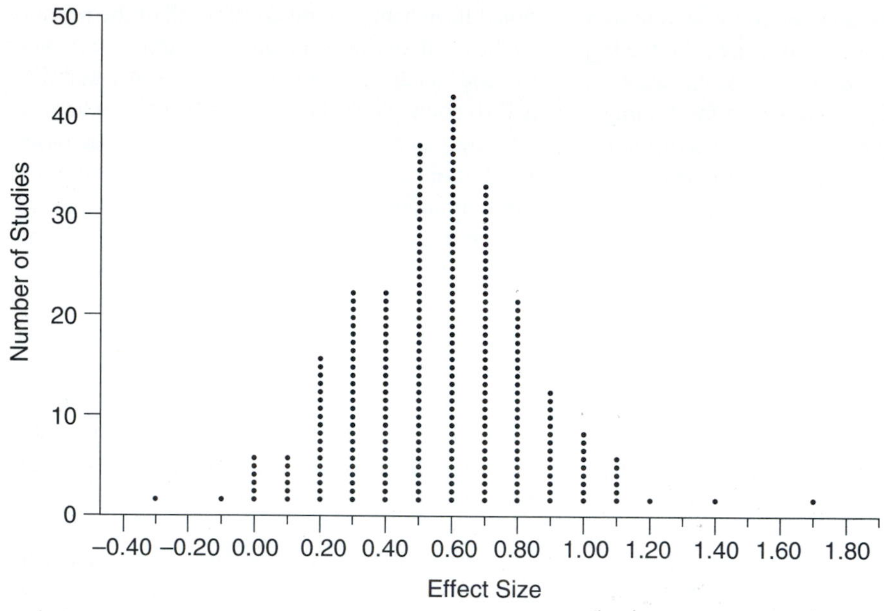

FIGURE 14.5 Illustrative example of normally distributed effect sizes indicating a single treatment outcome.

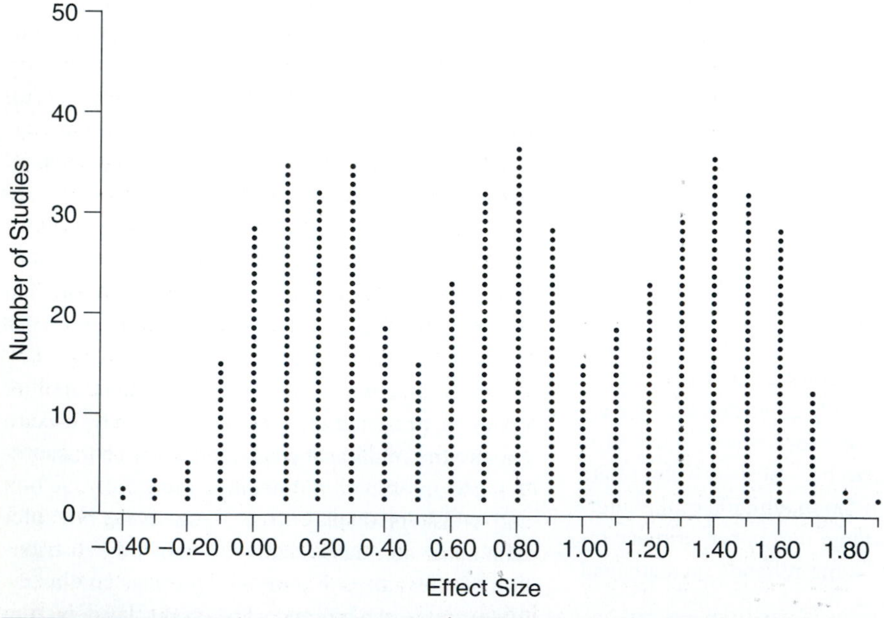

FIGURE 14.6 Illustrative example of effect sizes that are not normally distributed, indicating that there are clusters of treatment outcomes.

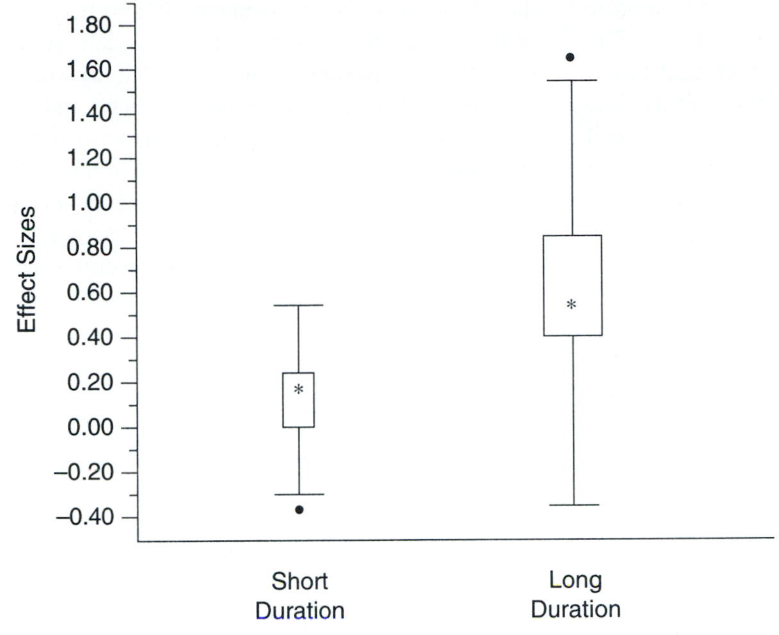

FIGURE 14.7 Illustrative example of box and whiskers plot depicting distributions associated with some primary-study characteristics.

or rectangle (i.e., hinges) marks off, roughly, the first and third quartiles, or approximately the mid-50% of the distribution. The asterisk represents the median with 25% of those inside the box on either side of it (median). In our example, the hinges (ends of the box or rectangle) for short duration of intervention are approximately .01 and .22. The median (represented by the asterisk) is approximately .18. The lines emanating from both ends of the box measure the distance to the "inner fence." The inner fence is one-and-one-half times the length of the box, or 150% of the "hinge" length (this length is arbitrarily chosen). The line at the end depicts the inner fence (–.24 and .52), and data points that lie outside the inner fences are considered outliers. Outliers should be looked at cautiously because they may be a function of some unexplainable factors such as measurement reporting errors, misprints, or miscalculations.

Inspection of Figure 14.7 reveals that there are only two outliers of concern. We could eliminate the outliers and recalculate the average effect size or, because of the small number, include them in the research synthesis. In this case, it would not really matter because there are relatively few outliers compared to the overall number of effect sizes. If there were a small number of effect sizes, it might be important to eliminate the outliers and recalculate the average effect size because they would have a greater effect on the outcome. Additionally, there is little overlap in the distributions of effect sizes for the short- and long-duration studies. This finding suggests that the duration of intervention has an effect on the intervention outcomes. Studies that employed longer treatments tend to produce more powerful intervention outcomes.

A statistical approach to determining whether the studies in a research synthesis share one common intervention outcome or whether outcomes are influenced by contextual factors is to test for the homogeneity of effect sizes. There are several methods for calculating a homogeneity statistic for the obtained effect sizes in a research synthesis (see Glass et al., 1981; Hedges & Olkin, 1985). The idea behind each of the homogeneity statistics is straightforward. If individual effect sizes vary little from the overall mean effect size, then the obtained homogeneity statistic will be small. Small observed values indicate homogeneity (sameness) among the obtained effect sizes. Homogeneity suggests that the obtained effect sizes were representative of one intervention outcome for the population. On the other hand, if the individual effect sizes vary dramatically from the overall mean effect size then the obtained homogeneity statistic will be large. Large observed values indicate significant heterogeneity among the obtained effect sizes. This finding indicates that we need to explore the relationship between study characteristics and intervention outcomes further.

Although tests of the homogeneity of obtained effect sizes in a research synthesis are useful, it is important to be cautious about accepting the absence of statistically significant heterogeneity as being definitive. A test of homogeneity may not be powerful enough to identify real differences in intervention outcomes. Thus, tests of homogeneity should be used as signals that there may be variation in intervention outcomes across studies rather than concluding that the obtained effect sizes are representative of one intervention outcome in the population. In other words, researchers should still explore the relationship between study characteristics and intervention outcomes when tests of homogeneity are statistically nonsignificant.

Finally, all of the standard inferential statistical methods such as any of the correlational techniques (e.g., Pearson's product moment correlation, point-biserial, and multiple regression) and analysis of variance are available to help relate study characteristics to intervention outcomes (see Glass et al., 1981; Hedges & Olkin, 1985). For example, researchers conducting research syntheses often correlate study characteristics with intervention outcomes. Smith and Glass (1977) employed correlation methods to relate study characteristics to intervention outcomes in their groundbreaking meta-analysis of the effectiveness of psychotherapy. Although many of the obtained correlations between study characteristics were generally small, some were statistically significant, suggesting (a) a relationship between the intelligence of clients and intervention outcomes; (b) a relationship between the similarity of the therapist and clients in terms of ethnicity, age, and social level and intervention outcomes; (c) a relationship between the reactivity of the dependent measure and intervention outcomes; and (d) a relationship between the age of clients and intervention outcomes.

Reporting the Results

Reporting the results of a research synthesis parallels doing so for primary research studies. Whether presenting the results of a narrative or quantitative review or some combination of the two, researchers should follow the standard presentation formation for primary research studies: (a) introduction, (b) method, (c) results, and (d) discussion (see Chapter 15 for an in-depth description of these article sections). Additionally, it is critical that the research synthesis be thorough and clearly written. Journal editors indicate that they seek clarity in these syntheses with regard to the purpose and problem definition, thoroughness and clarity in the presentation of methods and findings, and clarity in the researcher's conclusions (Becker, 1991). Specifically, research syntheses are typically evaluated by journal editors and reviewers on seven criteria: (a) quality of the literature reviewed, (b) significance of the topic, (c) potential impact of the review on research and practice, (d) contribution to the field, (e) appropriate length, (f) clarity of expression, and (g) balance and fairness (Murray & Raths, 1996).

Introduction. The goal of the introduction is to set the research synthesis within the field of inquiry. The introduction typically begins by describing the broad scientific question that is being addressed and its importance within the field of inquiry. The introduction should also indicate why the research synthesis is needed (e.g., it may be the first review of its kind, there may be some unresolved controversy in the field, previous research syntheses may have included only a portion of the primary studies). It is important that researchers specify the problem addressed by research syntheses in detail. Finally, the introduction should indicate what the critical research consumer will gain from the review and provide an overview of the research synthesis.

Method. The method section should describe the procedures to conduct the research synthesis in detail. Although the specific procedures may vary, method sections often include operational definitions of the concepts under review, a description of the literature search methods and scope, criteria for including and excluding primary studies, a description of the study characteristics and data gleaned from each of the primary studies, procedures for determining the accuracy of data collection methods (e.g., interrater agreement), and methods for determining the magnitude of the intervention effect and relating study characteristics to intervention outcomes. Additionally, if the specific procedures used in the research synthesis differ substantively from those published elsewhere, differences should be discussed in detail.

Results. The results section presents the findings of each aspect of the research synthesis. The results section typically begins with a description of the results of the synthesis (i.e., studies included in the research synthesis). Researchers sometimes include two lists of studies in the reference section. One list gives the primary studies used in the synthesis, and the second list presents the methodological or other articles referenced in the text. This format enables the critical research consumer to identify the primary studies included in the research synthesis with ease.

A results section should also include a description of the relevant study characteristics such as experimental conditions, participants, and dependent measures that are relevant to the purpose of the research synthesis. Researchers often provide summary tables or graphical presentations of the study characteristics to help the critical research consumer better understand the primary studies included. It is important to note that the amount of information that researchers present regarding study characteristics may depend on the journal space that editors allow.

Finally, the results section should present a detailed description of the primary findings. The primary findings should also be tabled or presented in a graphic format. Researchers sometimes include both the primary study characteristics and results on the same table. However, depending on the complexity of the research synthesis, researchers sometimes present the findings separately from the study characteristics. The results should include a description of both the pooled intervention outcomes (i.e., average intervention outcome) as well as relationships between study characteristics and intervention outcomes.

Discussion. The discussion section should set the findings of the research synthesis within the context of the field of inquiry. The focus of the discussion section should be related to the purpose of the review. For example, if the purpose was to assess the overall cost-effectiveness of a particular intervention, the discussion should focus on the economic impact of the intervention outcome. The discussion should clarify the implications of the findings regarding the relationship between study characteristics and intervention outcomes. Finally, the discussion should discuss the implications of the findings for future research.

Analysis of Data

Threats to the Validity of Research Syntheses. Research syntheses rely heavily on the conceptual and interpretive skills of researchers. Although recent developments have reduced the scope of error and bias associated with researchers conducting the research synthesis, all approaches are subject to the fallibility of the individuals conducting the review. Thus, it is critical that researchers and critical research consumers alike assess the validity of research syntheses because they are the main ways in which assessments are made about the accumulation of knowledge in a given field, impacting future research, policy, and practice. Research syntheses tend to have a greater impact on a field than does any one primary research study.

The validity of a research synthesis is dependent on the way in which it is conducted and disseminated. There are three points in time in the process of conducting a research synthesis when researchers can make errors that affect its validity: (a) searching and selecting primary research studies, (b) coding study characteristics, and (c) drawing conclusions. Dunkin (1996) details the topology of errors that researchers make in each of these points in time when conducting a research synthesis. Although it is difficult for critical research consumers to scrutinize research syntheses fully to ensure their validity, it is important to be aware that syntheses are *not* different from primary studies. They are also subject to error at every stage of their development and execution. Thus, researchers who conduct research syntheses need to avoid making these errors, and critical research consumers who use these syntheses should look closely to see if these errors have been made.

Errors Associated with Searching and Selecting Primary Research Studies. There are two types of errors that researchers can make when searching and selecting primary research studies. The first type of error centers on the exclusion of primary studies that fall within the declared scope of the review. The outcome of this error is that conclusions made by researchers conducting the research synthesis are not based on the entire defined field of inquiry. The inclusion of the missing primary research studies may contradict the findings of those based on the included studies. This type of error should become less of a problem as the tools available for conducting literature searches and developing bibliographies become more advanced. However, these advancements will not eliminate mistakes in the use of technologies made by researchers conducting research syntheses.

The second type of error focuses on the failure of researchers to discriminate between good and poor research. Researchers equally weight the findings from good and poor research. The outcome of this error is that conclusions are not balanced because the findings from good and poor research are given equal status. Weighting the findings from good research more heavily than those from poor research may lead to conclusions that contradict those made if good and poor research are given equal status. Weighting the findings from good research more heavily is important because not all research on the same phenomena is of equal quality.

Errors Associated with Coding Study Characteristics. The procedures used to code study characteristics is the second point in the review process at which errors can affect the validity of the research synthesis. This is the point at which the variety of errors made by researchers conducting the research synthesis is greatest (Dunkin, 1996). It is critical that researchers use procedures to ensure the accuracy of their procedures for coding study characteristics. There are four types of errors that researchers can make at this point in the review process. The first type of error centers on the inaccurate coding or recording of the study characteristics such as the sampling, methods, designs, procedures, and contexts of the primary research studies. For example, researchers will report the opening statement regarding the sample size and fail to recognize that attrition occurred. Errors in the coding of study characteristics can lead to the misclassification of the primary research studies so that they do not share the essential characteristics that are supposed to make them comparable to other studies. Making studies comparable is critical because one of the key aspects of conducting a research synthesis is to determine the relationship between study characteristics and intervention outcomes.

The second type of error focuses on double counting the findings from one primary research study, which gives it more weight in the research synthesis. This type of error occurs in two ways. First, many primary research studies include more than one intervention outcome. As mentioned earlier, researchers typically eliminate this problem by computing an average intervention outcome for the study. However, researchers may not compute an average intervention outcome in all cases. Second, a primary research study can be included more than once in a research synthesis because researchers often report the findings from a study several times. For example, it is not uncommon for researchers to first report the findings from a primary research study in a conference paper prior to publishing it in a peer-reviewed journal. Researchers often make this mistake because it is difficult to detect especially because titles and lists of authors are often changed. Thus, it is critical that researchers and critical research consumers alike look closely to ensure that multiple reporting of primary studies is not included in a research synthesis.

The third type of error centers on the failure of researchers to detect the faulty conclusions of the authors of primary research studies. Researchers of primary research studies do not always accurately or fully report the findings in their conclusions. Researchers conducting research syntheses risk continuing the misrepresentation of findings if they uncritically accept the conclusions of the authors of the primary research studies. The occurrence of this error can be contributed by the original authors, who may be biased to the extent of selectively incorporating only expected findings in their conclusions.

The final type of error focuses on the suppression of contrary findings. Primary research studies may contain findings that are contradictory to the conclusions which researchers conducting the research synthesis claim they support. This is not to say that the primary studies do not contain findings that support the conclusions of researchers conducting the research synthesis. Rather, the findings in the primary studies that contradict such conclusions may be suppressed or ignored.

Errors Associated with Drawing Conclusions. The conclusions drawn is the final point in the review process at which errors can affect the validity of the research synthesis. It is this point in time that the errors detailed earlier fully impact the research synthesis. Errors made at this point are a function of those made at earlier stages. All of the previous errors will affect the conclusions made by researchers. There is little question that valid conclusions cannot be made from inaccurate assessments of the primary studies included in the review or the exclusion of findings that are relevant to the phenomena under study.

WHEN SHOULD RESEARCHERS CONDUCT RESEARCH SYNTHESES?

Research syntheses are important in that they allow us to integrate large amounts of information. Recall from Chapter 1 that replications are critical to the scientific process. Research syntheses may allow us to combine the results of past investigations, many of which are replications. Questions referring to topics such as the effectiveness of certain types of instruction, limitations in our current knowledge level, or directions for future research may be answered with research syntheses. Finally, there are four instances when one would wish to complete a research synthesis: (a) to establish causal relationships between variables; (b) to determine the degree of relationship between two variables; (c) to develop and confirm theories; and (d) to assess the extent to which the findings from research can be generalized to a larger set of participants, experimental procedures, and situations beyond those of the original research studies.

DISCUSSION QUESTIONS

1. You are working on a committee at your school district charged with developing K–12 guidelines for homework. A colleague brings an unsystematic research synthesis for the committee to consider. Another member of the committee notices that you grimaced when the individual began to discuss the conclusions of the research synthesis and asks why you are

uncomfortable. Describe why you are uncomfortable placing confidence in the conclusions of the unsystematic research synthesis.

2. Describe to the members of the committee the difference between systematic and unsystematic research syntheses.
3. You are asked by the members of the committee about the advantages and disadvantages of conducting an unsystematic research synthesis on the effects of homework on the academic performance of K–12 students. How would you respond?
4. The committee decides to conduct a research synthesis on the effects of homework. Describe to the members of the committee the steps they should go through to conduct the research synthesis.
5. What types of research questions would you suggest the committee use to guide the research synthesis on the effects of homework on the academic performance of K–12 students?
6. You ask the members of the committee whether an exploratory research synthesis or a hypothesis-testing research synthesis should be conducted. A member of the committee is unsure of what the differences are between the two. Describe the differences between an exploratory research synthesis and a hypothesis-testing research synthesis.
7. As the committee begins to identify the literature to be included in the research synthesis, a colleague states that the committee could use a bibliography of articles on homework that he got from a presenter at a regional conference for elementary school teachers. Describe the disadvantages of restricting the research synthesis to those only included in the bibliography.
8. After this discussion, describe the process the committee should use to conduct an exhaustive search of the literature.
9. After the procedures for identifying the literature have been detailed, a member of the committee asks you what study characteristics should be examined. Describe the study characteristics that the committee should consider when reviewing each of the primary studies and why they should be related to the intervention outcomes.
10. As the committee is conducting the research synthesis, you raise the issue of ensuring its validity. Describe to the members of the committee the factors that might affect the validity of the research synthesis.

THE MORAL REASONING OF JUVENILE DELINQUENTS: A META-ANALYSIS

J. RON NELSON,[1] DEBORAH J. SMITH,[2] AND JOHN DODD[3]

To test the hypothesized immaturity of juvenile delinquents' moral reasoning, the results of 15 studies of the moral reasoning of juvenile delinquents were integrated quantitatively using meta-analysis. Hedges and Olkin (1985) methods were used to (a) compute effect sizes, (b) test the homogeneity of the obtained effect sizes, and (c) test the statistical significance of the pooled mean ef-

fect size. The results supported the hypothesis that the moral reasoning of juvenile delinquents is immature. It was concluded that several other issues are in need of investigation.

Researchers have investigated the moral reasoning of juvenile delinquents within a developmental framework (e.g., Foder, 1972; Kohlberg, 1969; Jurkovic, 1976). Kohlberg's theory of moral development and his concept of moral reasoning have been used in investigations of the delinquent conduct of adolescents (Jurkovic, 1980). These studies of moral reasoning have served to illuminate a previously ignored aspect of adolescent psychopathology.

Kohlberg (1958) assumed that moral reasoning plays a central role in moral action. Moral reasoning provides unity to the many complex processes (i.e., questions, doubts, judgments, and decisions) that compose moral action. From this perspective, moral action can be viewed as a criterion for measuring moral reasoning. On the basis of this perspective, researchers have hypothesized that the moral reasoning of juvenile delinquents is less mature than that of nondelinquents (e.g., Jurkovic, 1976; Kohlberg, 1958).

Two previous narrative reviews of the morality literature included the investigations of the moral reasoning of juvenile delinquents (Blasi, 1980; Jurkovic, 1980). However, neither specifically addressed the hypothesized immaturity of juvenile reasoning. Additionally, both Blasi (1980) and Jurkovic (1980) noted that design flaws (e.g., scoring procedures) common to a number of the studies limit the amount of confidence that can be placed in the findings of individual studies. The techniques of meta-analysis can be used to integrate quantitatively the findings of a group of studies and examine the effect of study characteristics of the findings (Hedges & Olkin, 1985). Therefore, the purpose of the present analysis was to integrate quantitatively, using the techniques of meta-analysis, the investigations of the hypothesized immaturity of juvenile delinquents' moral reasoning and to identify issues in need of investigation.

Manuscript received in final form October 31, 1989.

[1]Department of Special Education, Utah State University, Logan, Utah 84322–6500.

[2]Western Psychiatric Institute and Clinics, University of Pittsburgh, Pittsburgh, Pennsylvania.

[3]Institute of Habilitative Services, Eastern Montana College, Billings, Montana 59101.

METHOD

Selection of Studies

The literature examined was identified through a computer search of the complete *Exceptional Child Education Resources Abstracts, Dissertation Abstracts,* and *Psychological Abstracts.* Descriptors included morals, moral reasoning, juvenile delinquents, adolescents, adolescence, and youth. In addition, an ancestral search was conducted from the identified articles. Studies reviewed investigated the moral reasoning of juvenile delinquents and provided information needed to conduct the meta-analysis. With regard to this latter requirement, none of the studies reviewed was rejected.

Studies excluded from this review were those that failed to use an equivalent nondelinquent control group (Hawk & Peterson, 1974; Kanter, 1976) or investigated the moral reasoning of other subculture groups such as drug users (Alterman, Druley, Connolly, & Bush, 1978), psychopathic delinquents (Fodor, 1973), adolescents who exhibited withdrawn behaviors (Sigman, Ungerer, & Russell, 1983), or students with learning disabilities (Fincham, 1977).

The 15 studies identified, presented in chronological order in Table 1, provided a direct test of the hypothesized immaturity of juvenile delinquents' moral reasoning. Table 1 presents a description of the subjects, the basis for matching (e.g., race, intelligence, age), the measures of moral reasoning used, and the study outcome.

Classifying and Coding of Studies

Characteristics coded from each study included (a) number of subjects, (b) mean age of subjects,

TABLE 1 Studies of Relations between Moral Reasoning and Delinquency

STUDY	SUBJECTS	BASIS FOR MATCHING	MEASURE OF MORAL ORIENTATION	*d*
Betke (1944)	50 delinquents, 50 nondelinquents, mean age 13.8	Age, IQ, SES, geographic area	25 social-moral problems constructed by author	0.81
Kohlberg (1958)	12 delinquents, 12 nondelinquents, mean age about 16.0	Age, IQ, SES	9 dilemmas, Kohlberg interview, not blind	0.34
Ruma (1967)	30 delinquents, 30 nondelinquents, mean age about 16.0	Age, IQ, SES, geographic area	6 dilemmas, Kohlberg interview	0.43
Fodor (1972)	40 delinquents, 40 nondelinquents, mean age 15.0	Age, IQ, SES, mother's education	9 dilemmas, Kohlberg written, blind	1.19
Hudgins & Prentice (1973)	10 delinquents, 10 nondelinquents, mean age 15.4	Age, IQ, race, SES, geographic area	4 dilemmas, Kohlberg issue scoring	1.25
Jurkovic & Prentice (1974)	8 delinquents, 8 nondelinquents, mean age 15.0	Age, IQ, race, SES, geographic area, mother's education	4 dilemmas, Kohlberg issue scoring, blind	0.38
Miller, Zurnoff, & Stephens (1974)	16 delinquents, 16 nondelinquents, mean age 15.0	None	3 levels of moral judgement, 3-point system	0.86
Campagna & Harter (1975)	21 sociopaths, 23 normals, mean age 11.7	Age, IQ, SES, geographic area	4 dilemmas, Kohlberg interview, blind	1.68
Jurkovic (1976)	36 delinquents, 12 nondelinquents, mean age 15.0	Age, race, SES, social environment, length of institutionalization	3 dilemmas, Kohlberg issue scoring, blind	0.34
Schmidlin (1977)	60 delinquents, 30 nondelinquents, mean age 15.5	Age, IQ, race, SES, geographic area	Moral judgment scale/blind	0.51
Haviland (1977)	22 delinquents, 22 nondelinquents, mean age 12	Age, IQ,social, environment	3 stories of theft punitive restitutive reasoning	0.65
Kohlberg & Freundlich (1977)	20 delinquents, 14 nondelinquents, mean age 11.3	Age, IQ, SES	4 dilemmas, Kohlberg interview, not blind	0.24
Study 2	13 delinquents, 13 nondelinquents, mean age 14.9	Age, IQ, SES	9 dilemmas, Kohlberg interview, blind	1.01
Study 3	15 delinquents, 20 nondelinquents, mean age 15	Age, IQ, SES	9 dilemmas, Kohlberg interview, blind	0.96
Lee & Prentice (1988)	12 delinquents, 18 nondelinquents, mean age 16.05	Age, IQ, SES	2 dilemmas, Kohlberg interview, blind	0.79

(c) mean IQ of subjects, (d) percentage of male subjects, (e) date of publication, (f) publication form (i.e., journal article, dissertation, book, other published document), (g) whether researcher(s) included procedures to control for delinquents in their comparison group, (h) type of measure, (i) scoring procedures used (i.e., blind or not blind), and (j) basis for matching (e.g., IQ, age, race). These variables were coded by both the senior author and a colleague for 10 (67%) randomly selected investigations. Average agreement across all methodological features was 0.99, ranging from 0.98 to 1.00. Interrater agreement was calculated using the following formula: percentage of agreement = agreements between raters A and B divided by agreements and disagreements between rater A and B (Coutler, cited in Thompson, White, & Morgan, 1982). Disagreements were resolved through discussion between the raters.

Analysis

The unit of analysis in this meta-analysis was effect size (g), defined as the mean difference between experimental and comparison groups divided by the pooled sample standard deviation (see Hedges & Olkin, 1985). The g's computed for 11 of the studies were based on means and standard deviations, whereas g's for 4 of the studies were estimated from the probability (p) values (Kohlberg & Freundlich, 1977; Miller, Zumoff, & Stephens, 1974).

Because g possesses a bias with small sample size (i.e., overestimates the population effect size), a correction factor was applied (see Hedges & Olkin, 1985). Application of the correction factor removes the bias and converts the obtained g's to d's.

RESULTS

Study Characteristics

Before considering the hypothesized immaturity of the moral reasoning of juvenile delinquents, we examined the characteristics of the studies. Included were 673 subjects. The mean number of subjects per study was 48 and ranged from 16 to 100. The average age was 15.34 years (SD = 1.56), with a range from 11 to 17 years. Subjects' mean IQ fell into the average range (M = 90.27, SD = 4.82); however, IQ data were not available for 4 studies (Fodor, 1972; Kohlberg & Freundlich, 1977). Subject samples were either all male or all female (see Table 1). Three studies were published prior to the 1970s, 11 in the 1970s, and 1 in the 1980s. Eight studies were published documents (Betke, 1944; Campagna & Harter, 1975; Fodor, 1972; Haviland, 1977; Hudgins & Prentice, 1973; Jurkovic & Prentice, 1974; Lee & Prentice, 1988; Miller et al., 1974), 4 were dissertations (Jurkovic, 1976; Kohlberg, 1958; Ruma, 1967; Schmidlin, 1977), and 3 were unpublished papers (Kohlberg & Freundlich, 1977). Researchers in 11 studies failed to employ procedures to control for the possibility of delinquents in their comparison groups (Betke, 1944; Fodor, 1972; Haviland, 1977; Hudgins & Prentice, 1973; Kohlberg, 1958; Kohlberg & Freundlich, 1977; Lee & Prentice, 1988; Miller et al., 1974; Ruma, 1967). Kohlberg's interview was used as a measure of moral reasoning in 13 studies while researchers in the remaining 2 studies developed their own measures. Scoring was done blindly in only 9 studies. Subjects were matched on variety of factors in 13 studies, while subjects were not matched on any factors in the remaining two studies.

All of the correlations between effect size and study characteristics were nonsignificant ($p < .05$). The correlations between g's and study characteristics were as follows: (a) sample size (r = .03), (b) mean age (r = -.25), (c) mean IQ (r = .12), (d) an analysis of the association between gender and g was not conducted, (e) date of publication (η = .06), (f) source of publication (η = -.32), (g) control for delinquents in comparison group (r_{pbis} = .08), (h) measure of moral reasoning (r_{pbis} = -.16), (i) scoring (i.e., blind or not blind) (r_{pbis} = -.29), and (j) basis for matching (η = -.25).

Differences in Moral Reasoning

Before testing the null hypothesis that the population mean g equals zero, it was necessary to test the homogeneity of the obtained g's to determine whether they could be described as sharing a common population g. Calculation of a homogeneity statistic, Q, which has an approximate chi-square distribution with $k - 1$ degrees of freedom and where k is the number of effect sizes, provides a test of the homogeneity of the obtained g's (see Hedges & Olkin, 1985). The hypothesis that the population g's were statistically equivalent was not rejected, $Q(14) = 19.52$, $p < .05$, and the obtained g's were pooled and averaged.

With each study contributing a single g, a mean was computed with each of the g's weighted by the reciprocal of its variance (see Hedges & Olkin, 1985). This weighting procedure gives greater weight to g's that are more reliably estimated. The resulting mean was 0.74 (median = 0.79), indicating lower levels of moral reasoning for delinquents relative to nondelinquents. The 95% confidence interval (CI) for this mean, CI = .62 to .93, indicates that the mean d differed significantly from zero, which indicates exactly no effect. This statistical analysis provides evidence to support the hypothesis that the moral reasoning of juvenile delinquents is immature.

DISCUSSION

The results of the meta-analysis suggest that the moral reasoning of juvenile delinquents is lower relative to that of nondelinquents. The magnitude of the difference is substantial given that the measures of moral reasoning used in these studies are intended to measure fundamental, underlying structures of social thought rather than fine-grained descriptions of specific concepts and ideas (Schiaefli, Rest, & Thoma, 1985).

The results also suggest that differences in the methodologies employed failed to influence the findings. The lack of significant associations between study characteristics and the obtained mean g as well as the consistency of the g's across the studies provide evidence counter to Blasi's (1980) and Jurkovic's (1980) assertion that design flaws common to a number of the studies limit the amount of confidence that can be placed in the findings of individual studies.

Although the literature reviewed provides empirical support for the immaturity of juvenile delinquents' moral reasoning, it reflects a lack of emphasis on other important issues. First, there is need to clarify the association between categories (e.g., violent, nonviolent) of delinquent conduct and moral reasoning. Because authors failed to provide information regarding the type(s) of juvenile conduct, we were unable to examine this issue in this analysis. Kanter (1976) studied four categories of delinquent offenses (i.e., noneconomic violent, economic violent, economic nonviolent, and drug use) and found significant differences in moral reasoning among the groups. Although preliminary, the results of this study suggest that a more fine-grained analysis of the association between delinquent conduct and moral reasoning is possible. Similar types of studies would serve to clarify further the association between delinquent conduct and moral reasoning.

Next, the effects of personality variables, behavioral variables, and contextual variables on the moral reasoning of juvenile delinquents are needed. Although specific to females, Gilligan (1977) provides a provocative discussion regarding a variety of influences and their effect on moral reasoning. Clearly, further investigations are needed of the effect of these variables on moral reasoning.

Finally, there is a need for longitudinal studies to illuminate whether the moral reasoning of delinquents is fixated or whether it is progressing at slower rates than that of nondelinquents. Additionally, longitudinal studies would help to determine the effects of programs designed to modify the moral reasoning of juvenile delinquents.

REFERENCES

Alterman, A. I., Druley, K. A., Connolly. R., & Bush, D. (1978). A comparison of moral reasoning in drug addicts and nonaddicts. *Journal of Clinical Psychology, 34,* 790–794.

Betke, M. A. (1944). Defective moral reasoning and delinquency: A psychological study. *Catholic University of America Studies in Psychology and Psychiatry, 6*(4).

Blasi, A. (1980). Bridging moral cognition and moral action: A critical review of the literature. *Psychological Bulletin, 88,* 1–45.

Campagna, A. F., & Harter, S. (1975). Moral judgments in sociopathic and normal children. *Journal of Personality and Social Psychology, 31,* 199–205.

Fincham, F. (1977). A comparison of moral judgment in learning disabled and normal achieving boys. *Journal of Psychology, 96,* 153–160.

Fodor, E. M. (1972). Delinquency and susceptibility of social influence among adolescents as a function of moral development. *Journal of Social Psychology, 85,* 121–126.

Fodor, E. M. (1973). Moral development and parent behavior antecedents in adolescent psychopaths. *Journal of Genetic Psychology, 122,* 37–43.

Giligan, C. (1977). In a different voice. *Harvard Educational Review, 47,* 365–378.

Haviland, J. M. (1977). The punitive beliefs and behaviors of adolescent delinquent boys. *Developmental Psychology, 13,* 677–678.

Hawk, S., & Peterson, R. A. (1974). Do MMPI psychopathic deviancy scores reflect psychopathic deviancy or just deviancy? *Journal of Personality Assessment, 38,* 362–368.

Hedges, L., & Olkin, I. (1985). *Statistical methods for meta-analysis.* London: Academic Press.

Hudgins, W., & Prentice, N. M. (1973). Moral judgment in delinquent and nondelinquent adolescents and their mothers. *Journal of Abnormal Psychology, 82,* 145–152.

Jurkovic, G. J. (1976). The relationship of moral and cognitive development to dimensions of juvenile delinquency (Doctoral dissertation, University of Texas at Austin, 1975). *Dissertation Abstracts International, 36, 5262B.* (University Microfilms No. 76–8,054)

Jurkovic, G. J. (1980). The juvenile delinquent as a moral philosopher: A structural-developmental perspective. *Psychological Bulletin, 88,* 709–727.

Jurkovic, G. J., & Prentice, N. M. (1974). Dimensions of moral interaction and moral judgment in delinquent and nondelinquent families. *Journal of Consulting and Clinical Psychology, 42,* 256–262.

Kanter, J. E. (1976). The relationship between moral judgment and personality variables in adult offenders (Doctoral dissertation, Purdue University, 1975). *Dissertation Abstracts International, 36, 5262B-5263B.* (University Microfilms No. 76–7,088)

Kohlberg, L. (1958). *The development of modes of moral thinking and choice in the years ten to sixteen.* Unpublished doctoral dissertation, University of Chicago.

Kohlberg, L. (1969). Stage and sequence: The cognitive-developmental approach to socialization. In D. Goslin (Ed.), *Handbook of specialization theory* (pp. 347–480). New York: Rand McNally.

Kohlberg, L., & Freundlich, D. (1977). *Moral judgment in youthful offenders.* Unpublished manuscript, Harvard University.

Lee, M., & Prentice, N. M. (1988). Interrelations of empathy, cognition, and moral reasoning with dimensions of juvenile delinquency. *Journal of Abnormal Child Psychology, 16,* 127–139.

Miller, C. K., Zumoff, L., & Stephens, B. A. (1974). A comparison of reasoning skills and moral judgments in delinquent, retarded, and normal adolescent girls. *Journal of Psychology, 85,* 261–268.

Ruma, E. H. (1967). Conscience development in delinquents and non-delinquents: The relationship between moral judgment, guilt, and behavior (Doctoral dissertation, Ohio State University, 1967). *Dissertation Abstracts International, 28, 2631B.* (University Microfilms No. 67–16,331)

Schiaefli, A., Rest, J. R., & Thoma, S. J. (1985). Does moral education improve moral judgment? A meta-analysis of intervention studies using the defining issues test. *Review of Educational Research, 55*(3), 319–352.

Schmidlin, S. S. (1977). Moral judgment and delinquency: The effect of institutionalization and peer pressure (Doctoral dissertation, University of Florida, 1975). *Dissertation Abstracts International, 37, 3630B.* (University Microfilms No. 77–124)

Sigman, M., Ungerer, J. A., & Russell, A. (1983). Moral judgment in relation to behavioral and cognitive disorders in adolescents. *Journal of Abnormal Child Psychology, 11,* 503–512.

Thompson, R. H., White, K. R., & Morgan, D. P. (1982). Teacher-student interaction patterns in classrooms with mainstreamed mildly handicapped students. *American Educational Research Journal, 19,* 220–236.

FACTUAL QUESTIONS

1. What is the purpose of the research synthesis?
2. Why did researchers hypothesize that the moral reasoning of juvenile delinquents is less mature than that of nondelinquents?
3. How many previous research syntheses had been conducted on this topic?
4. What abstracts did the authors search to identify primary research studies?
5. What descriptors were used by the authors?
6. What types of studies were reviewed?
7. What types of studies were not reviewed?
8. What study characteristics did the authors extract from the primary studies?
9. What was the average effect size obtained?
10. Were any study characteristics related to the study outcomes?

DISCUSSION QUESTIONS

1. Does the introduction convince you that the article is going to present important new information?
2. What population of individuals would you be willing to generalize the results of this review of the literature? Explain.
3. Do you think the results have any relevance to professionals working with juvenile delinquents? Explain.
4. Do the authors describe the statistical procedures used adequately? Explain.
5. Are the procedures used to identify the articles adequately described?
6. Were the search strategies used by the authors of high quality? Explain.
7. Are the results presented in a clear and concise fashion? Explain.
8. Are the authors' conclusions consistent with the findings?
9. What threats to the validity of this review of the literature should critical research consumers be concerned about?
10. What is your opinion of the meta-analysis technique? State reasons for your opinion.

PART SEVEN

ACTION RESEARCH

CHAPTER 15 ACTION RESEARCH

Chapter 15

ACTION RESEARCH

MOVING FROM CRITICAL RESEARCH CONSUMER TO RESEARCHER

OBJECTIVES

After studying this chapter you should be able to

1. Describe what action research is.
2. Describe the characteristics of action research.
3. Describe how different research methods can be used in action research.
4. Explain why researchers must be aware of research ethics in research.
5. Describe what an institutional review board (IRB) is and why it functions.
6. Describe the Ethical Standards of the American Educational Research Association (AERA)
7. Describe the Ethical Principles of Psychologists and the Code of Conduct from the American Psychological Association (APA).
8. Explain the difference between refereed and nonrefereed journals.
9. Describe the concern over using politically-correct language.
10. Describe the contents of a research article.
11. Describe the process of submitting an article for publication.
12. Describe when one would conduct action research.
13. Critique an action research article.

OVERVIEW

We have described procedures that directly impact researchers and critical research consumers alike throughout this text. The focus has been on what researchers do and why. Our goal was to help you become aware of the complexities of research in such a way as to aid you in becoming a critical research consumer. But researchers are not the only ones capable of conducting research. When you become a critical research consumer, you can also begin to produce research. Thus, we now turn our attention to making critical research consumers actual researchers.

Becoming a "researcher" is difficult for many direct-care providers because of the sheer amount of time needed to conduct, write, and publish research findings. Many individuals see this as more of a burden than a benefit. However, the question to address is what type of research is a critical research consumer capable of doing given the constraints of his or her particular situation? We have to keep in mind that research informs practice. What are the necessary skills needed to conduct, write, and publish findings when critical research consumers are immersed in providing direct services to others? What must teachers, psychologists, and other care providers do to show that what they are doing is actually working?

This chapter describes the practice of action research. Action research is usually associated with qualitative methods; however, we believe this is short-sighted. Teachers, psychologists, and other professionals could use other research methods in an applied setting as well. Part of conducting any type of research is a concern with research ethics. Thus, research ethics are discussed. Additionally, if teachers, psychologists, and other professionals are interested in publishing the results of their action research, some understanding of the contents required for most articles and the publication process should be possessed. This chapter covers how to write a research article and how to go about getting it published. Finally, an illustrative action research investigation is presented at the end of the chapter for critique.

WHAT IS ACTION RESEARCH?

Action research has gained popularity in the last few years but has been around for some 50 years (Elden & Chisholm, 1993). Elden and Chisholm indicate that Kurt Lewin introduced the term "action research" in 1946. Lewin described action research as "a way of generating knowledge about a social system while, at the same time, attempting to change it" (p. 121). Action research (AR) may be conducted by a person in a particular situation or the persons in that setting have a major role in the design and implementation of the investigation.

For example, if research were conducted in the classroom, a teacher would be acting as the researcher. Action research could also involve the teacher helping a researcher design and conduct the investigation. In other words, the participants of action research can be involved in the research process *with* researchers. Additionally, professionals can collaborate to conduct action research such as when several teachers from a school district get together and discuss and actually pursue action research questions of interest (Caro-Bruce & McCreadie, 1994). This collaborative effort is different from having a researcher come into the classroom and take data without the help of the teacher. As described by Elden and Chisholm (1993):

> *Lewin (1946) and most subsequent researchers have conceived of AR as a cyclical inquiry process that involves diagnosing a problem situation, planning action steps, and implementing and evaluating outcomes. Evaluation leads to diagnosing the situation anew based on learnings from the previous activities cycle. A distinctive feature of AR is that the research process is carried out in collaboration with those who experience the problem or their representatives. The main idea is that action research uses a scientific approach to study important organizational or social problems with the people who experience them. (p. 124)*

Thus, when individuals plan for the collection of data, collect the data, and then evaluate or analyze the data to improve their situation, they are conducting action research.

Action research should also contain data that are collected frequently throughout the experimental period (e.g., grading period). For example, suppose a teacher was concerned with the effectiveness of her approach to teaching spelling in the third grade. The teacher could use her method of instruction as the independent variable and the percentage of words spelled correctly as the dependent measure. The teacher could then track the acquisition of spelling words throughout the semester. If the students' spelling skills improved, the teacher would be more confident in her instructional approach. If the students' performance did not improve greatly, the teacher would know this during the grading period and could make adjustments to her instructional approach. Data-based decision making is another term that has been used in fields such as special education and rehabilitation for this practice; that is, we make changes in how we teach (instruction) based on how our students are doing (assessment).

Although action research may be conducted to contribute to our understanding of a phenomenon, its sole purpose is not to control for threats to internal or external validity. The purpose of action research is primarily to determine what is occurring in a particular setting, how that something affects participants and/or professionals, and why that something occurs. The level of internal validity will usually be limited because the level of experimental control necessary to control for all threats to internal validity may not be possible. In addition, information on the external validity of a single investigation will also be limited because the variables to be taken into consideration (different participants, different teachers, different dependent variables/measures) will not be considered. The focus is on the particular context in which the research takes place.

Dimensions of Action Research

There are five dimensions of action research (Chisholm & Elden, 1993). These dimensions include (a) the complexity of the system levels (from less complex restricted to the particular group under study to most complex across societies); (b) the level of organization in the system (from loosely organized, where there are unclear values and unclear goals, to tightly organized, where there is clarity of roles and shared values); (c) the openness of the research process (from open, where the action research process is discovered, to closed, where the action research is predetermined); (d) the intended outcomes of the research (from basic, where there is a change in the key parameters within the system, to complex, where there is a change in the existing parameters of an organization); and (e) the role of the researcher (from collaboratively managed, where the decisions are made together with the researcher and system members, to researcher-dominated, where the researcher is in control of the project).

Thus, it is difficult to determine exactly what constitutes "pure" action research and what does not. The important consideration is that action research is not all the same, and action research investigations vary in important ways. For example, quantitative, qualitative, single-case, survey, historical, and program evaluation research methods can be used in action research.

WHAT ARE THE CHARACTERISTICS OF ACTION RESEARCH?

There are five characteristics of action research: (a) purposes and value choice, (b) contextual focus, (c) change-based data and sense making, (d) participation in the research process, and (e) knowledge diffusion (Elden & Chisholm, 1993). However, all of these characteristics must be present in an investigation for it to be considered action research. The extent to which each characteristic is present across investigations will vary.

Purposes and Value Choice

"Action research adds solving problems to the scientific enterprise. It rejects the idea that science is completely value free" (Elden & Chisholm, 1993, p. 126). Thus, the primary goal of action research is to solve problems in real-life situations. Also, action research indicates that those conducting the research usually have something at stake in the outcomes of that research. In action research, the obvious stake that teachers have is that their students learn what they need to learn to function in society. Additionally, teachers have an involvement with their students that prevents them from remaining totally objective and separated from their students. However, this situation can be seen as an advantage. When we realize that our values can and do affect how we see the world, we can take these values into consideration when interpreting research results. This realization is important for teachers and practitioners. Perhaps more important than anything else, action research can help practitioners understand what values they have and how those values affect what they are doing.

Contextual Focus

Action research is also context-bound—it occurs in the real world addressing real-life problems or situations. The problems or situations to be addressed in action research are defined by those already in the context such as classroom teachers. Action researchers set out to solve a problem or to answer a research question and then attempt to fit the results within a theory. This sequence of events is the reverse of much of quantitative research where the theory is developed first and the research is an attempt to verify predictions made based on the theory. The ultimate outcome of action research is the process through which the action researcher must go to obtain a solution. The gathering of data will allow action researchers to learn more about their settings and students/participants as well as themselves.

Change-Based Data and Sense Making

The data collected in action research is obtained in a systematic fashion similar to when researchers conduct field research. The goal of action researchers is to generate the data and then to make interpretations with the ultimate goal of making changes in their practice. Thus, the manner in which the data are collected must be logical and follow accepted methods of data gathering. For example, if action researchers were using qualitative methods, triangulation should be obtained. After the data are collected, action researchers should relate the findings to a theory or theories in much the same way as do conventional qualitative researchers. The data gathered by action researchers and the conclusions made based on the data can be as legitimate as data gathered by other researchers.

Participation in the Research Process

One way that can set action research apart from other forms of research is that action researchers are participants in the process. Action researchers are part of the contexts being investigated, and thus, are also being investigated. Unlike other research, action research can involve the investigation of one's self in a wider context. For example, if a classroom teacher is investigating how students react to new classroom rules using a qualitative research method, the teacher should measure how she responds to the changes in the rules as well. Additionally, since the teacher probably developed the rules with the help of the students, the teacher's action of setting up the new rules is under investigation. Thus, the teacher is determining how her actions affect others in the classroom context.

Knowledge Diffusion

A final characteristic of action research is that solutions to problems through the use of action research will be disseminated in some manner. The dissemination of the information obtained from action research occurs on a continuum. On one end, dissemination occurs when action researchers inform other teachers and/or staff of what was found. At the other end, action researchers determine how the problem and solution add to current knowledge and theory. Once that is done, action researchers will write up the results for publication (the process for this will be discussed later in this chapter). Somewhere in between, action researchers can present the findings at local, regional, or national meetings. The point here is that action research is typically disseminated in some form once the information has been gained and the solution to a problem has been found.

HOW ARE QUANTITATIVE METHODS USED IN ACTION RESEARCH?

The use of quantitative research designs in action research is not as common as in other research approaches since much of quantitative research will not necessarily incorporate all of the characteristics outlined before. Quantitative research methods usually require at least two groups of participants (e.g., two classrooms). It would be possible for two or more teachers to get together and design a quantitative research investigation and compare their respective classrooms, but the likeliness of this occurring is probably not high. Action research is usually conducted by one teacher in one classroom.

Teachers are also not likely to develop formal research hypotheses and approach the phenomenon in a deductive manner. Teachers are more likely to ask questions such as, "I wonder what would happen if...?" or "I wonder if what I do actually works?" It is also unlikely that most teachers and practitioners are as informed of educational and psychological theories as would be required normally to develop a hypothesis. This is not to say that teachers and practitioners are incapable of conducting quantitative research, but that quantitative research is not as adaptable to the day-to-day operations of the classroom environment.

A final difficulty of using quantitative research in the classroom by teachers is the need for ongoing data collection or assessment throughout the experimental period. Quantitative research requires at a minimum a posttest or pretest-posttest assessments. Unfortunately, a research design that calls for only a posttest or pretest and posttest assessments does not provide the information necessary to teachers. If teachers and practitioners are going to conduct action research, they are going to do so to help improve their own performance and/or the performance of the individuals they serve. For example, if teachers have access to only one assessment or measure after the grading period, it is too late to help the students. Ongoing assessments aid teachers in making needed adjustments throughout the grading period.

Quantitative research methods are not well suited to action research. They can of course be used and can provide comparative information because large groups of individuals can be studied and compared. The following research example illustrates this point.

Research Example

Snider and Crawford (1996) reported the results of a study conducted prior to the adoption of a new mathematics curriculum (i.e., Connecting Math Concepts) in a rural school district. The researchers wanted to compare the new curriculum to a traditional math textbook (i.e., published by Scott Foresman) to measure the most effective curriculum. The participants were students in the fourth grade and were randomly assigned to one of two fourth-grade classrooms. A teacher in each classroom was responsible for the delivery of instruction based on the particular curriculum. Each classroom received one of the two mathematics curricula. The researchers took pretest–posttest measures on the National Achievement Test (NAT), two curriculum-based measures based on each of the curricula, and experimenter-designed tests to assess recall of basic multiplication facts. The results demonstrated that there were no pretest differences between the two classrooms. However, there were statistically significant differences between the two classrooms favoring the new mathematics curriculum on most of the assessments and subtests of the NAT. The researchers concluded that the new mathematics curriculum was superior to the traditional one.

HOW ARE QUALITATIVE METHODS USED IN ACTION RESEARCH?

Qualitative methods seem to be ideally suited to action research. Qualitative research occurs in the natural context and requires ongoing or at least frequent contact with the participants. Additionally, qualitative research should not be driven by some preconceived hypothesis. Thus, action research is considered qualitative by many in the research field. Action researchers are able to generate a great deal of information about the individuals they serve and make decisions as time passes. They are not restricted to a single dependent variable; thus, action researchers can take into consideration a greater variety of variables than would be the case with quantitative research.

Those who wish to conduct action research using qualitative designs can be somewhat flexible in how they approach the research. Action researchers should have an idea of what they research. Many times, the research will be conducted to solve problems such as classroom disruptions. At other times, action research may be conducted to find out how the students like to be instructed. Once a reason for collecting data has been identified, action researchers should determine how the data are to be collected.

For example, in the classroom environment, an ethnographic-type approach, albeit on a much smaller scale, is acceptable. The teacher is part of the classroom culture. Participant observations can be conducted, and the teacher can collect field notes throughout the day or at the end of the day in the form of journal entries. The teacher can also use interviews to gain more specific information from specific students. Interviews with students who are especially open and honest can be extremely valuable. In order to gain triangulation, the teacher can ask the students as well as others in the setting such as instructional aides or peer tutors to make daily journal entries. Over a period of time, the information obtained by the teacher can aid in the improved management of the classroom and/or the improvement of the learning situation.

The main advantage of using qualitative research methods in action research is that the action researcher is already a part of the culture to be studied. The disruptions to daily activities are minimal since an outsider is not required. Additionally, the information gained will allow action researchers to reflect on critical variables in their environment. A potential problem is that qualitative research takes a large amount of effort to gather and assess the obtained data. Action researchers should have some skill in qualitative methods. Additionally, action researchers must be cautioned against making cause-and-effect claims using qualitative methods. Although action researchers may believe or hypothesize that one variable is responsible for another, the type of experimental rigor required to make such statements is difficult to achieve in such an applied context. In order to make cause-and-effect statements, additional constraints must be placed on those conducting the research and the participants. The following research example illustrates the use of a qualitative action research investigation.

Research Example

A study conduced by Goatley, Brock, and Raphael (1995) "examined the interactions of a diverse group of 5 fifth-grade students as they read and responded to the final novel in their reading program" (p. 357). The person responsible for the reading program (a book club) was the classroom teacher. The goal was to measure the meaning construction of three students from Chapter/Title 1, English as a Second Language, and special education programs, respectively. Specifically, the researchers wanted to determine the "students' participation in small-group lecture discussions and students' strategies for drawing on their own knowledge and the diverse knowledge of their peers in the social construction of meaning" (p. 357).

Therefore, the researchers wished to answer two questions, including the opportunities provided for student participation during student-led discussion groups and the opportunities available in student-led discussion groups for text interpretation. The researchers used ethnographic methods in the gathering of data including qualitative and sociolinguistic methods (i.e., interviews and written questionnaires, researchers' field notes, audiotaped discussions and transcripts of in-class activities, videotapes of student interactions and expressions during the activities, and students' written works). The data collection period lasted three weeks. The researchers analyzed the data by categorizing information and looking for patterns in the data, triangulating the data, and describing the situations involving reading. They found, among other things, that "learning opportunities were created and learning opportunities constructed" (p. 375). Also:

> *students' learning was facilitated through more knowledgeable members of the community and culture, with students turning to their book club peers and their teachers for assistance. When their understanding was impeded by information unavailable in the literature selection, students turned to these other sources of information. (p. 376)*

Finally, the researchers suggested, based on the results of the investigation, that the manner in which we approach the instruction of students with special needs should possibly change. They indicated that the facilitation of learning should be focused more on the integration of students into general classrooms where they can build off their knowledge of text through interactions with peers versus separate education settings.

HOW ARE SINGLE-CASE METHODS USED IN ACTION RESEARCH?

Although action research is considered by many to be the domain of qualitative methods, single-case research methods are also well-suited to applied settings. Teachers and practitioners can use single-case research methods to determine the effectiveness of behavior management procedures as well as skill development programs. However, they should be careful when determining the type of designs to use. The most basic design (i.e., A-B) can be used easily to assess a program. As you know by now, researchers are unable to determine causal effects using an A-B design. Action researchers will most likely not use the A-B-A design. This design is limited in terms of ethical concerns (see Chapter 10) as well as practical problems (i.e., returning to baseline levels). If action researchers are to use an experimental single-case design to determine a cause-and-effect relationship, they will most likely use a multiple-baseline design. Remember, single-case designs do not require single subjects but single entities. These single entities can contain several individuals such as groups of students. Other designs that can be used include the changing-criterion design and the alternating treatments design. The alternating treatments design could be used to compare two or more skill development or behavior management programs directly.

In order to use single-case designs in action research, action researchers must plan ahead. The independent and dependent variables must be determined and defined. The measures must be designed and checked for interobserver agreement by some other person in the setting such as a peer tutor, student, therapist, or instructional aide. Finally, data must be gathered on an ongoing basis.

There are several advantages of using single-case research methods in action research. First, data-based decisions can be made on an ongoing basis. Second, cause-and-effect relationships can be determined with most of the research methods. Finally, experimental control can be achieved with a small number of students.

A disadvantage of the single-case approach is that one or a small number of dependent variables are typically included. Other important information may be overlooked when action researchers focus on a single dependent variable. What could and probably should occur is to combine single-case methods with qualitative methods. Action researchers could collect objective data in a single-case fashion but also collect qualitative data through interviews and participant observations as long as the qualitative methods are being conducted throughout the baseline and intervention conditions.

The following research example illustrates the use of action research incorporating single-case methodology; additionally, qualitative information was gathered to assess the impact of the program on classroom personnel.

Research Example

The study conducted by Martella, Leonard et al. (1993) is a clear example of action research using a single-case design. In that investigation, a student teacher was involved in a classroom with a 12-year-old student with mild mental retardation who had a high level of disruptive behaviors. The classroom teacher and the student teacher developed the intervention package with the help of the other researchers. The classroom staff implemented the self-monitoring program, collected the data, and were involved in the interpretation of the results. The results demonstrated that the student's unwanted behaviors decreased when the self-monitoring program was implemented. The teacher and student teacher reported an improved classroom environment, and the student began to interact with other students appropriately on an increasing basis. Martella and colleagues concluded that the self-monitoring program aided in the improved student behavior.

HOW ARE SURVEY, HISTORICAL, AND PROGRAM EVALUATION METHODS USED IN ACTION RESEARCH?

The following research methods are not typically considered types of action research; however, we will describe how teachers and practitioners could use each method when conducting action research.

Survey Research

Teachers and practitioners can use surveys when they want to learn important information about students or parents that cannot be obtained in another fashion. For example, suppose a teacher wanted to determine the parents' levels of satisfaction with the social and/or academic progress of their children. A simple open-ended survey could be constructed that would allow the parents to describe areas of satisfaction and those in need of improvement. Another example might involve a secondary teacher who transitions students with impairments into employment situations. He may need to survey potential employers to prepare his students better for future employment situations. Finally, school counselors could distribute surveys to college recruiters to determine the expectations for college entrance from a number of college and universities. Thus, surveys could provide valuable information from sources that are critical in the lives of students.

Historical Research

Teachers and practitioners may use historical research when attempting to determine the best way to approach the education of certain students. For example, detailed information is kept in files for students with special needs as part of their individualized educational programs. Once information is obtained from this historical search, more informed plans for the educational future of these students can be made. Teachers may also wish to determine why a particular form of instruction is used today. Many educational practices seem to come and go in a cyclical pattern. Reading instruction is an example. A teacher may want to determine how students learned to read in the past and compare those methods with the current reading methods used today. This information can aid the teacher in understanding why she is expected to teach or facilitate reading in a certain manner.

Program Evaluation

We have all experienced program evaluations to some extent. The emphasis on standardized tests to measure the cognitive and intellectual achievement of students is an example of this. These standardized tests are measures of how the educational system is meeting the expectations of the community. Many action research investigations are a type of program evaluation but on a much smaller scale. For example, a teacher sets out to determine if his academic program is working as intended by looking at test scores; talking with students, parents, and other teachers; and making observations of the students during academic and social activities. In this way, he is conducting an evaluation of his program. Reflective teaching is essentially an activity in program evaluation, though not usually as formal. Therefore, program evaluations are used on an ongoing basis by teachers and practitioners who want to improve the academic, social, and behavioral performance of their students.

WHAT ARE THE ETHICAL PRINCIPLES AND CODES OF CONDUCT FOR RESEARCH?

Once we have determined that action research is warranted, ethical concerns should be considered. (*Note:* The following descriptions of ethical concerns are also pertinent to other types of research for all researchers. Ethical principles are presented here to aid action researchers in carrying out successful research projects.) All participants in an investigation have certain rights that must not be violated when conducting research. In many circumstances, the professionals conducting research will need to have the research approved by an institutional review board (IRB). An IRB is required to be established by any institution receiving federal funding. For instance, all public school districts across the country have IRBs. The sole purpose of an IRB is to protect the rights of persons involved in research. The IRB consists of a group of professionals who assess the level of risk to participants of an investigation and make sure that ethical safeguards are in place such as informed consent (discussed later). IRBs are required by the government for federally funded agencies under federal definitions and regulations governing research by such agencies. These definitions were developed in the 1960s and 1970s. In 1991, these definitions were updated in the "Federal Policy for the Protection of Human Subjects; Notices and Rules" published by the Federal Register.

The more action researchers know about research ethics, the better able they are to protect the rights of the participants. Thus, it would be fruitful for those interested in conducting research to be familiar with the "Ethical Standards of the American Educational Research Association" (AERA, 1992) and the "Ethical Principles of Psychologists and Code of Conduct" by the American Psychological Association (APA, 1997). The following are brief discussions of the concerns of the AERA and APA.

American Educational Research Association

The AERA ethical standards contain 45 standards that are organized into six topics. The topics include (a) responsibility to the field; (b) research populations, educational institutions, and the public; (c) intellectual ownership; (d) editing, reviewing, and appraising research; (e) sponsors, policy makers, and other users of research; and (f) students and student researchers. Individuals who are interested in conducting action research should read and understand the AERA standards. Table 15.1 presents the preambles for each of the six topics.

American Psychological Association

The American Psychological Association (APA) has put forth codes of conduct for psychologists. These codes can be modified to fit the ethical requirements for action researchers. The APA codes overlap to a certain extent with the AERA standards. The APA stresses eight ethical standards including (a) general; (b) evaluation, assessment, or intervention; (c) advertising and other public statements; (d) therapy; (e) privacy and confidentiality; (f) teaching, training supervision, research, and publishing; (g) forensic activities; and (h) resolving ethical issues. Standards (b), (e), (f), and (h) are especially relevant to the conduct of research.

As with the AERA standards, those who are interested in conducting action research should review the APA standards in depth. The APA also includes six general principles that should guide one who is considering conducting research. These principles include (a) competence, (b) integrity, (c) professional and scientific responsibility, (d) respect for people's rights and dignity, (e) concern for other's welfare, and (f) social responsibility. These principles are discussed in what follows.

Competence. Individuals conducting research should be competent to do so. Competence should be demonstrated in several areas. For example, if a teacher is going to attempt a classroom management system and wishes to demonstrate its effectiveness, the teacher should have the knowledge and skills necessary to implement the strategy. Similarly, if a teacher of mathematics plans on using a certain mathematics curriculum and conducts action research on the effects of the curriculum, the teacher should be well versed in that particular curriculum. The need for competence here is the same as the competence required as a teacher or practitioner in general. If teachers are to provide effective instruction, they should have the skills necessary that allow them to do so. Likewise, if psychologists are to provide counseling or assessment services, they should be skillful in the implementation of their services. Additionally, competence in using programs in a setting can determine the success the program achieves and, ultimately, the conclusions made by the teacher or practitioner. Teachers and practitioners are going to conduct action research for purposes described before. If teachers and practitioners are not competent in delivering the program, they may incorrectly conclude that the program was not effective when it could have been effective if a competent person was implementing it (Type II error).

Competence also refers to the use of adequate research methods. Teachers and practitioners (i.e.,

TABLE 15.1 Preambles from the Ethical Standards of the American Educational Research Association

I. Guiding Standards: Responsibilities to the Field (12 standards)

Preamble. To maintain the integrity of research, educational researchers should warrant their research conclusions adequately in a way consistent with the standards of their own theoretical and methodological perspectives. They should keep themselves well informed in both their own and competing paradigms where those are relevant to their research, and they should continually evaluate the criteria of adequacy by which research is judged.

II. Guiding Standards: Research Populations, Educational Institutions, and the Public (10 standards)

Preamble. Educational researchers conduct research within a broad array of settings and institutions, including schools, colleges, universities, hospitals, and prisons. It is of paramount importance that educational researchers respect the rights, privacy, dignity, and sensitivities of their research populations and also the integrity of the institutions within which the research occurs. Educational researches should be especially careful in working with children and other vulnerable populations. These standards are intended to reinforce and strengthen already existing standards enforced by institutional review boards and other professional associations.

III. Guiding Standards: Intellectual Ownership (2 standards)

Preamble. Intellectual ownership is predominantly a function of creative contribution. Intellectual ownership is not predominantly a function of effort expanded.

IV. Guiding Standards: Editing, Reviewing, and Appraising Research (6 standards)

Preamble. Editors and reviewers have a responsibility to recognize a wide variety of theoretical and methodological perspectives and, at the same time, to ensure that manuscripts meet the highest standards as defined in the various perspectives.

V. Guiding Standards: Sponsors, Policy Makers, and Other Users of Research (9 standards)

Preamble. Researchers, research institutions, and sponsors of research jointly share responsibility for the ethical integrity of research, and should ensure that this integrity is not violated. While it is recognized that these parties may sometimes have conflicting legitimate aims, all those with responsibility for research should protect against compromising the standards of research, the community of researchers, the subjects of research, and the users of research. They should support the widest possible dissemination and publication of research results. AERA should promote, as nearly as it can, conditions conducive to the preservation of research integrity.

VI. Guiding Standards: Students and Student Researchers (6 standards)

Preamble. Educational researchers have a responsibility to ensure the competence of those inducted into the field and to provide appropriate help and professional advice to novice researchers.

Source: Adapted from American Educational Research Association (1992). Ethical standards of the American Educational Research Association. *Educational Researcher, 21*(7), 23–26.

action researchers) should be competent in data collection and evaluation methods. If action researchers are unable to obtain adequate data and/or make reasonable conclusions based on the data, valuable information could be lost. Finally, it is critical that action researchers remain current with their chosen fields. For example, teachers should be aware of advances in education to determine if what they plan to investigate is part of best practice.

Integrity. Teachers and practitioners should be respectful of others. When conducting research, it is critical that action researchers respect the fact that the participants have rights that should be honored. Rosenthal (1994b) describes the concern of "hyperclaiming" when recruiting participants, or at least gaining the support of administrators and parents in the research project. Hyperclaiming is a problem when action researchers tell interested parties that the research is likely to achieve goals that are unlikely. For example, if a teacher wished to determine whether the reading program being used was successful in improving reading skills, a claim that the research will tell us how to best teach reading is not accurate. A single investigation with only one instructional method could not achieve this claim. It is more ethical to tell interested parties what will be obtained; in the example, we would expect the investigation to tell us whether or not the students exposed to the reading instruction demonstrated improved skills.

Teachers and practitioners should also be concerned with not coercing the individuals they are serving to become involved in the research project. These individuals should not be threatened in any way if they choose not to participate. Additionally, individuals participating in the study should not receive compensation that is excessive such as grants or large monetary payments for participating. Individuals should be allowed to not participate or to withdraw from research without any negative consequences.

Another concern related to integrity is what Rosenthal (1994b) called causism. Causism refers to making claims that a causal relationship will be found. In the preceding example, if the teacher claimed that the reading program definitely caused the improved reading performance, she would be making a claim that is most likely unfounded. At best, the teacher can state that the students' reading skills improved during the reading instruction. If the teacher wanted to determine if the reading program actually was responsible for the improvement, she would need to use a high constraint research method.

Professional and Scientific Responsibility. Action researchers should consult with other professionals on research-related concerns. For example, if there are other teachers in the school who have particular expertise in assessment, action researchers should seek out help from those individuals when designing the investigation. Additionally, action researchers must ensure that the research does not interfere with their normal responsibilities and with the progress of those they serve.

Respect for People's Rights and Dignity. Action researchers should always protect the rights of students involved in an investigation in terms of privacy, confidentiality, self-determination, and autonomy. It is not appropriate to distribute the assessment scores of students to individuals not associated with the education of these students. If data are collected as part of an action research investigation, teachers and practitioners must ensure that identifying information of participants does not go beyond the boundaries of the setting such as a classroom. For example, if a teacher were to make a presentation of the results of an investigation, actual names of the students should never be used.

Children and/or authorized adults should provide their consent to participate in the investigation. An institutional review board (IRB) will be concerned with the method of obtaining informed consent. Informed consent documents should be easy to read and understood by the parties. Table 15.2 shows an example informed consent letter to parents. This letter was used in a federally funded grant to prevent violent behaviors in schools in a midsize city in the Northwest. If parents are non-English speakers, the informed consent documents should be in their language. Teachers should be aware of cultural and individual differences such as gender, race, and religion when developing programs and obtaining informed consent. For example, a teacher wishing to determine the effectiveness of a social skills curriculum should be sensitive to cultural practices that may make some of the required skills objectionable.

Another concern has to do with deception. There may be times when researchers feel a need to deceive the participants to obtain the required

TABLE 15.2 Informed Consent Letter to Parents

Consent Letter Approved by Research Council
(Initial contact will be made by school official)

Dear Parent

I am writing to request your assistance in an evaluation of a project. The purpose of the project is to assess the effects of a school-based program to reduce disruptive behavior. The goal of the project is to provide teachers and others information with which to prevent these behaviors from occurring in schools.

(Child's name) has been chosen to participate in the project because *(Name of school official)* has informed me that you would be willing to allow your child to participate in the project. The project primarily will be assessing *(Child's name)*'s social adjustment and academic performance. The assessment procedures are standard practice and will be overseen by your child's teacher. Because *(Child's name)* and the other students in the classroom will be unaware of the purpose of the assessments, there is no discomfort or risk involved with *(Gender)* participation in the project.

(Child's name)'s participation in the project is voluntary and will not affect *(Gender)* education program in any way. You are free to withdraw your consent at any time. All information will remain anonymous. No identifying information shall be used at any stage of the project. No reports will contain information traceable to individual students and their families.

Additionally, please inform *(Child's name)* that you have given permission for *(Gender)* to take part in the project and that *(Gender)* can stop at any time.

Thank you for your voluntary participation in the project. Please sign and return this letter in the enclosed envelope. If you have any questions now or at any time, please feel free to call me at xxx-xxxx (work).

Thank you for your consideration.

Sincerely,

(researcher's name)

I ______________________ agree voluntarily to allow my child to participate in the project.

I ______________________ do not want my child to participate in the project.

---

data. For example, Martella, Marchand-Martella, and Agran (1992) used deception in several generalization assessments with individuals with developmental disabilities in employment settings. The researchers used contrived situations to make the environments look as if something in the environment could cause an injury (e.g., water on a kitchen floor). The participants were not told that the situations were simulated. The researchers assessed whether the participants responded in a manner that avoided an injury (although an injury actually had a low probability of occurring). The researchers received permission to use deception but only if there was an exceptionally low probability of injury and if the participants were debriefed afterward. The use of deception was unavoidable in the investigation since the occurrence of injuries is overall very low. Thus, the simulations helped to increase the frequency of potential injury-producing situations.

Deception should be used only if there is no other way to gather the data, and the data to be gathered are important to our knowledge and understanding of a phenomenon. Teachers and practitioners will rarely encounter situations where deception is needed. If these situations are encountered, appropriate permission from human rights committees, advocacy groups, parents, administrators, and so on should be sought.

Concern for Other's Welfare. Action researchers must be concerned with the welfare of the participants. Teachers and practitioners may be required to have a proposed research investigation reviewed by an institutional review board (IRB). According to Mordock (1995), IRBs in applied settings place more of an emphasis on the needs of participants than do university IRBs. A critical concern for the IRB is that the welfare of the students is considered. A concern will be the potential adverse effects on the students involved in the investigation. Action researchers should act to minimize the possibilities of harm to participants. For example, it would not be permissible to use a withdrawal design for problem behaviors in the classroom if a student has the potential to be harmful to himself or herself or to others.

Social Responsibility. Action researchers have a responsibility to inform others of their findings if those findings can contribute to educational practice. Those who inform others of the findings should follow accepted methods of dissemination. Rosenthal (1994b) cautions against several practices that may be viewed as unethical. First, fabricating data is a practice that cannot be tolerated. Fabricating data means "inventing" data or changing values of data to support a particular viewpoint. Another ethical problem is dropping data that contradict a researcher's theory or prediction. This practice is done when one eliminates or does not consider data that are not supportive.

One form of data dropping occurs when researchers reject data from outliers. In other words, when a single or small number of cases are quite different from the other cases, the data may be dropped because they are not representative of the overall sample. For example, suppose a teacher wants to determine how well a self-management strategy works in keeping students on task during a 20-minute daily academic activity. The teacher defines what on-task behavior means and sets out to measure the on-task rate of each student in the class. The teacher divides the class into four cooperative learning groups of five members per group. The self-management system is then presented to each group in a multiple-baseline fashion; that is, the first group receives the program, then the second, then the third, and so on. Throughout the self-management program, the teacher sees measurable improvement in the on-task duration of each of the groups. Few students are off-task; in fact, the average time on-task for each group was at least 18 minutes during the 20-minute daily activity by the end of the semester. The teacher concludes that the average student on-task rate improved when the self-management program was provided. However, there were two students in the first group and one in the third group who were off-task much more than the other children. In fact, by the end of the semester, the three students never exhibited 10 minutes of on-task behavior. There was no overall improvement in their on-task performance. Thus, the teacher deleted their data to come up with the reported 18 minutes of on-task time.

Rosenthal (1994b) indicated that data dropping may be acceptable, but the practice occurs more when the outliers are bad for the researcher's theory or expectations. Thus, Rosenthal indicated that if outliers are omitted from consideration, the researcher should point this out and possibly report in a footnote what the results would have been if the outliers were considered. Further, data dropping may also occur when one does not include a subset of data in the analysis (Rosenthal, 1994b). For example, suppose a teacher wished to determine the effects of improving the self-esteem of students through self-esteem-building exercises.

Thirty of the students went through the self-esteem-building exercises throughout the semester. The self-esteem of 20 of the children improved as assessed through journal entries of the students, but 10 of the children felt like failures throughout the term. If the teacher did not recognize the fact that many of the students did not feel good about themselves, but concluded that the self-esteem-building exercises helped improve the students' self-esteem, his ethics would be questionable. The teacher, ethically, should consider and comment on all of the students' perceptions, or at least, pick representative journal entries from all of the students.

Ethical Conduct of Action Researchers

Teachers and practitioners conducting action research should seek approval from an institutional review board to conduct the investigation. Under federal regulations, there are some exemptions for some types of research; however, these exemptions are not in effect for children/students. Therefore, teachers and practitioners should always consult with an administrator or supervisor before attempting a research project. Most importantly, teachers and practitioners should ensure that they are ethical in conducting the research. The participants' rights and welfare should be of primary concern. Also, teachers and practitioners should maintain professionalism when conducting the investigation as well as in their reporting of the results.

HOW DOES ONE WRITE A RESEARCH ARTICLE?

There may be times when teachers will want to write up the results of their action research because they see the information as being important for other professionals. The dissemination of the results of one's action research can help inform other professionals and aid in the improvement of their instruction. One journal in special education (i.e., *Teaching Exceptional Children [TEC]*) is intended for the dissemination of approaches that work in the classroom. Many of the authors are teachers, and teachers collaborate with college/university faculty as members of the journal's editorial board. Therefore, *TEC* encourages teachers to conduct action research and to publish their findings.

Once the decision has been made to disseminate the findings, action researchers will need to determine to which journal to send the manuscript. The journal decided on should be based on the readership. For example, if an action researcher wishes to have other secondary-level teachers read her report, she should target a journal that secondary teachers typically read. Another consideration action researchers must take into account is the requirements a journal may have for article submissions. Some journals may want a limited amount of jargon used. Others may like to have a certain type of data presented (i.e., quantitative versus qualitative). Journals will also require authors to submit a certain number of copies to the journal editor and to write in a certain style (e.g., APA style, *Publication Manual* 4th edition, 1994). Finally, if action researchers wish their article to be peer reviewed, they should seek out refereed journals. If they would rather their paper not be peer reviewed or wish to submit to a journal or magazine that does not have a peer review process, action researchers should seek out a nonrefereed publication.

Contents

Whether presenting the results of a narrative or quantitative review or some combination of the two, action researchers may follow the standard presentation format for primary research studies: (a) title page, (b) abstract, (c) introduction, (d) method, (e) results, (f) discussion, (g) references, and (h) additional sections such as tables, figures, footnotes, and acknowledgments. Numerous examples of research articles have been shown throughout this text. The following is a brief description of each of the sections of a research article that action researchers may wish to include in a write-up of their investigation. The length of each section will depend on two primary variables. First, length will depend on how much information the action researcher wishes to place in each section. Second, and probably more critical, the length of each section will depend on what the reviewers and/or editor deem to be acceptable. We have experienced having an editor request that a 30-page manuscript be cut down to 15 pages, with additional information presented in a section such as the method section. Please be aware, however, that the format and sections contained in all articles are not the same. The formats and sections vary across types of research methods used (e.g., qualitative or quantitative), journals, and purposes of the article (e.g., a formal research project description or an informal write-up of what was done).

Title Page. The title page is the first page of a manuscript. The title page should contain the title, action researcher's name, affiliation, and other information that may be required within a particular type of style (e.g., APA style) such as a running head. The title should be concise yet provide enough information to indicate the topic of the paper. The running head is an abbreviation of the title. Two or three words usually suffice. For example, if the title of the manuscript was "The Problem-Solving Training on the Work Safety Skills of Individuals in Supported Employment," the running head could be "Problem-Solving," or "Problem-Solving Skills," or "Work Safety," or what the action researcher feels is the main focus of the paper.

Abstract. The abstract is essentially a summarization of the entire paper. The abstract is usually the last major part of the paper written. Action researchers should be cautious about blocking sentences or paragraphs from parts of the paper and pasting these into the abstract. We have found that abstracts are best written after one reads the paper, sets the paper aside, and then attempts to describe the paper in one's own words. Abstracts are typically short, containing less than 150 words or are less than a half page in length. The abstract is typically a single paragraph that contains information about the topic, what was done, the results, and what will be contained in the discussion. The abstract usually does not contain any citations since it is only a summary of the paper.

Although the abstract is typically less than a page in length, it is a critical part of the paper. Many potential readers of an article will make a determination if they want to spend the time needed to read the entire article based on what is contained in the abstract. Therefore, the abstract should contain enough information and be written in an engaging style that will catch the reader's eye.

Introduction. The goal of the introduction is to set the research investigation within the field of inquiry. The introduction typically begins by describing the scientific question that is being addressed and its importance within the broad context of the field of inquiry. The introduction should also indicate why the research investigation is needed: Research on the phenomenon may be new to the literature; there may be some controversy in the field unresolved by research investigations; or the investigation replicates previous research in either a direct, systematic, or clinical manner. It is important that action researchers specify the problem addressed by the investigation in detail.

We have found that it is best to think of the focus of the information in the introduction as an inverted pyramid. At the top, the information is very broad. For example, if our investigation was on teaching individuals how to solve problems encountered on a daily basis, the beginning of the introduction could have a general description of what constitutes problem solving. As we move down the inverted pyramid, the topic becomes more focused. For example, we begin to focus on a certain type of problem-solving training such as a brainstorming or a generation of alternatives approach versus a single-solution approach to solving problems. Then we discuss weaknesses in the current research such as questions left unanswered (e.g., do individuals who go through a problem-solving program generalize or transfer the skills to "real-life" situations?). In essence, we need to justify the importance of the investigation or indicate what we are going to contribute to the literature. The final stage of the introduction is at the apex of the inverted pyramid. Here, we indicate what our research question or hypothesis is. We also indicate what the purpose of the investigation is, such as "The purpose of this investigation is to measure the generality of a problem-solving program from situations presented during training to actual problem situations." The purpose statement should inform the reader of what to expect in the rest of the paper.

Method. The method section should describe the procedures used to conduct the investigation in detail. Although the specific procedures may vary, method sections often include a description of the participants (e.g., characteristics, grade level, age, testing information such as intelligence), a description of the setting used in the investigation (e.g., the physical layout of a classroom), a description of the dependent variable (e.g., reading ability) and dependent measure (e.g., percentage of comprehension questions correct or participant attitudes of their reading performance), the measurement procedures (e.g., standardized tests given, types of interviews used, methods of observations, frequency of assessments), the procedures including the independent variable (e.g., reading method used, design utilized), and methods of analyzing the data (e.g., inferential statistical methods, qualitative interpretive methods, visual inspection of graphs).

Results. The results section presents the findings of each aspect of the review of the literature. The results section typically begins with a description of the results of the investigation (e.g., what was found statistically, what the triangulation methods found overall). Results sections should not include the action researcher's interpretation of the results. The results are presented in an objective manner informing the reader of what was found during the data analysis. The results section may include summary tables or graphical presentations of the results to help the reader better understand what was read. If figures or tables are used, the narrative is essentially a summarization of the figures or tables.

Discussion. The discussion section is possibly the most important section from a conceptual level. It is in this section that action researchers can make interpretations of their results (i.e., what do they mean?). Action researchers should set the findings of their investigation within the context of the field of inquiry. In other words, the results of the investigation are placed within the current knowledge of the field. Therefore, action researchers should revisit some of the information contained in the introduction. For example, suppose that the investigation was on the use of self-monitoring in the classroom to help decrease a student's inattentive behavior. In the introduction, the action researcher indicated that a great deal of research demonstrates that self-monitoring is effective with students who have behavior problems, but there is a lack of research on the effects of self-monitoring on attention difficulties in a classroom environment. In the discussion section, the action researcher would revisit this and indicate that we now have some information as to the effects of self-monitoring on maintaining attention in a classroom environment.

Another part of the discussion section to address are the weaknesses of the investigation. For example, suppose that in a qualitative investigation on whether students found a self-monitoring program helpful in maintaining their attention to a task, there was a problem with gaining multiple viewpoints for triangulation (e.g., if an aide forgot to keep a journal of student comments). Once difficulties are noted, the action researcher could indicate ways that these difficulties could be avoided in the future such as having a daily reminder or an aid to journal student comments.

Finally, the discussion should include the implications of the findings for future research. Action researchers should indicate where we go from here. Based on the knowledge action researchers have about the subject matter from the literature review for the introduction, they should have some idea of the weak areas in their research. Or they could indicate interesting related issues such as although self-monitoring has been shown to be effective for a wide range of behaviors, there is a paucity of investigations looking at the accuracy of how well students monitor their own behaviors.

The discussion section should be written in such a manner that captures the reader's attention.

It should prompt thoughts about where we go from here in terms of the topic of interest. Since this is the final narrative section of the paper, the discussion section should provide a summary of what was discussed previously in the article.

References. The reference section should contain all of the sources of information (e.g., articles, books, presentations) contained throughout the paper. Most references will come from the introduction. In a reference section, only those sources that are cited within the paper should be included.

Tables. As indicated earlier, tables may be included in the results section to display data in a visual format. Tables can also be placed in the method section to provide more detailed information about procedures or participants (e.g., intelligence scores, ages, settings). Tables should be as concise as possible. They should be organized in such a manner that makes them easy to read and interpret.

Figure Caption Page. If figures are used in the paper, the figures should contain identifying information. Essentially, a figure caption is a description of what is contained in the figure. These descriptions should be concise. Many journals require figure captions to be placed on a page separate from the figures themselves.

Figures. If figures are used in the paper, they should provide information that is easy to interpret. Many journals have standards that should be met for graphic displays of data. Action researchers should consult the journal or specific style guide for more information on graphing requirements such as those presented in Chapters 10 and 11.

Author Note. The final section of a paper is the author note section. This section is sometimes called the acknowledgment section. The author note section informs the reader of the action researcher's name, affiliation, and address where further information or reprints of the article can be obtained. This section may also contain acknowledgments to those individuals or agencies that helped with some part of the research either through funding (e.g., federal agencies), providing materials, assisting in writing the manuscript, or serving as consultants.

A Cautionary Note

When writing an article, politically correct language should be used. Action researchers should make a clear attempt not to offend individuals based on their gender, ethnicity, culture, or label. In order to keep from making unintended remarks, action researchers should follow these suggestions. First, individuals involved in investigations should be called participants rather than subjects. The term "participant" indicates that the individual is free to participate or not participate versus being "subjected" to a treatment.

Second, any overgeneralizations or stereotyping should be avoided. For example, if particular participants in a study are low readers, it would be inappropriate to indicate that low reading performance is expected for individuals from a particular ethnic group or gender.

Third, always use the label or description of an individual after the person, not before. For example, it not considered appropriate to say "the mentally ill" or "mentally retarded." It is considered more appropriate to say, "individuals with mental illness" or "individuals with mental retardation."

Finally, gender-specific language should be avoided or, if used, action researchers should justify its use. For example, always using he or his throughout the manuscript is not acceptable unless action researchers indicates that since they are discussing the topic of hyperactivity and since most children with hyperactivity are male, gender-specific language will be used. The use of he or she is an acceptable substitute if it is used sparingly since it can become awkward. Using a more generic pronoun such as, "the teacher is teaching the students" is preferable to "the teacher is teaching her students." According to the APA *Publication Manual* (1994), going back and forth between he and she indicates that he or she is generic, which is not true. A final alternative is to turn singular language into plural such as "a good teacher keeps the attention of her students" to "Good teachers keep the attention of their students."

HOW ARE ARTICLES SUBMITTED FOR PUBLICATION?

Once articles are written, action researchers then submit the manuscript to the editors for publication consideration. Journals will have different submission requirements such as page length and number of copies. Once articles are received, editors will determine if the articles are worth publishing if the journals are nonrefereed. If the journals are refereed, the editors will send the manuscripts to reviewers. Reviewers are either individuals who comprise editorial boards or outside "guest" reviewers who have little or no formal association with the journal. Reviewers are typically experts in the field of education or psychology and/or in the topic selected such as reading. The number of reviewers varies from journal to journal. Some journals have as many as five reviewers, and others may have as few as one or two. Reviews typically last approximately three months but can be much longer or shorter. Reviewers can be "blind" to the names of the action researchers (authors) or they may know the names of those who wrote the article. Reviewers will be looking at the things you studied throughout this text. Thus, if action researchers select journals that require a certain methodology (e.g., quantitative) and they complete different types of investigations (e.g., qualitative), the manuscripts may not be reviewed kindly. Reviewers will also be concerned with the internal and external validity of the investigation as well as the writing style.

Once the review process is finished, editors will collect the reviews and make their decision. The editors' job is to summarize the reviews for the authors. Researchers are typically sent copies of the reviews; they usually will not be informed of who reviewed their papers for publication. At least four decisions are possible. First, the editor may accept the manuscript as is; this is the exception rather than the rule. Second, the editor may recommend the manuscript for publication with revisions. Once the revisions are completed as specified by the editor, the manuscript is usually formally accepted. Third, the editor may recommend the manuscript be revised and resubmitted for review. If this occurs, the manuscript may need to go through the entire review process again. Finally, the editor may reject the manuscript for consideration of publication.

If a manuscript is rejected for publication, action researchers should be persistent and not give up. They should take the reviewers' suggestions and revise the manuscript. Then, they should submit the manuscript to another journal if they still believe it is worth publishing. Perseverance will pay off many times when attempting to get a manuscript in print. However, even if the manuscript does not get into a journal, action researchers should take the feedback as an opportunity to improve on future action research they may conduct. Most reviewers attempt to provide feedback in order to help authors. The difficulty is getting used to receiving feedback from people you do not know. Action researchers should not take ownership of the manuscript. They should look at the feedback not as criticism, but as an opportunity to learn and improve in the future research they may conduct.

WHEN SHOULD ONE CONDUCT ACTION RESEARCH?

The obvious advantage of action research is that teachers and practitioners can inform their own practice. For example, action research aids teachers in reflective teaching in that it helps them to determine how to improve instruction. Another advantage is with the concept of replications and external validity. It is acceptable to think of action research as a type of systematic or clinical replication process in that other persons are conducting the research, in different contexts (in applied settings) and with different participants. Additionally, the dependent measures may be different from those used by the researcher in the original investigation. Therefore, action research can be thought of as a way to expand our scientific knowledge to other situations and individuals, which is critical for a demonstration of external validity.

The opportunity for professionals in the field to publish is great. Teachers and practitioners working in applied settings should consider becoming involved in aiding in the advancement of our knowledge in some manner. The simplest way to do this is to stay current with the research in one's chosen profession. In order to do this, one must be a critical research consumer to become an adequate researcher. The second way to contribute to our knowledge of our profession is to conduct our own research. We have heard of many teachers who state that they teach one way or the other because they "know" it is the best way. If this is the case, then the possibility of validating one's belief is great. Additionally, the possibility of learning something new about how best to approach the instruction of students, which may be different from how one normally approaches instruction, can result.

If teachers and practitioners consider conducting research in their respective applied settings, they must be aware of ethical safeguards from their professional organizations, school districts, and building administrators. Once action researchers are confident that ethical safeguards have been satisfied, they can conduct the investigation. Once the investigation is completed, action researchers may wish to disseminate the findings. Dissemination can occur through several avenues such as presentations at local, regional, or national conferences or professional meetings; brief descriptions in newsletters; or through publications in nonrefereed or refereed journals. If action researchers feel that they would like to publish the results of the investigation, they should seek out an appropriate outlet and determine the journal's requirements. Finally, once the outlet has been determined, action researchers can write up the manuscript and submit it for publication.

The exciting part about writing and submitting our own work for publication is that we can obtain recognition for our work. Few things are more satisfying than to have a colleague read a paper you authored. More importantly, the feedback we can receive from the process of seeking to publish our own work can be critical to professional development. Other professionals will have an opportunity to view our work and thinking. We may have our thinking validated or criticized. Either way, we will receive feedback that will help shape our future thinking and cannot help but make us improved professionals.

DISCUSSION QUESTIONS

1. You go into a classroom and see the teacher collecting qualitative data. She says she wishes to see the students' perceptions of her classroom organization. You tell her that she is conducting action research. She asks you what that means since she has not heard the term before. What would you say?
2. The teacher then asks you how to tell action research from other forms of research. Describe to her the characteristics of action research.
3. The teacher wonders if qualitative research is the only form of action research. What would you tell her?
4. Another teacher hears your conversation and says that he thinks it is unethical to treat students as experimental subjects. You indicate that this is not a problem if one were informed about research ethics. Describe why teachers and practitioners should be aware of research ethics.
5. The second teacher asks you if there are any specific guidelines for conducting research. You mention the AERA and APA guidelines. How would you describe these guidelines?
6. Finally, the teachers ask if they should get permission to conduct research in their classrooms, and if so, from whom? What would you say?
7. A school psychologist visits a classroom in which you are teaching. She tells you that she gathered some data correlating students who have been identified as having a learning disability in reading with the type of reading instruction used in their respective classrooms. She tells you that some of her results were interesting and that others should have access to this information. After making sure that she followed appropriate ethical guidelines, you tell her that she should try to publish the data. She tells you that she has no idea what goes

into a research article. Describe the components of a research article for her.

8. Once you are finished describing the contents of the research article to the school psychologist, you go on to describe the publication process. How would you describe it?
9. While describing the publication process to the school psychologist, you mention the term "refereed journal." The school psychologist asks you what that means. Describe the difference between a refereed and nonrefereed journal.
10. Finally, you caution the school psychologist that she should be careful in the use of language in the paper. Describe the areas to which authors should pay particular attention.

DYADS AND DATA IN PEER COACHING

CYNTHIA O. VAIL
(CEC Georgia Federation) Associate Professor, Department of Special Education, University of Georgia, Athens

JENNIFER M. TSCHANTZ
Preschool Special Education Teacher, Madison County Schools, Danielsville, Georgia

ALICIA BEVILL
Preschool Special Education Teacher, Jackson County Schools, Jefferson, Georgia.

EARLY CHILDHOOD EDUCATORS IN ACTION

Private Preschools, Day Care, Head Start, Public Preschools

The world of early childhood education includes programs in many settings, and more and more of these community-based programs include young children both with and without disabilities.

In these inclusive programs, early childhood special educators collaborate and consult with other professionals with varied backgrounds. The minimal educational and experience requirements for early childhood teachers range from a high school education with no experience to a teaching certificate based on undergraduate or graduate coursework. Given this variability in teacher preparation, many teachers need collaborative support from early childhood special educators to meet the needs of their students with disabilities.

In this article, we share how we used peer coaching, a collaborative way to meet teachers' needs, in two different communities (see box page 545, "What Is Peer Coaching?"). One account (pp. 545–548), by Jennifer Tschantz, describes a *combination expert/reciprocal peer coaching method* used by an early childhood special educator with Head Start teachers. The second account (pp. 548–549), by Alicia Bevill, describes an *expert model* that is currently being field-tested by an early childhood special educator who is working with teachers in private and public preschool programs.

Box 1

WHAT IS PEER COACHING?

According to Joyce and Showers (1982), peer coaching involves teachers observing one another and giving specific feedback on teaching behaviors that need enhancement. Peer coaching can serve as a framework to guide the collaborative consultation process to bridge gaps in knowledge and skill among both professionals and paraprofessionals. Coaching by experts and reciprocal peer coaching are two coaching models (Ackland, 1991).

- Coaching by experts is more of a consultative model whereby professionals with specific expertise observe teachers and give them feedback and recommendations.
- Reciprocal peer coaching differs in that teachers observe one another in a collaborative manner, providing joint feedback.

Educators have successfully used both types of peer coaching models for both preservice and inservice teachers. (For more information on peer coaching, see Fishbaugh, 1997; Hendrickson, Gardner, Kaiser, & Riley, 1993; Kohler, McCullough, & Buchan, 1995; Miller, Harris, &, Watanabe, 1991; Morgan, Gustafson, Hudson, & Salzberg, 1992; Morgan, Menlove, Salzberg, & Hudson, 1994.)

COMBINATION EXPERT/RECIPROCAL PEER COACHING MODEL

The final task in fulfilling requirements for a master's degree in early childhood special education is conducting a research study. As I approached this task, I wanted my study to be practical—one that would not only add to the field of early childhood special education research but that would help me on a day-to-day basis.

Child-Directed Play—Facilitation Issues

As an early childhood special education teacher, I served children with special needs using a community-based model. Ten children with varying needs were spread across three Head Start classrooms. I spent approximately 3 hours per week in each of the classrooms working with the children during child-directed activities. I began to notice that during these periods, the Head Start teachers did not facilitate the children's play; rather, they interacted with the children on a limited basis (when children were arguing over a toy, answering children's questions, or praising work when brought to them).

I soon realized that the Head Start teachers had received limited training on child-directed/initiated instruction. My role as a consultant and collaborator was to share information about the students with special needs, answer questions, and help develop plans to embed individualized education program (IEP) goals and objectives into play. Before we could concentrate on embedding specific objectives, the teachers needed to facilitate play with all students.

A Nonthreatening Approach

To avoid the "turf' issues that arise whenever an outsider comes into a classroom, I decided to develop a nonthreatening method of imparting information about facilitative play to the Head Start teachers. Peer coaching was the perfect solution. My research question became, "Would peer coaching increase the rate of responsive teacher statements during a child-directed period in an inclusive preschool setting?"

The model I developed was both expert and reciprocal. I had expertise in specific teaching strategies to share with the Head Start teachers. However, rather than directly giving them advice, I wanted to foster an exchange of information through reciprocal observation and joint feedback. The focus was not specifically geared toward meeting the needs of children with disabilities only, but improving instructional strategies that are appropriate for all young children (Tschantz, 1995).

Dyads, Observations, and Discussions

We formed three peer coaching dyads, including myself and each of the Head Start teachers. Each Head Start teacher and I would observe each other for 15 minutes daily during the child-directed period. In addition, during individual peer-coaching sessions held twice a week, we would discuss the observations and target specific teaching strategies we wanted to improve.

During the initial peer-coaching sessions, I shared a list of effective teaching strategies. I provided definitions and examples and encouraged

(continued)

Box 1 Continued

discussions to obtain common understanding. This list included responsive statements, defined as the use of specific activity-related questions/comments or reflective statements made in the context of ongoing play. Other strategies included giving specific praise statements, giving reminders before transitioning, giving choices, stating rules in the positive, following through on directions, and embedding objectives. During these first sessions, I also introduced the teaching behavior plan forms (Figure 1), which included behaviors to improve or increase, examples of these behaviors, and space for anecdotal information from observations. Each of us completed the forms reciprocally. Each of us chose at least two behaviors to improve and together generated examples. Behaviors selected came from the teaching strategy list or were self-generated.

[Peer coaching] helped me to look at and evaluate my strengths and weaknesses. It helped me deal with and avoid behavior problems by actually sitting down with a peer teacher and figuring out positive solutions.

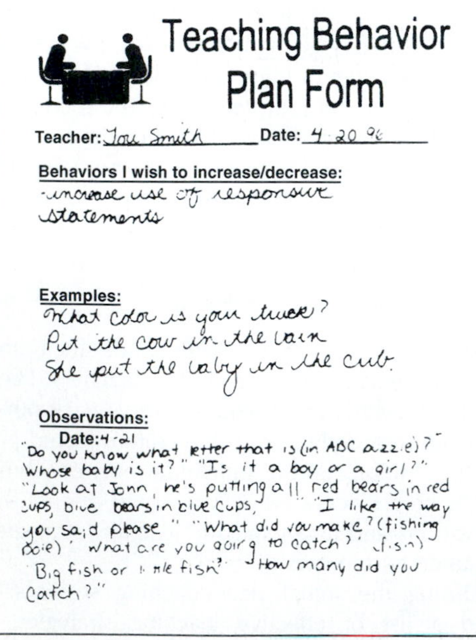

Teaching Behavior Plan Form

Teacher: Tou Smith Date: 4 20 96

Behaviors I wish to increase/decrease:
-increase use of responsive statements

Examples:
What color is your truck?
Put the cow in the barn
She put the baby in the cub.

Observations:
Date: 4-21
"Do you know what letter that is (in ABC puzzle)?" Whose baby is it?" "Is it a boy or a girl?" "Look at John, he's putting all red bears in red cups, blue bears in blue cups," "I like the way you said please" "What did you make? (fishing pole)" What are you going to catch?" (fish) Big fish or little fish? How many did you catch?"

FIGURE 1 Teaching behavior plan form.

Follow-Up and Decisions

During subsequent observations, each of us took anecdotal data on the behaviors selected during the peer-coaching sessions. For example, if the teacher selected "giving choices" as a teaching behavior to enhance, the observing teacher noted specific examples of when this behavior occurred or could have occurred. I also collected data on the Head Start teachers' rate of responsive statements.

After the initial session, each peer-coaching session consisted of the following:

- I verbally outlined what would occur during the session.
- The Head Start teacher reviewed her observation of me. With the Head Start teacher's input, I decided whether to continue working on the same behaviors or choose new ones. I always chose "increasing responsive statements" as one of my targeted behaviors because I wanted to model this behavior for them. I then developed a plan for improving my behaviors and documented it on the plan form, again defining the behavior, providing examples, and so forth.
- We switched roles. I gave anecdotal feedback on the Head Start teacher's chosen behaviors. I always offered specific feedback on responsive statements (e.g., defined responsive statements, gave examples, and reported rate observed).
- The Head Start teacher followed the same steps in developing her plan for improving teaching behaviors and documented it on the plan form.

To maintain a natural, comfortable dialogue, we followed a flexible sequence of these steps in each session.

Results? Positive!

The results of my study indicated that peer coaching was effective in increasing the rate of responsive statements made by all three teachers during a child-directed period (see Figure 2). This was wonderful news for the completion of my degree; but the positive feedback I received from the Head Start teachers on questionnaires was more important to me as a collaborative teacher. Teachers reported that peer coaching increased communication with the special educator, improved their effective teaching

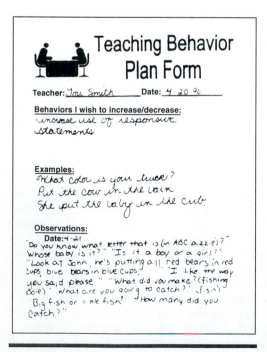

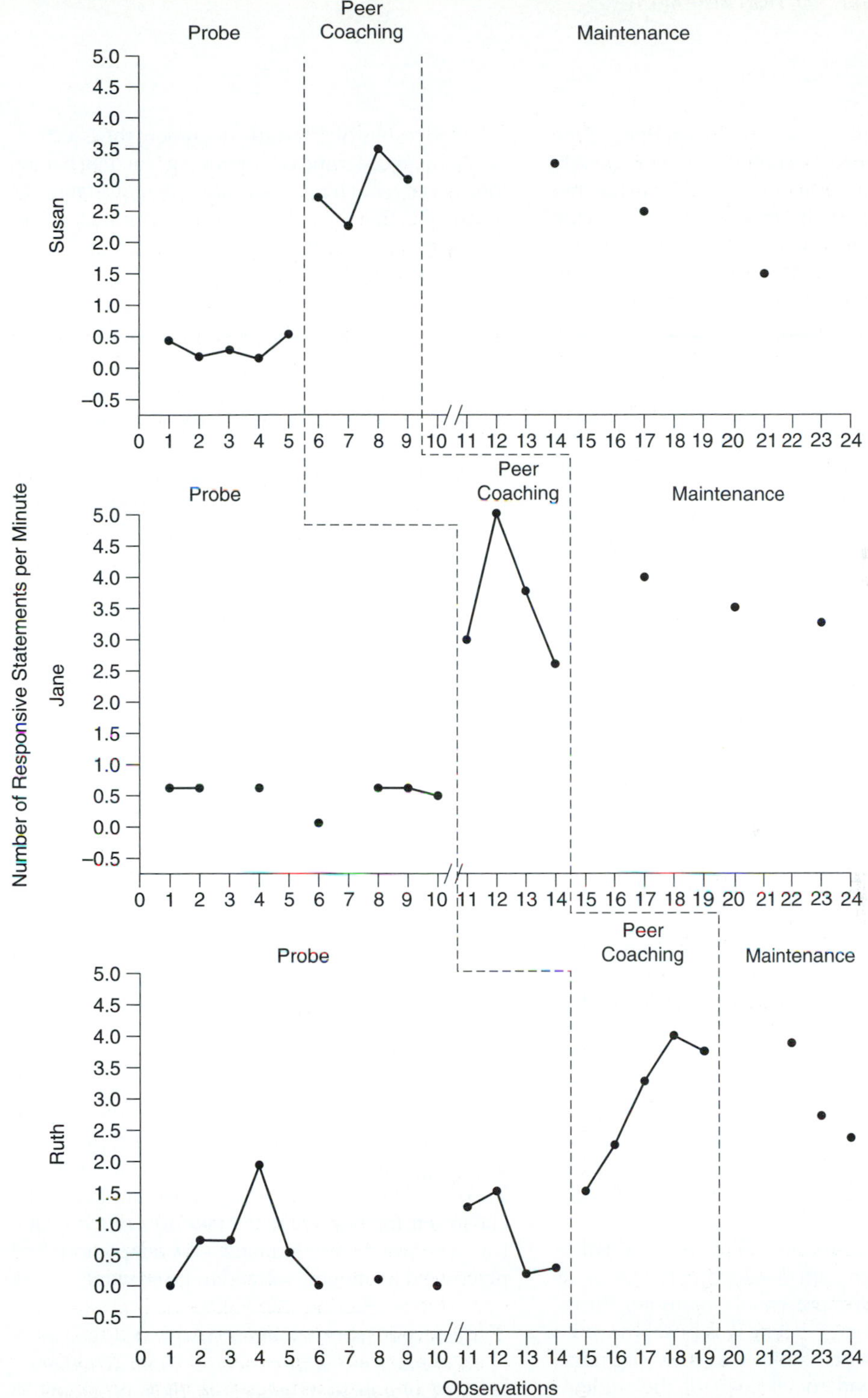

FIGURE 2 Rate of responsive teacher statements during a child-directed period.

(continued)

Box 1 Continued

strategies, and was not too time-consuming. One teacher stated that peer coaching was "very beneficial" in a nonintrusive manner, and it made her aware of the importance of "exactly what I say to the children." Most important, all three teachers indicated that they wished to continue peer-coaching sessions on at least a bimonthly basis.

The results of this study document the effectiveness of peer coaching on improving teaching behaviors. Peer coaching was also demonstrated as practical in that the entire study was conducted over an 8-week period. It was efficient in increasing effective teaching behaviors.

Box 2

EXPERT MODEL

As a preschool special education resource teacher, my role is to support students with significant developmental delays who are served in general preschool classrooms. Teachers in these community-based settings have a range of training and experience; but none has had formal training in the field of early childhood special education, and few have experience working with children with special needs. The support services I provide range from consultation with classroom teachers to direct service with students for a few hours each week. The 1996–97 school year was unusual, because several children who were previously served in self-contained special education preschool classes would now be included in regular preschool settings.

Inclusive Meetings for Adults

Before the school year began, I arranged individual meetings for four children on my caseload who would be served in a general preschool classroom. I invited all the adults who might be involved in serving the child, including teachers, therapists, paraprofessionals, parents, and administrators. The meetings took place during the first week of school, each lasting 30 minutes to an hour, with full attendance by all invited.

We all had concerns about how we could meet the needs of children with developmental delays, as well as their peers, in a preschool classroom. The recurring theme at every meeting was how we would address developmental concerns—the cognitive, language, motor, and social goals of the students with developmental delays. We discussed adaptations and purchased special materials and equipment. We scheduled support staff to serve children during times that we anticipated would be challenging for them, based on their delays.

Day 1 Arrives

By the first day of school, I felt that we had planned adequately for each child and that the groundwork had been laid for a successful school year. In some ways, I was correct in this assumption. The preschool service providers appeared to be comfortable including the students with special needs in their classrooms. They modified activities and tasks to allow successful participation and asked me for assistance when needed.

The preschool service providers appeared to be comfortable including the students with special needs in their classrooms.

Issues of Fairness and Time

Within 2 weeks, however, the situation in some settings took a turn for the worse. Classroom teachers and administrators began to contact me with concerns about whether the children we'd placed in their programs "belonged" there. They raised the issue of whether it was fair to the other children in the classroom for one child to "take too much of the teacher's time." I was stunned—the adaptations and plans we'd made had seemed to be working.

Classroom teachers and administrators began to contact me with concerns about whether the children we'd placed in their programs "belonged" there.

I made visits to the sites to observe students and speak directly with the teachers. I discovered that it was not the cognitive, language, or motor delays addressed on the students' IEPs that were causing such problems. In every case, it was students' troublesome behavior. The preschool classroom teachers were unprepared to work with students with challenging behavior. After observing and videotaping in the classrooms in question, I found that several students without identified delays were also exhibiting behaviors that interfered with learning.

Behavior Management Issues

In speaking with each of the preschool teachers, I discovered that none had experience in analyzing behavior or in behavior management beyond a basic "time-out" procedure. It was clear that training in these areas would benefit not only the students with special needs but the classroom as a whole.

We discussed several options, including inservice training on a teacher workday. Eventually, we decided that ongoing training and support in dealing with challenging behaviors was the best solution.

Planning Peer Coaching

We designed a plan of action that involved peer coaching between myself and each of the preschool teachers having difficulty with student behavior. This plan will be implemented over the course of the next several months to determine whether peer coaching between special and general educators will result in substantial changes in student behavior. Future research is also planned to examine whether teacher behavior will generalize to other students and whether changes in student behavior endure over time. Here are the steps of the model:

- The first step is pinpointing the target behavior. This step will be completed collaboratively between the special and preschool teacher and will yield a specific, observable definition of the behavior in question.
- The special educator will then guide the preschool teacher in conducting a functional analysis of the behavior.
- Once it has been determined that environmental factors are not causing or reinforcing the behavior, the special educator will use information from the functional analysis to suggest possible interventions.
- The final decision on which intervention to implement in the classroom will be left to the preschool teacher because he or she will ultimately be responsible for carrying out the plan.
- The preschool teacher will have the opportunity to role play and to observe the early childhood special educator carrying out the behavior management plan before implementing it on his or her own.
- Ongoing data will be collected to ensure that the preschool teacher is following the intervention plan as written, and feedback will be provided as necessary. The primary measure of this project will be the change in student behavior as a result of the intervention designed through peer coaching. Such information is needed to fill gaps in the literature, which has been primarily concerned with changes in teacher behavior and has examined the resulting change in student behavior as a secondary measure, if at all.

Peer coaching can be adapted to meet a variety of teacher needs in various settings. With the movement toward more inclusive environments and the changing roles of special educators, peer coaching could become a practical and powerful tool in increasing the communication and collaboration between general and special educators.

DISCUSSION

You may face barriers and challenges when trying to put peer coaching in action. A primary challenge is working with professionals or paraprofessionals with various levels of training and experience. They may operate from a philosophical position much different from your own. Because of these differences, individuals may view problems or situations from disparate perspectives. This challenge may be viewed as an advantage if professionals can collaborate and truly learn from one another. For example, a preschool teacher may bring a great wealth of expertise to a situation regarding the use of play as a context for learning from a Developmentally Appropriate Practice perspective (Bredekamp & Copple, 1997). The early childhood special educator can provide information related to how to embed individual objectives and evaluate progress within play. As these professionals work together they can become more knowledgeable and able to view situations from multiple perspectives. This will enhance their ability to provide constructive feedback to each other during the coaching process.

Another challenge inherent in peer coaching is the collaborative process. Many personnel preparation programs focus on teaching skill and content needed to work with children and spend little time on skills required for effective adult collaboration. Understanding various communication styles, how to overcome turf issues, and role release are a few of the critical variables related to successful collaboration and coaching. Staff development may help fill in training gaps regarding effective collaboration and facilitate successful peer coaching.

Finally, in order for the peer-coaching process to work, time set aside to collaborate is essential. This requires administrative support and creative scheduling. This becomes more challenging when working across settings such as child care, private preschool, and Head Start. Within child care settings there may be frequent staff turnover and schedule changes. We have faced these issues with the second model we described. Given the administrative support we have for our peer-coaching project, we hope that persistence, ongoing communication, and flexibility will help us overcome these staffing and scheduling barriers.

REFERENCES AND RESOURCES

Ackland, R. (1991). A review of the peer coaching literature. *Journal of Staff Development, 12,* 22–27.

Bredekamp, S., & Copple, C. (Eds.). (1997). *Developmentally appropriate practice in early childhood programs.* Washington, DC: National Association for the Education of Young Children.

Fishbaugh, M. S. E. (1997). *Models of Collaboration.* Boston: Allyn & Bacon.

Hendrickson, J. M., Gardner, N., Kaiser, A., & Riley, A. (1993). Evaluation of social integration coaching program in an integrated day-care setting. *Journal of Applied Behavior Analysis, 26,* 213–225.

Joyce, B., & Showers, B. (1982). The coaching of teaching. *Educational Leadership, 40,* 4–8.

Kohler, F. W., McCullough, K. M., & Buchan, K. A. (1995). Using peer coaching to enhance preschool teachers' development and refinement of classroom activities. *Early Education and Development. 6,* 215–239.

Miller, S. P., Harris, C., & Watanabe, A. (1991). Professional coaching: A method for increasing effective and decreasing ineffective teaching behavior. *Teacher Education and Special Education, 14,* 183–191.

Morgan, R. L., Gustafson, K. J., Hudson, P. J., & Salzberg, C. L. (1992). Peer coaching in a preservice special education program. *Teacher Education and Special Education, 15,* 249–258.

Morgan, R. L., Menlove, R., Salzberg, C. L., & Hudson, P. J. (1994). Effects of peer coaching on the acquisition of direct instruction skills with low-performing preservice teachers. *The Journal of Special Education, 28,* 59–76.

Tschantz. J. M. (1995). *The effects of peer coaching on the rate of facilitative teacher statements during a child-directed period in an inclusive preschool setting.* Unpublished master's thesis, University of Georgia, Athens.

Address correspondence to Cynthia O. Vail, Department of Special Education, 537 Aderhold Hall, University of Georgia. Athens, GA 30602 (e-mail: cvail@sage.coe.uga.edu).

FACTUAL QUESTIONS

1. What was the purpose of the article?
2. What is peer coaching?
3. Who were the students in the combination expert/reciprocal peer-coaching model?
4. Why was the nonthreatening approach, using joint feedback, important?
5. How were the dyads formed in the combination expert/reciprocal peer-coaching model?
6. In what type of classroom was the combination expert/reciprocal peer-coaching model used?
7. What was the type of design used in the combination expert/reciprocal peer-coaching model to assess its effectiveness? What were the results?
8. Who were the children in the expert model?
9. What were the concerns/issues involved in the expert model?
10. What were the steps in the expert model?

DISCUSSION QUESTIONS

1. Do you think the justification for peer coaching was adequate?
2. What are the differences in the two models?
3. Was the combination expert/reciprocal peer-coaching model explained in a manner that would allow for a teacher to replicate the procedure?
4. Are there any threats to the internal validity of the expert/reciprocal peer-coaching model study?
5. Are there threats to the external validity of the expert/reciprocal peer-coaching model study?
6. Do you think the results would convince others to use the model?
7. Was the expert model explained in a manner that would allow for a teacher to replicate the procedure?
8. How can peer coaching help professionals work together collaboratively?
9. What do you see as the advantages and disadvantages of each type of model?
10. How does this article differ from the other articles presented in the text?

Glossary

A-B design: A single-case design that combines the "A" condition or baseline/preintervention measurements with a "B" condition to determine the effectiveness of an intervention.

A-B-A/withdrawal design: A single-case design that combines the "A" condition or baseline/preintervention measurements with a "B" condition or intervention to determine the effectiveness of the intervention; the "B" condition is followed by a second "A" condition.

A-B-A-B design: A single-case design that combines the "A" condition or baseline/preintervention measurements with a "B" condition or intervention to determine the effectiveness of the intervention; the "B" condition is followed by a second "A" condition and ends with a return to the intervention "B."

A-B-C-B design: A single-case design that combines the "A" condition or baseline/preintervention measurements with a "B" condition or intervention; the first two conditions are followed by a "C" condition in which the intervention is changed to allow for the control of extra attention a participant may have received during the "B" condition.

Action research: Research that involves the application of the scientific method to everyday problems in the classroom or other applied setting; personnel are involved directly with the implementation of the research.

Alpha level: Statistical significance level chosen before data are gathered and analyzed for failing to accept (or to reject) the null hypothesis; also the Type I error rate.

Alternating treatments design: Also called the multielement design; a single-case design where the main purpose is to make comparisons between or among two or more conditions or interventions such as baseline and interventions(s) or multiple interventions; a secondary function is to determine experimental control.

Alternative hypothesis: Statements of statistically significant relationships between variables being studied or differences between values of a population parameter.

Analysis of covariance (ANCOVA): Used to control for initial differences between or among groups statistically before a comparison is made; makes groups equivalent with respect to one or more control variables (potential explanatory variables).

Analysis of variance (ANOVA): A powerful parametric test of statistical significance that compares the means of two or more sets of scores to determine whether the difference between them is statistically significant at the chosen alpha level.

Applied research: Research that attempts to solve real-life problems or study phenomena that directly impact what practitioners do or lay people do by using a theory developed through basic research.

Arithmetic mean (or average): Obtained by summing the scores for a data set and dividing by the number of participants or entities in that data set; takes into account all scores in the data set.

Attenuation: The lowering of the correlation coefficient because of the unreliability of the measure.

Authority: Information is gathered based on the views of "experts" in the field.

B-A-B design: A single-case design that combines the "B" condition or intervention with an "A" condition or baseline/preintervention; the "A" condition is followed by a second "B" condition.

Backward elimination multiple regression: This procedure starts with all of the independent variables in the regression model and sequentially removes them; researchers establish removal criteria rather than entry criteria; the independent variable with the smallest partial correlation with the dependent variable is examined first; if the independent variable meets established criteria for removal, it is removed from the regression model; if the independent variable does not meet the established criteria for removal, it remains in the regression model and the procedure stops.

Baseline: In single-case designs, "A" refers to the baseline; the level at which the participant performs a behavior without the intervention; the repeated measurement of a behavior under natural conditions.

Basic research: Research that focuses on more theoretical issues; conducted to help develop a new theory or refine an existing one.

Beta (β): Significance level for accepting (or failing to reject) the null hypothesis; also the Type II error rate.

Beta weights: Standardized regression coefficients (i.e., the regression coefficients that would have been obtained if each of the independent variables were equal to one another in terms of means and standard deviations) that enable direct comparisons of the relative relationship of each of the independent variables and the dependent variable.

Boolean rules: *See* logical operators.

Box and whiskers: A box and whiskers display uses a schematic box plot with some auxiliary features to depict the distribution of effect sizes.

Canonical correlation: Correlation procedure used in those cases in which researchers are interested in determining the relationship between a *set* of independent variables and a *set* of dependent variables.

Carryover effects: If an intervention has an effect on the other intervention irrespective of how the interventions were sequenced, the differences between the interventions may be minimal or nonexistent or may be greater than would occur otherwise; this result would not be because the interventions are equal in effectiveness or that one intervention was clearly less effective than the other, but because the effectiveness of one intervention improved or harmed the performance of the other intervention.

Case study research: A type of field-oriented investigation that involves an in-depth study of a single participant or group of participants; considered to be qualitative in nature.

Causal-comparative research: A type of research investigation used if the independent variable of interest cannot be manipulated or when it would be unethical to manipulate the independent variable.

Causism: Making claims that a causal relationship will be found.

Chain sampling: *See* snowball sampling.

Changing-criterion design: A single-case design that looks like an A-B design but includes "phase" lines (i.e., changes within the intervention condition); a criterion is established within each phase to reduce or increase some dependent variable in a stepwise manner.

Chi-square test (χ^2): A nonparametric test of statistical significance that compares the number of participants, objects, or responses, which fall into two or more categories each with two sets of data to determine whether the difference in the relative frequency of the two sets of data in a given category is statistically significant at the chosen alpha level.

Clinical replication: An investigation that involves the combination of two or more independent variables to form an intervention package.

Close-ended questions: In surveys or interviews, respondents are asked to select their answers from among those provided by the researchers.

Cluster sampling frames: In survey research, sampling frames in which the sampling is done in two or more stages (i.e., cluster sampling); in the first stage(s), researchers sample something other than the individuals to be surveyed; in one or more stages, these primary units are sampled from which a final sample is selected.

Coefficient of alienation: The proportion of variance of one variable that is *not* predictable from the variance of another variable; calculated as the square root of $1 - r^2$.

Coefficient of determination: The proportion of predictable variance obtained by squaring the obtained correlation coefficient r^2 and multiplying it by 100; allows one to state that a certain percentage of the variance of one variable is predictable from the variance of the other variable.

Coefficient of equivalence (or alternative or parallel forms reliability): A measure of the magnitude of the relationship between participants' scores on two analogous forms of the measurement device.

Coefficient of internal consistency: A measure indicating the magnitude of relationship between participants' scores on a single administration of the measurement device usually assessed by comparing two parts of a test (e.g., odd and even items).

Coefficient of stability (or test/retest reliability): A measure indicating the magnitude of relationship determined by administering the measurement device to a sample of individuals and then readministering the device to the same sample of individuals after some time delay.

Comparison group: In causal-comparative research, the group that does not possess the subject or organismic characteristic under study.

Complete observer observation: Similar to the types of observations used in single-case investigations; when one is a complete observer, there is an attempt to remain separated from the subject matter.

Complete participant observation: Observers become involved with the participants as if the observers were part of the group; the participants usually do not know they are being observed.

Concurrent validity: A type of criterion-related validity that determines the extent to which the measurement device may be used to estimate an individual's present standing on a criterion variable.

Confirming and disconfirming cases (sampling technique): In qualitative research, confirming and disconfirming cases involve the attempt to confirm what was found during the exploratory state of the investigation; once some conclusions have been drawn from the data (in field work or from other sources such as stakeholders), these conclusions should be confirmed or disconfirmed by sampling cases that will either confirm or disconfirm the earlier interpretations.

Constraint levels: The degree to which the researcher imposes limits or controls on any part of the research process; involves a continuum from low constraints to high constraints.

Construct validity: The extent to which a measurement device can be shown to measure a hypothetical construct.

Content validity: The representativeness of the sample of items included in the measurement device.

Contextual variable: Characteristics of the intervention and research methodology such as the duration of the intervention, who implemented the intervention (e.g., experimenter vs. practitioner), level of training, and type of experimental design or dependent variable that may affect the findings.

Contingency coefficient: Correlation coefficient that assesses the relationship between nominal variables.

Control group: In a controlled experiment, the group that receives no treatment or a treatment different from the experimental group.

Convenience sampling: Participants are selected for a sample because they are easy to access.

Convenience sampling frames: In survey research, sampling frames in which the sampling is done from a set of individuals who do something or go somewhere that enables researchers to administer a survey to them; this class of sampling frame differs from the exhaustive sampling frame in that there is not an advanced list from which researchers can sample; rather, the creation of the list or inventory of the members of the population and sampling occurs simultaneously.

Correlation coefficient: The statistic that is used to describe the relationship between two variables (is there a relationship between x and y?); a descriptive statistic; for a given sample represented with the italic letter r and the population value represented by the Greek letter ρ (rho).

Correlation ratio (η^2): The proportion of the total variability in the dependent variable that can be accounted for by knowing the value of the independent variable in correlational research.

Correlational research: A type of research investigation used to determine the strength of the relationship between/among variables; uses correlation as the statistical method.

Counterbalanced design: A quasi-experimental design in which two or more groups get the same independent variable(s), but the independent variable(s) is/are introduced in different orders.

Covariation: If a researcher applies an intervention to one behavior, there should not be a corresponding change in the other behavior (called covariation).

Criterion: In a changing-criterion design, the level set by the researcher that the participant must attain before moving on to a higher or lower level.

Criterion-referenced test: A test that compares a participant's score to some predetermined standard (criterion) or mastery level.

Criterion-related validity: The extent to which an individual's score on a measurement device is used to predict his or her score on another measurement device.

Criterion sampling: In qualitative research, setting a criterion of performance for individuals; those who meet or surpass the criterion will be included in the sample.

Criterion variable: In correlational research, the object of the research (dependent variable)—the variable about which researchers seek to discover more information.

Critical case sampling: Identifying critical cases that are particularly important for some reason.

Critical research consumer: An individual who is able to think critically about research and make conclusions based on the research findings.

Critical thinking: The ability to take a topic, consider both sides of the issue, and make an informed decision on the topic.

Curvilinear relationship: Nonlinear relationship between or among variables as noted on a scattergram used in correlational research.

Data-based decision making: A term used in fields such as special education and rehabilitation for making changes in how we teach (instruction) based on how our students are doing (assessment).

Data dropping: Data that contradict a researcher's theory or prediction are dropped from the study; outliers are dropped from the study; a subset of data is excluded from analysis.

Deductive logic: Moving from the general to the specific; involves the construction of a theory followed by testing parts of the theory to determine if the results of the testings uphold the theory.

Dependent variable: When trying to determine "if *X* caused *Y*," the "*Y*" would be the effect, and thus, the dependent variable; the variable that is affected by the independent variable (occurs or results from this other variable).

Descriptive research: *See* naturalistic research.

Descriptive statistics: Allows for the simple and parsimonious mathematical description of a data set, including central tendency, variation, and shape of the distribution.

Descriptive validity: The factual accuracy of the researcher's or observer's account; the concern here is whether the data gathered are contrived or distorted; others should be able to agree that the events or situations occurred.

Deviant case sampling: *See* Extreme case sampling.

Direct Instruction: A comprehensive system of instruction that focuses on active student involvement, mastery of skills, empirically validated curricula, and teacher-directed activities.

Directional hypothesis: The population parameter (e.g., mean) is stated to be greater or smaller than the other population parameter and then is tested by collecting and analyzing data.

Direct replication: An investigation conducted in the same manner as a previous experiment.

Discriminant function analysis: A type of multiple regression employed in those cases in which the dependent variable is nominal in nature; the goal is to identify the best set of independent variables that maximize the correct classification of participants/objects.

Distribution: Any set of scores that have been organized in such a way as to enable the shape of the data to be seen.

Document analysis: Popular method of data collection for qualitative researchers in which the data are presented as a permanent product; may include incident reports in a school, number and types of arrests on school grounds, or test scores and other information on student achievement.

Ecological validity: Concerned with the generalization of results to other environmental conditions.

Effect size: A statistic that provides an estimate of the magnitude of relationship or difference represented in a particular sample.

Efficiency evaluations: Assessments conducted to determine if the programs are conducted in a cost-effective way; deal with questions of cost.

Empiricism: Information is gathered by querying knowledge through the observation of our world; it is the information we gain from our senses.

Ethnographic research: A type of research investigation that involves the intense and in-depth study of a culture; a multitude of data collection methods are used to obtain as complete a picture as possible of the phenomenon under study.

Evaluative validity: The ability to make valid right or wrong statements.

Exhaustive sampling frames: In survey research, sampling frames in which the sampling is done from a more or less complete list of individuals of the population to be studied; this typically occurs when the population is small or clearly defined, and the list is used by researchers to select a sample.

Experimental control: Demonstrating that the independent variable produced changes in the dependent variable while decreasing the possibility of extraneous factors producing the results.

Experimental group: In a controlled experiment, the group that receives the treatment (independent variable).

Experimental research: A type of research investigation that is quantitative in nature, typically requiring a number of participants placed into one or several groups; also called group designed; the highest level of constraint research.

External criticism: The authenticity of the information obtained; has to do with the choice of sources historical researchers will read—they must be authentic.

External generalizability: The ability to generalize to other communities or groups.

External validity: Asks the question, "What is the generalizability of the results of a study?"

Extraneous variables: Factors that are not designed (unplanned) to be in a study that may influence the results.

Extreme case sampling: Also called deviant case sampling; focusing on cases that have important information because they are unusual or special in some way in qualitative research.

Fabricating data: "Inventing" data or changing values of data to support a particular viewpoint.

Factor analysis: Multivariate statistical method that is used to identify unobserved or latent variables; its purpose is to identify a structure or pattern within a set of variables.

Factorial experimental design: An experimental design used to assess the effects of two or more independent variables or the interaction of participant characteristics with the independent variable; used to determine whether the effect of a particular variable studied concurrently with other variables will have the same effect as it would when studied in isolation.

Field notes: Participant observations are recorded as facts or direct descriptions of what was seen and or overheard (this can also be in the form of audio recordings or the observer's thoughts about the events and interviews).

Forward selection multiple regression: The first variable entered into the regression model is the one with the largest positive or negative relationship with the dependent variable; if the first variable selected for entry meets the established criterion (alpha level established by the researcher) for inclusion in the model, forward selection continues; if the independent variable does not meet the criterion for inclusion in the model, the procedure terminates with no variables in the regression model; in this case, none of the independent variables is predictive of the dependent variable.

Fugitive literature: Primary sources of information used in research syntheses including dissertations, theses, course papers, paper presentations, technical reports, interim reports, and uncompleted research reports.

Functional relationship: When a change is produced in the independent variable (intervention), it is reliably followed by changes in the dependent variable.

General interview guide approach: This type of interview involves having an outline of topics to be covered during the interview; however, the order in which the topics is addressed is not set; the questions are not formulated beforehand; the purpose of outlines or guides is to aid interviewers in addressing each of the topics.

Generalizability (generalization): Ability to transfer results of an investigation to other situations/contexts/times.

Grounded theory: Theories developed once findings have been accumulated.

Historical research: Research that involves a systematic process of researching for data from the past that can help us understand what is going on now and what may occur in the future; geared to describe relations, correct inaccurate conclusions from other historical reports, or to explain what has occurred in the past.

History: May threaten the internal validity of a study when something other than the independent variable is occurring between the pretest and the posttest or during the implementation of the independent variable that may affect the participants' performance.

Homogeneity of variance: Score variances for the populations under study are equivalent (an assumption of parametric tests).

Homogeneous sampling: The opposite of maximum variation sampling in that participants similar to one another are selected to decrease the variation within the sample (in qualitative research).

Hyperclaiming: When researchers tell interested parties that the research they are conducting is likely to achieve specific goals that are unlikely.

Hypothesis: A prediction made by researchers about expected results in future investigations of the phenomenon.

Independent variable: When trying to determine "if *X* caused *Y*," the "*X*" would be what the researcher is manipulating or is interested in observing, and thus, the independent variable; the variable that produces changes in a dependent variable.

Inductive logic: Moving from the specific to the general; used in the formulation of theories after supporting research data are collected in a systematic fashion.

Inferential statistics: Allow for statistical inference; that is, researchers are able to generalize their results to the larger population or make an "inference" about the population based on the responses of the experimental sample.

Informal conversational interview: This type of interview usually occurs with the participant observation in the field and is the most open-ended interviewing method; it proceeds as a conversation in which interviewers ask spontaneous questions; there is no structured format, although interviewers should have some notion of the type of information they desire; in some instances, those being interviewed may be unaware of the interview.

Informed consent: Recruitment of participants should be voluntary and should include a complete understanding of the investigation, risks involved, and requirements imposed by the study; if the participants are underage or not competent to provide informed consent, a parent or legal guardian may provide this; informed consent provides the freedom to accept or decline participation in a study after making an informed decision.

Institutional review board (IRB): An IRB is required to be established by any institution receiving federal funding; the sole purpose of an IRB is to protect the rights of persons involved in research; it consists of a group of professionals who assess the level of risk to participants of an investigation and make sure that ethical safeguards are in place; are required by the government for federally funded agencies under federal definitions and regulations governing research by such agencies.

Instrumentation: May threaten the internal validity of a study when there are changes in the calibration of the instrument used in measurement.

Interaction effect: The effect of an independent variable on a dependent variable, which is influenced by one or more other independent variables.

Internal criticism: The accuracy of the information obtained; the documents are examined with the intent of making sure they are judged correctly.

Internal generalizability: The ability to generalize within the community or group being investigated to those not directly involved in the investigation.

Internal validity: Indicates a functional relationship between the independent variable and the dependent variable; addresses the question, "Did the treatment make the difference or was the change due to something else?"

Interobserver agreement: A direct measure of behavior where observers record the occurrence and nonoccurrence of specific behaviors and compare their findings.

Interpretative validity: Concerned with the subjective meanings of objects, events, and behaviors to the individuals engaged in and with the objects, events, and behaviors; specifically relevant to qualitative research.

Interval scale: Scale of measurement that provides equal intervals between equidistant points on a scale yet lacks an absolute zero point.

Intervention: The "B" or intervention condition is the time that the independent variable is in effect; the treatment.

Interview study: A study in which the researcher attempts to find out what is in or on someone else's mind (via interviewing).

Intuition: Information is gathered based on a "feeling" one gets about a topic.

Kendall coefficient of concordance: Correlation coefficient used when researchers want to establish the relationship among the rankings of several variables.

Kendall part rank correlation: Correlation coefficient used in those cases in which researchers want to control the influence of a third variable on the relationship between two variables; similar to the part correlation except that it is appropriate when the variables are measured on at least ordinal scales rather than interval or ratio scales.

Kendall's rank correlation coefficient: Referred to as τ, or tau; correlation coefficient that provides a measure of the disparity in the rankings between two variables and is computed by ranking the scores for each of the variables from smallest to largest and computing the Pearson product moment correlation coefficient on the ranks.

Kruskal–Wallis ANOVA: A nonparametric test of statistical significance that compares the medians or means of three or more sets of scores (at least ordinal scale).

Linear relationship: A straight line can be visualized in the middle of the values of scores running from one corner to another in a scattergram in correlational research.

Literature search: Gathering sources to use in an introduction of a journal article or in a research synthesis.

Logical operators: Terms used in a search strategy when conducting research syntheses that greatly affect the particular primary studies identified; bibliographic services provide guides to their services for these terms; for example, using OR in educational attainment OR academic ability OR academic aptitude OR academic achievement in a search would identify primary studies indexed using either of the terms or any combination of the terms; in contrast, using AND in educational attainment AND academic ability AND academic aptitude AND academic achievement in a search would identify only those primary studies indexed using all four of the terms.

Main effect: The effect of an independent variable by itself on a dependent variable.

Mann–Whitney *U* test: A nonparametric test of statistical significance that compares the medians or means of two sets of scores to determine whether the difference between them is statistically significant at the chosen alpha level.

Matching: Equating two or more groups of participants on a variable to rule out the variable's influence.

Maturation: May threaten the internal validity of a study when there is a passage of time where biological or psychological changes take place.

Maximum variation sampling: Capturing and describing the central themes or principle outcomes that cut across a great deal of participant or program variation.

Measurement error: Fluctuations in scores because the measurement device does not measure an attribute the same way every time; unknown and unrepeatable causes of variability in task performance over time and context.

Median: The point above and below which half of the scores fall; it is not affected by extreme scores in the data set.

Mode: The most commonly occurring score in a data set.

Mortality: May threaten the internal validity of a study when there is a differential loss of participants.

Multielement design: *See* Alternating treatments design.

Multiple-baseline design: A single-case design that involves a series of A-B designs; includes the placement of individual graphs on top of each other; can be used across participants, behaviors, or settings.

Multiple-probe design: Essentially multiple-baseline designs in which the measurements are not conducted on a frequent basis; overcomes the problem of using repeated measurements by probing (assessing) the behavior every so often; probes are also used in assessing generalization/transfer or maintenance of intervention effects; a single-case design.

Multiple regression: An extension of the correlation coefficient in which the overall and relative degree of relationship between a set of independent variables (nominal, ordinal, interval, or ratio in nature) and a dependent variable (interval or ratio in nature) is obtained.

Multitreatment design: Considered an associated design of the withdrawal design; it is a single-case design planned in such a way as to allow for the comparison of two or more interventions or the additive components of an intervention after baseline data are taken (e.g., A-B-A-C-A or A-B-A-B-BC-B-BC).

Narrative: A written representation of observed phenomena.

Naturalistic observation study: A study that involves observing participants in their natural settings; there is no attempt to manipulate what goes on in the setting and the observations are unobtrusive.

Naturalistic research: A type of research investigation that typically occurs in the participant's natural setting; typically considered qualitative in nature.

Needs assessment: Assessment to identify the level of existing needs within an organization or program; the goal is to look for potential, but unavailable, services for an identified population of individuals.

Nominal scale: Scale of measurement in which numbers simply act as identifiers, names, or labels.

Nondirectional hypothesis: A difference between two population parameters is stated but no direction is specified before collecting and analyzing the data.

Nonequivalent control-group design: A quasi-experimental design is similar to the pretest–posttest control group design except for the absence of the random selection of participants from a population and the random assignment of participants to groups.

Nonparametric test: A type of test of statistical significance that does not rely on assumptions such as the shape or variance of the population scores.

Nonparticipant observation study: A study in which the observer's presence is unknown to the participants.

Nonprobability sampling: The likelihood of any individual, object, or event of the population being selected is unknown.

Normal distribution: A purely theoretical distribution obtained by plotting theoretically obtained probabilities across the whole range of possible values from minus infinity to plus infinity along the horizontal axis.

Null hypothesis: Statements of valueless statistically significant relationships between variables being studied or differences between the values of a population parameter.

Observer-as-participant observation: Involves the observers remaining separate from the participants, but the participants are informed that they will be observed; these methods of observation overcome the ethical problem of complete observation; however, observers also risk reactivity on the part of the participants as a result of being aware that they are being observed.

Observer bias: Recording what was seen inaccurately because of a preexisting attitude or experience.

no intervention = baseline = 'A'

Observer drift: Occurs when observers change the way they employ the definition of behavior over the course of a study.

Observer effects: Problems that arise that may bias the reliability or validity of the data collected when observers are used.

One-group pretest–posttest design: A preexperimental design that differs from the one-shot case study in that a pretest measure is administered prior to the introduction of the independent variable.

One-shot case study: A preexperimental design in which an independent variable is introduced to a group of participants followed by the measurement of the dependent variable.

Open-ended questions: In surveys or interviews, the respondents are asked to provide their own answers to the questions.

Ordinal scale: Scale of measurement in which numbers represent a rank ordering of those objects/individuals of interest.

Outcome evaluation: Often referred to as summative evaluations because the primary goal is to develop summary statements and judgments about the program and its value.

Outlier: An individual or other entity whose score differs considerably from the scores obtained by the other participants or entities of the sample.

Parameter: Numerical description of a population's scores on some characteristic.

Parametric test: A type of test of statistical significance that makes certain assumptions about population parameters, including normal distribution of scores about the mean, equal population variances, and interval or ratio-scale data.

Part correlation: A correlation coefficient that establishes the relationship between two variables after the influence or effect of another variable has been removed from one of the variables but not both.

Partial correlation: Differs from the part correlation in that it enables researchers to establish the relationship between two variables after the influence or effect of a third variable has been removed from both.

Participant-as-observer observation: Involves observers engaging with the participants and also informing the participants of their intent to observe them.

Participant observation study: A study where the observer becomes personally acquainted with the participants.

Path analysis: Advanced statistic used to determine the amount of variance in a dependent variable that can be accounted for by a set of independent variables; in contrast to multiple regression, path analysis has the additional aim of determining whether the pattern of shared variances among the independent and dependent variables is consistent with particular causal pathways.

Phi coefficient: A correlation coefficient that assesses the relationship between nominal variables.

Pilot test: A "trial run" of an investigation to determine potential problems before an investigation is conducted formally; in survey research, finding out how the survey instrument works under realistic conditions.

Population: A group of potential participants, objects, or events to whom or to which researchers want to generalize the results of a study derived from a sample drawn from the population.

Population validity: The ability to generalize the results of a study from a sample to a larger group of individuals; includes two types—generalization across participants and interaction of personological variables and treatment effects.

Posttest-only control-group design: A true experimental design similar to the pretest–posttest-only control-group design with the exception that pretests of the dependent variable are not administered to the experimental and control groups.

Power: When we are able to detect a difference when one is actually present, or we correctly reject the null hypothesis; mathematically, Power = 1 – Type II error rate, or β.

Predictive validity: A type of criterion-related validity that determines the extent to which the measurement device may be used to estimate an individual's future standing on a criterion variable.

Predictor variable: In correlational research, the independent variable; variables in which participants' scores enable prediction of their scores on some criterion variable.

Preexperimental design: A research design that differs from true experimental designs and two of the quasi-experimental designs (i.e., counterbalanced and time series) in that it does not include a control group.

Pretest–posttest control group design: A true experimental design that includes measurement of the dependent variable before and after implementation of the independent variable.

Primary sources: Sources of information used in historical research, including oral testimony of individuals who were present at the time, documents, records, and relics; data come from sources who were present when the events took place; in research syntheses, descriptions of actual studies that are published in professional journals, dissertations, theses, government reports, foundation reports, and papers from scholarly meetings or conferences are also considered primary sources; "fugitive" literature is also regarded as a primary source.

Probability sampling: The likelihood of any one individual, object, or event of the population being selected is known.

Probability value: The level of significance actually obtained; indicated by the symbol *p*; a higher level of statistical significance corresponds to a lower *p* value.

Process evaluations: Assessment of the extent to which the program has been implemented, serves the identified population, and operates as expected.

Program evaluation: Provides feedback to those professionals who decide which social services are to be offered, design new programs, or make changes in existing approaches.

Proportion of nonoverlapping data (PND): An index of the magnitude of the intervention in reviews of research using single-case research; the number of data points that exceed the highest baseline data point in the expected direction divided by the total number of intervention data points in the intervention phase.

Qualitative research: Research in which the concern is with understanding the context in which behavior occurs, not just the extent to which it occurs; the assessment may be more subjective in that the dependent variables are not necessarily defined in observable terms; the data are collected in the natural setting; meanings and understandings are reached by studying cases intensively; inductive logic is used to place the resulting data in a theoretical context.

Quantitative research: Research involving an attempt to gather information in an objective manner; the research is usually conducted in a group format; quantitative research comes from a scientific-rational perspective; the method of gathering data is strictly prescribed, and the resulting data are subjected to a statistical analysis.

Quasi-experimental design: An experimental design in which participants are not randomly selected from the specified population nor randomly assigned to experimental and control groups.

Random assignment: Every individual, object, or event that comprises a sample has an equiprobability of being included in each group (treatment or control).

Random sample: Every individual, object, or event has an equiprobability of being included in the sample.

Range: The difference between the largest and smallest scores.

Ratio scale: Scale of measurement that provides equal intervals between equidistant points on a scale and has an absolute-zero point.

Rationalism: Information is gathered by interpreting or understanding the world around us through our reasoning processes.

Reactivity: Differences in interobserver agreement that result from observers being aware that their observations will be checked.

Refereed journal: A journal that accepts articles that have undergone a peer-review process; this process typically includes feedback from an editor and members of a review or editorial board.

Regression line (line of best fit): A line drawn on a scattergram to show the general relationship or trend in the data; provides an average statement about how a change in one variable affects another variable.

Reliability: Consistency of results over time.

Research question: If a study is not designed to test a hypothesis, a researcher may formulate a question to frame a study (e.g., "Does Direct Instruction produce high reading scores as compared to whole language instruction?").

Research synthesis: Pulling together the facts and findings from a group of related studies that are based on different (a) theoretical frameworks, (b) independent variables, (c) dependent measures, (d) research designs, and (e) data analysis procedures.

Response rate: The response rate is simply the number of people surveyed (or interviewed) divided by the number of individuals sampled multiplied by 100; the numerator includes all the individuals who were selected and did respond; the denominator includes all the individuals who were selected but did not respond for whatever reason.

Restriction of range: The variability (variance) of one variable is restricted or abbreviated and will reduce the correlation coefficient between the two variables.

Reversal design: A single-case design in which the researcher changes the level of participant behavior during the "B" condition such as reinforcing the behavior opposite of the desired one rather than simply removing the intervention.

Sample: A subset of the population.

Sampling error: A group's scores may be different each time the group is sampled; the difference between the characteristics of the sample and those of the population.

Sampling frames: The set of people (it is always people in the case of survey research) that has the chance to be selected, given the sampling procedure(s) used by researchers; the population or defined list from which the sample will be drawn.

Sampling politically important cases: A variation of the critical case strategy used in qualitative research; researchers attempt to select a politically sensitive site or conduct an analysis of a politically sensitive topic; in some cases, researchers may attempt to avoid the politically sensitive site or topic.

Science: The search for understanding of the world around us; the attempt to find order and lawful relations in the world; a method of viewing the world; the testing of our ideas in a public forum.

Scientific method: A method of gaining information which includes five steps: (a) identifying problem, (b) defining problem, (c) formulating hypothesis or research question, (d) determining observable consequences of hypothesis or research question, and (e) testing the hypothesis or attempting to answer the research question.

Scientific theory: A theory that is falsifiable or refutable; it must be able to be disproven.

Secondary sources: Sources of information used in historical research including reports from individuals who relay information from people who were present during the historical period, reports from individuals who have read information from the past, and books about the period under question such as history books and encyclopedias; in research syntheses, secondary sources cite, review, and organize the material from primary studies; that is, secondary sources are "once removed" from the actual research investigations; they include: (a) review journals, (b) periodicals, and (c) bibliographic services or abstract and citation archives.

Selection: May threaten the internal validity of a study if groups of individuals are selected in a differential manner.

Self-management: Procedures designed to help an individual change and/or maintain his or her own behavior (e.g., self instructions involve individuals talking themselves through tasks to complete them correctly and more efficiently).

Significance level (called alpha): This probability enables researchers to interpret how unlikely the difference might be due to sampling or measurement (chance) errors (symbolized α).

Simulation: The creation or re-creation of a situation to see how the participants will react under such circumstances.

Single-case research: A type of research investigation that relies on the intensive investigation of a single individual or a group of individuals; uses objective data collection techniques; may be thought of as a combination of qualitative and quantitative designs.

Snowball sampling: Also called chain sampling; involves asking others who would be a good choice to be involved in the sample.

Social validity: Research is considered to have social validity when society deems it to be important.

Solomon four-group design: A true experimental design that essentially combines the pretest–posttest control-group design and the posttest-only control-group design; two groups serve as experimental groups and two groups serve as control groups.

Spearman rank correlation coefficient: Referred to as ρ; the correlation coefficient that provides a measure of the disparity in the rankings between two variables and is computed by ranking the scores for each of the variables from smallest to largest and computing the Pearson product moment correlation coefficient on the ranks.

Stakeholders: People who have a vested interest in the design, implementation, and results of an investigation.

Standard deviation: Symbolized as *SD*; a statistic that describes how much the scores are spread out (distributed) around the mean; the larger the standard deviation, the more "spread out" the scores.

Standard error of measurement: An estimate of the variability of an individual's score if the measurement device was administered over and over again.

Standardized open-ended interview: This type of interview involves set topics similar to the general interview guide but also has predeveloped questions that researchers ask throughout the interview; each participant is exposed to the same topics and questions in the same order.

Standardized test: A test that has established procedures for administration, scoring, and interpretation for consistency across testing situations.

Static-group comparison design: A quasi-experimental design that is the same as the posttest-only control-group design except for the absence of the random selection of participants from a population and random assignment of participants to groups.

Statistical regression: May threaten the internal validity of a study if participants are selected who are extreme on some attribute.

Statistical significance: A difference between sets of scores may be so great that there is a likelihood, at some level of probability, that it is the result of one variable influencing another rather than a function of chance due to sampling or measurement error.

Statistical validity: Research is considered to have statistical validity if the results reach a certain level of confidence (pertains to the probability of obtaining the results of the investigation by chance and not some systematic variable).

Stepwise selection multiple regression: A combination of the forward selection and backward elimination procedures; stepwise selection is the most commonly used procedure; the first independent variable for consideration in the regression model is selected in the same manner as in the forward selection procedure; if the independent variable does not meet the established criteria for inclusion, the procedure is terminated with no independent variables in the regression model; if the independent variable meets the established criteria for inclusion in the regression model, the second independent variable is selected based on the highest partial correlation.

Structural equation modeling (LISREL): Statistical methodology that enables researchers to take a confirmatory approach to correlational research; includes the use of regression models to represent the causal relationships under study; LISREL stands for Linear Structural Relationships, a structural equation modeling computer program.

Survey research: The most widely used research method within and outside of the social sciences; used to identify how people feel, think, act, and vote; useful for collecting information from relatively large numbers of dispersed groups of people rather than a small number, as in the case of other research methods.

Syntheses: Involves organizing information, making conclusions, and, finally, making generalizations.

Systematic replication: An investigation that is conducted by a different researcher and/or person implementing the independent variable, involves participants with different characteristics from the original investigation, and/or is conducted in a different setting from the original experiment.

Systematic research syntheses: Parallel the methodologies used in original research studies in that researchers conducting research syntheses use a set of standard procedures to guide their efforts; in this way, the procedures used are much more systematic in nature.

Systematic variance: Variability we can account for between or among groups of people; this variability makes a group of individuals move in the same direction; may involve the independent variable or extraneous variables.

Tenacity: Information is gathered based on a persistence of a certain belief or way of thought for a long period of time.

Testing: May threaten the internal validity of the study when participants show improvement on a posttest simply due to the effects of taking the pretest.

Theoretical validity: Concerned with an *explanation* as well as a description and interpretation of an account; theories go beyond the data in that they attempt to provide an explanation for what is observed; one is concerned with taking descriptions and interpretations and constructing a grounded theory to help explain the phenomenon.

Theory: A simple guess in which the person stating the theory is making some prediction or explanation; a model derived to help understand a phenomenon; an explanatory system that describes the data gathered.

Time-series design: A quasi-experimental design that involves a series of repeated measurements of a group of research participants.

Triangulation: In qualitative research, the use of several kinds of methods or data, including using both quantitative and qualitative approaches; a combination of data collection methods (such as observation, interview, and document analyses) is used so that the strength of one method can compensate for a weakness of another method.

True experimental design: An experimental design that involves random selection of participants from the population to form a sample, random assignment of participants to experimental and control conditions, and equal treatment of both groups with the exception of the implementation of the independent variable.

***t* test:** A powerful parametric test of statistical significance that compares the means of two sets of scores to determine whether the difference between them is statistically significant at the chosen alpha level.

Type I error: Occurs when researchers reject the null hypothesis when it is true; that is, researchers conclude that any difference between sample groups was due to chance alone (called a false positive, or α).

Type II error: Occurs when researchers accept or fail to reject the null hypothesis when, in fact, there is a difference; that is, researchers conclude that the differences between groups were due to chance and/or systematic factors (a false negative, or β).

Typical case sampling: Selecting one or more typical cases for a sample; what is typical would be decided on by significant others (i.e., parents, teachers, community leaders, administrators, etc.) in the setting.

Unit of analysis: The focus of the research such as a group of individuals treated as one case or each individual case.

Unsystematic research syntheses: Few, if any, formal procedures and practices are used by researchers to review the literature for research syntheses.

Unsystematic variance: Variability within individuals and/or groups of individuals; it is essentially random; it may involve individual differences or measurement error.

Validity: The degree to which accurate inferences can be made based on the results of a study; relates to the question, "Does the measure assess what it purports to measure?"

Variability: The amount of dispersion or fluctuation in a set of scores.

Variable: A research expression for the construct or object of interest that varies in observable phenomena.

Variance: Calculated by squaring the standard deviation; a statistic that describes how much the scores are spread out (distributed) around the mean.

Vote counting: Method of integrating studies in a research synthesis; studies that provide information on the results of statistical significance testing are examined; three possible outcomes with regard to the relationship between the independent and dependent variables are noted: (a) the relationship is statistically significantly positive, (b) the relationship is statistically significantly negative, (c) there is no discernible relationship; the number of studies falling into each of these categories is tallied; if a majority of studies falls into any one of these three categories, this category is declared the winner; the category with the majority of studies is declared the winner because it is assumed that it provides the best estimate of the direction of the true relationship between the independent and dependent variables.

Whole-language approach: A philosophical approach to teaching and learning that emphasizes immersion (in the context of use), collaboration between learners and teachers, writing across the curriculum, and authentic materials and tasks.

Wilcoxon signed rank test: A nonparametric test of statistical significance that compares the medians or means of two sets of scores that are considered to be related in some fashion.

Withdrawal/A-B-A design: A single-case design that combines the "A" condition or baseline/preintervention measurements with a "B" condition or intervention to determine the effectiveness of the intervention; the "B" condition is followed by a second "A" condition.

References

Adams, M. J. (1992). *Beginning to read: Thinking and learning about print.* Cambridge, MA: The MIT Press.

Agran, M., Salzberg, C. L., & Martella, R. C. (1991). Expectancy effects in social validation methodology: Are there differential expectations for employees with mental retardation? *Research in Developmental Disabilities, 12,* 425–434.

Allen, S. J., & Kramer, J. J. (1990). Modification of personal hygiene and grooming behaviors with contingency contracting: A brief review and case study. *Psychology in the Schools, 27,* 244–251.

Allessi, G. F. (1980). Behavioral observation for school psychologists: Response-discrepancy model. *School Psychology Review, 9,* 31–45.

Alexander, P. A., Kulikowich, J. M., & Jetton, T. L. (1996). The role of subject-matter knowledge and interest in the processing of linear and nonlinear texts. *Review of Educational Research, 64,* 201–252.

American Educational Research Association. (1992). Ethical standards of the American Educational Research Association. *Educational Researcher, 21*(7), 23–26.

American Educational Research Association, American Psychological Association, & National Council on Measurement in Education. (1985). *Standards for educational and psychological testing.* Washington, DC: Authors.

American Psychological Association. (1994). *Publication manual of the American Psychological Association* (4th ed.). Washington, DC: Author.

American Psychological Association. (1997). *Ethical principles of psychologists and code of conduct.* Washington, DC: Author.

Anatasi, A. (1982). *Psychological testing* (5th ed.). New York: Macmillian.

Anderson, J. A. (1987). *Communication research: Issues and methods.* New York: McGraw-Hill.

Anderson, J. A., & Meyer, T. P. (1988). *Mediated communication: A social action perspective.* Newbury Park, CA: Sage.

Atkinson, P., & Hammersley, M. (1994). Ethnography and participant observation. In N. K. Denzin & Y. S. Lincoln (Eds.), *Handbook of qualitative research* (pp. 248–261). Thousand Oaks, CA: Sage.

Baer, D. M. (1977). Reviewer's comment: Just because it is reliable doesn't mean that you can use it. *Journal of Applied Behavior Analysis, 10,* 117–119.

Barlow, D. H., & Hersen, M. (1984). *Single case experimental designs: Strategies for studying behavior change* (2nd ed.). New York: Pergamon Press.

Becker, B. J. (1991). The quality and credibility of research reviews: What the editors say. *Personality and Social Psychology Bulletin, 17,* 267–272.

Billingsley, F., White, D. R., & Munson, R. (1980). Procedural reliability: A rationale and an example. *Behavioral Assessment, 2,* 247–256.

Bogdan, R. C., & Biklen, S. K. (1992) *Qualitative research for education: An introduction to theory and methods* (2nd ed.). Boston: Allyn & Bacon.

Bogdan, R., & Taylor, S. J. (1975). *Introduction to qualitative research methods: A phenomenological approach to the social sciences.* New York: Wiley.

Boneau, C. A. (1960). The effects of violations of assumptions underlying the *t* test. *Psychological Bulletin, 57,* 49–64.

Bornstein, R. F. (1990). Publication politics, experimenter bias and the replication process in social science research. *Journal of Social Behavior and Personality, 5*(4), 71–81.

Box, G. E. P., & Jenkins, G. M. (1970). *Time series analysis, forecasting, and control.* San Francisco: Holden-Day.

Bracht, G. H., & Glass, G. V. (1968). The external validity of experiments. *American Educational Journal, 5,* 437–474.

Brown, L. L., & Hammill, D. D. (1990). *Behavior rating profile* (2nd ed.). Austin, TX: PRO-ED.

Burchinal, M. R., Roberts, J. E., Nabors, L. A., & Bryant, D. M. (1996). *Child Development, 67,* 606–620.

Bybee, R. W., & Sund, R. B. (1990). *Piaget for educators* (2nd ed.). Prospect Heights, IL: Waveland.

Byrne, B. M. (1994). *Structural equation modeling with EQS and EQS/Windows: Basic concepts, applications, and programming.* Thousand Oaks, CA: Sage.

Caldwell, B. J. (1994). *Beyond positivism: Economic methodology in the twentieth century* (Rev. ed.). London: Routledge.

Campbell, D. T., & Stanley, J. C. (1963). *Experimental and quasi-experimental designs for research.* Boston: Houghton Mifflin.

Cannell, C., Groves, R., Magilary, L., Mathiowetz, N., & Miller, P. (1987). An experimental comparison of telephone and personal health interview surveys. *Vital and Health Statistics, Series 2,* 106. Washington, DC: Government Printing Office.

Caro-Bruce, C., & McCreadie, J. (1994). Establishing action research in one school district. *The Elementary School Journal, 95,* 33–40.

Carver, R. (1978). The case against statistical significance testing. *Harvard Educational Review, 48,* 378–399.

Carver, R. (1993). The case against statistical significance testing, revisited. *Journal of Experimental Education, 61*(4), 287–292.

Chiesa, M. (1994). *Radical behaviorism: The philosophy and the science.* Boston: Authors Cooperative.

Chisholm, R. F., & Elden, M. (1993). Features of emerging action research. *Human Relations, 46,* 275–297.

Christians, D. G., & Carey, J. W. (1989). The logic and aims of qualitative research. In G. H. Stempel III & B. H. Westley (Eds.). *Research methods in mass communication* (2nd ed., pp. 354–374). Englewood Cliffs, NJ: Prentice-Hall.

Cohen, J. (1990). Things I have learned (so far). *American Psychologist, 45,* 1304–1312.

Cohen, J., & Cohen, P. (1983). *Applied multiple regression/correlational analysis for the behavioral sciences.* Hillsdale, NJ: Lawrence Erlbaum.

Connors, R. J. (1992). Dreams and play: Historical method and methodology. In G. Kirsch & P. Sullivan (Eds.), *Methods and methodology in composition research* (pp. 15–36). Carbondale: Southern Illinois University.

Conoley, J. C., & Impara, J. C. (Eds.). (1994). *Supplement to the eleventh mental measurements yearbook.* Lincoln: The Buros Institute of Mental Measurements/University of Nebraska-Lincoln.

Cook, T. D., & Campbell, D. T. (1979). *Quasi-experimentation: Design and analysis issues for field settings.* Chicago: Rand McNally.

Cooper, H. M. (1989). *Integrating research: A guide for literature reviews* (2nd ed.). Newbury Park, CA: Sage.

Cooper, H., & Dorr, N. (1995a). Race comparisons on need for achievement: A meta-analytic alternative to Graham's narrative review. *Review of Educational Research, 65,* 483–508.

Cooper, H., & Dorr, N. (1995b). Narrative versus meta-analytic reviews: A rejoinder to Graham's comment. *Review of Educational Research, 65,* 515–517.

Cooper, H., & Hedges, L. V. (Eds.) (1994). *The handbook of research synthesis.* New York: Sage.

Cooper, J. O., Heron, T. E., & Heward, W. L. (1987). *Applied behavior analysis*. Columbus, OH: Merrill.

Cronbach, L. J. (1975). Beyond the two disciplines of scientific psychology. *American Psychologist, 30,* 116–127.

Dunkin, M. J. (1996). Types of error in synthesizing research in education. *Review of Educational Research, 66,* 87–98.

Ebey, T., Marchand-Martella, N., Martella, R., & Nelson, J. R. (1997). *Using parents as initial reading instructors for young children: A preliminary investigation.* Submitted for publication.

Edson, C. H. (1986). Our past and present: Historical inquiry in education. *The Journal of Thought, 21*(3), 13–27.

Educational Resources Information Center (1982). *ERIC processing manual* (Section 5: Cataloging). Washington, DC: Author.

Eisner, E. W. (1991). *The enlightened eye: Qualitative inquiry and the enhancement of educational practice.* Upper Saddle River, NJ: Merrill/Prentice Hall.

Elden, M., & Chisholm, R. F. (1993). Emerging varieties of action research: Introduction to the special issue. *Human Relations, 46,* 121–141.

Federal Register. (1991). Federal policy for the protection of human subjects; notices and rules, Part II. *Federal Register, 56,* 28001–28032.

Feigl, H. (1934/1996). The logical character of the principle of induction. In S. Sarkar (Ed.), *Science and philosophy in the twentieth century: Logical empiricism at its peak* (pp. 190–199). New York: Garland. (Reprinted from *Philosophy of science,* pp. 20–29, vol. 1, 1934.)

Feldt, L. S., & Brennan, R. L. (1989). Reliability. In R. L. Linn (Ed.), *Educational measurement* (3rd ed.) (pp. 235–271). Washington, DC: The American Council on Education and the National Council on Measurement in Education.

Ferguson, G. A. (1989). *Statistical analysis in psychology and education* (6th ed.). New York: McGraw-Hill.

Fetterman, D. M. (1989). *Applied social research methods series: Vol. 17. Ethnography step by step.* Newbury Park, CA: Sage.

Fetterman, D. M. (1991). *Using qualitative methods in institutional research.* San Francisco: Jossey-Bass.

Filion, F. (1975). Estimating bias due to nonresponse in mail survey. *Public Opinion Quarterly, 24,* 99–114.

Firby, P. (1993). Learning from the past. *Nursing Times, 89,* 32–33.

Fornell, C. (1982). *A second generation of multivariate analysis: Vol. 1. Methods.* New York: Praeger.

Fowler, F. J. (1993). *Survey research methods.* Newbury Park, CA: Sage.

Franklin, C., & Jordan, C. (1995). Qualitative assessment: A methodological review. *Families in Society, 76,* 281–295.

Gall, M. D., Borg, W. R., & Gall, J. P. (1996). *Educational research: An introduction* (6th ed.). White Plains, NY: Longman.

Gardner, H. (1993). *Frames of mind: The theory of multiple intelligences.* New York: Basic Books.

Gast, D. L., Wellons, J., & Collins, B. (1994). Home and community safety skills. In M. Agran, N. E. Marchand-Martella, & R. C. Martella (Eds.), *Promoting health and safety: Skills for independent living* (pp. 11–32). Baltimore: Paul H. Brookes.

Gast, D. L., & Wolery, M. (1988). Parallel treatment design: A nested single subject design for comparing instructional procedures. *Education and Treatment of Children, 11,* 270–285.

Gilgun, J. F. (1994). A case for case studies in social work research. *Social Work, 39,* 371–380.

Glaser B., & Strauss, A. L. (1967). *The discovery of grounded theory: Strategies for qualitative research.* Chicago: Aldine.

Glass, G. V. (1976). Primary, secondary, and meta-analysis of research. *Educational Researcher, 5,* 3–8.

Glass, G. V., McGaw, B., & Smith, M. L. (1981). *Meta-analysis in social research.* Beverly Hills, CA: Sage.

Glass, G. V., Willson, V. L., & Gottman, J. M. (1975). *Design and analysis of time-series experiments.* Boulder: Colorado University.

Goatley, V. J., Brock, C. H., & Raphael, T. E. (1995). Diverse learners participating in regular education "book clubs." *Reading Research Quarterly, 30,* 352–380.

Gold, R. L. (1969). Roles in sociological field observation. In G. J. McCall & J. L. Simmons (Eds.), *Issues in participant observation* (pp. 30–39). Reading, MA: Addison-Wesley.

Goto, S. T. (1996). School achievement from one Asian American perspective. *English Journal, 85,* 74–77.

Gould, S. J. (1981). *The mismeasure of man.* New York: Norton.

Graham, S. (1995). Narrative versus meta-analytic reviews of race difference in motivation. *Review of Educational Research, 65,* 509–514.

Graziano, A. M., & Raulin, M. L. (1993). *Research methods: A process of inquiry* (2nd ed.). New York: HarperCollins.

Greenwald, A. G. (1975). Consequences of prejudice against the null hypothesis. *Psychological Bulletin, 82,* 1–20.

Hall, R. V., & Fox, R. G. (1977). Changing-criterion designs: An alternative applied behavior analysis procedure. In B. C. Etzel, J. M. LeBlanc, & D. M. Baer (Eds.), *New developments in behavioral research: Theory, method, and application* (pp. 151–166). Hillsdale, NJ: Lawrence Erlbaum.

Hardman, M. L., Drew, C. J., & Egan, M. W. (1996). *Human exceptionality: Society, school, and family* (5th ed.). Boston: Allyn & Bacon.

Hart, S. N., & Pavlovic, Z. (1991). Children's rights in education: An historical perspective. *School Psychology Review, 20,* 345–358.

Hartman, D. P., & Hall, R. V. (1976). The changing-criterion design. *Journal of Applied Behavior Analysis, 9,* 527–532.

Hattie, J., & Marsh, H. W. (1996). The relationship between research and teaching: A meta-analysis. *Review of Educational Research, 66,* 507–542.

Hawkins, R. P., & Dotson, V. A. (1975). Reliability scores that delude: An Alice in Wonderland trip through misleading characteristics of interobserver agreement scores in interval recording. In E. Ramp & G. Semp (Eds.), *Behavior analysis: Areas of research and application* (pp. 359–376). Englewood Cliffs, NJ: Prentice Hall.

Hawkins, R. P., & Fabry, B. D. (1979). Applied behavior analysis and interobserver reliability: A commentary on two articles by Rirkimer and Brown. *Journal of Applied Behavior Analysis, 12,* 545–552.

Hayes, W. L. (1981). *Statistics* (3rd ed.). New York: Holt, Rinehart and Winston.

Hedges, L. V. (1987). How hard is hard science, how soft is soft science? *American Psychologist, 42,* 443–455.

Hedges, L. V., & Olkin, I. (1980). Vote-counting methods in research synthesis. *Psychological Bulletin, 88,* 359–369.

Hedges, L. V., & Olkin, I. (1985). *Statistical methods for meta-analysis.* Orlando, FL: Academic Press.

Hendrick, C. (1990). Replications, strict replications, and conceptual replications: Are they important? *Journal of Social Behavior and Personality, 5*(4), 41–49.

Herman, J. L., Morris, L. L., & Fitz-Gibbon, C. T. (1987). *Evaluator's handbook.* Newbury Park, CA: Sage.

Heward, W. L. (1996). *Exceptional children* (5th ed.). Columbus, OH: Merrill.

Hillocks, G., Jr. (1992). Reconciling the qualitative and quantitative. In R. Beach, J. L. Creeen, M. L. Kamil, & T. Shanahan (Eds.), *Multidisciplinary perspectives on literacy research* (pp. 57–65). Urbana, IL: National Conference on Research In English/ National Council of Teachers of English.

Horner, R. D., & Baer, D. M. (1978). Multiple-probe technique: A variation of the multiple baseline. *Journal of Applied Behavior Analysis, 11,* 189–196.

Hotelling, H. (1935). The most predictable criterion. *Journal of Educational Psychology, 26,* 139–142.

Howe, K., & Eisenhart, M. (1990). Standards for qualitative (and quantitative) research: A prolegomenon. *Educational Researcher, 19*(5), 2–9.

Huberty, C. J. (1987). On statistical testing. *Educational Researcher, 16*(8), 1–9.

Huberty, C. J. (1993). Historical orgins of statistical testing practices: The treatment of Fisher versus Neyman-Pearson views in textbooks. *Journal of Experimental Education, 61,* 317–333.

Hunter, J. E., Schmidt, F. L., & Jackson, G. B. (1982). *Meta-analysis: Cumulating research findings across studies.* Beverly Hills, CA: Sage.

Iwata, B. A., Vollmer, T. R., & Zarcone, J. R. (1990). The experimental (functional) analysis of behavior disorders: Methodology, applications, and limitations. In A. C. Repp & N. C. Singh (Eds.), *Perspectives on the use of nonaversive and aversive interventions for persons with developmental disabilities* (pp. 301–330). Sycamore, IL: Sycamore.

Jacob, E. (1988). Clarifying qualitative research: A focus on traditions. *Educational Researcher, 17,* 16–24.

Janowski, N. W., & Wester, F. (1991). The qualitative tradition in social science inquiry: Contributions to mass communication research. In K. B. Jensen & N. W. Jankowski (Eds.). *A handbook of qualitative methodoligies for mass communication research* (pp. 17–43). New York: Routledge.

Jensen, K. B., & Jankowski, N. W. (Eds.) (1991). *A handbook of qualitative methodologies for mass communication research. New York: Routledge.*

Jobber, D. (1984). Response bias in mail surveys: Further evidence. *Psychological Reports, 54,* 981–984.

Johnston, J. M., & Pennypacker, H. S. (1980). *Strategies and tactics of human behavioral research.* Hillsdale, NJ: Lawrence Erlbaum.

Joreskog, K., & Sorbom, D. (1986). *LISREL VI users manual.* Chicago: International Educational Services.

Kaestle, C. F. (1992). Standards of evidence in historical research: How do we know when we know? *History of Education Quarterly, 32,* 361–366.

Kamps, D. M., Leonard, B. R., Dugan, E. P., Boland, B., & Greenwood, C. R. (1991). The use of ecobehavioral assessment to identify naturally occurring effective procedures in classrooms serving students with autism and other developmental disabilities. *Journal of Behavioral Education, 1,* 367–397.

Kazdin, A. E. (1977). Artifact, bias, and complexity of assessment: The ABCs of reliability. *Journal of Applied Behavior Analysis, 10,* 141–150.

Kazdin, A. E. (1982). *Single-case research designs: Methods for clinical and applied settings.* New York: Oxford University Press.

Kazdin, A. E., & Hartman, D. P. (1978). The simultaneous treatment design. *Behavior Therapy, 9,* 912–922.

Kelly, M. B. (1977). A review of the observational data-collection and reliability procedures reported in the *Journal of Applied Behavior Analysis. Journal of Applied Behavior Analysis, 10,* 97–101.

Keppel, G. (1973). *Design and analysis: A researcher's handbook.* Englewood, CA: Prentice-Hall.

Kitchener, R. F. (1983). Changing conceptions of the philosophy of science and the foundations of developmental psychology. *Contributions to Human Development, 8,* 1–30.

Kochenderfer, B. J., & Ladd, G. W. (1996). Peer victimization: Cause or consequence of school maladjustment? *Child Development, 67,* 1305–1317.

Krahn, G. L., Hohn, M. F., & Kime, C. (1995). Incorporating qualitative approaches into clinical psychology research. *Journal of Clinical Child Psychology, 24,* 204–213.

Kratochwill, T. R., & Wetzel, R. J. (1977). Observer agreement, credibility, and judgment: Some considerations in presenting observer data. *Journal of Applied Behavior Analysis, 10,* 133–139.

Lamal, P. A. (1990). On the importance of replication. *Journal of Social Behavior and Personality, 5*(4), 31–35.

Lancy, D. F. (1993), *Qualitative research in education: An introduction to the major traditions.* New York: Longman.

Lazarus, B. D. (1993). Guided notes: Effects with secondary and post secondary students with mild disabilities. *Education and Treatment of Children, 16,* 272–289.

Lee, V. E., & Bryk, A. S. (1989). Effects of single-sex secondary schools: Response to Marsh. *Journal of Educational Psychology, 81,* 647–650.

Lewis, T. J., & Sugai, G. (1996). Descriptive and experimental analysis of teacher and peer attention and the use of assessment-based intervention to improve pro-social behavior. *Journal of Behavioral Education, 6,* 7–24.

Light, R. J., & Pillemer, D. B. (1984). *Summing up: The science of reviewing research.* Cambridge, MA: Harvard University Press.

Light, R. J., & Smith, P. V. (1971). Accumulating evidence: Procedures for resolving contradictions among different research studies. *Harvard Educational Review, 41,* 429–471.

Likins, M., Salzberg, C. L., Stowitschek, J. J., Lignugaris/Kraft, B., & Curl, R. (1989). Co-worker implemented job training: The use of coincidental training and quality-control checking on the food preparation skills of trainees with mental retardation. *Journal of Applied Behavior Analysis, 22,* 381–393.

Lincoln, Y. S., & Guba, E. G. (1985). *Natualistic inquiry.* Newbury, CA: Sage.

Lindlof, T. R. (1991). The qualitative study of media audiences. *Journal of Broadcasting & Electronic Media, 35,* 23–42.

Lindlof, T. R., & Meyer, T. P. (1987). Media use as ways of seeing, acting, and constructing culture: The tools and foundations of qualitative research. In T. R. Lindlof (Ed.), *Natural audiences: Qualitative research of media uses and effects* (pp. 1–30). Norwood, NJ: Ablex.

Lofland, J. (1971). *Analyzing social settings: A guide to qualitative observation and analysis* (2nd ed.). Belmont, CA: Wadsworth.

Mangione, T., Hingson, R., & Barret, J. (1982). Collecting sensitive data: A comparison of three survey strategies. *Sociological Methods and Research, 10,* 337–346.

Marchand-Martella, N. E., Huber, G., Martella, R. C., & Wood, W. S. (1996). Assessing the long-term maintenance of abduction prevention skills by disadvantaged preschoolers. *Education and Treatment of Children, 19,* 55–68.

Marchand-Martella, N. E., & Martella, R. C. (1990). The acquisition, maintenance, and generalization of first-aid skills by youths with handicaps. *Behavioral Residential Treatment, 5,* 221–237.

Marchand-Martella, N. E., Martella, R. C., Agran, M., & Young, K. R. (1991). Assessing the acquisition of first-aid treatments by elementary-aged children. *Child & Family Behavior Therapy, 13*(4), 29–43.

Marsh, H. W. (1989a). Effects of single-sex and coeducational high schools on achievement, attitudes, behaviors, and sex differences. *Journal of Educational Psychology, 81,* 70–85.

Marsh, H. W. (1989b). Effects of single-sex and coeducational schools: A response to Lee and Bryk. *Journal of Educational Psychology, 51,* 651–653.

Marshall, C., & Rossman, G. B. (1995). *Designing qualitative research* (2nd ed.). Thousand Oaks, CA: Sage.

Martella, R. C., Leonard, I. J., Marchand-Martella, N. E., & Agran, M. (1993). Self-monitoring negative statements. *Journal of Behavioral Education, 3,* 77–86.

Martella, R. C., & Marchand-Martella, N. E. (1995). Safety skills in vocational rehabilitation: A qualitative analysis. *Journal of Vocational Rehabilitation, 5,* 25–31.

Martella, R. C., Marchand-Martella, N. E., & Agran, M. (1992). Problem-solving to prevent work injuries in supported employment. *Journal of Applied Behavior Analysis, 25,* 637–645.

Martella, R. C., Marchand-Martella, N. E., Macfarlane, C. A., & Young, K. R. (1993). Improving the classroom behaviour of a student with severe disabilities via paraprofessional training. *British Columbia Journal of Special Education, 17,* 33–44.

Martella, R. C., Marchand-Martella, N. E., Young, K. R., & Macfarlane, C. A. (1995). Determining the collateral effects of peer tutor training on a student with severe disabilities. *Behavior Modification, 19,* 170–191.

Mason, R. O., McKenny, J. L., & Copeland, D. G. (1997, September). An historical method for MIS research: Steps and assumptions. *MIS Quarterly,* 307–319.

Mastropieri, M. A., Scruggs, T. E., Baken, J. P., & Brigham, F. J. (1996). A complex mnemonic strategy for teaching states and their capitals: Comparing forward and backward associations. *Learning Disabilities Research & Practice, 7,* 96–103.

Marx, M. H., & Hillix, W. A. (1963). *Systems and theories in psychology.* New York: McGraw-Hill.

Maxwell, J. A. (1992). Understanding and validity in qualitative research. *Harvard Educational Review, 62*(3), 279–300.

McNaughten, D., & Gabbard, C. (1993). Physical exertion and immediate mental performance of sixth-grade students. *Perceptual and Motor Skills, 77,* 1155–1159.

Meier, K. (1997, February 7). The value of replicating social-science research. *The Chronicle of Higher Education,* p. B7.

Mishler, E. G. (1990). Validation in inquiry-guided research: The role of exemplars in narrative studies. *Harvard Educational Review, 60,* 415–442.

Mitchell, J. V. (Ed.). (1983). *Tests in print.* Lincoln: University of Nebraska Press.

Mitchell, J. V. (Ed.). (1985). The mental measurements yearbook. Lincoln: University of Nebraska Press.

Moran, G., Dumas, J. E., & Symons, D. K. (1992). Approaches to sequential analysis and the description of contingency in behavioral interaction. *Behavioral Assessment, 14,* 65–92.

Mordock, J. B. (1995). Institutional review boards in applied settings: The role in judgments of quality and consumer protection. *Psychological Science, 6,* 320–321.

Murray, F. B., & Raths, J. (1996). Factors in peer review of reviews. *Review of Educational Research, 66,* 417–421.

Nelson, C. R. (1973). *Applied time series analysis for managerial forecasting.* San Francisco: Holden-Day.

Nelson, J. R. (1991, April). *An analysis of Utah's prereferral intervention policy.* Paper presented at the Annual American Education Research Association, Chicago.

Nelson, J. R. (1996a). *An evaluation of the Puffables smoking prevention program.* Unpublished evaluation report, Eastern Washington University, Cheney.

Nelson, J. R. (1996b). Designing schools to meet the needs of students who exhibit disruptive behavior. *Journal of Emotional and Behavioral Disorders, 4,* 147–161.

Nelson, J. R. (1996c). *Effectiveness of violence prevention programs for rural schools.* Evaluation report submitted to Educational Service District No. 101. Cheney: Eastern Washington University.

Nelson, J. R. (1996d, May). *Preventing escalating behavior chains in school settings.* Paper presented at the Annual Applied Behavior Analysis Conference, San Francisco.

Nelson, J. R., Drummond, M., Martella, R. C., & Marchand-Martella, N. E. (1997). The current and future outcomes of interpersonal social interactions: The views of students with behavioral disorders. *Behavioral Disorders, 22,* 141–151.

Nelson, J. R., Johnson, A., & Marchand-Martella, N. E. (1996). A comparative analysis of the effects of direct instruction, cooperative learning, and independent learning practices on the classroom behavior of students with behavioral disorders. *Journal of Emotional and Behavioral Disorders, 4,* 53–62.

Nelson, J. R., & Lignugaris/Kraft, B. (1989). A review of services provided students with learning disabilities in post-secondary institutions. *Exceptional Children, 56,* 246–265.

Nelson, J. R., Martella, R. C., & Galand, B. (in press). The effects of teaching school expectations and establishing a consistent consequence on formal office disciplinary actions. *Journal of Emotional and Behavioral Disorders.*

Nelson, J. R., Smith, D. J., & Dodd, J. M. (1994). The effects of learning strategy instruction on the completion of job applications by students with learning disabilities. *Journal of Learning Disabilities, 27,* 104–110.

Nelson, J. R., Smith, D. J., Young K. R., & Dodd, J. (1991). A review of self-management outcome studies conducted with students that exhibit behavioral disorders. *Behavioral Disorders, 16,* 169–179.

Neuliep, J. W., & Crandall, R. (1993a). Everyone was wrong: There are lots of replications out there. *Journal of Social Behavior and Personality, 8*(6), 1–8.

Neuliep, J. W., & Crandall, R. (1993b). Reviewer bias against replication research. *Journal of Social Behavior and Personality, 8*(6), 21–29.

Nicholls, J. G., & Nelson, J. R. (1992). Students' conceptions of controversial and noncontroversial knowledge. *Journal of Educational Psychology, 84*(2), 224–230.

Pajak, E. F., & Blase, J. J. (1984). Teachers in bars: From professional to personal self. *Sociology of Education, 57,* 164–173.

Patton, M. Q. (1987). *How to use qualitative methods in evaluation.* Newbury Park, CA: Sage.

Patton, M. Q. (1990). *Qualitative evaluation and research methods.* Newbury Park, CA: Sage.

Pauly, J. J. (1991). A beginner's guide to doing qualitative research in mass communication. *Journalism Monographs, 125.*

Peshkin, A. (1988). In search of subjectivity—One's own. *Educational Researcher, 17*(7), 17–22.

Pillemer, D. B. (1991). One- versus two-tailed hypothesis tests in contemporary educational research. *Educational Researcher, 20*(9), 13–17.

Pitman, M. A., & Maxwell, J. A. (1992). Qualitative approaches to evaluation: Models and methods. In M. D. LeCompte, W. L. Millory, & J. Preissle (Eds.), *The handbook of qualitative research in education* (pp. 729–770). San Diego: Academic Press/Harcourt Brace.

Popham, W. J. (1981). *Modern educational measurement.* Englewood Cliffs, NJ: Prentice Hall.

Popham, W. J. (1988). *Educational evaluation.* (2nd ed.). Englewood Cliffs, NJ: Prentice Hall.

Popper, K. R. (1957/1996). Philosophy of science: A personal report. In S. Sarkar (Ed.), *Science and philosophy in the twentieth century: Decline and obsolescence of logical empiricism* (pp. 237–273). New York: Garland. (Reprinted from *British philosophy in the mid-century: A Cambridge symposium,* pp. 155–191, by C. A. Mace (Ed.), 1957. New York: Macmillan Norwood Russe.)

Posavac, E. J., & Carey, R. G. (1997). *Program evaluation methods and case studies.* Upper Saddle River, NJ: Prentice Hall.

Potter, W. J. (1996). *An analysis of thinking and research about qualitative methods.* Mahwah, NJ: Lawrence Erlbaum.

Reid, J. B. (1970). Reliability assessment of observation data: A possible methodological problem. *Child Development, 41,* 1143–1150.

Richardson, M. W., & Kuder, G. F. (1939). The calculation of test reliability coefficients based on the method of rational equivalence. *Journal of Educational Psychology, 30,* 681–87.

Risley, T. R., & Wolf, M. M. (1972). Strategies for analyzing behavioral change over time. In J. Nesselroade & H. Reese (Eds.), *Life-span developmental psychology: Methodological issues* (pp. 175–183). New York: Academic Press.

Roethlisberger, F. J., & Dickson, W. J. (1939). *Management and the worker.* Cambridge, MA: Harvard University Press.

Rosenshine, B., & Meister, C. (1994). Reciprocal teaching: A review of the research. *Review of Educational Research, 64,* 479–530.

Rosenthal, R. (1978). Combining results of independent studies. *Psychological Bulletin, 85,* 185–193.

Rosenthal, R. (1979). The "file drawer problem" and tolerance for null results. *Psychological Bulletin, 86,* 638–641.

Rosenthal, R. (1984). *Meta-analytic procedures for social science research.* Beverly Hills, CA: Sage.

Rosenthal, R. (1990). Replication in behavioral research. *Journal of Social Behavior and Personality, 5*(4), 1–30.

Rosenthal, R. (1994a). Parametric measures of effect sizes. In H. M. Cooper & L. V. Hedges (Eds.), *The handbook of research synthesis* (pp. 231–243). New York: Sage.

Rosenthal, R. (1994b). Science and ethics in conducting, analyzing, and reporting psychological research. *Psychological Science, 5,* 127–134.

Rosnow, R. L., & Rosenthal, R. (1976). The volunteer subject revisited. *Australian Journal of Psychology, 28,* 97–108.

Sagan, C. (1996). *The demon-haunted world: Science as a candle in the dark.* New York: Ballantine Books.

Salvia, J., & Ysseldyke, J. E. (1995). *Assessment* (6th ed.). Boston: Houghton Mifflin.

Salzberg, C. L., Agran, M., & Lignugaris/Kraft, B. (1986). Behaviors that contribute to entry-level employment: A profile of five jobs. *Applied Research in Mental Retardation, 7,* 299–314.

Schatzman, L., & Strauss, A. L. (1973). *Field research: Strategies for a natural sociology.* Englewood Cliffs, NJ: Prentice Hall.

Schlinger, H. D. (1995). *A behavior analytic view of child development.* New York: Plenum.

Schwartz, H., & Jacobs, J. (1979). *Qualitative sociology: A method to the madness.* New York: The Free Press.

Scriven, M., & Roth, J. (1990). Special feature: Needs assessment. *Evaluation Practice, 11,* 135–140.

Scruggs, T. E., & Mastropieri, M. A. (1994). Successful mainstreaming in elementary science classes: A qualitative study of three reputational cases. *American Educational Research Journal, 31*(4), 785–812.

Scruggs, T. E., Mastropieri, M. A., & Casto, G. (1987). Reply to Owen White. *Remedial and Special Education, 8,* 40–42.

Scruggs, T. E., Mastropieri, M. A., Cook, S. B., & Escabar, C. (1985). Early intervention for children with conduct disorders: A quantitative synthesis of single-subject research. *Behavioral Disorders, 11,* 260–271.

Shaver, J. P. (1983). The verification of independent variables in teaching methods research. *Educational Research, 12,* 3–9.

Shaver, J. (1985). Chance and nonsense. *Phi Delta Kappan, 67*(1), 57–60.

Shaver, J. (1993). What statistical significance testing is, and what it is not. *Journal of Experimental Education, 61*(4), 293–316.

Sidman, M. (1960). *Tactics of scientific research: Evaluating experimental data in psychology.* New York: Basic Books.

Silverman, D. (1993). *Interpreting qualitative data: Methods for analysing talk, text, and interaction.* London: Sage.

Sindelar, P. T., Rosenberg, M. S., & Wilson, R. J. (1985). An adopted alternating treatments design for instructional research. *Education and Treatment of Children, 8,* 67–76.

Skinner, B. F. (1947/1972). Current trends in experimental psychology. In B. F. Skinner, *Cumulative record: A selection of papers* (3rd ed., pp. 295–313). New York: Appleton-Century-Crofts.

Skinner, B. F. (1963). Operant behavior. *American Psychologist, 18,* 503–515.

Slavin, R. E. (1994). *Educational psychology: Theory and practice.* Needham Heights, MA: Allyn & Bacon.

Smith, D. D., & Luckasson, R. (1995). *Introduction to special education: Teaching in an age of challenge* (2nd ed.). Boston: Allyn & Bacon.

Smith, D. J., Nelson, J. R., Young, K. R., & West, R. P. (1992). The effects of a self-management procedure on the classroom and academic behavior of students with mild handicaps. *School Psychology Review, 21,* 59–72.

Smith, J. K. (1983, March). Quantitative versus qualitative research: An attempt to clarify the issue. *Educational Researcher,* 6–13.

Smith, J. K., & Heshusius, L. (1986, January). Closing down the conversation: The end of the quantitative–qualitative debate among educational inquirers. *Educational Researcher,* 4–12.

Smith, M. L., & Glass, G. V. (1977). Meta-analysis of psychotherapy outcome studies. *American Psychologist, 32,* 752–760.

Snider, V. E., & Crawford, D. B. (1996). Action research: Implementing *Connecting Math Concepts. Effective School Practices, 15*(2), 17–26.

Stewart, K. G., & McLaughlin, T. F. (1992). Self-recording: Effects on reducing off-task behavior with a high school student with an attention deficit hyperactivity disorder. *Child & Family Behavior Therapy, 14*(3), 53–59.

Stock, W. A. (1994). Systematic coding for research synthesis (pp. 125–138). In H. Cooper & L. Hedges (Eds.), *The handbook of research synthesis.* New York: Sage.

Strauss, A., & Corbin, J. (1990). *Basics of qualitative research: Grounded theory procedures and techniques.* Newbury Park, CA: Sage.

Sulzer-Azaroff, B., & Mayer, R. G. (1991). *Behavior analysis for lasting change.* Fort Worth, TX: Holt, Rinehart and Winston.

Tan, A., Moore, D. W., Dixon, R. S., & Nicholson, T. (1994). Effects of training in rapid decoding on the reading comprehension of adult learners. *Journal of Behavioral Education, 4,* 177–189.

Tawney, J. W., & Gast, D. L. (1984). *Single subject research in special education.* Columbus, OH: Merrill.

Taylor, S., & Bogdan, R. (1984). *Introduction to qualitative research methods: The search for meanings.* New York: John Wiley.

Thomas, R. M. (1996). *Comparing theories of child development* (4th ed.). Pacific Grove, CA: Brooks/Cole.

Thompson, B. (1994). The concept of statistical significance testing (ERIC/AE Clearinghouse Digest #EDO-TM-94-1) *Measurement Update,* 4(1), 5–6 (ERIC Document Reproduction Service No. ED 366 654.)

Thompson, B. (1996). AERA editorial policies regarding statistical significance testing: Three suggested reforms. *Educational Researcher, 25*(2), 19–24.

Tripodi, T. (1994). *A primer on single-subject design for clinical social workers.* Washington, DC: National Association of Social Workers.

Tse, L. (1996). When an ESL adult becomes a reader. *Reading Horizons, 37,* 16–29.

Tufte, E. R. (1983). *The visual display of quantitative information.* Cheshire, CT: Graphics Press.

Tukey, J. W. (1977). *Exploratory data analysis.* Reading, MA: Addison-Wesley.

Tukey, J. W. (1991). The philosophy of multiple comparisons. *Statistical Science, 6,* 157–176.

Ulman, J. D., & Sulzer-Azaroff, B. (1975). Multielement baseline design in educational research. In E. Ramp & G. Semb (Eds.), *Behavior analysis: Areas of research and application* (pp. 377–391). Englewood Cliffs, NJ: Prentice Hall.

Weiner, E. A., & Stewart, B. J. (1984). *Assessing individuals: Psychological and educational tests and measurements.* Boston: Little, Brown.

Weinstein, C. S. (1990). Prospective elementary teachers' beliefs about teaching: Implications for teacher education. *Teaching and Teacher Education, 6,* 279–290.

Williams, R. L. (1974). Black pride, academic relevance, and individual achievement. In R. W. Tyler & R. M. Wolf (Eds.), *Crucial issues in testing* (pp. 219–231). Berkeley, CA: McCutchan.

Wimmer, R. D., & Dominick, J. R. (1991). *Mass media research* (3rd ed.). Belmont, CA: Wadsworth.

Wolcott, H. F. (1992). Posturing in qualitative research. In M. D. LeCompte, W. L. Millroy, & J. Preissle (Eds.), *The handbook of qualitative research in education* (pp. 3–52). San Diego: Academic Press.

Wolf, M. M. (1978). Social validity: The case of subjective measurement or how applied behavior analysis is finding its heart. *Journal of Applied Behavior Analysis, 11,* 203–214.

Wolf, M. M., & Risley, T. R. (1971). Reinforcement: Applied research. In R. Glaser (Ed.), *The nature of reinforcement* (pp. 310–325). New York: Academic press.

Wright, S. (1921). Correlation and causation. *Journal of Agricultural Research, 20,* 557–585.

Ysseldyke, J. E. (1977). Aptitude-treatment interaction research with first grade children. *Contemporary Educational Psychology, 2,* 1–9.

Zuriff, G. (1995). Continuity over change within the experimental analysis of behavior. In J. T. Todd & E. K. Morris (Eds.), *Modern perspectives on B. F. Skinner and contemporary behaviorism* (pp. 171–183). Westport, CT: Greenwood Press.

Name Index

Adams, M. J., 268
Agran, M., 380, 388, 407, 428, 431, 459, 536
Alexander, P. A., 491
Allen, S. J., 23, 412
Allessi, G. F., 81
American Educational Research Association (AERA), 533, 534
American Psychological Association (APA), 533
Anatasi, A., 69
Anderson, J. A., 259
Atkinson, P., 258, 291

Baer, D. M., 80, 368
Baken, J. P., 150
Barlow, D. H., 19, 23, 27, 29, 81, 333, 337, 364, 369, 373, 405, 419, 422, 423
Barret, J., 453
Becker, B. J., 512
Bevill, A., 544
Biklen, S. K., 78, 258, 282, 285, 327
Billingsley, F., 80
Blase, J. J., 267, 272, 273
Bogdan, R. C., 78, 258, 259, 261, 282, 285, 288, 296, 327
Boland, B., 344
Borg, W. R., 65, 109, 177, 366, 464
Bornstein, R. F., 24
Box, G. E. P., 151
Bracht, G. H., 47, 49, 56
Brennan, R. L., 65
Brigham, F. J., 150
Brock, C. H., 530
Brown, L. L., 64
Bryant, D. M., 227
Bryk, A. S., 100
Burchinal, M. R., 227, 228
Bybee, R. W., 22
Byrne, B. M., 223

Caldwell, B. J., 6, 9, 12, 13
Campbell, D. T., 38, 132, 136, 210, 219, 225, 332
Cannell, C., 453, 455
Carey, J. W., 260, 261
Carey, R. G., 470
Caro-Bruce, C., 526
Carver, R., 104
Casto, G., 507
Chiesa, M., 6, 8, 265
Chisholm, R. F., 526, 527
Christians, D. G., 260, 261
Cohen, J., 100, 216
Cohen, P., 216
Collins, B., 288
Conoley, J. C., 86
Cook, S. B., 507
Cook, T. D., 38, 132, 219, 225
Cooper, H. M., 491, 502, 505
Cooper, J. O., 84
Copeland, D. G., 461
Corbin, J., 258, 261, 262, 265, 295
Courson-Krause, P. S., 351
Crandall, R., 23, 27, 28
Crawford, D. B., 529
Cronbach, L. J., 68, 69, 89, 102
Curl, R., 422

Dickson, W. J., 51
Dixon, R. S., 343
Dodd, J. M., 134, 158, 478, 500, 516
Dominick, J. R., 261
Dorr, N., 502
Dotson, V. A., 84
Drew, C. J., 42
Drummond, M., 180, 183
Dumas, J. E., 152
Dunkin, M. J., 514

Ebey, T., 156
Edson, C. H., 460
Educational Resources Information Center (ERIC), 489
Egan, M. W., 42
Eisenhart, M., 256, 273, 300
Eisner, E. W., 77, 277, 296
Elden, M., 526, 527
Escabar, C., 507

Fabry, B. D., 80
Federal Register, 533
Feigl, H., 12
Feldt, L. S., 65
Ferguson, G. A., 141, 143, 177, 220
Fetterman, D. M., 274, 292
Filion, F., 456
Firby, P., 463
Fornell, C., 224
Fowler, F. J., 455
Fox, R. G., 406

Gabbard, C., 140
Galand, B., 300
Gall, J. P., 6, 65, 109, 177, 464
Gall, M. D., 6, 65, 109, 177, 464
Gardner, H., 10, 22
Gast, D. L., 288, 330, 332, 334, 347, 405, 410, 416, 417, 418, 419, 422
Gilgun, J. F., 282
Glaser, B., 264
Glass, G. V., 47, 49, 56, 151, 491, 499, 503, 512
Goatley, V. J., 530
Gold, R. L., 282
Goto, S. T., 299, 300
Gottman, J. M., 152
Gould, S. J., 65, 66
Graham, S., 502
Graziano, A. M., 13, 17
Greenwald, A. G., 499
Greenwood, C. R., 344

Groves, R., 453
Guba, E. G., 262

Hall, R. V., 405, 406
Hammersley, M., 258, 291
Hammill, D. D., 64
Hardman, M. L., 42
Hart, S. N., 468
Hartman, D. P., 405, 406, 421
Hattie, J., 490
Hawkins, R. P., 80, 84
Hayes, W. L., 104
Hedges, L. V., 102, 491, 505, 512
Hendrick, C., 25, 27, 28
Herman, J. L., 475
Heron, T. E., 84
Hersen, M., 19, 23, 27, 29, 81, 333, 337, 364, 369, 373, 375, 405, 419, 422, 423
Heshusius, L., 261
Heward, W. L., 42, 84
Hillix, W. A., 5
Hillocks, G., Jr., 77
Hingson, R., 453
Hohn, M. F., 264
Horner, R. D., 368
Hotelling, H., 219
Howe, K., 256, 273, 300
Huber, G., 382
Huberty, C. J., 102
Hunter, J. E., 505

Impara, J. C., 86
Iwata, B. A., 328

Jackson, G. B., 505
Jacob, E., 261
Jacobs, J., 260
Jankowski, N. W., 260, 262
Jenkins, G. M., 151
Jensen, K. B., 260, 262
Jetton, T. L., 491
Jobber, D., 456
Johnson, A., 423
Johnston, J. M., 11, 13
Joreskog, K., 223

Kaestle, C. F., 460
Kamps, D. M., 344
Kelly, M. B., 80
Keppel, G., 141, 143
Kime, C., 264
Kitchener, R. F., 11
Kochenderfer, B. J., 202, 228, 229, 230, 232
Krahn, G. L., 264
Kramer, J. J., 412
Kratochwill, T. R., 80
Kuder, G. F., 69

Ladd, G. W., 202, 228, 229, 230, 232
Lamal, P. A., 23, 25
Lancy, D. F., 260, 262
Lazarus, B. D., 347
Lee, V. E., 100
Leonard, B. R., 344
Leonard, I. J., 407, 428, 531
Lewis, T. J., 418
Light, R. J., 102, 491, 495, 499, 507
Lignugaris/Kraft, B., 422, 459, 494
Likins, M., 422
Lincoln, Y. S., 262
Lindlof, T. R., 259, 260, 262
Lofland, J., 259, 262
Luckasson, R., 42

Macfarlane, C. A., 298, 379
Magilary, L., 453
Mangione, T., 453
Marchand-Martella, N. E., 156, 180, 183, 298, 340, 351, 370, 379, 380, 382, 388, 407, 423, 428, 431, 536
Marsh, H. W., 100, 490
Marshall, C., 38, 77, 78, 462, 463
Martella, R. C., 156, 180, 183, 298, 300, 340, 351, 370, 379, 380, 382, 388, 428, 431, 459, 531, 536
Marx, M. H., 5
Mason, R. O., 461, 462, 463, 468
Mastropieri, M. A., 78, 79, 150, 302, 507
Mathiowetz, N., 453
Maxwell, J. A., 77, 78, 270, 271, 273, 277, 295, 296, 298
Mayer, R. G., 81
McCreadie, J., 526
McGaw, B., 491
McKenny, J. L., 461
McLaughlin, T. F., 344
McNaughten, D., 140
Meier, K., 23
Meister, C., 490, 506, 507
Meyer, T. P., 259, 260, 262
Miller, P., 7, 453
Mishler, E. G., 295
Mitchell, J. V., 453
Moore, D. W., 343
Moran, G., 152
Mordock, J. B., 537
Morgan, D., 388
Morris, L. L., 475
Munson, R., 80
Murray, F. B., 15, 512

Nabors, L. A., 227
Nelson, C. R., 152
Nelson, J. R., 134, 135, 138, 148, 152, 153, 155, 156, 158, 180, 181, 183, 300, 307, 382, 423, 476, 478, 494, 507, 516
Neuliep, J. W., 23, 27, 28
Nicholls, J. G., 181
Nicholson, T., 343

Olkin, I., 491, 503, 505, 512

Pajak, E. F., 267, 272, 273
Patton, M. Q., 258, 263, 267, 268, 269, 270, 275, 277, 278, 285, 287, 288, 290, 291
Pauly, J. J., 259, 262
Pavlovic, Z., 468
Pennypacker, H. S., 11, 12, 13
Peshkin, A., 285
Pillemer, D. B., 100, 102, 491, 499, 507
Pitman, M. A., 77, 277
Popham, W. J., 64, 474
Popper, K. R., 9
Posavac, E. J., 470
Potter, W. J., 257, 258, 266, 285, 286, 291, 293, 294, 296, 297, 298, 460, 461

Raphael, T. E., 530
Raths, J., 512

Raulin, M. L., 13, 17
Reid, J. B., 85
Richardson, M. W., 68, 69
Risley, T. R., 332, 333, 375
Roberts, J. E., 227
Roethlisberger, F. J., 51
Rosenberg, M. S., 422
Rosenshine, B., 490, 506, 507
Rosenthal, R., 24, 28, 29, 48, 491, 504, 505, 535, 537
Rosnow, R. L., 48
Rossman, G. B., 38, 77, 78, 462, 463
Roth, J., 472

Sagan, C., 4
Salvia, J., 76, 77
Salzberg, C. L., 388, 422, 459
Schatzman, L., 267, 290
Schlinger, H. D., 10
Schmidt, F. L., 505
Schmitt, B., 351
Schwartz, H., 260
Scriven, M., 472
Scruggs, T. E., 78, 79, 150, 302, 507
Shaver, J. P., 50, 104, 105
Sidman, M., 23, 27, 36, 418
Silverman, D., 38, 258, 295
Sindelar, P. T., 422
Skinner, B. F., 10, 103, 265
Slavin, R. E., 49
Smith, D. D., 42
Smith, D. J., 134, 158, 382, 478, 500, 516
Smith, J. K., 261
Smith, M. L., 512
Smith, P. V., 503
Snider, V. E., 529
Sorbom, D., 223
Stanley, J. C., 38, 332
Stewart, B. J., 69
Stewart, K. G., 344
Stock, W. A., 500
Stowitschek, J. J., 422
Strauss, A. L., 258, 261, 262, 264, 265, 267, 294, 295
Sugai, G., 418
Sulzer-Azaroff, B., 81, 418
Sund, R. B., 22
Symons, D. K., 152

Tan, A., 343
Tawney, J. W., 330, 332, 334, 347, 405, 410
Taylor, S., 77, 78, 259, 262
Thomas, R. M., 10
Thompson, B., 104
Tripodi, T., 329
Tschantz, J. M., 544
Tse, L., 298
Tufte, E. R., 330
Tukey, J. W., 104, 114, 178, 509

Ulman, J. D., 418

Vail, C. O., 544
Vollmer, T. R., 328

Weiner, E. A., 69
Weinstein, C. S., 73
Wellons, J., 288
West, R. P., 382
Wester, F., 261
Wetzel, R. J., 80
White, D. R., 80
Williams, R. L., 70
Willson, V. L., 151
Wilson, R. J., 422
Wimmer, R. D., 261
Wolcott, H. F., 282
Wolery, M., 417, 418, 419, 421, 422
Wolf, M. M., 57, 332, 375
Wood, W. S., 382
Wright, S., 221

Young, K. R., 298, 340, 379, 380, 382, 388, 500
Ysseldyke, J. E., 76, 77, 145

Zarcone, J. R., 328
Zuriff, G., 265

Subject Index

A-B design, 331–333, 338–339, 342, 350, 363–364, 366, 372–375, 378, 405, 409–412, 416, 531
  research example, 340–343
A-B-A design, 333–334, 350, 531. *See also* withdrawal design
  research example, 343–344
A-B-A-B design, 334, 344, 350
  research example, 344
A-B-C-B design, 335, 347
  research example, 347
  sample article, 351–357
action research, 23, 30, 525–551
  characteristics of, 527–528
  dimensions of, 527
  how historical methods are used, 532
  how program evaluation methods are used, 532
  how qualitative methods are used, 526, 529–530
  how quantitative methods are used, 528–529
  how single-case methods are used, 531
  how survey methods are used, 532
  qualitative research example, 530
  quantitative research example, 529
  sample article, 544–550
  single case research example, 531
adapted alternating treatments design (AATD), 422
advanced correlational procedures, 216
alternate forms reliability. *See* coefficient of equivalence
alternating treatments design (ATD), 405, 418–428, 531. *See also* multielement design
  analysis of data, 422–423, 428
  modifications of, 422
  research example, 423–424, 428
  skill acquisition programs, 421
  threats to external validity, 423
  threats to internal validity, 422–423
  when to use, 429–430
American Educational Research Association (AERA), 533
American Psychological Association (APA), 533
analysis of covariance (ANCOVA), 115, 147, 216
  using causal-comparative design, 177
  using non-equivalent control-group design, 149
  using posttest-only control-group design, 137
  using pretest–posttest control-group design, 134
analysis of variance (ANOVA), 114–115, 140, 216, 512
  repeated measures, 115
  multivariate, 115–116
  using causal-comparative design, 178
  using counterbalanced design, 149–150
  using factorial experimental design, 141
  using posttest-only control-group design, 137–138
  using Solomon four-group design, 140
analyst triangulation, 277–278
ANCOVA. *See* analysis of covariance
ANOVA. *See* analysis of variance
applied research, 22–24, 30, 35, 57, 337, 423
arithmetic mean, 56, 95–96. *See also* central tendency
attenuation, 213

B-A-B design, 334–335, 346, 350
  research example, 344–345
basic correlational procedures, 213–214
basic research, 22, 30, 47
beta weights, 218
bimodal distribution, 97
Boolean rules, 497–498

Canonical correlation, 219
carryover effects, 386, 422–423
case study, 20–21
causal-comparative research method, 7–8, 20, 115, 174–199, 201
  analysis of data, 177–180
  comparison with experimental research methods, 175, 201
  control for external validity threats, 179–180
  control for internal validity threats, 178–179
  not possible to manipulate independent variable, research example, 180
  prohibitive to assess changes in variable over time, research example, 181
  sample article, 183–195
  selection of groups, 176–177
  what to consider when designing a study, 176–180
  when to use, 182

cause-and-effect relationship, 19, 21, 298, 328, 458, 474, 531
in experimental designs, 157
in causal-comparative designs, 176
in correlational research, 225
in historical research, 461
in research syntheses, 490
central tendency, 95–96
measures of, 95
when to use the different measures, 96
chain sampling, 269. *See also* snowball sampling
chance factors, 99, 103–104, 112–113, 119
changing-criterion design, 405–407, 409
analysis of data, 407–412
research example, 412–413
sample article, 431–440
threats to external validity, 411–412
threats to internal validity, 407
when to use, 429–430
Chi-Square (χ^2), 115–118, 215–216
comparisons of relative frequencies, 116–118
goodness of fit test, 118
test for association between variables, 118
coders, 500–502
coding, 500–502, 507, 514–515
coefficient of alienation, 210
coefficient of determination, 209–210
coefficient of equivalence, 67–68, 80
coefficient of multiple correlation (R), 218
coefficient of stability, 66–67, 71, 80
combination single-case designs, 424–428
analysis of data, 428
research example, 428
threats to external validity, 428
threats to internal validity, 428
when to use, 430
comparison group, 134, 176
extreme groups method, 177
problem and solutions when using, 176–177
compensatory equalization of treatments, 46
compensatory rivalry by the control group, 45–46
complete observer observation, 283
complete participant observation, 282–283
concurrent validity, 76–77. *See also* criterion-related validity
confirming and disconfirming cases (sampling technique), 269
constraint levels, 4, 17–18
construct validity, 74–75
content validity, 75–76
contingency coefficient, 215–216
convenience sampling, 124–125, 267
in qualitative research, 270
in quantitative research, 132
correlation coefficient, 206, 263–265
factors affecting, 212–216
general interpretation of, 206–208
magnitude of, 209
negative correlation, 206–208, 215
Pearson product moment correlation coefficient, 206, 213–215
perfect correlation between variables, 206, 218
positive correlation, 206–208, 215
statistical significance of, 208–209
variance interpretation of, 209–210
zero correlation, 206–209
correlation ratio (eta coefficient), 212, 215
correlational research method, 7–8, 20–21, 175, 200–252
analysis of data, 203–227
comparison with the causal-comparative design, 201–202, 225, 226
control for external validity threats, 226–227
control for internal validity threats, 225–226
critical issues in, 202–203
exploring relationships research example, 227–228
forms of relationships, 205–206
issues in designing a study, 201–230
predictive research example, 228–230
sample article, 232–246
statistical procedures, 203, 206, 216–223
types of variables in, 201–202
when to use, 230
counterbalanced design, 149–150, 175
analysis of data, 149–150
control for external validity threats, 150
control for internal validity threats, 150
research example, 150–151
criterion-referenced tests, 177, 202, 348
criterion-related validity, 76–77
criterion sampling, 269
criterion variable, 202
critical case sampling, 268–269
critical thinking, 3–4, 9, 15
Cronbach's Coefficient Alpha, 68–69. *See also* coefficient of internal consistency
cubic relationship, 206
curvilinear relationship, 206, 212–214

Data-based decision making, 531
data sets, 95
  description of, 95–98
data sources triangulation, 277
dependent variable, 7, 17, 19, 106–107, 115, 255–256
descriptive research. *See* naturalistic research
descriptive statistics, 95, 206
descriptive validity, 270–271, 296
deviant case sampling, 268. *See also* extreme case sampling
diffusion of treatment, 45
discriminant function analysis, 219–220
distributions, 95
  bivariate frequency distribution, 203–206
  shape of, 97–98
  skewed, 96–97
  unimodal distribution, 97
  univariate frequency distribution, 95
document analysis, 276
  as sources of data for historical research, 463–464
  research example, 300
duration recording, 82–83
  formula, 83

Ecological validity, 49–56
effect sizes, 504–506
  as it relates to statistical significance, 504
  formula (Glass's Δ), 504
  homogeneity of, 511–512
  meaning of, 505–506
  parametric, 505
  problems associated with, 506–507
ethical principles and codes of conduct, 532–538
  Ethical Principles of Psychologists and Code of Conduct (APA), 533
  Ethical Standards of the American Educational Association (AERA), 533
  institutional review board (IRB), 532, 535, 537
  of action researchers, 538
ethnographic research, 21, 291–293
  features of, 293
  research example, 299–300
evaluative validity, 273
event recording, 82
  formula, 82
experiment, 130, 181
  control group, 131–132
  experimental (treatment) group, 130–133
experimental research methods, 18–20, 130–173, 502
  ability to control for threats to external validity, 134, 138, 140
  ability to control for threats to internal validity, 134, 138, 140
experimenter effects, 52–53
external criticism, 464–467
external generalizability, 273
external validity, 46–47
  general categories of, 47–56
extraneous variables, 38, 131
extreme case sampling, 268. *See also* deviant case sampling

Factor analysis, 220–221, 224
  interpretation, 221
  procedures, 221
factorial experimental design, 141–144
  analysis of data, 141–142
  control for external validity threats, 142
  control for internal validity threats, 142
  research example, 142–144
field-oriented studies, 282–300
fugitive literature, 493
functional relationship, 17, 38, 333, 335, 347

Generalization/generalizability, 25–27, 47, 120, 340, 418, 423
  across participants, 47–49
  from a qualitative perspective, 272–273, 297–298
graphs/graphical presentations, 330–331
  bar graphs, 331
  box and whiskers, 509
  condition change lines, 32, 362, 365
  data points and paths, 330–332, 337, 507–508
  histograms, 331
  horizontal (x) axis/abscissa, 95, 205, 330, 331, 332, 365
  methods of, 330–331
  multiple-baseline designs, 364
  plotting data, 95, 97, 205
  representations of effect sizes, 509–511
  scattergrams, 205, 212
  vertical (y) axis/ordinate, 205, 330, 332, 365
  withdrawal and associated designs, 509–511

Hawthorne effect, 50–51
historical research, 460–469, 532
  analysis of data, 464–468
  characteristics of, 461
  how designed, 462–469

historical research (*continued*)
purposes of, 461–462
research example, 468–469
threats to external validity, 464–467
threats to internal validity, 467–468
when to use, 469
history, 44, 332, 367, 411, 416
homogeneous group, 202
homogeneous sampling, 268
hypotheses, 5, 11, 12–13, 98–99
alternative, 99–102, 127, 176, 491
directional, 100–102, 109, 116, 118, 119, 127
in causal-comparative research, 174, 176
in correlational research, 202
in historical research, 462–463
in research syntheses, 495
nondirectional, 100–102, 118, 119, 127
null, 99–100, 101, 102, 104, 106–108, 110–111, 127
one-tailed, 100–102, 109
role of, 99
two-tailed, 100–102

Independent variable, 7, 18, 19, 20, 21, 27, 38, 42
inferences, 56, 64, 65–66, 78, 125, 223, 270, 328
inferential statistics, 57, 98–99, 127, 177
information gathering, 14–17
authority, 15–16
empiricism, 16
intuition, 15
rationalism, 16–17
tenacity, 14–15
instrumentation, 43, 152, 225
interaction effects, 140, 143, 216, 413
interaction of history and treatment effects, 54–55
interaction of personological variables and treatment effects, 49
interaction of time of measurement and treatment effects, 55–56
internal criticism, 467–468
internal generalizability, 272
internal validity, 38
threats to, 38–46
interobserver agreement, 64, 79–80, 531
factors that influence, 85–86
methods of establishing, 80–85
interpretive validity, 271, 296
interval recording, 83–85
formulas, 84
momentary time sampling, 83
partial-interval, 83
whole-interval, 83
interval scale, 94–95, 118, 127
interview study, 288
research example, 299
interviews, 257, 275–276, 288, 301, 452
as sources of data in historical research, 463
general interview guide approach, 289
informal conversational interview, 288–289
standardized open-ended, 289–290
types of questions, 290–291

John Henry effect, 45–46. *See also* compensatory rivalry by the control group

Kendall coefficient of concordance, 215
Kendall part rank correlation, 215
Kendall's rank correlation coefficient, 215
Kruskal-Wallis ANOVA, 119
using counterbalanced design, 150
using Solomon four-group design, 140
Kuder-Richardson method of rational equivalence, 68–69. *See also* coefficient of internal consistency

Latency recording, 82–83
formula, 83
line of best fit, 205–206. *See also* regression line
linear relationship, 215
logical operators, 497–500

Magnitude of relationship, 203, 209–210, 212
with multiple regression, 216
in research syntheses, 502–508
main effects, 139, 143, 216
Mann-Whitney U test, 118–119
using pretest–posttest control-group design, 134
using posttest-only control-group design, 137
using static-group comparison design, 144
MANOVA. *See* multivariate analysis of variance
maturation, 38–40, 67, 416–417
maximum variation sampling, 268
measurement, 63–85
goal of, 63
measurement devices, 66–80
factors to consider when assessing, 86–87
measurement error, 36–37, 66, 69–71, 102–103, 224
measurement of the dependent variable, 55, 133, 137, 145, 148, 150, 152, 153, 156
median, 96. *See also* central tendency
methods triangulation, 278–279
mode, 96. *See also* central tendency

mortality, 42–43
multielement design, 418. *See also* alternating treatments design
multiple-baseline designs, 363–404, 421, 424, 531
 across behaviors, 366
 across participants, 366
 across settings, 366–367
 advantages of using, 364–365, 369, 379
 analysis of data, 369–379
 disadvantages of using, 365–366, 369, 375, 378
 research example (across behaviors), 379–380
 research example (across participants), 380–382
 research example (across settings), 382
 sample article, 388–400
 threats to external validity, 379
 threats to internal validity, 369, 371
 when to use, 385–387
multiple-probe design, 367–369, 387, 430
 research example, 382–385
multiple regression, 216–217
 backward elimination, 217
 forward selection, 217
 interpretation of, 218–219
 statistical significance of, 219
 stepwise selection, 217–218
multiple treatment interference, 50–51, 418, 423
multitreatment design, 413–418, 421
 analysis of data, 416–418
 research example, 418
 threats to external validity, 418
 threats to internal validity, 416–417
 when to use, 430
multivariate analysis of variance (MANOVA), 115–116

Naturalistic observation study, 287
naturalistic research, 21
needs assessment, 472–473
nominal scale, 94
nonequivalent control-group design, 146–149, 475
 analysis of data, 147–148
 control for external validity threats, 148
 control for internal validity threats, 147–148
 research example, 148–149
nonparametric tests of statistical significance, 102, 109, 114, 116–119, 134, 138, 144, 156
nonparticipant observation study, 286–287, 298
nonprobability sampling, 124–125, 128
 convenience, 124–125
 opportunity, 125
 quota, 124
 volunteer, 125
normal distribution, 95, 97–98. *See also* unimodal distribution
novelty/disruption effects, 51–52

Observation studies, 282–285, 462
 research example, 298–299
observations, 16–17, 64, 85–86, 275, 276
 methods of analyzing in qualitative research, 284
 methods of in qualitative research, 282–285
observer-as-participant observation, 283
observer bias, 275, 284–285, 287
observer drift, 85
observer effects, 284, 287
one-group pretest-posttest design, 155–156
 analysis of data, 155–156
 control for external validity threats, 155, 156
 control for internal validity threats, 154, 156
 research example, 156
one-shot case study, 153–155
 analysis of data, 154–155
 control for external validity threats, 154–155
 control for internal validity threats, 154
 research example, 155
ordinal scale, 94, 118, 119
outcome evaluation, 474–475
outliers in data, 212–213, 537
 in box and whiskers plots, 511

Parallel forms reliability, 67. *See also* coefficient of equivalence
parallel treatments design (PTD), 422, 423
parametric tests of statistical significance, 102, 109, 111–116, 178
part correlation, 214
partial correlation, 214, 215, 217
path analysis, 221–223, 230
 limitation on causal inferences, 223
participant-as-observer observation, 283
participant observation study, 283
 field notes, 286
permanent product measures, 81
 formula, 81
phi coefficient, 215–216
population validity, 47–49, 119, 128
posttest-only control-group design, 136–138
 analysis of data, 137–138
 control for external validity threats, 138
 control for internal validity threats, 138
 research example, 138

posttest sensitization, 138
power, 108
  five methods of increasing, 108–111
predictive validity, 76–77. *See also* criterion-related validity
predictor variable, 201–202
preexperimental design, 131–132, 153, 270, 475
  types of, 153–156
  when to use, 157
pretest–posttest control-group design, 133–136
  analysis of data, 134
  control for external validity threats, 134
  control for internal validity threats, 134
  research example, 134–136
  sample article, 158–168
pretest sensitization, 53, 138, 139
primary sources of information, 463
  errors associated with searching and selecting, 514
  in historical research, 463
  in research syntheses, 493
probability sampling, 120–124, 128
  cluster, 123–124
  simple, 120–122
  stratified, 123
  systematic sampling, 122–123
  table of random numbers, 122
process evaluation, 473–474
program evaluation, 469–477, 532
  analysis of data, 476
  evaluation example, 476–477
  goal and objectives of, 470–471
  how conducted, 475–476
  types of, 471–475
  when to use, 477
projective tests, 69
proportion of nonoverlapping data (PND), 507–508

Quadratic relationship, 206
qualitative research, 6, 20–21, 38, 58, 77–79, 255–323, 327, 329, 461, 529–530
  analysis of data, 294–298
  analyzing research, 296–298
  characteristics of, 257–258
  data gathering procedures, 266–267
  differences between qualitative and quantitative research, 258–265, 281–282, 293, 294–296
  focus of research, 265
  nature of data, 263–264
  procedures, 265–270
  process of change, 264
  sample article, 302–321
  source of data, 258
  threats to external validity, 295–296
  threats to internal validity, 295
  type of reasoning, 264–265
  understanding in, 270–273
  when to use various designs, 300–301
quantitative research, 21, 64–66, 91–251, 528–529
quartic relationship, 206
quasi-experimental designs, 131, 144, 332
  common types, 144–153
  when to use, 157
questionnaires, 202

Random assignment, 157, 200
random sampling, 120–122, 123, 125. *See also* probability sampling
range, 97
ratio scale, 95, 213, 215, 219–220
reactivity, 85, 275, 276, 283, 287, 368–369
regression coefficient, 218
regression line, 206–208
regression models, 217–218, 224
relationships (between or among variables), 99, 132, 157, 201–211, 216, 219, 490
reliability, 23, 37, 64–73, 177, 226, 293
  evaluative criteria for judging qualitative research, 273–277
  in survey research, 456–457
  interpretation of reliability coefficients, 69
  issues in qualitative research, 77–79
  issues in quantitative research, 65–66
  relationship with sources of unsystematic measurement error, 69–71
  types of reliability coefficients, 66–69
replication, 23–29
  generalizability of findings, 25–27
  reliability of findings, 23–25
  types of, 27–29
  within a changing-criterion design, 410
research questions, 5, 11, 15, 30, 35, 56, 78
  in historical research, 462–463
  in qualitative research, 256, 266, 267, 278, 290, 296
  in research syntheses, 494–495
  in single-case research designs, 328
  in survey research, 456–457
research syntheses, 489–522
  analysis of data, 513–515

categories of, 491–492
coding, 500–502
considerations for conducting, 493–494
errors in conducting, 514–515
how to plan and execute, 494–515
purposes of, 490–491
reporting the results, 512–513
roles of, 489–490
sample article, 516–521
systematic, 491–492
threats to the validity of, 513–515
unsystematic, 491
when to use, 515
resentful demoralization of the control group, 44–45
restriction of range, 213
correction for, 213

Sample size, 111, 114, 125–126, 267, 503–504
formula, 126
sample variance, 97
sampling, 83, 119–126, 132
decisions, 125–126
in qualitative research, 267–270
in quantitative research, 124
issues, 120
methods, 119–125
using survey research, 450, 451–452
sampling error, 126–127
sampling frames, 454
convenience, 454
cluster, 454
the evaluation of, 454–455
exhaustive, 454
sampling politically important cases (sampling technique), 269–270
scales of measurement, 94–95
science, 4–5, 50, 174, 276, 340
purposes of, 6–8
scientific logic, 11–14
combination of logic forms, 13–14
deductive logic, 12–13
inductive logic, 11–12
scientific method, 5–6, 23, 461
five steps of, 5–6
scientific theory, 8–11, 29
good versus bad, 10
testability of, 10–11
secondary sources of information, 463
in historical research, 463
in research syntheses, 493
selection, 40–41, 126, 132, 157, 176–177, 272
selection by maturation interaction, 41
selection bias, 494
in research syntheses, 494
significance level, 104
alpha, 105, 107–109
errors made in interpretations, 104–105
probability value, 105
simulations, 287–288
single-case research designs, 19–20, 325–445, 531
combining studies using proportion of nonoverlapping data (PND), 507–508
similarities/differences as compared to qualitative research methods, 327–330
similarities/differences as compared to quantitative research methods, 327–330
snowball sampling, 269. *See also* chain sampling
social validity, 57–58
Solomon four-group design, 138–141
analysis of data, 139–140
control for external validity threats, 140
control for internal validity threats, 140
research example, 140–141
Spearman rank correlation coefficient, 215
split-half reliability, 68–69. *See also* coefficient of internal consistency
standard deviation, 57, 97–98, 126, 504–505
pooled (formula), 505
standard error of measurement, 71–72
formula, 72
standardized measurement devices (tests), 86, 202
static-group comparison design, 144–146
analysis of data, 144–145
control for external validity threats, 145
control for internal validity threats, 145
research example, 145–146
statistical regression, 41–42
statistical significance, 99–100, 102–104
as it relates to effect size, 504–507
combining significance tests (in research syntheses), 503–504
decisions made in, 103
in research syntheses, 502–504
of correlation coefficients, 208–209
tests for difference between variances, 116
types of methods, 111–119
statistical validity, 56–57
structural equation modeling (LISREL), 211, 223–225

survey research, 449–460, 532
  analysis of data, 458–459
  factors in choosing a survey method, 451–453
  how designed, 453–459
  purposes of, 450–451
  research example, 459
  sample article, 478–485
  threats to external validity, 458–459
  threats to internal validity, 458
  types of, 451–453
  when to use, 459–460
surveys, 202, 451–453, 532
  development of instruments, 456–458
  development of questions, 456–457
  piloting-testing, 458
  types of questions used, 456–457
systematic research syntheses, 491–492

T test, 100, 111–114, 116
  using causal-comparative design, 178
  using one-group pretest-posttest design, 155–156
  using one-shot case study, 154
  using static-group comparison design, 144
test-retest reliability, 66–67. *See also* coefficient of stability
testing, 43–44, 226
theoretical validity, 271–272, 296
theory, 8–9, 271, 300, 528
  disproving theories, 9–10
  grounded, 264–265
  testability of, 10–11
  developing theories from research syntheses, 490–491
theory/perspective triangulation, 278
time-series design, 151–153
  analysis of data, 151–152
  control for external validity threats, 152
  control for internal validity threats, 152
  research example, 152–153
triangulation, 277–279
  types of methods used, 277–279
true experimental designs, 131, 132–141
  common types, 133–141
  when to use, 156–157
Type I errors, 105–106
  relative seriousness of, 107–108
Type II errors, 106–107
  relative seriousness of, 107–108
typical case sampling, 268

Univariate frequency distribution, 95, 205
unsystematic research syntheses, 491–492

Validity, 64–65, 73–79
  consequential, 65–66
  evaluative criteria for judging qualitative research, 273–277
  from a qualitative perspective, 270
  in survey research, 456, 457
  issues in qualitative research, 77–79
  issues in quantitative research, 65–66
  of measurement devices, 73–77
  qualitative types of, 270–273
  quantitative types of, 74–77
variability, 19, 20, 36–38, 103
  sources of, 36–38
variance, 36–38, 58, 210, 222, 504
  systematic, 37–38
  unsystematic, 36–37
variation, 96–97
  measures of, 96–97
verification of the independent variable, 50, 180
vote counting procedure, 503, 504

Wilcoxon Signed Rank test, 119
withdrawal and associated designs, 325–362, 363
  advantages of using, 329, 330
  analysis of data, 337–340
  problems using, 334, 340, 347–350
  research examples, 340–347
  threats to external validity, 340
  threats to internal validity, 337–340
  when to use, 347–350
writing the research report/article, 538–541, 512–513
  contents of an article, 512–513, 538–541
  how articles are submitted for publication, 542
  in research syntheses, 512–513
  in action research, 538–541
  using politically correct/appropriate language, 541
  when to publish, 542–543